S0-BAH-650

ATLA BIBLIOGRAPHY SERIES

edited by Dr. Kenneth E. Rowe

1. *A Guide to the Study of the Holiness Movement,* by Charles Edwin Jones. 1974.
2. *Thomas Merton: A Bibliography,* by Marquita E. Breit. 1974.
3. *The Sermon on the Mount: A History of Interpretation and Bibliography,* by Warren S. Kissinger. 1975.
4. *The Parables of Jesus: A History of Interpretation and Bibliography,* by Warren S. Kissinger. 1979.
5. *Homosexuality and the Judeo-Christian Tradition: An Annotated Bibliography,* by Thom Horner. 1981.
6. *A Guide to the Study of the Pentecostal Movement,* by Charles Edwin Jones. 1983.
7. *The Genesis of Modern Process Thought: A Historical Outline with Bibliography,* by George R. Lucas, Jr. 1983.
8. *A Presbyterian Bibliography,* by Harold B. Prince. 1983.
9. *Paul Tillich: A Comprehensive Bibliography . . .,* by Richard C. Crossman. 1983.
10. *A Bibliography of the Samaritans,* by Alan David Crown. 1984.
11. *An Annotated and Classified Bibliography of English Literature Pertaining to the Ethiopian Orthodox Church,* by Jon Bonk. 1984.
12. *International Meditation Bibliography, 1950 to 1982,* by Howard R. Jarrell. 1984.
13. *Rabindranath Tagore: A Bibliography,* by Katherine Henn. 1985.
14. *Research in Ritual Studies: A Programmatic Essay and Bibliography,* by Ronald L. Grimes, 1985.
15. *Protestant Theological Education in America,* by Heather F. Day. 1985.
16. *Unconscious: A Guide to Sources,* by Natalino Caputi. 1985.
17. *The New Testament Apocrypha and Pseudepigrapha,* by James H. Charlesworth. 1987.
18. *Black Holiness,* by Charles Edwin Jones. 1987.
19. *A Bibliography on Ancient Ephesus,* by Richard Oster. 1987.
20. *Jerusalem, the Holy City: A Bibliography,* by James D. Purvis. 1988.
21. *An Index to English Periodical Literature on the Old Testament and Ancient Near Eastern Studies,* by William G. Hupper. Vol. I, 1987; Vol. II, 1988; Vol. III, 1990.
22. *John and Charles Wesley: A Bibliography,* by Betty M. Jarboe. 1987.
23. *A Scholar's Guide to Academic Journals in Religion,* by James Dawsey. 1988.
24. *The Oxford Movement and Its Leaders: A Bibliography of Secondary and Lesser Primary Sources,* by Lawrence N. Crumb. 1988.
25. *A Bibliography of Christian Worship,* by Bard Thompson. 1989.

An Index to English Periodical Literature on the Old Testament and Ancient Near Eastern Studies

Volume III

Compiled and Edited by

William G. Hupper

ATLA Bibliography Series, No. 21

The greatest obstacle to discovery is not ignorance—
it is the illusion of knowledge.
...Daniel J. Boorstin

The American Theological Library Association, and
The Scarecrow Press, Inc.
Metuchen, N.J., & London, 1990

Illustration from *Monument de Ninive* by M. P. E. Botta and M. E. Flandin, Paris 1849

British Library Cataloguing-in-Publication data available

Library of Congress Cataloging-in-Publication Data
(Revised for volume 3)

Hupper, William G.
An index to English periodical literature on the Old Testament and ancient Near Eastern studies.

(ATLA bibliography series; no. 21)
1. Bible. O.T.—Periodicals—Indexes. 2. Middle East—Periodicals—Indexes. I. American Theological Library Assoc iation. II. Title. III. Series.
Z 7772.A1H86 1987 [BS1171.2] 016.221 86-31448
ISBN 0-8108-1984-8 (v. 1)
ISBN 0-8108-2126-5 (v. 2)
ISBN 0-8108-2319-5 (v. 3)

Manufactured in the United States of America
Printed on acid-free paper

Table of Contents

Table of Contents

Table of Contents

Preface

With the production of Postscript fonts[1] which contain the necessary obscure diacritics (the lack of which made it necessary to produce the preceding volumes on a dot-matrix printer), Greek and Hebrew typefaces, as well as the ability to "bit-map" Egyptian hieroglyphics, *IEPLOT* Volume III has taken on a more professional appearance. Users should find this and succeeding volumes more readable.

As with any work of this magnitude, inevitable editorial *faux pas* occur despite all the careful attention one individual can apply. These include occasional page reference errors, chronological displacements, lapses of specific citations, and hopefully only isolated instances inaccurate of volume numbers. It was only after Volume II had gone to press that the important article on Ai by John A. Callaway[2] was discovered to have been left out. This and other articles will have to await the final volume to be properly included in the Additions and Corrections section.

The editor has followed the indirect recommendation of John Wright[3] including four more journals, two of which Wright was disappointed not to have found.[4] Incorporated in this and/or subsequent volumes are articles from *Imperial and Asiatic Quarterly Review, Journal of the Royal Anthropological Institute,*[5] *Journal of Christian Education,*[6] and *Viewpoint.*

---

1. Fonts used in preparation of this volume in addition to "Times" (an Adobe font) are: Semitica (a Postscript font containing a complete set of diacritics) compatible with "Times"; LaserGREEK; LaserHEBREW; and MacArabic; and MacHieroglyphics™ which are distributed by Linguist's Software.

2. Joseph A. Callaway, "New Evidence on the Conquest of ʿAi," *JBL* 87 (1968) 312-320.

3. John Wright's lengthy review of *IEPLOT* Volume I in *ABR* 37 (1988) pp. 68-71.

4. Incidentally, S. Yeivin's article "Religious and Cultural Trends in Jerusalem under the Davidic Dynasty," *VT* 3 (1953) 149-166, is found under §62 contrary to Wright's apparent "frustrated attempts" to locate it. (Wright, p. 71)

5. The suggestion by John Wright was indeed auspicious at this time as the incorporation of *JRAI* will allow users access to a large number of articles on anthropology under §170 of this volume. Unfortunately, several articles, including Kathleen M. Kenyon, "Excavations at Jericho," *JRAI* 84 (1954) 103-110, will also have to await the final volume for proper reference.

6. Special thanks to Mosher Library, Dallas Theological Seminary for providing some of the information necessary to complete *JCE*.

Further titles will not be included as it is deemed more expedient to proceed with publication, rather than additional research, lest the projected seven remaining volumes[7] require printing posthumously!

By the time this volume is in print, it will have been over twenty years since the original conception of this project. Little was known in the beginning of the scope of publications on Ancient Near Eastern Studies.[8] As with many endeavors of this type, it is a learning experience in which one attempts to rectify earlier mistakes and compensate for previous shortcomings by adding to, editing, reediting, and redefining divisions and sub-divisions. Wright's critique of certain sections of Volume I is well taken.[9] Revision was especially the dilemma with Volume III. The entire category of Art (§223-§229) was completely restructured and nearly every entry was physically rechecked from the journals in question in order to make the material more manageable. It is for just this reason of continual restructuring that the Table of Contents for the whole series cannot be reproduced in each volume as was suggested by Gorman.[10] At present the basic outline as found in the Introduction[11] in Volume I and Tables of Contents in individual volumes will have to suffice, with apologies to the users. The full Table of Contents for all the volumes will be duplicated in the index volume. It is sincerely hoped that Volumes IV and V will be ready for press in a shorter period of time than has been required for Volume III.

As with Volume II, places with the prefix "Tel" or "Tel el", etc. are located under the last word in the name (*e.g.* Tel al-Rimah is located under Rimah). Names beginning with Khirbet, Wadi, or Wady on the other hand are located under *K* and *W* respectively. Section 169, while covering "Science and the Bible" does not, save for a rare exception, contain articles on "Science and Religion". Section 230 "Assyriology" and 231 "Egyptology" are intentionally brief as the majority of articles are included in other sections which are more definitive in nature. It is hoped that the contents of this volume and others will spark additional interest in some subject to which previous references have been all but forgotten in some dusty archive.

Columbus Day, 1989

---

7. Somehow the reference in the preface of Volume II to Volumes IV and V being the high point of the series has been misinterpreted to mean that only five volumes will complete the work. Volumes VI and VII are now in the computer, and work continues to enter the estimated 40,000 remaining entries.

8. This has already been referred to at length in *IEPLOT* Volume I, xiv ff.

9. Wright, p. 70.

10. G. E. Gorman's review in *Riverina Library Review* 6, 3 (1989), p. 298f.

11. *IEPLOT* Volume I, p. xxi.

Periodical Abbreviations*

A

A&A	*Art and Archaeology; the arts throughout the ages* (Washington, DC, Baltimore, MD, 1914-1934)
A/R	*Action/Reaction* (San Anselmo, CA, 1967ff.)
A&S	*Antiquity and Survival* (The Hague, 1955-1962)
A(A)	*Anadolu (Anatolia)* (Ankara, 1956ff. [Subtitle varies; Volume 1-7 as: *Anatolia: Revue Annuelle d'Archeologie*]
AA	*Acta Archaeologica* (Copenhagen, 1930ff.)
AAA	*Annals of Archaeology and Anthropology* (Liverpool, 1908-1948; Suspended, 1916-1920)
AAAS	*Annales archéologiques arabes Syriennes. Revue d'Archéologie et d'Histoire* (Damascus, 1951ff.) [Volumes 1-15 as: *Les Annales archéologiques de Syrie* - Title Varies]
AAASH	*Acta Antiqua Academiae Scientiarum Hungaricae* (Budapest, 1951ff.)
AAB	*Acta Archaeologica* (Budapest, 1951ff.)
AAI	*Anadolu Araştirmalari Istanbul Üniversitesi Edebiyat Fakültesi eski Önasya Dilleri ve Kültürleri Kürsüsü Tarafindan Čikarilir* (Istanbul, 1955ff.) [Supersedes: *Jahrbuch für Kleinasiatische Forschungen*]
AAOJ	*American Antiquarian and Oriental Journal* (Cleveland, Chicago 1878-1914)
AASCS	*Antichthon. The Australian Society for Classical Studies* (Sydney, 1967ff.)
ABBTS	*The Alumni Bulletin [of] Bangor Theological Seminary* (Bangor, ME; 1926ff.)
ABenR	*The American Benedictine Review* (St. Paul, 1950ff.)
ABR	*Australian Biblical Review* (Melbourne, 1951ff.)
Abr-N	*Abr-Nahrain, An Annual Published by the Department of Middle Eastern Studies, University of Melbourne* (Melbourne, 1959ff.)
ACM	*The American Church Monthly* (New York, 1917-1939) [Volumes 43-45 as: *The New American Church Monthly*]

*All the journals indexed are listed in the Periodical Abbreviations even though no specific citation may appear in the present volume. Although the titles of many foreign language journals have been listed, only English Language articles are included in this index (except as noted). Articles from Modern Hebrew Language Journals are referred to by their English summary page.

Periodical Abbreviations

ACQ	*American Church Quarterly* (New York, 1961ff.) [Volume 7 on as: *Church Theological Review*]
ACQR	*The American Catholic Quarterly Review* (Philadelphia, 1876-1929)
ACR	*The Australasian Catholic Record* (Sydney, 1924ff.)
ACSR	*American Catholic Sociological Review* (Chicago, 1940ff.) [From Volume 25 on as: *Sociologial Analysis*]
ADAJ	*Annual of the Department of Antiquities of Jordan* (Amman, 1957ff.) [Volume 14 not published—destroyed by fire at the publishers]
AE	*Annales d'Ethiopie* (Paris, 1955ff.)
AEE	*Ancient Egypt and the East* (New York, London, Chicago, 1914-1935; Suspended, 1918-1919)
Aeg	*Aegyptus: Rivista Italiana di Egittologia e di Papirologia* (Milan,1920ff.)
AER	*American Ecclesiastical Review* (Philadelphia, New York, Cincinnati, Baltimore, 1889ff.) [Volumes 11-19 as: *Ecclesiastical Review*]
AfER	*African Ecclesiastical Review: A Quarterly for Priests in Africa* (Masaka, Uganda, 1959ff.)
Aff	*Affirmation* (Richmond, VA, 1966ff.) [Volume 1 runs from 1966 to 1980 inclusive]
AfO	*Archiv für Orientforschung; Internationale Zeitschrift für Wissenschaft vom Vorderen Orient* (Berlin, 1923ff.)
AfRW	*Archiv für Religionswissenschaft* (Leipzig, 1898-1941)
AHDO	*Archives d'histoire du droit oriental et Revue internationale des droits de l'antiquité* (Brussels, 1937-38, 1947-1951, *N.S.*, 1952-53)
AIPHOS	*Annuaire de l'institut de philologie et d'histoire orientales et slaves* (Brussels, 1932ff.)
AJ	*The Antiquaries Journal. Being the Journal of the Society of Antiquaries of London* (London, 1921ff.)
AJA	*The American Journal of Archaeology* (Baltimore, 1885ff.) [Original Series, 1885-1896 shown with *O. S;* Second Series shown without notation]
AJBA	*The Australian Journal of Biblical Archaeology* (Sydney, 1968ff.) [Volume 1 runs from 1968 to 1971 inclusive]
AJP	*The American Journal of Philology* (Baltimore, 1880ff.)
AJRPE	*The American Journal of Religious Psychology and Education* (Worcester, MA, 1904-1911)
AJSL	*The American Journal of Semitic Languages and Literatures* (Chicago, 1884-1941) [Volumes 1-11 as: *Hebraica*]
AJT	*American Journal of Theology* (Chicago, 1897-1920)
AL	*Archivum Linguisticum: A Review of Comparative Philology and General Linguistics* (Glasgow, 1949-1962)

Periodical Abbreviations

ALUOS	*The Annual of the Leeds University Oriental Society* (Leiden,1958ff.)
Amb	*The Ambassador* (Wartburg Theological Seminary, Dubuque, IA, 1952ff.)
AmHR	*American Historical Review* (New York, Lancaster, PA, 1895ff.)
AmSR	*American Sociological Review* (Washington, DC, 1936ff.)
Anat	*Anatolica: Annuaire International pour les Civilisations de l'Asie Anterieure* (Leiden, 1967ff.)
ANQ	*Newton Theological Institute Bulletin* (Newton, MA, 1906ff.) [Title varies as: *Andover-Newton Theological Bulletin; Andover-Newton Quarterly, New Series,* beginning 1960ff.]
Anthro	*Anthropos; ephemeris internationalis ethnologica et linguistica* (Salzburg, Vienna, 1906ff.)
Antiq	*Antiquity: A Quarterly Review of Archaeology* (Gloucester, England, 1927ff.)
Anton	*Antonianum. Periodicum Philosophico-Theologicum Trimestre* (Rome, 1926ff.)
AO	*Acta Orientalia ediderunt Societates Orientales Bœtava Donica, Norvegica* (Lugundi Batavorum, Havniæ, 1922ff.)
AOASH	*Acta Orientalia Academiae Scientiarum Hungaricae* (Budapest, 1950ff.)
AOL	*Annals of Oriental Literature* (London, 1820-21)
APST	*Aberdeen Philosophical Society, Transactions* (Aberdeen, Scotland, 1840-1931)
AQ	*Augustana Quarterly* (Rock Island, IL, 1922-1948)
AQW	*Anthropological Quarterly* (Washington, DC, 1928ff.) [Volumes1-25 as: *Primitive Man*]
AR	*The Andover Review* (Boston, 1884-1893)
Arch	*Archaeology* (Cambrige, MA, 1948ff.)
Archm	*Archaeometry. Bulletin of the Research Laboratory for Archaeology and the History of Art, Oxford University* (Oxford,1958ff.)
ARL	*The Archæological Review* (London, 1888-1890)
ArOr	*Archiv Orientální. Journal of the Czechoslovak Oriental Institute, Prague* (Vlašska, Czechoslovakia, 1929ff.)
AS	*Anatolian Studies: Journal of the British Institute of Archaeology at Ankara* (London, 1951ff.)
ASAE	*Annales du service des antiquités de l'Égypte* (Cairo, 1899ff.)
ASBFE	*Austin Seminary Bulletin. Faculty Edition* (Austin, TX; begins with volume 71*[sic]*, 1955ff.)

ASR	*Augustana Seminary Review* (Rock Island, IL, 1949-1967) [From volume 12 on as: *The Seminary Review*]
ASRB	*Advent Shield and Review* (Boston, 1844-45)
ASRec	*Auburn Seminary Record* (Auburn, NY, 1905-1932)
ASSF	*Acta Societatis Scientiarum Fennicae* (Helsinki, 1842-1926) [Suomen tideseura]
ASTI	*Annual of the Swedish Theological Institute (in Jerusalem)* (Jerusalem, 1962ff.)
ASW	*The Asbury Seminarian* (Wilmore, KY, 1946ff.)
AT	*Ancient Times: A Quarterly Review of Biblical Archaeology* (Melbourne, 1956-1961)
ATB	*Ashland Theological Bulletin* (Ashland, OH, 1968ff.)
ATG	*Advocate for the Testimony of God* (Richmond, VA, 1834-1839)
AThR	*The American Theological Review* (New York, 1859-1868) [*New Series* as: *American Presbyterian and Theological Review*, 1863-1868]
'Atiqot	*'Atiqot: Journal of the Israel Department of Antiquities* (Jerusalem, 1955ff.)
ATJ	*Africa Theological Journal* (Usa River, Tanzania, 1968ff.)
ATR	*Anglican Theological Review* (New York, Lancaster, Pa; 1918ff.)
AubSRev	*Auburn Seminary Review* (Auburn, NY, 1897-1904)
Aug	*Augustinianum* (Rome, 1961ff.)
AULLUÅ	*Acta Universitatis Lundensis. Lunds Universitets Årsskrift. Första Avdelningen. Teologi, Juridik och Humanistika Åmnen* (Lund, 1864-1904; *N. S.*, 1905-1964)
AUSS	*Andrews University Seminary Studies* (Berrien Springs, MI, 1963ff.)
AusTR	*The Australasian Theological Review* (Highgate, South Australia, 1930-1966)

B

B	*Biblica* (Rome, 1920ff.)
BA	*The Biblical Archaeologist* (New Haven; Cambridge, MA; 1938ff.)
Baby	*Babyloniaca Etudes de Philologie Assyro-Babylonienne* (Paris, 1906-1937)
BASOR	*Bulletin of the American Schools of Oriental Research* (So. Hadley, MA; Baltimore, New Haven, Philadelphia, Cambridge, MA;1919ff.)
BASP	*Bulletin of the American Society of Papyrologists* (New Haven, 1963ff.)

BAVSS	*Beiträge zur Assyriologie und vergleichenden semitischen Sprachwissenschaft* (Leipzig, 1889-1927)
BBC	*Bulletin of the Bezan Club* (Oxford, 1925-1936)
BC	*Bellamire Commentary* (Oxon., England; 1956-1968)
BCQTR	*British Critic, Quarterly Theological Review and Ecclesiastical Record* (London, 1793-1843) [Superseded by: *English Review*]
BCTS	*Bulletin of the Crozer Theological Seminary* (Upland, PA, 1908-1934)
Bery	*Berytus. Archaeological Studies* (Copenhagen, 1934ff.)
BETS	*Bulletin of the Evangelical Theological Society* (Wheaton, IL, 1958ff.)
BFER	*British and Foreign Evangelical Review, and Quarterly Record of Christian Literature* (Edinburgh, London, 1852-1888)
BH	*Buried History. Quarterly Journal of the Australian Institute of Archaeology* (Melbourne, 1964-65; 1967ff.)
BibR	*Biblical Repertory* (Princeton, NJ; New York, 1825-1828)
BibT	*The Bible Today* (Collegeville, MN, 1962ff.)
BIES	*Bulletin of the Israel Exploration Society* (Jerusalem, 1937-1967) [*Yediot*-ידיעות ארץ־ישראל החברה ועאקותיה לחקירת-Begun as: *Bulletin of the Jewish Palestine Exploration Society* through volume 15. English summaries discontinued from volume 27 on as translations published in: *Israel Exploration Journal*]
BIFAO	*Bulletin de l'institut français d'archéologie orientale au Caire* (Cairo, 1901ff.)
BJ	*Biblical Journal* (Boston, 1842-1843)
BJRL	*Bulletin of the John Rylands Library* (Manchester, 1903ff.)
BM	*Bible Magazine* (New York, 1913-1915)
BMB	*Bulletin du Musée de Byrouth* (Paris, 1937ff.)
BN	*Bible Numerics: a Periodical Devoted to the Numerical Study of the Scriptures* (Grafton, MA; 1904)
BO	*Bibliotheca Orientalis* (Leiden, 1944ff.)
BofT	*Banner of Truth* (London, 1955ff.)
BOR	*The Babylonian and Oriental Record: A Monthly Magazine of the Antiquities of the East* (London, 1886-1901)
BQ	*Baptist Quarterly* (Philadelphia, 1867-1877)
BQL	*Baptist Quarterly* (London, 1922ff.)
BQR	*Baptist Quarterly Review* (Cincinnati, New York, Philadelphia, 1879-1892)
BQRL	*The British Quarterly Review* (London, 1845-1886)
BR	*Biblical Review* (New York, 1916-1932)
BRCM	*The Biblical Review and Congregational Magazine* (London, 1846-1850)

BRCR *The Biblical Repository and Classical Review* (Andover, MA, 1831-1850) [Title varies as: *Biblical Repository; The Biblical Repository and Quarterly Observer; The American Biblical Repository*]

BRec *Bible Record* (New York, 1903-1912) [Volume 1, #1-4 as: *Bible Teachers Training School, New York City, Bulletin*]

BRes *Biblical Research: Papers of the Chicago Society of Biblical Research* (Amsterdam, Chicago, 1956ff.)

BS *Bibliotheca Sacra* (New York, Andover, Oberlin, OH; St. Louis, Dallas, 1843, 1844ff.)

BSAJB *British School of Archaeology in Jerusalem, Bulletin* (Jerusalem, 1922-1925)

BSOAS *Bulletin of the School of Oriental and African Studies. University of London* (London, 1917ff.)

BSQ *Bethel Seminary Quarterly* (St. Paul, MN; 1952ff.) [From Volume 13 on as: *Bethel Seminary Journal*]

BT *Biblical Theology* (Belfast, 1950ff.)

BTF *Bangalore Theological Forum* (Bangalore, India, 1967ff.)

BTPT *Bijdragen Tijdschrift voor philosophie en theologie* (Maastricht, 1938ff.) [Title varies as: *Bijdragen. Tijdschrift voor filosofie en theologie*]

BTr *Bible Translator* (London, 1950ff.)

BUS *Bucknell University Studies* (Lewisburg, PA; 1941ff.) [From Volume 5 on as: *Bucknell Review*]

BVp *Biblical Viewpoint* (Greenville, SC, 1967ff.)

BW *Biblical World* (Chicago, 1893-1920)

BWR *Bible Witness and Review* (London, 1877-1881)

BWTS *The Bulletin of the Western Theological Seminary* (Pittsburgh, 1908-1931)

BZ *Biblische Zeitschrift* (Paderborn, 1903-1939; *New Series,* 1957ff.) [*N.S.* shown without notation]

C

C&C *Cross and Crown. A Thomistic Quarterly of Spiritual Theology* (St. Louis, 1949ff.)

CAAMA *Cahiers archéologiques fin de l'antiquité et moyen age* (Paris, 1961ff.)

CAAST *Connecticut Academy of Arts and Sciences, Transactions* (New Haven, 1866ff.)

Carm *Carmelus. Commentarii ab instituto carmelitano editi* (Rome, 1954ff.)

CBQ *Catholic Biblical Quarterly* (Washington, DC; 1939ff.)

CC *Cross Currents* (West Nyack, NY; 1950ff.)

CCARJ *Central Conference of American Rabbis Journal* (New York,1953ff.)
CCBQ *Central Conservative Baptist Quarterly* (Minneapolis, 1958ff.) [From volume 9, #2 on as: *Central Bible Quarterly*]
CCQ *Crisis Christology Quarterly* (Dubuque, IA; 1943-1949) [Volume 6 as: *Trinitarian Theology*]
CD *Christian Disciple* (Boston, 1813-1823) [Superseded by: *Christian Examiner*]
CdÉ *Chronique d'Égypte* (Brussels, 1925ff.)
CE *Christian Examiner* (Boston, New York, 1824-1869)
Cent *Centaurus. International Magazine of the History of Science and Medicine* (Copenhagen, 1950ff.)
Center *The Center* (Atlanta, 1960-1965)
CFL *Christian Faith and Life* (Columbia, SC, 1897-1939) [Title varies: Original Series as: *The Bible Student and Religious Outlook,* volumes 1 & 2 as: *The Religious Outlook;* New Series as: *The Bible Student;* Third Series as: *The Bible Student and Teacher;* several volumes as: *Bible Champion*]
ChgoS *Chicago Studies* (Mundelein, IL; 1962ff.)
CJ *Conservative Judaism* (New York, 1945ff.)
CJL *Canadian Journal of Linguistics* (Montreal, 1954ff.)
CJRT *The Canadian Journal of Religious Thought* (Toronto, 1924-1932)
CJT *Canadian Journal of Theology* (Toronto, 1955ff.)
ClR *Clergy Review* (London, 1931ff.)
CM *The Clergyman's Magazine* (London, 1875-1897)
CMR *Canadian Methodist Review* (Toronto, 1889-1895) [Volumes 1-5 as: *Canadian Methodist Quarterly*]
CNI *Christian News from Israel* (Jerusalem, 1949ff.)
CO *Christian Opinion* (New York, 1943-1948)
Coll *Colloquium. The Australian and New Zealand Theological Review* (Auckland, 1964ff.) [Volume 1 through Volume 2, #1 as: *The New Zealand Theological Review*]
CollBQ *The College of the Bible Quarterly* (Lexington, KY, 1909-1965) [Break in sequence between 1927 and 1937, resumes in 1938 with volume 15 duplicated in number]
ColTM *Columbus Theological Magazine* (Columbus, OH; 1881-1910)
CongL *The Congregationalist* (London, 1872-1886)
CongML *The Congregational Magazine* (London, 1818-1845)
CongQB *The Congregational Quarterly* (Boston, 1859-1878)
CongQL *The Congregational Quarterly* (London, 1923-1958)
CongR *The Congregational Review* (Boston, Chicago, 1861-1871) [Volumes 1-6 as: *The Boston Review*]

Periodical Abbreviations

CongRL	*The Congregational Review* (London, 1887-1891)
ConstrQ	*The Constructive Quarterly. A Journal of the Faith, Work, and Thought of Christendom* (New York, London, 1913-1922)
Cont	*Continuum* (St. Paul, 1963-1970)
ContextC	*Context (Journal of the Lutheran School of Theology at Chicago)* (Chicago, 1967-1968)
ContR	*Contemporary Review* (London, New York, 1866ff.)
CovQ	*The Covenant Quarterly* (Chicago, 1941ff.) [Volume 1, #1 as: *Covenant Minister's Quarterly*]
CQ	*Crozer Quarterly* (Chester, PA; 1924-1952)
CQR	*Church Quarterly Review* (London, 1875-1968)
CR	*The Church Review* (New Haven, 1848-1891) [Title varies; Volume 62 not published]
CraneR	*The Crane Review* (Medford, MA; 1958-1968)
CRB	*The Christian Review* (Boston, Rochester; 1836-1863)
CRDSB	*Colgate-Rochester Divinity School Bulletin* (Rochester, NY; 1928-1967)
Crit	*Criterion* (Chicago, 1962ff.)
CRP	*The Christian Review: A Quarterly Magazine* (Philadelphia, 1932-1941)
CS	*The Cumberland Seminarian* (McKenzie, TN; Memphis; 1953-1970)
CSQ	*Chicago Seminary Quarterly* (Chicago, 1901-1907)
CSQC	*The Culver-Stockton Quarterly* (Canton, MO; 1925-1931)
CSSH	*Comparative Studies in Society and History: An International Quarterly* (The Hague, 1958ff.)
CT	*Christian Thought* (New York, 1883-1894)
CTJ	*Calvin Theological Journal* (Grand Rapids, 1966ff.)
CTM	*Concordia Theological Monthly* (St. Louis, 1930ff.)
CTPR	*The Christian Teacher [and Chronicle]* (London, 1835-1838; *N.S.*, 1838-1844 as: *A Theological and Literary Journal*) [Continues as: *The Prospective Review; A Quarterly Journal of Theology and Literature*)
CTSB	*Columbia Theological Seminary Bulletin* (Columbia, SC; Decatur, GA; 1907ff.) [Title varies]
CTSP	*Catholic Theological Society, Proceedings* (Washingon, DC; Yonkers, NY; 1948ff.)
CTSQ	*Central Theological Seminary Quarterly* (Dayton, OH; 1923-1931)
CUB	*Catholic University Bulletin* (Washington, DC; 1895-1914) [Volumes 1-20 only]

D

DDSR — *Duke Divinity School Review* (Durham, NC; 1936ff.) [Volumes 1-20 as: *The Duke School of Religion Bulletin;* Volumes 21-29 as: *Duke Divinity School Bulletin*]

DG — *The Drew Gateway* (Madison, NJ; 1930ff.)

DI — *Diné Israel. An Annual of Jewish Law and Israeli Family Law* ישואל שנתון למשפ ט עברי ולדיני משפחה ביראלדיני (Jerusalem, 1969ff.)

DJT — *Dialogue: A Journal of Theology* (Minneapolis, 1962ff.)

DownsR — *Downside Review* (Bath, 1880ff.)

DQR — *Danville Quarterly Review* (Danville, KY; Cincinnati; 1861-1864)

DR — *Dublin Review* (London, 1836-1968) [Between 1961 and 1964 as: *Wiseman Review*]

DS — *Dominican Studies. A Quarterly Review of Theology and Philosophy* (Oxford, 1948-1954)

DSJ — *The Dubuque Seminary Journal* (Dubuque, IA; 1966-1967)

DSQ — *Dubuque Seminary Quarterly* (Dubuque, IA; 1947-1949) [Volume 3, #3 not published]

DTCW — *Dimension: Theology in Church and World* (Princeton, NJ; 1964-1969) [Volumes 1 & 2 as: *Dimension* ; New format beginning in 1966 with full title, beginning again with Volume 1]

DTQ — *Dickinson's Theological Quarterly* (London, 1875-1883) [Superseded by *John Lobb's Theological Quarterly*]

DUJ — *The Durham University Journal* (Durham, 1876ff.; *N.S.*, 1940ff.) [Volume 32 of *O.S.* = Volume 1 of *N.S.*]

DUM — *Dublin University Magazine* (Dublin, London, 1833-1880)

DunR — *The Dunwoodie Review* (Yonkers, NY; 1961ff.)

E

EgR — *Egyptian Religion* (New York, 1933-1936)

EI — *Eretz-Israel. Archaeological, Historical and Geographical Studies* (Jerusalem, 1951ff.) מחקרים

ארץ־ישראל בידיעת הארץ ועתיקותיה

[English Summaries from Volume 3 on]

EJS *Archives européennes de Sociologie / European Journal of Sociology / Europäisches Archiv für Soziologie* (Paris, 1960ff.)
EN *The Everlasting Nation* (London, 1889-1892)
EQ *Evangelical Quarterly* (London, 1929ff.)
ER *Evangelical Review* (Gettysburg, PA; 1849-1870) [From Volume 14 on as: *Evangelical Quarterly Review*]
ERCJ *Edinburgh Review, or Critical Journal* (Edinburgh, London, 1802-1929)
ERG *The Evangelical Repository: A Quarterly Magazine of Theological Literature* (Glasgow, 1854-1888)
ERL *The English Review, or Quarterly Journal of Ecclesiastical and General Literature* (London, 1844-1853) [Continues *British Critic*]
ESS *Ecumenical Study Series* (Indianapolis, 1955-1960)
ET *The Expository Times* (Aberdeen, Edinburgh, 1889ff.)
ETL *Ephemerides Theologicae Lovanienses* (Notre Dame, 1924ff.)
Eud *Eudemus. An International Journal Devoted to the History of Mathematics and Astronomy* (Copenhagen, 1941)
Exp *The Expositor* (London, 1875-1925)
Exped *Expedition* (Philadelphia, 1958ff.) [Continues: *The University Museum Bulletin*]

F

F&T *Faith and Thought* (London, 1958ff.) [Supersedes: *Journal of the Transactions of the Victoria Institute, or Philosophical Society of Great Britain*]
FBQ *The Freewill Baptist Quarterly* (Providence, London, Dover, 1853-1869)
FDWL *Friends of Dr.Williams's Library (Lectures)* (Cambridge, Oxford, 1948ff.)
FLB *Fuller Library Bulletin* (Pasadena, CA; 1949ff.)
FO *Folia Orientalia* (Kraków, 1960ff.)
Focus *Focus. A Theological Journal* (Willowdale, Ontario, 1964-1968)
Folk *Folk-Lore: A Quarterly Review of Myth, Tradition, Institution & Custom being The Transactions of the Folk-Lore Society And Incorporating the Archæological Review and the Folk-Lore Journal* (London, 1890ff.)
Found *Foundations (A Baptist Journal of History and Theology)* (Rochester, NY; 1958ff.)
FUQ *Free University Quarterly* (Amsterdam-Centrum, 1950-1965)

G

GBT	*Ghana Bulletin of Theology* (Legon, Ghana; 1957ff.)
GJ	*Grace Journal* (Winona Lake, IN; 1960ff.)
GOTR	*Greek Orthodox Theological Review* (Brookline, MA; 1954ff.)
GR	*Gordon Review* (Boston; Beverly Farms, MA; Wenham, MA; 1955ff.)
GRBS	*Greek, Roman and Byzantine Studies* (San Antonio; Cambridge, MA; University, MS; Durham, NC; 1958ff.) [Volume1 as: *Greek and Byzantine Studies*]
Greg	*Gregorianum; Commentarii de re theologica et philosophica* (Rome, 1920ff.) [Volume 1 as: *Gregorianum; rivista trimestrale di studi teologici e filosofici*]
GUOST	*Glasgow University Oriental Society, Transactions* (Glasgow, 1901ff.)

H

H&T	*History and Theory: Studies in the Philosophy of History* (The Hague, 1960ff.)
HA	*Hebrew Abstracts* (New York, 1954ff.)
HDSB	*Harvard Divinity School Bulletin* (Cambridge, MA; 1935-1969)
Herm	*Hermathena; a Series of Papers on Literature, Science and Philosophy by Members of Trinity College, Dublin* (Dublin, 1873ff.) [Volumes 1-20; changes to issue number from #46 on]
HeyJ	*The Heythrop Journal* (New York, 1960ff.)
HJ	*Hibbert Journal* (London, Boston, 1902-1968)
HJAH	*Historia. Zeitschrift für alte Geschichte / Revue d'Histoire Ancienne / Journal of Ancient History / Rivista di Storia Antica* (Baden, 1950ff.)
HJud	*Historia Judaica. A Journal of Studies in Jewish History Especially in the Legal and Economic History of the Jews* (New York, 1938-1961)
HQ	*The Hartford Quarterly* (Hartford, CT; 1960-1968)
HR	*Homiletic Review* (New York, 1876-1934)
HRel	*History of Religions* (Chicago, 1961ff.)
HS	*Ha Sifrut. Quarterly for the Study of Literature* הספרוה רבעון למדע הספרות (Tel-Aviv, 1968ff.)
HSR	*Hartford Seminary Record* (Hartford, CT; 1890-1913)

HT	*History Today* (London, 1951ff.)
HTR	*Harvard Theological Review* (Cambridge, MA; 1908ff.)
HTS	*Hervormde Teologiese Studien* (Pretoria, 1943ff.)
HUCA	*Hebrew Union College Annual* (Cincinnati, 1904, 1924ff.)

I

IA	*Iranica Antiqua* (Leiden, 1961ff.)
IALR	*International Anthropological and Linguistic Review* (Miami, 1953-1957)
IAQR	*Asiatic Quarterly Review* (London, 1886-1966) [1st Series as: *Asiatic Quarterly Review,* (1886-1890); 2nd Series as: *The Imperial and Asiatic Quarterly and Oriental and Colonial Record,* (1891-1895); 3rd Series, (1896-1912); New Series, Volumes 1 & 2 as: *The Asiatic Quarterly Review* (1913); Volumes 3-48 (1914-1952) as: *Asiatic Review, New Series;* Volumes 49-59 (1953-1964) as: *Asian Review, New Series;* continued as: *Asian Review, Incorporating Art and Letters [and] the Asiatic Review, New Series,* Volumes 1-3 (1964-1966)]
ICHR	*Indian Church History Review* (Serampore, West Bengal, 1967ff.)
ICMM	*The Interpreter. A Church Monthly Magazine* (London, 1905-1924)
IEJ	*Israel Exploration Journal* (Jerusalem, 1950ff.)
IER	*Irish Ecclesiastical Record (A Monthly Journal under Episcopal Sanction)* (Dublin, 1864-1968)
IES	*Indian Ecclesiastical Studies* (Bangalore, India, 1962ff.)
IJA	*International Journal of Apocrypha* (London, 1905-1917) [Issues #1-7 as: *Deutero-Canonica,* pages unnumbered]
IJT	*Indian Journal of Theology* (Serampore, West Bengal, 1952ff.)
ILR	*Israel Law Review* (Jerusalem, 1966ff.)
Inter	*Interchange: Papers on Biblical and Current Questions* (Sydney, 1967ff.)
Interp	*Interpretation; a Journal of Bible and Theology* (Richmond, 1947ff.)
IPQ	*International Philosophical Quarterly* (New York, 1961ff.)
IR	*The Iliff Review* (Denver, 1944ff.)
Iran	*Iran: Journal of the British Institute of Persian Studies* (London, 1963ff.)
Iraq	*Iraq. British School of Archaeology in Iraq* (London, 1934ff.)
IRB	*International Reformed Bulletin* (London, 1958ff.)

IRM — *International Review of Missions* (Edinburgh, London, Geneva, 1912ff.)

Isis — *Isis. An International Review devoted to the History of Science and Civilization* (Brussels; Cambridge, MA; 1913ff.)

ITQ — *Irish Theological Quarterly* (Dublin, Maynooth, 1906ff.)

J

JAAR — *Journal of the American Academy of Religion* (Wolcott, NY; Somerville, NJ; Baltimore; Brattleboro, VT) [Volumes 1-4 as: *Journal of the National Association of Biblical Instructors;* Volumes 5-34 as: *Journal of Bible and Religion*]

JANES — *Journal of the Ancient Near Eastern Society of Columbia University* (New York, 1968ff.)

Janus — *Janus; Archives internationales pour l'Histoire de la Médecine et pour la Géographie Médicale* (Amsterdam; Haarlem; Leiden; 1896ff.)

JAOS — *Journal of the American Oriental Society* (Baltimore, New Haven, 1843ff.)

JAOSS — *Journal of the American Oriental Society, Supplements* (Baltimore, New Haven, 1935-1954)

JARCE — *Journal of the American Research Center in Egypt* (Gluckstadt, Germany; Cambridge, MA; 1962ff.)

JASA — *Journal of the American Scientific Affiliation* (Wheaton, IL, 1949ff.)

JBL — *Journal of Biblical Literature* (Middletown, CT; New Haven; Boston; Philadelphia; Missoula, MT; 1881ff.)

JC&S — *The Journal of Church and State* (Fresno, CA; 1965ff.)

JCE — *Journal of Christian Education* (Sydney, 1958ff.)

JCP — *Christian Philosophy Quarterly* (New York, 1881-1884) [From Volume 2 on as: *The Journal of Christian Philosophy*]

JCS — *Journal of Cuneiform Studies* (New Haven; Cambridge, MA;1947ff.)

JCSP — *Journal of Classical and Sacred Philology* (Cambridge, England, 1854-1857)

JEA — *Journal of Egyptian Archaeology* (London, 1914ff.)

JEBH — *Journal of Economic and Business History* (Cambridge, MA;1928-1932)

JEOL — *Jaarbericht van het Vooraziatisch-Egyptisch Gezelschap Ex Oriente Lux* (Leiden, 1933ff.)

JES — *Journal of Ethiopian Studies* (Addis Ababa, 1963ff.)

JESHO	*Journal of the Economic and Social History of the Orient* (Leiden, 1958ff.)
JHI	*Journal of the History of Ideas. A Quarterly Devoted to Intellectual History* (Lancaster, PA; New York;1940ff.
JHS	*The Journal of Hebraic Studies* (New York; 1969ff.)
JIQ	*Jewish Institute Quarterly* (New York, 1924-1930)
JJLP	*Journal of Jewish Lore and Philosophy* (Cincinnati, 1919)
JJP	*Rocznik Papirologii Prawniczej-Journal of Juristic Papyrology* (New York, Warsaw, 1946ff.) [Suspended 1947 & 1959-60]
JJS	*Journal of Jewish Studies* (London, 1948ff.)
JKF	*Jahrbuch für Kleinasiatische Forschungen* (Heidelberg, 1950-1953) [Superseded by *Anadolu Araştirmalari Istanbul Üniversitesi Edebiyat Fakültesi eski Önasya Dilleri ve Kültürleri Kürsüsü Tarafindan Čikarilir*]
JLTQ	*John Lobb's Theological Quarterly* (London, 1884)
JMUEOS	*Journal of the Manchester Egyptian and Oriental Society* (Manchester, 1911-1953) [Issue #1 as: *Journal of the Manchester Oriental Society*]
JMTSO	*Journal of the Methodist Theological School in Ohio* (Delaware, OH; 1962ff.)
JNES	*Journal of Near Eastern Studies* (Chicago, 1942ff.)
JP	*The Journal of Philology* (Cambridge, England; 1868-1920)
JPOS	*Journal of the Palestine Oriental Society* (Jerusalem, 1920-1948) [Volume 20 consists of only one fascicle]
JQR	*Jewish Quarterly Review* (London, 1888-1908; *N.S.*, Philadelphia, 1908ff.) [Includes 75th Anniversary Volume as: *JQR, 75th*]
JR	*Journal of Religion* (Chicago, 1921ff.)
JRAI	*Journal of the Royal Anthropological Institute of Great Britain and Ireland* (London, 1872-1965) [Volumes 1-69 as: *Journal of the Anthropological Institute* Continued as: *Man, N.S.*]
JRAS	*Journal of the Royal Asiatic Society of Great Britain and Ireland* (London, 1827ff.) [*Transactions,* 1827-1835 as *TRAS; Journal* from 1834 on: (Shown without volume numbers)]
JRelH	*Journal of Religious History* (Sydney, 1960ff.)
JRH	*Journal of Religion and Health* (Richmond, 1961ff.)
JRT	*Journal of Religious Thought* (Washington, DC; 1943ff.)
JSL	*Journal of Sacred Literature and Biblical Record* (London,1848-1868)
JSOR	*Journal of the Society of Oriental Research* (Chicago, 1917-1932)
JSP	*The Journal of Speculative Philosophy* (St. Louis, 1868-1893)

JSS	*Journal of Semitic Studies* (Manchester, 1956ff.)
JTALC	*Journal of Theology of the American Lutheran Conference* (Minneapolis, 1936-1943) [Volumes 1-5 as: *American Lutheran Conference Journal;* continued from volume 8, #3 as: *Lutheran Outlook* (not included)]
JTC	*Journal for Theology and the Church* (New York, 1965ff.)
JTLC	*Journal of Theology: Church of the Lutheran Confession* (Eau Claire, WI; 1961ff.)
JTS	*Journal of Theological Studies* (Oxford, 1899-1949; *N.S.*, 1950ff.)
JTVI	*Journal of the Transactions of the Victoria Institute, or Philosophical Society of Great Britain* (London, 1866-1957) [Superseded by *Faith & Thought*]
Jud	*Judaism. A Quarterly Journal of Jewish Life and Thought* (New York, 1952ff.)
JWCI	*Journal of the Warburg and Courtauld Institutes* (London,1937ff.)
JWH	*Journal of World History-Cahiers d'Histoire Mondiale -Cuadernos de Historia Mundial* (Paris, 1953ff.)

K

Kêmi	*Kêmi. Revue de philologie et d'archéologie égyptiennes et coptes* (Paris, 1928ff.)
Klio	*Klio. Beiträge zur alten Geschichte* (Leipzig, 1901ff.)
Kobez	*Kobez (Qobeṣ);* קובץ החברה העברית לחקירת ארץ־ישראל ועתיקתיה (Jerusalem, 1921-1945)
KSJA	*Kedem; Studies in Jewish Archaeology* (Jerusalem, 1942, 1945)
Kuml	*Kuml. Årbog for Jysk Arkæologisk Selskab* (Århus, 1951ff.)
Kush	*Kush. Journal of the Sudan Antiquities Service* (Khartoum, Sudan, 1953-1968)
KZ	*Kirchliche Zeitschrift* (St. Louis; Waverly, IA; Chicago; Columbus; 1876-1943)
KZFE	*Kadmos. Zeitschrift für vor-und frühgriechische Epigraphik* (Berlin, 1962ff.)

L

L	*Levant (Journal of the British School of Archaeology in Jerusalem)* (London, 1969ff.)
Lang	*Language. Journal of the Linguistic Society of America* (Baltimore, 1925ff.)
LCQ	*Lutheran Church Quarterly* (Gettysburg, PA; 1928-1949)
LCR	*Lutheran Church Review* (Philadelphia, 1882-1927)
Lěš	*Lěšonénu. Quarterly for the Study of the Hebrew Language and Cognate Subjects* לשוננו (Jerusalem, 1925ff.) [English Summaries from volume 30 onward]
LIST	*Lown Institute. Studies and Texts* (Brandeis University. Lown School of Near Eastern and Judaic Studies. Cambridge, MA; 1963ff.)
Listen	*Listening* (Dubuque, IA; 1965ff.) [Volume numbers start with "zero"]
LofS	*Life of the Spirit* (London, 1946-1964)
LQ	*The Quarterly Review of the Evangelical Lutheran Church* (Gettysburg, PA; 1871-1927; revived in1949ff.) [From 1878 on as: *The Lutheran Quarterly*]
LQHR	*London Quarterly and Holborn Review* (London, 1853-1968)
LS	*Louvain Studies* (Louvain, 1966ff.)
LSQ	*Lutheran Synod Quarterly* (Mankato, MN, 1960ff.) [Formerly *Clergy Bulletin* (Volume 1 of *LSQ* as *Clergy Bulletin,* Volume 20, #1 & #2)
LTJ	*Lutheran Theological Journal* (North Adelaide, South Australia, 1967ff.)
LTP	*Laval Theologique et Philosophique* (Quebec, 1945ff.)
LTQ	*Lexington Theological Quarterly* (Lexington, KY; 1966ff.)
LTR	*Literary and Theological Review* (New York; Boston, 1834-1839)
LTSB	*Lutheran Theological Seminary Bulletin* (Gettysburg, PA; 1921ff.)
LTSR	*Luther Theological Seminary Review* (St. Paul, MN; 1962ff.)
LWR	*The Lutheran World Review* (Philadelphia, 1948-1950)

M

Man *Man. A Monthly Record of Anthropological Science* (London,1901-1965; *N. S.,* 1966ff.) [Articles in original series referred to by *article* number not by *page* number - New Series subtitled: *The Journal of the Royal Anthropological Institute*]

ManSL *Manuscripta* (St. Louis, 1957ff.)

MB *Medelhavsmuseet Bulletin* (Stockholm, 1961ff.)

MC *The Modern Churchman* (Ludlow, England; 1911ff.)

McQ *McCormick Quarterly* (Chicago, 1947ff.) [Volumes 1-13 as: *McCormick Speaking*]

MCS *Manchester Cuneiform Studies* (Manchester, 1951-1964)

MDIÄA *Mitteilungen des deutsches Instituts für ägyptische Altertumskunde in Kairo* (Cairo, 1930ff.)

Mesop *Mesopotamia* (Torino, Italy, 1966ff.)

MH *The Modern Humanist* (Weston, MA; 1944-1962)

MHSB *The Mission House Seminary Bulletin* (Plymouth, WI; 1954-1962)

MI *Monthly Interpreter* (Edinburgh, 1884-1886)

MidS *Midstream (Council on Christian Unity)* (Indianapolis, 1961ff.)

Min *Ministry. A Quarterly Theological Review for South Africa* (Morija, Basutolan, 1960ff.)

Minos *Minos. Investigaciones y Materiales Para el Estudio de los Textos Paleocretenses Publicados Bajo la Dirección de Antonio Tovar y Emilio Peruzzi* (Salamanca, 1951ff.) [From Volume 4 on as: *Minos Revista de Filología Egea*]

MIO *Mitteilungen des Instituts für Orientforschung [Deutsche Akademie der Wissenschaften zu Berlin Institut für Orientforschung]* (Berlin, 1953ff.)

Miz *Mizraim. Journal of Papyrology, Egyptology, History of Ancient Laws, and their Relations to the Civilizations of Bible Lands* (New York, 1933-1938)

MJ *The Museum Journal. Pennsylvania University* (Philadelphia,1910-1935)

MMBR *The Monthly Magazine and British Register* (London, 1796-1843) [*1st Ser.,* 1796-1826, Volumes 1-60; *N.S.,* 1826-1838, Volumes 1-26; *3rd Ser.,* 1839-1843, Volumes 1-9, however, Volumes 7-9 are marked 95-97*[sic]*]

ModR	*The Modern Review* (London, 1880-1884)
Monist	*The Monist. An International Quarterly Journal of General Philosophical Inquiry* (Chicago; La Salle, IL; 1891ff.)
Mosaic	*Mosaic* (Cambridge, MA; 1960ff.)
MQ	*The Minister's Quarterly* (New York, 1945-1966)
MQR	*Methodist Quarterly Review (South)* (Louisville, Nashville, 1847-1861; 1879-1886; 1886-1930) [*3rd Ser.* as: *Southern Methodist Review;* Volume 52 (1926) misnumbered as 53; Volume 53 (1927) misnumbered as 54; and the volume for 1928 is also marked as 54]
MR	*Methodist Review* (New York, 1818-1931) [Volume 100 not published]
MTSB	*Moravian Theological Seminary Bulletin* (Bethlehem, PA; 1959-1970) [Volume for 1969 apparently not published]
MTSQB	*Meadville Theological School Quarterly Bulletin* (Meadville, PA;1906-1933) [From Volume 25 on as: *Meadville Journal*]
Muséon	*Le Muséon. Revue d'Études Orientales* (Louvain, 1882-1915;1930/32ff.)
MUSJ	*Mélanges de l'Université Saint-Joseph. Faculté orientale* (Beirut, 1906ff.) [Title varies]
Mwa-M	*Milla wa-Milla. The Australian Bulletin of Comparative Religion* (Parkville, Victoria, 1961ff.)

N

NB	*Blackfriars. A Monthly Magazine* (Oxford, 1920ff.) [From Volume 46 on as: *New Blackfriars*]
NBR	*North British Review* (Edinburgh, 1844-1871)
NCB	*New College Bulletin* (Edinburgh, 1964ff.)
NEAJT	*Northeast Asia Journal of Theology* (Kyoto, Japan, 1968ff.)
NEST	*The Near East School of Theology Quarterly* (Beirut, 1952ff.)
Nexus	*Nexus* (Boston, 1957ff.)
NGTT	*Nederduitse gereformeerde teologiese tydskrif* (Kaapstad, N.G., Kerk-Uitgewers, 1959ff.)
NOGG	*Nihon Orient Gakkai geppo* (Tokyo, 1955-1959) [Being the *Bulletin of the Society for Near Eastern Studies in Japan*-Continued as: *Oriento*]
NOP	*New Orient* (Prague, 1960-1968)

NPR	*The New Princeton Review* (New York, 1886-1888)
NQR	*Nashotah Quarterly Review* (Nashotah, WI; 1960ff.)
NT	*Novum Testamentum* (Leiden, 1955ff.)
NTS	*New Testament Studies* (Cambridge, England; 1954ff.)
NTT	*Nederlandsch Theologisch Tijdschrift* (Wageningen, 1946ff.)
NTTO	*Norsk Teologisk Tidsskrift* (Oslo, 1900ff.)
Numen	*Numen; International Review for the History of Religions* (Leiden, 1954ff.)
NW	*The New World. A Quarterly Review of Religion, Ethics and Theology* (Boston, 1892-1900)
NYR	*The New York Review. A Journal of The Ancient Faith and Modern Thought (St. John's Seminary)* (New York, 1905-1908)
NZJT	*New Zealand Journal of Theology* (Christchurch, 1931-1935)

O

OA	*Oriens Antiquus* (Rome, 1962ff.)
OBJ	*The Oriental and Biblical Journal* (Chicago, 1880-1881)
OC	*Open Court* (Chicago, 1887-1936)
ONTS	*The Hebrew Student* (Morgan Park, IL; New Haven; Hartford; 1881-1892) [Volumes 3-8 as: *The Old Testament Student;* Volume 9 onwards as: *The Old and New Testament Student*]
OOR	*Oriens: The Oriental Review* (Paris, 1926)
OQR	*The Oberlin Quarterly Review* (Oberlin, OH; 1845-1849)
Or	*Orientalia commentarii de rebus Assyri-Babylonicis, Arabicis, and Aegyptiacis, etc.* (Rome 1920-1930)
Or, N.S.	*Orientalia: commentarii, periodici de rebus orientis antiqui* (Rome, 1932ff.)
Oriens	*Oriens. Journal of the International Society of Oriental Research* (Leiden, 1948ff.)
Orient	*Orient. The Reports of the Society for Near Eastern Studies in Japan* (Tokyo, 1960ff.)
Orita	*Orita. Ibadan Journal of Religious Studies* (Ibadan, Nigeria, 1967ff.)
OrS	*Orientalia Suecana* (Uppsala, 1952ff.)
OSHTP	*Oxford Society of Historical Theology, Abstract of Proceedings* (Oxford, 1891-1968 [Through 1919 as: *Society of Historical Theology, Proceedings*]
Osiris	*Osiris* (Bruges, Belgium; 1936-1968) *[Subtitle varies]*
OTS	*Oudtestamentische Studiën* (Leiden, 1942ff.)

OTW	*Ou-Testamentiese Werkgemeenskap in Suid-Afrika, Proceedings of die* (Pretoria, 1958ff.) [Volume 1 in Volume 14 of: *Hervormde Teologiese Studies*]

P

P	*Preaching: A Journal of Homiletics* (Dubuque, IA; 1965ff.)
P&P	*Past and Present* (London, 1952ff.) *[Subtitle varies]*
PA	*Practical Anthropology* (Wheaton, IL; Eugene, OR; Tarrytown, NY; 1954ff.)
PAAJR	*Proceedings of the American Academy for Jewish Research* (Philadelphia, 1928ff.)
PAOS	*Proceedings of the American Oriental Society* (Baltimore, New Haven; 1842, 1846-50, 1852-1860) [After 1860 all proceedings are bound with *Journal*]
PAPA	*American Philological Association, Proceedings* (Hartford, Boston, 1896ff.) [*Transactions* as: *TAPA. Transactions* and *Proceedings* combine page numbers from volume 77 on]
PAPS	*Proceedings of the American Philosophical Society* (Philadelphia, 1838ff.)
PBA	*Proceedings of the British Academy* (London, 1903ff.)
PEFQS	*Palestine Exploration Fund Quarterly Statement* (London, 1869ff.) [From Volume 69 (1937) on as: *Palestine Exploration Quarterly*]
PEQ	*Palestine Exploration Quarterly* [See: *PEFQS*]
PER	*The Protestant Episcopal Review* (Fairfax, Co., VA; 1886-1900) [Volumes 1-5 as: *The Virginian Seminary Magazine*]
Person	*Personalist. An International Review of Philosophy, Religion and Literature* (Los Angeles, 1920ff.)
PF	*Philosophical Forum* (Boston, 1943-1957; *N.S.*, 1968ff.)
PHDS	*Perspectives. Harvard Divinity School* (Cambridge, MA; 1965-1967)
PIASH	*Proceedings of the Israel Academy of Sciences and Humanities* (Jerusalem, 1967ff.)
PIJSL	*Papers of the Institute of Jewish Studies, London* (Jerusalem,1964)
PJT	*Pacific Journal of Theology* (Western Samoa, 1961ff.)
PJTSA	*Jewish Theological Seminary Association, Proceedings* (New York, 1888-1902)

PP	*Perspective* (Pittsburgh, 1960ff.) [Volumes 1-8 as: *Pittsburgh Perspective*]
PQ	*The Presbyterian Quarterly* (New York, 1887-1904)
PQL	*The Preacher's Quarterly* (London, 1954-1969)
PQPR	*The Presbyterian Quarterly and Princeton Review* (New York, 1872-1877)
PQR	*Presbyterian Quarterly Review* (Philadelphia, 1852-1862)
PR	*Presbyterian Review* (New York, 1880-1889)
PRev	*The Biblical Repertory and Princeton Review* (Princeton, Philadelphia, New York, 1829-1884) [Volume 1 as: *The Biblical Repertory, New Series;* Volumes 2-8 as: *The Biblical Repertory and Theological Review*]
PRR	*Presbyterian and Reformed Review* (New York, Philadelphia, 1890-1902)
PSB	*The Princeton Seminary Bulletin* (Princeton, 1907ff.)
PSTJ	*Perkins School of Theology Journal* (Dallas, 1947ff.)
PTR	*Princeton Theological Review* (Princeton, 1903-1929)
PUNTPS	*Proceedings of the University of Newcastle upon Tyne Philosophical Society* (Newcastle upon Tyne, 1964-70)

Q

QCS	*Quarterly Christian Spectator* (New Haven, 1819-1838) *[1st Series* and *New Series* as: *Christian Spectator]*
QDAP	*The Quarterly of the Department of Antiquities in Palestine* (Jerusalem, 1931-1950)
QRL	*Quarterly Review* (London, 1809-1967)
QTMRP	*The Quarterly Theological Magazine, and Religious Repository* (Philadelphia, 1813-1814)

R

R&E	*[Baptist] Review and Expositor* (Louisville, 1904ff.)
R&S	*Religion and Society* (Bangalore, India, 1953ff.)
RAAO	*Revue d'Assyriologie et d'Archéologie Orientale* (Paris, 1886ff.)

RChR *The Reformed Church Review* (Mercersburg, PA; Chambersburg, PA; Philadelphia; 1849-1926) [Volumes 1-25 as: *Mercersburg Review;* Volumes 26-40 as: *Reformed Quarterly Review; 4th Series* on as: *Reformed Church Review*]

RCM *Reformed Church Magazine* (Reading, PA; 1893-1896) [Volume 3 as: *Reformed Church Historical Magazine*]

RdQ *Revue de Qumran* (Paris, 1958ff.)

RDSO *Rivista degli Studi Orientali* (Rome, 1907ff.)

RÉ *Revue Égyptologique* (Paris, 1880-1896; *N.S.*, 1919-1924)

RefmR *The Reformation Review* (Amsterdam, 1953ff.)

RefR *The Reformed Review. A Quarterly Journal of the Seminaries of the Reformed Church in America* (Holland, MI; New Brunswick, NJ; 1947ff.) [Volumes 1-9 as: *Western Seminary Bulletin*]

RÉg *Revue d'Égyptologie* (Paris, 1933ff.)

RelM *Religion in the Making* (Lakeland, FL; 1940-1943)

Resp *Response—in worship—Music—The arts* (St. Paul, 1959ff.)

RestQ *Restoration Quarterly* (Austin, TX; Abeline, TX; 1957ff.)

RFEASB *The Hebrew University / Jerusalem: Department of Archaeology. Louis M. Rabinowitz Fund for the Exploration of Ancient Synagogues, Bulletin* (Jerusalem, 1949-1960)

RHA *Revue Hittite et Asianique* (Paris, 1930ff.)

RIDA *Revue internationale des droits de l'antiquité* (Brussels, 1948ff.)

RJ *Res Judicatae. The Journal of the Law Students' Society of Victoria* (Melbourne, 1935-1957)

RL *Religion in Life* (New York, 1932ff.)

RO *Rocznik Orjentalistyczny. (Wydaje Polskie towarzystwo orjentalisyczne)* (Kraków, Warsaw, 1914ff.)

RP *Records of the Past* (Washington, DC; 1902-1914)

RR *Review of Religion* (New York, 1936-1958)

RS *Religious Studies* (London, 1965ff.)

RTP *Review of Theology and Philosophy* (Edinburgh, 1905-1915)

RTR *Recueil de travaux relatifs à la philologie et à l'archéologie egyptiennes et assyriennes* (Paris, 1870-1923)

RTRM *The Reformed Theological Review* (Melbourne, 1941ff.)

S

SAENJ	*Seminar. An Annual Extraordinary Number of the Jurist* (Washington, DC; 1943-1956)
SBAP	*Society of Biblical Archæology, Proceedings* (London, 1878-1918)
SBAT	*Society of Biblical Archæology, Transactions* (London, 1872-1893)
SBE	*Studia Biblica et Ecclesiastica* (Oxford, 1885-1903) Volume 1 as: *Studia Biblica*]
SBFLA	*Studii (Studium) Biblici Franciscani. Liber Annuus* (Jerusalem, 1950ff.)
SBLP	*Society of Biblical Literature & Exegesis, Proceedings* (Baltimore, 1880)
SBO	*Studia Biblica et Orientalia* (Rome 1959) [Being Volumes 10-12 respectively of *Analecta Biblica. Investigationes Scientificae in Res Biblicas*]
SBSB	*Society for Biblical Studies Bulletin* (Madras, India, 1964ff.)
SCO	*Studi Classici e Orientali* (Pisa, 1951ff.)
Scotist	*The Scotist* (Teutopolis, IL; 1939-1967)
SCR	*Studies in Comparative Religion* (Bedfont, Middlesex, England, 1967ff.)
Scrip	*Scripture. The Quarterly of the Catholic Biblical Association* (London, 1944-1968)
SE	*Study Encounter* (Geneva, 1965ff.)
SEÅ	*Svensk Exegetisk Årsbok* (Uppsala-Lund, 1936ff.)
SEAJT	*South East Journal of Theology* (Singapore, 1959ff.)
Sefunim	*Sefunim (Bulletin)* סינים [היפה] (Haifa, 1966-1968)
SGEI	*Studies in the Geography of Eretz-Israel* מחקרים בגיאוגרפיה של ארץ־ישראל (Jerusalem, 1959ff.) [English summaries in Volumes 1-3 only; continuing the *Bulletin of the Israel Exploration Society (Yediot)*]
SH	*Scripta Hierosolymitana* (Jerusalem, 1954ff.)
Shekel	*The Shekel* (New York, 1968ff.)
SIR	*Smithsonian Institute Annual Report of the Board of Regents* (Washington, DC; 1846-1964; becomes: *Smithsonian Year* from 1965 on]
SJH	*Seminary Journal* (Hamilton, NY; 1892)
SJT	*Scottish Journal of Theology* (Edinburgh, 1947ff.)
SL	*Studia Liturgica. An International Ecumenical Quarterly for Liturgical Research and Renewal* (Rotterdam, 1962ff.)

SLBR *Sierra Leone Bulletin of Religion* (Freetown, Sierra Leone; 1959-1966)
SMR *Studia Montes Regii* (Montreal, 1958-1967)
SMSDR *Studi e Materiali di Storia Delle Religioni* (Rome, Bologna, 1925ff.
SO *Studia Orientalia* (Helsinki, 1925ff.)
SOOG *Studi Orientalistici in Onore di Giorgio Levi Della Vida* (Rome, 1956)
Sophia *Sophia. A Journal for Discussion in Philosophical Theology* (Parkville, N.S.W., Australia, 1962ff.)
SP *Spirit of the Pilgrims* (Boston, 1828-1833)
SPR *Southern Presbyterian Review* (Columbia, SC; 1847-1885)
SQ/E *The Shane Quarterly* (Indianapolis, 1940ff.) [From Volume 17 on as: *Encounter*]
SR *The Seminary Review* (Cincinnati, 1954ff.)
SRL *The Scottish Review* (London, Edinburgh, 1882-1900; 1914-1920)
SS *Seminary Studies of the Athenaeum of Ohio* (Cincinnati, 1926-1968) [Volumes 1-15 as: *Seminary Studies*]
SSO *Studia Semitica et Orientalia* (Glasgow, 1920, 1945)
SSR *Studi Semitici* (Rome, 1958ff.)
ST *Studia Theologica* (Lund, 1947ff.)
StEv *Studia Evangelica* (Berlin, 1959ff.) [Being miscellaneous volumes of: *Text und Untersuchungen zur Geschichte der altchristlichen Literatur,* beginning with Volume 73]
StLJ *The Saint Luke's Journal* (Sewanee, TN; 1957ff.) [Volume 1, #1 as: *St. Luke's Journal of Theology*]
StMR *St. Marks Review: An Anglican Quarterly* (Canberra, A.C.T., Australia, 1955ff.)
StP *Studia Patristica* (Berlin, 1957ff.) [Being miscellaneous volumes of: *Text und Untersuchungen zur Geschichte der altchristlichen Literatur,* beginning with Volume 63]
StVTQ *St. Vladimir's Theological Quarterly* (Crestwood, NY; 1952ff. [Volumes 1-4 as: *St. Vladimir's Seminary Quarterly*]
Sumer *Sumer. A Journal of Archaeology in Iraq* (Bagdad, 1945ff.)
SWJT *Southwestern Journal of Theology* (Fort Worth, 1917-1924; *N.S.*, 1950ff.)
Syria *Syria, revue d'art oriental et d'archéologie* (Paris, 1920ff.)

T

T&C	*Theology and the Church / SÎN-HÁK kap kàu-Hōe (Tainan Theological College)* (Tainan, Formosa, 1957ff.)
T&L	*Theology and Life* (Lancaster, PA; 1958-1966)
TAD	*Türk tarih, arkeologya ve etnoğrafya dergisi* (Istanbul, 1933-1949; continued as: *Türk arkeoloji Dergisi,* (Ankara, 1956ff.)
TAPA	*American Philological Society, Transactions* (See: *PAPA*)
TAPS	*Transactions of the American Philosophical Society* (Philadelphia, 1789-1804; *N.S.*, 1818ff.)
Tarbiz	*Tarbiz. A quarterly review of the humanities;* תרביץ רעזן למדעי היהדות. שנת (Jerusalem, 1929ff.) [English Summaries from Volume 24 on only]
TB	*Tyndale Bulletin* (London, 1956ff.) [Numbers 1-16 as: *Tyndale House Bulletin*]
TBMDC	*Theological Bulletin: McMaster Divinity College* (Hamilton, Ontario, 1967ff.)
TE	*Theological Education* (Dayton, 1964ff.)
Tem	*Temenos. Studies in Comparative Religion* (Helsinki, 1965ff.)
TEP	*Theologica Evangelica. Journal of the Faculty of Theology, University of South Africa* (Pretoria, 1968ff.)
Text	*Textus. Annual of the Hebrew University Bible Project* (Jerusalem, 1960ff.)
TF	*Theological Forum* (Minneapolis, 1929-1935)
TFUQ	*Thought. A Quarterly of the Sciences and Letters* (New York, 1926ff.) [From Volume 15 on as: *Thought. Fordham University Quarterly*]
ThE	*Theological Eclectic* (Cincinnati; New York, 1864-1871)
Them	*Themelios, International Fellowship of Evangelical Students* (Fresno, CA; 1962ff.)
Theo	*Theology; A Journal of Historic Christianity* (London, 1920ff.)
ThSt	*Theological Studies* (New York; Woodstock, MD; 1940ff.)
TLJ	*Theological and Literary Journal* (New York, 1848-1861)
TM	*Theological Monthly* (St. Louis, 1921-1929)
TML	*The Theological Monthly* (London, 1889-1891)
TPS	*Transactions of the Philological Society* (London, 1842ff.) [Volumes 1-6 as: *Proceedings*]
TQ	*Theological Quarterly* (St. Louis, 1897-1920)

Tr — *Traditio. Studies in Ancient and Medieval History, Thought and Religion* (New York, 1943ff.)
Trad — *Tradition, A Journal of Orthodox Jewish Thought* (New York, 1958ff.)
TRep — *Theological Repository* (London, 1769-1788)
TRFCCQ — *Theological Review and Free Church College Quarterly* (Edinburgh, 1886-1890)
TRGR — *The Theological Review and General Repository of Religious and Moral Information, Published Quarterly* (Baltimore, 1822)
TRL — *Theological Review: A Quarterly Journal of Religious Thought and Life* (London, 1864-1879)
TT — *Theology Today* (Lansdown, PA; 1944ff.)
TTCA — *Trinity Theological College Annual* (Singapore, 1964-1969) [Volume 5 apparently never published]
TTD — *Teologisk Tidsskrift* (Decorah, IA; 1899-1907)
TTKB — *Türk Tarih Kurumu Belleten* (Ankara, 1937ff.)
TTKF — *Tidskrift för teologi och kyrkiga frågor (The Augustana Theological Quarterly)* (Rock Island, IL; 1899-1917)
TTL — *Theologisch Tijdschrift* (Leiden, 1867-1919) [English articles from Volume 45 on only]
TTM — *Teologisk Tidsskrift* (Minneapolis, 1917-1928)
TUSR — *Trinity University Studies in Religion* (San Antonio, 1950ff.)
TZ — *Theologische Zeitschrift* (Basel, 1945ff.)
TZDES — *Theologische Zeitschrift (Deutsche Evangelische Synode des Westens, North America)* (St. Louis, 1873-1934) [Continued from Volumes 22 through 26 as: *Magazin für Evangel. Theologie und Kirche;* and from Volume 27 on as: *Theological Magazine*]
TZTM — *Theologische Zeitblätter, Theological Magazine* (Columbus,1911-1919)

U

UC — *The Unitarian Christian* (Boston, 1947ff.) [Volumes 1-4 as: *Our Faith*]
UCPSP — *University of California Publications in Semitic Philology* (Berkeley, 1907ff.)
UF — *Ugarit-Forschungen. Internationales Jahrbuch für die Altertumskunde Syrien-Palästinas* (Neukirchen, West Germany; 1969ff.)
ULBIA — *University of London. Bulletin of the Institute of Archaeology* (London, 1958ff.)

UMB	*The University Museum Bulletin (University of Pennsylvania* (Philadelphia, 1930-1958)
UMMAAP	*University of Michigan. Museum of Anthropology. Anthropological Papers* (Ann Arbor, 1949ff.)
UnionR	*The Union Review* (New York, 1939-1945)
UPQR	*The United Presbyterian Quarterly Review* (Pittsburgh, 1860-1861)
UQGR	*Universalist Quarterly and General Review* (Boston, 1844-1891)
URRM	*The Unitarian Review and Religious Magazine* (Boston, 1873-1891)
USQR	*Union Seminary Quarterly Review* (New York, 1945ff.)
USR	*Union Seminary Review* (Hampton-Sidney, VA; Richmond; 1890-1946) [Volumes 1-23 as: *Union Seminary Magazine*]
UTSB	*United Theological Seminary Bulletin* (Dayton, 1905ff.) [Including: *The Bulletin of the Evangelical School of Theology; Bulletin of the Union Biblical Seminary,* later, *Bonebrake Theological Bulletin*]
UUÅ	*Uppsala Universitets Årsskrift* (Uppsala, 1861-1960)

V

VC	*Virgiliae Christianae: A Review of Early Christian Life and Language* (Amsterdam, 1947ff.)
VDETF	*Deutsche Vierteljahrsschrift für englisch-theologische Forschung und Kritik / herausgegeben von M. Heidenheim* (Leipzig, Zurich, 1861-1865) [Continued as: *Vierteljahrsschrift für deutsch – englisch- theologische Forschung und Kritik...* 1866-1873]
VDI	*Vestnik Drevnei Istoriĭ. Journal of Ancient History* (Moscow, 1946ff.) [English summaries from 1967 on only]
VDR	*Koinonia* (Nashville, 1957-1968) [Continued as: *Vanderbilt Divinity Review,* 1969-1971]
VE	*Vox Evangelica. Biblical and Historical Essays by the Members of the Faculty of the London Bible College* (London, 1962ff.)
Voice	*The Voice* (St. Paul, 1958-1960) [Subtitle varies]
VR	*Vox Reformata* (Geelong, Victoria, Australia, 1962ff.)
VT	*Vetus Testamentum* (Leiden, 1951ff.)
VTS	*Vetus Testamentum, Supplements* (Leiden, 1953ff.)

W

Way	*The Way. A Quarterly Review of Christian Spirituality* (London, 1961ff.)
WBHDN	*The Wittenberg Bulletin (Hamma Digest Number)* (Springfield, OH; 1903ff.) [Volumes 40-60 (1943-1963) only contain *Hamma Digest Numbers*]
WesTJ	*Wesleyan Theological Journal. Bulletin of the Wesleyan Theological Society* (Lakeville, IN; 1966ff.)
WLQ	*Wisconsin Lutheran Quarterly* (Wauwatosa, WI; Milwaukee;1904ff.) [Also entitled: *Theologische Quartalschrift*]
WO	*Die Welt des Orients . Wissenschaftliche Beiträge zur Kunde des Morgenlandes* (Göttingen, 1947ff.)
Word	*Word: Journal of the Linguistic Circle of New York* (New York, 1945ff.)
WR	*The Westminster Review* (London, New York, 1824-1914)
WSQ	*Wartburg Seminary Quarterly* (Dubuque, IA; 1937-1960) [Volumes 1-9, #1 as: *Quarterly of the Wartburg Seminary Association*]
WSR	*Wesleyan Studies in Religion* (Buckhannon,WV; 1960-1970) [Volumes 53-62 only*[sic]*]
WTJ	*Westminster Theological Journal* (Philadelphia, 1938ff.)
WW	*Western Watch* (Pittsburgh, 1950-1959) [Superseded by: *Pittsburgh Perspective*]
WZKM	*Wiener Zeitschrift für die Kunde des Morgenlandes* (Vienna, 1886ff.)

Y

YCCAR	*Yearbook of the Central Conference of American Rabbis* (Cincinnati, 1890ff.)
YCS	*Yale Classical Studies* (New Haven, 1928ff.)
YDQ	*Yale Divinity Quarterly* (New Haven, 1904ff.) [Volumes 30-62 as: *Yale Divinity News,* continued as: *Reflections*]
YR	*The Yavneh Review. A Religious Jewish Collegiate Magazine* (New York, 1961ff.) [Volume 2 never published]

Z

Z — *Zygon. Journal of Religion and Science* (Chicago, 1966ff.)

ZA — *Zeitschrift für Assyriologie und verwandte Gebiete* [Volumes 45 on as: *Zeitschrift für Assyriologie und vorderasiatische Archäologie]* (Leipzig, Strassburg, Berlin, 1886ff.)

ZÄS — *Zeitschrift für ägyptische Sprache und Altertumskunde* (Leipzig, Berlin, 1863ff.)

ZAW — *Zeitschrift für die alttestamentliche Wissenschaft* (Giessen, Berlin, 1881ff.)

ZDMG — *Zeitschrift der Deutschen Morgenländischen Gesellschaft* (Leipzig, Wiesbaden, 1847ff.)

ZDPV — *Zeitschrift des Deutschen Palästina-Vereins* (Leipzig, Wiesbaden, 1878ff.) [English articles from Volume 82 on only]

Zion — Zion. *A Quarterly for Research in Jewish History, New Series* ציון סדרה חדשה רבעון לחקר תולדוה ישראל (Jerusalem, 1935ff.) [English summaries from Volume 3 on only]

ZK — *Zeitschrift für Keilschriftforschung* (Leipzig, 1884-1885)

ZNW — *Zeitschrift für die neutestamentliche Wissenschaft und die Kunde des Urchristentums (...Kunde der älteren Kirche,* 1921—*)* (Giessen, Berlin, 1900ff.)

ZS — *Zeitschrift für Semitistik und verwandte Gebiete* (Leipzig, 1922-1935)

§168 2.5.5.7 Alphabetical Listing of Specific Cities and Places in the Near East, outside of Palestine - Geographical Studies (Alphabetical Listing)

A

Abana

*William Wright, "The Rivers of Damascus: Abana and Pharpar," *Exp, 5th Ser.*, 4 (1896) 290-297.

Abban

*Donald J. Wiseman, "Abban and Alalah," *JCS* 12 (1958) 124-129.

Abkhasia

*Yu. N. Voronov, "On the Localisation of the Coraxi and Their Fortress in Abkhasia," *VDI* (1968) #3, 142.

Aboo-habba

*†Theo. G. Pinches, "Remarks upon the Recent Discoveries of Mr. Rassam at Aboo-habba," *SBAP* 3 (1880-81) 109-111.

Abri Zumoffen

Dorothy Garrod and Diana Kirkbride, "Excavation of the Abri Zumoffen, a Paleolithic Rock-Shelter near Adlun, South Lebanon, 1958," *BMB* 16 (1961) 1-47.

*F. E. Zeuner, with the cooperation of I. W. Cornwall and Diana Kirkbride, "The Shore-Line Chronology of the Palaeolithic of Abri Zumoffen, Adlun Caves, Lebanon," *BMB* 16 (1961) 49-60.

Abu Dhabi

P. V. Glob, "Reconnaissance in Abu Dhabi," *Kuml* (1958) 164-165.

Tell Abu Huwam

Gus W. Van Beek, "The Date of Tell Abu Huwam, Stratum III," *BASOR* #138 (1955) 34-38.

Abu Shahrein

*J. E. Taylor, "Notes on Abu Shahrein and Tel el Lahm," *JRAS* (1855) 404-415.

Abusir

A. Wiedemann, "The Excavations at Abusir, Egypt," *SIR* (1903) 669-680.

Ludwig Borchard, "Excavations of the German Oriental Society Near Abusir," *RP* 3 (1904) 195-212. *(Trans. by Karl Hau.)*

Abydos

*F. Legge, "Recent Discoveries at Abydos and Negadah," *SBAP* 21 (1899) 183-193.

W. M. Flinders Petrie, "Excavations at Abydos," *Man* 2 (1902) #64.

W. M. Flinders Petrie, "Excavations at Abydos," *AAOJ* 25 (1903) 362-363.

*W. M. Flinders Petrie, "The Ten Temples of Abydos," *AAOJ* 26 (1904) 273-280.

Anonymous, "Discoveries at Abydos," *RP* 7 (1908) 307.

John Garstang, "Excavations at Abydos, 1909. Preliminary Description of the Principal Finds," *AAA* 2 (1909) 125-129.

*Wallace N. Stearns, "Deir el-Bahari and Abydos," *AJA* 16 (1912) 108.

Edouard Naville, "Egyptian Exploration Fund. The Excavations at Abydos," *AEE* 1 (1914) 103-104.

Edouard Naville, "Abydos," *JEA* 1 (1914) 2-8.

Abydos concluded

T. Eric Peet, "The Year's Work at Abydos," *JEA* 1 (1914) 37-39.

W. Leonard S. Loat, "The Ibis Cemetery at Abydos," *JEA* 1 (1914) 40.

*Edouard Naville, "Excavations at Abydos: The Great Pool and Tomb of Osiris," *JEA* 1 (1914) 159-167.

Thomas Wittemore, "The Ibis Cemetery at Abydos: 1914," *JEA* 1 (1914) 248-249.

Edouard Naville, "Excavations at Abydos," *SIR* (1914) 579-585.

W. Leonard S. Loat, "A Sixth Dynasty Cemetery at Abydos," *JEA* 9 (1923) 161-163.

H[enri] Frankfort, "Preliminary Report of the Expedition to Abydos 1925-6," *JEA* 12 (1926) 157-165.

H[enri] Frankfort, "The Cemeteries of Abydos: Work of the Season 1925-26," *JEA* 16 (1930) 213-219.

Labib Habachi, "A First Dynasty Cemetery at Abydos," *ASAE* 39 (1939) 767-774.

*Barry J. Kemp, "Abydos and the Royal Tombs of the First Dynasty," *JEA* 52 (1966) 13-22.

David O'Connor, "Abydos: A Preliminary Report of the Pennsylvania-Yale Expedition, 1967," *Exped* 10 (1967-68) #1, 10-23.

David O'Connor, "Abydos and the University Museum: 1898-1969," *Exped* 12 (1969-70) #1, 28-39.

Abyssinia

†Anonymous, "The Abyssinian Expedition," *QRL* 123 (1867) 510-533.

E. M. Clerke, "Abyssinia and its People," *DR, 3rd Ser.,* 12 (1884) 316-345. *[Original numbering as Vol. 95]*

Enno Littmann, "Preliminary Report of the Princeton University Expedition to Abyssinia," *ZA* 20 (1907) 151-182. (Contributions by R. Sundsfröm)

Abyssinia concluded

Samuel A. B. Mercer, "An Expedition to Abyssinia," *CJRT* 7 (1930) 371-375.

Accad see: Akkad

Acemhöyük

Nimet Özgüç, "Excavations at Acemhöyük," *A(A)* 10 (1966) 29-52.

*Nimet Özgüç, "New Light on the Dating of the Karum of Kanish and of Acemhöyük near Akeseray," *AJA* 72 (1968) 318-320.

Achaia

*Emily Townsend Vermeule, "The Mycenaeans in Achaia," *AJA* 62 (1958) 227.

Achmetha

*William F. Ainsworth, "The Achmethas or Ecbatanas of Western Asia," *SBAP* 15 (1892-93) 425-432.

Actium

*Colin N. Edmonson, "Augustus, Actium and Nicopolis," *AJA* 73 (1969) 235.

The Aegean

*C. Leonard Woolley, "Asia Minor, Syria and the Aegean," *AAA* 9 (1922) 41-56.

*John L. Myres, "The Geographical Background of the Aegean Civilization," *ArOr* 17 (1949) Part 2, 196-204.

A. J. B. Wace, "Aegean Prehistory: a Review," *Antiq* 32 (1958) 30-34. *(Review)*

The Aegean concluded

*James Mellaart, "The End of the Early Bronze Age in Anatolia and the Aegean," *AJA* 62 (1958) 9-33.

Aeolus

E. D. Phillips, "The Isle of Aeolus," *Antiq* 30 (1956) 203-208.

Africa

*H. Schlichter, "The African and Asiatic Coasts of the Indian Ocean in Antiquity," *IAQR, 2nd Ser.,* 2 (1891) 305-314.

*George A. Barton, "The Origins of Civilization in Africa and Mesopotamia, their Relative Antiquity and Interplay," *PAPS* 68 (1929) 303-312.

*G. D. Hornblower, "Prehistoric Egypt and North Africa," *Man* 30 (1930) #34.

S. H. Hooke, "Africa in the Bible," *GBT* 1 (1957-61) #2, 5-7.

*E. S. Higgs and D. R. Brothwell, "North Africa and Mount Carmel: Recent Developments," *Man* 61 (1961) #166.

Agathyrsi

*Robert Gordon Latham, "On the Name and Nation of the Dacian King Decebalus, with Notices of the Agathyrsi and Alani," *TPS* (1854) 109-113.

Aghaya Kaleh

H[ans] H[enning] von der Osten, "Aghaya Kaleh," *AJSL* 45 (1928-29) 275-278.

Aghrōpōs

†Wm. Wright, "The name Jirbās, Jerābees, and Jerāblus," *SBAP* 3 (1880-81) 58-59. *[Aghrōpōs]*

Agrigentum

*Niels Breitenstein, "Analacta Acragantina," *AA* 16 (1945) 113-153. *[Agrigentum]*

Ahlatli Tepecik

David Gordon Mitten and Gülden Yüğrüm, "Excavation At Ahlatli Tepecik The Gygean Lake, 1968," *TAD* 17 (1968) #1, 125-131.

Tell Ahmur

*Fritz Neugass, "Notes and Comments. Recent Excavations in Tello, Susa, and Syria," *A&A* 32 (1931) 137-138. [Til-Barsib (Tell Ahmur), pp. 1237-138]

Aï Khanum

Paul Bernard, "Aï Khanum on the Oxus: A Hellenistic City in Central Asia," *PBA* 53 (1967) 71-95.

Aintab

Anonymous, "Excavations Near Aintab," *RP* 11 (1912) 147.

Akabah

B. Weld, "Akabah: Its Position in Fact and History," *IER, 4th Ser.,* 22 (1907) 289-303.

Akkad

*[Paul Carus], "Accad and the Early Semites," *OC* 9 (1895) 4651-4654.

*J. Dyneley Prince, "Note on Akkad," *JBL* 25 (1906) 55-57.

*W[illiam] F[oxwell] Albright, "A Babylonian Geographical Treatise on Sargon of Akkad's Empire," *JAOS* 45 (1925) 193-245.

Akkad concluded

E[phraim] A. Speiser, "Some Factors in the Collapse of Akkad," *JAOS* 72 (1952) 97-101.

Robert M. Adams, "Settlements in Ancient Akkad," *Arch* 10 (1957) 270-273.

Akkuzulu Köy

Çetin Anlağan, "Akkuzulu Tumulus," *A(A)* 12 (1968) 7.

Akropotamos

George E. Mylonas, "The Site of Akropotamos and the Neolithic Period of Macedonia," *AJA* 45 (1941) 557-576.

Aksha

*Jean Vercoutter, "Preliminary Report of the Excavations at Aksha by the Franco-Argentine Archaeological Expedition, 1961," *Kush* 10 (1962) 109-117. [Notes relating to Inscriptions found at Aksha, by A. Rosenvasser, pp. 116-117]

*J[ean] Vercoutter, "Excavations at Aksha, September 1961-January 1962," *Kush* 11 (1963) 131-140. [Addenda (concerning inscriptions mentioned in this Report) by A. Rosenvasser, p. 140]

A. Rosenvasser, "Preliminary Report on the Excavations at Aksha by the Franco-Argentine Expedition, 1962-63," *Kush* 12 (1964) 96-101.

Aktab

Arno Poebel, "The City Aktab," *JAOS* 57 (1937) 359-367.

Alaca Höyök

Hamit Zübeyr Koşay, "The Results of the Excavations Made on behalf of the Turkish Historical Society at Alaca Höyük in the Summer of 1936," *TTKB* 1 (1937) 534-542.

Alahan

Michael R. E. Gough, "Report on Archaeological Work Carried out at Alahan in 1957," *TAD* 8 (1958) #2, 6-7.

Michael [R. E.] Gough, "Excavation at Alahan 1967," *TAD* 16 (1967) #1, 95-100.

Alalaḫ (Alalakh)

*Leonard Woolley, "North Syria as a Cultural Link in the Ancient World. *The Huxley Memorial Lecture for* 1942," *JRAI* 72 (1942) 9-18. [Alalakh (1780-1187 B.C.), pp. 9-17]

*Donald J. Wiseman, "Abban and Alalah," *JCS* 12 (1958) 124-129.

D[onald] J. Wiseman, "Some Aspects of Babylonian Influence at Alalaḫ," *Syria* 39 (1962) 180-187.

Alani

*Robert Gordon Latham, "On the Name and Nation of the Dacian King Decebalus, with Notices of the Agathyrsi and Alani," *TPS* (1854) 109-113.

Alashiya

*G. A. Wainwright, "Alashia = Alasa; and Asy," *Klio* 14 (1914-15) 1-36.

*H. R. Hall, "The Land of Alashiya and the Relation of Egypt and Cyprus Under the Empire. (1500-1100 B.C.)," *JMUEOS* #2 (1912-13) 33-45.

Alba Fucens

Fernand de Visscher, "Alba Fucens: A Roman Colony," *Arch* 12 (1959) 123-132.

Alexandria

Joseph Offord, "Alexandrian Archaeology," *AEE* 2 (1915) 57-58.

Alexandria concluded

*F. G. Vial, "What we owe to Alexandria," *IJA* #44 (1916) 7-9.

H. I. Bell, "Alexandria," *JEA* 13 (1927) 171-184.

E. Badian, "Ancient Alexandria," *HT* 10 (1962) 779-787.

*C. Bradford Welles, "The Discovery of Sarapis and the Foundation of Alexandria," *HJAH* 11 (1962) 271-298.

*C. Bradford Welles, "Sarapis and Alexandria, an Addendum," *HJAH* 12 (1963) 512.

Ali Kosh

Franke Hole and Kent V. Flannery, "Excavations at Ali Kosh, Iran, 1961," *IA* 2 (1962) 97-148.

Alishar Hüyük

Hans Henning von der Osten, "The Excavations at Alishar hüyük," *RHA* 1 (1930-32) 250-253.

Al-Mada'in

J. M. Fiey, "Topography of Al-Mada'in (Seleucia-Ctesphon area)," *Sumer* 23 (1967) 3-38.

Al Mina

*Sidney Smith, "The Greek Trade at Al Mina: A Footnote to Oriental History," *AJ* 22 (1942) 87-112.

*John Boardman, "Al Mina and Greek Chronology," *HJAH* 7 (1958) 250.

Altintepe

*Tahsin Özgüç, "Urartu and Altintepe," *Arch* 22 (1969) 256-263.

ʿAmārah West

*H. W. Fairman, "Preliminary Report on the Excavations at Sesebi (Sudla) and ʿAmārah West, Anglo-Egyptian Sudan, 1937-8," *JEA* 24 (1938) 151-156.

H. W. Fairman, "Preliminary Report on the Excavations at Amarah West, Anglo-Egyptian Sudan, 1938-9," *JEA* 25 (1939) 139-144.

H. W. Fairman, "Preliminary Report on the Excavations at Amarah West, Anglo-Egyptian Sudan, 1947-48," *JEA* 34 (1948) 3-11.

P. L. Shinnie, "Preliminary Report on the Excavations at ʿAmārah West, 1948-49 and 1949-50," *JEA* 37 (1951) 5-11.

El Amrah

D. Randall-MacIver, "A Prehistoric Cemetery at El Amrah in Egypt," *Man* 1 (1901) #40.

Tell el-Amarna

A. Crawford, "Tel el-Amarna, the Great Discovery," *PER* 5 (1891-92) 167-178.

Ludwig Borchardt, "Excavations at Tell el-Amarna, Egypt, in 1913-1914," *SIR* (1915) 445-457.

G[eorge] W. Gilmore, "The Excavations in Tel-el-Amrana," *HR* 72 (1916) 483-484.

J. G. Maxwell, "Correspondence: Tel El-Amarna," *IAQR* 16 (1920) 688-689.

H. R. Hall, "The Excavations at Tell El-Amarna," *IAQR* 17 (1921) 539-541.

T. Eric Peet, "Excavations at Tell el-Amarna: A Preliminary Report," *JEA* 7 (1921) 169-185.

T. Eric Peet, "Excavation at Tell el-Amarna," *Man* 21 (1921) #84.

H. R. Hall, "The Egyptian Exploration Society's Excavations at El-Amarna, 1921-1922," *IAQR* 18 (1922) 343-344.

Tell el-Amarna concluded

C. Leonard Woolley, "Excavations at Tell el-Amarna," *JEA* 8 (1922) 48-82.

F. G. Newton, "Excavations at El-ʿAmarnah, 1923-24," *JEA* 10 (1924) 289-305.

*J. Walter Johnshoy, "Studies in Biblical Archaeology," *TTM* 9 (1925-26) 116-135. [Egypt (Tell-el-Amarna), pp. 117-121]

T. Whittemore, "The Excavations at El-ʿAmarnah, Season 1924-5," *JEA* 12 (1926) 3-12.

H[enri] Frankfort, "Preliminary Report on the Excavations at Tel el-ʿAmarnah, 1926-7," *JEA* 13 (1927) 209-218.

H[enri] Frankfort, "Preliminary Report on the Excavations at El-ʿAmarnah, 1928-29," *JEA* 15 (1929) 143-149.

J. D. S. Pendlebury, "Preliminary Report of Excavations at Tell el-ʿAmarnah, 1930-1," *JEA* 17 (1931) 233-244.

J. D. S. Pendlebury, "Preliminary Report of Excavations at Tell el-ʿAmarnah, 1931-2," *JEA* 18 (1932) 143-149.

*E[dith] M.Guest, "Pathology and Art at El Amarna," *AEE* 18 (1933) 81-88.

J. D. S. Pendlebury, "Preliminary Report of Excavations at Tell el-ʿAmarnah, 1932-1933," *JEA* 19 (1933) 113-118.

J. D. S. Pendlebury, "Excavations at Tell el Amarna. 1932-33," *MDIAÄ* 4 (1933) 37.

J. D. S. Pendlebury, "Excavations at Tell el Amarna. Preliminary Report for the Seasons 1933-4," *JEA* 20 (1934) 129-136.

J. D. S. Pendlebury, "Preliminary Report of Excavations at Tell el-ʿAmarnah, 1934-1935," *JEA* 21 (1935) 129-135.

H. W. Fairman, "Topographical Notes on the Central City, Tell El-ʿAmarnah," *JEA* 21 (1935) 136-139.

*Jean Capart, "Tell el Amarna; the Name," *Man* 35 (1935) #216.

J. D. S. Pendlebury, "Summary Report on the Excavations at Tell El-ʿAmarnah, 1935-1936," *JEA* 22 (1936) 194-198.

al-ʿAmuq

*Henri de Contenson, "New Correlations Between Ras Shamra and al-ʿAmuq," *BASOR* #172 (1963) 35-40.

Amurru

*Albert T. Clay, "The Early Civilization of Amurru—The Land of the Amorites— Showing Amorite Influence on Biblical Literature," *JTVI* 57 (1925) 88-104. (Discussion and Communications, by T. G. Pinches, pp. 104-105; Theodore Roberts, p. 106; William Dale, pp. 106-107; W. Hoste, pp. 107-108; W. E. Leslie, pp. 108-109; G. B. Mitchell, pp. 109-111)

*H. M. Du Bose, "Amurru and the Genesis Stories," *BR* 11 (1926) 508-522.

Anaploga

*Patricia Lawrence, "The Protocorinthian and Corinthian Well at Anaploga," *AJA* 69 (1965) 170-171.

Anatolia

H[ans] H[enning] von der Osten, "Ancient Sites and Ruins in Central Anatolia," *AJA* 34 (1930) 55.

Winifred Lamb, "New Developments in Early Anatolian Archaeology," *Iraq* 11 (1949) 188-203.

*Samuel Noah Kramer, "A 'Fulbright' in Turkey," *UMB* 17 (1952-53) #2, 5-56. [Anatolian Archaeology: Two Outstanding Turkish Excavations, pp. 43-56]

*Albrecht Goetze, "The Linguistic Continuity of Anatolia as Shown by its Proper Names," *JCS* 8 (1954) 74-81.

C. A. Burney, "Northern Anatolia before Classical Times," *AS* 6 (1956) 179-203.

*James Mellaart, "The End of the Early Bronze Age in Anatolia and the Aegean," *AJA* 62 (1958) 9-33.

Anatolia concluded

C. A. Burney, "Eastern Anatolia in the Chalcolithic and Early Bronze Age," *AS* 8 (1958) 157-209.

*Peter J. Parr, "Palestine and Anatolia: A Further Note," *ULBIA* 1 (1958) 21-23.

Hans G. Guterbock, "The North-Central Area of Hittite Anatolia," *JNES* 20 (1961) 85-97.

‡Enver Bostancı, "Researches in South-East Anatolia. The Chellean and Acheulean Industry of Dülük and Kartal," *A(A)* 6 (1961-62) 111-162. [Bibliography, pp. 134-136]

Tahsin Özgüç, "Early Anatolian Archaeology in the Light of Recent Research," *A(A)* 7 (1963) 1-21.

Seton H. F. Lloyd, "Anatolia: An Archaeological Renaissance," *ULBIA* 5 (1965) 1-14.

*D. H. French, "Early Pottery Sites from Western Anatolia," *ULBIA* 5 (1965) 15-24.

Machteld J. Mellink, "Archaeology: Horizons New and Old. Anatolia: Old and New Perspectives," *PAPS* 110 (1966) 111-129.

Ian A. Todd, "Preliminary report on a Survey of Neolithic Sites in Central Anatolia," *TAD* 15 (1966) #2, 101-105.

D. H. French, "Prehistoric Sites in Northwest Anatolia. I. The İznik Area," *AS* 17 (1967) 49-100.

*James Mellaart, "Anatolian Trade with Europe and Anatolian Geography and Culture Provinces in the Late Bronze Age," *AS* 18 (1968) 187-202.

*Nimet Özgüç, "Assyrian Trade Colonies in Anatolia," *Arch* 22 (1969) 250-255.

Machteld J. Mellink, "The Early Bronze Age in Southwest Anatolia," *Arch* 22 (1969) 290-299.

D. H. French, "Prehistoric Sites in Northwestern Anatolia. II. The Balikesir and Akhisar/Manisa Areas," *AS* 19 (1969) 41-98.

*Briggs Buchanan, "The End of the Assyrian Colonies in Anatolia: The Evidence of the Seals," *JAOS* 89 (1969) 758-762.

Anazarbus

Michael Gough, "Anazarbus," *AS* 2 (1952) 85-105.

Anemurium

Elizabeth Alföldi, "Excavations and Restortion*[sic]* in Anemurium, 1966," *TAD* 15 (1966) #1, 5-12.

C. Leonard Smith, "Excavation report, eski Anamur *(Anemurium)* 1968," *TAD* 17 (1968) #2, 177-184.

Elizabeth Alföldi, Gerhard Huber, Altan Akat, and Peter Taylor, "Restoration work in the Odeon of Anemurium 1969," *TAD* 18 (1969) #2, 41-46.

Ankara

Seaton [H. F.] Lloyd, "British Institute of Archaeology at Ankara. Annual Report: 1953," *TAD* 6 (1956) #1, 29-34.

Antas

*Sabatino Moscati, "Antas: A New Punic Site in Sardinia," *BASOR* #196 (1969) 23-36.

Anthedon

*John C. Rolfe, "Discoveries at Anthedon in 1889," *AJA, O.S.,* 6 (1890) 96-107. [II. Report on Excavations at Anthedon, pp. 96-101]

Anti-Taurus

*Tahsin Özgüç, "Excavations at Fraktin near Develi and researches in Anti-Taurus region," *TTKB* 12 (1948) 266-267.

Antioch (Pisidian)

*David M. Robinson, "A Preliminary Report on the Excavations at Pisidian Antioch and at Sizma," *AJA* 28 (1924) 434-444.

Antioch (Pisidian) concluded

*David Moore Robinson, "The University of Michigan Excavations at Pisidian Antioch and at Sizma," *AJA* 29 (1925) 91.

*Glanville Downey, "The Political Status of Roman Antioch," *Bery* 6 (1939-41) 1-6.

*George Haddad, "The population of Antioch in the hellenistic-roman period," *AAAS* 1 (1951) 19-31.

Arthur Darby Nock, "The Praises of Antioch," *JEA* 40 (1954) 76-82.

*Glanville Downey, "The Size of the Population of Antioch," *TAPA* 89 (1958) 84-91.

Antioch-on-the-Orontes

W[illiam] A. Campbell, "The First Season of Excavation at Antioch on the Orontes," *AJA* 37 (1933) 115.

William A. Campbell, "Excavations at Antioch-on-the-Orontes," *AJA* 38 (1934) 201-206.

William A. Campbell, "The Third Season of Excavation at Antioch-on-the-Orontes," *AJA* 40 (1936) 1-9.

William A. Campbell, "The Fourth and Fifth Seasons of Excavation at Antioch-on-the-Orontes: 1935-1936," *AJA* 42 (1938) 205-217.

W[illiam] A. Campbell, "Archaeological Notes: The Sixth Season of Excavation at Antioch-on-the-Orontes: 1937," *AJA* 44 (1940) 417-427.

Frederick O. Waagé, "Antioch on the Orontes: Season of 1937," *AJA* 42 (1938) 126-127.

William A. Campbell, "The Seventh Campaign at Antioch-on-the-Orontes," *AJA* 43 (1939) 299.

Wachtang Z. Djobadze, "Report on Archeological activities in the Vicinity of Antakya," *TAD* 13 (1964) #1, 53-55. *[Antioch-on-the-Orontes]*

W[achtang Z.] Djobadze, "Second Preliminary Report on Excavations in the Vicinity of Antioch-on-the-Orontes," *TAD* 13 (1964) #2, 32-40.

Antinoë

*J. de M. Johnson, "Antinoë and its Papyri. Excavation by the Graeco-Roman Branch, 1913-14," *JEA* 1 (1914) 168-181.

Aphrodisias

Kenan T[evfik] Erim, "Excavations at Aphrodisias in Caria, 1961," *AJA* 66 (1962) 195-196.

Kenan T[evfik] Erim, "Excavations at Aphrodisias in Caria, 1963," *AJA* 68 (1964) 193-194.

K[enan] Tevfik Erim, "Aphrodisias 1965 Campaign," *TAD* 15 (1966) #1, 59-67.

Kenan T[evfik] Erim, "Aphrodisias 1966 Campaign," *TAD* 15 (1966) #2, 55-65.

Kenan T[evfik] Erim, "Excavations at Aphrodisias in Caria, 1966," *AJA* 71 (1967) 186-187.

Kenan T[evfik] Erim, "De Aphrodisiade," *AJA* 71 (1967) 233-243. *[Aphrodisias]*

Kenan T[evfik] Erim, "Aphrodisias results of the 1967 campaign," *TAD* 16 (1967) #1, 67-80.

Kenan T[evfik] Erim, "Excavations at Aphrodisias in Caria, 1967," *AJA* 72 (1968) 165.

Kenan T[evfik] Erim, "Aphrodisias Results of the 1968 Campaign," *TAD* 17 (1968) #1, 43-57.

Barbara Kadish, "Excavations of Prehistoric Remains at Aphrodisias, 1967," *AJA* 73 (1969) 49-65.

Kenan T[evfik] Erim, "The ninth Campaign of Excavations at Aphrodisias in Caria 1969," *TAD* 18 (1969) #2, 87-110.

Apliki

Joan du Plat Taylor, "A Late Bronze Age Settlement at Apliki, Cyprus," *AJ* 32 (1952) 133-167.

Apollonia

Arthur Kahn, "Apollonia: City of Statues," *Arch* 14 (1961) 161-165.

Donald White, "Excavations at Apollonia, Cyrenaica: Preliminary Report," *AJA* 70 (1966) 259-265.

John Griffiths Pedley, "Excavations at Apollonia, Cyrenaica: Second Preliminary Report," *AJA* 71 (1967) 141-147.

ʿAqar Qūf

Taha Baqir, "Excavations at ʿAqar Qūf 1942-1943," *Iraq* (1944) *Supplement,* 1-16.

Taha Baqir, "Iraq Government Excavations at ʿAqar Qūf. Second Interim Report, 1943-1944," *Iraq* (1945) *Supplement,* 1-15.

Taha Baqir, "Excavations at ʿAqar Qūf: Third Interim Report, 1944-5," *Iraq* 8 (1946) 73-93.

*E. Douglas Van Buren, "Excavations in Mesopotamia," *Or, N.S.,* 15 (1946) 497-503. [3. ʿAqar Qūf, pp. 501-503]

Ar-Ruád (Arpad/Arvad)

*(   ) Newbold, "On the Site of Caranus, and the Island of Ar-Ruád (الرواد), the Arvad or Arpad of Scripture," *JRAS* (1856) 32-36.

Arabia

*Anonymous, "The Historical Geography of Arabia; or, the Patriarchal Evidence of a Revealed Religion: A Memoir, with illustrative Maps," *QRL* 74 (1844) 325-358. *(Review)*

(   ) Gleiss, "The Biblical Geography of Arabia," *BRCM* 5 (1848-49) 165-183.

Anonymous, "Palgrave's Arabia," *CE* 79 (1865) 327-342. *(Review)*

Arabia cont.

*W. F. Prideaux, "On some recent Discoveries in South-Western Arabia," *SBAT* 2 (1873) 1-28.

A. H. Sayce, "Ancient Arabia," *ContR* 56 (1889) 901-907.

Fritz Hommel, "On the Historical Results of Eduard Glaser's Explorations in South Arabia," *AJSL* 6 (1889-90) 49-54.

Olaus Dahl, "The Early History of Arabia," *ONTS* 10 (1890) 153-159.

*A. G. Wright, "Syria and Arabia," *PEFQS* 27 (1895) 67-82.

*J. F. McCurdy, "Light on Scriptural Texts from Recent Discoveries. Arabia in the Old Testament," *HR* 33 (1897) 124-126.

Fritz Hommel, "Bearing of Arabian Archaeology on Bible and History," *HR* 41 (1901) 291-298.

[Paul Carus], "Arabian Pictures," *OC* 32 (1918) 466-475.

*W. W. Tarn, "Ptolemy II and Arabia," *JEA* 15 (1929) 9-25.

Raymond P. Dougherty, "The Sealand of Arabia," *JAOS* 50 (1930) 1-25.

R[aymond] P. Dougherty, "North Arabia and the Ancient Sealand," *JSOR* 15 (1931) 7-21.

Gus Van Beek, "Recovering the Ancient Civilization of Arabia," *BA* 15 (1952) 2-18. [Arabia and the Bible; The Excavations; The South Gate; The Temple; The Cemetery; Hajar bin Humeid]

*W[illiam] F[oxwell] Albright, "The Chronology of the Minaean Kings of Arabia," *BASOR* #129 (1953) 20-24.

William L. Reed, "The Bible and North Arabia," *SQ/E* 26 (1965) 143-153. [North Arabia—Home of Friend and Foe; Evidence from the Pentateuch; The Prophets and North Arabia; Treasures and Wisdom from North Arabia; North Arabia and the New Testament]

A[braham] Negev, "Oboda, Mampsis and Provincia Arabia," *IEJ* 17 (1967) 46-55.

P[eter] J. Parr, G. L. Harding, and J. E. Dayton, "Preliminary Survey in N. W. Arabia, 1968," *ULBIA* 8&9 (1968-69) 193-242.

Arabia concluded

*P[eter] J. Parr, "The Nabataeans and North-West Arabia," *ULBIA* 8&9 (1968-69) 250-252.

Brian Doe, "Southern Arabia," *ULBIA* 8&9 (1968-69) 256-258.

Aradus

*Greville J. Chester, "Notes on Raud (Aradus) and Adjacent Places in Northern Syria," *PEFQS* 7 (1875) 218-227.

ʿArâq el-Emîr

Paul W. Lapp, "Soundings at ʿArâq el-Emîr (Jordan)," *BASOR* #165 (1962) 16-34.

Paul W. Lapp, "The Second and Third Campaigns at ʿArâq el-Emîr," *BASOR* #171 (1963) 8-39.

Mount Ararat

*†Anonymous, "Morier's Second Journey through Persia to Constantinople," *MMBR* 45 (1818) 607-626 *(Review)* [Mount Ararat, p 622]

[B. B. Edwards], "Ascent of Mount Ararat," *BRCR* 7 (1836) 390-416.

H. G. O. Dwight, "Armenian Traditions about Mt. Ararat," *JAOS* 5 (1855-56) 189-191.

*Edgar J. Banks, "To the Summit of Mount Ararat," *OC* 27 (1913) 398-410.

Arcadia

Doro Levi, "Arcadia, an Early Greek Town: New Italian Excavations in Crete," *AAA* 12 (1925) 3-10.

Archanes

John A. Sakellarakis, "Minoan Cemeteries at Archanes," *Arch* 20 (1967) 276-281.

Ard El Naam

*Hishmaț Messiha, "Recent Excavations at Ard-El Naam Cairo 1957-1960 (Part I)," *ASAE* 59 (1966) 185-192. *[Part II not published]*

Argive Heraeum

Charles Waldstein, "Correspondence. Preliminary report from Prof. Waldstein on the excavations at the argive Heræum in 1893," *AJA, O.S.*, 9 (1894) 63-67.

Edward L. Tilton, "The Publication of the Results of the American Excavations at the Argive Heraeum," *AJA* 5 (1901) 6.

Bernadotte Perrin, "The 'Hiereiai' of Hellanicus and the Burning of the Argive Heraeum," *AJA* 5 (1901) 10-11.

Argo Island

*H. Jacquet-Grodon, C. Bonnet, and J. Jacquet, "Pnubs and the Temple of Tabo on Argo Island," *JEA* 55 (1969) 103-111.

Argolis

James M. Paton, "Report on Excavations Between Schenochori and Koutzopodi, Argolis, in 1893," *AJA, O.S.*, 429-436. (Note by Charles Waldestein, pp. 429, 436)

Argos

Carleton L. Brownson, "Papers of the American School of Classical Studies at Athens. II. Excavations at the Heraeum of Argos," *AJA, O.S.*, 8 (1893) 205-225.

Paul Courbin, "Discoveries at Ancient Argos," *Arch* 9 (1956) 166-174.

Arkhanes

John Sakellarakis, "Arkhanes 1965. Report on the excavations," *KZFE* 4 (1965) 177-180.

Armant

Robert Mond and Walter B. Emery, "A Preliminary Report on the Excavations at Armant," *AAA* 16 (1929) 3-12.

O. H. Myers and H. W. Fairman, "Excavations at Armant, 1929-31," *JEA* 17 (1931) 223-232.

Armenia

A. H. Sayce, "Recent Biblical Archaeology. Recent Discoveries in Armenia," *ET* 10 (1898-99) 471.

Bernard W. Henderson, "Controversies in Armenian topography," *JP* 28 (1901-03) 99-121.

Bernard W. Henderson, "Controversies in Armenian topography II," *JP* 28 (1901-03) 271-286.

T. B. Khungian, "Glimpses from Ancient Armenia," *AAOJ* 30 (1908) 270-275.

R. D. Barnett and W. Watson, "Russian Excavations in Armenia," *Iraq* 14 (1952) 132-147.

R. D. Barnett, "Further Russian Excavations in Armenia (1949-1953)," *Iraq* 21 (1959) 1-19.

*Vladimír Souček, "Tracing Ancient Cultures in Armenia," *NOP* 1 (1960) #6, 12-14.

Tall*[sic]* Arpa<u>ch</u>iyah

M. E. L. Mallowan and Cruikshank Rose, "Excavations at Tall*[sic]* Arpa<u>ch</u>iyah," *Iraq* 2 (1935) iii-xv, 1-178.

Arpad (See Ar-Ruàd)

Arpi

John Bradford, "The Ancient City of Arpi in Apulla," *Antiq* 31 (1957) 167-169.

Arsinoë

*Lysander Dickerman, "On Mr. Petrie's recent explorations in Hawara, Biahmu, and Arsinoë," *JAOS* 14 (1890) cxxvii-cxxix.

Arslantepe

Salvatore M. Puglisi, "Excavations of the Italian Mission at Arslantepe (Malatya). Season 1961," *TAD* 11 (1961) #2, 53-55.

Salvatore M. Puglisi, "Second report on the Excavations at Arslantepe (Malatya)," *TAD* 13 (1964) #1, 123-128.

Salvatore M. Puglisi, "Third Report on the Excavations at Arslantepe (Malatya)," *TAD* 13 (1964) #2, 41-48.

Paolo Emilio Pecorella, "Report on the 1967 Campaign at Arslantepe (Malatya)," *TAD* 16 (1967) #2, 173-176.

Ayba Palmieri, "Exvations*[sic]* at Arslantepe (Malatya) 1968," *TAD* 18 (1969) #1, 99-107.

Arvad (See Ar-Ruàd)

Arzawa

*John Garstang, "Notes on Hittite Political Geography," *AAA* 10 (1923) 21-26, 172-178. [III. Arzawa, pp. 21-26]

Aṣfûnul-Maṭâʿneh

*H. S. K. Bakry, "Aṣfûnul-Maṭâʿneh Sondages," *ASAE* 60 (1968) 37-53.

Ashkenaz

*Jehuda Rosenthal, "Ashkenaz, Sefarad, and Zarefat," *HJud* 5 (1943) 58-62.

(Western) Asia

*H. Schlichter, "The African and Asiatic Coasts of the Indian Ocean in Antiquity," *IAQR, 2nd Ser.*, 2 (1891) 305-314.

Western Asia concluded

*C[laude] R. Conder, "Discoveries in Western Asia," *SRL* 34 (1899) 236-259.

*Theophile G. Pinches, "Notes on Exploration in Western Asia," *JRAS* (1907) 1065-1070. [Babylonia; Niffer; Bismya; Asshur]

*Anonymous, "M. de Morgan on the Date of the Neolithic Age in Western Asia," *RP* 8 (1909) 267-268.

Felix V. Luschan, "The Early Inhabitants of Western Asia. *The Huxley Memorial Lecture for* 1911," *JRAI* 41 (1911) 221-244.

*Anonymous, "Archaeological Expeditions to the Near East and Asia. Season 1935-6," *AEE* 20 (1935) 92-96.

*W[illiam] F[oxwell] Albright, "Western Asia in the Twentieth Century B.C.: The Archives of Mari," *BASOR* #67 (1937) 26-30.

I. J. Gelb, "Studies in the Topography of Western Asia," *AJSL* 55 (1938) 66-85.

*M. B. Rowton, "The Woodlands of Ancient Western Asia," *JNES* 26 (1967) 261-277.

Asia Minor

H. J. Van Lennep, "Recent Archæological Explorations and Discoveries in Asia Minor," *JAOS* 9 (1869-71) lx.

*Claude R. Conder, "Notes on Perrot an Chipiez's 'Histoire de l'Art'. Vol IV—Sardinia, Judea, and Asia Minor," *PEFQS* 19 (1887) 107-110.

†Anonymous, "Professor Ramsay's *Asia Minor,*" *QRL* 175 (1892) 211-234. *(Review)*

†Anonymous, "Asia Minor Rediscovered," *QRL* 186 (1897) 64-87. *(Review)*

*George F. Barton, "Some Archaeological Notes on Asia Minor and Syria," *AJA* 7 (1903) 82-83.

Anonymous, "Report of the Cornell Expedition to Asia Minor," *RP* 7 (1908) 175-176.

Asia Minor concluded

Anonymous, "Work in Asia Minor by Professor Garstang," *RP* 7 (1908) 310.

Howard Crosby Butler, "Hellenistic Cities of Asia Minor. Preface," *A&A* 9 (1920) 155-156.

Anonymous, "Current Notes and News. American Excavations in Asia Minor," *A&A* 9 (1920) 203.

*C. Leonard Woolley, "Asia Minor, Syria and the Aegean," *AAA* 9 (1922) 41-56.

H[ans] H[enning] von der Osten, "Explorations in Hittite Asia Minor. A Preliminary Report," *AJSL* 43 (1926-27) 73-176.

H[ans] H[enning] von der Osten, "An Archaeological Trip in Asia Minor," *AJA* 31 (1927) 96.

John L. Myres, "Recent Archaeological Discoveries in Asia Minor," *Iraq* 6 (1939) 71-90.

George M. A. Hanfmann, "Archaeology in Homeric Asia Minor," *AJA* 52 (1948) 135-155. [Corrections, *AJA* 54 (1950) p. 203]

Machteld [J.] Mellink, "Archaeology in Asia Minor," *AJA* 59 (1955) 231-240; 62 (1958) 91-104

Machteld J. Mellink, Archaeology in Asia Minor," *AJA* 60 (1956) 369-384; 63 (1959) 73-85; 64 (1960) 57-69; 65 (1961) 37-52; 66 (1962) 71-85; 67 (1963) 173-190; 68 (1964) 149-166; 69 (1965) 133-149; 70 (1966) 139-159, 71 (1967) 155-174; 72 (1968) 125-147; 73 (1969) 203-227.

Machteld J. Mellink, Archaeology in Asia Minor: Addenda," *AJA* 70 (1966) 279-282.

*G. A. Wainwright, "The Teresh, the Etruscans and Asia Minor," *AS* 9 (1959) 197-213.

J. G. Macqueen, "Geography and History in Western Asia Minor in the Second Millennium B.C.," *AS* 18 (1968) 169-185.

Aşikli Hüyük

Ian A. Todd, "Aşikli Hüyük—A Protoneolithic Site in Central Anatolia," *AS* 16 (1966) 139-163.

Ian A. Todd, "The Dating of Aşikli Hüyük in Central Anatolia," *AJA* 72 (1968) 157-158.

Askut

Alexander Badawy, "Preliminary Report on the Excavations by the University of California at Askut (First Season, October 1962-January 1963)," *Kush* 12 (1964) 47-53.

Alexander Badawy, "Askut: A Middle Kingdom Fortress in Nubia," *Arch* 18 (1965) 124-131.

Alexander Badawy, "Archaeological Problems Relating to the Egyptian Fortress at Askut," *JARCE* 5 (1966) 23-27.

Asshur

Anonymous, "The Ancient Capital of Assyria," *MQR, 3rd Ser.,* 31 (1905) 789-790. *[Asshur]*

Anonymous, "A Comprehensive Account of the Excavations in Ashur from Sept, 18, 1903, to the end of February, 1905," *RP* 5 (1906) 15-24. *[Trans. and condensed by D. D. Luckenbill from the German Oriental Society reports]*

Anonymous, "Excavations in Ashur," *RP* 5 (1906) 86-89. *[Trans. and condensed by D. D. Luckenbill from the German Oriental Society reports]*

*Theophilus G. Pinches, "Aššur and Nineveh," *JTVI* 42 (1910) 154-174, 176. (Communication from A. Irving, pp. 174-175)

Theophilus G. Pinches, "The Discoveries by the German Expedition on the Site of Assur," *SBAP* 32 (1910) 41-54.

*Theophilus G. Pinches, "Aššur and Nineveh," *RP* 12 (1913) 23-41.

A. Leo Oppenheim, "The City of Assur in 714 B.C.," *JNES* 19 (1960) 133-147.

Assos

William Fenwick Harris, "The Publication of the Work of the Expedition to Assos in 1881-1883," *AJA* 5 (1901) 18-19.

Howard Crosby Butler, "The Investigations at Assos conducted by the Archaeological Institute of America," *A&A* 12 (1921) 17-26.

William Fenwick Harris, "Investigations at Assos," *A&A* 12 (1921) 39.

Assyria

†Anonymous, "Ancient Assyria," *WR* 51 (1849) 290-334.

*Anonymous, "On the Origin of the Name Assyria.—Gen. x: 10. 11," *SPR* 3 (1849-50) 630-637.

*†Anonymous, "Assyria and Babylon," *BFER* 2 (1853) 662-701. *(Review)*

Anonymous, "Assyrian History," *CE* 66 (1859) 183-201. *(Review)*

Anonymous, "Assyrian History," *JSL, 3rd Ser.*, 9 (1859) 332-348. *(Review)*

Anonymous, "Assyria and her Monuments," *BFER* 17 (1868) 751-776.

Anonymous, "Recent Assyrian Discoveries," *DUM* 84 (1874) 213-225.

*†Hormuzd Rassam, "Excavations and Discoveries in Assyria," *SBAP* 2 (1879-80) 3-4. (Remarks by J. Oppert, pp. 4-60)

Hormuzd Rassam, "Excavations and Discoveries in Assyria," *SBAT* 7 (1880-82) 37-58.

G[eorge] Rawlinson, "Biblical Topography No. III.—On the Chief Cities of Ancient Assyria," *MI* 3 (1885-86) 51-61.

*Morris Jastrow Jr., "On Palestine and Assyria in the Days of Joshua," *ZA* 7 (1892) 1-7.

W. W. Moore, "The Resurrection of Assyria," *USR* 4 (1892-93) 261-277.

*Hormuzd Rassam, "History of Assyrian and Babylonian Discoveries," *IAQR, 2nd Ser.*, 8 (1894) 86-101.

Assyria concluded

*Robert Francis Harper, "A Sketch of the Excavations in Babylonia and Assyria," *BW* 8 (1896) 23-29.

J. F. McCurdy, "Light on Scriptural Texts from Recent Discoveries. The Decline of Assyria," *HR* 33 (1897) 218-220.

*George L. Robinson, "Where Archaeological Investigation left off in Palestine and Assyria," *AJA* 21 (1917) 84.

Anonymous, "The Assyrian Expedition," *UMB* 4 (1932-33) 63-66, 102-103.

Anonymous, "Assyrian Expedition," *UMB* 5 (1934-35) #4, 27.

M. E. L. Mallowan, "Reflections on the History and Archaeology of Assyria," *Sumer* 7 (1951) 156-164.

W. J. Beasley, "Assyria and the Bible," *AT* 5 (1960-61) #3, 3-6. [Part 1. Layard's Search for a Lost Empire]

*William W. Hallo, "From Qarqar to Carchemish: Assyria and Israel in the Light of New Discoveries," *BA* 23 (1960) 34-61. (Correction, p. 132) [I. The Assyrian Resurgence (859-829); II. Revolt and Restoration (828-783); III. Assyria in Retreat (783-745); IV. Divide et Impera (745-705) V. Pax Assyriaca (705-648); VI. Decline and Fall (648-609)]

Astrabad

*M. Rostovtzeff, "The Sumerian Treasure of Astrabad," *JEA* 6 (1920) 4-27

Ast-Raset

G. A. Wainwright, "The Position of Ast-Raset," *JEA* 33 (1947) 58-62.

P. L. Shinnie, "A note on Ast-Raset," *JEA* 41 (1955) 128-129.

Aşvan

H. D[avid] French, "Aşvan Excavations 1968," *TAD* 17 (1968) #1, 71-73.

Aswan

†E. A. Wallis Budge, "Excavations made at Aswan by Major-General Sir F. Grenfell during the years 1885 and 1886," *SBAP* 10 (1887-88) 4-40.

(Lady) William Cecil, "Report on the Work done at Aswân," *ASAE* 4 (1903) 51-73.

(Lady) William Cecil, "Report of the Work done at Aswan during the first Months of 1904," *ASAE* 6 (1905) 273-283.

*Labib Habachi, "The Graffiti and Work of the Viceroys of Kush in the Region of Aswan," *Kush* 5 (1957) 13-36.

Asy

*G. A. Wainwright, "Alashia = Alasa; and Asy," *Klio* 14 (1914-15) 1-36.

Atchana-Alalakh

[C.] Leonard Woolley, "Excavations at Tal-Atchana, 1937," *AJ* 18 (1938) 1-28.

[C.] Leonard Woolley, "Excavations at Atchana-Alalakh, 1938," *AJ* 19 (1939) 1-37.

[C.] Leonard Woolley, "Excavations at Atchana-Alalakh, 1939," *AJ* 28 (1948) 1-19.

[C.] Leonard Woolley, "Excavations at Atchana-Alalakh, 1946," *AJ* 30 (1950) 1-21.

E. Douglas Van Buren, "Excavations at Atchana-alalakh," *Or, N.S.*, 17 (1948) 532-535.

Athens (includes articles on the Athenian Agora)

†Anonymous, "Bulwer's *Rise and Fall of Athens*," *ERCJ* 65 (1837) #132, 151-177. *(Review)*

*W. S. Tyler, "Athens, or Aesthetic Culture and the Art of Expression," *BS* 20 (1863) 152-180.

Athens cont.

W. A. Nichols, "Athens; The Grand Experiment," *CongR* 11 (1871) 172-184.

*A. J. Huntingdon, "Ancient Attica and Athens," *BQ* 11 (1877) 215-232.

*Thomas W. Ludlow, "The Harbors of Ancient Athens," *AJP* 4 (1883) 192-203.

Walter Miller, "Excavations upon the Akropolis at Athens," *AJA, O.S.,* 2 (1886) 61-65.

Walter Miller, "A History of the Akropolis at Athens," *AJA, O.S.,* 8 (1893) 473-556.

John L. Myres, "Pre-Mycenæan Athens," *Man* 1 (1901) #70.

*Mitchell Carroll, "Observations on the Harbors and Walls of Ancient Athens," *AJA* 8 (1904) 88-91. [I. Harbors; II. Site of Ancient Phalerum; III. The So-called Third Long Wall]

*Arthur Stoddard Cooley, "Archaeological Notes," *AJA* 9 (1905) 68-69. [Corinth; Athens; Syracuse; Rome]

Charles H. Weller, "The Situation of the Agraulion at Athens," *AJA* 12 (1908) 68-69.

C[harles] H. Weller, "Notes on Athenian Topography," *AJA* 16 (1912) 103-104. [Cynosarges; Asclepieum; Panathenaic Ship; Propylaea; Cecropium]

*Harold North Fowler, "The American School of Classical Studies at Athens," *A&A* 14 (1922) 171-260. [Researches on the Athenian Acropolos, pp. 233-246]

Anonymous, "Notes and Comments. Excavation of Athens Now Assured," *A&A* 24 (1927) 189-190.

Anonymous, "Notes and Comments. Greek Government Sanctions Agora Excavation," *A&A* 27 (1929) 47.

William Bell Dinsmoor, "Supplementary Excavation at the Entrance to the Acropolis, 1928," *AJA* 33 (1929) 101-102.

Athens cont.

T[heodore] Leslie Shear, "Notes and Comments. The Agora of Athens," *A&A* 30 (1930) 187-188.

T[heodore] Leslie Shear, "Notes and Comments. The Agora Excavations," *A&A* 32 (1931) 90-93.

Arthur Stanley Riggs, "Notes and Comments. The American Excavations in Athens," *A&A* 32 (1931) 88-90.

Walter Miller, "The Athenian Agora and the Northwest Slope of the Acropolis: I," *A&A* 32 (1931) 99-108.

Walter Miller, "The Athenian Agora and the Northwest Slope of the Acropolis: II," *A&A* 32 (1931) 175-183.

John Day, "Cape Colias Phalerum and the Phaleric Wall," *AJA* 36 (1932) 1-11. *[Topography of Athens]*

Elizabeth Pierce Blegen, "News Items from Athens," *AJA* 36 (1932) 60-64, 188-193, 351-361; 37 (1933) 152-159, 336-342, 491-495, 627-630; 38 (1934) 308-311, 469-476, 599-603; 39 (1935) 131-136, 267-270, 406-411, 615-620; 40 (1936) 145-153, 262-270, 371-377, 541-550; 46 (1942) 477-487.

Walter Miller, "The Athenian Agora and the Northwest Slope of the Acropolis: III," *A&A* 33 (1932) 20-23, 29.

Walter Miller, "The Athenian Agora and the Northwest Slope of the Acropolis: IV," *A&A* 33 (1932) 87-95.

T[heodore] Leslie Shear, "The Excavation of the Athenian Agora," *AJA* 36 (1932) 382-392.

T[heodore] Leslie Shear, "Progress of American Excavations in the Athenian Agora," *A&A* 34 (1933) 19-28.

Theodore Leslie Shear, "Discoveries in the Athenian Agora in 1933," *A&A* 34 (1933) 283-297.

Homer Thompson, "Activities in the American Zone of the Athenian Agora, Summer of 1932," *AJA* 37 (1933) 289-296.

T[heodore] Leslie Shear, "The Current Excavations in the Athenian Agora," *AJA* 37 (1933) 305-312; 40 (1936) 188-203.

Athens cont.

T[heodore] Leslie Shear, "The Latter Part of the Agora Campaign of 1933," *AJA* 37 (1933) 540-548.

Homer Thompson, "The Topography of the West Side of the Agora," *AJA* 39 (1935) 114.

T[heodore] Leslie Shear, "The Agora Excavations," *AJA* 39 (1935) 437-447.

T[heodore] Leslie Shear, "The Conclusion of the 1936 Campaign in the Athenian Agora," *AJA* 40 (1936) 403-414.

T[heodore] Leslie Shear, "Excavations in the Athenian Agora," *AJA* 41 (1937) 177-189.

T[heodore] Leslie Shear, "Latter Part of the 1937 Campaign in the Athenian Agora," *AJA* 42 (1938) 1-16.

T[heodore] Leslie Shear, "The 1938 Campaign in the Athenian Agora," *AJA* 43 (1939) 302-303.

T[heodore] Leslie Shear, "Discoveries in the Agora in 1939," *AJA* 43 (1939) 577-588.

Oscar Broneer, "Excavations on the Slopes of the Acropolis, 1939," *AJA* 44 (1940) 252-256.

Oscar Broneer, "Plato's Description of Early Athens in the Light of Archaeological Research," *AJA* 45 (1941) 92.

*Anthony E. Raubitschek, "Athens and Halikyai," *TAPA* 75 (1944) 10-14.

Homer A. Thompson, "Excavations in the Athenian Agora, 1947," *AJA* 52 (1948) 378-379.

Homer A. Thompson, "Excavations in the Athenian Agora, 1948," *AJA* 53 (1949) 145.

Homer A. Thompson, "Excavations in the Athenian Agora," *AJA* 52 (1948) 378-379.

†Homer A. Thompson, "Report on Excavations in the Athenian Agora," *AJA* 53 (1949) 368-372.

Athens cont.

Homer A. Thompson, "The Athenian Agora: 1949 Season," *Arch* 2 (1949) 184-185.

Homer A. Thompson, "The Athenian Agora: 1949," *AJA* 54 (1950) 257.

Oscar Broneer, "Athens in the Late Bronze Age," *Antiq* 30 (1956) 9-18.

Homer A. Thompson, "The Season's Work in the Athenian Agora, 1951," *AJA* 56 (1952) 177-178.

Homer A. Thompson, "*Excavations in* the Athenian Agora, 1952," *Arch* 5 (1952) 145-150.

Homer A. Thompson, "Excavations in the Athenian Agora, 1952," *AJA* 57 (1953) 21-25, 111.

Homer A. Thompson, "The Athenian Agora: *Excavation and Reconstruction,*" *Arch* 6 (1953) 142-146.

Homer A. Thompson, "The Season's Work in the Athenian Agora, 1953," *AJA* 58 (1954) 149.

Homer A. Thompson, "The Athenian Agora: 1954," *AJA* 59 (1955) 174.

Homer A. Thompson, "Activities in the Athenian Agora: 1955," *AJA* 60 (1956) 135-136.

Homer A. Thompson, "Activities in the Athenian Agora: 1957," *AJA* 62 (1958) 227.

*Stephen Foltiny, "Athens and the East Halstatt Region: Cultural Interrelations at the Dawn of the Iron Age," *AJA* 65 (1961) 283-297.

R. E. Wycherley, "The Pythion at Athens. Thucydides 2.15.4; Philostratos *Lives of the Sophists* 21.7," *AJA* 67 (1963) 75-79.

*Lawrence Waddy, "Did Strabo Visit Athens?" *AJA* 67 (1963) 296-300.

R. Ross Holloway, "Excavations Beside the Panathenaic Way," *AJA* 70 (1966) 191. *[Athens]*

Homer A. Thompson, "Activities in the Athenian Agora: 1966-67," *AJA* 72 (1968) 173-174.

Athens concluded

T[heodore] Leslie Shear Jr. *[sic]*, "Excavations in the Athenian Agora 1968," *AJA* 73 (1969) 245.

Tell Athrib (Athribis)

*R. Engelbach, "The treasure of Athribis (Benha)," *ASAE* 24 (1924) (1924) 178-185.

Alan Rowe, "Short report on excavations of the Institute of Archaeology, Liverpool at Athribis (Tell Atrib)," *ASAE* 38 (1938) 523-532.

Atlantis

*[W. M.] Flinders Petrie, "The Caucasian Atlantis and Egypt," *AEE* 9 (1924) 123-124.

Robert L. Scranton, "Lost Atlantis Found Again?" *Arch* 2 (1949) 159-162.

*Charles Seltman, "Life in Ancient Crete—II: Atlantis," *HT* 2 (1952) 332-343.

Atropatene

*David R. Milberg, "Parnasos," *JNES* 28 (1969) 62. [1. Atropatene]

Attica

*A. J. Huntingdon, "Ancient Attica and Athens," *BQ* 11 (1877) 215-232.

Avaris

W. C. Winslow, "On the identification of Avaris at Sān," *JAOS* 13 (1889) xcv.

Raymond Weill, "The Problem of the Site of Avaris," *JEA* 21 (1935) 10-25. *(Trans. by Ethel W. Burney)*

Ay Khanum

Richard N. Frye, "A Greek City in Afghanistan," *AJA* 70 (1966) 286. *[Ay Khanum]*

Anonymous, "Ay Khanum: a Hellenistic City in Central Asia," *Antiq* 41 (1967) 141-143.

Ayun Musa

Anonymous, "The Wells of Moses," *EN* 2 (1890) 29-30. *[Ayun Musa]*

Azerbaijan

T. Burton Brown, "Recent Archæological Work in Azarbaijan*[sic]*," *IAQR* 47 (1951) 60-77.

*David R. Milberg, "Parnasos," *JNES* 28 (1969) 62. [1. Atropatene]

B

Baalbek (See also: Coele-Syria)

Anonymous, "Sketches in Syria, &c. No. IV," *CongML* 19 (1836) 546-554. *[Balbec-Damascus]*

*Henry A. DeForest, "Notes on Ruins in Bŭḳaʻa and in the Belâd Ba'albek," *JAOS* 3 (1853) 349-366.

[Francis Wayland Dunn], "A Day at the Ruins of Baalbec," *FBQ* 15 (1867) 225-31.

Claude R. Conder, "State of the Ruins of Baalbek," *PEFQS* 5 (1873) 158-161.

Hugh Macmillan, "Baalbec," *LQHR* 98 (1902) 209-235.

Anonymous, "Baalbek," *MR* 84 (1902) 816-819.

F. J. Bliss, "The German Excavations at Baʻal bek," *PEFQS* 34 (1902) 168-175.

Baalbek concluded

*John P. Peters, "Palestinian Exploration. *Notes of a Vacation in Palestine in 1902.*," *JBL* 22 (1903) 15-31. [2. Baalbek, pp. 15-16]

R. Phene Spiers, "Baalbec," *PEFQS* 36 (1904) 58-64.

Lewis Bayles Paton, "The German Excavations at Baʿalbek," *A&A* 1 (1914-15) 121-128.

*Mortimer Wheeler, "Size and Baalbek," *Antiq* 36 (1962) 6-9.

R. Phene Spiers, "Baalbec," *PEFQS* 36 (1904) 58-64.

Lewis Bayles Paton, "The German Excavations at Baʿalbek," *A&A* 1 (1914-15) 121-128.

*Mortimer Wheeler, "Size and Baalbek," *Antiq* 36 (1962) 6-9.

Baal-Zephon

*C. W. Goodwin, "Notes by C. W. Goodwin," *ZÄS* 11 (1873) 12-15. [Baal-Zephon, p. 14]

Bābā Jān

*Clare Goff Meade, "Lūristān in the first half of the First Millennium B.C. A preliminary report on the first season's excavations at Bābā Jān, and associated surveys in the Eastern Pīsh-i-Kūn," *Iran* 6 (1968) 105-134.

Clare Goff [Meade], "Excavations at Bābā Jān 1967: Second Preliminary Report," *Iran* 7 (1969) 115-130.

Babylon (Babylonia)

†Anonymous, "Maurice on the Ruins of Babylon," *MMBR* 43 (1817) 622-628. *(Review)*

†Anonymous, "Present State of the Ruins of Babylon," *MMBR* 49 (1820) 151-154. *(Review)*

Babylon (Babylonia) cont.

*†Anonymous, "Sir R. Ker Porter's Travels in Georgia, Persia, Armenia, &c.," *MMBR* 53 (1822) 577-612. *(Review)* [The Ruins of Babylon, pp. 596-604]

†Anonymous, "Remains of Babylon," *ERCJ* 48 (1828) 185-219. *(Review)*

†Anonymous, "Keppel's Journey from India," *ERCJ* 47 (1828) 368-385. *(Review)* [The Ruins of Babylon, pp. 374-375]

[B. B. Edwards], "The Fall of Babylon and the present state of its Ruins," *BRCR* 8 (1836) 158-189.

*†Anonymous, "Assyria and Babylon," *BFER* 2 (1853) 662-701. *(Review)*

*†Anonymous, "Nineveh and Babylon," *DR* 35 (1853) 93-138. *(Review)*

*†Anonymous, "Layard's Second Expedition," *ERL* 19 (1853) 145-186. *(Review) [Babylon]*

*†Anonymous, "*Layard's* Discoveries in Nineveh and Babylon," *NBR* 19 (1853) 255-296. *(Review)*

*†Anonymous, "Layard's Nineveh and Babylon," *PQR* 2 (1853-54) 602-622. *(Review)*

*Anonymous, "Layard's New Discoveries at Nineveh and Babylon," *CRB* 19 (1854) 20-39. *(Review)*

*Anonymous, "The Ruins of Nineveh and Babylon," *FBQ* 2 (1854) 179-192. *(Review)*

*(   ) Collins, "Layard's Second Exploration," *MR* 36 (1854) 113-131. *(Review) [Nineveh and Babylon]*

H[enry] C. Rawlinson, "Notes on the Early History of Babylonia," *JRAS* (1855) 215-259.

Edward Hincks, "Babylon and Its Priest-Kings," *JSL, 3rd Ser.*, 8 (1858-59) 296-309.

*A. [H.] Sayce, "Ethnology of Early Chaldea—No. III," *JSL, 4th Ser.*, 6 (1864-65) 171-176. *[The Name "Babylon"]*

G. Smith, "Early History of Babylonia," *SBAT* 1 (1872) 28-92.

Babylon (Babylonia) cont.

*W. Chad Boscawen, "The Pre-Historic Civilisation of Babylonia," *JRAI* 8 (1878-79) 21-35.

*Theophilus G. Pinches, "On a Cuneiform Tablet relating to the Capture of Babylon by Cyrus and the Events which preceded and led to it," *SBAP* 2 (1879-80) 39-42.

*Theo. G. Pinches, "On a Cuneiform Tablet relating to the Capture of Babylon by Cyrus, and the Events which preceded and led to it," *SBAT* 7 (1880-82) 139-176.

*Theo. G. Pinches, "Some recent Discoveries bearing on the Ancient History and Chronology of Babylonia," *SBAP* 5 (1882-83) 6-12. (Remarks by J. Oppert, p. 12)

George Rawlinson, "The Biblical Notices of Babylon Illustrated from Profane Sources, Ancient and Modern," *CM* 16 (1883) 31-38, 105-113, 162-169, 228-236, 293-301, 347-356; 17 (1883) 34-42, 95-105, 163-171, 233-240, 294-302, 352-359.

Hormuzd Rassam, "Babylonian Cities," *JTVI* 17 (1883-84) 221-243. [(Discussion, pp. 243-246) (Appendix by W. St. Chad-Boscawen, pp. 247-253)]

H[ormuzd] Rassam, "Recent Discoveries of Ancient Babylonian Cities," *SBAT* 8 (1883-84) 172-197.

John Phelps Taylor, "The Wolfe Expedition to Babylonia," *AR* 2 (1884) 109-110.

F[ranz] Delitzsch, "A Walk through Ancient Babylon," *BFER* 34 (1885) 88-105. *(Trans. by M. and A. de Faye)*

G[eorge] Rawlinson, "Biblical Topography. No. II.—On the Early Cities of Babylonia," *MI* 2 (1885) 321-332.

†William Hayes Ward, "The Wolfe Expedition to Babylonia," *PAPA* 17 (1885) xxix-xxx.

Francis Brown, "The Wolfe Exploring Expedition to Babylonia," *PR* 7 (1886) 155-159.

John P. Peters, "Correspondence. Letter on the Babylonian Expedition," *AJA, O.S.*, 7 (1891) 472-475.

Babylon (Babylonia) cont.

*Fritz Hommel, "*Gišgalla-ki*—Babylon. *Ki-nu-nir-ki*—Borsippa," *SBAP* 15 (1892-93) 108-110.

*Owen C. Whitehouse, "Cyrus and the Capture of Babylon," *ET* 4 (1892-83) 396-402.

John P. Peters, "A Brief Statement concerning the Babylonian Expedition sent out under the auspices of the University of Pennsylvania," *JAOS* 15 (1893) cxlvi-cliii.

*Hormuzd Rassam, "History of Assyrian and Babylonian Discoveries," *IAQR, 2nd Ser.,* 8 (1894) 86-101.

†Anonymous, "The Earliest History of Babylonia," *QRL* 179 (1894) 338-364. *(Review)*

*Robert Francis Harper, "A Sketch of the Excavations in Babylonia and Assyria," *BW* 8 (1896) 23-29.

A. H. Sayce, "Recent Discoveries in Babylonia," *ContR* 71 (1897) 81-96.

Anonymous, "Early Babylonia," *MR* 79 (1897) 309-310.

*J. A. Selbie, "Cyrus and Deutero-Isaiah," *ET* 9 (1897-98) 407-408.

†Anonymous, "Babylonian Discoveries," *ERCJ* 187 (1898) 364-385.

*J. A. Selbie, "The Date of the Capture of Babylon by Cyrus," *ET* 10 (1898-99) 119-120.

*John D. Davis, "Belshazzar and the Fall of Babylon," *CFL, O.S.,* 3 (1899) 349-352.

Talcott Williams, "Field Report on the Babylonian Expedition conducted by the Babylonian Committee of the Department of Archaeology and Palaentology of the University of Pennsylvania," *AJA* 4 (1900) 157-160. [Compiled from the field reports of Dr. Haynes and the notes published by Dr. H. V. Hilprecht]

A. H. Sayce, "Notes," *SBAP* 22 (1900) 161. *[Babylonia]*

Anonymous, "Babylonian Explorations," *MR* 83 (1901) 137-138.

Babylon (Babylonia) cont.

J. H. Stevenson, "American Explorations in Babylonia," *MQR, 3rd Ser.,* 29 (1903) 672-685.

Anonymous, "Excavation of the Ruins of Babylon," *RP* 2 (1903) 3-15. *[Part I]*

Anonymous, "Excavation of the Ruins of Babylon. Part II," *RP* 2 (1903) 144-151. *(Trans. from the official German report)*

Anonymous, "Excavation of the Ruins of Babylon. Part III," *RP* 2 (1903) 185-189.

Anonymous, "Excavation of the Ruins of Babylon. Part IV," *RP* 2 (1903) 273-285.

Robert Francis Harper, "Exploration and Discovery in Babylonia," *AAOJ* 26 (1904) 177-179.

*V. Scheil, "Excavations made by the French in Susa and Babylonia, 1902-1903," *BW* 24 (1904) 146-152.

Anonymous, "Explorations in Babylonia," *MR* 86 (1904) 813-817.

Anonymous, "The Topography of Babylon," *MR* 86 (1904) 640-644.

Anonymous, "German Excavations in Babylon, 1901 and 1902," *RP* 3 (1904) 166-184. *(Trans. from German official Reports by Prof. Karl Hau)*

P. Volz, "What the Babylonian Excavations Teach Us," *LCR* 24 (1905) 319-336. *(Trans. by C. Theodore Benze)*

Anonymous, "The Rise and Fall of Babylon," *MQR, 3rd Ser.,* 31 (1905) 182-183.

*Carl Josef Grimm, "Babylonia, Glimpses of its Civilization and Culture," *LQ* 37 (1907) 377-384.

Anonymous, "Early History of Babylonia," *RP* 6 (1907) 304.

John Cameron, "A Visit to Babylon," *GUOST* 3 (1907-12) 12-15.

*Anonymous, "The Size of Babylon," *RP* 7 (1908) 261-262.

Babylon (Babylonia) cont.

S[tephen] Langdon, "Babylon in the Time of the Exile," *Exp, 7th Ser.*, 8 (1909) 82-96, 143-158.

Theophilus G. Pinches, "Discoveries in Babylonia and the Neighbouring Lands," *JTVI* 41 (1909) 99-121.

Theophilus G. Pinches, "Discoveries in Babylonia and the Neighboring Lands," *RP* 9 (1910) 94-112.

*Alan S. Hawkesworth, "Sardinia's Connection with Babylon," *OC* 25 (1911) 447.

Anonymous, "German Excavations at Babylon," *RP* 10 (1911) 116.

Theophilus G. Pinches, "Babylon from the Recent Excavations," *SBAP* 34 (1912) 83-106.

*Theophilus G. Pinches, "The Latest Discoveries in Babylonia," *JTVI* 46 (1914) 167-192, 196. (Discussion, pp. 192-196) [I. Creation-Stories; II. The Flood; III. Early Kings; IV. Abraham's Plough; V. The Newly-Discovered Tablets from Erech; VI. Tower of Babel at Babylon; Appendix. The Capture of Babylon by Cyrus, 539 B.C.]

*Lewis R. Freedman, "A Day at Babylon," *ContR* 110 (1916) 779-788.

Anonymous, "Babylonia, Ancient and Modern," *HR* 72 (1916) 316-317.

Theophilus G. Pinches, "The Last Days of Babylon's Independence," *ET* 28 (1916-17) 183-184.

*Julius J. Price, "Babylon in the Talmud," *ET* 28 (1916-17) 325-326.

*Theophilus G. Pinches, "From World-Domination to Subjection: The Story of the Fall of Nineveh and Babylon," *JTVI* 49 (1917) 107-131. [(Discussion, pp. 131-136) (Communications by J. W. Thistle, pp. 136-137; Andrew Craig Robinson, pp 137-140)]

David Gordon Lyon, "Recent Excavations at Babylon," *HTR* 11 (1918) 307-321.

A. T. Olmstead, "The Babylonian Empire," *AJSL* 35 (1918-19) 65-100.

S[tephen] Langdon, "Babylon and 'The Land Beyond the River'," *ET* 30 (1918-19) 461-463.

Babylon (Babylonia) cont.

*L[uther] T. Townsend, "Prehistoric Babylon, Nineveh and the Hittite Empire; their Bearing on the Theory of Evolution," *CFL, 3rd Ser.,* 25 (1919) 45-49.

Theophilus G. Pinches, "Babylon in the Days of Nebuchadrezzar," *JTVI* 52 (1920) 178-200, 205-208. (Discussion, pp. 200-205)

A. T. Olmstead, "Babylonia as an Assyrian Dependency," *AJSL* 37 (1920-21) 212-229.

*Raymond P. Dougherty, "Ancient Teimâ and Babylonia," *JAOS* 41 (1921) 458-459.

A. T. Olmstead, "The Rise and Fall of Babylon," *AJSL* 38 (1921-22) 73-96.

*Samuel A. B. Mercer, "The Hittites, Mitanni and Babylonia in the Tell el-Amarna Letters," *JSOR* 8 (1924) 13-28.

*H. R. Hall, "The Excavations of 1919 at Ur el—ʿObeid and Eridu, and the History of Early Babylonia (Brussels Conference 1923)," *Man* 25 (1925) #1.

Raymond P. Dougherty, "An Archaeological Survey in Southern Babylonia I.," *BASOR* #23 (1926) 15-28.

Raymond P. Dougherty, "An Archaeological Survey in Southern Babylonia II.," *BASOR* #25 (1927) 4-13.

P. J. Wiseman, "Babylon in the Days of Hammurapi and Nebuchadrezzar," *JTVI* 59 (1927) 121-135. (Remarks by Theophilus G. Pinches, pp. 135-136)

*Alan Rowe, "A Comparison of Egyptian and Babylonian Civilizations and their Influence on Palestine," *PAPS* 68 (1929) 313-319.

S. F. Hunter, "Babylonia during the Latter Half of the Jewish Exile," *NZJT* 2 (1932-33) 205-213.

Alex Heidel, "Babylon," *CTM* 6 (1935) 641-650.

E[phraim] A. Speiser, "Excavations in Northeastern Babylonia," *BASOR* #67 (1937) 2-6.

*P. E. v[an] d[er] Meer, "A Topography of Babylon," *Iraq* 5 (1938) 55-64.

Babylon (Babylonia) concluded

G. T. Manley, "Babylon on the Nile," *EQ* 16 (1944) 138-160.

*W. Glyn Evans, "Will Babylon be Restored?" *BS* 107 (1950) 335-342, 481-487.

M. B. Rowton, "The Date of the Hittite Capture of Babylon," *BASOR* #126 (1952) 20-24.

Albrecht Goetze, "The Date of the Hittite Raid on Babylon," *BASOR* #127 (1952) 21-26.

Joan Gorell, "Broad Walls." *AT* 2 (1957-58) #2, 10-11. *[Babylon]*

Joan Gorell, "*Babylon:* The Processional Way," *AT* 2 (1957-58) #3, 3-4.

J[oan] Gorell, "*Babylon:* The Ishtar Gate," *AT* 2 (1957-58) #4, 3-5.

Joan Gorell, "*Babylon:* Weighed and Found Wanting," *AT* 3 (1958-59) #4, 3-5.

*†John A. Brinkman, "A Preliminary Catalogue of Written Sources for a Political History of Babylonia: 1160-722 B.C.," *JCS* 16 (1962) 83-109.

Howard Wohl, "A Note on the Fall of Babylon," *JANES* 1 (1968-69) #2, 28-38.

Bactra

Rodney S. Young, "The South Wall of Balkh-Bactra," *AJA* 59 (1955) 267-276.

Badra

*Joan Oates, "First Preliminary Report on a Survey in the Region of Mandali and Badra," *Sumer* 22 (1966) 51-60.

Bad-Tibira

Vaughn E. Crawford, "The Location of Bad-Tibira," *Iraq* 22 (1960) 197-199.

Bahrain

*P. V. Glob, "Bahrain—Island of the Hundred Thousand Burial-Mounds," *Kuml* (1954) 100-105.

T. G. Bibby, "The Wells of the Bulls," *Kuml* (1954) 160-163. *[Bahrain]*

*P. V. Glob, "The Ancient Capital of Bahrain," *Kuml* (1954) 167-169. *[Ras al Qala'a]*

P. V. Glob, "The Danish Archaeological Bahrain-Expedition's Second Excavation Campaign," *Kuml* (1955) 190-193.

*P. V. Glob, "Snake Sacrifices in Bahrain's Ancient Capital. The Danish Archaeological Expedition's Fourth Campaign of Excavation," *Kulm* (1957) 125-127.

Baḥria Oasis

*Ahmed Fakhry, "Baḥria and Farafra Oases. A Preliminary Report," *ASAE* 38 (1938) 397-434.

*Ahmed Fakhry, "Baḥria and Farafra Oases. Second Preliminary Report," *ASAE* 39 (1939) 627-642.

*Ahmed Fakhry, "Baḥria and Farafra Oases. Third Preliminary Report," *ASAE* 40 (1940-41) 855-871.

Baiae

Richard M. Haywood, "'Let's Run Down to Baiae'," *Arch* 11 (1958) 200-205.

Balabish

G. A. Wainwright, "The Excavations at Balabish: Preliminary Notice," *JEA* 2 (1915) 202-203.

Baliḫ

M. E. L. Mallowan, "Excavations in the Baliḫ Valley, 1938," *Iraq* 9 (1947) 111-159.

Balkans

Stanley Casson, "A Royal Necropolis in the Balkans," *A&A* 32 (1931) 113-119.

Bampūr

Beatrice de Cardi, "The Bampur Sequence in the 3rd Millenium B.C.," *Antiq* 41 (1967) 33-41.

Beatrice de Cardi, "Excavations at Bampūr, S. E. Iran: A Brief Report," *Iran* 6 (1968) 135-155.

Barda-Balka

Naji al Asil, "Barda-Balka," *Sumer* 5 (1949) 205-206.

H. E. Wright Jr. and Bruce Howe, "Preliminary Report on the Soundings at Barda Balka," *Sumer* 7 (1951) 107-111.

Barghuthiat

*S[tephen] Langdon, "Excavations at Kish and Barghuthiat 1933, I. Sassanian and Parthian Remains in Central Mesopotamia," *Iraq* 1 (1934) 113-123.

Barkal

*George A. Reisner, "Note on the Harvard-Boston Excavations at El-Kurruw and Barkal in 1918-1919," *JEA* 6 (1920) 61-64.

Bashan

*[George H. Schodde], "Biblical Reserach Notes," *ColTM* 17 (1897) 117-121. [The Great Cities of Bashan, pp. 120-121]

Tell Basta

Shafik Farid, "Preliminary report on the Excavations of the Antiquities Department at Tell Basta (Season 1961)," *ASAE* 58 (1964) 85-98.

Batn el Hagar

Gordon W. Hewes, "Prehistoric Investigations on the West Bank in the Batn el Hagar by the University of Colorado Nubian Expedition," *Kush* 14 (1966) 25-43.

Bedḫet

Samuel A. B. Mercer, "The Original Bedḥet," *EgR* 1 (1933) 35-36.

Samuel A. B. Mercer, "Where in the Delta was Bedḥet?" *EgR* 1 (1933) 36-37.

Behnesa

*F. Cope Whitehouse, "MAR-Moeris, West of Exyrhyncus—Behnesa," *SBAP* 7 (1884-85) 112-120.

Belbaşi

Enver Y. Bostancı, "A New Upper Palaeolithic and Mesolithic Facies at Belbaşi Rock Shelter on the Mediterranean Coast of Anatolia," *TTKB* 26 (1962) 252-272.

Beldibi

Enver Y. Bostancı, "Researches on the Mediterranean Coast of Anatolia. A New Palaeolithic Site at Beldibi Near Antalya," *A(A)* 4 (1959) 129-178.

Beni-Hasan

John Garstang, "Excavations at Beni-Hassan*[sic]* (1902-1903-1904)," *ASAE* 5 (1904) 215-228.

John Garstang, "Excavations at Beni-Hasan, 1902-3," *Man* 3 (1903) #54, #74.

John Garstang, "Excavations at Beni-Hasan in Upper Egypt, (Second Season)," *Man* 4 (1904) #67.

Beqaʿa

*Henry A. DeForest, "Notes on Ruins in the Bŭka'a and the Belâd Ba'albek," *JAOS* 3 (1853) 349-366. [Beqaʿa]

*Diana Kirkbride, "Early Byblos and the Beqaʿa," *MUSJ* 45 (1969) 43-60.

Lorraine Copeland, "Neolithic village sites in the South Beqaʿa, Lebanon," *MUSJ* 45 (1969) 83-114.

Berenice Troglodytica

David Meredith, "Berenice Troglodytica," *JEA* 43 (1957) 56-70.

Beth-pelet

[W. M.] Flinders Petrie, "Beth-Phelet*[sic]*," *AEE* 13 (1928) 33-36.

[W. M.] Flinders Petrie, "Excavations at Beth-Pelet," *AEE* 13 (1928) 118-121.

*[W. M.] Flinders Petrie, "The Shepherd Kings of Palestine. Excavations at Beth-Pelet, II," *AEE* 14 (1929) 1-16.

Bethulia

*Charles C. Torrey, "The Site of 'Bethulia'," *JAOS* 20 (1899) 160-172.

Beycesultan

Seton Lloyd and James Mellaart, "Beycesultan Excavations," AS 5 (1955) 39-92.

Seton Lloyd and James Mellaart, "Beycesultan Excavations. Second Preliminary Report, 1955," *AS* 6 (1956) 101-135.

Seton Lloyd, "Beycesultan Excavations 1956," *TAD* 7 (1957) #1, 42-43.

Seton Lloyd, "Beycesultan Excavations 1957," *TAD* 8 (1958) #1, 12-13.

Beycesultan concluded

*Seton Lloyd and James Mellaart, "An Early Bronze Age Shrine at Beycesultan," *AS* 7 (1957) 27-36. *[= 3rd Preliminary Report]*

Seton Lloyd and James Mellaart, "Beycesultan Excavations. Fourth Preliminary Report, 1957," *AS* 8 (1958) 93-113.

Seton Lloyd, "Excavations at Beycesultan, 1958. I. A Middle Bronze Age Shrine," *AS* 9 (1959) 35-37 *[= 5th Preliminary Report]*

James Mellaart, "Excavations at Beycesultan, 1958. II. The Chalcolithic Sounding," *AS* 9 (1959) 38-47.

*David Stronach, "Excavations at Beycesultan, 1958. III. An Early Metal Hoard from Beycesultan," *AS* 9 (1959) 47-50.

Seton Lloyd, "Beycesultan, 1959: Sixth Prelminary Report," *AS* 10 (1960) 31-41.

Seton Lloyd, "Excavations-Beycesultan. Sixth Season 1959," *TAD* 10 (1960) #2, 26-27.

Machteld J. Mellink, "Beycesultan: A Bronze Age Site in Southwestern Turkey," *BO* 24 (1967) 3-9.

Beyşehir-Suğla

Ralph S. Solecki, "An archelogical*[sic]* reconnaisannce*[sic]* in the Beyşehir-Suğla area of south western Turkey," *TAD* 13 (1964) #1, 129-148.

William R. Farrand, "Geology and physiogrophy*[sic]* of the Beyşehir-Suğla depression, western, touros lake district, Turkey," *TAD* 13 (1964) #1, 149-154.

Biahmu

*Lysander Dickerman, "On Mr. Petrie's recent explorations in Hawara, Biahmu, and Arsinoë," *JAOS* 14 (1890) cxxvii-cxxix.

Tell Billah

E[phraim] A. Speiser, "University of Pennsylvania Museum-Baghdad School Expedition at Billah," *BASOR* #40 (1930) 11-14.

E[phraim] A. Speiser, "Letter of March 1 from Dr. Speiser to the Directors of the American School at Baghdad and the University Museum of Philadelphia," *BASOR* #42 (1931) 12-13. *[Tell Billah]*

Anonymous, "The Tell Billah Expedition," *UMB* 2 (1930-31) 79-85, 142-146.

Anonymous, "Notes and Comments. New Finds in Northern Mesopotamia," *A&A* 31 (1931) 283-284. *[Tell Billah]*

Anonymous, "The Expedition to Tell Billa[sic]* and Tepe Gawra," *UMB* 3 (1931-32) 59-64, 66.

Anonymous, "Developments at Tell Billa[sic]* and Tepe Gawra," *UMB* 3 (1931-32) 94-95.

Anonymous, "Excavations at Tell Billa[sic]* and Tepe Gawra," *UMB* 3 (1931-32) 126-172, 130.

E[phraim] A. Speiser, "The Excavation of Tell Billah: Letter from Dr. Speiser to the Directors of the American School of Oriental Research in Baghdad and the University Museum (October 30, 1931)," *BASOR* #44 (1931) 2-5.

*E[phraim] A. Speiser, "The Bearing of the Excavations at Tell Billah and at Tepe Gawra upon the Ethnic Problems of Ancient Mesopotamia," *AJA* 36 (1932) 29-35.

E[phraim] A. Speiser, "Tell Billah: Letter from Dr. Speiser to the Directors of the American School at Baghdad and the University Museum," *BASOR* #45 (1932) 32-33f.

*E[phraim] A. Speiser, "Reports from Professor Speiser on the Tell Billah and Tepe Gawra Excavations," *BASOR* #46 (1932) 1-9.

Anonymous, "Excavations at Tell Billa*[sic]*," *UMB* 4 (1932-33) 36-37.

*Charles Bache, "From Mr. Bache's First Report on the Joint Excavations at Tepe Gawra and Tell Billah, 1932-3," *BASOR* #49 (1933) 8-14.

Tell Billah concluded

Charles Bache, "From Mr. Bache's Reports on the Joint Excavation at Tell Billah," *BASOR* #50 (1933) 3-7.

Charles Bache, "Work of the Bagdad School, Tell Billah, " *BASOR* #51 (1933) 20-26.

Charles Bache, "The First Assyrian Level at Tell Billa*[sic]*," *MJ* 24 (1935) #1, 33-48.

Bisharin

C. G. Seligman, "Note on Bisharin," *Man* 15 (1915) #47.

Bismya

E. J. Banks, "Reports from the Work at Bismya," *BW* 24 (1904) 61-69.

*E. J. Banks, "Impressions from the Excavations by the Germans at Fara and Ahu Hatab," *BW* 24 (1904) 138-146. [Bismya]

Robert Francis Harper, "Exploration and Discovery. Report from Bismya," *AJSL* 20 (1903-04) 207-208, 260-268.

E. J. Banks, "Exploration and Discovery," *BW* 24 (1904) 377-384. [Report No. 24; Report No. 25—*(from Bismya)*]

Anonymous, "the Ancient City of Bismya," *MQR, 3rd Ser.,* 32 (1906) 385-386.

Boğazköy (Khattusas)

*G[eorge] E. White, "Visit to the Hittite Cities Eyuk and Boghaz Keoy," *JTVI* 33 (1901) 226-232. [(Notes by T. G. Pinches, pp. 232-236) (Discussion pp. 236-241)]

George E. White, "The Hittite Capital Boghaz-keuy*[sic]* and its Environs," *RP* 6 (1907) 245-253.

*W. G. Gilmore, "Boghaz-Köi and the Hittites," *HR* 73 (1917) 485-486.

Boğazköy (Khattusas) concluded

Hans G. Güterbock, "New Excavations at Böghazkoy, Capital of the Hittites," *Arch* 6 (1953) 211-216.

Kurt Bittel, "Boğazköy: The Excavations of 1967 and 1968," *Arch* 22 (1969) 276-279.

Borsippa

*Fritz Hommel, "Gišgalla-ki— Babylon. Ki-nu-nir-ki—Borsippa," *SBAP* 15 (1892-93) 108-110.

A. H. Sayce, "The Earliest Mention of Borsippa," *SBAP* 33 (1911) 6.

Bolu

Nezih Firatli, "Two Galatian Tumuli in the Vicinity of Bolu," *AJA* 69 (1965) 365-367.

Bottice

*Benjamin D. Meritt, "Inscriptional and Topographical Evidence for the Site of Spartolus and the Southern Boundary of Bottice," *AJA* 27 (1923) 334-339.

Bouto

[W.] M. Flinders Petrie, "The Towns of Uazit," *ASAE* 3 (1902) 286. *[Bouto]*

Bozokbağ

Yusuf Boysal, "A Report on the 1969[sic]* Turgut Excavations," *A(A)* 12 (1968) 81-93. [Researches in Bozokbağ, pp. 83-86]

Brak

*M. E. L. Mallowan, "Excavations at Brak and Chagar Bazar," *Iraq* 9 (1947) 1-259.

Brak concluded

*E. Douglas Van Buren, "Excavations at Brak and Chagar Bazar," *Or, N.S.*, 17 (1948) 248-255.

Buccino

R. Ross Holloway, "Excavations at Buccino: 1968," *AJA* 73 (1969) 199-201.

Buhen

Walter B. Emery, "A Preliminary Report on the Excavations of the Egypt Exploration Society at Buhen, 1958-59," *Kush* 8 (1960) 7-10.

Walter B. Emery, "A Preliminary Report on the Excavations of the Egypt Exploration Society at Buhen, 1959-60," *Kush* 9 (1961) 81-86.

W[alter] B. Emery, "Egypt Exploration Society: A Preliminary Report on the Excavations at Buhen, 1960-1," *Kush* 10 (1962) 106-108.

W[alter] B. Emery, "Egypt Exploration Society: Preliminary Report on the Excavations at Buhen, 1962," *Kush* 11 (1963) 116-120.

W[alter] B. Emery, "Egypt Exploration Society: Preliminary Report on the Excavations at Buhen, 1962-63," *Kush* 12 (1964) 43-46.

Bursakhanda

*A. H. Sayce, "Geographical Notes," *JRAS* (1921) 47-55. [The City of Bursakhanda, pp. 52-53]

Butera

Dinu Adamesteanu, "Butera—A Sicilian Town Through the Ages," *Arch* 10 (1957) 166-173.

Buto

*John A. Wilson, "Buto and Hierakonpolis in the Geography of Egypt," *JNES* 14 (1955) 209-236.

Byblos

*John P. Peters, "Palestinian Exploration. *Notes of a Vacation in Palestine in 1902.*," *JBL* 22 (1903) 15-31. [1. Byblos, p 15]

*Hugh G. Bevenot, "Ancient Lebanon and Byblos," *BS* 84 (1927) 203-224.

W[illiam] F[oxwell] Albright, "Dunand's New Byblos Volume: A Lycian at the Byblian Court," *BASOR* #155 (1959) 31-34. (Review)

Siegfreid H. Horn, "Byblos in Ancient Records," *AUSS* 1 (1963) 52-61.

C

Cabul

*T. K. Cheyne, "The Land of Cabul," *SBAP* 21 (1899) 177-179.

Caca Bey Madrasa

*Aydin Sayili and Walter Ruben, "Preliminary Report on the Results of the Excavations, made under the Auspices of the Turkish Historical Society, in the Caca Bey Madrasa of Kirsehir, Turkey," *TTKB* 11 (1947) 682-691.

Cairo

*J. A. Paine, "On the 'thesis' of Mr. Whitehouse affirming Cairo to be the Biblical Zoan and Tanis magna," *JAOS* 13 (1889) xiii-xvii.

*Hishmaṭ Messiha, "Recent Excavations at Ard-El Naam Cairo 1957-1960 (Part I)," *ASAE* 59 (1966) 185-192. *[No Part II]*

Calauria

J. Penrose Harland, "The Calaurian Amphictyony," *AJA* 29 (1925) 160-171.

Thomas Kelly, "The Calaurian Amphictyony," *AJA* 70 (1966) 113-121.

Campagna

Ralph Van Damen Magoffin, "The Roman Campagna," *A&A* 2 (1915) 35-45.

Carteia

Daniel E. Woods, "Excavations in Carteia, S. Spain, 1965-1967," *AJA* 73 (1969) 247-248. *[171 B.C.]*

Calneh

I. J. Gelb, "Calneh," *AJSL* 51 (1934-35) 189-191.

*W[illiam] F[oxwell] Albright, "a) The End of Calneh in Shinar," *JBL* 62 (1943) v-vi.

*A. S. Yahuda, "Calneh in Shinar," *JBL* 65 (1946) 325-327.

Can Hasan

David [H.] French, "Canhasan, Karaman: 1961," *TAD* 11 (1961) #1, 36-37.

D[avid] H. French, "Excavations at Can Hasan. First Preliminary Report, 1961," *AS* 12 (1962) 27-40.

David [H.] French, "Canhasan, Karaman: 1961," *TAD* 11 (1961) #1, 36-37.

D[avid] H. French, "Excavations at Can Hasan. First Preliminary Report, 1961," *AS* 12 (1962) 27-40.

David [H.] French, "Can Hasan, Karaman 1962," *TAD* 12 (1962-63) #1, 21-22.

D[avid] H. French, "Excavations at Can Hasan. Second Preliminary Report, 1962," *AS* 13 (1963) 29-42.

D[avid] H. French, "Excavations at Can Hasan. Third Preliminary Report, 1963," *AS* 14 (1964) 39-119.

D[avid] H. French, "Can Hasan 1963 and 1964," *TAD* 13 (1964) #2, 27-31.

Can Hasan concluded

D[avid] H. French, "Excavations at Can Hasan. Fourth Preliminary Report, 1964," *AS* 15 (1965) 87-94.

David H. French, "Can Hasan 1965," *TAD* 14 (1965) 147-150.

David H. French, "Excavations at Can Hasan, 1965. Fifth Preliminary Report," *AS* 16 (1966) 113-123.

David H. French, "Can Hasan 1966," *TAD* 15 (1966) #1, 69-73.

D[avid] H. French, "Excavations at Can Hasan, 1966. Sixth Preliminary Report," *AS* 17 (1967) 165-178.

D[avid] H. French, "Can Hasan-Karaman 1967," *TAD* 16 (1967) #1, 89-94.

D[avid] H. French, "Excavations at Can Hasan, 1967. Seventh Preliminary Report," *AS* 18 (1968) 45-53.

Caphtor

*Robert C. Horn, "The Philistines and Ancient Crete—Caphator, Keftiu, Crete," *RP* 12 (1913) 119-122.

*G. A. Wainwright, "The Septuagint's *Καππαδοκία* for Caphtor," *JJS* 7 (1956) 91-92.

*G. A. Wainwright, "Caphtor-Cappadocia," *VT* 6 (1956) 199-210.

Cappadocia

*G. A. Wainwright, "The Septuagint's *Καππαδοκία* for Caphtor," *JJS* 7 (1956) 91-92.

*G. A. Wainwright, "Caphtor-Cappadocia," *VT* 6 (1956) 199-210.

Richard P. Harper and İnci Bayburtluoğlu, "Preliminary Report on Excavations at şar Comana Cappadociae, in 1967," *TAD* 16 (1967) #2, 107-112.

Carchemish

Robert Francis Harper, "A Visit to Carchemish," *ONTS* 9 (1889) 308-309.

*D. G. Hogarth, "Hittite Problems and the Excavations of Carchemish," *PBA* 5 (1911-12) 361-375.

D. G. Hogarth, "Carchemish and its neighbourhood," *AAA* 2 (1909) 165-184.

*George W. Gilmore, "Hittite Civilization at Carchemish," *HR* 67 (1914) 438-441.

*A. H. Sayce, "Geographical Notes," *JRAS* (1921) 47-55. [Was Oropus the Classical Name of Carchemish? pp. 47-51]

*L. A. Waddell, "The 'Oropus' Title of Carchemish," *JRAS* (1922) 266-269.

C. Leonard Woolley, "The Name of Carchemish," *JRAS* (1922) 427-429.

*L. A. Waddell, "The Oropus or Europus Title of Carchemish," *JRAS* (1922) 580-588.

*A. H. Sayce, "The Classical Name of Carchemish," *JRAS* (1923) 409-410.

H. G. Guterbock, "Carchemish," *JNES* 13 (1954) 102-114.

Caria

Emily Vermeule, "The Early Bronze Age in Caria," *Arch* 17 (1964) 244-249.

Kenan T. Erim, "Excavations at Aphrodisias in Caria, 1965," *AJA* 70 (1966) 188.

Yusuf Boysal, "New Excavations in Caria," *A(A)* 11 (1967) 31-56.

Carteia

*Daniel E. Woods, "Excavations in Roman Carteia (Andalucia, Spain) and Talayotic Majorca (Baleares, Spain), 1965," *AJA* 70 (1966) 197-198.

Carthage

†Anonymous, "Recent Discoveries at Carthage," *DR* 49 (1861) 383-416. *(Review)*

†Anonymous, "Carthage," *ERCJ* 114 (1861) 69-98. *(Review)*

*Anonymous, "Phœnicia and Carthage," *PQR* 10 (1861-62) 291-326. *(Review)*

*†Anonymous, "Carthage and Tunis," *ERCJ* 155 (1882) 121-155. *(Review)*

Edward A. Freeman, "Carthage," *ContR* 58 (1890) 356-373.

Morris Jastrow Jr., "On the founding of Carthage," *JAOS* 15 (1893) lxx-lxxiii.

Philippe Berger, "The Excavation of Carthage," *SIR* (1898) 601-614.

*S[tanley] A. Cook, "Notes and Queries. 4. *Carthage and Gezer,*" *PEFQS* 38 (1906) 159-160.

Anonymous, "Discoveries at Carthage," *RP* 6 (1907) 342-343.

Anonymous, "Archaeological Notes and Comments. Legends of Carthage Declared to be Myths," *A&A* 14 (1922) 164.

Byron Khun de Prorok, "The Excavations of Carthage, 1921-1922," *A&A* 15 (1923) 38-45.

Anonymous, "Archaeological Notes and Comments. Excavations at Carthage," *A&A* 15 (1923) 51.

Anonymous, "Archaeological Notes and Comments. Digging up Old Carthage," *A&A* 15 (1923) 99.

Anonymous, "Archaeological Notes and Comments. Excavations at Carthage, 1923," *A&A* 17 (1924) 71.

Anonymous, "Archaeological Notes and Comments. Count de Prorok' s Third Season at Carthage," *A&A* 17 (1924) 245.

Byron Khun de Prorok, "Punic Carthage and the Excavations West of the Peninsula," *AJA* 28 (1924) 80.

Carthage concluded

George W. Gilmore, "The Archaeological Possibilites at Carthage," *HR* 87 (1924) 52.

(   ) Delattre, "Recent Excavations at Carthage," *A&A* 19 (1925) 44-45.

Francis W. Kelsey, "Carthage Ancient and Modern," *A&A* 21 (1926) 55-67.

Brandon Barringer, "Finding a Phoenician Colony. Part 1: The Search," *Exped* 3 (1960-61) #1, 2-6. *[Carthage]*

Brandon Barringer, "Finding a Phoenician Colony. Part 2: The Discovery," *Exped* 3 (1960-61) #1, 7-10. *[Carthage]*

Rhys Carpenter, "A Note on the Foundation Date of Carthage," *AJA* 68 (1964) 178.

David Neiman, "*Carchêdôn* = 'New City'," *JNES* 25 (1966) 42-47. *[Carthage]*

Çatal Hüyük

James Mellaart, "Çatalhöyük Excavations, 1961," *TAD* 11 (1961) #2, 49-52.

James Mellaart, "Excavations at Çatal Hüyük. First Preliminary Report, 1961," *AS* 12 (1962) 41-65.

James Mellaart, "Excavations at Çatal Höyük.*[sic]* Summary of Results," *TAD* 12 (1962-63) #1, 36-40.

James Mellaart, "Excavations at Çatal Höyük*[sic]* 1963," *TAD* 12 (1962-63) #2, 43-49.

*James Mellaart, "Deities and Shrines of Neolithic Anatolia: Excavations at Catal Huyuk, 1962," *Arch* 16 (1963) 29-38.

James Mellaart, "Excavations at Çatal Hüyük, 1962. Second Preliminary Report," *AS* 13 (1963) 43-103.

James Mellaart, "Excavations at Çatal Hüyük, 1963. Third Preliminary Report," *AS* 4 (1964) 39-119.

Çatal Hüyük concluded

Anonymous, "The Dawning of Village Life. The Australian Insitute of Archaeology supports an important dig at Catal Huyuk in Turkey," *BH* 1 (1964) #1, 16-20.

James Mellaart, "Çatal Hüyük West," *AS* 15 (1965) 135-156.

James Mellaart, "Çatal Hüyük, a Neolithic City in Anatolia," *PBA* 51 (1965) 201-213.

James Mellaart, "Excavations Çatal Hüyük, 1965. Fourth Preliminary Report," *AS* 16 (1966) 165-191.

Caucasus

*Hyde Clarke, "On the Egyptian Colony and Language in the Caucasus, and its Anthropological Relation," *JRAI* 3 (1873-74) 178-198. (Discussion, pp. 198-200)

W. E. D. Allen, "The Caucasus in Historical Literature," *IAQR* 23 (1927) 465-476.

W. E. D. Allen, "The Ancient Caucasus and the Origin of the Georgians," *IAQR* 24 (1928) 544-557.

*V. I. Avdief, "Egypt and Caucasus," *AEE* 18 (1933) 29-36.

Caunos

Baki Öğün, "Excavations at Caunos," *TTKB* 32 (1968) 150-160.

Cenchreae

John G. Hawthorne, "Cenchreae: Port of Corinth," *Arch* 18 (1965) 191-200.

Ceos (see also: Kea and Keos)

John L. Caskey, "Excavations at Agia Irini in Ceos," *AJA* 65 (1961) 187.

John L. Caskey, "Excavations at Ceos," *Arch* 16 (1963) 284-285.

Ceos concluded

John L. Caskey, "Excavations in Ceos 1963," *AJA* 68 (1964) 193.

John L. Caskey, "Excavations in Ceos 1964," *AJA* 69 (1965) 166.

Thomas W. Jacobson, "The Cemetery at Kephala in Ceos," *AJA* 68 (1964) 196.

John L. Caskey, "Ceos: 1964," *Arch* 17 (1964) 277-280.

Cephalonia

Anonymous, "Excavations on the Island of Cephalonia," *RP* 10 (1911) 240.

Cepi

Nikolai Sokolsky, "Excavations on the Taman Peninsula: The City of Cepi," *Arch* 18 (1965) 181-186.

Chagar Bazar

*M. E. L. Mallowan, "Excavations at Tall Chagar Bazar, and an Archaeological Survey of the Ḫabur Region, 1934-5," *Iraq* 3 (1936) 1-59.

*M. E. L. Mallowan, "Excavations at Tall Chagar Bazar, and an Archaeological Survey of the Ḫabur Region, 1936," *Iraq* 4 (1937) 91-154.

*M. E. L. Mallowan, "Excavations at Brak and Chagar Bazar," *Iraq* 9 (1947) 1-259.

*E. Douglas Van Buren, "Excavations at Brak and Chagar Bazar," *Or, N.S.*, 17 (1948) 248-255.

Chaironeia (Chaeronea)

*Arthur Stoddard Cooley, "The Macedonian Tomb and the Battlefield of Chaironeia," *RP* 3 (1904) 131-143.

Chaironeia (Chaeronea) concluded

N. G. L. Hammond, "The two battles of Chaeronea (338 B.C. and 86 B.C.)," *Klio* 31 (1938) 186-218.

W. Kendrick Prichett, "Observations on Chaironeia," *AJA* 62 (1958) 307-311.

Chaldea

*[D. M. Graham], "Researches in Chaldæa and Susiana," *FBQ* 5 (1857) 317-332. *(Review)*

*B. H. C., "Recent Researches in Chaldaea and Susiana," *JSL, 3rd Ser.*, 5 (1857) 372-386. *(Review)*

*William Hayes Ward, "Light on Scriptural Texts from Recent Discoveries. Chaldea and the Chaldeans," *HR* 30 (1895) 220-222. [Criticism by John D. Sands, p. 378]

Characene

Sheldon Arthur Nodelman, "A Preliminary History of Characene," *Bery* 13 (1959-60) 83-121.

Charax

*John Hansman, "Charax and Karkheh," *IA* 7 (1967) 21-58.

Chebar

*W. Francis Ainsworth, "The Two Captivities. The Habor and Cebar," *SBAP* 15 (1892-93) 70-72.

Chios

John Broadman, "The Island of Chios: Recent Discoveries," *Arch* 8 (1955) 245-251.

Choche (See also: Ctesiphon, Seleucia and Tell 'Umar)

*Mariangiola Cavallero, "The Excavations at Choche (presumed Ctesiphon) -Area 2," *Mesop* 1 (1966) 63-80.

*Maria Maddalena Negro Ponzi, "The Excavations at Choche (presumed Ctesiphon)-Area 1," *Mesop* 1 (1966) 81-88.

*Maria Maddalena Negro Ponzi, "The Excavations at Choche Area 1," *Mesop* 2 (1967) 41-47.

*Mariangiola Carnevale Cavallero, "The Excavations at Choche-Area 2," *Mesop* 2 (1967) 48-56.

Roberta Venco Ricciardi, "The Excavations at Choche: Seasons 1966, 1967 and 1968," *Mesop* 3&4 (1968-69) 57-68.

Choga Mami

Joan Oates, "Choga Mami 1967-68: A Preliminary Report," *Iraq* 31 (1969) 115-152.

Joan Oates, "A Preliminary Report on the First Season's Excavations at Choga Mami 1967-1968," *Sumer* 25 (1969) 138-139.

Chogha Mish

Helene J. Kantor, "The Excavations at Chogha Mish, Iran: The Prehistoric Periods," *AJA* 71 (1967) 190-191.

Tell Chūra

M. E. L. Mallowan, "Tell Chūra in Nordost-Syrien," *Iraq* 28 (1966) 89-95.

Cilicia (See also: Kizzuwadna and Mersin)

William Hayes Ward, "Light on Scriptural Texts from Recent Discoveries. V. Syrians and Assyrians in Cilicia," *HR* 25 (1893) 506-508.

*Hetty Goldman, "Preliminary Expedition to Cilicia, 1934, and Excavations at Gözlü Kule, Tarsus, 1935," *AJA* 39 (1935) 526-529.

Cilicia concluded

John Garstang, "Explorations in Cilicia. The Neilson Expedition: Preliminary Report," *AAA* 34 (1937) 53-68.

John Garstang, "Explorations in Cilicia. The Neilson Expedition: Preliminary Report II *(Concluded),*" *AAA* 25 (1938) 12-23.

*John Garstang, in collaboration with Seton Lloyd, G. M FitzGerald, Alison Dun, and Dorothy Marshall, "Excavations in Cilicia. The Neilson Expedition: Third Interim Report. Excavations at Mersin: 1937-38," *AAA* 25 (1938) 71-110. (Note by Miles Burkitt, pp. 106-110) *[A Note on a Stone Age Industry of Pre-Tell Halaf Age]*

*J[ohn] Garstang, "Explorations in Cilicia. The Neilson Expedition: Fourth Interim Report. Parts I and II *(concluded).* Excavations at Mersin: 1938-39," *AAA* 26 (1939-40) 38-50.

J[ohn] Garstang, "Discoveries in Cilicia," *PEQ* 71 (1939) 134-143.

*Miles Burkitt, "Explorations in Cilicia. Neilson Expedition: 1938-9. The Earlier Cultures at Mersin," *AAA* 26 (1939-40) 51-72.

*John Garstang, with contributions by Seton H. F. Lloyd, Richard Barnett, and G. M. FitzGerald, "Explorations in Cilicia. The Neilson Expedition: Fifth Interim Report. Parts III and IV. Explorations at Mersin: 1938-1939," *AAA* 26 (1939-40) 89-158.

M. V. Seaton-Williams, "Cilician Survey," *AS* 4 (1954) 121-174.

*C. J. Gadd, "Three Roman Parallels," *AfO* 18 (1957-58) 318. [1. Two Campaigns at Cilicia]

Machteld Mellink, "The Prehistory of Syro-Cilicia," *BO* 19 (1962) 219-226.

Machteld Mellink, "An Akkadian Illustration of a Campaign in Cilicia?" *A(A)* 7 (1963) 101-115.

Cnidus

T. Leslie Shear, "Cnidus," *A&A* 9 (1920) 197-200.

Coele-Syria (See also: Baʿalbek)

Abraham Shalit, "*Κοίλη Συρία* from the Mid-Fourth Century to the Beginning of the Third Century B.C.," *SH* 1 (1954) 64-77. *[Coele-Syria]*

Colophon

*Harold North Fowler, "The American School of Classical Studies at Athens," *A&A* 14 (1922) 171-260. [Excavations at Colophon, pp. 256-260]

Commagene

*L. W. King, "Kummukh and Commagene: A Study in North Syrian and Mesopotamian Geography," *JMUEOS* #2 (1912-13) 47-56.

Coppa Nevigata

T. E. Peet, "The Early Settlements of Coppa Nevigata and the Pre-history of the Adriatic," *AAA* 3 (1910) 118-133.

Corfu

Martin L. D'Ooge, "Excavations on the Island of Corfu by the Kaiser and Dr. Dörpfeld," *A&A* 1 (1914-15) 153-158.

Corinth

T. D. Seymour, "Note from Corinth," *AJA., O.S.,* 11 (1896) 196.

*Rufus B. Richardson, "Notes. Notes from Corinth," *AJA, O.S.,*11 (1896) 371-372.

A[rthur] S[toddard] Cooley, "The Excavations of the American School in Corinth," *AJA* 5 (1901) 30-31.

*Arthur Stoddard Cooley, "Archaeological Notes," *AJA* 9 (1905) 68-69. [Corinth; Athens; Syracuse; Rome]

David M. Robinson, "Terra-cotta 'Finds' at Corinth in 1903," *AJA* 9 (1905) 72.

Corinth cont.

*Arthur Stoddard Cooley, "Archaeological Notes," *AJA* 11 (1907) 52. [1. The American Excavations in Corinth]

Anonymous, "Work of American School at Corinth," *RP* 11 (1912) 103.

*Anonymous, "Current Notes and News. Saving the Excavations at Corinth," *A&A* 9 (1920) 50-51.

Carl W. Blegen, "Corinth in Prehistoric Times," *AJA* 24 (1920) 1-13. (Supplementary Note, p. 274)

*Harold North Fowler, "The American School of Classical Studies at Athens," *A&A* 14 (1922) 171-260. [The Excavations at Corinth, pp. 193-225]

Anonymous, "Archaeological Notes and Comments. Prehistoric Sites Near Corinth," *A&A* 15 (1923) 99-100.

Carl W. Blegen, "Corinth in Prehistoric Times," *AJA* 27 (1923) 151-163.

Anonymous, "Notes and Comments. Recent Discoveries at Corinth," *A&A* 20 (1925) 279.

Theodore Leslie Shear, "Excavations at Corinth in 1925," *AJA* 29 (1925) 381-397.

B. H. Hill, "Excavations at Corinth 1925: Preliminary Report," *AJA* 30 (1926) 44-49.

Oscar Broneer, "Excavations at Corinth 1925: Area North of Basilica," *AJA* 30 (1926) 49-57.

Theodore Leslie Shear, "Excavations in the Theatre District of Corinth in 1926," *AJA* 30 (1926) 444-463.

Theodore Leslie Shear, "Recent Excavations at Corinth," *A&A* 23 (1927) 109-115.

B. H. Hill, "Excavations at Corinth 1926," *AJA* 31 (1927) 70-79.

Benjamin D. Meritt, "Excavations at Corinth 1927: Preliminary Report," *AJA* 31 (1927) 450-461.

Corinth cont.

Oscar Broneer, "Excavations in the Odeum at Corinth, 1928," *AJA* 32 (1928) 447-473.

Theodore Leslie Shear, "Excavations in the Theatre District and Tombs of Corinth in 1928," *AJA* 32 (1928) 474-495.

Rhys Carpenter, "Researches in the Topography of Ancient Corinth—I," *AJA* 33 (1929) 345-360.

Theodore Leslie Shear, "Excavations in the Theatre District and Tombs of Corinth in 1929," *AJA* 33 (1929) 515-546.

Theodore Leslie Shear, "Excavations in the North Cemetery at Corinth in 1930," *AJA* 34 (1930) 403-431.

Richard Stillwell, "Corinth," *AJA* 37 (1933) 496.

Oscar Broneer, "Excavations in the Agora at Corinth, 1933," *AJA* 37 (1933) 554-572.

Oscar Broneer, "Excavations in Corinth, 1934," *AJA* 39 (1935) 53-75.

Richard Stillwell, "Excavations at Corinth, 1934-1935," *AJA* 40 (1936) 21-45.

Charles H. Morgan II, "Excavations at Corinth, 1935-1936," *AJA* 40 (1936) 466-484.

Charles H. Morgan II, "Excavations at Corinth, 1936-37," *AJA* 41 (1937) 539-552.

Charles H. Morgan II, "Excavations at Corinth, Autumn 1937," *AJA* 42 (1938) 362-370.

Charles H. Morgan II, "Excavations at Corinth, 1938," *AJA* 43 (1939) 255-267.

Charles H. Morgan II, "The Agora at Corinth," *AJA* 43 (1939) 301.

Saul S. Weinberg, "Excavations at Corinth, 1938-1939," *AJA* 43 (1939) 592-600.

*Josephine Harris, "Numismatic Reflections on the History of Corinth," *AJA* 44 (1940) 112.

Corinth concluded

Hazel Palmer, "Who Robbed the Graves?" *AJA* 54 (1950) 257. *[Corinth]*

Henry S. Robinson, "Excavation at Corinth, 1959-1960," *AJA* 65 (1961) 191-192.

*Rhys Carpenter, "'Once We Dwelt in Well-Watered Corinth'," *AJA* 67 (1963) 209.

Henry S. Robinson, "Excavations in Corinth, 1961-1962," *AJA* 67 (1963) 216-217.

Henry S. Robinson, "Excavations at Corinth, 1962-1964," *AJA* 69 (1965) 175.

Yvonne Schwartz, "Corinth: Excavation of Temple E, Northwest, 1965," *AJA* 70 (1966) 195.

James R. Wiseman, "Excavations in Corinth: The Gymnasium Area," *AJA* 70 (1966) 197.

James [R.] Wiseman, "Excavations at Corinth: The Gymnasium Area, 1966," *AJA* 71 (1967) 196-197.

Henry S. Robinson, "Excavations at Ancient Corinth, 1959-1963," *Klio* 46 (1966) 289-305.

Charles Kaufman Williams, "Excavations of the American School of Classical Studies, Corinth, Spring of 1966," *AJA* 71 (1967) 196.

Charles K[aufman] Williams, "Corinth, 1967, The Area immediately south of Temple Hill," *AJA* 72 (1968) 174.

Paul A. Clement, "Excavations at Poseidon's Sanctuary at the Isthmus of Corinth, 1967-1968," *AJA* 73 (1969) 233-234.

Charles K. Williams II, "Spring Excavations of the American School of Classical Studies at Corinth, 1968," *AJA* 73 (1969) 247.

James Wiseman, "Excavations at Corinth: The Gymnasium Area, 1967-1968," *AJA* 73 (1969) 247.

James Wiseman, "Ancient Corinth: The Gymansium Area," *Arch* 22 (1969) 216-225.

Corsica

Roger Grosjean, "Recent Work in Corsica," *Antiq* 40 (1966) 190-198.

Cosa

Frank E. Brown, "Cosa: Exploration in Etruria," *Arch* 2 (1949) 2-10.

L. Richardson Jr., "Excavations at Cosa in Etruria, 1948-1952," *Antiq* 27 (1953) 103-104.

L. Richardson Jr., "The Sixth Campaign of Excavations at Cosa—Temple B," *AJA* 58 (1954) 148.

Lawrence Richardson, "Cosa and Rome: Comitium and Curia," *Arch* 10 (1957) 49-55.

Frank E. Brown, "Excavations at Cosa, 1965-1968," *AJA* 73 (1969) 232.

Anna M. McCann, "Excavations of the Ancient Port at Cosa, 1968," *AJA* 73 (1969) 241-242.

Courtes

A. Taramelli, "Notes on the Necropolis of Courtes," *AJA* 5 (1901) 294-301.

Crete

*Anonymous, "Crete and the Cretans," *CE* 82 (1867) 224-246. *(Review)*

[Frederico Halbherr], "American Expedition to Krete Under Professor Halbherr," *AJA, O.S.*, 9 (1894) 538-544.

Frederico Halbherr, "Papers of the American School of Classical Studies at Athens. Report of the Expedition of the Institute to Crete," *AJA, O.S.*, 11 (1896) 525-538.

D. G. Hogarth, "The Exploration of Crete," *ContR* 78 (1900) 794-808.

Anonymous, "Excavation in Crete. Greek Civilization 3000 B.C.," *AAOJ* 23 (1901) 312-315.

William C. Winslow, "Recent Discoveries in Crete," *AJA* 5 (1901) 4-5.

Crete cont.

*(Miss) Harriet A. Boyd, "Houses and Tombs of the Geometric Period at Kavusi, Crete," *AJA* 5 (1901) 14-15.

Federico Halbherr, "Ruins of Unknown Cities at Haghios Ilias and Prinià," *AJA* 5 (1901) 393-403.

[A. J.] Evans and [D. G.] Hogarth, "The Cretan Exploration Fund: an Abstract of the Preliminary Report of the First Season's Excavations," *Man* 1 (1901) #2.

J. L. M[yers], "Abstract of the Report of the Committee of the British Association on Explorations in Crete," *Man* 1 (1901) #145.

Anonymous, "Cretan Discoveries," *MR* 83 (1901) 474-475.

*W. Boyd-Dawkins, "Remains of Animals found in the Dictæan Cave in 1901," *Man* 2 (1902) #114.

Anonymous, "Crete," *RP* 3 (1904) 92-94.

R. C. Bosanquet, "Excavations at Heleia (Palaikastro) and Praisos in Eastern Crete," *RP* 3 (1904) 376-377.

Anonymous, "Recent Excavations in Crete and Their Bearing on the Early History of the Ægean," *CQR* 61 (1905-06) 379-414.

Richard B. Seager, "Excavations on the Island of Mochlos, Crete, in 1908," *AJA* 13 (1909) 273-303.

*H. R. Hall, "The Discoveries in Crete and their Relation to the History of Egypt and Palestine," *SBAP* 31 (1909) 135-148, 221-238, 280-285, 311-318.

Anonymous, "Minoan Crete," *ERCJ* 211 (1910) 457-479. *(Review)*

(Miss) Edith H. Hall, "American Excavations in Crete in 1910," *AJA* 15 (1911) 73-74.

Anonymous, "Excavations on Crete," *RP* 10 (1911) 239, 296.

*Charles H. Hawes, "Cretan Anthropometry," *AJA* 15 (1912) 65-67.

E[dith] H. Hall, "Mediterranean Section. The Cretan Expedition," *MJ* 3 (1912) 39-44.

Crete concluded

Anonymous, "Work on the Island of Crete," *RP* 11 (1912) 280.

*Robert C. Horn, "The Philistines and Ancient Crete—Caphator, Keftiu, Crete," *RP* 12 (1913) 119-122.

Anonymous, "Discoveries in Crete," *MR* 95 (1913) 302-306.

Anonymous, "Discoveries in Crete," *RP* 13 (1914) 115-116.

‡J[ohn] L. Myers, "The Cretan Labyrinth: A Retrospective of Ægean Research. *The Huxley Memorial Lecture for* 1933," *JRAI* 63 (1933) 269-312. [Bibliography, pp. 308-312]

Sp. Marinatos, "Volcanic Destruction of Minoan Crete," *Antiq* 13 (1939) 425-439.

*Charles Seltman, "Life in Ancient Crete—I: Minos," *HT* 2 (1952) 231-242.

*Charles Seltman, "Life in Ancient Crete—II: Atlantis," *HT* 2 (1952) 332-343.

*V. E. G. Kenna, "Ancient Crete and the Use of the Cylinder Seal," *AJA* 72 (1968) 321-336.

Harriett Boyd Hawes, "Memoirs of a Pioneer Excavator in Crete," *Arch* 18 (1965) 94-101.

Harriett Boyd Hawes, "Part II: Memoirs of a Pioneer Excavator in Crete," *Arch* 18 (1965) 268-276.

*Roland F. Willetts, "The Second International Cretological Congress," *KZFE* 5 (1966) 162-163.

*Keith Branigan, "Further Light on Prehistoric Relations between Crete and Byblos," *AJA* 71 (1967) 117-121.

Crotona

*Anonymous, "Plan to Excavate Locri and Crontona," *RP* 6 (1907) 270-271.

Ctesiphon (See also: Choche, Seleucia and Tell ʿUmar)

Oscar Reuther, "The German Excavations at Ctesiphon," *Antiq* 3 (1928) 434-451.

George A. Barton, "Dr. Waterman's Excavation at Tel Omar (Ctesiphon)," *BASOR* #30 (1928) 6-8.

Giorgio Gullini, "First Report of the Results of the First Excavation Campaign at Seleucia and Ctesiphon (1st Octoper[sic]*—17th December 1964)," *Sumer* 20 (1964) 63-65.

*Giorgio Gullini, "First Preliminary Report of Excavations at Selucia and Ctesiphon - Season 1964, Foreword," *Mesop* 1 (1966) 3-6.

*Giorgio Gullini, "Problems of an Excavation in Northern Babylon," *Mesop* 1 (1966) 7-38 *[Area of Seleucia and Ctesiphon]*

*Mariangiola Cavallero, "The Excavations at Choche (presumed Ctesiphon)-Area 2," *Mesop* 1 (1966) 63-80.

*Maria Maddalena Negro Ponzi, "The Excavations at Choche (presumed Ctesiphon)-Area 1," *Mesop* 1 (1966) 81-88.

*Giorgio Gullini, "Second Preliminary Report of the Excavations at Seleucia and Ctesiphon - Season 1965, Foreword," *Mesop* 2 (1967) 7-8.

*Maria Maddalena Negro Ponzi, "The Excavations at Choche Area 1," *Mesop* 2 (1967) 41-47. *[Tell ʿUmar]*

*Mariangiola Carnevale Cavallero, "The Excavations at Choche-Area 2," *Mesop* 2 (1967) 48-56.

*Giorgio Gullini, "Third Preliminary Report of the Excavations at Seleucia and Ctesiphon-Seasons 1966, 1967, 1968. Foreword," *Mesop* 3&4 (1968-69) 7-10.

Cunaxa

†W. F. Ainsworth, "The Battle of Cunaxa," *SBAP* 7 (1884-85) 28-30.

†H. Rassam, "The Battle of Cunaxa," *SBAP* 7 (1884-85) 50-52.

Cush (See also: Kush)

*A[ngus] C[rawford], "Notes—Archæological, Historical, Critical, Etc.," *PER* 12 (1898-99) 346-348. [Cush, pp. 347-348]

*Claude R. Conder, "Notes on New Discoveries," *PEFQS* 41 (1909) 266-275. [Cush, p. 266]

*J. W. Jack, "Recent Biblical Archaeology," *ET* 52 (1940-41) 112-115. [Cush and Cushan-Rishathaim, pp. 114-115]

B. G. Haycock, "The Kingship of Cush in the Sudan," *CSSH* 7 (1964-65) 461-480.

Cutha

Edgar James Banks, "Cutha," *BW* 22 (1903) 60-64.

Cyinda

R. H. Simpson, "A Note on Cyinda," *HJAH* 6 (1957) 503-504.

Cyme

Freya Stark, "Cyme: The Phrygian Mood," *HT* 4 (1954) 598-604.

Cyprus

*Augustus C. Merriam, "Troy and Cyprus," *PAPA* 7 (1875) 19-21. *[Bound with Transactions, but paged separately]*

*Bayard Taylor, "Discovered Treasures of Ephesus, Cyprus and Mycenæ," *DTQ* 4 (1878) 213-226.

C[laude] R. Conder, "Antiquities of Cyprus," *SRL* 23 (1894) 126-143. *(Review)*

Paul V. C. Baur, "Post-Myceanaean Influence in Cyprus," *AJA* 7 (1903) 74-75.

*Joseph Offord, "Archaeological Notes on Jewish Antiquities. LI. *Cyprus and Mizraim,*" *PEFQS* 50 (1918) 138-139.

Cyprus cont.

Einar Gjerstad, "The Swedish Excavations in Cyprus," *Antiq* 2(1928) 189-191.

Arthur J. Evans, "Mycenæan Cyprus as Illustrated in the British Museum Excavations," *JRAI* 30 (1900) 199-220.

Anonymous, "The Cyprus Expedition," *UMB* 3 (1931-32) 22-23, 118-121; 5 (1934-35) #2, 40.

E[dith] H. D[othan], "The Cyprus Expedition," *UMB* 4 (1932-33) 12-16.

G[eorge] H. McF[adden], "The Cyprus Expedition," *UMB* 5 (1934-35) #4, 11-13.

P. Dikaios, "New Light on Prehistoric Cyprus," *Iraq* 7 (1940) 69-83.

Harry Luke, "Cyprus: An Historical Retrospect," *IAQR* 40 (1944) 417-423.

T. B. Mitford, "The Character of Ptolemaic Rule in Cyprus," *Aeg* 33 (1953) 80-90.

*John Barns, "Cimon and the first Athenian Expedition to Cyprus," *HJAH* 2 (1953-54) 163-176.

Saul S. Weinberg, "Exploring the Early Bronze Age in Cyprus," *Arch* 9 (1956) 112-121.

J. Du Plat Taylor, "Late Cypriot III in the Light of Recent Excavations," *PEQ* 88 (1956) 22-37.

*Ruth Amiran, "Palestine, Syria and Cyprus in the MB I Period," *EI* 5 (1958) 84*.

Vassos Karageorghis, "Notes on some Mycenaean survivals in Cyprus during the first millenium*[sic]* B.C.," *KZFE* 1 (1962) 71-77.

Judy Birmingham, "The Chronology of Some Early and Middle Iron Age Cypriot Sites," *AJA* 67 (1963) 15-42.

*Einar Gjerstad, "Supplementary Notes on Finds from Ajia Irini in Cyprus," *MB* #3 (1963) 3-40.

K. Nicolaou, "Archaeological News from Cyprus, 1966," *AJA* 71 (1967) 399-406.

Cyprus concluded

*Hans G. Guterbock, "The Hittite Conquest of Cyprus Reconsidered," *JNES* 26 (1967) 73-81.

K. Nicolaou, "Archaeological News from Cyprus, 1967," *AJA* 72 (1968) 369-382.

Vassos Karageorghis, "Late Bronze Age news from Cyprus (1967-1968)," *KZFE* 7 (1968) 100-102.

*Heinz Geiss, "The First International Congress of Cypriot Studies," *KZFE* 8 (1969) 162-164.

Cyrenaica

Theresa Howard Carter, "Reconnaissance in Cyrenaica," *Exped* 5 (1962-63) #3, 18-27.

Donald White, "Excavations at Apollonia Cyrenaica: Preliminary Report," *AJA* 70 (1966) 259-265.

Cyrene

Anonymous, "Preliminary Work in the Excavation of Cyrene," *RP* 10 (1911) 16.

Anonymous, "Explorations at Cyrene," *RP* 11 (1912) 105.

*S. Applebaum, "A Lamp and Other Remains of the Jewish Community of Cyrene," *IEJ* 7 (1957) 154-162.

*L. H. Jeffery, "The Pact of the First Settlers of Cyrene," *HJAH* 10 (1961) 139-147.

David Crownover, "Discoveries in Cyrene," *Exped* 5 (1962-63) #3, 28-31.

Cyzicus

Arthur E. Henderson, "Survey of Cyzicus," *RP* 3 (1904) 355-364.

Anonymous, "The City of Cyzicus," *MQR, 3rd Ser.*, 32 (1906) 378-380.

D

Dabnarti

Jay W. Ruby, "Preliminary Report of the University of California Expedition to Dabnarti, 1963," *Kush* 12 (1964) 54-56.

Dadassas

*John Garstang, "The Hulaya River Land and Dadassas: A Crucial Problem in Hittite Geography," *JNES* 3 (1944) 14-37.

Dahshur

M. Basta, "Excavations in the Desert Road at Dahshur," *ASAE* 60 (1968) 57-63.

Damascus

J. L. Porter, "The Rivers of Damascus," *JSL, 2nd Ser.*, 4 (1853) 245-262; 6 (1854) 235-236.

J. L. Porter, "The Rivers of Damascus. Article II," *JSL, 2nd Ser.*, 5 (1853-54) 45-57.

John Hogg, "On the Rivers of Damascus," *JSL, 2nd Ser.*, 5 (1853-54) 216-217.

*†Anonymous, "The Rev. J. L. Porter 's Damascus and Palmyra," *TLJ* 10 (1857-58) 146-158. (Review)

*G[eorge] Rawlinson, "Biblical Topography. VI.—Sites connected with the History of Abraham—Harran, Damascus, Hebron," *MI* 4 (1886) 241-252. [Part IV not published]

*A. Lowy, "On the Origin of the Name Dameshek (Damascus)," *SBAP* 11 (1888-89) 237.

Anonymous, "Damascus," *EN* 2 (1890) 36-37.

Damascus concluded

E. W. G. Masterman, "Damascus, the Oldest City in the World," *BW* 12 (1898) 71-85.

E. W. Gurney Masterman, "The Rivers of Damascus," *ET* 13 (1901-02) 215-220, 477.

R. J. Robinson, "Damascus: The Pearl of the Desert," *BW* 33 (1909) 152-159.

*J. E. Hanauer, "Damascus Notes," *PEFQS* 44 (1912) 40-45.

F. G. Newton, "Notes on Damascus. 1. *Roman Arch, North of North Gate, in Temple Enclosure Wall,*" *PEFQS* 48 (1916) 33-35.

E[phraim] A. Speiser, "'Damascus' as Ša-imērišu," *JAOS* 71 (1951) 256-257.

Cyrus H. Gordon, "Damascus in Assyrian Sources," *IEJ* 2 (1952) 174-175.

Robert North, "The Damascus of Qumran Geography," *PEQ* 87 (1955) 34-48.

Dar-Al-Imara

Mohamed Ali Mustafa, "Dar-Al-Imra at Kufa," *Sumer* 13 (1957) 207-208.

Deeba-Korti

J[ean] de Heinzelin, "Survey in the Deeba-Korti Area," *Kush* 15 (1967-68) 59-69.

Defenneh

*J. N. Fradenburgh, "'The Palace of the Jew's Daughter'," *MR* 72 (1890) 765-766. *[Defenneh-Jer. 3:16]*

el-Deir

*Tewfik Boulos, "Report on excavatons carried out at Sheikh Nassir and el-Deir, near Abydos," *ASAE* 37 (1937) 243-256.

Deir el-Bahari

†Samuel Birch, "Remarks on the recent discoveries at the Deir-el-Bahari," *SBAP* 4 (1881-82) 5-6.

Alfred H. Kellogg, "Note on the 'Find' at Deir-el-Bahari," *PR* 4 (1883) 152-160.

Edouard Naville and H. R. Hall, "Excavations at Deir el-Bahari, 1905-6," *Man* 6 (1906) #64.

Edouard Naville, "Excavations at Deir el-Bahari (1906-7)," *Man* 7 (1907) #102.

*Wallace N. Stearns, "Deir el-Bahari and Abydos," *AJA* 16 (1912) 108.

I. E. S. Edwards, "Lord Dufferin's Excavations at Deir El-Baḥri and the Clandeboye Collection," *JEA* 51 (1965) 16-28.

Deir el-Ḳala

Laurence M. Angus, "Roman Remains at Deir el-Ḳala, Lebanon," *PEFQS* 52 (1920) 158-161.

Deir el-Madina

B. Bruyère, "New details for insertion in the Theban 1/1000 scale maps.—I. Deir el-Madina," *ASAE* 25 (1925) 174-177. (Note by R. Engelbach, p. 174)

Delos

Anonymous, "Excavations on the Island of Delos during 1906," *RP* 6 (1907) 223-224.

Joseph Offord, "Archaeological Notes. IV. *The Jewish Community at Delos,* " *PEFQS* 47 (1915) 201-203.

Charlotte R. Long, "Reply to M. Gallet de Santerre,"*AJA* 65 (1961) 65-66. *[Delos]*

Delphi

Charles Seltman, "Delphi I: Pythian Apollo," *HT* 1 (Aug., 1951) 14-23.

Charles Seltman, "Delphi II: The Other God," *HT* 1 (Sept., 1951) 13-22.

*W. G. Forrest, "Colonisation and the Rise of Delphi," *HJAH* 6 (1957) 160-175.

Demetrias

Roland G. Kent, "The City Gates of Demetrias," *AJA* 9 (1905) 166-169.

Dendereh (Dendrá)

Axel Persson, "The Swedish Excavations at Dendrá, Greece," *A&A* 25 (1928) 277-284, 291, 300.

Ray Anita Slater, "Dendereh and the University Museum 1898-1970," *Exped* 12 (1969-70) #4, 15-20.

Dêr

*Seton Lloyd, "Recent Discoveries of the Iraq Directorate of Antiquities," *PEQ* 75 (1943) 105-109. (Additional note by S. W. Perowne, p. 109) *[Tell Dêr, pp. 108-109]*

Taha Baqir and Ali Mustafa, "Iraq Government Sounding at Dêr," *Sumer* 1 (1945) #2, 37-54.

Tell Al-Dhiba'i

M. A. Mustafa, "Soundings at Tell Al-Dhiba'i*[sic]*," *Sumer* 5 (1949) 173-186.

Lamia al-Gailani, "Tell edh-Dhiba'i," *Sumer* 21 (1965) 33-40.

*Abdul Kareem Abdullah, "The Paramount God and the Old Name of Al-Dhiba'i," *Sumer* 23 (1967) 189-192.

Tell-edh-Dhiyab

*E[phraim] A. Speiser, "An Important Discovery," *BASOR* #27 (1927) 11-12. *[Tell-edh-Dhiyab]*

Didyma

E. Baldwin Smith, "Didyma," *A&A* 9 (1920) 187-195.

Dilmun

S[amuel] N[oah] Kramer, "Dilmun, the Land of the Living," *BASOR* #96 (1944) 18-28.

P. B. Cornwall, "On the Location of Dilmun," *BASOR* #103 (1946) 3-11.

Diyala Basin

Thorkild Jacobsen, "Summary of Report by the Diyala Basin Archaeological Project June 1, 1957 to June 1, 1958," *Sumer* 14 (1958) 79-89.

Dog River

G. Frederick Wright, "Inscriptions at Dog River, Syria," *RP* 5 (1906) 3-5.

*Dorothy Mackay and E. S. Kennedy, "Report of the Excavation of cave near the mouth of the Dog River. North of Beirut," *BMB* 13 (1956) 53-71.

Domuztepe

U. Bahadir Alkim, "The Results of the Recent Excavations at Domuztepe," *TTKB* 16 (1952) 238-250.

Dongola Reach

Anthony E. Marks, T. R. Hays, and Jean de Heinzelin, "Preliminary Report of the South Methodist University Expedition in the Dongola Reach," *Kush* 15 (1967-68) 165-192.

Dorginarti

*James Knudstad, "Serra East and Dorginarti. A Preliminary Report on the 1963-64 Excavations of the University of Chicago Oriental Institute Sudan Expedition," *Kush* 14 (1966) 165-186.

Dra Abu el-Naga

Lanny Bell, "Return to Dra Abu el-Naga," *Exped* 11 (1968-69) #3, 26-37.

Dura-Europos

Anonymous, "Notes and Comments. Yale Receives Antiquities from Excavations in Doura," *A&A* 30 (1930) 142. *[Dura-Europos]*

J. M. Unvala, "Doura-Eropos*[sic]*," *BSOAS* 6 (1930-32) 133-149.

*Fritz Neugass, "Notes and Comments. Recent Excavations in Tello, Susa and Syria," *A&A* 32 (1931) 137-138. [Doura-Europos*[sic]*, p. 138]

Clark Hopkins, "The Season 1934-35 at Dura," *AJA* 39 (1935) 293-299.

Clark Hopkins, "Yale Excavations at Dura-Europos, 1934-1935," *AJA* 40 (1936) 123.

Frank E. Brown, "The Campaign of 1936-37 at Dura-Europos," *AJA* 42 (1938) 127.

J. W. Crowfoot, "Dura-Europos," *Antiq* 19 (1945) 113-121.

Alfred R. Bellinger, "Seleucid Dura," *Bery* 9 (1948-49) 51-67.

J[otham] J[ohnson], "The Dura Air Photographs," *Arch* 3 (1950) 158-161.

Margaret Deanesly, "Dura-Europos," *CQR* 168 (1967) 5-10.

E

Eanna

*Joseph Poplicha, "The Biblical Nimrod and the Kingdom of Eanna," *JAOS* 49 (1929) 303-317.

Ecbatanas

*William F. Ainsworth, "The Achmethas or Ecbatanas of Western Asia," *SBAP* 15 (1892-93) 425-432.

Edassa (Urfa)

J. B. Segal, "Report on an Expedition to Edassa (Urfa), Turkey, August-September 1959," *TAD* 10 (1960) #2, 28-29.

Ed-Dêr

A. H. Sayce, "Excavations at Ed-Dêr," *ASAE* 6 (1905) 159-167.

Eden

*W[illiam] F[oxwell] Albright, "The Location of the Garden of Eden," *AJSL* 39 (1922-23) 15-31.

*George S. Duncan, "Notes and Comments. The Location of Eden," *A&A* 27 (1929) 92.

*George S. Duncan, "The Biblical and Archaeological Location of Eden," *AJA* 33 (1929) 103-104.

*G[eorge] Rawlinson, "Biblical Topography. No. 1.—The Site of Paradise," *MI* 1 (1884-85) 401-410. *[Eden]*

*C. H. Toy, "Notice of F. Delitzch's views as to the alleged site of Eden," *JAOS* 11 (1885) lxxii-lxxiii.

Edri

[Leslie Porter], "The Ruins of an Ancient City at Edri," *MQR, 3rd Ser.,* 33 (1907) 611-612.

Ehnasya

W. M. Flinders Petrie, "Excavations at Ehnasya," *Man* 4 (1904) #77.

Egypt

†Meirion, "Name of Egypt," *MMBR* 6 (1798) 258-259.

†Anonymous, "Dr. White's Ægyptiaca. Part I.," *BCQTR* 17 (1801) 565-572; 18 (1801) 131-136.

†Anonymous, "Antiquities of Egypt," *QRL* 19 (1818) 391-424. *(Review)*

*†Anonymous, "Belzoni's Discoveries in Egypt and Nubia," *BCQTR, N.S.,* 14 (1820) 561-580. *(Review)*

†Anonymous, "Belzoni's Researches in Egypt," *MMBR* 50 (1820-21) 643-658. *(Review)*

†Anonymous, "Belzoni's Operations and Discoveries in Egypt, &c.," *QRL* 24 (1820-21) 139-169. *(Review)*

Anonymous, "Researches in Egypt," *MMBR* 60 (1825-26) 32-35.

*†Anonymous, "Egypt and Thebes," *QRL* 53 (1835) 103-142. *(Review)*

†Anonymous, "The Chevalier Bunsen's *Ancient Egypt* ," *ERCJ* 83 (1846) 391-430. *(Review)*

†Anonymous, "Bunsen *on Egypt,*" *QRL* 78 (1846) 145-174. *(Review)*

O. T. D., "Egypt's Place in Universal History," *BRCM* 5 (1848-49) 377-404. *(Review)*

C. C., "Ancient Egypt," *WR* 50 (1848-49) 208-233. *(Review)*

*†Anonymous, "Discoveries in Picture Writing," *BQRL* 12 (1850) 70-110. *(Review)*

Anonymous, "Egypt and its Monuments," *MR* 32 (1850) 130-147. *(Review)*

C. D., "Egypt," *JSL, 1st Ser.,* 7 (1851) 257-291. *(Review)*

F. W. H., "Egypt as It Is," *CE* 52 (1852) 51-68. *(Review)*

Anonymous, "Lepsius' Letters from Egypt, &c.," *CTPR, 3rd Ser.,* 9 (1853) 449-467. *(Review)*

*R. S. P., "Egypt, Ethiopia, and the Peninsula of Sinai," *JSL, 2nd Ser.,* 6 (1854) 314-330. *(Review)*

Egypt cont.

Anonymous, "Bunsen's Egypt," *DUM* 46 (1855) 273-281. *(Review)*

†Anonymous, "Bunsen's Egypt," *BQRL* 23 (1856) 334-360. *(Review)*

[Edward Young] Hincks, "Bunsen's Egypt," *DUM* 54 (1859) 20-32. *(Review)*

*†Anonymous, "Bunsen's Egypt and the Chronology of the Bible," *QRL* 105 (1859) 382-421. *(Review)*

W. W., "Bunsen's Egyptian History," *JSL, 3rd Ser.,* 10 (1859-60) 53-71. *(Review)*

†Anonymous, "Palmer's Egyptian Chronicles," *DR* 52 (1862) 25-51. *(Review)*

Anonymous, "Clark's Illustrations of Egypt," *CongR* 4 (1864) 273-282. *(Review)*

Anonymous, "Bunsen's Egypt," *CE* 88 (1867) 305-335. *(Review)*

[George T. Day], "Sketches of Egypt," *FBQ* 15 (1867) 133-150.

*J. E. Howard, "Egypt and the Bible," *JTVI* 10 (1876-77) 340-377. [(Appendices, pp. 377-379) (Discussion, pp. 379-385)]

Reginald Stuart Poole, "Ancient Egypt," *ContR* 34 (1878-79) 304-321, 570-581, 741-762; 35 (1879) 107-120, 237-250.

*P. Thomson, "Nebuchadnezzar's Conquest of Egypt. confirmed from a contemporary Hieroglyphic Inscription," *Exp., 1st Ser.,* 10 (1879) 397-403.

†Anonymous, "Egypt," *LQHR* 52 (1879) 286-327. *(Review)*

*†Anonymous, "Egypt and Sacred Chronology," *LQHR* 53 (1879-80) 265-310. *(Review)*

R. P. Greg, "II. The Palæolithic Age in Egypt," *JRAI* 10 (1880-81) 428-429.

Reginald Stuart Poole, "Ancient Egypt in Its Comparative Relations. Lectures Delivered at the Royal Institution in February and March, 1881," *ContR* 39 (1881) 804-820; 40 (1881) 45-62, 282-299, 361-377.

Egypt cont.

*Villers Stuart, "Note on some Egyptian Antiquities," *JRAI* 12 (1882-83) 324-236.

John W. Dawson, "A Naturalist's Visit to Egypt," *JCP* 3 (1883-84) 278-290, 576-582.

*George Rawlinson, "The Biblical Notices of Egypt Illustrated from Profane Sources," *CM* 18 (1884) 37-46, 98-106, 159-167, 288-296, 359-367; 19 (1884) 41-48, 105-113, 158-166, 223-231, 297-305, 347-354.

Howard Osgood, "Egypt Before B.C. 2000," *ONTS* 5 (1884-85) 161-166, 213-219.

†F. Cope Whitehouse, "Remarks," *SBAP* 8 (1885-86) 201-210. [Researches in the Moeris Bais; The Wadi Moeleh; Dionysius and the Dier Moeleh; Meredis Lacus on the Ptolemaic Maps; Hanes-Heracleopolis; Behnesa]

†Anonymous, "The Voice of Memnon," *ERCJ* 164 (1886) 263-283. *(Review)*

W. M. Flinders Petrie, "A Season's Results in Egypt," *BOR* 1 (1886-87) 151-154.

J. Leslie Porter, "Egypt: Physical, Historical, Literary, and Social," *JTVI* 20 (1886-87) 15-35. (Discussion, pp. 35-36)

F. C. H. Wendel, "Erman's Egypt," *AJSL* 5 (1888-89) 110-114. *(Review)*

Farley B. Goddard, "Correspondence. Letter from Egypt," *AJA, O.S.*, 6 (1890) 122.

*J. N. Fradenburgh, "Recent Explorations in Egypt," *MR* 72 (1890) 818-834. [I. Pithom; II. Goshen; III. San—Tanis—Zoan; IV. Tahpanhes; V. Naukratis; VI. Bubastis; VII. Important Discoveries]

*Edward Hull, "Sketch of the Geographical History of Egypt and the Nile Valley," *JTVI* 24 (1890-91) 307-334.

W. W. Moore, "Daybreak on the Nile," *USR* 2 (1890-91) 88-97.

W. W. Moore, "Otherworldiness in Ancient Egypt," *USR* 2 (1890-91) 166-178.

Egypt cont.

W. W. Moore, "Some Recent Explorations in Egypt," *USR* 3 (1891-92) 184-195.

*E. Amélineau, "Some Geographical Identifications in Egypt," *IAQR, 2nd Ser.,* 3 (1892) 328-345. [I. *ΜΕΝΕΛΙΑΤΟΥ*, II. *ΓΑΒΑΣΕΟΣ*, III. *ΑΓΝΟΥ*, IV. *ΗΛΕΑΠΧΙΑ*, V. *ΝΙΚΕΤΟΥ*, VI. *ΠΤΕΝΕΤΩ*, VII. HEROOPOLIS]

W. St. C[had] Boscawen, "A Season's Work in Egypt," *BOR* 6 (1892-93) 236-239.

Anonymous, "Recent Works on Egypt," *CQR* 39 (1894-95) 474-501. *(Review)*

*W. M. Flinders Petrie, "Egypt and Israel," *ContR* 69 (1896) 617-627.

J. E. Quibell, "On the date of the period in Egypt called Neolithic, Libyan and New Race," *ZÄS* 35 (1897) 134-140.

F. A. Walker, "Herodotus. I.—How Far His Remarks bearing on Egyptian Geology are reliable in the Light of Recent Egyptian Research," *JTVI* 31 (1897-98) 57-65. (Discussion, pp. 66-71)

*Grant Bey, "The Climate of Egypt in Geological, Prehistoric, and Ancient Historic Times," *JTVI* 32 (1898-99) 87-105.

*A. H. Sayce, "Notes," *SBAP* 22 (1900) 77-79. *[Egypt]*

Geo. St. Clair, "New Light on Egypt," *WR* 154 (1900) 187-189. *(Review)*

Benjamin Ide Wheeler, "The Archaeological Work now in Progress under the Auspices of the University of California," *AJA* 5 (1901) 19-20. *[Egypt]*

Charles S. Myers, "Note on the Early Dynastic Period in Egypt," *Man* 2 (1902) #51.

Howard Carter, "Report on General Work done in the Southern Inspectorate," *ASAE* 4 (1903) 43-50. [§I. Biban el-Molouk; §II. Drah Abou'l Neggeh; §III. Sheikh Abd el Goornah; §IV. Palace of Medinet-Habu; §V. Kouft]

Egypt cont.

*Howard Carter, "Report of Work done in Upper Egypt," *ASAE* 4 (1903) 171-180. [III. Excavations: 1. Continuation of the excavations of Amenhotep III Palace—Medinet-Habou; 2. Excavation of Biban El Hareem; 3. Excavation at Sheikh Abdel Goorneh; 4. Excavation at Biban El-Moluk; 5. A small excavation in the Assasif. Western Thebes; 6. Excavations at the Ramesseum by the Service, pp. 175-178]

*Walter Melville Patton, "Ancient Egypt and Syria," *BS* 60 (1903) 92-108.

W. M. Flinders Petrie, "The Ancient Civilization of Egypt," *JTVI* 35 (1903) 9-11. (Discussion, pp. 12-13)

William E. Curtis, "Ancient Cities of Egypt," *AAOJ* 26 (1904) 77-84. [Alexandria; Cairo and Its University; Stone Towers; Memphis; Mastabah of Ti; Rock-Hewn Tombs]

Anonymous, "Ancient Egypt," *QRL* 200 (1904) 48-75. *(Review)*

N. de Garis Davies, "The Work of the Archaeological Survey of Egypt," *BW* 23 (1904) 382-384.

*Howard Carter and G. Legrain, "Report on Work done in Upper Egypt (1903-1904)," *ASAE* 6 (1905) 112-129. [VII. Deir el Bahri; VIII. Sheikh Abd-el-Goorneh; IX. Medinet Habou; X. Kouft; XI. Negadeh; XII. Gobbet-el-Howa (Aswan)]

John Garstang, Note upon Excavations made in 1904-05," *Man* 5 (1905) #79. *[Egypt]*

Dow Covington, "Mastaba mound Excavations," *ASAE* 6 (1905) 193-218.

Anonymous, "The Latest from Egypt," *MR* 87 (1905) 646-648.

*M[elvin] G[rove] Kyle, "Egyptological Notes," *RP* 4 (1905) 32. *[Two Egypts]*

George A. Reisner, "The Work of the Hearst Egyptian Expedition of the University of California in 1903-4," *RP* 4 (1905) 131-141.

Joseph Offord, "Egypt Under the Earlier Dynasties," *AAOJ* 28 (1906) 266-269.

W. C. Winslow, "Petrie's Work in the Delta," *AAOJ* 28 (1906) 304-305.

Egypt cont.

J. Lieblein, "Observations on the Ancient History of Egypt," *SBAP* 28 (1906) 29-32.

Melvin Grove Kyle, "Archeological Department: A Season in Egypt," *CFL, 3rd Ser.,* 9 (1908) 10-13.

Anonymous, "Late Discoveries in Egypt," *MR* 90 (1908) 307-311.

Anonymous, "Progress of Excavations in Egypt," *RP* 7 (1908) 122-123.

[A. H. Sayce(?)], "Recent Discoveries in Egypt," *SBAP* 30 (1908) 72-74.

Henry Proctor, "Ancient Egypt," *AAOJ* 31 (1909) 163-166.

Anonymous, "'New Light on Ancient Egypt'," *CFL, 3rd Ser.,* 11 (1909) 19-20. *(Review)*

*H. R. Hall, "The Discoveries in Crete and their Relation to the History of Egypt and Palestine," *SBAP* 31 (1909) 135-148, 221-238, 280-285, 311-318.

D. Randall MacIver, "The Egyptian Section. The Eckley B. Coxe Junior Expedition," *MJ* 1 (1901) 4, 22-28.

C. L[eonard] Woolley, "Egyptian Section. The Eckley B. Coxe Expedition," *MJ* 1 (1910) 42-48.

H. de Morgan, "Report on Excavations made in Upper Egypt during the winter 1907-1908," *ASAE* 12 (1912) 25-50.

Camden M. Cobern, "The Latest Excavations in Egypt," *HR* 66 (1913) 352-357.

*Camden M. Cobern, "Archaeological Notes," *HR* 65 (1913) 464-465. [Notes from the Nile, p. 465]

E. P. Wilkins, "Napoleon's Egypt," *MJ* 4 (1913) 56-62.

Aylward M. Blackman, "The Archaeological Survey: Report for 1913, 1914," *JEA* 1 (1914) 41-42, 182-184. *[Egypt]*

G. H. Richardson, "The World's Debt to Egypt," *OC* 28 (1914) 303-317.

Egypt cont.

Anonymous, "The Eckley B. Coxe, Jr. Egyptian Expedition," *MJ* 6 (1915) 63-84.

Stanley A. Cook, "Notes and Queries. *The Eastern Frontier of Egypt*," *PEFQS* 48 (1916) 100-102.

Clarence S. Fisher, "The Eckley B. Coxe Jr. Egyptian Expedition," *MJ* 8 (1917) 211-237.

*L[uther] T. Townsend, "Prehistoric Egypt—Its Bearing on the Theory of Evolution," *CFL, 3rd Ser.*, 25 (1919) 1-7.

Warren R. Dawson, "British Archæology in Egypt," *IAQR* 15 (1919) 627-630.

A. H. Sayce, "The Date of the Middle Empire," *AEE* 6 (1921) 102-103. (Note by [W. M.] F[linders] P[etrie], p. 103)

*H. R. Hall, "Egypt and the External World in the Time of Akhenaten," *JEA* 7 (1921) 39-53.

C. G. Seligman, "The Older Palæolithic Age in Egypt," *JRAI* 51 (1921) 115-153.

*W. J. Phythian-Adams, "*Aiguptos:* a Derivation and Some Suggestions," *JPOS* 2 (1922) 94-100.

Ludlow S. Bull, "The Work of the Metropolitan Museum in Eygpt 1907-1923," *A&A* 16 (1923) 211-230; 17 (1924) 19-42.

G. W. Murray, "Egypt: The Palæolithic Age," *Man* 23 (1923) #13.

M. A. Murray, "General Results of the Season's Excavations in Egypt," *Man* 23 (1923) #63.

Anonymous, "The Egyptian Expedition: Lord Carnarvon in Egypt," *MJ* 14 (1923) 19-20.

*[W. M.] Flinders Petrie, "The Caucasian Atlantis and Egypt," *AEE* 9 (1924) 123-124.

*Warren R. Dawson, "Tutankhamen: Egypt and Asia," *IAQR* 20 (1924) 154-168. *(Review)*

Egypt cont.

*W[illiam] F[oxwell] Albright, "Egypt and the Early History of the Negeb," *JPOS* 4 (1924) 131-161.

Samuel A. Mercer, "Some Recent Books on Egypt," *JSOR* 8 (1924) 167-181.

William Dale, "Egypt in the Days of Akhenaten and Tutakhamen," *JTVI* 56 (1924) 11-20. (Discussion, p. 20)

E Marion Smith, "Naukratis, a Chapter in the History of the Hellenization of Egypt," *JSOR* 10 (1926) 119-207.

I. G. Matthews, "A Visit to the Land of the Pharaohs," *CQ* 4 (1927) 413-433

Anonymous, "Notes and Comments. Neolithic Settlement in the Nile Delta," *A&A* 27 (1929) 280-281.

[W. M.] Flinders Petrie, "The Age of Egypt," *AEE* 14 (1929) 33-42.

*J. H. Dunbar, "Betwixt Egypt and Nubia," *AEE* 14 (1929) 108-117.

William F. Albright, "The Egyptian Empire in Asia in the Twenty-first Century B.C.," *JPOS* 8 (1928) 223-256.

*W. J. Perry, "Sumer and Egypt," *Man* 29 (1929) #18.

H. H. F. Jayne, "A New Expedition to Egypt," *MJ* 20 (1929) 114-118.

*K. S. Sandford and A. J. Arkell, "The Relation of Palæolithic Man to the History and Geology of the Nile Valley in Egypt," *Man* 29 (1929) #50.

*Alan Rowe, "A Comparison of Egyptian and Babylonian Civilizations and their Influence on Palestine," *PAPS* 68 (1929) 313-319.

*G. D. Hornblower, "Prehistoric Egypt and North Africa," *Man* 30 (1930) #34.

Anonymous, "The Egyptian Expedition," *UMB* 1 (1930) #1, 5-6; # 2, 5-7.

Anonymous, "The Museum's Egyptian Expedition," *UMB* 1 (1930) #3, 7-10.

*[W. M.] Flinders Petrie, "A Revision of History," *AEE* 16 (1931) 1-20.

Egypt cont.

*R. Engelbach, "Notes of Inspection," *ASAE* 31 (1931) 132-143. [I. The Road to El-Quṣeir; II. Myos Hormos and the Imperial Porphyry Quarries]

James H. Breasted, "The Predynastic Union of Egypt," *BIFAO* 30 (1931) 709-724.

Anonymous, "The Coxe Egyptian Expedition," *UMB* 3 (1931-32) 111, 114-115.

Anonymous, "Notes and Comments. Recent Excavation in Egypt," *A&A* 34 (1933) 162-164.

*V. I. Avdief, "Egypt and the Caucasus," *AEE* 18 (1933) 29-36.

M. A. Murray, "China and Egypt," *AEE* 18 (1933) 39-42.

*T. H. Gaster, "Ras Shamra and Egypt," *AEE* 19 (1934) 33-37.

[W. M.] Flinders Petrie, "Changes in the Egyptian Coast," *AEE* 20 (1935) 52-54.

W. Leonard, "A Glimpse of Egypt," *ACR* 13 (1936) 25-39.

C. R. Williams, "News Items from Egypt: The Season of 1935 to 1936 in Egypt," *AJA* 40 (1936) 551-556.

S. R. K. Glanville, "Some Recent Excavations in Egypt," *Antiq* 10 (1936) 77-85.

Charles A. Bachatly, "Two hitherto unknown Prehistoric sites in Upper Egypt," *Man* 36 (1936) #14. [Mousterian site at Nagʿ el-Deir; Capsian station at Khôr Hardân]

C. R. Williams, "News Items from Egypt. The Season of 1936 to 1937 in Egypt," *AJA* 41 (1937) 629-637.

*Naphtali Lewis, "*ΜΕΡΙΣΜΟΣ ΑΝΑΚΕΧΩΡΗΚΟΤΩΝ:* An Aspect of the Roman Oppression in Egypt," *JEA* 23 (1937) 63-75.

H. I. Bell, "Roman Egypt from Augustus to Diocletian," *CdÉ* 13 (1938) 347-363.

Egypt cont.

G. A. Wainwright, "Thoughts on Three Recent Articles," *JEA* 24 (1938) 39-64. [*ΜΕΡΙΣΜΟΣ ΑΝΑΚΕΧΩΡΗΚΟΤΩΝ,* pp. 63-64]

*C. C. McCown, "Two Years' Achievements in Palestinian Archaeology," *RL* 8 (1939) 97-108. [The Egyptian Border, p. 102]

*Dows Dunham, "Romano-Coptic Egypt and the Culture of Meroë," *AJA* 46 (1942) 122.

*R. Engelbach, "An essay on the advent of the dynastic race in Egypt and its consequences," *ASAE* 42 (1943) 193-221.

Ahmed Fakhry, "A report on the Inspectorate of Upper Egypt," *ASAE* 46 (1947) 25-54.

Wm. Arndt, "Egypt—A Land of the Past," *CTM* 18 (1947) 454-456.

G. A. Wainwright, "Pharonic Survivals between Lake Chad and the West Coast," *JEA* 35 (1949) 170-175.

F. Addison, "Archaeological Discoveries on the Blue Nile," *Antiq* 24 (1950) 12-24.

*Hermann Ranke, "The Egyptian Collection of the University Museum," *UMB* 15 (1950) #2/3, 5-109. [A Sketch of the Geography and History of Egypt, pp. 7-15]

David Meredith, "The Roman Remains in the Eastern Desert of Egypt," *JEA* 38 (1952) 94-111.

Alan Rowe, "A Contribution to the Archaeology of the Western Desert," *BJRL* 36 (1953-54) 128-145, 484-500.

David Meredith, "The Roman Remains in the Eastern Desert of Egypt *(continued),*" *JEA* 39 (1953) 95-106.

*John A. Wilson, "Buto and Hierakonpolis in the Geography of Egypt," *JNES* 14 (1955) 209-236.

S. Yeivin, "The Extent of Egyptian Domination in Hither Asia under the Middle Bronze Kingdom," *EI* 4 (1956) III-IV.

Egypt cont.

*D. G. Reder, "Ancient Egypt, a Center of Agriculture," *JWH* 4 (1957-58) 801-817.

*Labib Habachi, "God's fathers and the role they played in the history of the first intermediate period," *ASAE* 55 (1958) 167-190.

Shehata Adam, "Recent discoveries in the Eastern Delta (Dec. 1950-May 1955)," *ASAE* 55 (1958) 301-324.

Mary Neely, "A Broken Reed—The Legendary Greatness of Egypt," *ABR* 7 (1959) 66-68.

*E. Badian, "Egypt under the Ptolemies," *HT* 10 (1960) 451-459.

David Crownover, "Amelia Edwards and the New Aswan Dam," *Exped* 4 (1961-62) #3, 24-27.

Eva L. R. Meyerowitz, "Ghana and Ancient Egypt," *Man* 61 (1961) #137.

Hjalmar Larsen, "Finds from Badarian and Tasian Civilizations," *MB* #1 (1961) 9-19.

Zbyněk Žába, "Czechoslovak Discoveries in Egypt," *NOP* 2 (1962) #2, 6-10.

T[orgny] Säve-Söderbergh, "Preliminary Report of the Scandinavian Joint Expedition. Archaeological Survey between Faras and Gamai, January-March 1961," *Kush* 10 (1962) 76-103.

*S. Truesdell Brown, "The Greek Sense of Time in History as suggested by their Accounts of Egypt," *HJAH* 11 (1962) 257-270.

Thomas W. Africa, "Herodotus and Diodorus on Egypt," *JNES* 12 (1963) 254-258.

T[orgny] Säve-Söderbergh, "Preliminary Report of the Scandinavian Joint Expedition: Archaeological Investigations between Faras and Gemai, November 1961-March 1962," *Kush* 11 (1963) 47-69.

*Jaroslav Černý, "The Contribution of the Study of Unofficial and Private Documents to the History of Pharonic Egypt," *SSR* 7 (1963) 31-57.

*Miriam Lichtheim, "Ancient Egypt: A Survey of Current Historiography," *AmHR* 69 (1963-64) 30-46.

Egypt concluded

H. S. Smith, "Egypt and C14 Dating," *Antiq* 38 (1964) 32-37.

William Kelly Simpson, "The Pennsylvania-Yale Expedition to Egypt: Preliminary Report for 1963: Toshka and Arminna (Nubia)," *JARCE* 3 (1964) 15-23.

*William C. Hayes, "Most Ancient Egypt," *JNES* 23 (1964) 73-114, 145-192, 217-274. [Chapter I. The Formation of the Land; Chapter II. Paleolithic Man in Egypt; Chapter III. The Neolithic and Chalcolitic Communities of Northern Egypt]

T[orgny] Säve-Söderbergh, "Preliminary Report of the Scandinavian Joint Expedition: Archaeological Investigation between Faras and Gemai, November 1962-March 1963," *Kush* 12 (1964) 19-39.

George T. Scanlon, "Fusṭāṭ Expedition: Preliminary Report 1965," *JARCE* 5 (1966) 83-112.

J. Gwyn Griffiths, "Hecataeus and Herodotus on 'A Gift of the River'," *JNES* 25 (1966) 57-61. *[Egypt]*

George T. Scanlon, "Fusṭāṭ Expedition: Preliminary Report 1965 Part II," *JARCE* 6 (1967) 65-86.

David O'Connor, "Field Work in Egypt," *Exped* 11 (1968-69) #1, 27-30.

River of Egypt

H. Bar-Deroma, "The River of Egypt (Nahal Mizraim)," *PEQ* 92 (1960) 37-56.

Elam

G[eorge] Rawlinson, "Biblical Topography. V.—Elam, its Chief City, and its Chief River," *MI* 3 (1885-86) 217-227.

John P. Peters, "The Eldest Son of Shem," *HR* 52 (1906) 248-251, 335-339. *[Elam]*

*P. M. Sykes, "The Ancient History of Persia (Elam, Media, and the Rise of the Achæmenian Dynasty)," *IAQR* 7 (1915) 125-147.

Elam concluded

*Arno Poebel, "The Name of Elam in Sumerian, Akkadian, and Hebrew," *AJSL* 48 (1931-32) 20-26.

Elateia

Saul S. Weinberg, "A Neolithic Site at Elateia," *AJA* 65 (1961) 193.

Elbatana

*David R. Milberg, "Parnasos," *JNES* 28 (1969) 62. [1. Elbatana]

Plain of Elbistan

*Tahsin Ozgüç, "Archaeological journeys in the plain of Elbistan and the excavation of Kara-höyük," *TTKB* 12 (1948) 232-237.

Elea (Velia)

*Pellegrino Claudio Sestieri, "Greek Elea—Roman Velia," *Arch* 10 (1957) 2-10.

Elephantine

Anonymous, "The Elephantine Cave," *AAOJ* 2 (1879-80) 165-166.

M. J. Lagrange, "The Jewish Military Colony of Elephantine Under the Persians," *NYR* 3 (1907-08) 129-144.

*John Merlin Powis Smith, "The Jewish Temple at Elephantine," *BW* 31 (1908) 448-459.

*William Hayes Ward, "An Appendix to the Book of Nehemiah," *HR* 55 (1908) 24-27. *[Elephantine]*

*A. F. R. Platt, "The Origin of the Name of the Island of Elephantine," *SBAP* 30 (1908) 206-207.

*Hermann Gunkel, "The Jâhû Temple in Elephantine," *Exp, 8th Ser.,* 1 (1911) 20-39.

Elephantine cont.

*A. H. Sayce, "The Jewish Garrison and the Temple at Elephantine," *Exp, 8th Ser.*, 2 (1911) 97-116.

*A. H. Sayce, "The Jews and their Temple at Elephantine," *Exp, 8th Ser.*, 2 (1911) 417-434.

Parke P. Flournoy, "The Long Hidden Treasures of Elephantinê," *RP* 10 (1911) 170-179.

*Henry Preserved Smith, "Light on Some Ancient History," *MTSQB* 6 (1911-12) #2, 11-23. *[Elephantine]*

*P[arke] P. Flournoy, "Elephantine, and The Priest Code Theory," *USR* 24 (1912-13) 285-295.

Anonymous, "A Jewish Colony in Egypt," *HR* 81 (1921) 280-281. *[Elephantine] (Review)*

Parke P. Flournoy, "The Long Hidden Treasures of Elephantine," *BR* 13 (1928) 553-568.

*R. Engelbach, "A Coptic Ostracon mentioning Iēb (Elephantine)," *ASAE* 38 (1938) 47-52.

*U[mberto] Cassuto, "The Gods of the Jews of Elephantine," *KSJA* 2 (1945) VI.

*Emil G. Kraeling, "New Light on the Elephantine Colony," *BA* 15 (1952) 50-67. [Yeb and Syene; Elephantine in Egyptian History; An Archaeological Mystery Story; First Published Elephantine Discoveries; Preparation of the Wilbour Papyri; Contents of the Papyri; Nos. 9-13 and Their Historical Importance; Origin of the Jewish Colony of Elephantine; The Restoration of the Jewish Temple]

A. Sachs, "The Answer to a Puzzle," *BA* 15 (1952) 89. *[Reference to previous article by Kraeling]*

Cyrus H. Gordon, "The Origin of the Jews at Elephantine," *JNES* 14 (1955) 56-58.

Labib Habachi, "Hekaib: The Deified Governor of Elephantine," *Arch* 9 (1956) 8-15.

Elephantine cont.

E. C. B. MacLaurin, "Date of the Foundation of the Jewish Colony at Elephantine," *JNES* 27 (1968) 89-96.

Eleusis

K. Kourouniotes, "The Excavations at Eleusis," *A&A* 32 (1931) 3-15.

George E. Mylonas, "Eleusis in the Bronze Age," *AJA* 36 (1932) 104-117.

George E. Mylonas and K. Kourouniotes, "Excavations at Eleusis, 1932," *AJA* 37 (1933) 217-288.

George E. Mylonas, "Excavations at Eleusis in 1932," *AJA* 37 (1933) 110.

George Mylonas, "Eleusiniaka," *AJA* 40 (1936) 122, 415-431.

John Travlos, "The Topography of Eleusis," *AJA* 52 (1948) 376-377.

*George Mylonas, "The Cemetery of Eleusis and the New Grave Circle of Mycenae," *AJA* 59 (1955) 172-173.

George E. Mylonas, "Excavations at Eleusis, 1955-1956," *AJA* 61 (1957) 185.

Elim

Anonymous, The Seventy Palm-trees of Elim," *CongML* 14 (1831) 481-482.

Elis

Jerome Sperling, "Explorations in Elis, 1939," *AJA* 46 (1942) 77-89.

Elishah

C[laude] R. Conder, "Notes by C. R. Conder, R. E. II. Alosha Elishah," *PEFQS* 24 (1892) 44-45. *[Elishah]*

*Joseph Offord, "Archaeological Notes on Jewish Antiquities. XXXV. *The Home Country of one of the Toldoth, Beni Noah*," *PEFQS* 49 (1917) 142-143. *[Elishah]*

Emer

Albrecht Goetze, "The Syrian Town of Emer," *BASOR* #147 (1957) 22-27.

Emirler

Yusuf Boysal, "A Report on the 1969[sic]* Turgut Excavations," *A(A)* 12 (1968) 81-93. [Work in the Region of Emirler, pp. 86-87]

Enkomi

*Sara A. Immerwahr, "The Latest Elements in the Enkomi Tombs," *AJA* 50 (1946) 402.

G. F. A. Schaeffer, "Enkomi," *AJA* 52 (1948) 165-177.

Porphyrios Dikaios, "Recent Excavations at Enkomi by the Department of Antiquities of Cyprus," *AJA* 57 (1953) 106, 280.

Enoch

*A. H. Sayce, "Recent Biblical Archaeology. The City of Enoch," *ET* 13 (1901-02) 178-179. *[Khanak?]*

Ephesus

Anonymous, "Ephesus, Pagan and Christian," *DUM* 74 (1869) 377-402.

F. A. Paley, "The Ruins of Ephesus," *ACQR* 2 (1877) 460-474.

Anonymous, "Mr. Wood's Discoveries at Ephesus," *BQRL* 65 (1877) 366-391. *(Review)*

†Anonymous, "Wood's *Discoveries at Ephesus*," *ERCJ* 145 (1877) 204-228. *(Review)*

*Bayard Taylor, "Discovered Treasures of Ephesus, Cyprus, and Mycenæ," *DTQ* 4 (1878) 213-226.

*David M. Robinson, "Pergamum and Ephesus," *A&A* 9 (1920) 157-170.

Einar Gjerstad, "Studies in Archaic Greek Chronology. II. Ephesus," *AAA* 24 (1937) 15-34.

Ephesus concluded

Alfons Wotschitzky, "Ephesus: Past, Present and Future of an Ancient Metropolis," *Arch* 14 (1961) 205-212.

Ephyra (Kichyros)

*Sotirios I. Dakaris, "The Dark Palace of Hades," *Arch* 15 (1962) 85-93. *[Ephyra (or Kichyros)] (Trans. by John L. Caskey)*

Epidaurus

*Charles Newton Smiley, "Epidaurus and Greek and Roman Medicine," *A&A* 7 (1918) 121-130.

Episkopi

Saul S. Weinberg, "The Missouri Cyprus Expedition: Preliminary Excavations of an Early Cypriot Settlement," *AJA* 60 (1956) 181-182. *[Episkopi]*

Erbaba

Jacques Bordaz, "A Preliminary Report of the 1969 Excavations at Erbaba, a neolithic site near Beyşehir, Turkey," *TAD* 18 (1969) #2, 59-64.

Erech

Theophilus G. Pinches, "Glimpses of Life in Erech," *ET* 25 (1913-14) 420-423.

Raymond P. Dougherty, "The Antiquity of Erech," *BS* 86 (1929) 382-391.

Eridu

*H. R. Hall, "Ur and Eridu: The British Museum Excavations of 1919," *JEA* 9 (1923) 177-195.

*H. R. Hall, "The Excavations of 1919 at Ur el-â Obeid and Eridu, and the History of Early Babylonia (Brussels Conference 1923)," *Man* 25 (1925) #1.

Eridu concluded

Naji al-Asil, "Eridu," *Sumer* 3 (1947) 3.

Naji al-Asil, "Eridu. A Preliminary Communication on the First Season's Excavations. January-March 1947. Foreword," *Sumer* 3 (1947) 84.

Seton Lloyd, "Eridu. A Preliminary Communication on the First Season's Excavations January-March 1947. I. Introduction," *Sumer* 3 (1947) 85-95.

Fuad Safar, "Eridu. A Preliminary Communication on the First Season's Excavations January-March 1947. II. History of Eridu," *Sumer* 3 (1947) 95-100.

Fuad Safar, "Eridu. A Preliminary Communication on the First Season's Excavations January-March 1947. III. Excavations," *Sumer* 3 (1947) 100-111.E. Douglas Van Buren, "Excavations at Eridu," *Or, N.S.,* 17 (1948) 115-119.

Seton Lloyd and Fuad Safar, "Eridu. A Preliminary Communication on the Second Season's Excavations 1947-48," *Sumer* 4 (1948) 115-125.

Charlotte M. Otten, "Note on the Cemetery of Eridu," *Sumer* 4 (1948) 125-127.

E. Douglas Van Buren, "Discoveries at Eridu," *Or, N.S.,* 18 (1949) 123-124.

Fuad Safar, "Eridu. A Preliminary Report on the Third Season's Excavations, 1948-49," *Sumer* 6 (1950) 27-33.

*Seton Lloyd, "Ur-Al 'Ubaid, 'Uqaid and Eridu: An Interpretation of Some Evidence from the Flood-Pit," *Iraq* 22 (1960) 23-31.

*Joan Oates, "Ur and Eridu, the Prehistory," *Iraq* 22 (1960) 32-50.

*Kent V. Flannery and Henry T. Wright, "Faunal Remains from 'Hut Sounding' at Eridu, Iraq," *Sumer* 22 (1966) 61-63.

Erythraean Sea

W. H. Scoff, "The name of the Erythraean Sea," *JAOS* 33 (1913) 349-362.

Eski Anamur (Anemurium)

C. Leonard Smith, "Excavation Report Eski Anamur (Anemurium)," *TAD* 16 (1967) #1, 137-144.

Esna

*John Garstang, "Excavations at Hierakonopolis, at Esna, and in Nubia," *ASAE* 8 (1907) 132-148.

Eretria

*Charles Waldestein, Rufus B. Richardson, Andrew Fossum, and Carleton L. Brownson, "Papers of the American School of Classical Studies at Athens. Excavations by the American School at Eretria, 1891," *AJA, O.S.*, 7 (1891) 233-280. [I. Introductory Note, pp. 233-235; II. Inscriptions Discovered at Eretria, 1891, pp. 246-253; III. Excavations in the Theatre of Eretria, pp. 253-257; IV. The State-Building of the Theatre at Eretria, pp. 257-266; V. The Theatre at Eretria, Orchestra and Cavea, pp. 266-280]

John Pickard, "Papers of the American School of Classical Studies at Athens. Excavations by the American School at Eretria in 1891," *AJA, O.S.*, 7 (1891) 371-389. [VI. A Topographical Study of Eretria] (Introductory Note by Charles Waldstein, p. 371)

Etham

*Edouard Naville, "Hebraeo-Aegyptiaca. III," *SBAP* 37 (1914) 208-214. *[Etham]*

Ethiopia

†Anonymous, "Geography of Ethiopia," *ERCJ* 41 (1824-25) 181-194. *(Review)*

*Anonymous, "The Highlands of Ethiopia," *CRB* 9 (1844) 396-415.

*R. S. P., "Egypt, Ethiopia, and the Peninsula of Sinai," *JSL, 2nd Ser.*, 6 (1854) 314-330. *(Review)*

Anonymous, "Discoveries in Ethiopia," *HR* 80 (1920) 134.

Ethiopia concluded

*G. A. Reisner, "The Meroitic Kingdom of Ethiopia: A Chronological Outline," *JEA* 9 (1923) 34-77.

*G. A. Reisner, "The Meroitic Kingdom of Ethiopia: Additional Note," *JEA* 9 (1923) 157-160.

G. W. Gilmore, "'Candace' and the Kingdom of Ethiopia," *HR* 87 (1924) 138-139.

Ernest Zyhlarz, "The Countries of the Ethiopian Empire of Kash (Kush) and Egyptian Old Ethiopia in the New Kingdom," *Kush* 6 (1958) 7-38. *(Trans. by M. Jackson)*

Ernst Hammerschmidt, "A Brief History of German Contributions to the Study of Ethiopia," *JES* 1 (1963) #2, 30-48.

Ephraim Isaac, "The Hebraic Molding of Ethiopian Culture," *Mosaic* 6 (1965) #1, 8-15.

Etruria

*Tenney Frank, "On Rome's conquest of Sabinum, Picenum and Etruria," *Klio* 11 (1911) 367-381.

*Hugh Hencken, "Syracuse, Etruria and the North: Some Comparisons," *AJA* 62 (1958) 259-272.

*Giovanni Colonna, "The Sanctuary at Pyrgia In Etruria," *Arch* 19 (1966) 11-23. *(Trans. by Lionel Casson)*

Pamela Hemphill, "An Archaeological Survey of Southern Etruria," *Exped* 12 (1969-70) #2, 31-39.

Euboea

*Franklin P. Johnson, "The 'Dragon-Houses' of Southern Euboea," *AJA* 29 (1925) 398-412.

*L. H. Sackett, "The British School Excavations at Xeropolis (Lefkandi) in Euboea," *AJA* 70 (1966) 194-195.

Euboea concluded

Thomas W. Jacobsen, "Recent Surface Exploration in Euboia*[sic]*," *AJA* 70 (1966) 191.

Eupatorium

D. S. Rayevsky, "The Site of Ancient Eupatorium," *VDI* (1968) #3, 133.

Euphrates River and Valley

Anonymous, "The Euphrates Expedition," *DUM* 36 (1850) 379-392. *(Review)*

†Anonymous, "The Euphrates Expedition," *ERCJ* 92 (1850) 436-467. *(Review)*

†Anonymous, "Chesney's Survey of the Euphrates," *ERL* 14 (1850) 13-37. *(Review)*

*†Anonymous, "The Expedition for the Survey of the Rivers Euphrates and Tigris," *WR* 53 (1850) 332-348.

*Francis Brown, "Euphrates and Tigris," *PR* 3 (1882) 399-400.

G. H. Emerson, "The Latest Discoveries in the Tigro-Euphrates Valley," *UQGR, N.S.*, 28 (1891) 389-405.

*R. O. Faulkner, "The Euphrates Campaign of Tuthmosis III," *JEA* 32 (1946) 39-42.

*Evelyn Howell, "River Control in Mesopotamia," *QRL* 237 (1922) 68-84. *[Euphrates]*

Maurits N. van Loon, "New Sites in the Euphrates Valley," *Arch* 22 (1969) 65-68.

Eyuk

*G. E. White, "Visit to the Hittite Cities Eyuk and Boghaz Keoy," *JTVI* 33 (1901) 226-232. [(Note by T. G. Pinches, pp. 232-236) (Discussion, pp. 236-241)]

Ezbet Rushdi

Sheḥata Adam, "Report on the Excavations of the Department of Antiquities at Ezbet Rushdi," *ASAE* 56 (1959) 207-226.

F

Failaka

Erling Albrectsen, "Alexander the Great's Visiting Card," *Kuml* (1958) 186-189. *[Failaka]*

Fara

*E. J. Banks, "Impressions from the Excavations by the Germans at Fara and Abu Hatab," *BW* 24 (1904) 138-146.

Anonymous, "German Excavations in Fara," *RP* 3 (1904) 233-243. *(Translated and condensed from the offical reports of the German Oriental Society by Prof. Karl Hau)*

Anonymous, "The Expedition at Fara," *UMB* 2 (1930-31) 186-187.

Erich Schmidt, "Excavations at Fara, 1931," *MJ* 22 (1931) 193-246.

Farafra Oasis

*Ahmed Fakhry, "Baḥria and Farafra Oases. A Preliminary Report," *ASAE* 38 (1938) 397-434.

*Ahmed Fakhry, "Baḥria and Farafra Oases. Second Preliminary Report," *ASAE* 39 (1939) 627-642.

*Ahmed Fakhry, "Baḥria and Farafra Oases. Third Preliminary Report," *ASAE* 40 (1940-41) 855-871.

Tell El-Farâ'în

M. V. Seaton-Williams, "The Tell El-Farâ'în Expedition 1964-1965," *JEA* 51 (1965) 9-15.

Tell El-Farâ'în concluded

Veronica Seaton-Williams, "The Town of the Cobra Godess of Lower Egypt," *Arch* 19 (1966) 208-213. *[Tell el-Farâ'în]*

M. V. Seaton-Williams, "The Tell el-Farâ'în Expedition 1966," *JEA* 52 (1966) 163-171.

M. V. Seaton-Williams, "The Tell el-Farâ'în Expedition 1967," *JEA* 53 (1967) 146-155.

M. V. Seaton-Williams, "The Tell el-Farâ'în Expedition 1968," *JEA* 55 (1969) 5-22.

Dorothy Charlesworth, "Tell El Farâ'in: The Industrial Site, 1968," *JEA* 55 (1969) 23-30.

(The) Fayoum

*F. Cope Whitehouse, "Lake Moeris and recent explorations in the Desert near the Fayoum," *SBAP* 4 (1881-82) 124-135.

H. W. Seaton-Kerr, "Discovery of a neolithic Settlement in the W. desert N. of the Fayoum," *ASAE* 6 (1905) 185-187.

G. Canton-Thompson and E. W. Gardner, "Research in the Fayum," *AEE* 11 (1926) 1-4.

(Miss) E. A. Gardner and (Miss) G. Caton-Thompson, "The Recent Geology and Neolithic Industry of the Northern Fayum Desert," *JRAI* 56 (1926) 301-323. [I. The Recent Geology of the Northern Fayum Desert, (by E. A. Gardner), pp. 301-307; II. The Neolithic Industry of the Northern Fayum Desert. *Being the substance of a Paper Read to Section H of the British Association, Oxford,* 1926, (by G. Caton-Thompson), pp. 309-323]

W. [M.] Flinders Petrie, "Observations on 'The Recent Geology and Neolithic Industry of the Northern Fayum Desert,' by Miss E. W. Gardiner, M. A., and Miss G. Caton-Thompson, F.R.G.S.," *JRAI* 56 (1926) 325-327. [The History of the Fayum Lake]

G. Canton Thompson, "Recent Excavations in the Fayum," *Man* 28 (1928) #69.

(The) Fayoum concluded

Ahmed Fakhry, "A fortnight's digging at Medinet-Qûta (Fayoum)," *ASAE* 40 (1940-41) 897-909.

Firakdin

Nimet Özgüç, "Finds at Firakdin," *TTKB* 19 (1955) 301-307.

Fraktin

Tahsin Özgüç, "Excavations at Fraktin near Develi and researches in Anti-Taurus," *TTKB* 12 (1948) 266-267.

G

Galatia

*Ronald Syme, "Galatia and Pamphylia under Augustus: the Governorships of Piso, Qurinius and Silvanus," *Klio* 27 (1934) 122-148.

Gargara

*Joseph Thacher Clarke, "Gargara, Lamponia and Pionia: Towns of Troad," *AJA, O.S.,* 4 (1888) 291-319.

Garigliano River

S. Dominic Ruegg, "Excavations in the Garigliano River, 1967," *AJA* 72 (1968) 172.

Gašga

*John Garstang, "Notes on Hittite Political Geography," *AAA* 10 (1923) 21-26, 172-178. [III. Gašga, pp. 177-179]

Gaul

*J. Wells, "Cicero and the Conquest of Gaul," *QRL* 230 (1918) 361-379. *(Review)*

Gebel Adda

Nicholas B. Millet, "Gebel Adda. Preliminary Report for 1963," *JARCE* 2 (1963) 147-165.

Nicholas B. Millet, "Gebel Adda Expedition. Preliminary Report, 1963-1964," *JARCE* 3 (1964) 7-14.

Nicholas B. Millet, "Gebel Adda Preliminary Report, 1965-66," *JARCE* 6 (1967) 53-63.

Gebel Gorod

*Michael Schiff Giorgini, "Sedeinga, 1964-65," *Kush* 14 (1966) 244-258. [Gebel Gorod, p. 261]

Gebel Silsila (Gebel es-Silsilah)

A. H. Sayce, "Excavations at Gebel Silsila," *ASAE* 8 (1907) 97-105.

Ricardo A. Caminos, "Surveying Gebel es-Silsilah," *JEA* 41 (1955) 51-57.

Gebelen

*Willoughby G. Fraser, "El Kab and Gebelen," *SBAP* 15 (1892-93) 494-500.

Cape of Gelidonya

*George F. Bass, "Report of the Underwater Excavation at Cape of Gelidonya," *TAD* 11 (1961) #1, 7-9.

Gerga

G. E. Bean, "Gerga in Caria," *AS* 19 (1969) 179-182.

Ghirza

Byron Khun de Prorok, "Ghirza: Mystery City of the Sahara," *A&A* 31 (1931) 15-17, 46.

Gibraltar

*W. L. H. Duckworth, "Cave Exploration at Gibraltar in 1911," *JRAI* 42 (1912) 515-528.

*Dorothy A. E. Garrod, L. H. Dudley Buxton, G. Elliot Smith, and Dorothea M. A. Bate, "Excavation of a Mourterian Rock-Shelter at Devil's Tower, Gibraltar," *JRAI* 58 (1928) 33-113. [I—Archæology and Geology, by Dorothy A. E. Garrod, pp. 34-56; Appendix A: Report on Sands, by R. C. Spiller, p. 56; II.—Human Remains, by L. H. Dudley Buxton, pp. 57-85; III.—The Endocranial Cast, by G. Elliot Smith, pp. 86-91; IV.—The Animal Remains, by Dorothea M. A. Bate, pp. 92-110; Appendix B: Note on Fossil Voles, by Martin A. C. Hinton, pp. 110-111; Appendix C: Fossil Mollusca, by Paul Fischer, pp. 111-113]

Girsu

*Ira Maurice Price, "H. De Genouillac on *'Lagash'* and *'Girsu'*," *JAOS* 57 (1937) 309-312.

Gish-ban (ki)

W. St. Chad Boscawen, "Gish-ban (ki)," *BOR* 8 (1895-1900) 161-164.

Giza

G. A. Reisner and C. S. Fisher, "Preliminary Report on the work of the Harvard—Boston Expedition in 1911-13," *ASAE* 13 (1914) 227-252. *[Egypt, cemetery west of Cheops' Pyramid]*

H. Junker, "The Austrian Excavations, 1914. Excavations of the Vienna Imperial Academy of Sciences at the Pyramids of Gizah," *JEA* 1 (1914) 250-253.

Clarence S. Fisher, "Excavations at Gizeh. The Eckley B. Coxe, Jr., Expedition to Egypt," *MJ* 8 (1917) 46-52.

[George A. Reisner], "Notes and Comments. Dr. Reisner's Discovery at Ghizeh," *A&A* 21 (1926) 299-300.

Selim Hasan, "Excavations at Gezeh," *AEE* 15 (1930) 23-24.

*G[eorge] A. Reisner, "Note on Overbuilding and Intrusive Burials at Gīzah," *JEA* 23 (1937) 260.

Godin Tepe

Louis D. Levine, "Excavations at Godin Tepe, Iran, 1965-1967," *AJA* 73 (1969) 240-241.

*T. Cuyler Young Jr., "The Chronology of the Late Third and Second Millennia in Central Western Iran as Seen from Godin Tepe," *AJA* 73 (1969) 287-291.

Göksu Valley

D. H. French, "Prehistoric Sites in the Göksu Valley," *AS* 15 (1965) 177-201.

Gordion

Rodney S. Young, "The Excavations at Yassihuyuk-Gordion, 1950," *Arch* 3 (1950) 196-201.

Rodney S. Young, "Progress at Gordion, 1951-52," *UMB* 17 (1952-53) #4, 3-39.

Rodney S. Young, "Gordion: Achaemenian and Phrygian Levels," *AJA* 58 (1954) 150-151.

Rodney S. Young, "Gordion: Preliminary Report, 1953," *AJA* 59 (1955) 1-18.

Rodney [S.] Young, "Gordion—1955 Results," *AJA* 60 (1956) 182.

Rodney S. Young, "The Campaign of 1955 at Gordion: Preliminary Report," *AJA* 60 (1956) 249-266.

Rodney S. Young, "Discoveries at Gordion 1956," *Arch* 9 (1956) 263-267.

Rodney S. Young, "Phrygian Gordion," *AJA* 61 (1957) 187-188.

Rodney S. Young, "Gordion 1956: Preliminary Report," *AJA* 61 (1957) 319-331.

Rodney S. Young, "Gordion Excavations, 1956," *TAD* 7 (1957) #1, 26-38. [The Küçük Höyük; The Höyük; The Cemetery]

Gordion concluded

Rodney S. Young, "The Gordion Campaign of 1957: Preliminary Report," *AJA* 62 (1958) 139-154.

Rodney S. Young, "Gordion report 1957," *TAD* 8 (1958) #1, 33-44.

G. Roger Edwards, "The Gordion Campaign of 1958: Preliminary Report," *AJA* 63 (1959) 263-268.

G. Roger Edwards, "Gordion Report, 1958," *TAD* 9 (1959) #1, 12-13.

Rodney S. Young, "The Gordion Campaign of 1959: Preliminary Report," *AJA* 64 (1960) 227-243.

Rodney S. Young, "Gordion 1959," *TAD* 10 (1960) #1, 60-63.

Rodney S. Young, "The 1961 Campaign at Gordion," *AJA* 66 (1962) 153-168.

G. Roger Edwards, "Gordion: 1962," *Exped* 5 (1962-63) #3, 42-48.

Rodney S. Young, "The 1963 Campaign at Gordion," *AJA* 68 (1964) 279-292.

Rodney S. Young, "The Gordion Campaign of 1965," *AJA* 70 (1966) 267-278.

Rodney S. Young, "The Gordion Campaign of 1967," *AJA* 72 (1968) 231-241.

Rodney S. Young, "Operation Gordion," *Exped* 11 (1968-69) #1, 16-19.

Gortyna

Antonio Taramelli, "Gortyna," *AJA* 6 (1902) 101-165.

Goshen

*Edward Robinson, "The Land of Goshen, and the Exodus of the Israelites," *BRCR, N.S.*, 3 (1840) 306-324.

Daniel Hy. Haigh, "גשן Goshen," *ZÄS* 7 (1869) 47.

Goshen concluded

F. Cope Whitehouse, "Where is the Land of Goshen?" *CT* 2 (1884-85) 351-367

A. C[rawford], "Goshen Identified," *PER* 1 (1886-87) 78-82.

[F.] Cope Whitehouse, "Where was the Land of Goshen," *Exp, 4th Ser.*, 8 (1893) 337-348.

*Alan H. Gardiner, "The Supposed Egyptian Equivalent of the Name of Goshen," *JEA* 5 (1918) 218-223.

*George B. Michell, "The Land of Goshen and the Exodus," *JTVI* 67 (1935) 231-241, 244-246. (Discussion, pp. 241-244)

Gozan (See also: Tell Halaf)

*B[enjamin] Maisler, "The Israelite Exiles at Gozan," *BIES* 15 (1949-50) #3/4, III.

W[illiam] F[oxwell] Albright, "The Date of the Kapara Period at Gozan (Tell Halaf)," *AS* 6 (1956) 75-85.

Gözlü Kule

*Hetty Goldman, "Preliminary Expedition to Cilicia, 1934, and Excavations at Gözlü Kule, Tarsus, 1935," *AJA* 39 (1935) 526-549.

Hetty Goldman, "Excavations at Gözlü Kule, Tarsus, 1936," *AJA* 41 (1937) 262-286.

Hetty Goldman, "Excavations at Gözlü Kule, Tarsus, 1937," *AJA* 42 (1938) 30-54.

Hetty Goldman, "Excavations at Gözlü Kule, Tarsus, 1938," *AJA* 44 (1940) 60-86.

Greece

†Anonymous, "Mitford's History of Greece," *BCQTR* 9 (1797) 581-586; 10 (1797) 37-44. *(Review)*

Greece cont.

Anonymous, "The History of Greece. By William Mitford Esq. Vol. IV.," *ERCJ* 12 (1808) 478-517. *(Review)*

†Anonymous, "Mitford's *History of Greece,*" *QRL* 25 (1821) 154-174. *(Review)*

†Anonymous, "Thirlwall's *History of Greece,*" *ERCJ* 62 (1835-36) 83-108. *(Review)*

Anonymous, "Ancient and Modern Greece," *BRCR, N.S.,* 7 (1842) 441-467. *(Review)*

†Anonymous, "Grote's History of Greece," *ERCJ* 84 (1846) 343-377. *(Review)*

†Anonymous, "Grote's *History of Greece,*" *QRL* 78 (1846) 133-144; 86 (1849-50) 384-415; 99 (1856) 60-105. *(Review)*

C. C. F., Grote's History of Greece," *CE* 48 (1850) 292-301. *(Review)*

Anonymous, "Grote's History of Greece," *DUM* 35 (1850) 753-765. *(Review)*

†Anonymous, "Grote's *History of Greece,*" *ERCJ* 91 (1850) 118-152. *(Review)*

†Anonymous, "History of Greece," *QRL* 88 (1850-51) 41-69. *(Review)*

†Anonymous, "Grote's History of Greece," *BQRL* 13 (1851) 289-331. *(Review)*

J. T. Champlin, "Grote's Greece," *CRB* 16 (1851) 481-505. *(Review)*

†Anonymous, "Grote's *History of Greece,*" *ERCJ* 94 (1851) 204-228. *(Review)*

†Anonymous, "The Greeks and their Language," *PQR* 1 (1852-53) 259-275. *(Review)*

†Anonymous, "Greece during the Macedonian Period," *NBR* 21 (1854) 425-450. *(Review)*

†Anonymous, "Grote's Greece," *DUM* 45 (1855) 477-490. *(Review)*

Greece cont.

†Anonymous, "Grote's *History of Greece. Vols. IX. X. XI.*," *ERCJ* 98 (1855) 425-447. *(Review)*

George Frederick Holmes, "Greece and its History," *MQR* 9 (1855) 38-61. *(Review)*

†Anonymous, "*Grote's* History of Greece," *NBR* 25 (1856) 141-172. *(Review)*

Anonymous, "*A History of Greece,*" *LQHR* 7 (1856-57) 51-71. *(Review)*

N. L. F., "Grote's History of Greece," *CE* 62 (1857) 55-73. *(Review)*

W. Martin Leake, "Greek Archæology and Topography," *JCSP* 4 (1857-60) 239-254.

†Anonymous, "History of Greece," *BQRL* 61 (1875) 43-68. *(Review)*

†Anonymous, "Cox's *History of Greece,*" *ERCJ* 141 (1875) 242-272. *(Review)*

Courtney Kenny, "Cox's History of Greece," *TR* 12 (1875) 424-435. *(Review)*

Edward A. Freeman, "Greek Cities under Roman Rule," *ContR* 46 (1884) 687-703.

†Anonymous, "Recent Discoveries in Greece," *QRL* 159 (1885) 298-322. *(Review)*

†Anonymous, "Naucratis and the Greeks in Egypt," *QRL* 164 (1886) 66-96. *(Review)*

Augustus C. Merriam, "Correspondence. Letter from Greece," *AJA, O.S.,* 4 (1888) 47-57.

Cecil Smith, "*Recent Archæological Research.* No. IV.—Greek Archæology in Modern Times," *ARL* 3 (1889) 297-315.

†Anonymous, "Dr. Schliemann's last Excavations," *ERCJ* 175 (1892) 399-434. *(Review)*

A. J. Evans, "'The Oldest Civilisation of Greece: Mr. Hall and "H"'," *Man* 1 (1901) #138.

Greece cont.

Anonymous, "The Dawn of Greece," *QRL* 194 (1901) 218-243. *(Review)*

Anonymous, "The Future of Greek History," *QRL* 195 (1902) 79-97. *(Review)*

George Frederick Wright, "The Oldest Civilization of Greece," *RP* 1 (1902) 195-204.

P. Kabbadias, "Prehistoric Archæology in Greece," *Man* 4 (1904) #112.

A. J. B. Wace, J. P. Droop, and M. S. Thompson, "Early Civilization in Northern Greece," *AAA* 1 (1908) 118-130.

A. J. B. Wace, J. P. Droop, and M. S. Thompson, "Further Report on Early Civilization in Northern Greece," *AAA* 1 (1908) 131-134.

David M. Robinson, "Recent Archaeological Work in Greece," *AJA* 12 (1908) 67-68.

A. J. B. Wace, and M. S. Thompson, "Early Civilization in Northern Greece: Preliminary Report on Excavations in 1909," *AAA* 2 (1909) 149-158.

'Darley Dale', "Ancient and Modern Greece," *IER, 5th Ser.*, 11 (1918) 39-49.

C[arl] W. Blegen, "Excavations in Greece in 1921," *A&A* 13 (1922) 209-216.

*Harold North Fowler, "The American School of Classical Studies at Athens," *A&A* 14 (1922) 171-260. [Excavations of Classic Sites, pp. 184-191; Excavations of Pre-Hellenic Sites, pp. 226-232]

*Allen B. West and Benjamin D. Meritt, "Cleon's Amphipolitan Campaign and the Assessment List of 421," *AJA* 29 (1925) 59-69.

Carl W. Blegen, "The Coming of the Greeks: 2. The Geographical Distribution of Prehistoric Remains in Greece," *AJA* 32 (1928) 146-154.

Arthur Stanley Riggs, "The Flowering of Greece," *OC* 45 (1931) 705-724.

Clark Hopkins, "The Early History of Greece," *YCS* 2 (1931) 115-183.

Greece cont.

Martin P. Nilsson, "New Aims in Prehistoric Greek Archaeology," *AJA* 44 (1940) 106.

Oscar Broneer, "Archaeology in Greece Today," *AJA* 49 (1945) 416-419. [Olympia, Corinth, Crete, Athens]

Anonymous, "Greece 1951," *Arch* 4 (1951) 130-135.

Eugene Vanderpool, "News Letter from Greece," *AJA* 57 (1953) 281-286; 58 (1954) 231-241; 59 (1955) 223-229; 60 (1956) 267-274; 61 (1957) 281-285; 62 (1958) 321-325; 63 (1959) 279-283; 64 (1960) 265-271; 65 (1961) 299-303; 66 (1962) 389-391; 67 (1963) 279-283; 68 (1964) 293-295; 69 (1965) 353-357.

Homer A. Thompson, "Athens and the Hellenistic Princes," *PAPS* 97 (1953) 254-261.

*Raymond V. Schoder, "Air Views of Greece and Rome," *AJA* 57 (1953) 110.

A. J. B. Wace, "The History of Greece in the third and second Millenniums B.C.," *HJAH* 2 (1953-54) 74-94.

G. E[rnest] Wright, "New Discoveries in Greece," *BA* 17 (1954) 47-48.

*RaymondV.Schoder, "Air Views of Greece and Rome,"*AJA* 57(1953) 110.

A. J. B. Wace, "The History of Greece in the third and second Millenniums B.C.," *HJAH* 2 (1953-54) 74-94.

G. E[rnest] Wright, "New Discoveries in Greece," *BA* 17 (1954) 47-48.

R. M. Cook, "Archaeological Argument: Some Principles," *Antiq* 34 (1960) 177-179. *[Greece]*

Emily Townsend Vermeule, "New Mycenaean Discoveries in Western Greece," *AJA* 65 (1961) 193.

Perry A. Bialor and Michael H. Jameson, "Paleolithic in the Argolid," *AJA* 66 (1962) 181-182.

William A. McDonald, "Archaeological Prospecting in Greek Lands," *Arch* 17 (1964) 112-121.

Greece concluded

Raymond V. Schoder, "Some Major Greek Sites from the Air," *AJA* 69 (1965) 175.

Miriam Ervin, "News Letter from Greece," *AJA* 71 (1967) 293-306.

Miriam Ervin, "News Letter from Greece," *AJA* 72 (1968) 265-278.

Miriam Ervin, "News Letter from Greece: Addendum," *AJA* 72 (1968) 381-382.

*H. H. Lamb, "Climatic Changes during the Course of Early Greek History," *Antiq* 42 (1968) 231-233.

William G. Loy, "The Land of Nestor: A Method of Resource Analysis," *AJA* 73 (1969) 241.

Miriam Ervin, "News Letter from Greece," *AJA* 73 (1969) 341-357.

H

Ha'il

Willaim L. Reed and Fred V. Winnett, "Report on the Archaeological Expedition to Ha'il in Northern Saudi Arabia (1967)," *BASOR* #188 (1967) 2-3.

Habor

*W. Francis Ainsworth, "The Two Captivities. The Habor and Chebar," *SBAP* 15 (1892-93) 70-76.

Ḫabur

*M. E. L. Mallowan, "Excavations at Tall Chagar Bazar, and an Archaeological Survey of the Ḫabur Region, 1934-5," *Iraq* 3 (1936) 1-59.

*M. E. L. Mallowan, "Excavations at Tall Chagar Bazar, and an Archaeological Survey of the Ḫabur Region. Second Campaign, 1936," *Iraq* 4 (1937) 91-154.

Hacilar

James Mellaart, "Excavations at Hacilar: First Preliminary Report," *AS* 8 (1958) 127-156.

James Mellaart, "Hacilar-Burdur Excavations 1957," *TAD* 8 (1958) #1, 17-18.

James Mellaart, "Excavations at Hacilar: Second Preliminary Report," *AS* 9 (1959) 51-65.

James Mellaart, "Hacilar-Burdur Excavations 1958," *TAD* 9 (1959) #1, 23-24.

James Mellaart, "Excavations at Hacilar: Third Preliminary Report," *AS* 10 (1960) 83-104.

James Mellaart, "Excavations at Hacilar, 1959," *TAD* 10 (1960) #1, 67-68.

James Mellaart, "Hacilar Excavations 1960," *TAD* 11 (1961) #1, 29-34.

James Mellaart, "Excavations at Hacilar: Fourth Preliminary Report," *AS* 11 (1961) 39-75.

Hadhramaut

Gus W. Van Beek, Glen H. Cole, and Albert Jamme, "An Archaeological Reconnaissance in Hadhramaut, South Arabia—A Preliminary Report," *SIR* (1963) 521-545.

Haghios Kosmas

George E. Mylonas, "Excavations at Haghios Kosmas," *AJA* 38 (1934) 186-187; 38 (1934) 258-279.

Tell Halaf (See also: Gozan)

Anonymous, "German Excavations at Tell Halaf," *RP* 9 (1910) 60.

Anonymous, "Excavations at Telhalef," *RP* 11 (1912) 148.

John L. Myres, "Excavations at Tell Halaf, Northern Mesopotamia," *AAA* 2 (1909) 139-144. *(Review)*

Halieis

John H. Young, "A Migrant City in the Peloponnesus," *Exped* 5 (1962-63) #3, 2-11. *[Halieis]*

Michael H. Jameson, "Halieis: Excavations at Porto Cheli," *AJA* 71 (1967) 190.

*Thomas W. Jacobsen, "Investigations of Porto Cheli-Halieis, 1967," *AJA* 72 (1968) 167.

Sarah Dublin, "A Greek Acropolis and Its Goddess," *Exped* 11 (1968-69) #2, 26-29. *[Halieis]*

*Michael H. Jameson, "Halieis—Porto Cheli, 1968," *AJA* 73 (1969) 238.

Halikyai

*Anthony E. Raubitschek, "Athens and Halikyai," *TAPA* 75 (1944) 10-14.

Hama

Harald Ingholt, "Archaeological Notes. The Danish Expedition at Hama on the Orontes," *AJA* 46 (1942) 469-476.

P. J. R. Modderman, "On a Survey of Palaeolithic Sites Near Hama," *AAAS* 14 (1964) 51-66.

Hamath

Hyde Clarke, "Khita," *PEFQS* 12 (1880) 210-211. *[Hamath]*

George L. Robinson, "The Entrance to Hamath," *BW* 32 (1908) 7-18.

Tell El-Ḥammeh

Nelson Glueck, "Tell El-Ḥammeh," *AJA* 39 (1935) 321-330.

Hana

C. H. W. Johns, "The Kingdom of Hana," *SBAP* 31 (1909) 292-294.

Harageh

Rex Engelbach, Battiscombe Gunn, and Duncan Willey, "British School of Archaeology in Egypt. Harageh, 1913-14," *AEE* 1 (1914) 101-102.

Haran

H. B. Hackett, "Biblical Notes. 1. Situation of Haran," *BS* 24 (1867) 176-179.

*[Stephen D. Peet], "The Journey of Jacob," *AAOJ* 3 (1880-81) 151-152. *(Editorial) [Haran]*

*G[eorge] Rawlinson, "Biblical Topography. VI.—Sites connected with the History of Abraham—Harran, Damascus, Hebron," *MI* 4 (1886) 241-252. *[Part IV not published]*

Wm. Francis Ainsworth, "Haran in Mesopotamia," *SBAP* 13 (1890-91) 385-391.

W. Taylor Smith, "Haran in Very Early Times," *ET* 3 (1891-92) 208-209.

P. E. Kretzmann, "Where was Haran, or Charran?" *CTM* 6 (1935) 218-219.

Anonymous, "Excavations at Haran," *AT* 2 (1957-58) #4, 11, *continued on p. 10.*

Hare Nome

R. O. Faulkner, "The Rebellion at the Hare Nome," *JEA* 30 (1944) 61-63.

Tell el-Ḥarîrī (See: Mari)

Tell Harmal

Sidney Smith, "Excavations at Tell Harmal I. Diniktim," *Sumer* 2 (1946) #2, 19-21.

Taha Baqir, "Tell Harmal. A Preliminary Report," *Sumer* 2 (1946) #2, 24-30.

Taha Baqir, "Excavations at Harmal," *Sumer* 4 (1948) 137-138.

Harran

Seton Lloyd and William Brice, "Harran," *AS* 1 (1951) 77-111. (Note by C. J. Gadd, pp. 108-110)

Hasanlu

Robert H[arris] Dyson Jr., "Iran 1957: Iron Age Hasanlu," *UMB* 22 (1958) #2, 25-32.

Robert H. Dyson Jr., "Digging in Hasanlu, 1958," *Exped* 1 (1958-59) #3, 4-17.

Robert H. Dyson Jr., "The Death of a City," *Exped* 2 (1959-60) #3, 2-11. *[Hasanlu]*

*Robert H. Dyson Jr., "Hasanlu and Early Iran," *Arch* 13 (1960) 118-129.

Robert H. Dyson Jr., "New Discoveries at Hasanlu, Iran, in 1960 and 1962," *AJA* 67 (1963) 210.

*Robert H. Dyson Jr., "Problems of Protohistoric Iran as Seen from Hasanlu," *JNES* 24 (1965) 193-217.

Ḫaššam

*Sidney Smith, "Ursu and Ḫaššam," *AS* 6 (1956) 35-43.

Tell Hassuna

Seton Lloyd and Faud Safar, "Tell Hassuna: Excavations by the Iraq Government Directorate General of Antiquities in 1943 and 1944, with prefatory remarks by Robert J. Braidwood," *JNES* 4 (1945) 255-289.

*E. Douglas Van Buren, "Excavations in Mesopotamia," *Or, N.S.*, 15 (1946) 497-503. [1. Tell Hassuna, pp. 497-499]

Hatay Province

Muzaffer [Süleyman] Şenyürek, "New Researches in the Hatay Province," *TTKB* 22 (1958) 443.

Hatra

Faud Safar, "Hatra and the First Season of Excavation 1951. Part I," *Sumer* 8 (1952) 3-16. *[Part II not published as such]*

Anonymous, "The Archaeological Discoveries at Hatra in the Fourth Season of Excavation (1954)," *Sumer* 10 (1954) 84-85.

Hawara

*Lysander Dickerman, "On Mr. Petrie's recent explorations in Hawara, Biahmu, and Arsinoë," *JAOS* 14 (1890) cxxvii-cxxix.

Hearion

Anonymous, "Hearion," *RP* 3 (1904) 56.

Hecatompylos

*John Hansman, "The Problems of Qūmis," *JRAS* (1968) 111-139. *[Hecatomylos?]*

Helice

Spyriodon N. Marinatos, "Helice: A Submerged Town of Classical Greece," *Arch* 13 (1960) 186-193.

Heliopolis (See: On)

*Melvin Grove Kyle, "Professor Petrie's Excavations at Heliopolis, The Biblical On," *BS* 69 (1912) 553-564.

Hellenion

Anonymous, "Africa:—Egypt," *RP* 2 (1903) 317. *[Hellenion]*

Helwan

Zaki Y. Saad, "Preliminary report on the Royal Excavations at Helwan (1942)," *ASAE* 41 (1942) 405-409.

Zaki Y. Saad, "Preliminary report on the Royal Excavations at Helwan (1942). (Plan)," *ASAE* 42 (1943) 357.

Heraeum

G. A. Harrer, "Excavations at the Argive Heraeum 1925," *AJA* 29 (1925) 413-433.

Herakleion

*Eugene Vanderpool, "The Deme of Marthon and the Herakleion," *AJA* 70 (1966) 319-323.

Herakleopolis

*Percy E. Newberry, "The Tree of the Herakleopolite Nome," *ZÄS* 50 (1912) 78-79.

W. M. Flinders Petrie, "Discoveries at Herakleopolis," *AEE* 6 (1921) 65-69.

Herculaneum

George Shelvocke, "An Account of the Subterraneous Town in the Neighbourhood of Naples, lately discovered," *MMBR* 16 (1803) 13-15. *[Herculaneum]*

Anonymous, "Excavations at Herculaneum," *MQR, 3rd Ser.*, 31 (1905) 389-390.

A[rthur] S[tanley] R[iggs], "Notes and Comments. The New Excavations at Herculaneum," *A&A* 30 (1930) 93-94.

*Charles Seltman, "A mine of statues," *HT* 1 (Jan., 1951) 34-42. *[Herculaneum]*

Charles F. Mullett, "Englishmen Discover Herculaneum and Pompeii," *Arch* 10 (1957) 31-38.

Hermopolis

M. Kamal, "Excavations of the Antiquities Department (1942) in the so-called 'Agora' of Hermopolis (Ashmunein)," *ASAE* 46 (1947) 289-295.

Labib Habachi, "Notes on the Delta Hermopolis, capital of the XVth Nome of Lower Egypt," *ASAE* 53 (1955) 441-480.

Alexander Badawy, "The Cemetery at Hermopolis West: A Fortnight of Excavation," *Arch* 11 (1958) 117-122.

Heroon-polis

*C. W. Goodwin, "Notes by C. W. Goodwin," *ZÄS* 11 (1873) 12-15. [3. Heron and Heroon-polis, pp. 13-14]

Heroöpolis

*C. R. Gillett, "Pithom—Heroöpolis—Succoth," *AR* 8 (1887) 82-92.

*E. Amélineau, "Some Geographical Identifications in Egypt," *IAQR, 2nd Ser.*, 3 (1892) 328-345. [VII. HEROOPOLIS, pp. 342-345]

Hierakonpolis

Anonymous, "Egyptian Excavations," *RP* 4 (1905) 319. *[Hierakonpolis]*

*John Garstang, "Excavations at Hierakonpolis, at Esna, and in Nubia," *ASAE* 8 (1907) 132-148.

*John A. Wilson, "Buto and Hierakonpolis in the Geography of Egypt," *JNES* 14 (1955) 209-236.

*Barry J. Kemp, "Excavations at Hierakonpolis Fort, 1905: A Preliminary Note," *JEA* 49 (1963) 24-28.

Hierothesion

Theresa Goell, "The Excavation of the 'Hierothesion' of Antiochus I of Commagene on Nemrud Dugh(1953-1956),"*BASOR* #147(1957) 4-22.

Hilar

Ellsworth Huntington, "The Hittite Ruins of Hilar, Asia Minor," *RP* 2 (1903) 131-140.

Ḥimyar

Léon Legrain, "In the Land of the Queen of Sheba," *AJA* 38 (1934) 329-338. *[Ḥimyar]*

Hermann von Wissman, "Ḥimyar, Ancient History," *Muséon* 77 (1964) 429-499.

Hissarlik

Daniel Quinn, "Archaeological Excavations at Hissarlik," *ACQR* 29 (1904) 482-492.

Ḥiṭân Shenshef

G. W. Murray, "Note on the Ruins of Ḥiṭân Shenshef, near Berenice," *JEA* 12 (1926) 166-167.

Mount Horeb

*J. Stow, "Mount Horeb," *PEFQS* 23 (1891) 178-182. (Note by C. R. Conder, p. 182) [Correction, *PEFQS* 24 (1892) p. 47]

Chas. Fox, "The Latitude of Mount Horeb," *PEFQS* 25 (1893) 63-67.

*W. J. Phythian-Adams, "The Volcanic Phenomena of the Exodus," *JPOS* 12 (1932) 86-103. *[Mt. Horeb]*

Horoztepe

Burhan Tezcan, "New Finds from Horoztepe," *A(A)* 5 (1960) 29-46.

Tahsin Özvüç, "New Finds from Horoztepe," *A(A)* 8 (1964) 1-17.

Hoyucek

Muzaffer Süleyman Şenyürek, E. Şenyürek, Hikki Gultekin, and Ahmet Dönmez, "The Test Excavation at Hoyucek, in the Vicinity of Larisa," *TTKB* 14 (1950) 496-504.

Mount Hymettos

Rodney S. Young, "Archaeological Notes: Excavations on Mount Hymettos, 1939," *AJA* 44 (1940) 1-9.

I

Igdyr

R. D. Barnett, "The Urartian Cemetery at Igdyr," *AS* 13 (1963) 153-198.

Ikaria

[A. L. Frothingham Jr.], "The Excavations in Ikaria by the American Classical School at Athens," *AJA, O.S.*, 4 (1888) 44-46.

*Carl D. Buck, "Discoveries in the Deme of Ikaria, 1888," *AJA. O.S.*, 5 (1889) 135-181. [IV. Chronological Report of Excavations, pp. 154-158; V. Topography of the Ikarian District, pp. 158-165; VI. Architectural Remains, pp. 165-181]

Ilios

†Anonymous, "Schliemann's Ilios," *ERCJ* 153 (1881) 514-547. *(Review)*

Tell Ingharra

P. R. S. Moorey, "A Reconsideration of the Excavations on Tell Ingharra (East Kish), 1923-33," *Iraq* 28 (1966) 18-51.

Iolkos

Demetrios R. Theochares, "Iolkos—Whence Sailed the Argonauts," *Arch* 11 (1958) 13-18.

Ionia

†Anonymous, "The Ionian Islands," *QRL* 29 (1823) 86-116. *(Review)*

Ekrem Akurgal, "The Early Period of the Golden Age of Ionia," *AJA* 66 (1962) 369-379.

Iran

*Louis H. Gray, "The Kings of Early Iran according to the Sidrā Rabbā," *ZA* 19 (1905-06) 272-287.

T. J. Arne, "The Swedish Archaeological Expedition to Iran 1932-1933," *AA* 6 (1935) 1-48.

Donald E. McCown, "The Material Culture of Early Iran," *JNES* 1 (1942) 424-449.

Robert H. Dyson Jr., "Iran, 1956," *UMB* 21 (1957) #1, 27-39.

*Robert H. Dyson Jr., "Hasanlu and Early Iran," *Arch* 13 (1960) 118-129.

R.J.Braidwood,"The Iranian Prehistoric Project,1959-1960," *IA* 1(1961)3-7.

*Robert H. Dyson Jr., "Ninth Century Men in Western Iran," *Arch* 17 (1964) 3-11.

*Robert H. Dyson Jr., "Problems of Protohistoric Iran as Seen from Hasanlu," *JNES* 24 (1965) 193-217.

C[lare Meade] Goff, L. B. de Cardi, H. Luschey, R. H. Dyson, Jr., M. B. Nicol, P. E. L. Smith, T. Cuyler Young Jr., E. Negahban, D. B. Whitehouse, R. Ghirshman, D. Huff, Joseph R. Caldwell, C. S. Smith, J. Deshayes, P. Delougaz, "Survey of Excavations in Iran During 1965-66," *Iran* 5 (1967) 133-149. [Bābā Jān Tepe; Bāmpūr; Bard e Nechandeh; Bīsitūn; Dahān-i-Ghulāmān; Dinkha Tepe; Dorudzan; Ghar-i-Khar and Ganj-i Dareh; Gordin Tepe; Haft Tepe; Rashi; Siraf; Suse *[French Text]*; Takht-i-Suleiman *[German Text]*; Tal-i Iblīs; Metallurgical Archaeology; Tepes Kalwali and War Kabud; Tureng Tépé *[French Text]*; Choga Mish]

Iran concluded

Clare Meade Goff, P. E. L. Smith, T. Cuyler Young Jr., E. Negahban, David Stronach, D. B. Whitehouse, R. Ghirshman, J. Deshayes, Wolfram Kleiss, C. C. Lamberg-Karlovsky, Paul Gotch, "Survey of Excavations in Iran During 1966-67," *Iran* 6 (1968) 157-171. [I. Excavation Reports: Bābā Jān; Ganj Dareh Tepe; Gordin Tepe; Haft Tepe; Tepe Nūsh-i-Jān and Shahr-i-Kōmis; Sīrāf; Suse et Masjid-i Solaiman; Travaux de la Delegation archeologique Française en Iran—Hiver 1966/1967 *[French Text];* II. Survey Reports: Das Deutsche Archäologische Institut, Teheran *[German Text];* Survey and Excavations in the Kirman Area; A Survey of the Persepolis Plain and Shiraz Area; III. Notes]

Robert H. Dyson Jr., "A Decade in Iran," *Exped* 11 (1968-69) #2, 39-47.

*Edith Porada, "Iranian Art and Archaeology: A Report of the Fifth International Congress, 1968," *Arch* 22 (1969) 54-65. [The Emergence of Early Farming Communities; Early Farming Communities and Their External Relations; Early Farming Communities of Western Iran; The Elamites; Grey Wares and the Problem of Indo-Europeans in Iran; The Early Iron Age, Marlik Culture and Hasanlu v; Anatolian and Urartian Remains The Context of the Luristan Bronzes and Finds of the Median Period; Achaemenid Architecture]

*Clare L. Goff, L. Vanden Berghe, Frank Hole, Murray B. Nicol, Henry T. Wright, Ezat O. Negahban, C. A. Burney, Robert H. Dyson Jr., Oscar White Muscarella and Mary M. Voigt, Maurizio Tosi, David Whitehouse, M.-J. Steve, C. C. Lamberg-Karlovsky, R. B. R. Kearton, Wolfram Kleiss, Ralph S. Solecki, Theodore A. Wertime, Paul Gotch, Dietrich Huff, "Survey of Excavations in Iran, 1967-8," *Iran* 7 (1969) 169-193 [I. Excavation Reports: Bābā Jān; Bāni Surmah; Choga Sefīd; Darvāzeh Tepe; Tepe Farukhābād; Haft Tepe; Haftavān Tepe; Ḥasanlū Project 1968: Hajji Firuz, Dinkat Tepe, Se Girdan, Qalatgah; Kaluraz, Kangavar, Shahr-i Sokhte; Sīrāf; Suse *[French Text];* Tepe Yaḥyā; II. Survey Reports: Archaeological Service of Iran: the discovery of an Assyrian relief; Survey in Azerbaijan; Survey in Western Azerbaijan; Survey of Man's fire-using industries in Afghanistan, Iran and Turkey; The Persepolis Plain and Shiraz; Field Survey 2; Takht-i Suleiman *[German Text]*]

*George F. Dales and Louis Flam, "On Tracking Woolly Kullis and the Like," *Exped* 12 (1969-70) #1, 15-23. *[Iran]*

Iraq

E. G. H. Kraeling, "Current Notes and Comments. Excavations in Iraq," *A&A* 17 (1924) 287; 19 (1925) 109.

George A. Barton, "Our Excavation in Iraq," *BASOR* #18 (1925) 1-11.

Anonymous, "Notes and Comments. Palæolithic Discoveries in Northern Iraq," *A&A* 27 (1929) 90.

George A. Barton, "Archaeological News from Iraq," *BASOR* #33 (1929) 11-12.

E[phraim] A. Speiser, "Reports from our Expeditions in Iraq," *BASOR* #41 (1931) 19-27.

H[enri] Frankfort, "The Work of the Oriental Institute of Iraq," *AJA* 37 (1933) 529-539.

*Charles Arden-Close, "Sir Aurel Stein's Explorations of the Roman Frontiers in Iraq and Trans-jordan," *PEQ* 73 (1941) 18-21.

P. J. Wiseman, "Iraq," *JTVI* 75 (1943) 104-105.

Seton Lloyd, "Note on War-Time Archaeological Activity in Iraq," *Sumer* 1 (1945) #1, 5-11.

Seton Lloyd, "Priorities of post-war Excavation," *Sumer* 1 (1945) #2, 3-14. *[Iraq]*

Seton Lloyd, "A Note on Prehistoric Research," *Sumer* 3 (1947) 26-28. *[Iraq]*

‡Gurgis Awad, "Bibliography of Excavations in Iraq (1939-1946)," *Sumer* 3 (1947) 30-35.

Samuel Noah Kramer, "Iraqi Excavations During the War Years," *UMB* 13 (1947-48) #2, 1-29.

Naji al-Asil, "Recent Archaeological Activities in Iraq," *Sumer* 6 (1950) 3-5.

Naji al-Asil, "Archaeological Research in Iraq and International Exchanges Between Archaeological Museums and Institutions," *Sumer* 6 (1950) 111-114.

Iraq concluded

Robert J. Braidwood, "From Cave to Village in Prehistoric Iraq," *BASOR* #123 (1951) 12-18.

‡Gurgis Awad, "Bibliography Relating to Excavations in Iraq, 1947-1951," *Sumer* 8 (1952) 90-100.

*W. Rees Williams, "The Origin of the Al Batin and the Al Dibdibba," *Sumer* 8 (1952) 217-218. *[Iraq]*

‡Gurgis Awad, "Bibliography Relating to Excavations in Iraq, 1952-1954," *Sumer* 11 (1955) 61-70.

*H. E. Wright Jr., "Geological Aspects of the Archaeology of Iraq," *Sumer* 11 (1955) 83-90.

Naji al Asil, "Recent Archaeological Activity in Iraq," *Sumer* 12 (1956) 3-7.

*Robert M. Adams, "Survey of Ancient Water Courses and Settlements in Central Iraq," *Sumer* 14 (1958) 101-103.

H. J. Lenzen, "The E-Anna District After Excavations in the winter of 1958-1959," *Sumer* 16 (1960) 3-11. *[Iraq]*

Georges Roux, "Recently Discovered Ancient Sites in the Hammar Lake District (Southern Iraq)," *Sumer* 16 (1960) 20-31.

‡Gurgis Awad, "Bibliography of Excavations in Iraq, 1955-1959," *Sumer* 16 (1960) 48-74.

T. Cuyler Young Jr., "Survey in Western Iran, 1961," *JNES* 25 (1966) 228-239.

*Jeffrey Orchard, "Recent Restoration Work in Iraq," *Iraq* 24 (1962) 73-77.

Jeffrey Orchard, "Recent Archaeological Activity in Iraq: A Review," *Iraq* 25 (1963) 104-109.

Henry T. Wright, "A Note on a Paleolithic Site in the Southern Desert," *Sumer* 22 (1966) 101-106. *[Iraq]*

Ischia

Jonkvrouwe M. W. Stoop, "Some Observations on the Recent Excavations on Ischia," *A&S* 1 (1955-56) 255-267.

Isin

S[tephen] Langdon, "The Location of Isin," *JRAS* (1922) 430-431.

Issus

*William Hayes Ward, "The Ship-yard at Ancient Issus," *JBL* 5 (1885) 84.

Isthmia

Oscar Broneer, "The University of Chicago Excavations at Isthmia," *AJA* 57 (1953) 105.

Oscar Broneer, "Excavation of Isthmia, 1957-1958," *AJA* 63 (1959) 187.

Italy

A. L. Frothingham Jr., "Note from Italy," *AJA, O.S.,* 11 (1896) 197-204.

Guido Calza, "Art and Archaeology in Italy in 1921,"*A&A* 13 (1922) 217-230.

Anonymous, "Notes and Comments. Italy Opens Excavation Field to Foreigners," *A&A* 30 (1930) 94-95.

Anna Schellkopf, "Italica," *A&A* 31 (1931) 275-282.

*Edith Hall Dohan, "Archaeological Evidence for an Etruscan Invasion of Italy," *AJA* 46 (1942) 119.

Ithaca

†Anonymous, "Gell's Geography and Antiquities of Ithaca," *BCQTR* 32 (1808) 21-28. *(Review)*

Anonymous, "Discovery of the Homeric City of Ithaca," *RP* 6 (1907) 159.

Ithaca concluded

Anonymous, "Location of the Homeric Ithaca," *RP* 10 (1911) 115.

Alexander Shewan, "Ithaka," *Antiq* 1 (1927) 402-411.

William Dörpfeld, Ancient Ithaca," *A&A* 27 (1929) 51-57.

W. A. Heurtley, "Excavations in Ithaca," *Antiq* 5 (1931) 103-105.

J. L. Myres, "Recent Discoveries in Ithaca by Members of the British School of Archaeology in Athens," *AJA* 42 (1938) 121-122.

Itj-Towy

William K. Simpson, "Studies in the Twelfth Egyptian Dynasty: I-II," *JARCE* 2 (1963) 53-63. [I. The Residence of Itj-Towy]

Iulis

*Irwin L. Merker, "The Harbor of Iulis," *AJA* 72 (1968) 383-384.

J

Jarmo

*F. Basmachi, "Supplementary Report on the Excavations at Tell Mattarah and Qal'at Jarmo," *Sumer* 4 (1948) 134-136. *[Supplements-Arabic article in same volume]*

*Robert J. Braidwood, "Jarmo: A Village of Early Farmers in Iraq," *Antiq* 24 (1950) 189-195.

Robert J. Braidwood, "The Iraq-Jarmo Project of the Oriental Institute of the University of Chicago, Season 1954-1955," *Sumer* 10 (1954) 120-138.

Anonymous, "The Iraq-Jarmo Project: 1954-5," *Antiq* 30 (1956) 113-115.

Anonymous, "The Oldest Villages in the World," *AT* 3 (1958-59) #2, 6. *[Jarmo]*

The Jaulan

G. Schumacher, "The Jaulan," *PEFQS* 20 (1888) [numbered separately as: pp. 1-128, 129-304 in the *January* and *April* issues]

Javan

*Charles C. Torrey, "'Yāwān' and 'Hellas' as Designations of the Seleucid Empire," *JAOS* 25 (1904) 302-311. [יָוָן= Javan; היונים]

*A. H. Sayce, "Geographical Notes," *JRAS* (1921) 47-55. *[Javan]*

Jebel Musa

*(   ) G., "Jebel Musa and Er Raheh," *JSL, 3rd Ser.,* 13 (1861) 435-440.

Jerf Ajla

B. Schroeder, "The lithic material from Jerf Ajla. A Preliminary Report," *AAAS* 16 (1966) #2, 201-210.

Jezireh

Carl H. Kraeling, "Report on a sounding in the Jezireh, May 25-26, 1962," *AAAS* 2 (1952) 252-258.

Joppa

*Hans Goedicke, "The Capture of Joppa," *CdÉ* 48 (1968) 291-223.

Tell Judadiah

Robert J. Braidwood, "A Correction," *AJA* 43 (1939) 378-379. *[Tell Judadiah]*

K

El Kab

*G. Willoughby Fraser, "El Kab and Gebelen," *SBAP* 15 (1892-93) 494-500.

James Henry Breasted, "Exploration and Discovery: Excavations of the Egyptian Research Account at El Kab. (Illustrated)," *BW* 9 (1897) 219-220.

J. E. Quibell, "Exploration and Discovery: The Egyptian Research Account at El Kab," *BW* 9 (1897) 380-381.

A. H. Sayce and Somers Clarke, "Report on certain Excavations made at El-Kab during the Years 1901, 1902, 1903, 1904," *ASAE* 6 (1905) 239-272.

Somers Clarke, "El-Kâb and the Great Wall," *JEA* 7 (1921) 54-79.

*Somers Clarke, "El-Kâb and its Temples," *JEA* 8 (1922) 16-40.

Anthony Kriesis, "On the Enclosure Walls of El Kab," *AJA* 53 (1949) 261-262.

Kadesh (on Orontes)

*Henry George Tomkins, "The Campaign of Rameses II in his fifth year against Kadesh on Orontes," *SBAT* 7 (1880-82) 390-406.

†H[enry] G[eorge] Tomkins, "The Campaign of Rameses II in his fifth year against Kadesh on the Orontes," *SBAP* 4 (1881-82) 6-7. (Remarks by William Wright, pp. 8-9)

Henry George Tomkins, "Kadesh on Orontes," *PEFQS* 14 (1882) 47-50.

William Wright, "Kadesh on the Orontes," *PEFQS* 14 (1882) 132.

C[laude] R. Conder, "Notes. *Kadesh on Orontes,*" *PEFQS* 14 (1882) 155; 15 (1883) 100-101.

C[laude] R. Conder, "The Battle of Kadesh," *PEFQS* 22 (1890) 309-310.

Kadesh (on Orontes) concluded

George L. Robinson," Modern Kadesh, or 'Ain Kadîs," *BW* 17 (1901) 327-337.

*Claude R. Conder, "Notes on New Discoveries," *PEFQS* 41 (1909) 266-275. [Kadesh, Kedeshah, p. 269]

Anonymous, "The Battle of Kadesh," *MR* 101 (1918) 790-795.

*A. H. Burne, "Some Notes on the Battle of Kadesh. Being a Military Commentary on Professor J. H. Breasted's Book, *The Battle of Kedesh* (University of Chicago Press, 1903)," *JEA* 7 (1921) 191-195.

*H. L Ginsberg, "An Ancient Name of the Syrian Desert," *BIES* 6 (1938-39) #2, III. *[Kadesh]*

R. O. Faulkner, "The Battle of Kadesh," *MDIÄA* 16 (1958) 93-111.

*Alan R. Schulman, "The *N ʿrn* at the Battle of Kadesh," *JARCE* 1 (1962) 47-53.

B. Oded, "Two Assyrian References to the Town of Qadesh on Orontes," *IEJ* 14 (1964) 272-273.

Hans Goedicke, "Considerations on the Battle of Ḳadesh," *JEA* 52 (1966) 71-80.

Kadesh Barnea

C[laude] R. Conder, "Note on Kadesh Barnea," *PEFQS* 13 (1881) 60-61.

H. Clay Trumbull, " A Visit to "Ain Qadis: The Supposed Site of Kadesh-barnea," *PEFQS* 13 (1881) 208-212.

Nathaniel Schmidt, "Kadesh Barnea," *JBL* 29 (1910) 61-76.

George Adam Smith, "Some Remarks on Professor Schmidt's Article *Kadesh Barnea*," *JBL* 29 (1910) 196-197.

Camden M. Cobern, "Kadesh-Barnea—The Oasis Where the Israelites Camped for Thirty-Eight Years," *HR* 67 (1914) 261-267.

Kadesh Barnea concluded

Camden M. Cobern, "Kadesh-Barnea—The Lost Oasis of the Sinaitic Peninsula," *HR* 67 (1914) 347-354.

Camden M. Cobern and J. D. Crace, "Dr. H. Clay Trumbull and Kadesh-barnea," *PEFQS* 48 (1916) 97-100.

I. O. Nothstein, "Kadesh-Barnea," *AugQ* 7 (1928) 167-168.

*J. R. Porter, "The Role of Kadesh-Barnea in the Narrative of the Exodus," *JTS* 44 (1943) 139-143.

M. Dothan, "The Fortress at Kadesh-Barnea," *IEJ* 15 (1965) 134-151.

Anonymous, "Kadesh Barnea Investigated," *BH* 1 (1964) #3, 24.

H. Bar-Deroma, "Kadesh-Barneʿa," *PEQ* 96 (1964) 101-134.

Kaniş

*Tahsin Özgüç, "Report on a work-shop belonging to the late phase of the Colony Period (Ib)," *TTKB* 19 (1955) 77-80. *[Kaniş]*

Kara-höyük

*Tahsin Özgüç, "Archaeological journeys in the plain of Elbistan and the excavation of Kara-höyük," *TTKB* 12 (1948) 232-237.

U. Bahadir Alkim and Handan Alkim, "Excavations at Gedikli (Karahüyük) First Preliminary—Report," *TTKB* 30 (1966) 27-57.

Karamania

*G. A. Wainwright, "Keftiu and Karamania (Asia Minor)," *AS* 4 (1954) 33-48.

Karanis

A. E. R. Boak, "The University of Michigan's Excavations at Karanis: 1924-5," *JEA* 12 (1926) 19-21.

Louise A. Shier, "A Roman Town in Egypt," *AJA* 53 (1949) 146. *[Karanis]*

Karataş-Semayük

Machteld J. Mellink, "Excavations at Karataş-Semayük in Lycia," *AJA* 68 (1964) 197.

Machteld J. Mellink, "Excavations at Karataş-Semayük in Lycia, 1963," *AJA* 68 (1964) 269-278.

Machteld [J.] Mellink, "Report on the first campaign of Excavations at Karataş,—Semayük September 15-November 17, 1963," *TAD* 13 (1964) #1, 97-102.

Machteld J. Mellink, "Excavations at Karataş-Semayük," *TAD* 13 (1964) #2, 49-57.

Machteld J. Mellink, "Excavations at Karataş-Semayük in Lycia, 1964," *AJA* 69 (1965) 171; 241-251

Machteld J. Mellink, "Excavations at Karataş-Semayük 1965," *TAD* 14 (1965) 223-230.

Machteld J. Mellink, "Excavations at Karataş-Semayük in Lycia, 1965," *AJA* 70 (1966) 245-255.

Machteld J. Mellink, "Excavations at Karataş-Semayük 1966," *TAD* 15 (1966) #2, 73-80.

Machteld J. Mellink, "Excavations at Karataş-Semayük 1966," *AJA* 71 (1967) 251-267.

Machteld J. Mellink, "Excavations of Karataş-Semayük 1967," *TAD* 16 (1967) #1, 107-112.

Machteld J. Mellink, "Excavations at Karataş-Semayük in Lycia, 1967," *AJA* 72 (1968) 243-259.

Machteld J. Mellink, "Excavations at Karataş-Semayük 1968," *TAD* 17 (1968) #2, 145-150.

Machteld J. Mellink, "Excavations at Karataş-Semayük in Lycia, 1968," *AJA* 73 (1969) 319-331.

Machteld J. Mellink, "Excavations at Karataş-Semayük 1969," *TAD* 18 (1969) #2, 137-139.

Karatepe

Halet Çambel, "Karatepe. An archaeological introduction to a recently discovered Hittite site in southern Anatolia," *Oriens* 1 (1948) 147-162.

U. Bahadir Alkim, "Excavations at Karatepe," *TTKB* 12 (1948) 249-255.

*Franz Steinherr, "Karatepe, the Key to the Hittite Hieroglyphics," *Arch* 2 (1949) 177-180.

*Julian Obermann, "New Discoveries at Karatepe. A Complete Text Of The Phoenician Royal Inscription From Cilicia," *CAAST* 38 (1949) 1-50.

U. Bahadir Alkim, "Third Season's Work at Karatepe," *TTKB* 13 (1949) 371-374. *[No English article published on "*Second *Season's Work" - This article may be misnumbered, cf. second article at top of page]*

*J. J. Mellink, "Karatepe: More light on the dark ages," *BO* 7 (1950) 141-150.

U. Bahadir Alkim, "Karatepe: Third Campaign," *TTKB* 14 (1950) 542-565.

U. Bahadir Alkim, "Karatepe: Fourth Campaign," *TTKB* 14 (1950) 655-659.

U. Bahadir Alkim, "The Fifth Season's Work at Karatepe," *TTKB* 14 (1950) 680-682.

*Anonymous, "Summary of Archaeological Research in Turkey, 1949-1950," *AS* 1 (1951) 9-20. [Explorations of Ancient Roads passing Karatepe, by Alkim U. Bahadir, pp. 19-20, (Note by W. M. Calder, p. 20)]

U. Bahadir Alkim, "The Sixth season's work at Karatepe," *TTKB* 16 (1952) 134-136.

U. Bahadir Alkim, "Karatepe: Seventh Campaign," *TTKB* 16 (1952) 620-624.

U. Bahadir Alkim, "The Eighth Season's Work at Karatepe," *TTKB* 16 (1952) 625-628.

Karkheh

*John Hansman, "Charax and Karkheh," *IA* 7 (1967) 21-58.

Karnak

A. H. Sayce, "Discoveries at Karnak," *SBAP* 21 (1899) 141.

A[ngus] C[rawford], "Karnak," *PER* 13 (1899-1900) 171-172

*A. H. Sayce, "Recent Biblical Archaeology. The City of Enoch," *ET* 13 (1901-02) 178-179. *[Khanak?]*

*A. H. Sayce, "Notes from Egypt," *SBAP* 24 (1902) 86. *[Excavations at Karnak]*

Anonymous, "New Discoveries at Karnak," *RP* 4 (1905) 96.

Anonymous, "Discoveries at Karnak," *RP* 4 (1905) 156-157.

*Anonymous, "Methods of Work at Karnak," *RP* 7 (1908) 258. *[Archaeological Methods]*

Shehata Adam and Farid El-Shaboury, "Report on the work of Karnak during the seasons 1954-55 and 1955-56," *ASAE* 56 (1959) 35-52.

*M. Abdul-Qader Muhammed, "Recent finds," *ASAE* 59 (1966) 143-155. [Karnak: Third Pylon; Amenophis III; Sobek-Hotep; Nebpeḥtire Aḥmosis; Amenophis I; Tuthmosis II; Tuthmosis IV; The Sacred Lake; The Theban Necropolis: The Temple of Amenophis III; The Tomb of Kheruef]

H. S. K. Bakry, "Reconstruction of the Third Pylon at Karnak," *ASAE* 60 (1968) 7-14.

Kas

*A. H. Sayce, "Geographical Notes," *JRAS* (1921) 47-55. [Kas and Kusa, p. 54]

Katna

*Ch. Virolleaud, "The Syrian Town of Katna and the Kingdom of Mitanni," *Antiq* 3 (1929) 312-317.

Kato Zakro

Leon Pomerance, "Excavations at Kato Zakro, 1964-1965," *AJA* 70 (1966) 193-194.

Leon Pomerance, "Excavations at Kato Zakro, 1966," *AJA* 71 (1967) 193.

Kavousi

Harriett A. Boyd, "Excavations at Kavousi, Crete in 1900," *AJA* 5 (1901) 125-158.

Kawa

L. P. Kirwan, "Preliminary Report of the Oxford University Excavations at Kawa, 1935-1936," *JEA* 22 (1936) 199-211.

Kayalidere

Seton Lloyd and C. A. Burney, "Excavations at the Urartian Citadel of Kayalidere (1965 Season)," *TAD* 14 (1965) 217-222.

C. A. Burney, "A First Season of Excavation at the Urartian Citadel of Kayalidere," *AS* 16 (1966) 55-111.

Kazaphani

J. R. Stewart, "Kazaphani," *AAA* 28 (1948) 5-7.

Kea (see also: Ceos and Keos)

John L. Caskey, "Excavations at Kea, 1961," *AJA* 66 (1962) 195.

*Frederick R. Matson, "Could Pottery Have Been Made at Kea?" *AJA* 71 (1967) 191. *[Keos]*

Kebeleh

G. E. Wickens, "A Brief Note on the Recently Discovered Tora City of Kebeleh," *Kush* 15 (1967-68) 310-313.

Kef Kalesi

Emin Bilgiç and Baki Öğün, "Excavations at Kefi Kales of Adilcevaz, 1964," *A(A)* 8 (1964) 93-124.

Emin Bilgiç and Baki Öğün, "Second Season Excavations at Kef Kalesi of Adilcavez (1965)," *A(A)* 9 (1965) 11-28.

Keftiu

*Robert C. Horn, "The Philistines and Ancient Crete—Caphator, Keftiu, Crete," *RP* 12 (1913) 119-122.

G. A. Wainwright, "Asiatic Keftiu," *AJA* 56 (1952) 196-212.

*G. A. Wainwright, "Keftiu and Karamania (Asia Minor)," *AS* 4 (1954) 33-48.

Kenchreai

Edwin S. Ramage, "Excavations at Kenchreaf, *[sic]* 1963," *AJA* 68 (1964) 198-199.

Edwin S. Ramage, "Excavations at Kenchreai, 1964," *AJA* 69 (1965) 173-174.

Robert Scranton, "Kenchreai—1968," *AJA* 73 (1969) 245.

Keos (see also: Ceos and Kea)

John L. Caskey, "Excavations in Keos, 1966," *AJA* 71 (1967) 184-185.

*J. E. Coleman, "Excavations at Kephala in Ceos," *AJA* 71 (1967) 185.

*Frederick R. Matson, "Could Pottery Have Been Made at Kea?" *AJA* 71 (1967) 191. *[Keos]*

Keos concluded

John L. Caskey, "Excavations in Keos, 1967," *AJA* 72 (1968) 163.

Kephala

*J. E. Coleman, "Excavations at Kephala in Ceos," *AJA* 71 (1967) 185.

Kerkenes Dagh

Erich F. Schmidt, "Test Excavations in the City on Kerkenes Dagh," *AJSL* 45 (1928-29) 221-274. *[Asia Minor]*

Kerma

George Reisner, "Excavations at Kerma (Dongola-Province) I. A report on the Egyptian Expedition of Harvard University and the Boston Museum of Fine Arts 1913," *ZÄS* 52 (1914) 34-39.

George Reisner, "Excavations at Kerma II. A report on the Harvard-Boston Excavations 1913-1914," *ZÄS* 52 (1914) 40-49.

Khafâjeh

*Patrick Railton, "Some Remains of the Ancient Near East," *JMUEOS* #18 (1932) 55-59. *[Khafâje]*

*E[phraim] A. Speiser, "New Discoveries at Tepe Gawra and Khafaje," *AJA* 41 (1937) 190-193.

E[phraim] A. S[peiser], "Khafaje, 1937," *UMB* 6 (1935-37) #6, 14-18.

*E[phraim] A. Speiser, "Progress on the Joint Expedition to Mesopotamia," *BASOR* #70 (1938) 3-10. [Khafâjeh, pp. 7-10]

*Arthur J. Tobler, "Progress of the Joint Expedition to Mesopotamia," *BASOR* #71 (1938) 18-23. *[Khafâjeh]*

Khalbi

*Albrecht Goetze, "The City of Khalbi and the Khapiru People," *BASOR* #79 (1940) 32-34.

Khana

H. G. Tomkins, "Khiana or Khâna," *SBAP* 19 (1897) 113-114.

A. H. Sayce, "A New Date from the Kingdom of Khana," *SBAP* 34 (1912) 52.

Khan-Sheikhoun

*Fritz Neugass, "Notes and Comments. Recent Excavations in Tello, Susa and Syria," *A&A* 32 (1931) 137-138. [Khan-Sheikhoun, p. 138]

El Khargeh

C. S. Myers, "El Khargeh: Four Photographs from the Oasis of El Khargeh with a Brief Description of the District," *Man* 1 (1901) #91.

G. Caton-Thompson, "Prehistoric Research Expedition to Kharga Oasis, Egypt," *Man* 31 (1931) #91.

G. Caton-Thompson, "The Royal Anthropological Institute's Prehistoric Research Expedition to Kharga Oasis, Egypt," *Man* 32 (1932) #158.

Khatâ'na-Qantîr

Labib Habachi, "Khatâ'na-Qantîr: Importance," *ASAE* 52 (1952-54) 443-562.

Khattusas (See: Boğazköy)

Khor Rori (Dhofar)

*Ray L. Cleveland, "The Sacred Stone Circle of Khor Rori (Dhofar)," *BASOR* #155 (1959) 29-31.

Khorsabad

*Gordon Loud, "An Architectural Formula for Assyrian Planning Based on the Results of Excavations at Khorsabad," *RAAO* 33 (1936) 153-160.

Kichyros

*Sotirios I. Dakaris, "The Dark Palace of Hades," *Arch* 15 (1962) 85-93. *[Ephyra (or Kichyros)] (Trans. by John L. Caskey)*

Killara

*Benjamin D. Meritt, "Towns of Asia Minor," *AJP* 58 (1937) 385-391. *[Killara]*

Kirkuk

Anonymous, "Excavations at Kirkuk," *UMB* 1 (1930) #2, 10-14.

Anonymous, "The Kirkuk Excavations," *UMB* 1 (1930) #3, 6-7.

Anonymous, "Important Finds at Kirkuk," *UMB* 1 (1930) #4, 10-14.

*Anonymous, "Developments at Kirkuk," *UMB* 2 (1930-31) 187, 189-190. *[Note of a tablet found at Kirkuk making mention of a place name "Ibla" in Syria!]*

Edward Chiera, "Excavations near Kirkuk," *CQ* 3 (1926) 217-222.

Kirsehir

*Aydin Sayili and Walter Ruben, "Preliminary Report on the Results of the Excavation, made under the Auspices of the Turkish Historical Society, in the Caca Bey Madrasa of Kirsehir, Turkey," *TTKB* 11 (1947) 682-691.

Kirrha

*(Miss) Sylvia Benton, "No Tin from Kirrha in Phokis," *Antiq* 38 (1964) 138.

Kish

Stephen Langdon, "The Field Museum-Oxford University Joint Expedition at Kish, 1926-7," *A&A* 24 (1927) 103-111.

Kish concluded

Stephen Langdon, "Excavating Kish: The Cradle of Civilization, 1927-1928," *A&A* 26 (1928) 155-168.

Henry Field, "The Field Museum-Oxford University Joint Expedition at Kish," *AJA* 34 (1930) 54.

S[tephen] Langdon, "Excavations at Kish, 1928-29," *JRAS* (1930) 601-610.

Henry Field, "The Field Museum-Oxford University Joint Expedition at Kish -I," *A&A* 31 (1931) 243-252.

Henry Field, "The Field Museum-Oxford University Joint Expedition at Kish: II," *A&A* 31 (1931) 323-334.

*S[tephen] Langdon, "Excavations at Kish and Barghuthiat 1933, I. Sassanian and Parthian Remains in Central Mesopotamia," *Iraq* 1 (1934) 113-123.

*Albrecht Goetze, "Early Kings of Kish," *JCS* 15 (1961) 105-111.

Seton Lloyd, "Back to Ingharra: Some Further Thoughts on the Excavations at East Kish," *Iraq* 31 (1969) 40-49.

Ḳizzuwadna (See also: Cilicia)

*Sidney Smith, "Ḳizzuwadna and Ḳode," *JEA* 8 (1922) 45-47.

*John Garstang, "Notes on Hittite Political Geography," *AAA* 10 (1923) 21-26, 172-178. [II. Kizzuwadna, pp. 172-177]

*Sidney Smith, "Ḳizzuwadna," *JEA* 10 (1924) 104-115.

A. H. Sayce, "The Site of Kizzuwadna," *AAA* 12 (1925) 173-174.

*L. A. Mayer and J. Garstang, "Kizzuwadna and other Hittite States," *JEA* 11 (1925) 23-35.

Knidos

Iris Cornelia Love, "Knidos-Excavations in 1967," *TAD* 16 (1967) #2, 133-159.

Knidos concluded

Iris C[ornelia] Love, "Knidos-Excavations in 1968," *TAD* 17 (1968) #2, 123-143.

Iris Cornelia Love, "Knidos Excavations, 1968,"*AJA* 73 (1969) 241.

Knossos

*A[rthur] J. Evans, "The Neolithic Settlement at Knossos and its Place in the History of Early Ægean Culture," *Man* 1 (1901) #146.

A[rthur] J. Evans, "Excavations at Knossos in Crete," *Man* 2 (1902) #53.

Anonymous, "Excavations at Knossos," *MR* 87 (1905) 304-306.

*William Ridgeway, "Minos the Destroyer rather than the Creator of the so-called 'Minoan' Culture of Cnossos," *PBA* 4 (1909-10) 97-129.

Joan [D.] Evans, "Sir Arthur Evans and Knossos," *Arch* 3 (1950) 134-139.

*J. Walter Graham, "Phaistos—*Second Fiddle to Knossos?*" *Arch* 10 (1957) 208-214.

*Emily Vermeule, "The Fall of Knossos and the Palace Style," *AJA* 67 (1963) 195-199.

J[oan] D. Evans, "Excavations in the Neolithic Mound of Knossos 1958-60," *ULBIA* 4 (1964) 34-60.

*Sinclair Hood, "'Last Palace' and 'Reoccupation' at Knossos," *KZFE* 4 (1965) 16-44.

*Mervyn R. Popham, "The Palace of Knossos: its destruction and reoccupation reconsidered," *KZFE* 5 (1966) 17-24.

Kokkinovrisi

Noel Robertson, "Excavation at Kokkinovrisi near Corinth, 1962-63," *AJA* 68 (1964) 200.

Kom El-Dikka

Jadwiga Kipinska and Henry Riad, "Trial Pits at Kom El-Dikka in Alexandria," *ASAE* 59 (1966) 99-108.

Kôm el-Ḥisn

A. Hamada and M. El-Amir, "Excavations at Kôm el-Ḥisn: season 1943," *ASAE* 46 (1947) 101-111.

A. Hamada and Sh. Farid, "Excavations at Kôm el-Ḥisn (season 1945)," *ASAE* 46 (1947) 195-205.

Guy Brunton, "The dating of the cemetery at Kôm el-Hisn," *ASAE* 46 (1947) 143-145.

A. Hamada and Sh. Farid, "Excavations at Kom*[sic]* el-Ḥisn, Third season 1946," *ASAE* 48 (1948) 299-308.

A. Hamada and Sh. Farid, "Excavations at Kôm el-Ḥisn fourth season 1947," *ASAE* 50 (1950) 367-379.

Kom el-Kharaz

A. Hamada and Sh. Farid, "A Graeco-Roman Cemetery at Kom el-Kharaz," *ASAE* 48 (1948) 327-332.

Kôm el-Wist

Labib Habachi, "Finds at Kôm el-Wist," *ASAE* 47 (1947) 285-291.

Kom Ombo

*Howard Carter, "Report of Work done in Upper Egypt," *ASAE* 4 (1903) 171-180. [II. Komo Ombo, pp. 172-175]

Komistratos

*Benjamin D. Meritt, "Towns of Asia Minor," *AJP* 58 (1937) 385-391. *[Komistratos]*

Koptos

W. St. Chad Boscawen, "The Beginnings of Egyptian Civilization. The Exploration of Prof. Petrie at Koptos," *BOR* 7 (1892-93) 234-239.

Kor

H. S. Smith, "Kor: Report on the Excavations of the Egypt Exploration Society at Kor, 1965," *Kush* 14 (1966) 187-243.

Korucutepe

Maurits Van Loon and Giorgio Buccellak, "The 1968 Excavation at Korucutepe Near Elâziğ," *TAD* 17 (1968) #1, 79-82.

Maurits Van Loon and Hans G. Güterbock, "The 1969 excavation at Korucutepe near Elâziğ," *TAD* 18 (1969) #2, 123-128.

Koszylowce

Ion Nestor, "Some Notes on Koszylowce," *AAA* 22 (1935) 185-188.

Kouklia

T. B. Mitford, "Excavations at Kouklia (Old Paphos), Cyprus, 1950," *AJ* 31 (1951) 51-66.

Kourion

Anonymous, "Kourion—The Late Bronze Age Settlement," *UMB* 7 (1937-39) #1, 15-18.

G[eorge] H. McF[ayden], "Excavations at Kourion," *UMB* 7 (1937-39) #2, 3-17.

J[ohn] F[ranklin] D[aniel], "Kourion: The Late Bronze Age Settlement," *UMB* 7 (1937-39) #3, 14-21.

John Franklin Daniel, "Excavations at Kourion: The Late Bronze Age Settlement—Provisional Report," *AJA* 42 (1938) 261-275.

Kourion concluded

John Franklin Daniel, "Kourion, Cyprus, in the Late Bronze Age," *AJA* 44 (1940) 105.

J[ohn] F[ranklin] D[aniel], "Kourion—Past Achievements and Future Plans," *UMB* 13 (1947-48) #3, 7-15.

Kourion-Bamboula

*S[aul] S. Weinberg, "Kourion-Bamboula: The Late Bronze Age Architecture," *AJA* 56 (1952) 178.

Ksâr 'Akil

J. Franklin Ewing, "Preliminary Note on the Excavations at the Palaeolithic Site of Ksâr 'Akil, Republic of Lebanon," *Antiq* 21 (1947) 186-196.

Robert J. Braidwood, H. E. Wright Jr., and J. Franklin Ewing, "Ksâr 'Akil: Its Archeological Sequence and Geological Setting," *JNES* 10 (1951) 113-122.

Ḳuë

*J. W. Jack, "Recent Biblical Archaeology," *ET* 53 (1941-42) 367-370. [Archæology and the Biblical Text: 4. The Land of Ḳuë, p. 369]

Kufä

'Ali Muhammad Mustafä, "Preliminary Report on the Excavations in Kufä during the Third Season," *Sumer* 19 (1963) 36-65. *[Trans. by Christel Kessler)*

Kültepe

Isabel Frances Dodd, "Kul Tepe," *RP* 8 (1909) 93-96.

Tahsin Özgüç, "Excavations at Kültepe 1954, finds on level Ib," *TTKB* 19 (1955) 64-72.

Kültepe concluded

Tahsin Özgüç, "Excavations at Kültepe, level II finds," *TTKB* 19 (1955) 453-461.

*Nimet Özgüç, "New Light on the Dating of the Karum of Kanish and of Acemhöyük near Akeseray," AJA 72 (1968) 318-320. *[Kültepe]*

Kumma

*Jean Vercoutter, "Semna South Fort and the Records of Nile Levels at Kumma," *Kush* 14 (1966) 125-164.

Kummukh

*L. W. King, "Kummukh and Commagene: A Study in North Syrian and Mesopotamian Geography," *JMUEOS* #2 (1912-13) 47-56.

Kurdistan

Anonymous, "Rich's Researches in Koordistan[sic]* and Nineveh," *DUM* 8 (1836) 17-26. *(Review)*

Robert J. Braidwood, "A Preliminary Note on Prehistoric Excavations in Iraqi Kurdistan 1950-1951," *Sumer* 7 (1951) 99-104.

Linda S. Braidwood, "*Early Food Producers:* Excavations in Iraqi Kurdistan," *Arch* 5 (1952) 157-164.

Kürigin Kaleh

H. H. von der Osten and T. George Allen, "The Ancient Settlement at Kürigin Kaleh in Asia Minor," *AJSL* 43 (1926-27) 288-296.

El-Kurruw

*George A. Reisner, "Note on the Harvard-Boston Excavations at El-Kurruw and Barkal in 1918-1919," *JEA* 6 (1920) 61-64.

Kusa

*A. H. Sayce, "Geographical Notes," *JRAS* (1921) 47-55. [Kas and Kusa, p. 54]

Kush (See also: Cush)

Dows Dunham, "Notes on the History of Kush 850 B.C.-A.D. 350," *AJA* 50 (1946) 378-388.

H. F. C. Smith, "The Transfer of the Capital of Kush from Napata to Meroë," *Kush* 3 (1955) 20-25.

Kussar

*A. H. Sayce, "The Original Home of the Hittites and the Site of Kussar," *JRAS* (1928) 257-264.

Kuššara (Kuşşara)

Julius Lewy, "Old Assyrian Evidence Concerning Kuššara and its Location," *HUCA* 33 (1962) 45-57.

Julius Lewy, "Old Assyrian Evidence concerning 'Kuşşara' and its Location," *AAI* 2 (1965) 305-315.

Kutha

*H. Rassam, "Recent Discoveries of Ancient Babylonian Cities," *SBAP* 5 (1882-83) 83-84. *[Kutha]*

Kuwait

P. V. Glob, "Investigations in Kuwait," *Kuml* (1958) 169-171.

L

Labranda

Gösta Saflund, "The Swedish Excavations at Labranda, 1953," *TAD* 6 (1956) #1, 45-46.

Lagash

Ira M. Price, "Some Light from Ur Touching Lagash," *JAOS* 50 (1930) 150-158.

*Ira Maurice Price, "H. De Genouillac on *'Lagash'* and *'Girsu'*," *JAOS* 57 (1937) 309-312.

T. Fish, "URÚ.ki," *JJS* 1 (1956) 206-215. *[Lagash]*

A. G. Kifishin, "The Western Quarters of Lagash," *VDI* (1968) #3, 84-85.

Tel el Lahm

*J. E. Taylor, "Notes on Abu Shahrein and Tel el Lahm," *JRAS* (1855) 404-415. [Tel el Lahm, pp. 412-413]

Faud Safar, "Soundings at Tell Al-Lahm," *Sumer* 5 (1949) 154-164.

Lahun

Guy Brunton, "The British School at Lahun," *AEE* 1 (1914) 49-51.

Lambaesis

George H. Allen, "The So-called Praetorium in the Roman Legionary Camp at Lambaesis," *AJA* 12 (1908) 71-72.

Lamponia

*Joseph Thacher Clarke, "Gargara, Lamponia and Pionia: Towns of Troad," *AJA, O.S.*, 4 (1888) 291-319.

Larissa

*G. B., "Date of the Capture of Larissa," *JSL, 3rd Ser.*, 7 (1858) 192-193.

Larsa

G. W. Gilmore, "Life in Larsa 4,000 Years Ago," *HR* 75 (1918) 314, 333, 400, 432. *(Review)*

Latamne

J. D[esmond] Clark, "The middle acheulian occupation site at Latamne," *AAAS* 16 (1966) #2, 31-74.

J. Desmond Clark and A. van Dusen Eggers, "Further excavations (1965) at the middle acheulian occupation site at Latamne, Northern Syria: General Results, Definitions and Interpretations," *AAAS* 16 (1966) #2, 75-113.

Latium

Jotham Johnson, "The Hill Forts of Latium," *AJA* 58 (1954) 146-147.

Lebanon

*Asad Rustum, "New Traces of the Old Lebanon Forest," *PEFQS* 54 (1922) 68-71.

Cameron Mackay, "The Land of the Lost Boundary," *CQR* 116 (1933) 1-23. *[Lebanon]*

*Cameron Mackay, "The Lebanon Watershed," *CQR* 166 (1965) 278-291.

Lorraine Copeland and Peter J. Wescombe, "Inventory of Stone-Age Sites in Lebanon," *MUSJ* 41 (1965) 29-175. [Part One: West-Central Lebanon]

Lorraine Copeland and Peter J. Wescombe, "Inventory of Stone-Age Sites in Lebanon. Part two: North, South and East-Central Lebanon," *MUSJ* 42 (1966) 1-174.

Roger Saidah, "Archaeology in the Lebanon, 1968-1969," *Bery* 18 (1969) 119-142.

Lebanon concluded

*‡Jinan Mudarres, "Syria and Lebanon in Antiquity: Bibliography for 1968," *Bery* 18 (1969) 143-158.

Lechaeum

Joseph W. Shaw, "A Foundation in the Inner Harbor at Lechaeum," *AJA* 73 (1969) 370-372.

Lefkandi

*L. H. Sackett, "The British School Excavations at Xeropolis (Lefkandi) in Euboea," *AJA* 70 (1966) 194-195.

L. Hugh Sackett, "Lefkandi in Euboea: The Results of Three Seasons' Excavations," *AJA* 72 (1968) 172.

Leptis Magna

Theresa Howard Carter, "Western Phoenicians at Lepcis[sic]* Magna," *AJA* 69 (1965) 123-132.

Eric Read, "Leptis Magna—Pushing Back the Sands of Time," *ContR* 209 (1966) 73-77.

Lerna

John L. Caskey, "A Preclassical Site at Lerna in the Argolid," *AJA* 57 (1953) 105.

John L. Caskey, "An Early Settlement at the Spring of Lerna," *Arch* 6 (1953) 99-102.

John L. Caskey, "Lerna 1953," *Arch* 7 (1954) 28-30.

John L. Caskey, "Excavations at Lerna, 1956," *AJA* 61 (1957) 182-183.

John L. Caskey, "Excavations at Lerna, 1957," *AJA* 62 (1958) 222.

*John L. Caskey, "Supplementary Excavations at Lerna and Eutresis," *AJA* 63 (1959) 187.

Lerna concluded

*John L. Caskey, "Lerna, The Cyclades, and Crete," *AJA* 64 (1960) 183.

J. L. Caskey, "Lerna in the Early Bronze Age," *AJA* 72 (1968) 313-316.

Lesbos

*Jerome D. Quinn, "Cape Phokas, Lesbos—Site of an Archaic Sanctuary for Zeus, Hera and Dionysus?" *AJA* 65 (1961) 391-393.

Levant

*W[illem] J. van Liere and H[enri] de Contenson, "Holocene Environment and Early Settlement in the Levant," *AAAS* 14 (1964) 125-128.

Libya

*D. Newbold, "Rock-pictures and Archaeology in the Libyan Desert," *Antiq* 2 (1928) 261-291.

Anthony de Cosson, "Notes on the Baḥrēn, Nuwēmisah, and El-Aʿreg Oases in the Libyan Desert," *JEA* 23 (1937) 226-229.

Carl H. Kraeling, "Now and Then in Libya," *JAOS* 80 (1960) 104-111.

Byron Khun de Prorok, "Recent Explorations and Discoveries in the Libyan Desert 1926-27-28. I. Where Alexander the Great was Proclaimed God," *A&A* 26 (1928) 177-184.

Byron Khun de Prorok, "Recent Explorations and Discoveries in the Libyan Desert 1926-27-28. II: Mysteries of the North African Sands and Lakes," *A&A* 26 (1928) 237-245.

Lilybaeum

*G. Aldo Ruggieri, "Motya and Lilybaeum," *Arch* 10 (1957) 131-136.

Lishanum

*William F. Edgerton, "Lishanum, Patesi of Marad," *AJSL* 38 (1921-22) 141.

Lisht

Anonymous, "Egyptian Work of the Metropolitan Museum," *RP* 6 (1907) 340. *[Excavations at Lisht]*

Locri

*Anonymous, "Plan to Excavate Locri and Crotona," *RP* 6 (1907) 270-271.

Alfonso de Franciscis, "Ancient Locri," *Arch* 11 (1958) 206-212.

Locris

W. A. Oldfather, "Studies in the History and Topography of Locris. I," *AJA* 20 (1916) 32-61.

W. A. Oldfather, "Studies in the History and Topography of Locris. II," *AJA* 20 (1916) 154-172.

Lucania

Paola Zancani Montuoro and Umberto Zanotti-Bianco, "Excavations at the Heraeum of Lucania," *AJA* 42 (1938) 441-444.

*A. W. Van Buren, "Campania and Lucania in 1953," *Arch* 7 (1954) 104-111.

Lūristān

Henrik Thrane, "Archaeological Investigations in Western Luristan. Preliminary Report of the Second Danish Archaeological Expedition to Iran," *AA* 35 (1964) 153-169.

*Clare Goff Meade, "Lūristān in the first half of the First Millennium B.C. A preliminary report on the first season's excavations at Bārā Jān, and associated surveys in the Eastern Pīsh-i-Kūn," *Iran* 6 (1968) 105-134.

Luxor

S. Yeivin, "The Mond Excavations at Luxor: Report on the Operations," *AAA* 13 (1926) 3-16.

Lycia

J. Imbert, "Some Results of Prof. Benndorf's Last Visit to Lycia," *BOR* 7 (1893-94) 161-163.

Donat Sampson, "Austrian Explorations in Lycia," *ACQR* 27 (1902) 277-294.

*J. C. Keene, "The Lycian Cities of the Xanthus River Valley," *A&A* 35 (1934) 99-108.

M

Ma'adi

Anonymous, "Egyptian University. Faculty of Arts. The Excavations of the Egyptian University at Ma'adi," *AEE* 17 (1932) 108-109.

Mustapha Amer, "The Excavations of the Egyptian University in the Prehistoric Site at Maadi, near Cairo," *JRAI* 66 (1936) 65-69.

Guy Brunton, "A first dynasty cemetery at Maadi," *ASAE* 39 (1939) 419-424.

Macedonia

A. J. B. Wace and M. S. Thompson, "Prehistoric Mounds in Macedonia," *AAA* 2 (1909) 159-164.

Stanley Casson, "Excavations in Macedonia," *AJ* 6 (1926) 59-72.

W. A. Heurtley, "Prehistoric Macedonia," *Anitq* 3 (129) 318-323.

W. A. Heurtley, "Prehistoric Macedonia. What has been done and what remains to be done," *Man* 31 (1931) #211.

Macedonia concluded

*George E. Mylonas, "The Site of Akropotamos and the Neolithic Period of Macedonia," *AJA* 45 (1941) 557-576.

*Homer L. Thomas, "Troy, Macedonia and the North," *AJA* 63 (1959) 191.

Magan

*W[illiam] F[oxwell] Albright, "Magan, Meluḫa, and the Synchronism between Menes and Narâm-Šin," *JEA* 7 (1921) 80-86.

*W[illiam] F[oxwell] Albright, "New Light on Magan and Meluḫa," *JAOS* 42 (1922) 317-322.

G. A. Wainwright, "Early Magan," *Anitq* 37 (1963) 307-308.

*M. E. L. Mallowan, "The Mechanics of Ancient Trade in Western Asia. Reflections on the location of Magan and Meluḫḫa," *Iran* 3 (1965) 1-7.

*Edmond Sollberger, "The Problem of Magan and Meluhha," *ULBIA* 8&9 (1968-69) 247-249. (Discussion, p. 250)

Makan

*Daniel Hy Haigh, "Makan and Miluχ," *ZÄS* 12 (1874) 53-55.

Makhmur Plain

Mahamud El Amin and M. E. L. Mallowan, "Soundings in the Makhmur Plain," *Sumer* 5 (1949) 145-153; 6 (1950) 55-68.

Malatya District

Salvatore M. Puglisi and Alba Palmieri, "Researches in the Malatya District 1965-1966," *TAD* 15 (1966) #2, 81-100.

Mallorca

Daniel E. Woods, "Excavations in Mallorca," *AJA* 63 (1959) 192.

Malta

John Worthington, "Excavations in Malta," *AJA, O.S.*,1 (1885) 404.

Thomas Ashby, Themistocles Zammit, and Giuseppe Despott, "Excavations in Malta in 1914," *Man* 16 (1916) #1, #14.

G. Despott, "Excavations Conducted at Ghar Dalam (Malta) in the Summer of 1917," *JRAI* 48 (1918) 214-221.

*L. H. Dudley Buxton, "Personal and Place Names in Malta," *Man* 21 (1921) #91.

T[hemistocles] Zammit, "The Archaeology of the Maltese Islands," *A&A* 15 (1923) 79-84.

G. Despott, "Excavations at Ghar Dalam (Dalam Cave), Malta," *JRAI* 53 (1923) 18-35.

*Arthur Keith, "Neanderthal Man in Malta. *with an account of the survey of Dalam Cave (Ghar Dalam)* by Mr. George Sinclair," *JRAI* 54 (1924) 251-275. ["Ghar Dalam and the Eurafrican Land Bridge," by George Sinclair with some additions by Arthur Keith, pp. 261-275]

T[hemistocles] Zammit, "The Prehistoric Remains of the Maltese Islands," *Antiq* 4 (1930) 55-79.

D. Randall-MacIver, "Prehistoric Antiquities of Malta," *Anitq* 9 (1935) 204-208.

H. Braun, "Antiquities of Malta," *Man* 46 (1946) #89.

L. Bernabò Brea, "Malta and the Mediterranean," *Antiq* 34 (1960) 132-137.

John D. Evans, "Malta and the Mediterranean," *Antiq* 34 (1960) 218-220.

Mandali

*Joan Oates, "First Preliminary Report on a Survey in the Region of Mandali and Badra," *Sumer* 22 (1966) 51-60.

Joan Oates, "Prehistoric Investigations Near Mandali, Iraq," *Iraq* 30 (1968) 1-20.

MAR-Moeris

*F. Cope Whitehouse, "MAR-Moeris, West of Oxyrhyncus—Behnesa," *SBAP* 7 (1884-85) 112-120.

Marathon

J. W. Blakesley, "Attempt at an explanation of some Difficulties in the currently received account of the Battle of Marathon," *TPS* (1854) 1-10.

*Harris Gary Hudson, "The Shield Signal at Marathon," *AmHR* 42 (1936-37) 443-459.

Stuart E. P. Atherley, "The Battle of Marathon: An Essay in Historical Detection," *HT* 2 (1952) 443-450.

*Elizabeth MacNeil Boggess, "Ancient Horsemanship and Marathon," *AJA* 70 (1966) 183.

*Eugene Vanderpool, "The Deme of Marthon and the Herakleion," *AJA* 70 (1966) 319-323.

Mards

J. Halévy, "The Nation of the Mards," *BOR* 4 (1889-90) 73-79.

Mari

W[illiam] F[oxwell] Albright, "Mâri on the Upper Euphrates or in Eastern Babylonia?" *AJSL* 41 (1924-25) 282-283.

*W[illiam] F[oxwell] Albright and R. P. Dougherty, "From Jerusalem to Bagdad down the Euphrates II. From Aleppo to Baghdad," *BASOR* #21 (1926) 11-21. [The Search for Ancient Mari, pp. 15-18]

I. J. Gelb, "Mari," *AJSL* 52 (1934-35) 43-44.

Hugh Pope, "Mari: A Long-Lost City," *DR* 204 (1939) 322-337.

*Frederic G. Kenyon, "Ras Shamra and Mari: Recent Archaeological Discoveries Affecting the Bible," *JTVI* 73 (1941) 81-92, 96. [(Discussion, p. 92) (Communications by H. S. Curr, pp. 92-94; P. J. Wiseman, pp. 94-95; Norman S. Denham, pp. 95-96)]

Mari concluded

*George E. Mendenhall, “Mari,” *BA* 11 (1948) 1-19. [The Palace; The Royal Archives; The History of Mari; Mari and the Patriarchs] *[Tell el-Ḥarîrī]*

Barbara E. Morgan, “The Destruction of Mari by Hammurabi,” *MCS* 1 (1951) 35-36.

A. Leo Oppenheim, “The Archives of the Palace of Mari,” *JNES* 11 (1952) 129-139.

*J. N. Schofield, “Some Archaeological Sites and the Old Testament. Mari and the Old Testament,” *ET* 66 (1954-55) 250-252.

*Lester J. Kuyper, “Israel and Her Neighbors,” *RefR* 10 (1956-57) #3, 11-20. [Mari, pp. 16-17]

*E[phraim] A. Speiser, “Census and Ritual Expiation in Mari and Israel,” *BASOR* #149 (1958) 17-25.

*C. L. Gibson, “Life and Society at Mari and in Old Israel,” *GUOST* 18 (1959-60) 15-29.

*A[braham] Malamat, “Mari and the Bible: Some Patterns of Tribal Organization and Institutions,” *JAOS* 82 (1962) 143-150.

Marlik Tepe

*E. O. Negahban, “A Brief Report on the Excavation of Marlik Tepe and Pileh Qal 'eh,” *Iran* 2 (1964) 13-19.

Marmarica

Oric Bates, “Semitic Traces in Marmarica,” *SBAP* 37 (1915) 201-207.

Marseilles

Fernand Benoit, “The New Excavations at Marseilles,” *AJA* 53 (1949) 237-240.

Masawwarat es-Sufra

*P. D. Scott-Moncrieff, "The Ruined Sites at Masawwarat es-Sufra and Naga," *SBAP* 30 (1908) 192-203.

Massalia

*Yu. B. Tsifkin, "The Tin Route and the Northern Trade of Massalia," *VDI* (1968) #3, 104.

Mattarah

*F. Basmachi, "Supplementary Report on the Excavations at Tell Mattarah and Qal'at Jarmo," *Sumer* 4 (1948) 134-136.

Robert J. Braidwood, Linda Braidwood, James G. Smith, and Charles Leslie, "Matarrah: A Southern Variant of the Hassunan Assemblage, Excavated in 1948," *JNES* 11 (1952) 1-75.

Tell el-Mazâr

*Warren J. Moulton, "A Visit to Qarn Sartabeh," *BASOR* #62 (1936) 14-18. *[Tell el-Mazâr]*

Mecyberna

George E. Mylonas, "Excavations at Mecyberna, the Port Town of Olynthos," *AJA* 43 (1939) 304-305.

George E. Mylonas, "Excavations at Mecyberna, 1934, 1938," *AJA* 47 (1943) 78-87.

Media

*P. M. Sykes, "The Ancient History of Persia (Elam, Media, and the Rise of the Achæmenian Dynasty)," *IAQR* 7 (1915) 125-147.

Mediterranean Sea

†Anonymous, "The Mediterranean Sea," *ERCJ* 106 (1857) 356-382. *(Review)*

*Edward Hull, "On the Physical Conditions of the Mediterranean Basin, which have Given Rise to a Community of Some Species of Fresh-Water Fishes in the Nile and the Jordan Basins," *JTVI* 31 (1897-98) 111-120. (Discussion, p. 121)

Meluẖa

*W[illiam] F[oxwell] Albright, "Magan, Meluẖa, and the Synchronism between Menes and Narâm-Šin," *JEA* 7 (1921) 80-86.

*W[illiam] F[oxwell] Albright, "New Light on Magan and Meluẖa," *JAOS* 42 (1922) 317-322.

*M. E. L. Mallowan, "The Mechanics of Ancient Trade in Western Asia. Reflections on the location of Magan and Meluẖẖa," *Iran* 3 (1965) 1-7.

*Edmond Sollberger, "The Problem of Magan and Meluhha," *ULBIA* 8&9 (1968-69) 247-249. (Discussion, p. 250)

Memphis

*G[eorge] Rawlinson, "Biblical Topography. VIII.—Further Egyptian Sites—Memphis, Thebes, Migdol, Syene," *MI* 4 (1886) 453-463.

A. Wiedemann, "The Age of Memphis," *SBAP* 9 (1886-87) 184-190.

Anonymous, "Egyptian Research Account. Proposed Excavation at Memphis," *RP* 6 (1907) 268-269.

Joseph Offord, "Professor Petrie's Excavations at Memphis," *AAOJ* 31 (1909) 213-215.

W. M. Flinders Petrie, "Memphis and Its Foreigners," *RP* 8 (1909) 131-136.

Thomas Nicol, "The Recovery of Memphis," *LQHR* 116 (1911) 95-108. *(Review)*

W. M. Flinders Petrie, "The Excavation of Memphis," *RP* 10 (1911) 3-14.

Memphis concluded

Anonymous, "Work at Memphis," *RP* 11 (1912) 239.

Anonymous, "The Eckley B. Coxe, Jr. Expedition," *JEA* 3 (1915) 45-47. *[Memphis]*

Mustapha el Amir, "The *ΣΗΚΟΣ* of Apis at Memphis. A Season of Excavations at Mīt Rahīnah in 1941," *JEA* 34 (1948) 51-56.

Rudolf Anthes, "A First Season of Excavating in Memphis," *UMB* 20 (1956-57) #1, 3-25.

Rudolf Anthes, "The Mit Rahineh (Memphis) Excavation 1956," *AJA* 61 (1957) 181.

*Rudolf Anthes, "Memphis (Mit Rahineh) in 1956," *UMB* 21 (1957) #2, 3-34.

Mende

*Benjamin D. Meritt, "Scione, Mende, and Torone," *AJA* 27 (1923) 447-460.

Mendes (See also: Tell el Rubʿa)

Bernard V. Bothmer, "Excavation at Mendes, 1964," *AJA* 69 (1965) 165.

Donald P. Hansen, "Mendes 1964," *JARCE* 4 (1965) 31-37.

Donald P. Hansen, "Excavations at Mendes in Egypt, 1965," *AJA* 70 (1966) 191.

Anonymous, "Biblical Research and Discovery. Findings of Radical Criticism Again Reversed," *CFL, O.S.*, 2 (1898) 72. *[Mendes]*

Meribath-Kadesh

Stanley A. Cook, "Notes on Old Testament History, V, Meribath-Kadesh," *JQR* 18 (1905-06) 739-760.

Merimda

E. J. Baumgartel, "What Do We Know About the Excavations at Merimda?" *JAOS* 85 (1965) 502-511.

Meroë

A. H. Sayce, "Meroë," *AAA* 3 (1910) 53-56.

J[ohn] Garstang, "Preliminary Note on an Expedition to Meroë in Ethiopia," *AAA* 3 (1910) 57-70.

John Garstang, "Second Interim Report on the Excavation at Meroë in Ethiopia. Part I. Excavations," *AAA* 4 (1911-12) 45-52.

A. H. Sayce, "Second Interim Report on the Excavations at Meroë in Ethiopia. Part II. The Historical Results," *AAA* 4 (1911-12) 53-65.

*R. C. Bosanquet, "Second Interim Report on the Excavations at Meroë in Ethiopia. Part III. On the Bronze Portrait-head," *AAA* 4 (1911-12) 66-71.

John Garstang, "Third Interim Report on the Excavations at Meroë," *AAA* 5 (1912-13) 73-82.

John Garstang, "Fourth Interim Report on the Excavations at Meroë. 1. Historical," *AAA* 6 (1913-14) 1-8.

W. S. George, "Fourth Interim Report on the Excavations at Meroë. 2. Architectural and General Results," *AAA* 6 (1913-14) 9-21.

John Garstang, "Fifth Interim Report on the Excavations at Meroë. 1. General Results," *AAA* 7 (1914-16) 1-10.

W. J. Phythian-Adams, "Fifth Interim Report on the Excavations at Meroë. 2. Detailed Examination," *AAA* 7 (1914-16) 11-22.

*Dows Dunham, "Romano-Coptic Egypt and the Culture of Meroë," *AJA* 46 (1942) 122.

G. A. Wainwright, "The Date of the Rise of Meroë," *JEA* 38 (1952) 75-77.

Basil Davidson, "The Mystery of Meroe," *HT* 8 (1958) 386-393.

Mersin (See also: Cilicia and Kizzuwadna)

*John Garstang, in collaboration with Seton Lloyd, G. M FitzGerald, Alison Dun, and Dorothy Marshall, "Excavations in Cilicia. The Neilson Expedition: Third Interim Report. Excavations at Mersin: 1937-38," *AAA* 25 (1938) 71-110. (Note by Miles Burkitt, pp. 106-110) *[A Note on a Stone Age Industry of Pre-Tell Halaf Age]*

*J[ohn] Garstang, "Explorations in Cilicia. The Neilson Expedition: Fourth Interim Report. Parts I and II *(concluded)*. Excavations at Mersin: 1938-39," *AAA* 26 (1939-40) 38-50.

*Miles Burkitt, "Explorations in Cilicia. Neilson Expedition: 1938-9. The Earlier Cultures at Mersin," *AAA* 26 (1939-40) 51-72.

*John Garstang, with contributions by Seton H. F. Lloyd, Richard Barnett, and G. M. FitzGerald, "Explorations in Cilicia. The Neilson Expedition: Fifth Interim Report. Parts III and IV. Explorations at Mersin: 1938-1939," *AAA* 26 (1939-40) 89-158.

John Garstang, "Archaeological Notes. The Discoveries at Mersin and Their Significance," *AJA* 47 (1943) 1-14.

*J. Kaplan, "A Suggested Correlation Between Stratum IX, Jericho, and Stratum XXIV, Mersin," *JNES* 28 (1969) 197-199.

Mesha

*Samuel Krauss, "Service Tree in Bible and Talmud in Modern Palestine," *HUCA* 1 (1924) 179-217. *[Mesha]*

Mešek

Morris Jastrow Jr., "Mešek and Tabal[sic]*," *AJSL* 13 (1896-97) 217.

Mesopotamia

*Justin Perkins, "Miscellanies IV. Late Discoveries in Persia and Mesopotamia," *JAOS* 3 (1853) 490-491.

William Willcocks, "Mesopotamia: Past, present and future," *SIR* (1909) 401-416.

Mesopotamia cont.

Anonymous, "Excavations in Mesopotamia," *MR* 92 (1910) 804-807.

Anonymous, "The Future of Mesopotamia," *MR* 102 (1919) 128-133.

Anonymous, "Archaeological Notes and Comments. Archaeologists Take Up Work in Tigris and Euphrates Valleys," *A&A* 14 (1922) 164.

R. A. MacLean, "Some Ancient Sites in Mesopotamia," *AJA* 24 (1920) 80-81.

L. H. Dudley Buxton, "Recent Excavations in Mesopotamia," *Man* 23 (1923) #54.

Edward Chiera, "Recent Excavations in Mesopotamia," *CQ* 2 (1925) 462-467.

*L. A. Waddell, "Dynasty of Haryashwa or the Sumerian Uruash ('Ur-Nina') as Imperial Kings of Kish, Erek and Lagash in Mesopotamia About 3100-2900 B.C.," *IAQR* 21 (1925) 676-682.

W[illiam] F[oxwell] Albright, "Notes on the Topography of Ancient Mesopotamia," *JAOS* 46 (1926) 220-230.

L. H. Dudley Buxton, "Excavations in Mesopotamia," *Man* 26 (1926) #29.

S[tephen] Langdon, "Recent Excavations in Mesopotamia, 1918-1926," *ET* 38 (1926-27) 70-77.

*George A. Barton, "The Origins of Civilization in Africa and Mesopotamia, their Relative Antiquity and Interplay," *PAPS* 68 (1929) 303-312.

*E[phraim] A. Speiser, "On Some Important Synchronisms in Prehistoric Mesopotamia," *AJA* 36 (1932) 465-471.

*E[phraim] A. S[peiser], "First Steps in Mesopotamian Archaeology," *BASOR* #52 (1933) 15-18.

Anonymous, "Mesopotamian Excavations," *UMB* 5 (1934-35) #1, 27.

*M. E. L. Mallowan, "A Mesopotamian Trilogy," *Antiq* 13 (1939) 159-170. *(Review)*

Mesopotamia concluded

*T. Fish, "The Place of the Small State in the Political and Cultural History of Ancient Mesopotamia," *BJRL* 18 (1944) 83-98.

*E. Douglas Van Buren, "Excavations in Mesopotamia," *Or, N.S.,* 15 (1946) 497-503. [1. Tell Hassuna; 2. Tell Uqair; 3. ʿAqar Quf]

V. Gordon Childe, "Mesopotamian Archaeology: a review," *Antiq* 22 (1948) 198-200. *(Review)*

*M. E. L. Mallowan, "Mesopotamia and Syria. Unity and Diversity of the Earliest Civilizations," *Sumer* 5 (1949) 1-7.

*Roger T. O'Callaghan, "Notes on Mesopotamian History," *CBQ* 12 (1950) 132-135.

C. J. Gadd, "Geographical History of the Mesopotamian Plains," *RAAO* 48 (1954) 28-29.

A. M. Beek and P. Buringh, "Statement Concerning Archaeology and Soil Survey in Mesopotamia," *Sumer* 11 (1955) 143-144.

*Hans Helbaek, "Ecological Effects of Irrigation in Ancient Mesopotamia," *Iraq* 22 (1960) 186-196.

J. J. Finkelstein, "Mesopotamia," *JNES* 21 (1962) 73-92.

Robert H. Punke, "The Fertile Crescent—Mesopotamia," *BibT* #4 (1963) 208-217.

*Stanley D. Walters, "The Development of Civilization in Ancient Mesopotamia," *JASA* 17 (1965) 68-73.

George Giacumakis Jr., "Letters to the Editor. Civilization in Ancient Mesopotamia," *JASA* 18 (1966) 31.

Edwin Yamauchi, "Letters to the Editor. Civilization in Ancient Mesopotamia," *JASA* 18 (1966) 31-32.

Messenia

William A. McDonald, "Exploration and Excavation in Messenia: 1958-59," *AJA* 64 (1960) 188.

Messenia concluded

William A. McDonald, "Surface Exploration in Messenia: 1962," *AJA* 67 (1963) 214-215.

R. Hope Simpson, "University of Minnesota Messenian Expedition, 1963," *AJA* 68 (1964) 196.

R. Hope Simpson, "University of Minnesota: Exploration in Messenia 1964-1966," *AJA* 71 (1967) 194.

Metapa

W. A. Oldfather, "The Location of Metapa," *AJA* 33 (1929) 405-406.

Meydûm

F. L. Griffith, "Notice of Mêdûm by W. M. Flinders Petrie," *SBAP* 14 (1891-92) 484-487. *(Review)*

Anonymous, "Notes and Comments. University of Pennsylvania Museum to Excavate at Medum, Egypt," *A&A* 28 (1929) 95.

Anonymous, "Notes and Comments. The University of Pennsylvania Museum's Excavations at Meydum," *A&A* 29 (1930) 140-141.

Anonymous, "Report from Mr. Rowe at Meydum," *UMB* 1 (1930) #4, 7-10.

Anonymous, "Excavations at Meydûm," *UMB* 2 (1930-31) 190-194.

Alan Rowe, "Excavations of the Eckley B. Coxe, Jr., Expedition at Meydûm, Egypt, 1929-30," *MJ* 22 (1931) 5-84.

Midian

*Anonymous, "The Land of Midian and its Mines," *PEFQS* 10 (1878) 141-145.

Migdol

*G[eorge] Rawlinson, "Biblical Topography. VIII.—Further Egyptian Sites—Memphis, Thebes, Migdol, Syene," *MI* 4 (1886) 453-463.

Miletus

Anonymous, "German Excavations Near Miletus," *RP* 8 (1909) 214.

*Howard Crosby Butler, "Miletus, Priene and Sardis," *A&A* 9 (1920) 171-186.

Miluχ

*Daniel Hy Haigh, "Makan and Miluχ," *ZÄS* 12 (1874) 53-55.

El Mina

*Leonard Woolley, "North Syria as a Cultural Link in the Ancient World. *The Huxley Memorial Lecture for* 1942," *JRAI* 72 (1942) 9-18. [El Mina (1180-320 B.C.), p. 17]

Minos

R. C. Bosanquet, "The Realm of Minos," *ERCJ* 236 (1922) 49-70.

Sidney Smith, "Middle Minoan I-II and Babylonian Chronology," *AJA* 49 (1945) 1-24.

*Charles Seltman, "Life in Ancient Crete—I: Minos," *HT* 2 (1952) 231-242.

*Chester G. Starr, "The Myth of the Minoan Thalassocracy," *HJAH* 3 (1954-55) 282-291.

*John L. Caskey, "Crises in the Minoan-Mycenaean World," *PAPS* 113 (1969) 433-449.

Minturnae

Anonymous, "Progress at Minturno," *UMB* 3 (1931-32) 176-178.

Anonymous, "Excavations at Minturno," *UMB* 3 (1931-32) 18-20, 22.

Anonymous, "The Minturno Expedition," *UMB* 3 (1931-32) 56, 58-59, 91-94.

Minturnae concluded

Jotham Johnson, "The Excavation of Minturnae," *A&A* 33 (1932) 283-293.

Anonymous, "The Expedition to Minturnæ," *UMB* 4 (1932-33) 115, 135-139.

*Jotham Johnson, "City Planning at Minturnae," *AJA* 37 (1933) 110.

J[ohn Story] J[enks], "The Road from Rome," *UMB* 6 (1935-37) #2, 57-65. *[Minturnæ]*

Minya

J. Penrose Harland, "Life in a Minyan Village," *Arch* 1 (1948) 94-103.

Mirgissa

Noel F. Wheeler, "Diary of the Excavation of Mirgissa Fort 14 November 1931 to 3 February 1932 *By the Harvard University—Museum of Fine Arts Expedition,*" *Kush* 9 (1961) 87-179. (Forward by Dows Dunham, p. 87)

Jean Vercoutter, "Excavations at Mirgissa—I (October- December 1962)," *Kush* 12 (1964) 57-62.

Jean Vercoutter, "Excavations at Mirgissa—II (Oct. 1963-March 1964)," *Kush* 13 (1965) 62-73.

Jean Vercoutter, "Excavations at Mirgissa—III," *Kush* 15 (1967-68) 269-279.

Misthia

A. S. Hall, "The Site of Misthia," *AS* 9 (1959) 119-124.

Mitanni

*Samuel A. B. Mercer, "The Hittites, Mitanni and Babylonia in the Tell el-Amarna Letters," *JSOR* 8 (1924) 13-28.

*Ch. Virolleaud, "The Syrian Town of Katna and the Kingdom of Mitanni," *Antiq* 3 (1929) 312-317.

Mizraim

*John Taylor, "Mizraim or Muzri?" *ET* 7 (1895-96) 405-409.

*Joseph Offord, "Archaeological Notes on Jewish Antiquities. LI. *Cyprus and Mizraim,*" *PEFQS* 50 (1918) 138-139.

Lake Moeris

*†F. Cope Whitehouse, "Lake Moeris and recent explorations in the Desert near the Fayoum," *SBAP* 4 (1881-82) 124-135.

†F. Cope Whitehouse, "Researches in the Moeris Basin," *SBAP* 5 (1882-83) 169-176.

F. C[ope] Whitehouse, "On the Hieroglyphic Evidence that Lake Mœris extended to the west of Behnesa," *JAOS* 11 (1885) ccvi-ccvii.

*Alan H. Gardiner and H. I. Bell, "The Name of Lake Moeris," *JEA* 29 (1943) 37-50.

Charles F. Nims, "Additional Demotic Evidence on the *ḥōnĕ* of Mi-wēr," *JEA* 33 (1947) 92. *[Lake Moeris]*

Mohenjo-Daro

[W. M.] Flinders Petrie, "Mohenjo-Daro," *AEE* 17 (1932) 33-40.

Morgantina

*T. V. Buttrey Jr., "The Morgantina Excavations Excavations and Date of the Roman Denarius," *AJA* 66 (1962) 195.

Motya

Anonymous, "Phœnician Settlement on Motya," *RP* 8 (1909) 124.

*G. Aldo Ruggieri, "Motya and Lilybaeum," *Arch* 10 (1957) 131-136.

B. S. J. Isserlin, E. Macnamara, J. N. Coldstream, G. Pike, J[oan] du Plat Taylor, and A. M. Snodgrass, "Motya, a Phoenician-Punic Site near Marsala, Sicily. Preliminary report of the Leeds-London-Fairleigh Dickinson Excavation, 1961-1963," *ALUOS* 4 (1962-63) 84-131.

Motya concluded

Joan du Plat Taylor, "Motya: A Phoenician Trading Settlement in Sicily," *Arch* 17 (1964) 91-100.

B. S. J. Isserlin, "Schiemann at Motya," *Antiq* 42 (1968) 144-148.

Mozia

Anonymous, "Phœnician Town on the Island of San Panteleo," *RP* 6 (1907) 119. *[Mozia]*

Tell Al-Mubaddad

Walid Yasin, "A Note on Three Samarra-Halaf Sites in the Tikril Area," *Sumer* 24 (1968) 117-119. [3. Tell Al-Mubaddad, p. 118]

Mugharat el-Bezez

Dorothy A. E. Garrod, "Mugharat el-Bezez, Adlun: Interim Report, July 1965," *BMB* 19 (1966) 5-9.

Mugharet el-Kebarah

F. Turville-Petrie, "Excavations in the Mugharet el-Kebarah," *JRAI* 62 (1932) 271-276.

Muqeyer

J. E. Taylor, "Notes on the Ruins of Muqeyer," *JRAS* (1855) 260-276.

*J. E. Taylor, "Notes on Abu Shahrein and Tel el Lahm," *JRAS* (1855) 404-415 [Muqeyer, pp. 414-415]

(Tell) Mureybiṭ

Maurits van Loon, "First results of the 1965 excavations at Tell Mureybat*[sic]* near Meskene," *AAAS* 16 (1966) 211-217.

(Tell) Mureybiṭ concluded

*Maurits van Loon, "The Oriental Institute Excavations at Mureybiṭ, Syria: Preliminary Report on the 1965 Campaign, Part I: Architecture and General Finds," *JNES* 27 (1968) 265-281.

*James H. Skinner, "The Oriental Institute Excavations at Mureybiṭ, Syria: Preliminary Report on the 1965 Campaign, Part II: Chipped Stone Finds," *JNES* 27 (1968) 282-290.

Muṣaṣ(ṣ)ir

Albrecht Gœtze, "Muṣaṣ(ṣ)ir," *RAAO* 46 (1952) 158-159.

Musawwarat es Sufra

Fritz Hintze, "Preliminary Report on the Excavations at Musawwarat es Sufra, 1960-1 by the Institute of Egyptology, Humboldt University, Berlin," *Kush* 10 (1962) 170-202.

F[ritz] Hintze, "Musawwarat es Sufra: Preliminary Report on the Excavations of the Institute of Egyptology, Humboldt University, Berlin, 1961-62 (Third Season)," *Kush* 11 (1963) 217-226. *(Trans. by H. P. T. Hyde)*

Fritz Hintze, "Musawwarat es Sufra: Report of the Excavations on the Institute of Egyptology, Humboldt University, Berlin, 1963-1966," *Kush* 15 (1967-68) 283-298.

El-Mutabbaq

*Julian Reade, "El-Mutabbaq and Umm Rus," *Sumer* 20 (1964) 83-89.

Muzri

*John Taylor, "Mizraim or Muzri?" *ET* 7 (1895-96) 405-409.

Mycenae

*J. P. Mahaffy, "On the Date of the Capture of Mycenæ by the Argives," *Herm* 3 (1877-79) 60-66.

Mycenae cont.

*Bayard Taylor, "Discovered Treasures of Ephesus, Cyprus, and Mycenæ," *DTQ* 4 (1878) 213-226.

†Anonymous, "Dr. Schliemann's Exploration of Mycenæ," *ERCJ* 147 (1878) 220-256. *(Review)*

*Anonymous, "Homer Illustrated by Recent Discovery," *CQR* 7 (1878-79) 392-421. *[Mycenæ]*

Anonymous, "The Mycenæan Age," *CQR* 53 (1901-02) 331-351.

Rufus Byam Richardson, "A Quarter Century of Mycenology," *AJA* 8 (1904) 84-86.

M. Thompson, "The Distribution of Mycenean Remains and the Homeric Catalogue," *AAA* 4 (1911-12) 128-139.

J. P. Droop, "Mycenae, 1921-1923: Legitimate and Illegitimate Criticism," *AAA* 13 (1926) 43-48.

A[lan] J. B. Wace, "Mycenae," *Antiq* 10 (1936) 405-416.

A[lan] J. B. Wace, "Excavations at Mycenae, 1952," *AJA* 57 (1953) 111.

Alan J. B. Wace, "New Light on Homer—*Excavations at Mycenae, 1952*," *Arch* 6 (1953) 75-81.

Alan J. B. Wace, "Excavations at Mycenae 1952," *PAPS* 97 (1953) 248-253.

Alan J. B. Wace, "New Discoveries at Mycenae 1953," *AJA* 58 (1954) 150.

Alan J. B. Wace, "New Discoveries at Mycenae 1954," *AJA* 59 (1955) 174-175.

*L. R. Palmer, "Homer and Mycenae: I Heroic Greek Society," *HT* 7 (1957) 367-372.

*L. R. Palmer, "Homer and Mycenae: II The Last Days of Pylos," *HT* 7 (1957) 436-442.

George E. Mylonas, "Excavations at Mycenae, 1958," *AJA* 63 (1959) 190.

M. S. F. Hood, "Schliemann's Mycenae Albums," *Arch* 13 (1960) 61-65.

Mycenae concluded

Emily Townsend Vermeule, "The Fall of the Mycenaean Empire," *Arch* 13 (1960) 66-75.

George E. Mylonas, "Excavations at Mycenae 1959-1961," *AJA* 66 (1962) 199.

*Emmett L. Bennett Jr., "Third International Colloquium for Mycenaean Studies," *KZFE* 1 (1962) 79-81.

*Carl W. Blegen and Mabel Lang, "The Palace of Nestor Excavations of 1962," *AJA* 67 (1963) 155-162. *[Mycenae]*

George E. Mylonas, "Excavations at Mycenae, 1962," *AJA* 67 (1963) 215-216.

*Emmett L. Bennett Jr., "Fourth International Colloquium of Mycenaean Studies," *KZFE* 4 (1965) 169-170.

Charles G. Higgins, "Possible Disappearance of Mycenaean Coastal Settlements of the Messenian Peninsula," *AJA* 70 (1966) 23-29.

George E. Mylonas, "Excavations at Mycenae, 1965," *AJA* 70 (1966) 193.

*A. Bartoněk, "The Mycenaean Symposium of Brno 13th-14th April 1966," *KZFE* 5 (1966) 163-165.

*W[illam] C. Brice, "The Fourth Edinburgh Minoan-Mycenaean Symposium," *KZFE* 5 (1966) 166-168.

*William S. Woodard, "The Later History of Grave Circle A at Mycenae," *AJA* 72 (1968) 174-175.

*William C. Brice, "The First Conference of the British Association for Mycenaean Studies," *KZFE* 7 (1968) 178-179.

*John L. Caskey, "Crises in the Minoan-Mycenaean World," *PAPS* 113 (1969) 433-449.

Mykenai

*Wilhelm, Dörpfeld, "Letter from Greece," *AJA, O.S.*, 5 (1889) 331-336. *[Mykenia]*

Mykonos

John S. Belmont and Colin Renfrew, "Two Prehistoric Sites on Mykonos," *AJA* 68 (1964) 395-400.

N

Naga

*P. D. Scott-Moncrieff, "The Ruined Sites at Masawwarat es-Sufra and Naga," *SBAP* 30 (1908) 192-203.

Naga-ed-Dêr

George A. Reisner, "Work of the Expedition of the University of California at Naga-ed-Der," *ASAE* 5 (1904) 105-109.

Albert M. Lythgoe, "The Egyptian Expedition of the University of California: An Early Prehistoric Cemetery at Naga ed Dêr," *AJA* 9 (1905) 79.

Anonymous, "'The Fulfillment of the Field-Worker's Prayer'," *A&A* 35 (1934) 43. *[Naga-ed Dêr]*

Peter J. Ucko, "The Predynastic Cemetery N 7000 at Naga-ed Dêr," *CdÉ* 42 (1967) 345-353.

Nag el-Kelebat

Tewfik Boulos, "Report on Excavation at Nag el-Kelebat," *ASAE* 7 (1906) 1-3.

Nahor

William Hayes Ware, "Light on Scriptural Texts from Recent Discoveries. The City of Nahor," *HR* 28 (1894) 315-317.

Nahr Malka

*T. G. Pinches, "An Early Mention of the Nahr Malka," *JRAS* (1917) 735-740.

Napata-Meroë

D. M. Dixon, "The Origin of the Kingdom of Kush (Napata-Meroë)," *JEA* 50 (1964) 121-132.

Naṣḫana

*Z. Vilnay, "Miscellany," *BIES* 10 (1942-44) #2/3, IV. [(a) Naṣḥana = Ṣalḥana in Syria]

Naucratis

Ernest A. Gardner, "Excavations at Naukratis," *AJA, O.S.*, 2 (1886) 180-181.

Anonymous, "The Discovery of Naukratis," *NPR* 1 (1886) 143-145.

Einar Gjerstad, "Studies in Archaic Greek Chronology. I. Naucratis," *AAA* 21 (1934) 67-84.

Tell Al Na'ur

*Walid Yasin, "A Note on Three Samarra-Halaf Sites in the Tikril Area," *Sumer* 24 (1968) 117-119. [2. Tell Al Na'ur, pp. 117-118]

Negadah

*F. Legge, "Recent Discoveries at Abydos and Negadah," *SBAP* 21 (1899) 183-193.

Nemea

Carl W. Blegen, "Notes and Comments. Excavations at Nemea Concluded," *A&A* 24 (1927) 189.

Carl W. Blegen, "Excavations at Nemea 1926," *AJA* 31 (1927) 421-440.

J. Penrose Harland, "The Excavations of Tsoungiza, the Prehistoric Site of Nemea," *AJA* 32 (1928) 63.

Charles K. Williams, "Excavations at Nemea, 1962," *AJA* 68 (1964) 201-202.

Charles K. Williams, "Nemea, 1964," *AJA* 69 (1965) 178-179.

Neša

Hildegard Lewy, "Neša," *JCS* 17 (1963) 103-104. *[Kaniš = Neša (?)]*

Nile River (Valley)

*Anonymous, "Nubia and the Nile," *DUM* 43 (1854) 475-492. *(Review)*

*John Hogg, "On the Supposed Antiquity of the Alluvium of the Nile and Man's Existence," *JSL, 3rd Ser.*, 9 (1859) 386-388.

Anonymous, "Egyptology, Oriental Travel and Discovery," *BFER* 13 (1864) 628-640. *(Review) [Discovery of the Source of the Nile River]*

†Anonymous, "The Source of the Nile," *BQRL* 41 (1865) 152-169. *(Review)*

Anonymous, "The Solution of the Nile Problem," *DUM* 68 (1866) 101-106. *(Review)*

†Anonymous, "Baker's *Exploration of the Albert Nyanza*," *ERCJ* 124 (1866) 151-184. *(Review) [Nile River Sources]*

†Anonymous, "Baker's *Albert Nyanza*," *QRL* 120 (1866) 155-171. *(Review) [Source of the Nile River]*

Anonymous, "Sources of the Nile," *SPR* 18 (1867-68) 451-472. *(Review)*

Francis R. Conder, "The Nile and Its Work," *SRL* 15 (1890) 252-285.

Nile River (Valley) concluded

*Edward Hull, "Sketch of the Geological History of Egypt and the Nile Valley," *JTVI* 24 (1890-91) 307-334.

*Alan H. Gardiner, "The Egyptian name of the Nile," *ZÄS* 45 (1908) 140-141. *[ḥʿpr]*

*K. S. Sandford and A. J. Arkell, "The Relation of Palæolithic Man to the History and Geology of the Nile Valley in Egypt," *Man* 29 (1929) #50.

*G. Ch. Aalders, "The Biblical Deluge and the Inundation by the Nile," *EQ* 6 (1934) 127-136.

Donald A. Mackenzie and W. B. Stevenson, "The Colours of the Nile," *GUOST* 8 (1936-37) 1-5.

J. H. Plumb, "The Search for the Nile," *HT* 2 (1952) 738-745.

O. G. S. Crawford, "Field Archaeology of the Middle Nile Region," *Kush* 1 (1953) 2-29; 6 (1958) 170-171. *[4th to 5th Cataracts]*

*G. J. Verwers, Hans-Åke Nordström, H. T. B. Hall, "Archaeological Survey on the West Bank of the Nile," *Kush* 10 (1962) 10-75. [Introduction, pp. 10-18; The Survey from Faras to Gezira Dabarosa, pp. 19-33; Excavations and Survey in Faras, Argin and Gezira Dabarosa, pp. 34-58; A Note on the Cattle Skulls Excavated at Faras, pp. 58-61]

William W. Y. Adams and Hans-Åke Nordström, "The Archaeological Survey of the West Bank of the Nile: Third Season, 1961-62," *Kush* 11 (1963) 10-46.

*Rhodes W. Fairbridge, "Nile Sedimentation above Wadi Halfa during the last 20,000 years," *Kush* 11 (1963) 96-107.

Jurgen von Beckerath, "The Nile Level Records at Karnak and their Importance for the History of the Libyan Period (Dynasties XXII and XXIII)," *JARCE* 5 (1966) 42-55.

*Jean Vercoutter, "Semna South Fort and the Records of Nile Levels at Kumma," *Kush* 14 (1966) 125-164.

Nimrud

Anonymous, "The Nimrud Excavation," *Sumer* 5 (1949) 209-210.

M. E. L. Mallowan, "Excavations at Nimrud. 1949-1950," *Iraq* 12 (1950) 147-183.

M. E. L. Mallowan, "Excavations at Nimrud. 1949 Season," *Sumer* 6 (1950) 101-102.

M. E. L. Mallowan, "Excavations at Nimrud (Kalḫu), 1950," *Sumer* 7 (1951) 49-54.

M. E. L. Mallowan, "Excavations at Nimrud (Kalḫu), 1951," *Iraq* 14 (1952) 1-23.

M. E. L. Mallowan, "Excavations at Nimrud (Kalḫu), 1952," *Iraq* 15 (1953) 1-42.

M. E. L. Mallowan, "Excavations at Nimrud (Kalḫu), 1953," *Iraq* 16 (1954) 59-163.

M. E. L. Mallowan, "Excavations at Nimrud (Kalḫu), 1955," *Iraq* 18 (1956) 1-21.

*David Oates and J. H. Reid, "The Burnt Palace and the Nabu Temple; Nimrud, 1955," *Iraq* 18 (1956) 22-39.

M. E. L. Mallowan, "Excavations at Nimrud (Kalḫu), 1956," *Iraq* 19 (1957) 1-25.

M. E. L. Mallowan, "Excavations at Nimrud (Kalḫu), 1957," *Iraq* 20 (1958) 101-108.

M. E. L. Mallowan, "Excavations at Nimrud (Kalḫu), 1958," *Iraq* 21 (1959) 93-97.

David Oates and Joan Oates, "Nimrud 1957: the Hellenistic Settlement," *Iraq* 20 (1958) 114-157.

David Oates, "The Excavations at Nimrud (Kalḫu)," *Iraq* 23 (1961) 1-14.

David Oates, "The Excavations at Nimrud (Kalḫu), 1962," *Iraq* 25 (1963) 6-37.

Nimrud concluded

David Oates, "Nimrud 1961. 2nd Summary Report," *Sumer* 17 (1961) 117-120.

David Oates, "The Excavations at Nimrud (Kalḫu), 1961," *Iraq* 24 (1962) 1-25.

Anonymous, "With an Open Bible at Nimrud. Some Comments on Professor Mallowan's Excavation Report," *BH* 3 (1967) #1, 25-29.

Helene J. Kantor, "Nimrud and its Remains: A Review Article," *Arch* 21 (1968) 92-99. *(Review)*

Nineveh

*†Anonymous, "The Chronology of the Sieges of Nineveh rectified," *MMBR* 10 (1800) 5-7.

*†Anonymous, "Rich's Researches in Koordistan and Nineveh," *DUM* 8 (1836) 17-26. *(Review)*

[B. B. Edwards], "Ruins of Ancient Nineveh," *BRCR* 9 (1837) 139-159.

[W. A.] Schmid, "Recent Discoveries at Nineveh, under the direction of the French Consul, M. Botta," *BRCM* 1 (1846) 13-15. *(Trans. from Ziet. für Geschichtswissenshaft)*

Anonymous, "Further Discoveries at Nineveh," *BRCM* 2 (1846) 365-370.

Anonymous, "Nineveh and its Remains," *QRL* 84 (1848-49) 106-153. *(Review)*

*†Anonymous, "Nineveh and the Bible," *BQRL* 9 (1849) 399-442. *(Review)*

T. H. W., "Discovery of the Ancient Nineveh," *CE* 47 (1849) 1-31. *(Review)*

Anonymous, "Nineveh," *DUM* 33 (1849) 411-429. *(Review)*

Anonymous, "Nineveh and its Remains," *MR* 31 (1849) 577-594. *(Review)*

†Anonymous, "*Layard's* Nineveh and its Remains," *NBR* 11 (1849) 209-253. *(Review)*

Nineveh cont.

†Anonymous, "Layard's Nineveh," *TLJ* 2 (1849-50) 501-521. *(Review)*

Anonymous, "Nineveh and its Remains," *CRB* 15 (1850) 111-130. *(Review)*

†Anonymous, "Nineveh and its Remains," *DR* 28 (1850) 354-398. *(Review)*

*Justin Perkins, "Journal of a Tour from Oroomiah to Mosul, through the Koordish Mountains, and a Visit to the Ruins of Nineveh," *JAOS* 2 (1851) 69-119.

C. D., "Nineveh," *JSL, 1st Ser.,* 7 (1851) 1-34. *(Review)*

*†Anonymous, "Nineveh and Babylon," *DR* 35 (1853) 93-138. *(Review)*

*†Anonymous, "Layard's Second Expedition," *ERL* 19 (1853) 145-186. *(Review) [Nineveh]*

*†Anonymous, "*Layard's* Discoveries in Nineveh and Babylon," *NBR* 19 (1853) 255-296. *(Review)*

*†Anonymous, "Layard's Nineveh and Babylon," *PQR* 2 (1853-54) 602-622. *(Review)*

*Anonymous, "Layard's New Discoveries at Nineveh and Babylon," *CRB* 19 (1854) 20-39. *(Review)*

*(   ) Collins, "Layard's Second Exploration," *MR* 36 (1854) 113-131. *(Review) [Nineveh and Babylon]*

Felix Jones, "Topography of Nineveh, illustrative of the Maps of the chief Cities of Assyria; and the general Geography of the Country intermediate between the Tigris and Upper Zab," *JRAS* 15 (1855) 297-397.

G. B., "The Probable Date of the Fall of Nineveh," *JSL, 3rd Ser.,* 7 (1858) 144-159.

Anonymous, "Nineveh: the Historians and the Monuments," *BFER* 8 (1859) 874-894.

Anonymous, "Nineveh: The Historians and the Monuments," *CRB* 24 (1859) 432-457.

Nineveh cont.

*R. E. Trywhitt, "Ptolemy's Chronology of Babylonian Reigns conclusively vindicated; and the date of the Fall of Nineveh ascertained; with Elucidations of Connected points in Assyrian, Scythian, Median, Lydian, and Israelite History," *JRAS* (1861) 106-149.

Dwight W. Marsh, "On the Ruins of Ancient Nineveh," *JAOS* 7 (1862) xlvii.

*J. W. Bosanquet, "On the Date of the Fall of Nineveh and the Beginning of the Reign of Nebuchadnezzer at Babylon, B.C. 581," *SBAT* 2 (1873) 147-178.

George Smith, "Account of Recent Excavations and Discoveries made on the Site of Nineveh," *SBAT* 3 (1874) 446-464.

W. W. Taylor, "The Discoveries at Nineveh. Their Force in Confirming the Historical Statements of the Scriptures," *OBJ* 1 (1880) 124-134.

O. D. Miller, "'On the True Site of Nineveh'," *UQGR, N.S.*, 17 (1880) 474-480.

George Smith, "The Library at Nineveh," *ONTS* 3 (1883-84) 352-353.

Porter C. Bliss, "On the True Site of Nineveh," *JAOS* 11 (1885) xxv-xxvi.

William Hayes Ward, "Light on Scriptural Texts from Recent Discoveries. That Bloody City," *HR* 29 (1895) 411-413. *(Review)*

*William Hayes Ward, "Light on Scriptural Texts from Recent Discoveries. Sennacherib and the Destruction of Nineveh," *HR* 30 (1895) 505-506.

*J. F. McCurdy, "Light on Scriptural Texts from Recent Discoveries. *The Book of Nahum and the Fall of Nineveh,*" *HR* 33 (1897) 408-411.

Christopher Johnston, "The Fall of Nineveh," *JAOS* 22 (1901) 20-22.

Anonymous, "Ancient Nineveh," *RP* 3 (1904) 55-56.

*Anonymous, "Nina and Nineveh," *RP* 4 (1905) 61.

*Theophilus G. Pinches, "Nina and Nineveh," *SBAP* 27 (1905) 69-79, 155.

Anonymous, "Ancient Nineveh," *RP* 5 (1906) 379.

Nineveh cont.

Paul Haupt, "Xenophon's Account of the Fall of Nineveh," *JAOS* 28 (1907) 99-107.

*Anonymous, "Nineveh and the Cylinder of Sennacherib," *CFL, 3rd Ser.*, 12 (1910) 333-335.

*Anonymous, "Sennacherib Building his Capital at Nineveh. From the New Octagonal Cylinder in the British Museum," *CFL, 3rd Ser.*, 12 (1910) 429-430.

*W. S[t] C[had] Boscawen, "The Making of Nineveh. The Great Cylinder of Sennacherib," *IAQR, 3rd Ser.*, 30 (1910) 314-335.

*Theophilus G. Pinches, "Aššur and Nineveh," *JTVI* 42 (1910) 154-174, 176. (Communication by A. Irving, pp. 174-175)

*Theophile G. Pinches, "Sennacherib's Campaigns on the North-West and his Work at Nineveh," *JRAS* (1910) 387-411.

*Theophilus G. Pinches, "Aššur and Nineveh," *RP* 12 (1913) 23-41.

*Theophilus G. Pinches, "From World-Domination to Subjection: The Story of the Fall of Nineveh and Babylon," *JTVI* 49 (1917) 107-131. [(Discussion, pp. 131-136) (Communications by J. W. Thistle, pp. 136-137; Andrew Craig Robinson, pp. 137-140)]

*L[uther] T. Townsend, "Prehistoric Babylon, Nineveh and the Hittite Empire; their Bearing on the Theory of Evolution," *CFL, 3rd Ser.*, 25 (1919) 45-49.

C. J. Gadd, "The Fall of Nineveh," *PBA* 10 (1921-23) 473-485.

W. B. Stevenson, "Newly Discovered Account of the Fall of Nineveh," *GUOST* 5 (1923-28) 14-15.

Anonymous, "When was Nineveh Destroyed?" *Exp, 9th Ser.*, 1 (1924) 53-54.

*George W. Gilmore, "What One Babylonian Tablet Has Done," *HR* 91 (1926) 135. *[Nineveh]*

Oswald T. Allis, "The Fall of Nineveh," *PTR* 22 (1924) 465-477.

Nineveh concluded

*G. R. Driver, "Some Recent Discoveries in Babylonian Literature," *Theo* 8 (1924) 2-13, 67-79, 123-130, 190-197. [II.—The Fall of Nineveh, pp.67-79]

Cranston Earl Goddard, "A Tradition Current in the Third Century B.C.," *JBL* 46 (1927) 106-110. *[Nineveh]*

*R. Campbell Thompson and R. W. Hamilton, "The British Museum Excavations on the Temple of Ishtar at Nineveh, 1930-31," *AAA* 19 (1932) 55-116.

R. Campbell Thompson and M. E. L. Mallowan, "The British Museum Excavations at Nineveh, 1931-32," *AAA* 20 (1933) 71-186.

R. W. Hutchinson, "The Nineveh of Tacitus," *AAA* 21 (1934) 85-88.

W. J. Beasley, "Assyria & the Bible. Part 2: Nineveh in Modern Times," *AT* 5 (1960-61) #3, 7-11.

Tariq [A.] Madhloum, "Excavations at Nineveh. A Preliminary Report (1965-1967)," *Sumer* 23 (1967) 76-81.

T[ariq] A. Madhloum, "Nineveh. The 1967-1968 Campaign," *Sumer* 24 (1968) 45-52.

*H. W. F. Saggs, "Nahum and the Fall of Nineveh," *JTS, N.S.*, 20 (1969) 220-225.

T[ariq] A. Madhloum, "Nineveh. The 1968-1969 Campaign," *Sumer* 25 (1969) 43-58.

Ninus

*A. H. Sayce, "The Classical Name of Carchemish," *JRAS* (1923) 409-410. *[Ninus(?)]*

Nippur

Robert F. Harper, "The Expedition of the Babylonian Exploration Fund. Excavations at Niffer*[sic]* During the Season of 1889," *BW* 1 (1893) 135-137.

Nippur cont.

John P. Peters, "Some Recent Results of the University of Pennsylvania Excavations at Nippur, Especially of the Temple Hill," *AJA, O.S.*, 10 (1895) 13-46.

Theophilus G. Pinches, "Requests and Replies," *ET* 9 (1897-98) 463-464. *[Nippur]*

Anonymous, "Literary Discoveries at Nippur," *HR* 40 (1900) 259-260.

A[lbert] T. Clay, "Hilprecht's Discoveries at Nippur," *ET* 14 (1902-03) 322-324.

John P. Peters, "The University of Pennsylvania's Expedition to Babylonia. Exploration of Nippur," *RP* 2 (1903) 35-46.

Albert T. Clay, "Professor Hilprecht's Recent Excavations at Nippur," *RP* 2 (1903) 47-62.

*John P. Peters, "The Nippur Library," *JAOS* 26 (1905) 145-164.

William Cruickshank, "Nippur," *ET* 24 (1912-13) 186-187.

*H. F. Lutz, "Nin-Uraš and Nippur," *JAOS* 42 (1922) 210-211.

T. Fish, "The Sumerian City of Nippur in the Period of the Third Dynasty of Ur," *Iraq* 5 (1938) 157-179.

L[eon] Legrain, "Nippur Fifty Years Ago," *UMB* 13 (1947-48) #4, 1-33.

Seton Lloyd, "The Nippur Expedition," *Sumer* 5 (1949) 98.

Donald E. McCown, "Nippur, Season of 1948," *Sumer* 5 (1949) 99-101.

Francis R. Steele, "Nippur Today," *UMB* 14 (1949-50) #1, 1-21.

Donald E. McCown, "Excavation at Nippur," *Sumer* 6 (1950) 99-100.

D[onald] McC[own], "Nippur: The Holy City," *UMB* 16 (1951-52) #2, 5-19.

Donald E. McCown, "Recent Finds at Nippur: A Great City of Ancient Mesopotamia," *Arch* 5 (1952) 70-75.

Nippur concluded

Donald E. McCown, "Excavations at Nippur, 1948-50," *JNES* 11 (1952) 169-176.

Donald E. McCown, "The Fourth Season of the Joint Expedition to Nippur," *Sumer* 10 (1954) 89-90.

Richard C. Haines, "The Latest Report in the Progress of the Excavations at Nippur," *Sumer* 11 (1955) 107-109.

Vaughn E. Crawford, "Nippur, the Holy City," *Arch* 12 (1959) 74-83.

Richard C. Haines, "A Report of the Excavations at Nippur during 1960-1961," *Sumer* 17 (1961) 67-70.

James E. Knudstad, "A Report on the 1964-1965 Excavations at Nippur," *Sumer* 22 (1966) 111-114.

James [E.] Knudstad, "A Preliminary Report on the 1966-67 Excavations at Nippur," *Sumer* 24 (1968) 95-106.

Nisa

*Paul W. Wallace, "A Reidentification of the Boiotian City Salganeus and a Suggested Location of the Homeric Nisa," *AJA* 73 (1969) 246.

Nod

Anonymous, "Old Testament Documents and the Cuneiform," *HR* 72 (1916) 55. *[Nod]*

A. H. Sayce, "The Land of Nod," *SBAP* 38(1916) 6-10.

Tall-i-Nokhodi

Clare Goff, "Excavations at Tall-i-Nokhodi," *Iran* 1 (1963) 43-70.

Clare Goff, "Excavations at Tall-i-Nokhodi, 1962," *Iran* 2 (1964) 41-52.

Nubia

*†Anonymous, "Belzoni's Discoveries in Egypt and Nubia," *BCQTR, N.S.*, 14 (1820) 561-580. *(Review)*

*Anonymous, "Nubia and the Nile," *DUM* 43 (1854) 475-492. *(Review)*

Anonymous, "Nubian Excavations," *RP* 6 (1907) 271.

Anonymous, "Second Coxe Expedition to Nubia," *RP* 7 (1908) 297-303.

F. Ll. Griffith, "Oxford Excavations in Nubia," *AAA* 8 (1921) 1-18, 65-104; 9 (1922) 67-124; 10 (1923) 73-171; 11 (1924) 115-125, 141-178; 12 (1925) 57-172; 13 (1926) 17-37, 49-93; 14 (1927) 57-116; 15 (1928) 63-88.

*J. H. Dunbar, "Betwixt Egypt and Nubia," *AEE* 14 (1929) 108-117.

W[alter] B. Emery, "Preliminary Report of the Work of the Archæological Survey of Nubia, 1929-1930," *ASAE* 30 (1930) 117-128.

W[alter] B. Emery, "Preliminary Report of the Work of the Archaeological Survey of Nubia, 1930-1931," *ASAE* 31 (1931) 70-80.

J. H. Dunbar, "A Town in Old Nubia," *AEE* 17 (1932) 14-24.

Walter B. Emery, "Preliminary report of the work of the Archaeological Survey of Nubia 1931-1932," *ASAE* 32 (1932) 38-46.

*R. Engelbach, "The quarries of the Western Nubian Desert. A preliminary report," *ASAE* 33 (1933) 65-74.

W[alter] B. Emery, "Preliminary report of the work of the Archaeological Survey of Nubia (1932-1934)*[sic]*," *ASAE* 33 (1933) 201-207.

L. P. Kirwan, "The Oxford University Excavations at Nubia, 1934-1935," *JEA* 21 (1935) 191-198.

*R. Engelbach, "The Quarries of the western Nubian desert and the ancient road to Tushka," *ASAE* 38 (1938) 369-390.

T[orgny] Säve-Söderbergh, "The Nubian Kingdom of the Intermediate Period," *Kush* 4 (1956) 54-61.

*Zbyněk Žába, "Ancient Nubia Calls for Help," *NOP* 1 (1960) #3, 6-9.

Nubia cont.

John O. Brew, "The Threat to Nubia," *Arch* 14 (1961) 268-276.

William Kelly Simpson, "Nubia: The University Museum-Yale University Expedition," *Exped* 4 (1961-62) #2, 29-39.

William Kelly Simpson, "Nubia: 1962 Excavations at Toshka and Arminna," *Exped* 4 (1961-62) #4, 37-46.

William Y. Adams, P. E. T. Allen, G. J. Verwers, "Archaeological Survey of Sudanese Nubia," *Kush* 9 (1961) 7-43. [Introduction, pp. 7-10; The Aerial Survey of Sudanese Nubia, pp. 11-14; Trial Excavations in the Faras Region, pp. 15-29]

William Kelly Simpson, "The Pennsylvania-Yale Excavations in Nubia," *AJA* 67 (1963) 217.

Ralph S. Soleki, Jean de Heinzelin, Robert L. Stigler, Anthony E. Marks, Roland Paepe, and Jean Guichard, "Preliminary Statement of the Prehistoric Investigations of the Columbia University Nubian Expedition in Sudan, 1961-62," *Kush* 11 1963) 70-92.

William Y. Adams, "Post-Pharaonic Nubia in the Light of Archaeolgy. I," *JEA* 50 (1964) 102-120.

Fred Wendorf, R. D. Daugherty, and John Waechter, "The Museum of New Mexico-Columbia University Nubian Expedition: The 1962-63 Field Programme*[sic]*," *Kush* 12 (1964) 12-18.

William Y. Adams, "Post-Pharaonic Nubia in the Light of Archaeology. II," *JEA* 51 (1965) 160-178. *[Part III not applicable]*

Henry T. Irwin and Joe Ben Wheat, "Report of the Palaeolithic Section University of Colorado Nubian Expedition," *Kush* 13 (1965) 17-23.

Fred Wendorf, Joel L. Shiner, Anthony E. Marks, Jean de Heinzelin, and Waldemar Chmielewski, "The Combined Prehistoric Expedition: Summary of the 1963-64 Field Season," *Kush* 13 (1965) 28-55. *[Nubia]*

A. J. Mills and Hans-Åke Norström, "The Archaeological Survey from Gemai to Dal. Preliminary Report on the Season 1964-65," *Kush* 14 (1966) 1-15. *[Nubia]*

Nubia concluded

Fred Wendorf, Joel L. Shiner, Anthony E. Marks, Jean de Heinzelin, Waldemar Chmielewski, and Romuald Schild, "The 1965 Field Season of the Southern Methodist University," *Kush* 14 (1966) 16-24. *[Nubia]*

Roy L. Carlson, "A Neolithic Site in the Murshid District, Nubia," *Kush* 14 (1966) 53-62.

Gerald E. Kadish, "Old Kingdom Egyptian Activity in Nubia: Some Reconsiderations," *JEA* 52 (1966) 23-33.

Roy L. Carlson and John S. Sigstad, "Paleolithic and Late Neolithic Sites Excavated by the Fourth Colorado Expedition," *Kush* 15 (1967-68) 51-58. *[Nubia]*

Torgny Säve-Söderbergh, "Preliminary Report of the Scandinavian Joint Expedition. Archaeological Investigations Between Faras and Gemmai—November 1963–March 1964," *Kush* 15 (1967-68) 211-250. *[Nubia]*

John A. Wilson, "The Nubian Campaign: An Exercise in International Archaeology," *PAPS* 111 (1967) 268-271.

William Y. Adams, "Invasion, Diffusion, Evolution?" *Antiq* 42 (1968) 194-215. *[Nubia]*

Labib Habachi, "The Deluge in Lower Nubia," *Arch* 22 (1969) 196-203.

Nuzi (See also: Yargon Teppe)

Anonymous, "Notes and Comments. Nuzi Destroyed about 2000 B.C.?" *A&A* 25 (1928) 308.

Anonymous, "The Expedition at Nuzi," *UMB* 2 (1930-31) 111-115.

Anonymous, "Excavations at Nuzi," *UMB* 2 (1930-31) 146-147.

Robert H. Pfeiffer, "The Harvard Excavations at Nuzi (Kirkuk) During 1928-29," *AJA* 34 (1930) 54.

R. F. S. Starr, "Notes from the Excavation at Nuzi," *BASOR* #38 (1930) 3-8.

Robert H. Pfeiffer, The Excavations at Nuzi: Preliminary Report of the Fourth Campaign," *BASOR* #42 (1931) 1-7.

Nuzi concluded

R. F. S. Starr, "Notes on the Tracing of Mud-Brick Walls," *BASOR* #58 (1935) 18-27.

*Robert H. Pfeiffer, "Nuzi and the Hurrians: The excavations at Nuzi (Kirkuk, Iraq) and their contribution to our knowledge of the history of the Hurrians," *SIR* (1935) 535-558.

Sidney Smith, "The City Nuzu," *Antiq* 12 (1938) 425-431.

J. N. Schofield, "Some Archaeological Sites and the Old Testament. Nuzu," *ET* 66 (1954-55) 315-318.

*E[phraim] A. Speiser, "Nuzi or Nuzu?" *JAOS* 75 (1955) 52-55.

*Lester J. Kuyper, "Israel and Her Neighbors," *RefR* 10 (1956-57) #3, 11-20. [Nuzu, pp. 18-20]

O

Tell el Obeid

*H. R. Hall, "The Discoveries at Tell el 'Obeid in Southern Babylonia and Some Egyptian Comparisons," *JEA* 8 (1922) 241-257.

C. Leonard Woolley, "Excavations at Tel el Obeid," *AJ* 4 (1924) 329-346.

C. L[eonard] Woolley, "The Excavations at Tel el Obeid," *MJ* 15 (1924) 237-251.

*E[phraim] A. Speiser, "An Important Discovery," *BASOR* #27 (1927) 11-12. *[Tell-el-Obeid]*

Olympia

[Stephen D. Peet], "The Discoveries at Olympia," *AAOJ* 3 (1880-81) 145-150. *[Editorial]*

Alfred Emerson, "Letter from Olympia," *AJA, O.S.,* 3 (1887) 95-97.

Anonymous, "Work at Olympia," *RP* 7 (1908) 259.

Olympia concluded

*Charles Newton Smiley, "Olympia and Greek Athletics," *A&A* 10 (1920) 177-189.

John Boardman, "Recent Discoveries at Olympia," *Antiq* 30 (1956) 222-223.

Mt. Olympos

W. Kendrick Pritchett, "Xerxes' Route over Mount Olympos," *AJA* 65 (1961) 369-375.

Olynthos

David M. Robinson, "A Preliminary Report on the Excavations at Olynthos," *AJA* 33 (1929) 53-76.

George E. Mylonas, "Neolithic Settlement at Olynthus," *AJA* 33 (1929) 98.

David Moore Robinson, "The Residential Districts and the Cemeteries at Olynthos," *AJA* 36 (1932) 118-138.

*David M. Robinson, "A Typical Block of Houses at Olynthos with an Account also of Three Hoards of Coins," *AJA* 37 (1933) 111-113.

David M. Robinson, "The Third Campaign at Olynthos," *AJA* 39 (1935) 210-247.

David M. Robinson and George E. Mylonas, "The Fourth Campaign at Olynthos," *AJA* 43 (1939) 48-77.

*Alex Boëthius, "Ancient Town Architecture and the New Material from Olynthus," *AJP* 69 (1948) 396-407.

*R. E. Wycherley, "Notes on Olynthus and Selinus," *AJA* 55 (1951) 231-236.

David M. Robinson, "Olynthus—*The Greek Pompeii*," *Arch* 5 (1952) 228-235.

Oman

Karen Frifelt, "Archaeological investigations in the Oman peninsula: A preliminary report," *Kuml* (1968) 170-175.

Tel Omar (See also: Opis)

*V. K. Richards, “The Toledo-Michigan-Cleveland Expedition,” *A&A* 33 (1932) 42-47. *[Tel Omar (Opis)]*

Tell Om Harb

C. C. Edgar, “Report on an excavation at Tell Om Harb,” *ASAE* 11 (1911) 164-169.

On (See also: Heliopolis)

*Melvin Grove Kyle, “Professor Petrie’s Excavations at Heliopolis, the Bibical On,” *BS* 59 (1912) 553-564.

Alan Rowe, “The Famous Solar City of On,” *PEQ* 94 (1962) 133-142. [I. Introduction; II. The Pharaoh, Joseph and His Family, *On* ‘City-of-the-Column(s)’, Etc.; III. The Evolution of the Earliest Egyptian Columns including the *Iwn* (Plate XXX, A, B, C)]

Onias

*William Copley Winslow, “Important Discoveries by Dr. Petrie,” *RP* 5 (1906) 191-192. *[Onias]*

William Copley Winslow, “Petrie’s Work in the Delta,” *RP* 5 (1906) 239-240. *[Onias]*

Ophir

*Joseph W. Jenks, “On Ophir and Sheba,” *PAOS* (May, 1869) iv.

*Joseph W. Jenks, “On Ophir and Sheba,” *JAOS* 9 (1871) liv.

*Alex. Mackenzie Cameron, “The Identity of Ophir and Taprobane, and their Site indicated,” *SBAT* 2 (1873) 267-288.

*Anonymous, “Goldfields: Ancient and Modern,” *WR* 120 (1883) 378-408. *(Review)* [Ophir, p. 391]

James Hastings, “About Ophir,” *ET* 7 (1895-96) 380.

Ophir concluded

G[eorge] H. S[chodde], "The Biblical Ophir," *ColTM* 22 (1902) 382-384.

*J. D. Murphy, "Ancient Commerce with East Africa and the 'Ophir' of King Solomon," *ACQR* 28 (1903) 157-173.

*Walter Eugene Clark, "The Sandalwood and Peacocks of Ophir," *AJSL* 36 (1919-20) 103-119.

W[illiam] F[oxwell] Albright, "Ivory and Apes of Ophir," *AJSL* 37 (1920-21) 144-145.

H. Hirschfeld, "Note on Ophir," *JRAS* (1924) 260.

Thomas Price, "'Sofala, Thought Ophir…'," *GUOST* 20 (1963-64) 23-37.

Opis (See also: Tell Omar)

*J. F. MacMichael, "On the Sites of Sittake and Opis, as given in Professor Rawlinson's History of Herodotus. Vol. I. p. 261, Note 5," *JP* 4 (1872) 135-145.

*V. K. Richards, "The Toledo-Michigan-Cleveland Expedition," *A&A* 33 (1932) 42-47. *[Tel Omar (Opis)]*

Opous

Carl W. Blegen, "The Site of Opous," *AJA* 30 (1926) 401-404.

Orontes River

W. J. van Liere, "The pleistocene and stone age of the Orontes river," *AAAS* 16 (1966) #2, 7-29.

Oropus

*A. H. Sayce, "Geographical Notes," *JRAS* (1921) 47-55. [Was Oropus the Classical Name of Carchemish? pp. 47-51]

*L. A. Waddell, "The 'Oropus' Title of Carchemish," *JRAS* (1922) 266-269.

Oropus concluded

*L. A. Waddell, "The Oropus or Europus Title of Carchemish," *JRAS* (1928) 580-588.

Ostia

Guido Calza, "Roman Necropolis Brought to Light Near Ostia," *A&A* 30 (1930) 169-170.

Anonymous, "The Significance of Ostia and the Insula Sarca," *A&A* 30 (1930) 173-175.

Adrian Burnel, "Ostia: Roman satellite town," *HT* 5 (1955) 18-23.

P

Paestum

Amedeo Maiuri, "The Excavation of Paestum," *A&A* 32 (1931) 161-165.

Pellegrino Claudio Sestieri, "The Antiquities of Paestum," *Arch* 7 (1954) 206-213.

Pagasæ

Anonymous, "Ancient City of Pagasæ," *RP* 8 (1909) 125.

Pakhuwa

John Garstang, "The Location of Pakhuwa," *AAA* 28 (1948) 48-54.

Palaiokastro

R. C. Bosanquet, "A Mycenæan Town and Cemeteries at Palaiokastro," *Man* 2 (1902) #119.

Palmyra

*†Anonymous, "The Rev. J. L. Porter's Damascus and Palmyra," *TLJ* 10 (1857-58) 146-158. *(Review)*

C[laude] R. Conder, "The Native Name of Palmyra," *PEFQS* 22 (1890) 307.

*William L. Reed, "Caravan Cities of the Near East," *CollBQ* 35 (1958) #3, 1-16. [Palmyra-Bride of the Desert, pp. 4-8]

Pamphylia

*Ronald Syme, "Galatia and Pamphylia under Augustus: the Governorships of Piso, Quirinius and Silvanus," *Klio* 27 (1934) 122-148. [I. The Status of Pamphylia, pp. 122-127]

Panakton

Irwin L. Merker, "Panakton," *AJA* 69 (1965) 171.

Papremis

Jaroslav Černý, "The Name of the Town of Papremis," *ArOr* 20 (1952) 86-89.

Paran

A. H. Sayce, "Recent Biblical Archaeology. Paran and Hagar's Well," *ET* 13 (1901-02) 66.

Parthia

Selah Merrill, "Parthia the Rival of Rome," *BS* 31 (1874) 365-377.

Pasargadae

David Stronach, "Excavations at Pasargadae: First Preliminary Report," *Iran* 1 (1963) 19-42.

*David Stronach, "Excavations at Pasargadae: Second Preliminary Report," *Iran* 2 (1964) 21-39.

Pasargadae concluded

David Stronach, "Excavations at Pasargadae: Third Preliminary Report," *Iran* 3 (1965) 9-40.

*R. D. Barnett, "ʿAnath, Baʿal and Pasargadae," *MUSJ* 45 (1969) 405-422.

Pazarlik

John M. Cook, "Exploration at Pazarlik, 1959," *TAD* 10 (1960) #1, 16-17.

J[ohn] M. Cook, "Pazarlik, 1960," *TAD* 11 (1961) #1, 15-17.

Pekiin

*I. Ben-Zevil, "Discoveries at Pekiin," *PEFQS* 62 (1930) 210-213.

Pella

Photios Petsas, "New Discoveries at Pella—Birthplace and Capital of Alexander," *Arch* 11 (1958) 246-254.

Photios Petsas, "Ten Years at Pella," *Arch* 17 (1964) 74-84.

Peloponnese

William A. McDonald and Richard Hope Simpson, "Prehistoric Habitation in Southwestern Peloponnese," *AJA* 65 (1961) 221-260.

William A. McDonald and Richard Hope Simpson, "Further Exploration in Southwestern Peloponnese: 1962-1963," *AJA* 68 (1964) 229-245.

*Frank J. Frost, "Some Underwater Sites in the Peloponnesus," *AJA* 72 (1968) 165.

William A. McDonald and Richard Hope Simpson, "Further Explorations in Southwestern Peloponnese: 1964-1968," *AJA* 73 (1969) 123-177.

Perachora

*Charles A. Robinson Jr., "Topographical Notes on Perachora, with Special Reference to Xenophon's Account of the Corinthian War, 390 B.C.," *AJA* 31 (1927) 96.

Perea

R. L. Steward, "The Land Beyond the Jordan," *CFL, N.S.*, 2 (1900) 270-276. *[Perea]*

Pergamum

*David M. Robinson, "Pergamum and Ephesus," *A&A* 9 (1920) 157-170.

Persepolis

Thomas Forwythe Nelson, "Site of Ancient Persepolis," *RP* 6 (1907) 131-137.

Anonymous, "The Persepolis Discoveries," *A&A* 34 (1933) 87-92, 112.

M. E. L. Mallowan, "Persepolis: a review," *Antiq* 29 (1955) 141-146. *(Review)*

Arthur Upham Pope, "Persepolis as a Ritual City," *Arch* 10 (1957) 123-130.

R. D. Barnett, "Persepolis," *Iraq* 19 (1957) 55-72.

*George Woodcock, "Persia and Persepolis," *HT* 17 (1967) 236-241.

*George Woodcock, "Persia and Persepolis: II," *HT* 17 (1967) 301-307.

Persia

†Anonymous, "Malcolm's *History of Persia,*" *QRL* 15 (1816) 236-292. *(Review)*

*Justin Perins, "Miscellanies IV. Late Discoveries in Persia and Mesopotamia," *JAOS* 3 (1853) 490-491.

Ernest Babelon, "Recent archaeological discoveries in Persia," *AJA, O.S.*, 2 (1886) 61-64.

C. E. Biddulph, "The Physical Geography of Persia," *IAQR, 2nd Ser.*, 4 (1892) 43-48.

*Ellsworth Huntington, "Climate and History of Eastern Persia and Sistan," *RP* 4 (1905) 205-219.

Persia concluded

John P. Peters, "Excavations in Persia," *HTR* 8 (1915) 82-93.

*P. M. Sykes, "The Ancient History of Persia (Elam, Media, and the Rise of the Achæmenian Dynasty)," *IAQR* 7 (1915) 125-147.

Oscar Reuther, "Recent discoveries in Persia: a review," *Antiq* 4 (1930) 421-424. *(Review)*

Anonymous, "Announcing a Joint Persian Expedition," *UMB* 2 (1930-31) 109-111.

Anonymous, "The Joint Expedition to Persia," *UMB* 3 (1931-32) 14-17, 82, 122-124, 126; 5 (1934-35) #3, 86-87.

Anonymous, "The Persian Expedition," *UMB* 4 (1932-33) 5-9, 31-36.

Anonymous, "A New Expedition to Persia," *UMB* 4 (1932-33) 140-142.

*George Woodcock, "Persia and Persepolis," *HT* 17 (1967) 236-241.

*George Woodcock, "Persia and Persepolis: II," *HT* 17 (1967) 301-307.

Persian Gulf

P. V. Glob, "Archeological Investigations in Four Arab States," *Kuml* (1959) 238-239. *[Kuwait, Bahrain, Qatar, Abu Dhabi]*

P. V. Glob, "Danish Archeologists in the Persian Gulf," *Kuml* (1960) 212-213.

Geoffrey Bibby, "Arabian Gulf archeology," *Kuml* (1964) 101-111. [The Eighth Campaign of the Danish Archeological Expedition 1961/62; Bahrain, Abu Dhabi; The Ninth Campaign of the Danish Archeological Expedition 1962/63; Bahrain, Qatar, Abu Dhabi, Saudi Arabia]

Geoffrey Bibby, "Arabian Gulf Archeology," *Kuml* (1965) 144-152. [The Tenth Campaign of the Danish Archeological Expedition 1964; Bahrain, Qatar, Abu Dhabi, Saudi Arabia, Gulf of Oman Coast]

Geoffrey Bibby, "Arabian Gulf Archeology. The Eleventh Archeological Expedition 1965," *Kuml* (1966) 90-95. [Bahrain; Abu Dhabi; Saudi Arabia]

Persian Gulf concluded

Beatrice de Cardi, "A preliminary report of field survey in the northern Trucial States," *Kuml* (1969) 215-217. [Ras al-Khaimah; The Batina coast]

Persis

Aurel Stein, "An Archaeological Tour in the Ancient Persis," *Iraq* 3 (1936) 111-225.

Phaistos

Antonio Taramelli, "A Visit to Phaestos," *AJA* 5 (1901) 418-436.

*J. Walter Graham, "Phaistos—*Second Fiddle to Knossos?*" *Arch* 10 (1957) 208-214.

Phalerum

*Mitchel Carroll, "Observations on the Harbors and Walls of Ancient Athens," *AJA* 8 (1904) 88-91. [II. Phalerum, pp. 90-91]

*John Day, "Phalerum and the Phaleric Wall," *TAPA* 59 (1928) 164-178.

Pharpar River

*William Wright, "The Rivers of Damascus: Abana and Pharpar," *Exp, 5th Ser.*, 4 (1896) 290-297.

Philae

Charles de Wolf Brower, "Philae," *RP* 3 (1904) 259-268.

G. B. Gordon, "Egyptian Section. Philae, the Forsaken," *MJ* 2 (1911) 5-10.

Philus

Henry S. Washington, "Excavations at Phlius*[sic]* in 1892," *AJA* 27 (1923) 438-449.

Carl W. Blegen, "Excavations at Philus, 1924," *A&A* 20 (1925) 23-33.

Phocis

Anonymous, "Mounds in Phocis, Greece," *RP* 7 (1908) 260.

Phoenicia

*Anonymous, "Phœnicia and Carthage," *PQR* 10 (1861-62) 291-326. *(Review)*

†Anonymous, "Phœnician Antiquities," *ERCJ* 163 (1886) 193-230. *(Review)*

C[laude] R. Conder, "The Pre-Semitic Element in Phœnicia," *ARL* 1 (1888) 91-101.

Cameron Mackay, "The Phœnix Land," *CongQL* 27 (1949) 134-142. *[Phoenicia]*

*Richard D. Barnett, "Phoenicia and the Ivory Trade," *Arch* 9 (1956) 87-97.

*W[illiam] F[oxwell] Albright, "Remarks on the Chronology of Early Bronze IV-Middle Bronze IIA in Phoenicia and Syria-Palestine," *BASOR* #184 (1966) 26-35.

Phileh Qalʻeh

E. O. Negahban, "A Brief Report on the Excavation of Marlik Tepe and Phileh Qalʻeh," *Iran* 2 (1964) 13-19.

Picenum

*Tenney Frank, "On Rome's conquest of Sabinum, Picenum and Etruria," *Klio* 11 (1911) 367-381.

Pionia

*Joseph Thacher Clarke, "Gargara, Lamponia and Pionia: Towns of Troad," *AJA, O.S.*, 4 (1888) 291-319.

Piraeus

John Day, "The *ΚΩΦΟΣ ΛΙΜΗΝ* of the Piraeus," *AJA* 31 (1927) 441-449.

Pi-Raʿmesse-mi-Amūn

Alan H. Gardiner, "The Delta Residence of the Ramessides," *JEA* 5 (1918) 127-138, 179-200, 242-271. *[Pi-Raʿmesse-mi-Amūn]*

*Alan H. Gardiner, "Tanis and Pi-Raʿmesse: A Retraction," *JEA* 19 (1933) 122-128.

Pīsh-i-Kūn

*Clare Goff Meade, "Lūristān in the first half of the First Millennium B.C. A preliminary report on the first season's excavations at Bābā Jān, and associated surveys in the Eastern Pīsh-i-Kūn," *Iran* 6 (1968) 105-134.

Pisidia

*G. E. Bean, "Notes and Inscriptions from Pisidia. Part I," *AS* 9 (1959) 67-117.

*G. E. Bean, "Notes and Inscriptions from Pisidia. Part II," *AS* 10 (1960) 43-82.

W. M. Ramsay, "Res Antolicae," *Klio* 23 (1929-30) 239-255. [III. Ecce Iterum Pisidia]

Pithekoussai

*Giorgio Buchner, "Pithekoussai: Oldest Greek Colony in the West," *Exped* 8 (1965-66) #4, 5-12.

Pithom

*†Anonymous, "On Pithom and Raamses," *MMBR* 40 (1815-16) 496-498.

Stanley Lane-Poole, "The Discovery of Pithom-Succoth," *BQRL* 78 (1883) 108-119.

Anonymous, "The Recovery of Pithom-Succoth. A Sketch of the Recent Remarkable Excavations and Discoveries in Egypt," *CongL* 12 (1883) 845-853.

*Alfred H. Kellogg, "The Discovery of Pithom-Succoth and the Exodus Route," *PR* 4 (1883) 838-845.

Anonymous, "The Excavations at Pithom," *JTVI* 18 (1884-85) 95-98.

*M. E., "M. Naville and the Exodus," *Exp, 3rd Ser.,* 1 (1885) 399-400. *(Review) [Pithom]*

G. Lansing, "Pithom, 'the Treasure City'," *MI* 3 (1885-86) 32-50.

C. R. Gillett, "Pithom," *JBL* 6 (1886) Part 2, 69-78.

*G[eorge] Rawlinson, "Biblical Topography. VII.—Egyptian Sites—Zoan and Pithom," *MI* 4 (1886) 321-331.

*Anonymous, "Pithom and the Route of the Exodus," *NPR* 1 (1886) 142-143.

C. R. Gillett, "Pithom: Naville and His Reviewers," *ONTS* 6 (1886-87) 139-145. *(Review)*

*C. R. Gillett, "Pithom—Heroöpolis—Succoth," *AR* 8 (1887) 82-92.

L. Dickerman, "On Naville's Identification of the city Pithom," *JAOS* 13 (1889) x-xi.

Wm. C. Winslow, "On Naville's Identification of Pithom," *JAOS* 13 (1889) xi-xiii.

W. W. Moore, "The Discovery of Pithom," *PQ* 3 (1889) 243-255.

M[elvin] G[rove] Kyle, "Bricks without Straw at Pithom. A Re-examination of Naville's Works," *RP* 8 (1909) 304-307.

Pithom concluded

[Melvin Grove Kyle(?)], "Another Word about the 'Bricks without Straw'," *RP* 9 (1910) 73. *[Pithom]*

Melvin Grove Kyle, "Bricks without Straw at Pithom:—A Re-examination of Naville's Work," *CFL, 3rd Ser.,* 12 (1910) 98-102.

*Joseph Offord, "Archaeological Notes on Jewish Antiquities. LVIII. *The Semitic Name of Pithom,*" *PEFQS* 51 (1919) 182-184.

*Harold M. Weiner, "Pithom and Ramses," *AEE* 8 (1923) 75-77.

*E. P. Uphill, "Pithom and Raamses: Their Location and Significance," *JNES* 27 (1968) 291-316; 28 (1969) 15-39.

Plataia

Charles Waldstein, "Papers of the American School of Classical Studies at Athens. Discoveries in Plataia, 1889," *AJA, O.S.,* 5 (1889) 439-442. [II. Report on Excavations at Plataia in 1889]

*Charles Waldstein, H. S. Washington, and W. Irving Hunt, "Discoveries in Plataia in 1890," *AJA, O.S.,* 6 (1890) 445-475. [I. General Report on the Excavations, pp. 445-448; II. Detailed Report on the Excavations, pp. 448-452; III. Description of the Site and Walls of Plataia, pp. 452-462; IV. Notes on the Battlefield of Plataia, pp. 463-475]

W. Kendrick Pritchett, "New Light on Plataia," *AJA* 61 (1957) 9-28.

Pnubs

*H. Jacquet-Grodon, C. Bonnet, and J. Jacquet, "Pnubs and the Temple of Tabo on Argo Island," *JEA* 55 (1969) 103-111.

Poggio Civitate

Kyle Meredith Phillips Jr., "Poggio Civitate," *Arch* 21 (1968) 252-261.

Polatli

Seton Lloyd and Nuri Görkçe, "Excavations at Polatli. *A New Investigation of Second and Third Millennium Stratigraphy in Anatolia,*" *AS* 1 (1951) 21-75.

Pollentia

Daniel E. Woods, "Excavations in Alcudia, Mallorca (Baleares)," *AJA* 62 (1958) 228. *[Pollentia]*

Pontus

William G. Fletcher, "The Pontic Cities of Pompey the Great," *TAPA* 70 (1939) 17-29.

Porto Cheli-Halieis (See also: Halieis)

*Thomas W. Jacobsen, "Investigations of Porto Cheli-Halieis, 1967," *AJA* 72 (1968) 167.

Praesos

Frederico Halbherr, "Report on the Researches at Praesos," *AJA* 5 (1901) 371-392.

R. C. Bosanquet, "Report on Excavations at Præsos in Eastern Crete," *Man* 1 (1901) #148.

Priene

Anonymous, "Discoveries at Prienè," *MR* 84 (1902) 479-483.

*Howard Crosby Butler, "Miletus, Priene and Sardis," *A&A* 9 (1920) 171-186.

Prostanna

M. H. Ballance, "The Site of Prostanna," *AS* 9 (1959) 125-128.

Prosymna

*Carl W. Blegen, "Prosymna: Remains of Post-Mycenaean Date," *AJA* 43 (1939) 410-444.

Ptolemais

*Carl H. Kraeling, "Excavations at Tolmeita (Ptolemais) in Libya, 1956," *AJA* 61 (1957) 184.

Punt

*Edouard Naville, "The Land of Punt and the Hamites," *JTVI* 57 (1925) 190-203. (Discussion, pp. 203-207)

William Stevenson Smith, "The Land of Punt," *JARCE* 1 (1962) 59-61.

Pylos

*K. Kourouniotis and Carl W. Blegen, "Archaeological Notes: Excavations at Pylos, 1939," *AJA* 43 (1939) 557-576.

W. A. McDonald, "Where Did Nestor Live?" *AJA* 46 (1942) 538-545. *[Pylos]*

*Bedřich Hronzý, "A_2-Lu Jaluka = The Capital of the Empire of Pylos = Ancient Name of Pylos?" *JJP* 6 (1952) 15.

Carl W. Blegen, "The Palace of Nestor. Excavations at Pylos, 1952," *AJA* 57 (1953) 59-64.

Carl W. Blegen, "Excavations at Pylos, 1953," *AJA* 58 (1954) 27-32.

S. Marinatos, "Excavations near Pylos, 1956," *Antiq* 31 (1957) 97-100. *(Trans. by John Boardman)*

L. R. Palmer, "Homer and Mycenae II: The Last Days of Pylos," *HT* 7 (1957) 436-442.

Carl W. Blegen, "Nestor's Pylos," *PAPS* 101 (1957) 379-385.

John Chadwick, "The Two Provinces of Pylos," *Minos* 7 (1961-63) 125-141.

Pylos concluded

John E. Coleman, "Salvage Excavations at Pylos in Elis," *AJA* 73 (1969) 234.

W. K[endrick] Pritchett, "The Battle of Pylos and Sphacteria," *AJA* 68 (1964) 198.

William P. Donovan, "Excavations at Nestor's Pylos: The Cemetery," *AJA* 71 (1967) 186.

D. A. Was, "The Kingdom of Pylos. Its Topography and Defence," *Anat* 3 (1969-70) 147-176.

Q

Tell Qalinj Agha (Erbil)

*Behnam Abu al-Soof, "Short Sounding at Tell Qalinj Agha (Erbil)," *Sumer* 22 (1966) 77-82.

Behnam Abu Al-Soof[sic]*, "More Soundings at Tell Qalinj Agha (Erbil)," *Sumer* 23 (1967) 69-75.

*Behnam Abu al-Soof, "Excavations at Tell Qalinj Agha (Erbil) Summer, 1968," *Sumer* 25 (1969) 3-42.

Qantîr

Mahmud Hamza, "Excavations of the Department of Antiquities at Qantîr (Faqus District) (Season May 21st-July 7th, 1928)," *ASAE* 30 (1930) 31-68.

Qaṣr al-Ḥayr al-Sharqi

Oleg Grabar, "Qaṣr al-Ḥayr al-Sharqi,"*AAAS* 15 (1965) #2, 107-120. *[Part I]*

Oleg Grabar, "Qaṣr al-Ḥayr al-Sharqi: Preliminary Report on the First Season of Excavations," *AAAS* 16 (1966) #1, 29-46. *[Part II]*

Qaṣr Ibrîm

J. Martin Plumley, "Qaṣr Ibrîm 1963-1964," *JEA* 50 (1964) 1-5.

J. Martin Plumley, "Qaṣr Ibrîm 1966," *JEA* 52 (1966) 9-12.

J. Martin Plumley, "Qaṣr Ibrîm December 1966," *JEA* 53 (1967) 3-5.

Qataban

*W[illiam] F[oxwell] Albright, "The Chronology of Ancient South Arabia in the Light of the First Campaign of Excavation in Qataban," *BASOR* #119 (1950) 5-15.

*A. Jamme, "A New Chronology of the Qatabanian Kingdom," *BASOR* #120 (1950) 26-27.

Qarn Sartabeh

*Warren J. Moulton, "A Visit to Qarn Sartabeh," *BASOR* #62 (1936) 14-18. *[Tell el-Mazâr]*

Qatar

P. V. Glob, "Reconnaissance at Qatar," *Kuml* (1956) 201-202.

P. V. Glob, "Prehistoric Discoveries in Qatar," *Kuml* (1957) 175-178.

*Viggo Nielsen, "The Al Wusail Mesolithic Flint Sites at Qatar," *Kuml* (1961) 181-184.

*Hans Jørgen Madsen, "A Flint Site in Qatar," *Kuml* (1961) 197-201.

Holger Kapel, "Stone Age discoveries in Qatar," *Kuml* (1964) 148-155.

Qau-el-Kebir

W. M. Flinders Petrie, "The British School at Qau," *AEE* 8 (1923) 44-45. *[Qau-el-Kebir]*

[W. M.] Flinders Petrie, "The British School in Egypt. Excavations at Qau," *AEE* 9 (1924) 16-17. *[Qau-el-Kebir]*

Qūmis

*John Hansman, "The Problems of Qūmis," *JRAS* (1968) 111-139. *[Hecatompylos?]*

R

Raamses

*†Anonymous, "On Pithom and Raamses," *MMBR* 40 (1815-16) 496-498.

Howard Carter, "Report on Work done at Ramesseum during the years 1900-1901," *ASAE* 2 (1901) 193-195.

*Harold M. Weiner, "Pithom and Ramses," *AEE* 8 (1923) 75-77.

G. Ernest Wright, "Two Misunderstood Items in the Exodus-Conquest Cycle," *BASOR* #86 (1942) 32-35. [2. The "Store-City" Raamses, pp. 34-35]

H. H. Rowley, "Two Observations," *BASOR* #87 (1942) 40. *[II. Raamses]*

*E. P. Uphill, "Pithom and Raamses: Their Location and Significance," *JNES* 27 (1968) 291-316; 28 (1969) 15-39.

Raiyān-Moeris

F. Cope Whitehouse, "The Raiyān-Moeris and the Ptolemaic Maps," *SBAP* 15 (1892-93) 77-87.

Ras al 'Amiya

David Stronach, "The Excavations at Ras al 'Amiya," *Iraq* 23 (1961) 95-137.

Ras al Qala'a

*P. V. Glob, "The Ancient Capital of Bahrain," *Kuml* (1954) 167-169. *[Ras al Qala'a]*

*T. G[eoffrey] Bibby, "The Hundred-Meter Section," *Kuml* (1957) 152-163. *[Ras al Qala'a]*

Ras Shamra (See: Ugarit)

Rayy

Anonymous, "Excavations at Rayy," *UMB* 5 (1934-35) #4, 25-26.

Anonymous, "The Persian Expedition," *UMB* 5 (1934-35) #5, 41-49. *[Rayy]*

E[phraim A.] S[peiser], "Rayy Research 1935...Part I," *UMB* 6 (1935-37) #3, 79-87.

E[phraim A.] S[peiser], "Rayy Research, 1935, Part II," *UMB* 6 (1935-37) #4, 133-136.

Razzaza

*Caesar Voûte, "A Prehistoric Find Near Razzaza (Karbala Liwa). Its Significance for the Morphological and Geological History of the Abu Dibbis Depression and Surrounding Area," *Sumer* 13 (1957) 135-148.

Red Sea

J. G. Malcolmson, "Note on the Saltiness of the Red Sea," *JRAS* (1837) 214-216.

*Lyman Coleman, "The Great Crevasse of the Jordan and of the Red Sea," *BS* 24 (1867) 248-262.

Owen C. Whitehouse, "Requests and Replies," *ET* 2 (1890-91) 23. *[The Location of the Red Sea]*

Edward Hull, "Requests and Replies," *ET* 7 (1895-96) 461. *[The Location of the Red Sea]*

J. S. King, "The Red Sea: Why so Called?" *JRAS* (1898) 617-618.

*Sarah F. Hoyt, "The Name of the Red Sea," *JAOS* 32 (1912) 115-119.

Joseph Offord, "The Red Sea *(Yam Suph)*," *PEFQS* 52 (1920) 176-181.

J. J. Hess, "Suez and Clysma," *JEA* 14 (1928) 277-279. *[Red Sea]*

Red Sea concluded

*Howard H. Scullard, "The Passage of the Red Sea," *ET* 42 (1930-31) 55-61.

John Robert Towers, "The Red Sea," *JNES* 18 (1959) 150-153.

N. H. Snaith, "יַם־סוּף: The Sea of Reeds: The Red Sea," *VT* 15 (1965) 395-398.

Reqaqnah

John Garstang, "Excavations at Reqaqnah in Upper Egypt," *Man* 2 (1902) #50.

Rhages

Anonymous, "Notes and Comments. Joint Archaeological Expedition to Excavate Rhages, Persia," *A&A* 35 (1934) 46.

Rhodes

Anonymous, "Asia Minor:—Rhodes," *RP* 2 (1903) 254-255.

*R. E. Wycherley, "Hippodamus and Rhodes," *HJAH* 13 (1964) 135-139.

Gregory Konstantinopoulos, "Rhodes: New Finds and Old Problems," *Arch* 21 (1968) 115-123. *(Trans. by J. Walter Graham)*

Tell Rifaʿat

M. V. Seton Williams, "Preliminary Report on the Excavations at Tell Rifaʿat," *Iraq* 23 (1961) 68-87.

M. V. Seton-Williams, "The Excavations at Tell Rifa'at*[sic]*, 1964: Second Preliminary Report," *AAAS* 17 (1967) 69-84.

M. V. Seton-Williams, "The Excavations at Tell Rifaʿat, 1964: Second Preliminary Report," *Iraq* 29 (1967) 16-33.

Tell al-Rimah

David Oates, "Excavations at Tell al-Rimah. A Summary Report," *Sumer* 19 (1963) 69-77.

Theresa Howard Carter, "Excavations at Tell al-Rimah, 1964. Preliminary Report," *BASOR* #178 (1965) 40-69.

David Oates, "The Excavations at Tell al-Rimah, 1964," *Iraq* 27 (1965) 62-80.

David Oates, "The Excavations at Tell al-Rimah, 1965," *Iraq* 28 (1966) 122-139.

Theresa Howard Carter, "Tell al-Rimah: The Campaigns of 1965 and 1966," *Arch* 20 (1967) 282-289.

David Oates, "The Excavations at Tell al-Rimah, 1966," *Iraq* 29 (1967) 70-96.

David Oates, "The Excavations at Tell al-Rimah, 1967," *Iraq* 30 (1968) 115-138.

Riotinto

*Immanuel Ben Dor, "Phoenicians in Spain and Excavations at Riotinto, 1966," *AJA* 71 (1967) 183. *[Tarshsish]*

Rome

†Anonymous, "Bankes's History of Rome," *BCQTR, N.S.*, 12 (1819) 131-150. *(Review)*

†Anonymous, "Niebuhr's *History of Rome*," *WR* 11 (1829) 353-388. *(Review)*

†Anonymous, "Niebuhr's *History of Rome*," *ERCJ* 51 (1830) 358-396. *(Review)*

†Anonymous, "Drumann's *Genealogical History of Rome*," *QRL* 56 (1836) 332-367. *(Review)*

†Anonymous, "Rome, Ancient and Modern, and its Environs," *CTPR, 3rd Ser.*, 1 (1845) 562-576. *(Review)*

Rome cont.

†Anonymous, "Merivale's *Rome under the Empire*," *ERCJ* 92 (1850) 57-94. *(Review)*

†Anonymous, "Ancient Rome," *QRL* 99 (1856) 415-451. *(Review)*

Anonymous, "Glimpses of Cæsarean Rome," *DUM* 62 (1863) 275-282.

E. A. F., "The Primæval Archæolgy of Rome," *BQRL* 60 (1874) 127-158. *(Review)*

†Anonymous, "Recent Discoveries in Art and Archæology in Rome," *QRL* 144 (1877) 46-81. *(Review)*

†Anonymous, "Recent Excavations in Rome,"*ERCJ* 149 (1879) 321-354; 170 (1889) 479-512. *(Review)*

Samuel Ball Platner, "Recent Excavations in the Roman Forum," *AJA* 5 (1901) 20.

G. Sergi, "Primitive Rome," *Monist* 14 (1903-04) 161-176. *(Trans. by Ira W. Howerth)*

Rodolfo Lanciani, "Notes from Rome," *RP* 3 (1904) 377-379.

Anonymous, "Discoveries in the Roman Forum," *RP* 5 (1904) 378.

*Arthur Stoddard Cooley, "Archaeological Notes," *AJA* 9 (1905) 68-69. *[Corinth; Athens; Syracuse; Rome]*

Arthur Fairbanks, "Excavations in the Roman Forum during 1904," *AJA* 9 (1905) 74.

Walter Dennison, "The Latest Excavations in the Roman Forum," *RP* 4 (1905) 171-179.

*Anonymous, "Excavations on the Palatine," *RP* 6 (1907) 270.

Anonymous, "Finds at Rome," *RP* 6 (1907) 340.

Thomas Ashby, "The Rediscovery of Rome," *QRL* 209 (1908) 101-122. *(Review)*

J. O. Kinnaman, "Some Puzzles of Roman Archaeology," *AAOJ* 30 (1908) 3-9.

Rome cont.

J. O. Kinnaman, "Prehistoric Rome," *AAOJ* 31 (1909) 30-40.

Anonymous, "Finds Near the Mons Janiculum, Rome," *RP* 8 (1909) 173-175.

J. O. Kinnaman, "Roman Archaeology," *AAOJ* 33 (1911) #2, 30-36, 155-159, 214-219; 34 (1912) 21-27.

Arthur L. Frothingham, "The Real Explanation of the Founding and Early Growth of the City of Rome," *AJA* 16 (1912) 109-110.

Esther Boise Van Deman, "The Neronian Sacra Via," *AJA* 27 (1923) 383-424.

Thomas Ashby, "Archæological and Topographical Research near Rome, 1908-1928," *QRL* 251 (1928) 281-296. *(Review)*

Thomas Ashby, "Archæological and Topographical Research near Rome, 1908-1928. Part II.," *QRL* 252 (1929) 97-109. *(Review)*

A. W. Van Buren, "News Items from Rome," *AJA* 36 (1932) 361-367; 37 (1933) 497-508; 38 (1934) 477-490; 39 (1935) 508-521; 40 (1936) 378-388; 41 (1937) 386-494; 42 (1938) 407-423.

Inez Scott Rybert, "The Esquiline Necropolis in the Fifth Century," *AJA* 41 (1937) 100-106.

Henry T. Rowell, "Rome," *AJA* 50 (1946) 289-290.

*Raymond V. Schoder, "Air Views of Greece and Rome," *AJA* 57 (1953) 110.

A. W. Van Buren, "News Letter from Rome," *AJA* 58 (1954) 323-331; 59 (1955) 303-314; 60 (1956) 389-400; 61 (1957) 375-386; 62 (1958) 415-427; 63 (1959) 383-394; [Erratum, *AJA* 64 (1960) p. 218]; 64 (1960) 359-364; 65 (1961) 377-388; 66 (1962) 393-401; 67 (1963) 397-409; 68 (1964) 371-385; [Errata, *AJA* 69 (1965) p. 198]; 70 (1966) 349-361; 71 (1967) 395-398; 69 (1965) 359-364.

Aline Abaecherli Boyce, "The Foundation and Birthday of Rome *in Legend and History*," *Arch* 7 (1954) 9-14.

Richard Krautheirmer, Wolfgang Frankl, and Gugliemo Gatti, "Excavations at San Lorenzo f.l.m. in Rome, 1957," *AJA* 62 (1958) 379-382.

Rome concluded

Harold Mattingly, "Rome and the Great Social War," *HT* 8 (1958) 275-278.

*Lawrence Richardson, "Cosa and Rome: Comitium and Curia," *Arch* 10 (1957) 49-55.

D. F. Jones, "Rome and her British Clients," *HT* 14 (1964) 350-357.

Einar Gjerstad, "Cultural History of Early Rome. Summary of Archaeological Evidence," *AA* 36 (1965) 1-41.

Frank E. Brown, "New Soundings in the Regia," *AJA* 70 (1966) 184-185. *[Rome]*

Tell el Rub'a (See also: Mendes)

Donald P. Hansen, "Mendes 1965 and 1966. I. *The Excavations at Tell el Rub'a*," *JARCE* 6 (1967) 5-16.

*Christine L. Soghor, "Mendes 1965 and 1966. II. *Inscriptions at Tell el Rub'a*," *JARCE* 6 (1967) 16-32.

Rub' al Khali

*Henry Field, "Carbon-14 Date for a 'Neolithic' Site in the Rub' al Khali," *Man* 60 (1960) #214.

S

Sabinum

*Tenney Frank, "On Rome's conquest of Sabinum, Picenum and Etruria," *Klio* 11 (1911) 367-381.

Sai

J[ean] Vercoutter, "Excavations at Sai 1955-7: A Preliminary Report," *Kush* 6 (1958) 144-169.

Sais

*Percy E. Newberry, "To what Race did the Founders of Sais belong?" *SBAP* 28 (1906) 68-75.

Sakce Gözü

*J. du Plat Taylor, M. V. Seton-Williams, and J. Waechter, "The Excavations at Sakce Gözü," *Iraq* 12 (1950) 53-138.

*J. Waechter, Sabahat Gögüs, and Veronica Seton-Williams, "The Sakce Gözü Cave Site 1949," *TTKB* 15 (1951) 193-201.

Sakje-Geuzi

John Garstang, "Excavations at Sakje-Geuzi, in North Syria: Preliminary Report for 1908," *AAA* 1 (1908) 97-117.

John Garstang, "Second Interim Report on the Excavations at Sakje-Geuzi, in North Syria, 1911," *AAA* 5 (1912-13) 63-72.

John Garstang, W. J. Phythian-Adams, and V. Seton-Williams, "Third Report on the Excavations at Sakje-Geuzi, 1908-1911 I. General Survey," *AAA* 24 (1937) 119-140.

Salamis

Paul W. Wallace, "Psyttaleia and the Triophies of the Battle of Salamis," *AJA* 73 (1969) 293-303.

Salganeus

*Paul W. Wallace, "A Reidentification of the Boiotian City Salganeus and a Suggested Location for the Homeric Nisa," *AJA* 73 (1969) 246.

Ṣalḫana

*Z. Vilnay, "Miscellany," *BIES* 10 (1942-44) #2/3, IV. [(a) Naṣḫana = Ṣalḫana in Syria]

Saliagos

Colin Renfrew and J. D. Evans, "Saliagos: A Neolithic Site in the Cyclades," *Arch* 21 (1968) 262-271.

Ṣaḳḳārah

Walter B. Emery, "Recent Discoveries at Ṣaḳḳārah," *JEA* 24 (1938) 243.

Jasper Y. Brinton, "New Finds at Sakkarah," *Arch* 2 (1949) 142-145.

Salamis

J. W. Blakesley, "On the Position and Tactics of the Contending Fleets in the Battle of Salamis," *TPS* 6 (1852-53) 101-115.

W. Kendrick Pritchett, "Toward a Restudy of the Battle of Salamis," *AJA* 63 (1959) 251-262.

N. G. L. Hammond, "On *Salamis:* Letter to the Editor," *AJA* 64 (1960) 367-368.

Salvador

A. J. Arkell, "A Prehistoric Site at Salvador, Near Tummo, between Hoggar and Tibesti," *Kush* 12 (1964) 291-292.

Sam'al

W. St. Chad Boscawen, "Recent German Oriental Explorations. The Land of Sam'al," *BOR* 5 (1891) 145-152.

Sāmarrā

A. Sachs, "Another Occurrence of the Alleged Ancient City of Sāmarrā," *JAOS* 57 (1937) 419-420.

Samosata

Theresa Goell, "Report of Preliminary Excavation at Samosata," *AJA* 70 (1966) 189.

Samothrace

Karl Lehmann-Hartleben, "Observations in Samothrace," *AJA* 42 (1938) 126.

Karl Lehmann-Hartleben, "Excavations in Samothrace," *AJA* 43 (1939) 133-145.

Karl Lehmann-Hartleben, "Recent Discoveries in Samothrace," *AJA* 44 (1940) 107.

Karl Lehmann-Hartleben, "Preliminary Report on the Second Campaign of Excavation in Samothrace," *AJA* 44 (1940) 328-358.

Karl Lehmann [-Hartleben], "Samothrace—*Seventh Campaign of Excavations, 1952*," *Arch* 6 (1953) 30-35.

Elsbeth B. Dusenbery, "A Samothracian Necropolis," *Arch* 12 (1959) 163-170.

Elsbeth B. Dusenbery, "Excavations in the South Necropolis at Samothrace, 1962," *AJA* 67 (1963) 210.

Phyliss Lehmann, "The Floral Central Akroteria of the Hieron in Samothrace," *AJA* 67 (1963) 214.

Elsbeth B. Dusenbery, "The South Necropolis of Samothrace," *Arch* 17 (1964) 185-192.

James R. McCredie, "Excavations on Samothrace, 1963-1964," *AJA* 69 (1965) 171.

James R. McCredie, "Excavations on Samothrace 1965-1966," *AJA* 71 (1967) 191-192.

Elsbeth B. Dusenbery, "Samothrace: The South Necropolis," *Arch* 20 (1967) 116-122.

Samothrace concluded

James R. McCredie, "Excavations on Samothrace; 1967-1968," *AJA* 73 (1969) 242.

San el-Hager

*E. A. Cerny, "Archaeological Corner. San el-Hager (Tanis), Egypt," *CBQ* 1 (1939) 264-266.

Santorini

Leon Pomerance, "The Final Collapse of Santorini—1400 B.C. or 1200 B.C.?" *AJA* 73 (1969) 244.

Saparda

O. E. Hagen, "The geographical situation of Saparda," *BOR* 3 (1888-89) 31-35.

Saqqâra

J. E. Quibell, "Excavations at Saqqara," *AEE* 2 (1915) 6-8.

*Cecil M. Firth, "Excavations of the Department of Antiquities at the Step Pyramid, Saqqara (1924-1925)," *ASAE* 25 (1925) 149-159.

Cecil M. Firth, "Preliminary Report on the excavations at Saqqara (1925-1926)," *ASAE* 26 (1926) 97-101.

C[ecil] M. Firth, "Excavations of the Service des Antiquités at Saqqara (November 1926-April 1927)," *ASAE* 27 (1927) 105-111.

C[ecil] M. Firth, "Excavations of the Service des Antiquités at Saqqara (October 1927-April 1928)," *ASAE* 28 (1928) 81-88.

C[ecil] M. Firth, "Excavations of the Department of Antiquities at Saqqara (October 1928 to March 1929)," *ASAE* 29 (1929) 64-70.

Saqqâra concluded

C[ecil] M. Firth, "Report on the Excavations of the Department of Antiquities at Saqqara (November, 1929-April, 1930)," *ASAE* 30 (1930) 185-189.

C[ecil] M. Firth, "Excavations of the Department of Antiquities at Saqqara, 1930-1931," *ASAE* 31 (1931) 45-48.

Selim Bey Hassan, "Excavations at Saqqara (1937-1938)," *ASAE* 38 (1938) 503-522.

Zaki Y. Saad, "A preliminary report on the Excavations at Saqqara, 1939-1940," *ASAE* 40 (1940-41) 675-693.

Zaki Y. Saad, "Preliminary report on the Royal Excavations at Saqqara, 1941-1942," *ASAE* 41 (1942) 381-393.

Zaki Y. Saad, "Preliminary report on the excavations of the Department of Antiquities at Saqqara 1942-43," *ASAE* 43 (1943) 449-457.

W. B. Emery, "Preliminary Report on the Excavations at North Saqqâra 1964-1965," *JEA* 51 (1965) 3-8.

W. B. Emery, "Preliminary Report on the Excavations at North Saqqâra 1965-6," *JEA* 52 (1966) 3-8.

W. B. Emery, "Preliminary Report on the Excavations at North Saqqâra 1966-7," *JEA* 53 (1967) 141-145.

W. B. Emery, "Preliminary Report on the Excavations at North Saqqâra 1968," *JEA* 55 (1969) 31-35.

Saraçhane

[R.] Martin Harrison and Nezih Firath, "Excavations of Saraçhane in Istanbul 1965," *TAD* 16 (1967) #1, 81-88.

R. Martin Harrison and Nezih Firath, "Excavations at Saraçhane in Istanbul 1968," *TAD* 18 (1969) #2, 191-198.

Sardinia

*Claude R. Conder, "Notes on Perrot and Chipiez's 'Histoire de l'Art'. Vol. IV.—Sardinia, Judea, and Asia Minor," *PEFQS* 19 (1887) 107-110.

Anonymous, "Sardinian Archæology," *A&A* 6 (1907) 218-219.

*Alan S. Hawkesworth, "Sardinia's Connection with Babylon," *OC* 25 (1911) 447.

Sardis

Howard Crosby Butler, "First Preliminary Report of the American Excavations at Sardes*[sic]* in Asia Minor," *AJA* 14 (1910) 401-413.

Howard Crosby Butler, "Second Preliminary Report of the American Excavations at Sardes*[sic]* in Asia Minor," *AJA* 15 (1911) 445-458.

Howard Crosby Butler, "Third Preliminary Report on the American Excavations at Sardes*[sic]* in Asia Minor," *AJA* 16 (1912) 465-479.

Anonymous, "Excavations at Sardis," *RP* 11 (1912) 104; 12 (1913) 102-103.

Howard Crosby Butler, "Fourth Preliminary Report on the American Excavations at Sardes*[sic]* in Asia Minor," *AJA* 17 (1913) 471-478.

Howard Crosby Butler, "Fifth Preliminary Report on the American Excavations at Sardes*[sic]* in Asia Minor," *AJA* 18 (1914) 425-437.

*Joseph Offord, "Archaeological Notes on Jewish Antiquities. XXXVIII. *Sardis the Site of Sepharad,*" *PEFQS* 49 (1917) 183-184.

*Howard Crosby Butler, "Miletus, Priene and Sardis," *A&A* 9 (1920) 171-186.

Theodore Leslie Shear, "Sixth Preliminary Report on the American Excavations at Sardes*[sic]* in Asia Minor," *AJA* 26 (1922) 389-409.

*George W. Gilmore, "The Archaeological World," *HR* 85 (1923) 393-394. [Excavations at Sardis, p. 394]

Anonymous, "Recent Excavations at Sardis," *AT* 3 (1958-59) #4, 7, 10.

Sardis cont.

George M. A. Hanfmann, "Excavations at Sardis, 1958," *BASOR* #154 (1959) 5-35.

George M. A. Hanfmann and A. Henry Detweiler, "Report on the First Campaign At Sardis, 1958," *TAD* 9 (1959) #1, 14-19.

George M. A. Hanfmann and A. Henry Detweiler, "New Explorations at Sardis," *Arch* 12 (1959) 53-61.

George M. A. Hanfmann, "Excavations at Sardis—1959," *AJA* 64 (1960) 185.

George M. A. Hanfmann, "Excavations at Sardis, 1959," *BASOR* #157 (1960) 8-43.

George M. A. Hanfmann, "Excavations at Sardis—1960," *AJA* 65 (1961) 189-190.

George M. A. Hanfmann and A. Henry Detweiler, "Report on the Excavations at Sardis in 1959," *TAD* 10 (1960) #1, 21-38.

George M. A. Hanfmann and A. Henry Detweiler, "From the Heights of Sardis," *Arch* 14 (1961) 3-11.

George M. A. Hanfmann, "The Third Campaign at Sardis. (1960)," *BASOR* #162 (1961) 8-49.

George M. A. Hanfmann and A. Henry Detweiler, "Report on the Third Campaign at Sardis, 1960," *TAD* 11 (1961) #1, 18-22.

George M. A. Hanfmann, "Excavations at Sardis, 1961," *AJA* 66 (1962) 197.

George M. A. Hanfmann and A. Henry Detweiler, "The Fourth Campaign at Sardis (1961)," *TAD* 11 (1961) #2, 40-45.

George M. A. Hanfmann, "The Fourth Campaign at Sardis (1961)," *BASOR* #166 (1962) 1-57.

Henry A. Detweiller and David Gordon Mitten, "The Sixth Campaign at Sardis 1963," *TAD* 12 (1962-63) #2, 8-23.

Sardis cont.

George M. A. Hanfmann, "Excavations at Sardis, 1962," *AJA* 67 (1963) 212.

George M. A. Hanfmann and A. Henry Detweiler, "Excavations at Sardis in 1962," *TAD* 12 (1962-63) #1, 26-33.

George M. A. Hanfmann, "The Fifth Campaign at Sardis (1962)," *BASOR* #170 (1963) 1-65.

David Gordon Mitten, "Excavations at Sardis, 1963," *AJA* 68 (1964) 197-198.

George M. A. Hanfmann, "The Sixth Campaign at Sardis (1963)," *BASOR* #174 (1964) 3-58.

George M. A. Hanfmann and A. Henry Detweiler, "Excavations at Sardis in 1964," *TAD* 13 (1964) #2, 58-80.

George M. A. Hanfmann, "Excavations at Sardis, 1964," *AJA* 69 (1965) 168.

Noel Robertson, "Lydian Levels beside the Pactolus at Sardis," *AJA* 69 (1965) 174-175.

George M. A. Hanfmann, "The Seventh Campaign at Sardis," *BASOR* #177 (1965) 2-37.

George M. A. Hanfmann, A. Henry Detweiler, and D[avid] G. Mitten, "Excavations at Sardis, 1965," *TAD* 14 (1965) 151-160.

George M. A. Hanfmann, "Excavations at Sardis, 1965," *AJA* 70 (1966) 190-191.

George M. A. Hanfmann and A. Henry Detweiler, "Sardis Through the Ages," *Arch* 19 (1966) 90-98.

David Gordon Mitten, "A New Look at Ancient Sardis," *BA* 29 (1966) 38-68.

Sardis concluded

*George M. A. Hanfmann, "The Eighth Campaign at Sardis (1965)," *BASOR* #182 (1966) 2-8. [Special reports by G. F. Swift Jr., "'Lydian Trench' and the 'House of Bonzes Area'", pp. 8-34; D. G. Mitten, "The Synagogue and Vicinity," pp. 34-45; and Julian Whittlesey, "Application of Stero Photogrammetry in Archaeological Excavations," pp. 46-54]

George M. A. Hanfmann and A. Henry Detweiler, "Excavations At Sardis in 1966," *TAD* 15 (1966) #1, 75-87.

George M. A. Hanfmann, "Excavations at Sardis, 1966," *AJA* 71 (1967) 188-189.

*George M. A. Hanfmann, "The Ninth Campaign at Sardis (1966)," *BASOR* #186 (1967) 17-52. [Special report by G. F. Swift Jr., (continued from No. 186) "'Lydian Trench' Area: the Deep Pit," pp. 31-52]

George M. A. Hanfmann, "The Ninth Campaign at Sardis (1966)," *BASOR* #187 (1967) 9-32. [Special report by L. J. Majewski, "Evidence for the Interior Decoration of the Synagogue, pp. 32-62]

George M. A. Hanfmann, A. Henry Detweiler, and David G. Mitten, "Excavations at Sardis-1967," *TAD* 16 (1967) #2, 75-87.

George M. A. Hanfmann, "Excavations at Sardis, 1967," *AJA* 72 (1968) 165-166.

George M. A. Hanfmann, "The Tenth Campaign at Sardis (1967)," *BASOR* #191 (1968) 2-41. [Special Reports by D. G. Mitten, "Prehistoric Survey of Gygen Lake and Excavations at Ahlatli Tepecik," pp. 7-10; A. Ramage, "City Area; Pactolus North, pp. 10-41]

David Gordon Mitten, "Excavations At Sardis 1968," *TAD* 17 (1968) #1, 111-124.

David Gordon Mitten, "Excavations at Sardis, 1968," *AJA* 73 (1969) 243.

G[eorge] M. A. Hanfmann and D[avid] G. Mittten, "Sardis Campaign of 1968: A Summary," *JNES* 28 (1969) 271-272.

George M. A. Hanfmann, "Excavations at Sardis-1969," *TAD* 18 (1969) #1, 61-75.

Saras Plain

A. J. Mills, "The Archaeological Survey from Gemai to Dal – Report on the 1965-1966 Season," *Kush* 15 (1967-68) 200-210. *[Saris Plain]*

Satrianum

R. Ross Holloway, "Excavations at Satrianum, 1966," *AJA* 71 (1967) 59-62.

R. Ross Holloway, "Excavations at Satrianum, 1967," *AJA* 72 (1968) 119-120.

Sawâma

T. Wittemore, "The Sawâma Cemeteries," *JEA* 1 (1914) 246-247.

Tell es-Sawwan

Faisal El-Wailly and Behnam Abu es-Soof, "Excavations at Tell es-Sawwan. First Preliminary Report (1964)," *Sumer* 21 (1965) 17-32.

Ghanim Wahida, "Excavations of the Third Season at Tell as-Sawwan*[sic]*, 1966," *Sumer* 23 (1967) 167-178.

Behnam Abu al-Soof, "Tell es-Sawwan. Excavations of the Fourth Season (Spring, 1967)," *Sumer* 24 (1968) 3-15.

Khalid Ahmad al-A'dami, "Excavations at Tell es-Sawwan (Second Season)," *Sumer* 24 (1968) 57-94.

Scione

*Benjamin D. Meritt, "Scione, Mende, and Torone," *AJA* 27 (1923) 447-460.

Scythia

Francis W. Newman, "On Scythia and the surrounding countries, according to Herodotus," *TPS* 1 (1842-44) 77-80.

Sedeinga

Michela Schiff Giorgini, "Premierè Campagne de Fouilles a Sedeinga, 1963-1964," *Kush* 13 (1965) 112-128. [English Summary-The First Seasons of Excavations at Sedeinga 1963-1964, pp. 128-130]

*Michela Schiff Giorgini, "Sedeinga, 1964-5," *Kush* 14 (1966) 244-258. [English Summary, pp. 259-261]

*Michela Schiff Giorgini, "Soleb—Sedeinga. Resume Des Travaux De La Mission Hendant Les Trois Compagnes Automne 1965-Printeps 1968," *Kush* 15 (1967-68) 251-265. [English Summary—Soleb-Sedeinga: Summary of work accomplished by the mission during the three campaigns Autumn 1965—Spring 1968, pp. 266-268]

Tell Selenkaḫiye

Maurits Van Loon, "First Results of the 1967 Excavations at Tell Selenkaḥiye," *AAAS* 18 (1968) 21-34.

Seleucia

Leroy Waterman, "Professor Waterman's Work at Seleucia," *BASOR* #35 (1929) 25-27.

Leroy Waterman, "Recent Excavations at Seleucia-on-the-Tigris," *AJA* 37 (1933) 113-114.

W. A. Campbell, "The First Campaign at Seleucia Pieria," *AJA* 42 (1938) 126.

Giorgio Gullini, "First Report of the Results of the First Excavation Campaign at Seleucia and Ctesiphon (1st Octoper[sic]*—17th December 1964)," *Sumer* 20 (1964) 63-65.

*Giorgio Gullini, "First Preliminary Report of Excavations at Selucia and Ctesiphon-Season 1964, Foreword," *Mesop* 1 (1966) 3-6.

*Giorgio Gullini, "Problems of an Excavation in Northern Babylon," *Mesop* 1 (1966) 7-38 *[Area of Seleucia and Ctesiphon]*

Seleucia Pieria

W. A. Campbell, "The First Campaign at Seleucia Pieria," *AJA* 42 (1938) 126.

Selinus

*R. E. Wycherley, "Notes on Olynthus and Selinus," *AJA* 55 (1951) 231-236.

Semna

*Jean Vercoutter, "Semna South Fort and the Records of Nile Levels at Kumma," *Kush* 14 (1966) 125-164.

Sendschirli

*Morris Jastrow Jr., "The Excavations at Sendschirli and some of their Bearings on the Old Testament," *BW* 3 (1894) 406-416

Sepharad

*Joseph Offord, "Archaeological Notes on Jewish Antiquities. XXXVIII. *Sardis the Site of Sepharad,*" *PEFQS* 49 (1917) 183-184.

*Jehuda Rosenthal, "Ashkenaz, Sefarad, and Zarefat," *HJud* 5 (1943) 58-62.

*David Neiman, "Sefarad: The Name of Spain," *JNES* 22 (1963) 128-132.

Serbal

*Philip Schaff, "Disputed Scripture Localities," *PRev* 54 (1878) Part 1, 851-884. [Serbal or Sinai? pp. 861-868]

Serâbît

Kirsopp Lake, "The Serâbît Expedition of 1930: I. Introduction," *HTR* 25 (1932) 95-100.

Serâbît concluded

*A. Barrois, "The Serâbît Expedition of 1930: II. The Mines of Sinai," *HTR* 25 (1932) 101-121.

*Silva New, "The Serâbît Expedition of 1930: III. The Temple of Hator," *HTR* 25 (1932) 122-129.

Serra East

*James Knudstad, "Serra East and Dorginarti. A Preliminary Report on the 1963-64 Excavations of the University of Chicago Oriental Institute Sudan Expedition," *Kush* 14 (1966) 165-186.

Serra Orlando

Richard Stillwell and Erik Sjöqvist, "Excavations at Serra Orlando. Preliminary Report," *AJA* 61 (1957) 151-159.

Erik Sjöqvist, "Excavations at Serra Orlando (Morgantina). Preliminary Report II," *AJA* 62 (1958) 155-162. [Appendix by George A. Stamires, pp. 162-164]

Richard Stillwell, "Excavations at Serra Orlando 1958. Preliminary Report III," *AJA* 63 (1959) 167-173. [Erratum, p. 328]

Erik Sjöqvist, "Excavations at Morgantina (Serra Orlando) 1959: Preliminary Report IV," *AJA* 64 (1960) 125-135.

Richard Stillwell, "Excavations at Morgantina (Serra Orlando) 1960: Preliminary Report V," *AJA* 65 (1961) 277-281.

Erik Sjöqvist, "Excavations at Morgantina (Serra Orlando) 1961: Preliminary Report VI," *AJA* 66 (1962) 135-143.

Richard Stillwell, "Excavations at Morgantina (Serra Orlando) 1962: Preliminary Report VII," *AJA* 67 (1963) 163-171. (Addendum, p. 330)

Erik Sjöqvist, "Excavations at Morgantina (Serra Orlando) 1963: Preliminary Report VIII," *AJA* 68 (1964) 137-147.

Richard Stillwell, "Excavations at Morgantina (Serra Orlando) 1966: Preliminary Report IX," *AJA* 71 (1967) 245-250.

Sérvia

W. A. Heurtley, "Excavations at Sérvia in Western Macedonia," *AJ* 12 (1932) 227-238.

Sesebi

A. M. Blackman, "Preliminary Report on the Excavation at Sesebi, Northern Province, Anglo-Egyptian Sudan, 1936-7," *JEA* 23 (1937) 145-151.

*H. W. Fairman, "Preliminary Report on the Excavations at Sesebi (Sudla) and ʿAmārah West, Anglo-Egyptian Sudan, 1937-8," *JEA* 24 (1938) 151-156.

A. J. Arkell, "The Name of Sesebi," *JEA* 27 (1941) 159.

Setia

Henry H. Armstrong, "Studies at Setia," *AJA* 17 (1913) 92.

Tell Shalfahat

*Walid Yasin, "A Note on Three Samarra-Halaf Sites in the Tikril Area," *Sumer* 24 (1968) 117-119. [1. Tell Shalfahat, p. 117]

Shahrein

*J. E. Taylor, "Notes on Abu Shahrein and Tel el Lahm," *JRAS* (1855) 404-415.

Shahriyar

T. Burton-Brown, "Excavations in Shahriyar, Iran," *Arch* 15 (1962) 27-31.

Shamiram-alti

*L. W. King, "The Prehistoric Cemetery at Shamiram-alti near Van in Armenia," *SBAP* 34 (1912) 198-204.

Shanidar Cave

Ralph S. Solecki, "A Paleolithic Site in the Zagros Mountains of Northern Iraq, Report on a Sounding at Shanidar Cave, Part I," *Sumer* 8 (1952) 127-161.

Ralph S. Solecki, "A Paleolithic Site in the Zagros Mountains of Northern Iraq, Report on a Sounding at Shanidar Cave, Part II," *Sumer* 9 (1953) 60-93.

*Ralph S. Solecki, "The Shanidar Cave Sounding, 1953 Season with Notes Concerning the Discovery of the First Paleolithic Skull in Iraq," *Sumer* 9 (1953) 229-232.

Ralph S. Solecki, "Shanidar Cave, a Paleolithic Site in Northern Iraq," *SIR* (1954) 389-425.

Ralph S. Solecki, "Shanidar Cave, a Palaeolithic Site in Northern Iraq, its Relationship to the Stone Age Sequence of Iraq," *Sumer* 11 (1955) 14-38.

Ralph S. Solecki, "A Postscript to the Shanidar Cave Report, 1955," *Sumer* 11 (1955) 124.

Ralph S. Solecki, "The 1956 Season at Shanidar," *Sumer* 13 (1957) 165-171.

Ralph S. Solecki, "The 1956-1957 Season at Shanidar," *Iraq* 14 (1958) 104-108.

Shaqadud

K.-H. Otto, "Shaqadud: A New Khartoum Neolithic Site outside the Nile Valley," *Kush* 11 (1963) 108-115.

Shaṭṭer Rigāl

*H. E. Winlock, "The Court of King Neb-Ḥepet-Rēʿ Mentu-Ḥotpe at Shaṭṭer Rigāl," *AJSL* 57 (1940) 137-161.

Sheba

*Joseph W. Jenks, "On Ophir and Sheba," *PAOS* (May, 1868) iv.

*Joseph W. Jenks, "On Ophir and Sheba," *JAOS* 9 (1871) liv.

Fritz Hommel, "The Land of Frankincense. The Home of the Wise Men from the East and the Country of the Queen of Sheba," *HR* 55 (1908) 344-349.

Sheikh Abd el Gurneh

*Robert Mond and Walter B. Emery, "Excavations at Sheikh Abd el Gurneh," *AAA* 14 (1927) 13-34.

Tell Sheikh Nareddin

C. C. Edgar, "Report on the demolition of Tell Sheikh Nareddin," *ASAE* 13 (1914) 122-124.

Sheikh Nassir

*Tewfik Boulos, "Report on excavations carried out at Sheikh Nassir and el-Deir, near Abydos," *ASAE* 37 (1937) 243-256.

(Tell) Shemshara

Joergen Laessoe[sic]*, "The Old-Babylonian Archive Discovered at Tell Shemshara," *Sumer* 13 (1957) 216-218.

Harald Ingholt, "The Danish Dokan Expedition," *Sumer* 13 (1957) 214-215. *[Tell Shimshara[sic]]*

J[oergen] Laessoe[sic]*, "The Second Shemshara Archive," *Sumer* 16 (1960) 12-19.

Shengavit

*Ruth Amiran, "Yanik Tepe, Shengavit, and the Khirbet Kerek Ware," *AS* 15 (1965) 165-167.

Tell-esh-Shihab

Anonymous, "Egypt," *RP* 3 (1904) 123-124. *[Tell-esh-Shihab]*

Shinar

*W[illiam] F[oxwell] Albright, "Shinar-Šangār and Its Monarch Amraphel," *AJSL* 40 (1923-24) 125-133.

I. O. Northstein, "In the Land of Shinar," *AugQ* 7 (1928) 42-43.

I. J. Gelb, "Shanhar," *AJSL* 53 (1936-37) 253-255.

Shur

Charles R. Gillett, "Shur and the 'Egyptian Wall'," *PR* 8 (1887) 310-315.

Shushan

William Hayes Ward, "Light on Scriptural Texts from Recent Discoveries. Shushan, the Palace," *HR* 27 (1894) 509-511.

Sicily

†Anonymous, "Smyth—Sicily and its Islands," *QRL* 30 (1823-24) 382-403. *(Review)*

†Anonymous, "Ancient Sicily," *QRL* 175 (1892) 319-347. *(Review)*

J. B. Bury, "Freeman's History of Sicily," *SRL* 19 (1892) 26-54. *(Review)*

J. B. Bury, "Freeman's History of Sicily, Vol. III," *SRL* 20 (1892) 300-321. *(Review)*

Norman E. Henry, "Classic Sicily," *A&A* 3 (1916) 143-147.

*J. Penrose Harland, "Aegean Influence in Sicily in the Bronze Age," *AJA* 33 (1919) 106-107.

*H. D. Westlake, "Athenian Aims in Sicily 427-424 B.C. *A Study in Thucydidean Motivation,*" *HJAH* 9 (1960) 385-402.

Sicily concluded

Piero Nicola Gargallo, "Exploring Off the Coast of Sicily," *Arch* 15 (1962) 193-197. (In collaboration with Lionel Casson)

Siena

Kyle Meredith Phillips Jr., "Excavations in the Province of Siena, 1964," *AJA* 69 (1965) 172-173.

Sigeion

Jerome Sperling, "The Site of Sigeion," *AJA* 40 (1936) 122-123.

Sikyon

*W. J. McMurtry and M. L. Earle, "Papers of the American School of Classical Studies at Athens. Excavations at the Theatre of Sikyon," *AJA, O.S.*, 5 (1889) 286-292. [I. General Report of the Excavations; II. Supplementary Report of the Excavations]

Sinai (Mount and Peninsula) [See also: Suez]

(   ) H., "Lepsius on the Peninsula of Sinai," *BRCM* 4 (1847-48) 23-37.

*(   ) L., "Sacred Geography. Passage of the Red Sea.—Position of Mount Sinai," *BRCM* 5 (1848-49) 38-54.

*R. S. P., "Egypt, Ethiopia, and the Peninsula of Sinai," *JSL, 2nd Ser.*, 6 (1854) 314-330. *(Review)*

*Anonymous, "Sinai and Palestine," *DUM* 48 (1856) 313-329. *(Review)*

*†Anonymous, "Sinai, Palestine, and Mecca," *ERCJ* 104 (1856) 363-399. *(Review)*

*†Anonymous, "Stanley's Sinai and Palestine," *TLJ* 9 (1856-57) 397-411. *(Review)*

W. O., "The Sinai Question," *JSL, 4th Ser.*, 1 (1862) 193-194. *[Mt. Sinai]*

Sinai cont.

Henry Crossley, "The Topography of The Sinaitis," *JSL, 4th Ser.*, 1 (1862) 432-438.

Anonymous, *"The Comparative Geography of Palestine and the Sinaitic Peninsula,"* *LQHR* 28 (1867) 404-452. *(Review)*

Anonymous, "The Peninsula of Sinai," *ThE* 5 (1868) 129-155. *(Article IX. pages misnumbered!)*

*Trelawney Saunders, "On the Desert of Tih," *PEFQS* 1 (1869) 133-136. *[Sinai]*

*E. H. Palmer, "The Desert of Tih and the Country of Moab," *PEFQS* 3 (1871) 3-73. (Index, pp. 77-80) *[Sinai]*

*E. H. Palmer, "The Desert of Tih," *PEFQS* 3 (1871) 73-76. *[Sinai]*

*Philip Schaff, "Disputed Scripture Localities," *PRev* 54 (1878) Part 1, 851-884. [Serbal or Sinai? pp. 861-868]

F. W. Holland, "The Topography of the Sinaitic Peninsula," *JTVI* 14 (1880-81) 2-11. (Discussion, pp. 11-15)

A. H. Sayce, "Where was Mount Sinai?" *IAQR, 2nd Ser.*, 6 (1893) 149-158.

*Claude R. Conder, "Sinai and Syria Before Abraham," *PEFQS* 25 (1893) 167-177.

Edward Hull, "Where is Mount Sinai," *JTVI* 31 (1897-98) 39-47, 50-51, 55. [(Discussion, pp. 48-50) (Communications by W. Arthur, pp. 51-54; R. Collins, 54-55)]

R. Campbell Thompson, "Note on Sinaitic Antiquities," *Man* 5 (1905) #54.

W. M. Flinders Petrie, "The Sinai Expedition, 1904-5," *Man* 5 (1905) #64.

R. Campbell Thompson, "Note on the Antiquities of Sinai," *Man* 5 (1905) #73.

Anonymous, "The Discovery of Sinai," *MQR, 3rd Ser.*, 31 (1905) 386-387.

Anonymous, "Sinaitic Peninsular Excavations," *RP* 4 (1905) 223-224.

Sinai concluded

James Baikie, "Petrie's Researches in Sinai," *ET* 27 (1905-06) 524-528.

P. A. Gordon Clark, "Sinai," *ET* 18 (1906-07) 46.

Edward Hull, "'Researches in Sinai,' by W. M. Flinders Petrie," *JTVI* 39 (1907) 23-40. *(Review)*

E. Oberhummer, "The Sinai Problem," *SIR* (1912) 669-677.

Charles M. Watson, "The Desert of the Wanderings," *PEFQS* 46 (1914) 18-23. *[Sinai]*

C. Leonard Woolley, "The Desert of the Wanderings. Report of the Survey by the Palestine Exploration Fund," *PEFQS* 46 (1914) 58-66. *[Sinai]*

*S. E. Newcombe, "The Survey of Sinai and South Palestine," *PEFQS* 46 (1914) 128-133.

Anonymous, "'The Desert of Wanderings'," *HR* 69 (1915) 455-456.

Anonymous, "The Desert of the Exodus," *MR* 98 (1916) 299-304.

Ditlaf Nielsen, "The Site of the Biblical Mount Sinai," *JPOS* 7 (1927) 187-208.

W. J. Phythian-Adams, "The Mount of God," *PEFQS* 62 (1930) 135-149; 192-209.

*[W. M.] Flinders Petrie, "Recent Discoveries in the Syria and Sinai. Season 1934-35," *AEE* 20 (1935) 15-18.

W[illiam] F[oxwell] Albright, "Exploring in Sinai with the University of California African Expedition," *BASOR* #109 (1948) 5-20.

Anonymous, "Researches in the Sinai Peninsula," *AT* 1 (1956-57) #4, 14.

Y. Aharoni, "Recent Discoveries in the Sinai Peninsula: A Preliminary Note," *A&S* 2 (1957) #2/3, 287-296.

*Henry Wansbrough, "Event and Interpretation. II. Desert Encounter," *ClR* 52 (1967) 929-937. [Sinai, pp. 935-936]

Sinim

*T[errien] de Lacouperie, "The Sinim of Isaiah, not the Chinese," *BOR* 1 (1886-87) 45-48.

*T. K. Cheyene, "The Land of Sinim in Isaiah," *BOR* 1 (1886-87) 182.

*C[laude] R. Conder, "Notes on Bible Geography. IV. *Sinim*," *PEFQS* 37 (1905) 74.

Sinjar

Seaton Lloyd, "Some Ancient Sites in the Sinjar District," *Iraq* 5 (1938) 123-142.

Seaton Lloyd, "Iraq Government Soundings at Sinjar," *Iraq* 7 (1940) 13-21.

Sinope

David M. Robinson, "Ancient Sinope," *PAPA* 37 (1905) xxv-xxvii.

David M. Robinson, "Ancient Sinope. First Part," *AJP* 27 (1906) 125-153.

David M. Robinson, "Ancient Sinope. Second Part," *AJP* 27 (1906) 245-279.

Sippara

*Francis Brown, "סְפַרְוַיִם," *PR* 3 (1882) 169.

Francis Brown, "Sippara," *PR* 3 (1882) 400.

*H. Rassam, "Recent Discoveries of Ancient Babylonian Cities," *SBAP* 5 (1882-83) 83-84. *[Sippara]*

Theo. G. Pinches, "The Antiquities found by Mr. H. Rassam at Abu-Habbah (Sippara)," *SBAT* 8 (1883-84) 164-171.

William Hayes Ward, "Sippara," *AJSL* 2 (1885-86) 79-86.

[Wm. H.] Ward, "On the location of Sippara," *JAOS* 13 (1889) lxxiii-lxxiv.

Sīrāf

David Whitehouse, "Excavations at Sīrāf: First Preliminary Report," *Iran* 6 (1968) 1-22.

David Whitehouse, "Excavations at Sīrāf: Second Interim Report," *Iran* 7 (1969) 39-62.

Sistan

*Ellsworth Huntington, "Climate and History of Eastern Persia and Sistan," *RP* 4 (1905) 205-219.

Sittake

*J. F. MacMichael, "On the Sites of Sittake and Opis, as given in Professor Rawlinson's History of Herodotus. Vol. I. p. 261, Note 5," *JP* 4 (1872) 135-145.

Siva Oasis

Anonymous, "The Siva Oasis," *RP* 4 (1905) 61-62.

Siwa

Ahmed Fakhry, "The Necropolis of 'Gabal el-Môta' at Siwa," *ASAE* 40 (1940-41) 779-799.

Sizma

*David M. Robinson, "A Preliminary Report on the Excavations at Pisidian Antioch and Sizma," *AJA* 28 (1924) 434-444.

*David Moore Robinson, "The University of Michigan Excavations at Pisidian Antioch and Sizma," *AJA* 29 (1925) 91.

*David M. Robinson, "The Discovery of a Prehistoric Site at Sizma," *AJA* 31 (1927) 26-50.

Smyrna

George Horton, "Smyrna: 'The Infidel City'," *A&A* 11 (1921) 145-154.

G. E. Bean, "A. The Defences of Hellenistic Smyrna," *AAI* 1 (1955) 43-52.

Soleb

Michela Schiff Giorgini, "Soleb Campagna 1959-60," *Kush* 9 (1961) 182-196. [English Summary p. 197]

Michela Schiff Giorgini, "Soleb Campagna 1960-1," *Kush* 10 (1962) 152-167. [English Summary, pp. 168-169]

Michela Schiff Giorgini, "Soleb—Campagnes 1961-63," *Kush* 12 (1964) 87-94. [English Summary, pp. 94-95]

*Michela Schiff Giorgini, "Soleb—Sedeinga. Resume Des Travaux De La Mission Hendant Les Trois Campagnes Automne 1965-Printemps 1968," *Kush* 15 (1967-68) 251-265. [English Summary—Soleb-Sedeinga: Summary of work accomplished by the mission during the three campaigns Autumn 1965—Spring 1968, pp. 266-268]

Solygeia

Nicholas M. Verdelis, "A Sanctuary at Solygeia," *Arch* 15 (1962) 184-192. *(Trans. by Oscar Broneer)*

Sotria

P. Dikaios, "Trial Excavations at Sotria, Site Teppés on Behalf of the University Museum Cyprus Expedition," *UMB* 13 (1947-48) #3, 16-23. [Foreword by John Franklin Daniels]

Spain

Paul Baur, "Pre-Roman Antiquities of Spain," *AJA* 11 (1907) 51, 182-193.

*David Neiman, "Sefarad: The Name of Spain," *JNES* 22 (1963) 128-132.

Spain concluded

*Daniel E. Woods, "Excavations in Roman Carteia (Andalucia, Spain) and Talayotic Majorca (Baleares, Spain), 1965," *AJA* 70 (1966) 197-198.

*Immanuel Ben Dor, "Phoenicians in Spain and Excavations at Riotinto, 1966," *AJA* 71 (1967) 183. *[Tarshsish]*

Sparta

Nicholas E. Crosby, "The Topography of Sparta," *AJA, O.S.*, 8 (1893) 335-373.

Charles Waldstein and Z. M. Paton, "Papers of the American School of Classical Studies at Athens. Report on Excavations at Sparta in 1893," *AJA, O.S.*, 8 (1893) 410-426.

*N. E. Crosby, "Notes. The topography of Sparta and the building of Epimenides," *AJA, O.S.*, 9 (1894) 212-213.

*Arthur Stoddard Cooley, "Archaeological Notes," *AJA* 11 (1907) 52. [2. The British Excavations Near Sparta]

Anonymous, "Work at Sparta," *RP* 8 (1909) 124.

Spartolus

*Benjamin D. Meritt, "Inscriptional and Topographical Evidence for the Site of Spartolus and the Southern Boundary of Bottice," *AJA* 27 (1923) 334-339.

Spina

Sabine Gova, "Spina Rediviva," *Arch* 13 (1960) 208-214.

Srr

*Henry G. Fischer, "Varia Aegyptiaca. 10. The Land of *Srr*," *JARCE* 2 (1963) 50.

Stamata

*Charles Waldstein, "Papers of the American School of Classical Studies at Athens. Report on Excavations near Stamata in Attika," *AJA. O.S.*, 5 (1889) 423-425. [II. Report on Excavations and Sculptures]

Subat-Samas

*Hildegard Lewy, "Subat-Samas and Tuttul," *Or, N.S.*, 27 (1958) 1-18.

Suberde

Jacques Bordaz, "Suberde, An Early Neolithic Site in Southwestern Turkey: Some Preliminary Results," *AJA* 70 (1966) 183-184.

Jacques Bordaz, "The Suberde excavations, Southwestern Turkey: An interim Report," *TAD* 17 (1968) #2, 43-71.

Succoth

*C. R. Gillett, "Pithom—Heroöpolis—Succoth," *AR* 8 (1887) 82-92.

*Edouard Naville, "Hebraeo-Aegyptiaca. III," *SBAP* 37 (1904) 208-214. *[Succoth]*

Sudan

*Anonymous, "Isaiah's Knowledge of the Sudan," *CFL, 3rd Ser.*, 11 (1909) 200.

*Anonymous, "Isaiah's Knowledge of the Sudan," *RP* 8 (1909) 218-219.

*A. J. Arkell, "Varia Sudanica," *JEA* 36 (1950) 24-40.

*Rosalind Moss, "The Ancient Name of Serra (Sudan)," *JEA* 36 (1950) 41-42.

‡Dows Dunham, "The Harvard-Boston Archaeological Expedition in the Sudan. A Progress Report on Publication," *Kush* 3 (1955) 70-74. *[Bibliography]*

Suez

William Andrews, "Suez and its Desert," *PEFQS* 11 (1879) 48-51.

Sultantepe

Seton Lloyd and Nuri Gokçe, "Sultantepe. *Anglo-Turkish Joint Excavations, 1952,*" *AS* 3 (1953) 27-51.

Seton Lloyd, "Sultantepe," *AS* 4 (1954) 101-110.

Sumer

*W. J. Perry, "Sumer and Egypt," *Man* 29 (1929) #18.

*T. Fish, "Religion and Community at Sumer," *JMUEOS* #23 (1942) 13-15.

Francis I. Anderson, "The Early Sumerian City-State in Recent Soviet Historiography," *Abr-N* 1 (1959-60) 56-61.

Susa

W. St. Chad Boscawen, "Recent Explorations at Susa. M. de Morgan's Expedition," *BOR* 9 (1901) 25-30.

*W. St. Chad Boscawen, "Explorations at Susa," *IAQR, 3rd Ser.,* 12 (1901) 330-356.

Anonymous, "Discoveries at Susa," *MR* 84 (1902) 140-143.

J. de Morgan, "J. De Morgan's Work in Persia," *RP* 1 (1902) 231-245. *[Susa]*

*V. Scheil, "Excavations made by the French in Susa and Babylonia, 1902-1903," *BW* 24 (1904) 146-152.

Anonymous, "Excavations in Susa," *MQR, 3rd Ser.,* 32 (1906) 384-385.

Anonymous, "Work at Susa," *RP* 7 (1908) 261.

Anonymous, "Excavations at Susa," *HR* 83 (1922) 394.

Susa concluded

*J. M. Unvala, "Ancient Sites in Susiana," *RAAO* 25 (1928) 83-93. [Two monuments of the Partho-Roman period recently discovered at Susa, pp. 88-90]

*Fritz Neugass, "Notes and Comments. Recent Excavations in Tello, Susa and Syria," *A&A* 32 (1931) 137-138. [Susa, p. 137]

R. de Mecquenem, "Excavations at Susa (Persia)," *Antiq* 5 (1931) 330-344.

*Louis Le Breton, "The Early Periods at Susa, Mesopotamian Relations," *Iraq* 19 (1957) 79-124.

Robert H. Dryson Jr., "Early Work on the Acropolis at Susa," *Exped* 10 (1967-68) #4, 21-34.

Susiana

*B. H. C., "Recent Researches in Chaldaea and Susiana," *JSL, 3rd Ser.*, 5 (1857) 372-386. *(Review)*

J[ochaim(?)] D. Ménant, "The French Expedition to Susiana," *AJA, O.S.*, 3 (1887) 87-93.

*J. M. Unvala, "Ancient Sites in Susiana," *RAAO* 25 (1928) 83-93. [Aiwan-i-Kerkhah; Masjid-i-Suleiman; Qala-i-Madresse; The Ātashgāh of Isfahan; Two monuments of the Partho-Roman period recently discovered at Susa, pp. 88-90]

Sybaris

Donald Freeman Brown, "In Search of Sybaris," *AJA* 58 (1954) 144.

Donald Freeman Brown, "In Search of Sybaris: 1962," *Exped* 5 (1962-63) #2, 40-47.

Donald Freeman Brown, "Sybaris 1962," *AJA* 67 (1963) 209.

Froelich Rainey, "The Search for Sybaris," *Exped* 11 (1968-69) #2, 10-13.

Froelich Rainey, "The Location of Archaic Greek Sybaris," *AJA* 73 (1969) 261-273.

Syracuse

*Arthur Stoddard Cooley, "Archaeological Notes," *AJA* 9 (1905) 68-69. *[Corinth; Athens; Syracuse; Rome]*

*Hugh Hencken, "Syracuse, Etruria and the North: Some Comparisons," *AJA* 62 (1958) 259-272.

Sybaris

*Elizabeth K. Ralph, "The Electronic Detective and the Case of the Missing City," *Exped* 7 (1964-65) #2, 4-8. *[Sybaris]*

Syene

*G[eorge] Rawlinson, "Biblical Topography. VIII.—Further Egyptian Sites—Memphis, Thebes, Migdol, Syene," *MI* 4 (1886) 453-463.

Syria

*J. W. C., "Late Important Discoveries in Syria and the Holy Land," *DUM* 42 (1853) 364-382.

*Anonymous, "Recent Researches in Syria and Palestine," *ThE* 3 (1886) 46-48.

*Anonymous, "Recent Travels and Explorations in Syria," *BQRL* 58 (1873) 144-167. *(Review)*

*Greville J. Chester, "Notes on Ruad (Aradus) and Adjacent Places in Northern Syria," *PEFQS* 7 (1875) 218-227.

D. Temple, "Glimpses at the Syria of the Present [Adapted from the *Juedische Literaturblatt of Magdeburg*]," *ONTS* 2 (1882-83) 208-210.

†H[enry] G[eorge] Tomkins, "The Ancient Geography of Northern Syria," *SBAP* 5 (1882-83) 58-62.

*†Anonymous, "Heth and Moab," *ERCJ* 159 (1884) 457-485. *(Review) [Syria]*

Syria cont.

*Henry George Tomkins, "A Paper on the Topography of Northern Syria, with special reference to the Karnak Lists of Thothmes III," *SBAP* 7 (1884-85) 160-163.

*Henry George Tomkins, "A paper On the Topography of Northern Syria, with special reference to the Karnak Lists of Thothmes III," *SBAT* 9 (1886-93) 227-254.

*Henry George Tomkins, "The Karnak Lists of Thothmes III, relating to Northern and Southern Syria," *SBAT* 9 (1886-93) 255-280. (Index to Places in the Lists, pp. 481-484)

Henry George Tomkins, "Notes on the Geography of Northern Syria and some Neighbouring Lands, viewed from the Assyrian side," *BOR* 3 (1888-89) 2-6, 41-46.

*C[laude] R. Conder, "Sinai and Syria Before Abraham," *PEFQS* 25 (1893) 167-177.

*A. G. Wright, "Syria and Arabia," *PEFQS* 27 (1895) 67-82.

Howard Crosby Butler, "Report of an American Archaeological Expedition in Syria, 1899-1900," *AJA* 4 (1900) 415-440.

Anonymous, "Discoveries in Syria," *MR* 83 (1901) 640-641.

*Walter Melville Patton, "Ancient Egypt and Syria," *BS* 60 (1903) 92-108.

*Samuel Ives Curtiss, "Researches in Syria and Palestine Conducted in the Summer of 1903," *BW* 23 (1904) 91-103.

George C. Doolittle, "Neglected Archaeological Ruins in Coelesyria," *RP* 3 (1904) 227-233. *[Syria]*

*Henry Proctor, "The Bible and Syrian Archæology," *AAOJ* 27 (1905) 197-199.

Howard Crosby Butler and Enno Littmann, "Preliminary Report of the Princeton University Expedition to Syria," *AJA* 9 (1905) 389-410.

Anonymous, "The Princeton Expedition to Syria," *MR* 88 (1906) 484-487.

Syria cont.

Howard Crosby Butler, "The Princeton University Archæological Expedition to Syria," *PAPS* 46 (1907) 182-186.

A. H. Sayce, "Notes on an Unexplored District of Northern Syria," *SBAP* 33 (1911) 171-179.

*Anonymous, "Archaeological Notes," *HR* 65 (1913) 464-465. [Exploration in Syria, p. 464]

*J. Dyneley Prince, "The Babylonian Equations for Syria," *AJSL* 30 (1913-14) 212-218.

*C. Leonard Woolley, "Asia Minor, Syria and the Aegean," *AAA* 9 (1922) 41-56.

R. A. MacLean, "The Syrian Desert: from Amman to Ramadie," *AJA* 28 (1924) 76.

*Louis C. West, "Commerical Syria under the Roman Empire," *TAPA* 55 (1924) 159-189.

Anonymous, "Syria," *Antiq* 1 (1927) 223-226.

F. A. Schaeffer, "The French Excavations in Syria," *Antiq* 4 (1930) 460-466.

*Fritz Neugass, "Notes and Comments. Recent Excavations in Tello, Susa and Syria," *A&A* 32 (1931) 137-138.

*Millar Burrows, "Palestinian and Syrian Archaeology in 1931," *AJA* 36 (1932) 64-73. [III. Syria, pp. 71-73]

*N. D. Mironov, "Aryan Vestiges in the Near East of the Second Millenary B.C.," *AO* 11 (1932-33) 140-217. [III. Palestine and Syria (Amarna Letters), pp. 171-185]

T. P. O'Brien, "A Cholcolithic Site in North Syria," *Man* 33 (1933) #182.

*W[illiam] F[oxwell] Albright, "Excavations During 1933 in Palestine, Transjordan and Syria," *AJA* 38 (1934) 191-199.

W[illiam] F[oxwell] Albright, "Archaeological News from Syria," *BASOR* #54 (1934) 24-27.

Syria cont.

*S. Yeivin, "A New Egyptian Source for the History of Palestine and Syria," *JPOS* 14 (1934) 194-239.

*[W. M.] Flinders Petrie, "Recent Discoveries in Syria and Sinai. Season 1934-35," *AEE* 20 (1935) 15-18.

*W[illiam] F[oxwell] Albright, "A Summary of Archaeological Research during 1934 in Palestine, Transjordan and Syria," *AJA* 39 (1935) 137-148. [Syria, pp. 144-148]

*W[illiam] F[oxwell] Albright, "Archaeological Exploration and Excavation in Palestine and Syria, 1935," *AJA* 40 (1936) 154-167.

[William Foxwell] Albright, "Syria in the 3rd and 4th Millennia," *Antiq* 10 (1936) 88-89.

C. W. McEwan, "The Syrian Expedition of the Oriential Institute of the University of Chciago," *AJA* 41 (1937) 8-16.

*W[illiam] F[oxwell] Albright and Nelson Glueck, "Archaeological Exploration and Excavation in Palestine, Transjordan, and Syria during 1936," *AJA* 41 (1937) 146-153.

*Nelson Glueck, "Archaeological Exploration and Excavation in Palestine, Transjordan, and Syria during 1937," *AJA* 42 (1938) 165-176.

*Nelson Glueck, "Nabataean Syria and Nabataean Transjordan," *JPOS* 18 (1938) 1-6.

*Nelson Glueck, "Archaeological Exploration and Excavation in Palestine, Transjordan and Syria during 1938," *AJA* 43 (1939) 146-157.

James L. Kelso, "Biblical Archaeology Coming Out of Syria," *BS* 96 (1939) 38-41.

*Nelson Glueck, "Nabataean Syria," *BASOR* #85 (1942) 3-8.

*Leonard Woolley, "North Syria as a Cultural Link in the Ancient World," *Man* 43 (1943) #19.

*M. E. L. Mallowan, "Mesopotamia and Syria. Unity and Diversity of the Earliest Civilizations," *Sumer* 5 (1949) 1-7.

Syria concluded

Glanville Downey, "The Occupation of Syria by the Romans," *TAPA* 82 (1951) 149-163.

*Ruth Amiran, "Palestine, Syria and Cyprus in the MB I Period," *EI* 5 (1958) 84*.

Anonymous, "Syria: Its Little-Known Wonders," *IAQR* 58 (1962) 200-203.

Willem J. van Liere and Henri de Contenson, "A Note on Five Early Neolithic Sites in Inland Syria," *AAAS* 13 (1963) 175-209.

*W[illiam] F[oxwell] Albright, "Remarks on the Chronology of Early Bronze IV-Middle Bronze IIA in Phoenicia and Syria-Palestine," *BASOR* #184 (1966) 26-35.

*George Buccellati, "Cities and nations of ancient Syria, an essay on political institutions with special reference to the Israelite kingdoms," *SSR* 26 (1967) 1-264.

*‡Jinan Mudarres, "Syria and Lebanon in Antiquity: Bibliography for 1968," *Bery* 18 (1969) 143-145.

T

Tabara

Sinclair Hood, "Excavations at Tabara, 1948-49," *AS* 1 (1951) 113-147.

Tabo

Charles Maystre, "Excavations at Tabo, Argo Island, 1965-1968: Preliminary Report," *Kush* 15 (1967-68) 193-199.

Tahpanhes

Francis Brown, "Notes on Biblical Archæology. Tahpanhes," *AJA, O.S.,* 2 (1886) 430-431.

Lysander Dickerman, "Mr. Petrie's Discoveries at the Biblical Tahpanhes," *ONTS* 10 (1890) 279-281.

Talayotic Majorca

*Daniel E. Woods, "Excavations in Roman Carteia (Andalucia, Spain) and Talayotic Majorca (Baleares, Spain), 1965," *AJA* 70 (1966) 197-198.

Tanis (See also: San el-Hager)

*F. C. Whitehouse, "On the thesis, Zoan is Tanis magna, a suburb of Memphis, and not San el-Hagar or Tanis parva on the Delta," *JAOS* 11 (1885) ccxv-ccxviii.

*J. A. Paine, "On the 'thesis' of Mr. Whitehouse, affirming Cairo to be the Biblical Zoan and Tanis magna," *JAOS* 13 (1889) xiii-xvii.

*Alan H. Gardiner, "Tanis and Pi Ra'messe: A Retraction," *JEA* 19 (1933) 122-128.

*E. A. Cerny, "Archaeological Corner. San el-Hager (Tanis), Egypt," *CBQ* 1 (1939) 264-266.

Tanta

Hakim [effendi] Abou-Seif, "Report on the inspectorate of Tanta from September 1923 to January 1925," *ASAE* 24 (1924) 146-150.

Taprobane

*Alex. Mackenzie Cameron, "The Identity of Ophir and Taprobane, and their Site indicated," *SBAT* 2 (1873) 267-288.

Taramptos

*Benjamin D. Meritt, "Towns of Asia Minor," *AJP* 58 (1937) 385-391. *[Taramptos]*

Tarkhan

W. M. Flinders Petrie, "A Cemetery of the Earliest Dynasties," *Man* 12 (1912) #73. *[Tarkhan]*

Tarkhan concluded

W. M. Flinders Petrie, "Tarkhan," *RP* 13 (1914) 3-25.

Tar Kshaife

Ralph S. Solecki, "Tar Kshaife. A Possible Prehistoric Station near Ukhaidher, Iraq," *Sumer* 10 (1954) 62-64.

Tarrha

Thomas S. Buechner, "Excavations at Tarrha (Crete)," *AJA* 64 (1960) 183.

Tarshish

P. le Page Renouf, "Where was Tarshish?" *SBAP* 16 (1893-94) 104-108, 138-141, 307.

*William F. Ainsworth, "Tarshish—Phoenicia or Tarsus?" *SBAP* 16 (1893-94) 300-306. (Remarks by P. le P. Renouf, p. 307)

W. W. Covey-Crump, "The Situation of Tarshish," *JTS* 17 (1915-16) 280-290.

A. H. Sayce, "Recent Biblical Archaeology. Tarshish," *ET* 13 (1901-02) 179-180.

*Immanuel Ben Dor, "Phoenicians in Spain and Excavations at Riotinto, 1966," *AJA* 71 (1967) 183. *[Tarshish]*

Tarsus

*William F. Ainsworth, "Tarshish—Phoenicia or Tarsus?" *SBAP* 16 (1893-94) 300-306. (Remarks by P. le P. Renouf, p. 307)

J. P. Arendzen, "Tarsus," *IER, 5th Ser.,* 26 (1925) 337-349.

Tawilan

S. H. Horn, "The Excavations at Tawilan, Nr. Petra," *ADAJ* 12&13 (1967-68) 53-55.

Telke Tepe

Silva Lake, "A Prehistoric Mound—Telke Tepe," *JBL* 60 (1941) xi.

Tell Taya

J. E. Reade, "Tell Taya (1967): Summary Report," *Iraq* 30 (1968) 234-264.

Telloh

*Anonymous, "The Head of Gudea and Other Finds at Telloh," *RP* 4 (1905) 127-128.

*Fritz Neugass, "Notes and Comments. Recent Excavations in Tello, Susa and Syria," *A&A* 32 (1931) 137-138.

Thorkild Jacobsen, "A Survey of the Girsu (Telloh) Region," *Sumer* 25 (1969) 103-109.

Telul eth-Thalathat

Namio Egami, "The Preliminary Report of the Excavations at Telul Ath-Thalathat*[sic]*," *Sumer* 13 (1957) 5-11.

Namio Egami, Toshihiko Sono, and Kiyoharu Horiuchi, "Brief Report of the Third Season's Excavations at Tell II of Telul eth-Thalathat and Some Observations," *Sumer* 22 (1966) 1-16.

Têmâ

*Raymond P. Dougherty, "Ancient Teimâ and Babylonia," *JAOS* 41 (1921) 458-459.

Raymond P. Dougherty, "A Babylonian City in Arabia," *AJA* 34 (1930) 296-312. *[Têmâ]*

Raymond P. Dougherty, "Têmâ's Place in the Egypto-Babylonian World of the Sixth Century B.C.," *Miz* 1 (1933) 140-143.

Tepe Gawra

George A. Barton, "Dr. Speiser's Excavation of Teppe Gawra," *BASOR* #29 (1928) 12-15.

*E[phraim] A. Speiser, "Traces of the oldest cultures of Babylon and Assyria," *AfO* 5 (1928-29) 162-164.

Anonymous, "Tepe Gawra, a New Site," *UMB* 2 (1930-31) 141-142.

E[phraim] A. Speiser, "The Excavation of Tepe Gawra: Letter from Dr. Speiser to the President of the Dropsie College and the Directors of the American School in Baghdad and the University Museum (November 1, 1931)," *BASOR* #44 (1931) 5-8.

E[phraim] A. Speiser, "Letter of February 28 from Dr. Speiser to the President of Dropsie College and the Director of the American School at Baghdad," *BASOR* #42 (1931) 10-12. *[Tepe Gawra]*

E[phraim] A. Speiser, "Tepe Gawra," *BASOR* #43 (1931) 19-21.

*Anonymous, "Expedition to Tell Billa and Tepe Gawra," *UMB* 3 (1931-32) 59-64, 66.

*Anonymous, "Developments at Tell Billa and Tepe Gawra," *UMB* 3 (1931-32) 94-95.

*Anonymous, "Excavations at Tell Billa and Tepe Gawra," *UMB* 3 (1931-32) 126-127, 130.

*E[phraim] A. Speiser, "The Bearing of the Excavations at Tell Billa and at Tepe Gawra upon the Ethnic Problems of Ancient Mesopotamia," *AJA* 36 (1932) 29-35.

E[phraim] A. Speiser, "The Joint Excavation at Tepe Gawra," *AJA* 36 (1932) 564-568.

*E[phraim] A. Speiser, "Reports from Professor Speiser on the Tell Billah and Tepe Gawra Excavations," *BASOR* #46 (1932) 1-9.

E[phraim] A. Speiser, "The Joint Excavation at Tepe Gawra," *BASOR* #47 (1932) 17-23.

*Charles Bache, "From Mr. Bache's First Report on the Joint Excavations at Tepe Gawra and Tell Billah, 1932-3," *BASOR* #49 (1933) 8-14.

Tepe Gawra cont.

Anonymous, "Tepe Gawra Excavations," *UMB* 5 (1934-35) #5, 34-36.

Charles Bache, "A Report from Mr. Bache on the Tepe Gawra Expedition," *BASOR* #57 (1935) 12-18.

Charles Bache, "Tepe Gawra 1934-1935," *AJA* 39 (1935) 185-188.

E[phraim] A. Speiser, "The Season's Work at Tepe Gawra," *BASOR* #58 (1935) 4-5.

Charles Bache, "The Joint Assyrian Expedition: Letters from Mr. Bache," *BASOR* #58 (1935) 5-9.

J[ohn Story] J[enks], "The Great Mound," *UMB* 5 (1934-35) #6, 63-68, 70. *[Tepe Gawra]*

C[halres] B[ache], "Gawra XII," *UMB* 6 (1935-37) #3, 93-97.

E[phraim] A. Speiser, "An International Business Center at*[sic]* 3000 B.C.," *AJA* 40 (1936) 125. *[Tepe Gawra]*

M. E. L. Mallowan, "Tepe Gawra," *Antiq* 10 (1936) 441-447.

Charles Bache, "Report on the Joint Excavation of Tepe Gawra in Assyria," *BASOR* #61 (1936) 5-61.

Charles Bache, "The Joint Assyrian Expedition," *BASOR* #62 (1936) 6-9. *[Tepe Gawra]*

E[phraim] A. Speiser, "On Some Recent Finds at Tepe Gawra," *BASOR* #62 (1936) 10-14.

E[phraim] A. Speiser, "First Report on the Current Assyrian Campaign," *BASOR* #64 (1936) 4-9. *[Tepe Gawra]*

E[phraim] A. Speiser, "Progress of the Joint Assyrian Expedition," *BASOR* #65 (1937) 2-8. *[Tepe Gawra]*

E[phraim] A. Speiser, "Three Reports on the Joint Assyrian Expedition," *BASOR* #66 (1937) 2-19. *[Tepe Gawra]*

*E[phraim] A. Speiser, "New Discoveries at Tepe Gawra and Khafaje," *AJA* 41 (1937) 190-193.

Tepe Gawra concluded

*E[phraim] A. Speiser, "Progress on the Joint Expedition to Mesopotamia," *BASOR* #70 (1938) 3-10. [Tepe Gawra, pp. 4-7]

*Arthur J. Tobler, "Progress on the Joint Expedition to Mesopotamia," *BASOR* #71 (1938) 18-23. *[Tepe Gawra]*

E[phraim] A. Speiser, "Closing the gap at Tepe Gawra," *SIR* (1939) 437-445.

E. Douglas Van Buren, "A Lesson in Early History: Tepe Gawra," *Or., N.S.*, 20 (1951) 443-452.

Tepe Guran

Jørgen Meldgaard, Peder Mortensen, and Henrik Thrane, "Excavations at Tepe Guran, Luristan. Preliminary Report of the Danish Archaeological Expedition to Iran 1963," *AA* 34 (1963) 97-133.

Tepe Hissar

E[rich] F. Schmidt, "Tepe Hissar: Excavations of 1931. The Joint Expedition to Persia of the University Museum and the Pennsylvania Museum of Art," *MJ* 23 (1932) 323-483.

Erich F. Schmidt, "The Joint Expedition to Persia," *AJA* 37 (1933) 303-304. *[Tepe Hissar]*

D. H. Gordon, "The Chronology of the Third Cultural Period at Tepe Hissar," *Iraq* 13 (1951) 40-61.

Tepe Nūsh-i Jāh

David Stronach, "Excavations at Tepe Nūsh-i Jāh, 1967," *Iran* 7 (1969) 1-20.

Thāj

H. R. P. Dickson and V. P. Dickson, "Thaj and Other Sites," *Iraq* 10 (1948) 1-8.

Thāj concluded

James T. Mandaville, "Thāj: A Pre-Islamic Site in Northeastern Arabia," *BASOR* #172 (1963) 9-20.

Thasos

Jean Pouilloux, "Thasos: *Cultural Crossroads,*" *Arch* 8 (1955) 198-204.

Thebes (Egypt)

*†Anonymous, "Egypt and Thebes," *QRL* 53 (1835) 103-142. *(Review)*

Edw. Hincks, "The Assyrian sacking of Thebes," *ZÄS* 4 (1866) 1-3, 20.

*G[eorge] Rawlinson, "Biblical Topography. VIII.—Further Egyptian Sites—Memphis, Thebes, Migdol, Syene," *MI* 4 (1886) 453-463.

†Anonymous, "The Plain of Thebes," *ERCJ* 186 (1897) 454-482. *(Review)*

Robert [M.] Mond, "Report of Work done in the Gebel esh-sheikh Abd-el-Kurneh at Thebes," *ASAE* 5 (1904) 97-104.

Robert M. Mond, "Report on Work in the Necropolis of Thebes during the Winter of 1903-1904," *ASAE* 6 (1905) 65-96.

Percy E. Newberry, "Topographical notes on Western Thebes collected in 1830, by Joseph Bonomi," *ASAE* 7 (1906) 78-86.

E. Mackay, "Report of the excavations and other work carried out in the necropolis of Thebes for the Department of Antiquities by Robert Mond, Esq., of Combe Bank, Sevenoaks, Kent, England, during the year beginning March 9th, 1913," *ASAE* 14 (1914) 88-96.

*Howard Carter, "A Tomb prepared for Queen Hatshepsuit and other Recent Discoveries at Thebes," *JEA* 4 (1916) 107-118.

*Warren R. Dawson, "The Necropolis of Ancient Thebes. A Rescue from Oblivion," *IAQR* 17 (1921) 181-184, 339-342.

*M. A. Murray, "The Derivation of the Name Thebes," *AEE* 9 (1924) 55.

Thebes (Egypt) concluded

J. H. Cole, "Notes on the recent survey of the Theban Necropolis," *ASAE* 24 (1924) 151-156.

R. Engelbach, "Addendum to survey report of the maps of the Theban Necropolis," *ASAE* 24 (1924) 157-158.

Twefik Boulos, "Valley of the Kings. Thebes," *ASAE* 46 (1947) 263-264.

*Labib Habachi, "Clearance of the area to the east of Luxor Temple and discovery of some objects," *ASAE* 51 (1951) 447-468. *[Thebes]*

Charles F. Nims, "Places about Thebes," *JNES* 14 (1955) 110-123.

Lanny Bell, "The Work of the University Museum at Thebes," *Exped* 10 (1967-68) #2, 38-47.

Thebes (Greece)

Anonymous, "Excavations at Thebes, Greece," *RP* 6 (1907) 218.

*Sarantis Symeonoglou, "Mycenaean Pottery and other Finds from Thebes," *AJA* 73 (1969) 245-246.

*James Wiseman, "Epaminondas and the Theban Invasions," *Klio* 51 (1969) 177-199.

Thera

Spyridon Marinatos, "Archaeological Report from Thera," *AJA* 72 (1968) 168.

Thermopylai

W. Kendrick Pritchett, "New Light on the Thermopylai," *AJA* 62 (1958) 203-213.

Thermos

Georgios Soteriades, "The Greek Excavations at Thermos," *RP* 1 (1902) 173-181. *(Trans. by Arthur Stoddard Cooley)*

Thessaly

Anonymous, "Work of A. J. B. Wace in Thessaly," *RP* 8 (1909) 266.

Thîs

A. H. Sayce, "On the Site of Thîs," *SBAP* 7 (1884-85) 171-178.

Thisbe

*F. J. Tarbell and J. C. Rolfe, "Discoveries at Thisbe in 1889," *AJA, O.S.,* 6 (1890) 112-120. [I. Report on Excavations, pp. 112-113]

Thomu

*A. H. Sayce, "Notes on Assyrian and Egyptian History. An Aramaic Ostracon," *SBAP* 30 (1908) 13-19. *[Part V, Thomu, p. 18]*

Thrace

Anonymous, "Mounds in Thrace," *RP* 6 (1907) 159.

V. Gordon Childe, "Some Affinities of Chalcolithic Culture in Thrace," *Man* 23 (1923) #2.

Sönmez Kantman, "Trakya ve Marmara kiyi Bölgesi Paleolitik Yerleşme Yerleri Araştirma Plânlamasi," *AAI* 3 (1969) 37-43. [English Summary, pp. 41-42] *[Thrace]*

Thurii

Oliver C. Colburn, "A Habitation Area of Thurii," *Exped* 9 (1966-67) #3, 30-38.

Tiber River

*Leicester B. Holland and Louise Adams Holland, "The Tiber in Primitive Commerce," *AJA* 54 (1950) 261-262.

Tigisis

*Martin L. Rouse, "Procopius's African Monument of Joshua's Conquest of Canaan: *Narrative of a visit to the Site,*" *JTVI* 34 (1902) 234-250. (Discussion, pp. 251-251) *[Tigisis]*

Tigris River

*†Q. P., "Etymology of Tigris," *MMBR* 13 (1802) 204.

*†Anonymous, "The Expedition for the Survey of the Rivers Euphrates and Tigris," *WR* 53 (1850) 332-348.

*Francis Brown, "Euphrates and Tigris," *PR* 3 (1882) 399-400.

*Evelyn Howell, "River Control in Mesopotamia," *QRL* 237 (1922) 68-84. *[Tigris]*

Desert of Tih

*Trelawney Saunders, "On the Desert of Tih," *PEFQS* 1 (1869) 133-136.*[Sinai]*

*E. H. Palmer, "The Desert of Tih and the Country of Moab," *PEFQS* 3 (1871) 3-73. (Index, pp. 77-80) *[Sinai]*

*E. H. Palmer, "The Desert of Tih," *PEFQS* 3 (1871) 73-76. *[Sinai]*

Til-Barsib

M. E. L. Mallowan, "The Syrian City of Til-Barsib," *Antiq* 11 (1937) 328-339.

Tilki Tepe

Edward Bowen Reilly, "Test Excavations at Tilki Tepe (1937)," *TAD* 4 (1940) 156-165.

Tilmum (Tilwum)

*A. H. Sayce, "The Archaeological Analysis of the Book of Genesis. The Dilmun of the Cuneiform Inscriptions," *ET* 18 (1906-07) 234. *[Tilmum or Tilwum]*

Tell Timai

Edward L. Ochsenschlager, "Mendes 1965 and 1966. III. *The Excavations at Tell Timai*," *JARCE* 6 (1967) 32-51.

Tirqan

*Sidney Smith, "Assyriological Notes," *JRAS* (1928) 849-875. [Three Cities called Tirqan, pp. 868-875]

Tiryns

Scott B. Rathbun, "Progress of Archaeological Research," *CR* 47 (1886) 179-212. *[Tiryns] (Review)*

†Anonymous, "Schliemann's Tiryns," *QRL* 162 (1886) 108-132. *(Review)*

*Wilhelm Dörpfeld, "Letter from Greece," *AJA, O.S.,* 5 (1889) 331-336. *[Tiryns]*

Anonymous, "Older City at Tiryns," *RP* 6 (1907) 270.

R. V. D. M[agoffin], "Current Notes and News. New Discoveries in Tiryns," *A&A* 3 (1916) 237-238.

Tirynthia Semata

Franz J. Tritsch, "Tirynthia Semata," *KZFE* 7 (1968) 124-137.

Tol-e-Bakun

E[phraim A.] S[peiser], "Tol-e-Bakun: Prehistoric Mound Near Persepolis," *UMB* 7 (1937-39) #3, 27-28.

Tolfa-Allumiere

Mario A. Del Chiaro, "An Archaeological-Topographical Study of the Tolfa-Allumiere District: Preliminary Report," *AJA* 66 (1962) 49-55.

Tolmeita (Ptolemais)

*Carl H. Kraeling, "Excavations at Tolmeita (Ptolemais) in Libya, 1956," *AJA* 61 (1957) 184.

Topakli

Luigi Polacco, "Topakli Campaign of excavation 1968," *TAD* 17 (1968) #2, 165-175.

Toprak Kale

R. D. Barnett, "The Excavations of the British Museum at Toprak Kale, near Van," *Iraq* 12 (1950) 1-43.

R. D. Barnett, "The Excavations at Toprak Kale, Near Van—Addenda," *Iraq* 16 (1954) 3-22.

Torone

*Benjamin D. Meritt, "Scione, Mende, and Torone," *AJA* 27 (1923) 447-460.

Torre Mordillo

G. Roger Edwards, "Torre Mordillo: 1967," *Exped* 11 (1968-69) #2, 30-35.

Toukh el-Qaramous

C. C. Edgar, "Report on an Excavation at Toukh el-Qaramous," *ASAE* 7 (1906) 205-212.

Toumba of Vardino

W. A. Heurtley, R. W. Hutchinson, and W. B. C. Buchanan, "Report on an Excavation at Toumba of Vardino, Macedonia," *AAA* 12 (1925) 15-36.

Tripoli

Alfred Emerson, "Letter from Tripoli," *AJA, O.S.,* 3 (1887) 93-94.

E. C. B. MacLaurin, "A Possible Phoenician Site Near Tripoli," *PEQ* 101 (1969) 40-41.

Tripolitania

Guido Calza, "Sabratha and Leptis Magna: The Glories of Roman Tripolitania," *A&A* 20 (1925) 211-221.

Troad

*Joseph Thacher Clarke, "Gargava, Lamponia and Pionia: Towns of Troad," *AJA, O.S.,* 4 (1888) 291-319.

Jerome W. Sperling, "Topographical Researches in the Troad," *AJA* 39 (1935) 116.

Lake Trogitis

W. M. Ramsay, "Res Antolicae," *Klio* 22 (1928-29) 369-383. [The Elimination of Lake Trogitis (Seidi-Sheher), pp. 369-375; II. Oroanda: Ager Oroandicus: Tractus Oroandicus. A. The Oroandeis in 189 ante Christum; B. Oura; C. Ager Oroandicus (Orindicus?) and the Campaign of Servillius Isauricus]

W. M. Calder, "Lake Trogitis," *Klio* 23 (1929-30) 88-91.

W. M. Ramsay, "Trogitis or Soghal Göl (Marsh-Lake), also called Seidi-Sheher-Göl, Kara-Viran-Göl," *Klio* 23 (1929-30) 98-99.

Troy

†Anonymous, "Mr. Bryant's Observations on the Plain of Troy," *BCQTR* 9 (1797) 535-547, 591-603. *(Review)*

†Anonymous, "Bryant's Dissertation on the War of Troy," *BCQTR* 9 (1797) 604-605. *(Review)*

†Anonymous, "Morritt and Francklin's Remarks on Troy," *BCQTR* 16 (1800) 418-424. *(Review)*

†Anonymous, "Gell's Topography of Troy," *BCQTR* 25 (1805) 349-361. *(Review)*

Anonymous, "The Topography of Troy, with Drawings and Descriptions. By William Gell Esq.," *ERCJ* 6 (1805) 257-283. *(Review)*

†Anonymous, "Acland's Plains of Troy," *QRL* 66 (1840) 355-374. *(Review)*

*T. B. Browne, "Troy and Homer," *ContR* 12 (1869) 481-499.

J. M. Van Benschoten, "Troy and Dr. Schliemann's Discoveries," *PAPA* 6 (1874) 28-29. *[Bound with Transactions, but paged separately]*

Frederick Vinton, "The Disentombment of Troy," *PQPR* 3 (1874) 349-354.

*Augustus C. Merriam, "Troy and Cyprus," *PAPA* 7 (1875) 19-21. *[Bound with Transactions, but paged separately]*

F. A. Paley, "Homeric Troy: Its Site and Remains," *ACQR* 1 (1876) 539-559.

*Anonymous, "Homer Illustrated by Recent Discovery," *CQR* 7 (1878-79) 392-421.

†Anonymous, "Schliemann's *Ilios: The Site of Homer's Troy*," *QRL* 152 (1881) 205-239. *(Review)*

†Anonymous, "The First and Last War of Troy," *QRL* 157 (1884) 169-186. *(Review)*

Carus Sterne, "The Northern Origin of the Story of Troy. Attested by the Pitcher of Tragliatella," *OC* 32 (1918) 449-466, 522-546.

*(Miss) Ida C. Thallon, "Some Balkan and Danubian Connections of Troy," *AJA* 23 (1919) 67-68.

Troy cont.

Paul Haupt, "Philological and Archeological Studies," *AJP* 45 (1924) 238-259. [7. The Hittite Name of Troy, pp. 252-255]

W. M. Ramsay, "Homer and the Troad," *QRL* 247 (1926) 266-284. *(Review)*

Winfred Lamb, "The Site of Troy," *Antiq* 6 (1932) 71-81.

Carl W. Blegen, "Excavations at Troy 1932," *AJA* 36 (1932) 431-451.

Anonymous, "Notes and Comments. Where Was Troy?" *A&A* 34 (1933) 103.

Anonymous, "Notes and Comments. 'Where Was Troy?'," *A&A* 34 (1933) 219.

Charles Vellay, "Where Was Troy?" *A&A* 34 (1933) 313-318. *(Trans. by Arthur Stanley Riggs)*

Carl W. Blegen, "Excavations at Troy 1933," *AJA* 38 (1934) 223-248.

Carl W. Blegen, "Excavations at Troy, 1934," *AJA* 39 (1935) 6-34.

Carl W. Blegen, "Excavations at Troy, 1935," *AJA* 39 (1935) 550-587.

W. F. J. Knight, "Myth and Legend at Troy," *Folk* 46 (1935) 98-121.

Carl W. Blegen, "Excavations at Troy, 1936," *AJA* 41 (1937) 17-51.

Carl W. Blegen, "Excavations at Troy, 1937," *AJA* 41 (1937) 553-597.

John L. Caskey, "New Material from Troy VIIb," *AJA* 42 (1938) 121.

Carl W. Blegen, "Excavations at Troy, 1938," *AJA* 43 (1939) 204-228.

Jerome Sperling, "The Identification of the Site of Troy," *AJA* 43 (1939) 300.

*Carl W. Blegen, "The Foreign Relations of Troy in the Bronze Age," *AJA* 46 (1942) 121.

John L. Caskey, "The Middle Bronze Age at Troy," *AJA* 50 (1946) 401-402.

*Homer L. Thomas, "Troy, Macedonia, and the North," *AJA* 63 (1959) 191.

Troy concluded

*James Mellaart, "Notes on the Architectural Remains of Troy I and II," *AS* 9 (1959) 131-162.

Carl Nylander, "The Fall of Troy," *Antiq* 37 (1963) 6-11.

*George F. Bass, "Troy and Ur: Gold Links Between Two Ancient Capitals," *Exped* 8 (1965-66) #4, 26-39.

*George F. Bass, "A New Tie between Troy IIg and the Royal Cemetery at Ur," *AJA* 71 (1967) 183.

Tubal

Morris Jastrow Jr., "Mešek and Tabal[sic]*," *AJSL* 13 (1896-97) 217.

Tuttul

*Hildegard Lewy, "Subat-Samas and Tuttul," *Or, N.S.,* 27 (1958) 1-18.

Tuna

Tewfik effendi Boulos, "Report on Some Excavations at Tuna," *ASAE* 10 (1909) 285-286.

Tunis

*†Anonymous, "Carthage and Tunis," *ERCJ* 155 (1882) 121-155. *(Review)*

Tunisia

Arthur Stoddard Cooley, "A Roman City in Tunisia," *A&A* 5 (1917) 21-31.

Tura

Ali El-Khouli, "A Preliminary Report on the Excavations at Tura, 1963-64," *ASAE* 60 (1968) 73-76.

Tureng Tepe

Jean Deshayes, "New Evidence for the Indo-Europeans from Tureng Tepe, Iran," *Arch* 22 (1969) 10-17.

Turgut

Yusuf Boysal, "A Report on the 1969[sic]* Turgut Excavations," *A(A)* 12 (1968) 81-93.

Turkey

Ellsworth Huntington, "The Prehistoric Mounds of Eastern Turkey," *RP* 1 (1902) 163-171.

Thomas Whittemore, "Archaeology During the Republic in Turkey," *AJA* 47 (1943) 164-170.

Şevket Aziz Kansu, "Stone Age Cultures in Turkey," *AJA* 51 (1947) 227-232.

Afet İnan, "Contributions to Turkish history through the research activities of the archaeological sections of the Turkish Historical Society, between 1943-1948 X.," *TTKB* 13 (1949) 479-495. *(Trans. by Ahmet E. Uysal)*

*Anonymous, "Summary of Archaeological Research in Turkey, 1949-1950," *AS* 1 (1951) 9-20. [Karatepe, by U. Bahadır Alkım, pp. 9-10; Kültepe, by Tahsin Özgüç, pp. 10-11; Gordion, by Rodney Young, pp. 11-12; The Hüyük (tell) pp. 12-14; Labranda, by A. Persson, pp. 14-15; Side (Eski Antalya), p. 15; Old Smyrna, by Ekrem Akurgal and John Cook, p. 16; Claros, by Louis Robert, pp. 17-18; Other Activities of the French Institute; Classical and Post-Classical Cilicia; Explorations of Ancient Roads passing Karatepe, by Alkim U. Bahadir, pp. 19-20, (Note by W. M. Calder, p. 20)]

Anonymous, "Summary of Archaeological Work in Turkey During 1951," *AS* 2 (1952) 11-24. [Harran, 1. Aşaği Yarimca, 2. Sultantepe; Kültepe, by Nimet Özgüç; Side, by A. M. Mansel; Claros, by L. Robert; Yazilikaya in Phrygia, by A. Gabriel; Explorations in Lycia; Xanthos in Lycia, by P. Demargne; Karatepe, by U. Bahadır Alkım; Gordion, by Rodney Young and G. R. Edwards; Old Smyrna (Bayrakli); Labranda]

Turkey cont.

*Samuel Noah Kramer, "A 'Fulbright' in Turkey," *UMB* 17 (1952-53) #2, 5-56. [Background and Purpose, pp. 5-8]

Anonymous, "Summary of Archaeological Work in Turkey, 1952," *AS* 3 (1953) 9-13. [I. Boğazköy, by K. Bittel; Side, by Arif Müfid Mansel; Phrygian Tombs at Myrlaca, Near Bursa; Explorations in Lycia; The Palace of the Emperors at Istanbul; Karatepe, by U. Bahadır Alkım]

Anonymous, "Summary of Archaeological Work in Turkey in 1953," *AS* 4 (1954) 13-20. [Alanya; Arsameia Nymphaios, by F. K. Dörner; Claros, by L. Robert; Gordion, by Rodney Young; Istanbul (Hagia Sophia and the Kahriye Cami) by Paul A. Underwood; Karatepe, by Halet Çambel; Kültepe, by Tahsin Özgüç; Side and Perge, by A. M. Mansel; Yazilikaya, by A. Gabriel]

James Mellaart, "Preliminary Report on a Survey of Pre-Classical Remains in Southern Turkey," *AS* 4 (1954) 175-240.

Anonymous, "Summary of Archaeological Work in Turkey in 1954," *AS* 5 (1955) 23. [Arsameia on the Nymphaios, by F. K. Dörner; Nemrud Dagh, by Theresa Goell; Boğazköy, by K. Bittel; Claros, by Louis Robert; Karatepe, Halet Çambel; Kültepe-Kanesh, by Tahsin Özgüç; Fraktin, by Tahsin Özgüç; Phokaia, by Ekrem Akurgal; Propontis, by Ekrem Akurgal; Side, by A. M. Mansel; Sinope, by Ekrem Akurga; Xanthos, by A. Gabriel]

Anonymous, "Summary of Archaeological Work in Turkey in 1955," *AS* 6 (1956) 17-26. [Gordion, by Rodney Young; Claros, by Louis Robert; Kültepe, by Tahsin Özgüç]

Anonymous, "Summary of Archaeological Work in Turkey in 1956," *AS* 7 (1957) 15-25. [Gordion, by Rodney Young; Kültepe, by Tahsin Özgüç; Boğazköy, by K. Bittel; Side and Perge, 1955-6, by Arif Müfit Mansel; Miletus, 1955, by C. Weickert; Explorations in Caria, by G. E. Bean]

Rodney Young, K. Bittel, Tahsin Özgüç, Franz Miltner, M. Louis Robert, Carl Weickert, Arif Müfit Mansel, and H. T. Bossert, "Summary of Archaeological Research in Turkey in 1957," *AS* 8 (1958) 17-33. [Gordion; Boğazköy; Kültepe; Horoztepe; Ephesus; Claros; Miletus; Misis; Mersin; Explorations in Lycia and Pisidia]

Turkey cont.

Muzaffer [Süleyman] Şenyürek, and Enver Bostancı, "Preliminary historic Researches in the Hatay Province," *TTKB* 22 (1958) 157-166. *[Turkey]*

*Muzaffer [Süleyman] Şenyürek, and Enver Bostancı, "The Palaeolithic Cultures of the Hatay Province," *TTKB* 22 (1958) 191-210. *[Turkey]*

G. Roger Edwards, K. Bittel, Franz Miltner, Louis Robert, George M. A. Hanfmann, A. Henry Detweiler, Tahsin Özgüç, Sedat Alp, and Nezih Firath, "Summary of Archaeological Research in Turkey in 1958," *AS* 9 (1959) 15-33. [Gordion; Boğazköy; Ephesus; Claros; Sardis; Kültepe; Karahöyük; Istanbul and Izmit; Archaeological Survey of the Konya Plain]

Rodney Young, Thomas Beran, Louis Robert, G. M. A. Hanfmann, A. H. Detweiler, and Tahsin Özgüç, "Summary of Archaeological Research in Turkey in 1959," *AS* 10 (1960) 17-29. [Gordion; Boğazköy; Claros; Sardis; Kültepe; Altintepe; Four Early Christian Monasteries in Central Lycia; The Troad and Western Anatolia]

R. M. Harrison, "Summary of Research in Turkey as Fellow of the British Institute of Archaeology at Ankara, 1959-60," *TAD* 10 (1960) #2, 25.

*Thomas Beran, Tahsin Özgüç, Hâmit Z. Koşay; G. M. A. Hanfmann, A. H. Detweiler, J. M. Cook, and Miss Joan du Plat Taylor, "Summary of Archaeological Research in Turkey in 1960," *AS* 11 (1961)15-27. [Boğazköy; Kültepe and Altintepe; Pulur; Sardis; Pazarlik; Other Classical Sites in Anatolia; Underwater Expedition off Cape Gelidonya]

Rodney Young, Thomas Beran, and G. M. A. Hanfmann, "Summary of Archaeological Research in Turkey in 1961," *AS* 12 (1962) 17-26. [Gordion; Boğazköy; Sardis]

*G. Roger Edwards, P. Neve, Tahsin Özgüç, E. Boehringer, R. Naumann, G. M. A. Hanfmann, U. Bahadır Alkım, and Nimet Özgüç, "Summary of Archaeological Research in Turkey in 1962," *AS* 13 (1963) 19-28. [Gordion; Boğazköy; Kültepe-Kaniš; Altintepe; Pergamon; Didyma; Sardis; Underwater Excavations at Yassi Ada; Muskebi-Dirmil; Tilmen Hüyük; Acemhöyük]

Turkey cont.

*Tahsin Özgüc, Nimet Özgüc, Emil Bilgiç, U. Bahadir Alkim, Kenan T. Erim, R. Naumann, George Bass, J. Birmingham, D. C. Biernoff, and D. H. French, "Recent Archaeological Research in Turkey," *AS* 14 (1964) 21-37. [Altintepe; Kültepe; Acemhöyük; Van and its Enviorons; Tilmen Hüyük; Aphrodisias in Caria; Ilica; Miletus; Underwater Excavations at Yassi Ada; Surface Finds from Various Sites; Prehistoric Settlement in Muğla Vilayet]

U. Bahadır Alkım, "The Road from Sam'al to Asitawandawa: *Contributions to the Historical Geography of the Amanus Region*," *AAI* 2 (1965) 1-45.

Handan Alkim, "Explorations and Excavations in Turkey, 1963," *JEOL* #18 (1964) 345-382.

U. Bahadır Alkım, "Archaeological Activities in Turkey (1962)," *Or, N.S.*, 33 (1964) 500-512.

*P. Neve, Tahsin Özgüç, Nimet Özgüç, Baki Ögün, U. Bahadır Alkım, Jacques Bordaz, Winfried Orthmann, George Bass, Ian A. Todd, and D. H. French, "Recent Archaeological Research in Turkey," *AS* 15 (1965) 23-39. [Boğazköy, 1964; Excavations at Kültepe-Kaniş; Altintepe, 1964; The Acemhöyük Excavations, 1964; Excavations at Adilcavaz, 1964; Exploration and Excavations in the District of Islahiye; Suberde Excavations, 1964; Excavations in Ilica in 1964; Underwater Excavations at Yassi Ada; Surface Finds from Various Sites]

*P. Neve, Tahsin Özgüç, Nimet Özgüç, Emin Bilgiç, U. Bahadır Alkım, Jacques Bordaz, R. Naumann, R. M. Harrison, Machteld Mellink, Kenan T. Erim, F. K. Dörner, G. M. A. Hanfmann, George F. Bass, Ian A. Todd, and D. H. French, "Recent Archaeological Research in Turkey," *AS* 16 (1966) 25-53. [Boğazköy; Kültepe-Kaniş; Altintepe; Acemhöyük; Adilcevaz, 1965; Gedikli (Karahüyük); Suberde; Didyma; Myrelaion (Istanbul); Saraçhane (Istanbul); Karataş-Semayük; Aphrodisias, 1964 and 1965; Arsameia on the Nymphaios, 1963-5; Sardis; Underwater Survey; Surface Finds from Various Sites; Central Anatolia; Further Discoveries in Thrace; Anatolian Pottery in the Aegean Area by Ian A. Todd]

Handan Alkim, "Explorations and Excavations in Turkey, 1964," *Anat* 1 (1967) 1-43.

Turkey cont.

*H. Hauptmann, H. Z. Koşay, Tahsin Özgüç, Nimet Özgüç, G. M. A. Hanfmann, G. Kleiner, F., Eichler, R. Naumann, H. Weber, U. Bahadır Alkım, Oktay Aslanapa, Machteld Mellink, and D. H. French, "Recent Archaeological Research in Turkey," *AS* 17 (1967) 25-36. [Boğazköy; Alaca Höyük; Kültepe-Kanish; Altintepe; Acemhöyük; Sardis; Miletus, 1966; Ephesus, 1966; Myrelaion (Istanbul), 1966; Myus; Temple of Apollo Smintheus; Chryse; The Troad; Gedikli (Karhüyük); Iznik, 1963-66; Karataş-Semayük, 1966; Anatolian Pottery in the Aegean Area]

Handan Alkim, "Explorations and Excavations in Turkey, 1965 and 1966," *Anat* 2 (1968) 1-76.

Machteld Mellink, U. Bahadır Alkım, H. Z. Koşay; K. Bittel; P. Meriggi, Baki Öğün, Afif Erzen, F. K. Dörner, G. M. A. Hanfmann, Kenan T. Erim, H[enri] Metzger; Doro Levi, Iris Cornelia Love, [F.] Eichler, Arif Müfid Mansel, and Nezih Firath, "Recent Archaeological Research in Turkey," *AS* 18 (1968) 21-43. [Karataş-Semayük, 1967; İslâhiye Region: I. Gedikla; II. Kirişkal Hüyük; Alaca Hüyük, 1967; Boğazköy, 1967; Topakli and Aslantepe; Kef Kalesi (Adilcevaz),1967; Çavuştepe, 1967; Sardis, 1967; Aphrodisias, 1967; Letoon, Xanthos, Iasos, 1967; Preliminary Excavations at Knidos in Caria; Ephesus, 1967; Perge, 1967; Sondages at Kaunos; Koşay; Erzen; Finds in Izmit and its Neighbourhood; Archaeological Researches in the Uşak Region in 1966 and 1967]

Muvaffak Uyanik, "Prehistoric Research in South-East Turkey," *TTKB* 32 (1968) 94-95.

U. Bahadır Alkım, "The Amanus Region in Turkey: New Light on the Historical Geography and Archaeology," *Arch* 22 (1969) 280-289.

*İrem Acaroğlu, "The Keban Project; Salvage Archaeology in Turkey," *Arch* 22 (1969) 319-320.

Hâmit [Z.] Koşay, "Pulur in the Keban Region," *Arch* 22 (1969) 320-321.

Hâmit Z. Koşay, "Alaca Höyük: Campaign of 1968," *Arch* 22 (1969) 322.

Turkey concluded

*Machteld Mellink, Hâmit Zübeyir Koşay, U. Bahadır Alkım, Dott.saa Alba Palmieri, P. Neve, A. Erzen, Raci Temizer, M. Olivier Pelon, Burhan Tezcan, Yusuf Boysal, G. M. A. Hanfmann, D. G. Mitten, Fr. K. Dörner, Kenan T. Erim, Arif Müfid Mansel, Iris Cornelia Love, F. Eichler, Henri Metzger, Leonard C. Smith, G. Kleiner, Nezih Firath, Doğan Kuban, and George F. Bass, "Recent Archaeological Research in Turkey," *AS* 19 (1969) 5-26. [Karataş-Semayük, 1968; Pulur (Sakyol), 1968; Islâhiye Region; Arsalantepe (Malatya), 1968; Alach Hüyük; Boğazköy, 1968; Çavuştepe, Van; Eskiyapar; Porsuk; Ulukişla; Göllüdağ; Necropolis at Çömlekçi Köy near Bodrum; Sardis, 1968; Arsamelia on the Nymphaios, 1968; Aphrodisias, 1968; Kutluca (Bithynia), 1968; Knidos, 1968; Ephesus, 1968; Didyma; Letoon, Xanthos, 1968; The Troad; Eski Anamur (Anemurium), 1968; Miletus, 1968; Perge (Pamphylia), 1968; Region of İzmit, 1968; Kalenderhane Camisi; Selçikler (Sebaste), 1968; Underwater Expedition; Istanbul (Saraçhane), 1968; Saqqara (Egypt)]

Handan Alkim, "Explorations and Excavations in Turkey, 1967 and 1968," *Anat* 3 (1969-70) 1-91.

Tuscany

Kyle Meridith Phillips Jr., "Bryn Mawr College Excavations in Tuscany, 1966," *AJA* 71 (1967) 133-139.

Kyle Meridith Phillips Jr., "Bryn Mawr College Excavations in Tuscany, 1967," *AJA* 72 (1968) 121-124. [Erratum, p. 300]

Kyle Meridith Phillips Jr., "Bryn Mawr College Excavations in Tuscany, 1968," *AJA* 73 (1969) 333-339.

Tusculum

Clara S. Streeter, "Tusculum, and the Villa of Cicero," *A&A* 11 (1921) 163-168.

Tyndaris

*R. Ross Holloway, "Tyndaris: Last Colony of the Sicilian Greeks," *Arch* 13 (1960) 246-250.

U

'Ubaid

*Seton Lloyd, "Ur-Al, 'Ubaid, 'Uqair and Eridu: An Interpretation of Some Evidence from the Flood-Pit," *Iraq* 22 (1960) 23-31.

Ugarit (Ras Shamra)

*Fritz Neugass, "Notes and Comments. Recent Excavations in Tello, Susa and Syria," *A&A* 32 (1931) 137-138. [Ras-Shamra, p. 138]

René Dussaud, "Ras Shamra," *AAA* 21 (1934) 93-98.

*T. H. Gaster, "Ras Shamra and Egypt," *AEE* 19 (1934) 33-37.

*Zellig S. Harris, "Ras Shamra: Canaanite civilization and language," *SIR* (1937) 479-502.

T. H. Gaster, "Ras Shamra," *Antiq* 13 (1939) 304-319.

C. F. A. Schaeffer, "Ras Shamra-Ugarit," *Antiq* 13 (1939) 356-359.

J. Philip Hyatt, "Canaanite Ugarit—Modern Ras Shamra," *BA* 2 (1939) 1-2.

*E. A. Cerny, "Archaeological Corner," *CBQ* 1 (1939) 166-168. [Ras Shamra, p. 168]

*H. H. Rowley, "Ras Shamra and the Habiru Question," *PEQ* 72 (1940) 90-94.

*J. W. Jack, "Recent Biblical Archaeology," *ET* 52 (1940-41) 454-458. [Shipping at Ugarit (Ras Shamra), pp. 456-457]

*Frederic G. Kenyon, "Ras Shamra and Mari: Recent Archaeolgical Discoveries Affecting the Bible," *JTVI* 73 (1941) 81-92, 96. [(Discussion, p. 92) (Communications by H. S. Curr, pp. 92-94; P. J. Wiseman, pp. 94-95; Norman S. Denham, pp. 95-96)]

C. F. A. Schaeffer, "Excavations at Ras Shamra in North Syria," *Man* 42 (1942) #47.

*H. L. Ginsberg, "Ugaritic Studies and the Bible," *BA* 8 (1945) 41-58.

Ugarit concluded

*William Foxwell Albright, "The Old Testament and Canaanite Language and Literature," *CBQ* 7 (1945) 5-31. [II. The Discovery and Excavation of Ras Shamra, pp. 7-9]

John Gray, "The Excavation of Ras Shamrā, Past and Present," *ET* 64 (1952-53) 205-208, 227-229.

John Gray, "Some Archaeological Sites and the Old Testament. Ugarit: A Canannite Metropolis of the Bronze Age," *ET* 66 (1954-55) 326-330.

*Lester J. Kuyper, "Israel and Her Neighbors," *RefR* 10 (1956-57) #3, 11-20. [Ras Shamra or Ugarit, pp. 11-16]

Wayne Weissenbuehler, "Ras Shamra (Ugarit)," *Amb* 10 (1960-61) #5, 3-15.

*Henri de Contenson, "New Correlations Between Ras Shamra and al-ʿAmuq," *BASOR* #172 (1963) 35-40.

*A[nson] F. Rainey, "A Canaanite at Ugarit," *IEJ* 13 (1963) 43-45.

*Henry de Contenson, "A Further Note on the Chronology of Basal Ras Shamra," *BASOR* #175 (1964) 47-48.

*A[nson] F. Rainey, "Ugarit and the Canaanites Again," *IEJ* 14 (1964) 101.

Michael C. Astour, "New Evidence on the Last Days of Ugarit," *AJA* 69 (1965) 253-258.

A[nson] F. Rainey, "The Kingdom of Ugarit," *BA* 28 (1965) 102-125.

M[ax] E. L. Mallowan, "Ugarit," *Antiq* 40 (1966) 29-32.

Tell ʿUmar (ʿUmayr) [See also: Choche, Ctesiphon and Seleucia]

Antonio Invernizzi, "The Excavations at Tell ʿUmayr," *Mesop* 1 (1966) 39-62; 2 (1967) 9-32.

Antonio Invernizzi, "The Trial Trench in CVI, 14/24," *Mesop* 2 (1967) 33-40. *[Tell ʿUmayr]*

*Maria Maddalena Negro Ponzi, "The Excavations at Choche Area 1," *Mesop* 2 (1967) 41-47. *[Tell ʿUmayr]*

Tell 'Umar ('Umayr) concluded

Antonio Invernizzi, "The Excavations at Tell 'Umayr," *Mesop* 3&4 (1968-69) 11-28.

Antonio Invernizzi, "Excavations in Squares CVI 69/70/79/80 (The Archives Building)," *Mesop* 3&4 (1968-69) 29-38.

Giorgio Gullini, "Trial Trench on the Canal," *Mesop* 3&4 (1968-69) 39-42.

Germana Graziosi, "Excavations in Squares CLXXI, 54/55/56/64/65/66 (Porticoed Street)," *Mesop* 3&4 (1968-69) 43-52.

Mariamaddalena Negro Ponzi, "Excavations in Squares X 6/ XXX 96 ('Agora')," *Mesop* 3&4 (1968-69) 53-56.

Umm el-Biyara

*William H. Morton, "Umm el-Biyara," *BA* 19 (1956) 26-36. [Description; The Pottery; The Buildings; The Cisterns; The Petroglyphs]

Umm Rus

*Julian Reade, "El-Mutabbaq and Umm Rus," *Sumer* 20 (1964) 83-89.

Upî

Samuel I. Feigin, "Upî near Ishchali," *JAOS* 59 (1939) 106-107.

Tell Uqair

*Seton Lloyd and Faud Safar, "Tell Uqair: Excavations by the Iraq Government Directorate of Antiquities in 1940 and 1941," *JNES* 2 (1943) 131-158. [Introduction by H. Frankfort, pp 132-134; Archaic Texts of Uqair, pp. 155-158.]

*Seton Lloyd, "Recent Discoveries of the Iraq Directorate of Antiquities," *PEQ* 75 (1943) 105-109. (Additional Note by S. W. Perowne, p.109) *[Tel al 'Uqair]*

*E. Douglas Van Buren, "Excavations in Mesopotamia," *Or, N.S.,* 15 (1946) 497-503. [2. Tell Uqair, pp. 499-501]

Tell Uqair concluded

*Seton Lloyd, "Ur-Al, 'Ubaid, 'Uqair and Eridu: An Interpretation of Some Evidence from the Flood-Pit," *Iraq* 22 (1960) 23-31.

Ur

Francis Brown, "Ur Kasdim," *JBL* 7 (1887) Part 2, 46-57.

James W. Redhouse, "Modern Name of 'Ur of the Chaldees'," *JRAS* (1890) 822-823.

A. H. Sayce, "Modern Name of Ur of the Chaldees," *JRAS* (1891) 479.

Anonymous, "Ur of the Chaldees," *MR* 77 (1895) 965-968.

*Hormuzd Rassam, "Abraham and the Land of his Nativity," *SBAP* 20 (1898) 70-92. *[Ur]*

Edgar James Banks, "The Proposed Excavation of the Babylonian Ruin Mugheir, or Ur of the Chaldees, the Birthplace of Abraham," *AJA* 4 (1900) 155-156.

John P. Peters, "Excavations of Mugheir," *AJA* 4 (1900) 156-157. *[Ur]*

A. H. Sayce, "Recent Bibilical Archaeology. Ur of the Chaldees," *ET* 13 (1901-02) 64-66.

Paul Haupt, "Kir = Ur of the Chaldees," *JBL* 36 (1917) 93-99.

*George W. Gilmore, "The Archaeological World," *HR* 85 (1923) 393-394. [Ur of the Chaldees, p. 394]

*H. R. Hall, "Ur and Eridu: The British Museum Excavations of 1919," *JEA* 9 (1923) 177-195.

Anonymous, "The Mesopotamian Expedition: Ur of the Chaldees," *MJ* 14 (1923) 9-18.

G. B. Gordon, "The Excavations at Ur," *MJ* 14 (1923) 249-265.

G[eorge] W. G[ilmore], "'They went forth...from Ur of' the Chaldees," *HR* 88 (1924) 102-104.

C. Leonard Woolley, "The Expedition to Ur," *MJ* 15 (1924) 5-27.

Ur cont.

C. Leonard Woolley, "The Excavations at Ur, 1923-1924," *AJ* 5 (1925) 1-20.

C. Leonard Woolley, "The Excavations at Ur, 1924-1925," *AJ* 5 (1925) 347-402.

C. Leonard Woolley, "The Expedition to Ur," *MJ* 16 (1925) 27-55.

*H. R. Hall, "The Excavations of 1919 at Ur el-'Obeid and Eridu, and the History of Early Babylonia (Brussels Conference 1923)," *Man* 25 (1925) #1.

Leon Legrain, "The Joint Expedition to Ur of the Chaldees," *MJ* 16 (1925) 81-124.

Anonymous, "The Joint Expedition to Ur," *MJ* 16 (1925) 202-203.

[C. Leonard Woolley], "Notes and Comments. Dr. Woolley Reports from Ur of the Chaldees," *A&A* 21 (1926) 245-247.

C. Leonard Woolley, "The Excavations at Ur, 1925-6," *AJ* 6 (1926) 365-401.

*Theophilus G. Pinches, "Notes on the Discoveries at Ur and Tel al-Obeid, and the Worship of the Moon-God," *JTVI* 58 (1926) 32-54, 59-62. (Discussion, pp. 54-59)

Leon Legrain, "The Pilgrim of the Moon at Ur of the Chaldees. Concerning the Fourth Campaign of the Joint Expedition of the Museum of the University of Pennsylvania and the British Museum," *MJ* 17 (1926) 245-272.

C. Leonard Woolley, "Notes and Comments. This Winter's Discoveries at Ur," *A&A* 23 (1927) 187-189.

C. Leonard Woolley, "The Excavations at Ur, 1926-7," *AJ* 7 (1927) 385-423.

Anonymous, "Ur of the Chaldees," *Antiq* 1 (1927) 341-342, 482.

Leon Legrain, "The Expedition at Ur of the Chaldees," *MJ* 18 (1927) 121-157.

Ur cont.

[C. Leonard Woolley], "Remarkable New Discoveries at Ur Reported by Dr. Leonard Woolley," *A&A* 25 (1928) 157, 202-203.

C. Leonard Woolley, "Excavations at Ur, 1926-7. Part II," *AJ* 8 (1928) 1-29.

C. Leonard Woolley, "Excavations at Ur, 1927-8," *AJ* 8 (1928) 415-448.

*H. R. Hall, "The Discoveries at Ur, and the Seniority of the Sumerian Civilization," *Antiq* 2 (1928) 56-68.

*T. Fish, "The City of Ur and Its God Nanna(r) in the Third Dynasty of Ur," *BJRL* 12 (1928) 336-346.

G. Walter Fiske, "Where Abraham went to Church," *HR* 95 (1928) 180-182. *[Ur]*

Anonymous, "Excavations at Ur," *JRAS* (1928) 148-149.

C. Leonard Woolley, "Excavatons at Ur, 1927-8," *JRAS* (1928) 635-642.

*S[tephen] Langdon, "Ibi-Sin and the fall of the kingdom of Ur," *RAAO* 20 (1928) 49-51. [Correction, *RAAO* 21 (1914) pp. 37-38]

Anonymous, "Notes and Comments. The Lesson of Ur," *A&A* 27 (1929) 189.

C. Leonard Woolley, "Excavations at Ur, 1928-9," *AJ* 9 (1929) 305-343.

[C. Leonard Woolley], "The Flood Draws Steadily Nearer," *A&A* 29 (1930) 184-185. *[Ur]*

[C. Leonard Woolley], "Notes and Comments. The Walls and Waters of Ur," *A&A* 29 (1930) 232-233.

C. Leonard Woolley, "The Ur Excavations," *Antiq* 4 (1930) 223-225.

C. Leonard Woolley, "Excavation at Ur, 1929-30," *JRAS* (1930) 879-887.

*C. Leonard Woolley, "Excavations at Ur, 1929-30," *MJ* 21 (1930) 81-105. [Appendix: Tablets and Seal-Impressions, by E. Burrows, pp. 106-107]

Henry Charles Suter, "The Antiquities of Ur," *MR* 113 (1930) 878-887.

Ur cont.

C. Leonard Woolley, "Excavations at Ur, 1930-1," *AJ* 11 (1931) 343-381.

C. Leonard Woolley, "Excavations at Ur, 1930-31," *MJ* 22 (1931) 247-282.

C. Leonard Woolley, "Excavations at Ur, 1931-2," *AJ* 12 (1932) 355-392.

C. Leonard Woolley, "Excavations at Ur, 1931-32," *MJ* 23 (1932) 193-248.

C. Leonard Woolley, "Report on the Excavations at Ur, 1932-33," *AJ* 13 (1933) 359-383.

C. Leonard Woolley, "The Excavations at Ur, 1933-4. Being the Report of the Joint Expedition of the British Museum and of the University of Pennsylvania to Mesopotamia," *AJ* 14 (1934) 355-378.

E[phraim] A. Speiser, "Ur Excavations: A Review," *Antiq* 8 (1934) 448-452.*(Review)*

Anonymous, "The Joint Expedition to Ur," *UMB* 1 (1930) #1, 6; #2, 7-10; #3, 6.

Anonymous, "Mr. Woolley's Report from Ur," *UMB* 1 (1930) #4, 5-6.

Anonymous, "The Ur Finds, Season of 1929-30," *UMB* 2 (1930-31) 38-39.

Anonymous, "A Report from Ur," *UMB* 2 (1930-31) 88, 90; 3 (1931-32) 109-111.

Anonymous, "Excavations at Ur," *UMB* 2 (1930-31) 166-170; 182-186; 3 (1931-32) 172-174.

Anonymous, "The Joint Expedition to Ur," *UMB* 3 (1931-32) 79; 4 (1932-33) 62-63, 99-102; 5 (1934-35); #2, 35-36; #3, 79-83, 86.

Anonymous, "Notes and Comments. End of the Ur Excavations," *A&A* 35 (1934) 141-142.

T. Fish, "The World of Ur III," *BJRL* 23 (1939) 215-227.

D. L. Cracknell, "Abraham and Ur: Ur, Metropolis of Mesopotamia," *AT* 4 (1959-60) #3, 11-13.

M. E. L. Mallowan, "Memories of Ur," *Iraq* 22 (1960) 1-19.

Ur concluded

*Seton Lloyd, "Ur-Al, 'Ubaid, 'Uqair and Eridu: An Interpretation of Some Evidence from the Flood-Pit," *Iraq* 22 (1960) 23-31.

*Joan Oates, "Ur and Eridu, a Prehistory," *Iraq* 22 (1960) 32-50.

H. W. F. Saggs, "Ur of the Chaldees: A Problem of Identification," *Iraq* 22 (1960) 200-209.

J. A. Brinkman, "Ur: 721-605 B.C.," *Or, N.S.*, 34 (1965) 241-258. *(Review)*

*George F. Bass, "Troy and Ur: Gold Links Between Two Ancient Capitals," *Exped* 8 (1965-66) #4, 26-39.

*George F. Bass, "A New Tie between Troy IIg and the Royal Cemetery at Ur," *AJA* 71 (1967) 183.

J. A. Brinkman, "Ur: 'The Kassite Period and the Period of the Assyrian Kings'," *Or, N.S.*, 38 (1969) 310-348. *(Review)*

Urartu

*Tahsin Özgüç, "Urartu and Altintepe," *Arch* 22 (1969) 256-263.

Ursu

*Sidney Smith, "Ursu and Ḫaššum," *AS* 6 (1956) 35-43.

Uruk

Walter Andrae, "The Story of Uruk," *Antiq* 10 (1936) 133-145.

Robert McC. Adams, "Uruk-Warka Area," *Sumer* 23 (1967) 203-209.

Utica

Byron Khun de Prorok, "The Excavations of Ancient Utica," *A&A* 20 (1925) 37-39.

Uz

Friedrich Delitzsch, "The Land of Uz," *ONTS* 4 (1884-85) 417-420.

V

Van

*F. A. Molony, "The Noachian Deluge and its Probable Connection with Lake Van," *JTVI* 68 (1936) 43-53. 64-65. (Discussion and Communications, pp. 54-64)

Robert H. Pfeiffer, "The Excavations at Van in 1939," *BASOR* #78 (1940) 31-32.

C. A. Burney, "Urartian Fortresses and Towns in the Van Region," *AS* 7 (1957) 37-53.

Velia

Amedeo Maiuri, "Velia: The First Official Italian Recognition and Exploration May-September 1927," *A&A* 31 (1931) 37-46.

*Pellegrino Claudio Sestieri, "Greek Elea—Roman Velia," *Arch* 10 (1957) 2-10.

*L. B. Kreitner, "Archaeological Notes. A Greek Arch and Parmenides' Head: *A report on Velia-Elea*," *HT* 18 (1968) 129, 131.

Vetulonia

A. L. F[rothingham] Jr., "Vetulonia and Early Italic Archæology," *AJA, O.S.,* 4 (1888) 175-180.

Vrokastro

(Miss) Edith H. Hall, "Excavations at Vrokastro, Crete, 1912," *AJA* 17 (1913) 91-92.

Edith H. Hall, "Excavations at Vrokastro, Crete, in 1912," *A&A* 1 (1914-15) 33-36.

W

Wadi Arabah

*G. W. Murray, "A New Empire(?) copper mine in the Wadi ʿAraba," *ASAE* 51 (1951) 217-218.

*K. Morgan, "*The Wadi Arabah:* Solomon's Mines," *AT* 5 (1960-61) #1, 9-12.

*K. Morgan, "*The Wadi Arabah:* Solomon's Industrial Port," *AT* 5 (1960-61) #2, 2-6.

*Anonymous, "Solomon's Mines," *AT* 5 (1960-61) #3, 14-16. *[Wadi Arabah]*

Wady el Kittar

Dow Covington, "Report on a summary Exploration of Wady el Kittar," *ASAE* 9 (1908) 97-104.

Wàdi el-Natrûn

Ahmed Fakhry, "Wàdi el-Natrûn," *ASAE* 40 (1940-41) 837-848.

Wadi el-Rayyān

Ahmed Fakhry, "Wadi el-Rayyān," *ASAE* 46 (1947) 1-19.

Wadi Hadhramaut

Gus W. Van Beek, "An Archaeological Survey in Wadi Hadhramaut, South Arabia," *AJA* 67 (1963) 218.

Wady Sheykh

*Elise Baumgärtel, "The Flint Quarries of Wady Sheykh," *AEE* 15 (1930) 103-108.

Wadi Sirhan

Nelson Glueck, "Wadi Sirhan in North Arabia," *BASOR* #96 (1944) 7-17.

Wadi Tharthar

A. J. Young, "Two Ancient Sites at Wadi Tharthar," *Sumer* 19 (1963) 109-111.

Wādi Umm Sidrah

*G. W. Murray, "The Archaic Hut in Wādi Umm Sidrah," *JEA* 25 (1939) 38-39.

Warka

Julius Jordan, "The Excavatons at Warka (Mesopotamia)," *Antiq* 4 (1930) 109-111. *(Trans. by Roland G. Austin)*

R. North, "Status of the Warka Expedition," *Or, N.S.,* 26 (1957) 185-256.

Heinrich J. Lenzen, "New Discoveries at Warka in Southern Iran," *Arch* 17 (1964) 122-131.

X

Xanthus River Valley

*J. C. Keene, "The Lycian Cities of the Xanthus River Valley," *A&A* 35 (1934) 99-108.

Xeropolis (See also: Lefkandi)

*L. H. Sackett, "The British School Excavations at Xeropolis (Lefkandi) in Euboea," *AJA* 70 (1966) 194-195.

Y

Yabroud

*W. R. Farrand, "Geology, Climate and Chronology of Yabrud Rockshelter I," *AAAS* 15 (1965) #1, 35-50.

Ralph S. Solecki and Rose L. Solecki, "New data from Yabroud, Syria. Preliminary Report of the Columbia University Archaeological Investigations," *AAAS* 16 (1966) #2, 121-153.

Tel-el-Yahoudieh

Lewis T. Hayter, "Some Remarks on Excavations made in Tel-el-Yahoudee (the Mound of the Jew) near Cairo, and on some Antiquities brought therefrom and now in the British Museum," *SBAP* 2 (1879-80) 31-33.

Lewis T. Hayter, "Tel-el-Yahoudeh (the Mound of the Jew)," *SBAT* 7 (1880-82) 177-192.

†Lewis T. Hayter, "Notes on the Tel-el-Yahoudeh," *SBAP* 4 (1881-82) 89-90.

*William Copley Winslow, "Important Discoveries by Dr. Petrie," *RP* 5 (1906) 191-192. *[Tel-el-Yehudiyeh]*

C. C. Edgar, "Tomb-stones from Tell el Yahoudieh," *ASAE* 19 (1919) 216-224.

*G. R. H. Wright, "Tell el-Yehūhīyah and the Glacis," *ZDPV* 84 (1968) 1-17.

Yanik Tepe

C. A. Burney, "Excavations at Yanik Tepe, North-West Iran," *Iraq* 23 (1961) 138-153.

C. A. Burney, "The Excavations at Yanik Tepe, Azerbaijan, 1961. Second Preliminary Report,"*Iraq* 24 (1962) 134-152.

C. A. Burney, "The Excavations at Yanik Tepe, Azerbaijan, 1962: Third Preliminary Report," *Iraq* 26 (1964) 54-61.

Yanik Tepe concluded

*Ruth Amiran, "Yanik Tepe, Shengavit, and the Khirbet Kerak Ware," *AS* 15 (1965) 165-167.

Yorgan Teppe (See also: Nuzi)

David G. Lyon, "The Joint Expedition of Harvard University and the Baghdad School at Yargon Tepa*[sic]* near Kirkuk," *BASOR* #30 (1928) 1-5.

Robert H. Pfeiffer, "Yorgan Teppe. Preliminary Report the Excavations During 1928-29," *BASOR* #34 (1929) 2-7

Yarim Tepe

Nicolai Merpert and Rauf Munchajev, "The Investigation of the Soviet Archaeological Expedition in Iraq in the Spring 1969. Excavations at Yarim Tepe. First Preliminary Report," *Sumer* 25 (1969) 125-131.

Yassi Ada

*George F. Bass, "Underwater Excavations at Yassi Ada 1962-1963," *TAD* 13 (1964) #1, 41-51.

Z

Zakro

D. G. Hogarth, "Exploration at Zakro in Eastern Crete," *Man* 1 (1901) #147.

George Huxley, "The Ancient Name of Zakro," *GRBS* 8 (1967) 85-87.

Zawi Chemi Shanidar

Ralph Solecki and Meyer Rubin, "The Dating of Zawi Chemi Shanidar, an early Neolithic village in Northern Iraq," *Sumer* 14 (1958) 131-133.

Rose L. Solecki, "The 1960 Season at Zawi Chemi Shanidar," *Sumer* 17 (1961) 124-125.

Zawiet Abu

Tewfik Boulds, "Digging at Zawiet Abu Mossallam," *ASAE* 19 (1919) 145-148.

Zincirli

David Ussishkin, "'Der Alte Bau' in Zincirli," *BASOR* #189 (1968) 50-53.

Zinjirli

Robert Francis Harper, "A Visit to Zinjirli," *ONTS* 8 (1888-89) 183-184.

Ziwiyeh

Robert H. Dyson Jr., "Archaeological Scrap: Glimpses of History at Ziwiye," *Exped* 5 (1962-63) #3, 32-37.

Robert H. Dyson Jr., "Test Excavations at Ziwiyeh, 1964," *AJA* 70 (1966) 188.

Zoan

*F. C. Whitehouse, "On the thesis, Zoan is Tanis magna, a suburb of Memphis, and not San el-Hagar or Tanis parva on the Delta," *JAOS* 11 (1885) ccxv-ccxviii.

William C. Wilson, "The Exploration at Zoan," *CR* 47 (1886) 407-416. *(Review)*

*G[eorge] Rawlinson, "Biblical Topography. VII—Egyptian Sites—Zoan and Pithom," *MI* 4 (1886) 321-331.

*J. A. Paine, "On the 'thesis' of Mr. Whitehouse, affirming Cairo to be the Biblical Zoan and Tanis magna," *JAOS* 13 (1889) xiii-xvii.

Zubediyah

*Stuart A. Harris and Robert M. Adams, "A Note on Canal and Marsh Stratigraphy Near Zubediyah," *Sumer* 13 (1957) 157-162.

Zygouries

D[avid] M. R[obinson], "Discovery of a New Prehistoric Site in Greece at Zygouries," *A&A* 12 (1921) 38-39.

C. W. Blegen, "Excavations at Zygouries, Greece, 1921," *A&A* 15 (1923) 85-89.

§169 *2.5.6 Science and the Bible (Includes Studies on Creation and Evolution) [See also: The Historical Reliability of the Old Testament - General Studies →]*

†Anonymous, "Howard's History of the Earth," *BCQTR* 10 (1797) 101-115. *(Review)*

†B. J. C., "Traces of Modern Geological Theories in Ancient Authors," *MMBR* 27 (1809) 538-539.

Anonymous, "The Bible, a Key to the Phenomena of the Natural World," *PRev* 1 (1829) 101-120.

*Anonymous, "The Mosaic History Accordant with the Existing State of Things," *PRev* 1 (1829) 189-209.

†Anonymous, "Sacred History of the World," *BCQTR, 4th Ser.,* 12 (1832) 64-88. *(Review)*

†Anonymous, "The Analogy of Revelation and Science," *BCQTR, 4th Ser.,* 15 (1834) 411-434. *(Review)*

*Edward Hitchcock, "The Connection between Geology and the Mosaic History of Creation," *BRCR* 5 (1835) 439-451; 6 (1835) 261-332.

*Anonymous, "Geology considered with Reference to Natural Theology," *QRL* 56 (1836) 31-64. *(Review)*

Anonymous, "Epoch of the Creation," *LTR* 4 (1837) 526-538.

†Anonymous, "Scriptural Difficulties of Geology," *DR* 16 (1844) 345-373. *(Review)*

†Anonymous, "Natural History of Creation," *ERCJ* 82 (1845) 1-85. *(Review)*

G. W. M., "Geology.—Its Facts and its Influences," *UQGR* 2 (1845) 5-21.

W. F., "Geology and the Scripture," *UQGR* 2 (1845) 349-384.

Anonymous, "Scriptural Evidences for Creation," *BRCM* 3 (1847) 81-94.

†Anonymous, "The Pre-Adamite Earth," *BQRL* 5 (1847) 387-411. *(Review)*

Anonymous, "The Pre-Adamite Earth," *BRCM* 3 (1847) 161-173. *(Review)*

*J. W. Ward, "The Consistency of the Eternal Purposes of God with the Free Agency of Men," *BS* 4 (1847) 77-95.

M. Jacobs, "The Consistency of the Discoveries of Geology with the Teachings of Revelation," *ER* 1 (1849-50) 363-390.

*M. N., "Genesis and Geology; or an Investigation into the Reconciliation of the Modern Doctrines of Geology with the Declarations of Scripture," *JSL, 1st Ser.,* 6 (1850) 261-291.

D. Martindale, "Footprints of the Creator," *MQR* 5 (1851) 489-516.

Anonymous, "The Harmony of Revelation, and Natural Science; with Especial Reference to Geology.—Number I.," *SPR* 5 (1851-52) 93-111.

Anonymous, "The Harmony of Revelation, and Natural Science; with Especial Reference to Geology.—Number II.," *SPR* 5 (1851-52) 284-315.

Anonymous, "The Harmony of Revelation, and Natural Science;—Number III.," *SPR* 5 (1851-52) 461-495.

*[David N. Lord], "Genesis, and the Geological Theory of the Age of the Earth," *TLJ* 4 (1851-52) 529-614.

[David N. Lord], "The Theory of which Geologists found their Deduction of the great age of the World," *TLJ* 5 (1852-53) 1-74.

[David N. Lord], "The Sources from which the Materials of the present Crust of the Earth were derived," *TLJ* 5 (1852-53) 177-233.

[David N. Lord(?)], "Answers to the Objections of Geologists," *TLJ* 5 (1852-53) 292-312.

†[David N. Lord], "Dr. Hitchcock's Religion of Geology," *TLJ* 5 (1852-53) 353-403. *(Review)*

*Anonymous, "Science and Revealed Religion," *FBQ* 1 (1853) 280-295.

†[David N. Lord], "Dr. J. P. Smith on the Geological Theory," *TLJ* 5 (1852-53) 588-613; 6 (1853-54) 1-33. *(Review)*

*†[David N. Lord], "Hugh Miller's Lecture on Genesis and Geology," *TLJ* 7 (1854-55) 119-144. *(Review)*

*(   ) M., "Theology, Philology, Geology," *JSL, 3rd Ser.,* 2 (1855-56) 66-81; 3 (1856) 184-188.

[David N. Lord(?)], "Geology and the Bible," *TLJ* 8 (1855-56) 108-115.

James D. Dana, "Science and the Bible," *BS* 13 (1856) 80-129. *(Review)*

Tayler Lewis, "Letter from Prof. Lewis," *BS* 13 (1856) 471-476. *[Reply to James D. Dana's Review (above)]*

James D. Dana, "Science and the Bible. Number II.," *BS* 13 (1856) 631-656. *(Review)*

*Anonymous, "The Bearing of the Geological Theory of the Age of the World on the Inspiration of the Bible," *TLJ* 9 (1856-57) 251-270.

†Anonymous, "Typical Forms and Special Ends in Creation," *TLJ* 9 (1856-57) 270-299. *(Review)*

†Anonymous, "The Bible and Science," *PQR* 5 (1856-57) 642-654. *(Review)*

James D. Dana, "Science and the Bible," *BS* 14 (1857) 388-413, 461-524.

[George T. Day], "Miller's Testimony of the Rocks," *FBQ* 5 (1857) 293-317. *(Review)*

Anonymous, "The Progress of Science, and its Connection with Scripture," *MQR* 11 (1857) 44-73.

†Anonymous, "H. Miller's Bearing of Geology on Natural and Revealed Religion," *TLJ* 10 (1857-58) 97-145. *(Review)*

Hugh Miller, "The Testimony of the Rocks," *SPR* 10 (1857-58) 463-473.

Anonymous, "Geological Speculation, and the Mosaic Account of Creation," *SPR* 10 (1857-58) 534-573.

†[David N. Lord(?)], "Dr. Hitchcock's Rational Cosmology," *TLJ* 11 (1858-59) 353-386. *(Review)*

H. M. G., "Mr. Hugh Miller's 'Geology in its Bearings upon the Two Theologies, Natural and Revealed'," *JSL, 3rd Ser.,* 8 (1858-59) 413-427. *(Review)*

A. Tholuck, "What is the Result of Science with Regard to the Primitive World?" *ER* 10 (1858-59) 400-454; 11 (1859-60) 110-125, 289-300. *(Trans. by T. J. Lehmann)*

*D. C. M'Laren, "The Facts of Geology consistent with the Revealed History of Creation," *TLJ* 12 (1859-60) 133-151. (Errata, p. 352)

W. Barrows, "Moses and the Geologists," *AThR* 2 (1860) 457-482.

†Anonymous, "Darwin on the Origin of Species," *BQRL* 31 (1860) 398-421. *(Review)*

Anonymous, "The Religion of Geology," *BS* 17 (1860) 673-709. *(Review)*

Anonymous, "Darwin's Origin of Species," *CE* 68 (1860) 449-464. *(Review)*

†Anonymous, "Darwin on the Origin of Species," *DR* 48 (1860) 50-81. *(Review)*

†Anonymous, "Darwin *on the Origin of Species,*" *ERCJ* 111 (1860) 487-532. *(Review)*

Anonymous, "*On the Origin of Species.* By Charles Darwin," *LQHR* 14 (1860) 281-308. *(Review)*

†Anonymous, "Darwin's Origin of Species," *QRL* 108 (1860) 225-264. *(Errata on insert following Table of Contents)*

Anonymous, "Darwin on the Origin of Species," *TLJ* 13 (1860-61) 101-148. *(Review)*

*[R. B. Jenness], "The Two Histories of Creation—How Reconciled," *FBQ* 9 (1861) 121-145.

W. C. Wilson, "Darwin on the Origin of Species," *MR* 43 (1861) 605-627. *(Review)*

A. Essick, "The Two Records of Creation; or the Bible and Geology," *ER* 13 (1861-62) 173-198.

Anonymous, "Geology and the Bible," *SPR* 14 (1861-62) 246-274.

P. A. Chadbourne, "Final Cause of Varieties," *BS* 21 (1864) 348-362.

Andrew P. Peabody, "The Bearing of Modern Scientific Theories on the Fundamental Truths of Religion," *BS* 21 (1864) 710-724.

*Anonymous, "Conflicts of Revelation and Science—The Science of the Bible Phenomenal," *DQR* 4 (1864) 339-361.

*[Enoch Pond], "Geology and Revelation," *FBQ* 12 (1864) 173-191.

Denis Wortman, "Resume of the Geological Argument," *AThR, N.S.,* 3 (1865) 613-640.

George Warington, "A Sketch of the Existing Relations between Science and Scripture," *JTVI* 1 (1866-67) 85-102. (Discussion, pp. 102-114)

Charles Mountford Burnett, "On the Difference between the Scope of Science and that of Revelation as Standards of Truth," *JTVI* 1 (1866-67) 115-136. (Discussion, pp. 136-146)

Evan Hopkins, "On the General Character of Geological Formations," *JTVI* 1 (1866-67) 303-318. (Discussion, pp. 318-322)

John Kirk, "On the Past and Present Relations of Geological Science to the Sacred Scripture,"*JTVI* 1 (1866-67) 331-379. (Discussion, pp. 379-381)

Anonymous, "Geology and Revelation," *IER, 1st Ser.,* 3 (1866-67) 121-134, 241-261, 358-374; 4 (1867-68) 49-66, 169-187, 326-341, 373-385; 5 (1868-69) 49-73, 193-223.

J. Brodie, "On the Lessons taught us by Geology in relation to the Nature of God," *JTVI* 1 (1866-67) 382-388.

*C. H. Hitchcock, "Relations of Geology to Theology," *BS* 24 (1867) 363-388, 429-481.

George Warington, "On the Credibility of Darwinism," *JTVI* 2 (1867-68) 39-62. (Discussion, pp. 85-125)

James Reddie, "On the Credibility of Darwinism," *JTVI* 2 (1867-68) 63-85. [(Discussion, pp. 85-125), (Note, p. 125-128)]

James Reddie, "On Geological Chronology, and the Cogency of the Arguments by which some Scientific Doctrines are supported. (In reply to Professor Huxley's Address delivered at Sion College on 21st Nov. 1867.)," *JTVI* 2 (1867-68) 299-337. [(Discussion, pp. 337-371) (Notes, pp. 371-376) (Abstract of Huxley's Address, pp. 377-386)]

Heman Lincoln, "Development *versus* Creation," *BQ* 2 (1868) 257-274.

L. Sternberg, "Geology and Moses," *ER* 19 (1868) 138-153.

J. H. Wheatley, "On Life, with some Observations on its Origin," *JTVI* 3 (1868-69) 26-45. (Discussion, pp. 45-59)

R. Laming, "On the Immediate Derivation of Physical Science from the Great First Cause," *JTVI* 3 (1868-69) 174-191. (Discussion, pp. 191-202)

*C. McCausland, "On some Uses of Sacred Primeval History," *JTVI* 3 (1868-69) 447-458. (Discussion, pp. 458-471)

C. A. Row, "On the Relation of Reason to Philosophy, Theology, and Revelation," *JTVI* 3 (1868-69) 472-502. (Discussion pp. 502-516)

†[James Bowling Mozley], "The Argument of Design," *QRL* 127 (1869) 134-176. *(Review)*

*John Kirk, "On the Doctrine of Creation according to Darwin, Agassiz, and Moses," *JTVI* 4 (1869-70) 45-66. (Discussion, pp. 66-85)

J. H. Wheatley, "Life—Brief Remarks on Its Origins. Being an Examination of Some Modern Opinions," *JTVI* 4 (1869-70) 163-184. (Discussion, pp. 184-198)

G. Henslow, "On Certain Analogies between the Methods of Deity in Nature and in Revelation," *JTVI* 4 (1869-70) 262-273. (Discussion, pp. 273-293)

Anonymous, "Dr. Molloy on Geology and Revelation," *DR, N.S.,* 14 (1870) 403-417. *(Review) [Original numbering as Vol. 66]*

Anonymous, "Harmony of Revealed Truths and Geological Facts," *DUM* 75 (1870) 477-490.

S. R. Pattison, "On Geological Proofs of Divine Action," *JTVI* 5 (1870-71) 231-246. (Discussion, pp. 246-263)

Samuel Adams, "Darwinism," *CongR* 11 (1871) 233-253, 338-361.

Anonymous, "Genesis and Geology," *CR* 23 (1871) 343-358. *(Review)*

Anonymous, "Evolution and Faith," *DR, N.S.,* 17 (1871) 1-40. *(Review) [Original numbering as Vol. 69]*

†Anonymous, "Darwin's *Descent of Man,* " *QRL* 131 (1871) 47-90. *(Review)*

J. R. Leebody, "The Theory of Evolution, and its Relation to Religious Thought," *BFER* 21 (1872) 1-35.

Frederic Gardiner, "Darwinism," *BS* 29 (1872) 240-289.

John Bascom, "Evolution as Advocated by Herbert Spencer," *PQPR* 1 (1872) 496-515.

J. G. C., "Darwinism," *IER, N.S.,* 9 (1872-73) 337-361.

H. H. Howorth, "Strictures on Darwinsim," *JRAI* 2 (1872-73) 21-37. [Part I.—On Fertility and Sterility]

E. Nisbet, "Darwinism," *BQ* 7 (1873) 69-87, 204-227.

*James A. Lyon, "The Contrast Between Man and the Brute Creation Establishes the Divine Origin of the Scriptures," *PQPR* 2 (1873) 726-737.

H. Charlton Bastian, "The Evolution Hypothesis, and the Origin of Life," *ContR* 23 (1873-74) 528-544, 703-720.

H. H. Howorth, "Strictures on Darwinsim. Part II.—The Extinction of Types," *JRAI* 3 (1873-74) 208-228. (Discussion, pp. 228-229)

F. Bateman, "On Darwinism Tested by Recent Researches in Language," *JTVI* 7 (1873-74) 73-91. (Appendix, pp. 92-95)

C. R. Bree, "On Darwinism and Its Effects upon Religious Thought," *JTVI* 7 (1873-74) 253-270. (Discussion, pp. 270-285)

J. E. Howard, "On 'Scientific Facts and Christian Evidence'," *JTVI* 7 (1873-74) 324-343. [(Notes, pp. 344-347) (Discussion, pp. 347-354)]

G. W. Weldon, "Law of Creation—Unity of Plan, Variety of Form," *JTVI* 7 (1873-74) 355-374. (Discussion, pp. 374-387)

C. H. T[oy], "Does the Bible Anticipate Modern Science?" *BQ* 8 (1874) 97-99.

M. Charles Lévégue, "The Sense of the Beautiful in Brutes. Psychological Darwinism and Comparative Psychology," *PQPR* 3 (1874) 126-142. *(Translated from Revue des Deux Mondes)*

J. G. G., "Evolution," *ERG, 6th Ser.,* 1 (1874-75) 141-148.

J. G. G., "Evolution and God," *ERG, 6th Ser.,* 1 (1874-75) 192-201, 233-243.

H. H. Howorth, "Strictures on Darwinism. Part III.—On Gradual Variations," *JRAI* 4 (1874-75) 101-119. (Discussion, pp. 119-121)

Andrew Taylor, "Geological Evidence against Evolution," *BFER* 24 (1875) 60-82.

S. H. Carpenter, "The Philosophy of Evolution," *BQ* 9 (1875) 149-164.

George F. Wright, "Recent Books Bearing upon the Relation of Science to Religion," *BS* 32 (1875) 537-555.[No. I.—The Nature and Degree of Scientific Proof]

T. R., "The Argument from Design and the Theory of Evolution," *CongL* 4 (1875) 728-735.

*Otto Zöckler, "The Biblical Account of Creation and Natural Science," *DTQ* 1 (1875) 1-17.

George B. Cheever, "The Philosophy of Evolution. Some of the Methods and Results of the Examples of Scientific Reasoning by Darwin and Spencer, Huxley and Tyndall," *PQPR* 4 (1875) 121-157. *(Review)*

H. Alleyne Nicholson, "On the Bearing of certain Palaeontological Facts upon the Darwinian Theory of the Origin of Species, and of Evolution in General," *JTVI* 9 (1875-76) 207-231. [(Discussion, pp. 231-236) (Note by J. W. Dawson, pp. 236-237)]

Herbert Spencer, "The Comparative Psychology of Man," *JRAI* 5 (1875-76) 310-315. (Discussion, pp. 315-316)

George Dering Wolff, "Modern Physicists and the Origin of Man," *ACQR* 1 (1876) 126-147.

George F. Wright, "Recent Works Bearing on the Relation of Science to Religion," *BS* 33 (1876) 448-493. [No. II.—The Divine Method of Producing Living Species]

George F. Wright, "Recent Works Bearing on the Relation of Science to Religion," *BS* 33 (1876) 656-694.[No. III.—Objections to Darwinism, and the Rejoinders of its Advocates]

X. C. S. P., "Positivism and Evolution," *ACQR* 2 (1877) 598-613.

George F. Wright, "Recent Works Bearing on the Relation of Science to Religion," *BS* 34 (1877) 355-385. [IV.—Concerning the True Doctrine of Final Cause or Design in Nature]

A. M. Kirsch, "Professor Huxley on Evolution," *ACQR* 2 (1877) 644-664.

George F. White, "The Darwinian Hypothesis, and the Design in Nature," *DTQ* 3 (1877) 404-419.

*†Anonymous, "The Book of Genesis and Science," *LQHR* 48 (1877) 52-66. *(Review)*

J. S. Beekman, "The Development Theory," *PQPR* 6 (1877) 603-608.

E. R. Craven, "The Inductive Sciences of Nature and the Bible," *PQPR* 6 (1877) 673-688.

†John Evans, "On the Antiquity of Man," *JRAI* 7 (1877-78) 149-151.

David Howard, "On the Structure of Geological Formations as Evidence of Design," *JTVI* 11 (1877-78) 382-393. (Discussion, pp. 393-400)

Frederic Gardiner, "The Bearing of Recent Scientific Thought upon Theology," *BS* 35 (1878) 46-75.

James McCosh, "Geology and Scripture," *DTQ* 4 (1878) 534-543.

D. W. Simon, "Science and Philosophy," *Exp, 1st Ser.,* 8 (1878) 321-346.

John T. Duffield, "Evolution Respecting Man, and the Bible," *PRev* 54 (1878) Part 1, 150-177.

Paul A. Chadbourne, "Design in Nature," *PRev* 54 (1878) Part 1, 272-303.

Laurens P. Hickok, "Evolution from Mechanical Force," *PRev* 54 (1878) Part 1, 567-605.

J. W. Dawson, "Evolution and the Apparition of Animal Forms," *PRev* 54 (1878) Part 1, 662-675.

*Andrew P. Peabody, "Science and Revelation," *PRev* 54 (1878) Part 1, 760-783.

J. E. Howard, "Creation and Providence, with Special Reference to the Evolutionist Theory," *JTVI* 12 (1878-79) 191-228, 238-242. [(Appendix, pp. 229-236) (Remarks by John Walter Lea, pp. 236-238)]

Edward F. X. McSweeny, "The Logic of Evolution," *ACQR* 4 (1879) 551-580.

†Anonymous, "The Fallacies of Evolution," *ERCJ* 150 (1879) 219-253. *(Review)*

*J. W. Dawson, "Points of Contact Between Science and Revelation," *PRev* 55 (1879) Part 2, pp. 579-606.

J. Robinson, "Evolution, Viewed in Relation to Theology," *BQR* 72 (1880) 78-98. *(Review)*

George Frederic Wright, "Recent Books Bearing upon the Relation of Science to Religion," *BS* 37 (1880) 48-76. [V.—Some Analogies between Calvinism and Darwinism]

A. K. McMurchy, "Biblical Genesis and Development of Life," *DTQ* 6 (1880) 22-27.

*H. E. D[ennehy], "Revelation, Geology, the Antiquity of Man," *IER, 3rd Ser.*, 1 (1880) 185-193, 260-272.

Anonymous, "Evolution," *MQR, 2nd Ser.*, 2 (1880) 649-661.

J. H. McIlvaine, "Evolution in Relation to Species," *PR* 1 (1880) 611-630.

*J. W. Dawson, "The Antiquity of Man and the Origin of the Species," *PRev* 56 (1880) Part 2, 383-398.

Joseph Le Conte, "Evolution in Relation to Materialism," *PRev* 57 (1881) Part 1, 149-174.

M. C. Read, "Evolution," *AAOJ* 3 (1880-81) 35-38.

S. Fitzsimons, "A Glance at the Conflict between Religion and Science," *ACQR* 6 (1881) 1-18.

*St. George Mivart, "Intellect and Evolution," *BQRL* 74 (1881) 298-332.

*F. D. Hoskins, "Evolution and the Christian Doctrine of the Fall," *CR* 36 (1881) 25-40. *[Volume actually listed as No. 135]*

Stanley Leathes, "The Bible and Modern Science," *CM* 13 (1881) 257-268.

Henry Calderwood, "The Relations of Moral Philosophy to Speculation Concerning the Origin of Man," *PRev* 57 (1881) Part 2, 288-302.

Joseph Le Conte, "Illustrations of a Law of Evolution of Thought," *PRev* 57 (1881) Part 2, 373-393.

Charles F. Deems, "The Cry of 'Conflict'," *JCP* 1 (1881-82) #2, Article #1, 1-24.

C. A. Young, "Astronomical Facts and Fancies for Philosophical Thinkers," *JCP* 1 (1881-82) #2, Article #2, 1-22.

Alexander Winchell, "The Speculative Consequences of Evolution," *JCP* 1 (1881-82) #3, Article #1, 1-30.

*J. H. McIlavine, "Science and Revelation," *JCP* 1 (1881-82) #3, Article #2, 1-24.

John Bascom, "The Gains and Losses of Faith from Science," *JCP* 1 (1881-82) #4, Article I, 1-16.

Leonard Marsh, "The Practical Determination of Species," *BS* 39 (1882) 51-73.

John A. Earnest, "Evolution and the Scriptures," *LQ* 12 (1882) 88-105.

J. S. Stahr, "The Genesis of the Earth," *RChR* 29 (1882) 611-628.

*S. R. Pattison, "The Age of Man Geologically Considered," *JCP* 2 (1882-83) 471-486.

W. S. Duncan, "The Probable Region of Man's Evolution," *JRAI* 12 (1882-83) 513-525. (Discussion, p. 525)

J. Hassell, "The Theory of Evolution taught by Haeckel, and held by his followers, Examined and Shown to be not Proven," *JTVI* 16 (1882-83) 249-282. (Discussion, pp. 282-290)

St. George Mivart, "A Limit to Evolution," *ACQR* 8 (1883) 193-221.

James Croll, "Evolution by Force Impossible: a New Argument against Materialism," *BQR* 77 (1883) 35-71.

Henry Wace, "The Present Position of Evolution and Its Bearings on Christian Faith," *Exp* 4 (1883) 19-33.

James McCosh, "A Symposium on Evolution. Is the Darwinian Theory of Evolution Reconcilable with the Bible? If so, with what Limitations? No. I," *HR* 8 (1883-84) 229-235.

Joseph T. Duryea, "A Symposium on Evolution. Is the Darwinian Theory of Evolution Reconcilable with the Bible? If so, with what Limitations? No. II," *HR* 8 (1883-84) 282-288.

Alexander Winchell, "A Symposium on Evolution. Is the Darwinian Theory of Evolution Reconcilable with the Bible? Is so, with what Limitations? No. III," *HR* 8 (1883-84) 345-349.

Francis L. Patton, "A Symposium on Evolution. Is the Darwinian Theory of Evolution Reconcilable with the Bible? If so, with what Limitations? No. IV," *HR* 8 (1883-84) 404-411.

Henry Ward Beecher, "A Symposium on Evolution. Is the Darwinian Theory of Evolution Reconcilable with the Bible? If so, with what Limitations? No. V," *HR* 8 (1883-84) 470-472.

Jesse B. Thomas, "A Symposium on Evolution. Is the Darwinian Theory of Evolution Reconcilable with the Bible? If so, with what Limitations? No. VI," *HR* 8 (1883-84) 529-534.

John P. Gulliver, "A Symposium on Evolution. Is the Darwinian Theory of Evolution Reconcilable with the Bible? If so, with what Limitations? No. VII," *HR* 8 (1883-84) 591-597.

J. M. Buckley, "A Symposium on Evolution. Is the Darwinian Theory of Evolution Reconcilable with the Bible? If so, with what Limitations? No. VIII," *HR* 8 (1883-84) 644-647.

William J. Harsha, "Darwinism and the Dakota Group," *PR* 4 (1883) 131-138.

W. Powell James, "On the Argument from Design in Nature, with some Illustrations from Plants," *JTVI* 17 (1883-84) 71-90. (Discussion, pp. 90-97)

Charles F. Deems, "Is There any Theory of Evolution Proven?" *HR* 8 (1883-84) 709-715.

*Charles B. Warring, "The Agreement of Science with *Genesis* I," *JCP* 3 (1883-84) 173-195.

C. A. Gordon, "Climatic Influences as Regards Organic Life," *JTVI* 17 (1883-84) 33-55. (Discussion pp. 55-69)

C. A. Gordon, "On Certain Theories of Life," *JTVI* 17 (1883-84) 142-166. (Discussion, pp. 166-170)

John Eliot Howard, "On Certain Definitions of Matter," *JTVI* 17 (1883-84) 171-189.

G. G. Stokes, "On the Absence of Real Opposition between Science and Revelation," *JTVI* 17 (1883-84) 195-204. (Discussion, pp. 204-219)

Edmund Beckett, "How Did the World Evolve Itself?" *JTVI* 17 (1883-84) 282-310. (Discussion, pp. 310-317)

F. H. Johnson, "Theistic Evolution," *AR* 1 (1884) 363-381.

Eustace Conder, "The Harmony of Science and Revelation," *CongL* 13 (1884) 803-813.

J. Murphy, "Darwinism," *IER, 3rd Ser.,* 5 (1884) 584-594.

J. Murphy, "Evolution and Faith," *IER, 3rd Ser.,* 5 (1884) 756-767.

James Woodrow, "Evolution," *SPR* 35 (1884) 341-368.

J. P. Landis, "Matter—Eternal or Created?" *ONTS* 4 (1884-85) 145-151.

Lyman Abbott, "Evolution and Theology," *AR* 4 (1885) 561-567.

*James D. Dana, "Creation; or, the Biblical Cosmology in the Light of Modern Science," *BS* 42 (1885) 201-224. *(Review)*

Heman Lincoln, "Science not Supreme, but Subordinate," *BS* 42 (1885) 225-250.

F. H. Johnson, "Instinct and Natural Selection," *BS* 42 (1885) 431-452.

Enoch F. Burr, "Astronomical Mysteries," *BS* 42 (1885) 453-469.

A. Pflueger, "Some Mistakes of Scientists," *ColTM* 5 (1885) 145-154, 225-236.

John S. Vaughan, "Faith and Evolution: A Further Consideration on the Question," *IER, 3rd Ser.*, 6 (1885) 409-424.

J. Murphy, "Faith and Evolution," *IER, 3rd Ser.*, 6 (1885) 481-496.

Alexander Stewart, "Evolution," *MI* 2 (1885) 422-438.

D. H. Hill, "Darwinism," *MQR, 2nd Ser.*, 7 (1885) 417-431.

D. H. Hill, "Natural Selection," *MQR, 2nd Ser.*, 7 (1885) 565-574.

*J. Hassell, "Was Primeval Man a Savage?" *JTVI* 19 (1885-86) 193-208. (Discussion, pp. 208-211)

W. R. Benedict, "Theism and Evolution," *AR* 6 (1886) 337-350, 607-622.

Abraham Coles, "A Half-Hour with the Evolutionists," *BFER* 35 (1886) 346-366.

*S. R. Pattison, "The Age of Man Geologically Considered," *ColTM* 6 (1886) 302-320.

William Dawson, "The Present Status of the Darwinian Theory of Evolution," *HR* 11 (1886) 373-381.

*H. P. Laird, "The Ancient Oracle," *RChR* 33 (1886) 301-320. *(Creation/Evolution)*

[John] Duns, "The Theory of Natural Selection and the Theory of Design," *JTVI* 20 (1886-87) 37-47, 60. [(Discussion, pp. 47-57) (Remarks by E. Beckett pp, 58-59and C. Popham Miles, p. 59)]

*E. A. Davies, "Bible Account of Creation in the Light of Modern Science," *CT* 5 (1887-88) 296-305.

B. W. Fielder, "Design versus Chance," *MQR, 3rd Ser.*, 3 (1887-88) 166-178.

Edmund Montgomery, "Cope's Theology of Evolution," *OC* 1 (1887-88) 160-164, 217-220, 274-277, 300-303.

E. D. Cope, "Montgomery on the Theology of Evolution," *OC* 1 (1887-88) 285-288, 358-361.

Eddy James, "Thoughts on Evolution," *OC* 1 (1887-88) 463-464.

E. D. Cope, "Evolution and Idealism," *OC* 1 (1887-88) 655-657.

J. H. Hyslop, "Evolution and Ethical Problems," *AR* 9 (1888) 348-366.

*Chas. S. Robinson, "Evolution as a Theory of Creation," *HR* 16 (1888) 123-127.

Anonymous, "The Prophet of Natural Selection," *LQHR* 70 (1888) 93-114. *(Review)*

Anonymous, "The Sting of Darwinism," *LQHR* 70 (1888) 337-345.

†Anonymous, "Darwin's Life and Letters," *QRL* 166 (1888) 1-30. *(Review)*

*†Anonymous, "The Mammoth and the Flood," *QRL* 166 (1888) 112-129. *(Review)*

Samuel Z. Beam, "Evolution as a Failure," *RChR* 35 (1888) 494-512.

Thomas Hill, "Creation is Revelation," *CT* 6 (1888-89) 121-134.

"Veritas", "Evolution and the Origin of Life," *MQR, 3rd Ser.*, 5 (1888-89) 219-241.

C. Walker, "The Uniformity of Nature," *BS* 46 (1889) 245-261.

Anonymous, "Re-examination of Darwin's Theory of Coral Islands," *BS* 46 (1889) 377-381.

*G. Frederick Wright, "The Glacial Period and Noah's Deluge," *BS* 46 (1889) 466-474.

G. Frederick Wright, "The Affinity of Science for Christianity," *BS* 46 (1889) 701-720.

Edwin de Lisle, "The Evolutionary Hypothesis," *DR, 3rd Ser.*, 21 (1889) 51-70. *[Original numbering as Vol. 104]*

B[enjamin] B. Warfield, "Darwin's Arguments Against Christianity and Against Religion," *HR* 17 (1889) 9-16.

W. J. Scott, "'A Biological Thermidor.'," *MQR, 3rd Ser.*, 6 (1889) 24-38.

Francis H. Smith, "Thoughts on the Discord and Harmony Between Science and the Bible," *CT* 7 (1889-90) 1-19.

Joseph J. Smith, "Is There Any Scientific Evidence of the Creation of Matter?" *CT* 7 (1889-90) 394-397.

C. Stanilan Wake, "Deity and the Universe.—A Controversy. I. God in Evolution," *OC* 3 (1889-90) 1997-2000.

Alfred Cave, "The Conflict between Religion and Science," *AR* 14 (1890) 441-452.

St. George Mivart, "Darwinism," *DR, 3rd Ser.*, 23 (1890) 33-74. *(Review) [Original numbering as Vol. 106]*

Joseph Parker, "The New Genesis: A Scientific Memo," *HR* 19 (1890) 416-420.

James McCann, "The Bible and Science," *TML* 4 (1890) 415-425.

George W. King, "Professor Huxley's Latest Polemic Against the Christian Faith," *CT* 8 (1890-91) 436-448.

E. D. McCreardy, "Three Decades of Evolution," *MQR, 3rd Ser.*, 9 (1890-91) 79-100.

*Anonymous, "Dana on Genesis and Science," *BS* 48 (1891) 171-174.

John Henry Hopkins, "Two Points on Evolution," *CR* 60 (1891) 78-80.

Charles Chapman, "Darwinism and Revelation as Now Related," *ET* 3 (1891-92) 263-266.

G. Frederick Wright, "Adjustments Between the Bible and Science," *BS* 49 (1892) 153-156.

*John Thomas Gulick, "Evolution and the Fall of Man," *BS* 49 (1892) 516-519.

*Charles B. Warring, "Professor Huxley Versus Genesis I," *BS* 49 (1892) 638-649.

Thomas Hughes, "A Baby's Footprint and Other Vestiges," *ACQR* 18 (1893) 19-41.

John Ming, "The Idea of Evolution," *ACQR* 18 (1893) 762-778.

William North Rice, "Twenty-five Years of Scientific Progress," *BS* 50 (1893) 1-35.

Frank Hugh Foster, "Evolution and the Evangelical System of Doctrine," *BS* 50 (1893) 408-428.

V. M. Olyphant, "The Relations of Biblical Facts and Science Regarding God and Man to Universal Truth," *BW* 2 (1893) 92-96.

William Caven, "The Testimony of Physical Science to the Truth of Scripture," *HR* 25 (1893) 395-401.

S. C. Wells, "Relations of the Bible to Scientific Methods," *LQ* 23 (1893) 578-585.

G. Frederick Wright, "The Bible and Science," *CT* 11 (1893-94) 325-344.

D. S. Martin, George Macloskie, W. W. McLane, "Discussing Prof. Wright's Paper," *CT* 11 (1893-94) 344-355.

James E. Poindexter, "Evolution and Creation," *PER* 7 (1893-94) 25-44.

St. George Mivart, "The Newest Darwinism," *ACQR* 19 (1894) 673-690.

*J. A. Zahm, "The Mosaic Hexaemeron in the Light of Exegesis and Modern Science," *AER* 10 (1894) 161-227. [I. Moses and Science; II. Allegorism and Literalism; III. St. Gregory of Nyssa and the Nebular Hypothesis; IV. St. Augustine and Evolution (exegesis old and new); V. Modern Theories of Cosmogony]

Jacob Cooper, "Is Adaptation Possible Without Design?" *BS* 51 (1894) 117-130.

G. Frederick Wright, "The Adaptations of Nature to the Highest Wants of Man," *BS* 51 (1894) 206-230.

G. Frederick Wright, "The Adaptations of Nature to the Intellectual Wants of Man," *BS* 51 (1894) 560-586.

J. A. Buck, "Evolution as a Science—Is There any Truth in It?" *PER* 8 (1894-95) 224-228.

*Hamilton M. Bartlett, "Evolution and the Idea of God," *PER* 8 (1894-95) 563-570.

G[eorge] Macloskie, "Common Errors as to the Relation of Science and Faith," *PRR* 6 (1895) 98-107.

R. B. Girdlestone, "On Scientific Research and Biblical Study," *JTVI* 29 (1895-96) 25-35. [(Discussion, pp. 35-41) (Communication by Hastings C. Dent, p. 42)]

G. J. Romanes, "The Darwinism of Darwin, and of the Post-Darwinian Schools," *Monist* 6 (1895-96) 1-27.

R. J. M., "The Creed of Science—or Agnostic Evolution as a Religion," *ACQR* 21 (1896) 518-540.

Jesse B. Thomas, "Some Recent Revision of Scientific Judgment Concerning Bible Statements," *HR* 31 (1896) 14-19.

G. B. Strickler, "The Bible and Science," *USR* 8 (1896-97) 253-255.

John B. Hogan, "Christian Faith and Modern Science," *ACQR* 22 (1897) 382-398.

*D. W. Simon, "Evolution and the Fall of Man," *BS* 54 (1897) 1-20.

G. Frederick Wright, "The Paradoxes of Science," *BS* 54 (1897) 205-231.

W. Douglas Mackenzie, "Evolution Theories and Christian Doctrine," *BS* 54 (1897) 542-562.

Henry Morton, "Science and the Supernatural," *BS* 54 (1897) 568-570.

Owen Scott, "Rocks and Revelation," *BW* 9 (1897) 112-121.

†Anonymous, "The Warfare of Science with Theology," *ERCJ* 186 (1897) 357-380. *(Review)*

William W. McLane, "The Case of Theology versus Science," *HR* 34 (1897) 8-13.

E. Gaynor, "Sir Robert S. Ball on Evolution," *IER, 4th Ser.*, 1 (1897) 243-260.

M. M. Kinard, "The Ethics of Evolution," *LCR* 16 (1897) 34-51.

A. E. Deitz, "Evolution as Taught in the Scriptures," *LQ* 27 (1897) 210-216.

Moncure D. Conway, "The Evolution of Evolution," *OC* 11 (1897) 498-502.

W. T. Freeman, "About a Separate Creation," *WR* 148 (1897) 580-589.

St. George Mivart, "What Makes a Species," *ACQR* 23 (1898) 28-44.

George C. Hungerford Pollen, "Is Geology a Science?" *ACQR* 23 (1898) 399-423.

Jacob Cooper, "Creation: or, The Transmutation of Energy," *BS* 55 213-243.

J. W. Dawson, "Creative Development and Evolution," *Exp, 5th Ser.,* 7 (1898) 43-56.

J. W. Dawson, "Spencer and Argyll on 'Organic Evolution'," *Exp, 5th Ser.,* 7 (1898) 179-187.

J. W. Dawson, "Creative Development and Spontaneous Evolution," *Exp, 5th Ser.,* 7 (1898) 308-320.

John W. Diggle, "The Faith of Science," *Exp, 5th Ser.,* 7 (1898) 439-455.

*G. Frederick Wright, "The First Chapter of Genesis and Modern Science," *HR* 35 (1898) 392-399.

Otto Pfleiderer, "Evolution and Theology," *NW* 7 (1898) 413-429.

George Macloskie, "Theistic Evolution," *PRR* 9 (1898) 1-22.

A. G., "Evolution in History," *TQ* 2 (1898) 180-197.

Walter Kidd, "Creation or Evolution," *JTVI* 32 (1898-99) 178-205. {[Discussion, pp. 206-212] [Communications by F. R. Tennant, pp. 212-214] [Notes by W. H. Turton, p. 214; Robert P. C. Corfe, pp. 214-215; [W. E.(?)] Gladstone, pp. 215-216]}

George Macloskie, "Common Errors as to the Relations of Science and Faith," *JTVI* 32 (1898-99) 217-228. (Discussion, pp. 229-233)

A. L. Cortie, "The Origin of the Solar System," *ACQR* 24 (1899) #96, 19-27.

James J. Walsh, "Life in Modern Biology," *ACQR* 24 (1899) #96, 124-141.

E. Gaynor, "Darwinism," *IER, 4th Ser.,* 6 (1899) 147-166.

G. Frederick Wright, "The Evolutionary Fad," *BS* 57 (1900) 303-316.

Jesse B. Thomas, "The Stampede into Evolution," *HR* 40 (1900) 304-309.

G. Ferries, "Science and Faith," *ET* 12 (1900-01) 390-394, 501-505.

A. S. Packard, "Lamarck's Views on the Evolution of Man, on Morals, and on the Relation of Science to Religion," *Monist* 11 (1900-01) 30-49.

S. Fitzsimons, "The Rise and Fall of Evolution by Natural Selection," *ACQR* 26 (1901) 87-107.

S. Fitzsimons, "The True Critical Test of Natural Selection," *ACQR* 26 (1901) 559-582.

B[enjamin] B. W[arfield], "Editorial Notes," *CFL, N.S.,* 4 (1901) 1-8. *[Creation versus Evolution]*

Edmund T. Shanahan, "The Fallacy in Evolution," *CUB* 7 (1901) 257-275.

Edmund T. Shanahan, "The Language of Evolution—I," *CUB* 7 (1901) 411-430.

G. Matheson, "Scientific Lights on Religious Problems. VIII. Is God a Present Guide," *Exp, 6th Ser.,* 4 (1901) 262-273.

J. Arthur Thomson, "The Present Aspects of the Evolution Theory," *LQHR* 95 (1901) 324-346. *(Review)*

H. W. Conn, "Some Questions that Evolution Does Not Answer," *MR* 83 (1901) 31-45.

G. Ferries, "Science and Faith," *ET* 13 (1901-02) 32-35. [III. Advantages derived from the Interaction of Religion and Science]

Frederick W. Sardeson, "Reaction between Natural Science and Religion," *BS* 59 (1902) 557-574.

Edmund T. Shanahan, "The Language of Evolution—II," *CUB* 8 (1902) 35-57.

*Peter Coffey, "The Hexahemeron and Science," *IER, 4th Ser.,* 12 (1902) 141-162, 249-271.

Oliver Lodge, "The Outstanding Controversy between Science and Faith," *HJ* 1 (1902-03) 46-61.

Oliver Lodge, "The Reconciliation between Science and Faith," *HJ* 1 (1902-03) 209-227.

George Macloskie, "The Origin of New Species and Man," *BS* 60 (1903) 261-276.

G. Frederick Wright, "The Revision of Geological Time," *BS* 60 (1903) 578-582.

*Charles B. Warring, "Miracle, Law, Evolution," *BS* 60 (1903) 750-764.

Charles B. Warring, "The Missing Link Between Theology and Modern Science," *HR* 46 (1903) 174-177.

E. A. Selley, "The Nebular Theory and Divine Revelation," *IER, 4th Ser.*, 13 (1903) 335-349, 418-429.

N. Murphy, "The Nebular Theory and Divine Revelation," *IER, 4th Ser.*, 13 (1903) 456-457.

E. A. Selley, "'The Nebular Theory and Divine Revelation'," *IER, 4th Ser.*, 13 (1903) 567-568.

Cavaliere Gugliemo Jervis, "The Glorious Revelation Touching the Creation of the World," *JTVI* 35 (1903) 156. *[(Summary only, Edward Hull) (Trans. by Martin L. Rouse)]*

William Hallock Johnson, "Evolution and Theology To-day," *PTR* 1 (1903) 403-422.

George Macloskie, "The Outlook of Science and Faith," *PTR* 1 (1903) 597-615.

J. Arthur Harris, "The Origin of Species by Mutation. Historical Review," *Monist* 14 (1903-04) 641-671.

Samuel Zane Batten, "The Logic of Evolution," *AJT* 8 (1904) 470-486.

G. F. Whidborne, "The Genesis of Nature," *JTVI* 36 (1904) 16-55. [(Discussion, pp. 55-62) (Communications by D. Biddle, pp. 62-63; J. Rate, pp. 63-64; C. Godfrey Ashwin, pp. 64-65)]

G[eorge] Macloskie, "Mosaism and Darwinism," *PTR* 2 (1904) 425-441.

Walter Lloyd, "The Bible, Science, and Education," *WR* 162 (1904) 56-64.

L[uther] T. Townsend "The Collapse of Evolution," *CFL, 3rd Ser.,* 2 (1905) 8-28.

H. D. Jenkins, "Evolution Pro and Con," *CFL, 3rd Ser.,* 3 (1905) 139-142.

W. A. Lambert, "Modern Science and Biblical Criticism," *CFL, 3rd Ser.,* 3 (1905) 420-423.

William Cowper Conant, "Profits of the Evolution Theory: A Brief Review," *CFL, 3rd Ser.,* 3 (1905) 460-462. *(Review)*

W. M. Lisle, "The New Evolution," *CFL, 3rd Ser.,* 3 (1905) 423-427.

*George Macloskie, "Creation as Illustrated by Evolution," *USR* 17 (1905-06) 89-100.

*George Macloskie, "The Creation of Man. (Sequel to Article on Creation as Illustrated by Evolution.)," *USR* 17 (1905-06) 235-246.

William Wood Smyth, "The Bible in the Light of Modern Science," *JTVI* 38 (1906) 212-215.

J. Arthur Harris, "The Experimental Data of the Mutation Theory," *Monist* 16 (1906) 254-293.

Hugh M. Scott, "Has Scientific Investigation Disturbed the Basis of Faith?" *PTR* 4 (1906) 433-453.

F. R. Tennant, "Points of Contact Between Theology and Science," *ICMM* 3 (1906-07) 18-41, 114-125, 285-295.

*Charles Reed Zahniser, "Evolution and the Fall," *BW* 29 (1907) 41-44.

Alexander Patterson, "Does the Bible Teach Science?" *CFL, 3rd Ser.,* 7 (1907) 206-309.

*D. Gath Whitley, "Science and Scripture," *LQHR* 108 (1907) 315-317. *(Review)*

John T. Gulick, "False Biology and Fatalism," *BS* 65 (1908) 358-367.

Gabriel Campbell, "Evolution and the Miraculous," *BS* 65 (1908) 572-585.

W. B. Riley, "The Theory of Evolution and False Theology," *CFL, 3rd Ser.,* 9 (1908) 36-42.

*Herbert William Magoun, "The Glacial Epoch and the Noachian Deluge," *BS* 66 (1909) 217-242, 431-457.

[George Frederick Wright (?)], "The Mistakes of Darwin and His Would-be Followers," *BS* 66 (1909) 332-343.

G. L. Young, "Relation of Evolution and Darwinism to the Question of Origins," *CFL, 3rd Ser.,* 11 (1909) 38-48.

George Frederick Wright, "The Mistakes of Darwin and His Would-be Followers," *CFL, 3rd Ser.,* 10 (1909) 333-337.

E. J. Gwynn, "The Bible, or Evolution, Which?" *CFL, 3rd Ser.,* 11 (1909) 74-76. *(Editorial)*

E. J. Gwynn, "Darwinian Evolution or Genesis—Which?" *CFL, 3rd Ser.,* 11 (1909) 295-303.

E. B. Poulton, "The Centenary of Darwin: Darwin and his Modern Critics," *QRL* 211 (1909) 1-38. *(Review)*

*F. R. Tennant, "The Influence of Darwinism upon Theology," *QRL* 211 (1909) 418-440. *(Review)*

John M. Macfarlane, "The Legacy Left Us by Darwin and His Collaborators," *RChR, 4th Ser.,* 13 (1909) 378-401.

Anonymous, "A Study in Evolution," *ET* 21 (1909-10) 115-116.

Borden P. Bowne, "Darwin and Darwinism," *HJ* 8 (1909-10) 122-138.

*C. H. Parez, "Short Studies and Correspondence. Men of Science and Genesis," *ICMM* 6 (1909-10) 105-106.

*Herbert William Magoun, "The Glacial Epoch and the Noahian Deluge," *BS* 67 (1910) 105-119, 204-229.

Simon FitzSimons, "Father Wassman on Evolution," *ACQR* 35 (1910) 12-48.

J. B. McGovern, "W. E. Gladstone and T. H. Huxley," *HR* 59 (1910) 16-19.

*Thomas W. Galloway, "Does Evolutionary Philosophy Offer Any Constructive Argument for the Reality of God?" *HTR* 3 (1910) 500-510.

John I. Swander, "The Merits and Mistakes of Darwinism," *RChR, 4th Ser.*, 14 (1910) 200-215.

*Henry Proctor, "Evolution and Genesis," *AAOJ* 33 (1911) 151-154.

*Robert Paterson, "Scientific Difficulties in a Section of Paul's Teaching. I. *Evolution: Creation in Genesis,*" *HR* 62 (1911) 15-21.

*Walter Foxon, "Does the Doctrine of Evolution Destroy the Teaching of Genesis 1:1-2:3," *HR* 62 (1911) 346-353.

R. E. Froude, "Is Darwinism Played Out?" *DR* 151 (1912) 241-255.

*Clark Wissler, "The Doctrine of Evolution and Anthropology," *AJRPE* 6 (1913) 223-237.

William Patten, Ray Moulton, Henry Fairfield Osborn, T. P. Mall, S. W. Williston, Albert P. Mathews, Jacques Loeb, John M. Coulter, E. G. Conklin, C. M. Child, Frank R. Lillie, Edward B. Wilson, Charles B. Davenport, "Has Evolution 'Collapsed'?" *BW* 41 (1913) 75-79.

Wm. M. M'Pheeters, "'Has Evolution Collapsed? A Symposium by Scientists'," *CFL, 3rd Ser.*, 16 (1913) 221-223.

Joseph Hutcheson, "Bergson's Creative Evolution," *HR* 65 (1913) 191-196.

Andrew C. Zenos, "Regarding Evolution," *HR* 65 (1913) 456-457.

Alexander Turnbull, "Regarding Evolution," *HR* 66 (1913) 168.

J. Arthur Thomson, "The Biological Control of Life," *ET* 25 (1913-14) 102-109.

G. Frederick Wright, "Present Aspects of the Relation between Science and Revelation," *BS* 71 (1914) 513-533.

W. Breitenbach, "Fifty Years in the Service of the Evolutionary Theory," *OC* 28 (1914) 74-92.

*L[uther] T. Townsend "The First Man. How Man Did Not Originate," *CFL, 3rd Ser.*, 19 (1915) 56-61.

*Warren Upham, "Geologic and Archaeologic Time," *BS* 72 (1915) 421-432.

Ukichi Kawaguchi, "The Doctrine of Evolution and the Conception of God," *AJT* 19 (1915) 550-576.

*L[uther] T. Townsend, "The First Man, According to Evolution," *CFL, 3rd Ser.,* 20 (1915) 154-157.

Paul Elmer More, "Evolution and the Other World," *HTR* 8 (1915) 339-356.

Charles Caverno, "Louis Agassiz and Charles Darwin: A Synthesis," *BS* 73 (1916) 137-140.

L. T. Townsend, "Transmutation of Species, A Delusion," *CFL, 3rd Ser.,* 21 (1916) 3-8.

L. T. Townsend, "Sterility of Hybrids," *CFL, 3rd Ser.,* 21 (1916) 104-107.

L. T. Townsend, "Everything After Its Kind," *CFL, 3rd Ser.,* 21 (1916) 59-62.

L. T. Townsend, "Artificial Culture and Breeding," *CFL, 3rd Ser.,* 21 (1916) 156-161.

L. T. Townsend, "Rudimentary Organs and Unused Structures, Employed in Support of Evolution," *CFL, 3rd Ser.,* 21 (1916) 212-215, 262-266.

L. T. Townsend, "Similarities of Organic Structures and Other Similarities Wrongly Employed in Support of Evolution," *CFL, 3rd Ser.,* 22 (1916) 24-29.

L. T. Townsend, "Similarities of Organic Structures and Other Similarities Wrongly Employed in Support of Evolution. Second Paper," *CFL, 3rd Ser.,* 22 (1916) 68-72.

L. T. Townsend, "Missing and Hypothetical Links," *CFL, 3rd Ser.,* 22 (1916) 116-119.

L. T. Townsend, "Missing and Hypothetical Links. Second Paper," *CFL, 3rd Ser.,* 22 (1916) 161-166.

Arthur Keith, "Presidental Address. On Certain Factors concerned in the Evolution of Human Races," *JRAI* 46 (1916) 10-34.

L. T. Townsend, "The Theory of Evolution; Its Incompetence," *CFL, 3rd Ser.,* 23 (1917) 157-164.

L. T. Townsend, "Disagreements Among Evolutionists," *CFL, 3rd Ser.*, 23 (1917) 209-216.

L. T. Townsend, "Scientific Opinion Opposed to Evolution," *CFL, 3rd Ser.*, 23 (1917) 259-265.

*L. T. Townsend, "Historical Geology, Historical Anthropology, and the Theory of Evolution," *CFL, 3rd Ser.*, 24 (1918) 251-253, 294-296.

*C. Sprenger, "The Evolution Theory in its Bearing on Theology and Ethics," *TZDES* 46 (1918) 281-285.

George McCready Price, "A Closed Question Reopened," *BR* 4 (1919) 426-454. *[Creation vs. Evolution]*

*Thomas J. Agius, "Genesis and Evolution," *IER, 5th Ser.*, 13 (1919) 441-453.

O. A. Tingelstad, "The Theory of Evolution Today," *TTM* 2 (1919) 161-201.

Laird Wingate Snell, "'Create Evolution' and the Christian Faith," *ATR* 2 (1919-20) 255-289.

G. Frederick Wright, "Genesis and Science," *CFL, 3rd Ser.*, 26 (1920) 2-4.

Anonymous, "'Scientific Bluff'," *CFL, 3rd Ser.*, 26 (1920) 85-86.

Anonymous, "Higher Criticism—Evolution," *CFL, 3rd Ser.*, 26 (1920) 493-495.

Herbert Booth Smith, "Has Evolution Overthrown the Bible?" *CFL, 3rd Ser.*, 27 (1921) 301-307.

A. C. Dixon, "The Origin of Life," *CFL, 3rd Ser.*, 27 (1921) 323-324.

W. H. Griffith Thomas, "Evolution and the Supernatural," *BS* 79 (1922) 184-208.

William Jennings Bryan, "The Menace of Darwinism," *CFL, 3rd Ser.*, 28 (1922) 181-198.

H. W. Clough, "The Bible *vs.* Evolution," *CFL, 3rd Ser.*, 28 (1922) 589-590.

Frederic J. Gurney, "Evolution, the Bible and Religion," *HR* 84 (1922) 103-109.

Cephas C. Bateman, "'Evolution, the Bible and Religion'," *HR* 84 (1922) 426.

*William Jennings Bryan, "God and Evolution. I. Moses vs. Darwin," *HR* 83 (1922) 446-452.

S. Parker Cadman, "God and Evolution. II. Darwin's Theory of Natural Selection," *HR* 83 (1922) 452-456.

Alfred T. Schofield, "Some Difficulties of Evolution," *JTVI* 54 (1922) 80-91. [(Discussion, pp. 91-94) (Communications by J. E. H. Thompson, p. 94; W. Woods-Smyth, p. 95)]

J. C. F. Rupp, "The Rule of Authority in Religious Thought," *LCR* 41 (1922) 336-352. *[Creation vs. Evolution]*

*Ismar J. Peritz, "The Biblical Account of Creation and Evolution," *MR* 105 (1922) 960-968.

William Brenton Greene Jr., "Yet Another Criticism of the Theory of Evolution," *PTR* 20 (1922) 537-561.

George McCready Price, "The Fossils and Age-Markers in Geology," *PTR* 20 (1922) 585-615.

Edmond G. A. Holmes, "The Idea of Evolution and the Idea of God," *HJ* 21 (1922-23) 227-247.

*N. H. Williams, "'The Idea of Evolution and the Idea of God'," *HJ* 21 (1922-23) 386-388.

William Wallace Everts, "Science Ignorant of Origins," *BS* 80 (1923) 174-185.

George McCready Price, "The New Catastrophism in Geology," *BS* 80 (1923) 209-236.

Leander S. Keyser, "The Theory of Evolution up to Date," *BS* 80 (1923) 471-490.

A. C. Dixon, "The Menace of Evolution," *CFL, 3rd Ser.,* 29 (1923) 28-30.

*Harold W. Clark, "The New Genesis," *CFL, 3rd Ser.,* 29 (1923) 40-41. *[Paraphrase of Genesis 1 based on the evolutionary theory]*

L[eander] S. K[eyser], "Who's Who in Evolution," *CFL, 3rd Ser.*, 29 (1923) 73-75.

L[eander] S. K[eyser], "The *Non-Sequitur* in Evolution," *CFL, 3rd Ser.*, 29 (1923) 128-129.

Dyson Hague, "The Christian and Evolution," *CFL, 3rd Ser.*, 29 (1923) 134-139.

C. V. Dunn, "Mr. Bryan and His Critics," *CFL, 3rd Ser.*, 29 (1923) 321-330, 413-417, 489-496.

L[eander] S. K[eyser], "Darwinism and Evolution," *CFL, 3rd Ser.*, 29 (1923) 390-391.

D[avid] S. K[ennedy], "Revelation and Evolution," *CFL, 3rd Ser.*, 29 (1923) 398-399.

*W. B. Riley, "Do Genesis and Geology Agree?" *CFL, 3rd Ser.*, 29 (1923) 431-437.

W. M. McPheeters, "Evolution: Its Effects: Is Mr. Bryan an Idle Alarmist?" *CFL, 3rd Ser.*, 29 (1923) 562-563.

J. F. Lawson, "Learned and Fashionable Substitute for Story of Creation," *CFL, 3rd Ser.*, 29 (1923) 620-625.

L[eander] S. Keyser, "A Mixture of Science and Conjecture: An Analysis of an Evolutionist's Logical Processes," *CFL, 3rd Ser.*, 29 (1923) 625-629.

L[eander] S. Keyser, "'The Misconceptions of an Evolutionist' Some Critical Remarks on Both His Manner and His Matter," *LQ* 53 (1923) 82-102.

James Dunlop, "The Evolution of Evolution," *R&E* 20 (1923) 169-187.

W. Lee Rector, "The Import of Organic Evolution," *SWJT* 7 (1923) #2, 10-23.

W. Lee Rector, "The Defects of Theistic Evolution," *SWJT* 7 (1923) #3, 36-47.

L[eander] S. Keyser, "Vulnerable Points in the Theory of Evolution," *TZDES* 51 (1923) 109-117.

Dunbar H. Ogden, "The Bible and Evolution," *USR* 35 (1923-24) 253-261.

*William Hallock Johnson, "Evolution and the Fall," *BR* 9 (1924) 371-386.

D[avid] J[ames] B[urrell], "Evolution," *CFL, 3rd Ser.,* 30 (1924) 241-244.

Joseph D. Wilson, "The New Geology," *CFL, 3rd Ser.,* 30 (1924) 278-279, 457-458. *(Review)*

L[eander] S. Keyser, "Some So-Called 'Proofs' Critically Examined," *CFL, 3rd Ser.,* 30 (1924) 322-326.

George McCready Price, "What's So and what Isn't about Evolution: Darwinism Theory Fades as Scientific Knowledge Increases," *CFL, 3rd Ser.,* 30 (1924) 326-330.

D[avid] J[ames] B[urrell], "Some Facts about Darwin and his Theory," *CFL, 3rd Ser.,* 30 (1924) 441-445.

L[eander] S. Keyser, "Was the Horse Evolved?" *CFL, 3rd Ser.,* 30 (1924) 495-497.

Eduard König, "The Modern Science of Religion and the Evolutionary Theory," *CFL, 3rd Ser.,* 30 (1924) 510-513. [Anonymous notes, pp. 494-495] *(Trans. by E. W. Hammer)*

Leander S. Keyser, "The Hall of the Age of Man As Described by Drs. Osborn and Greagory," *CFL, 3rd Ser.,* 30 (1924) 516-519.

George McCready Price, "Botany Refutes Evolution," *CFL, 3rd Ser.,* 30 (1924) 587-589.

Philip Mauro, "Why Evolution is a Religious Dogma," *CFL, 3rd Ser.,* 30 (1924) 636-638.

George McCready Price, "What Botanists Are Doing as to Organic Evolution," *CFL, 3rd Ser.,* 30 (1924) 641-645.

Edward B. Pollard, "Some Fundamental Doctrines in the Light of Evolution," *CQ* 1 (1924) 66-84.

George McCready Price, "Geology and Its Relation to Scripture Revelation," *JTVI* 56 (1924) 97-115, 121-123. (Discussion and Communications, pp. 115-121)

T. E. Savage, "Science and the Bible," *OC* 38 (1924) 129-141.

Floyd E. Hamilton, "The Evolutionary Hypothesis in the Light of Modern Science," *PTR* 22 (1924) 420-446.

E. Hove, "Evolutionism," *TTM* 7 (1924) 182-196.

William Colcord Woods, "The Present Status of Evolution," *ACM* 16 (1924-25) 98-118.

Leander S. Keyser, "Creation versus Evolution," *BS* 82 (1925) 276-298.

L. Franklin Gruber, "The Physical Universe: Finite or Infinite?" *BS* 82 (1925) 307-313.

George McCready Price, "Outlawed Theories," *CFL, 3rd Ser.,* 31 (1925) 134-142.

Leander S. Keyser, "What is the Lure of It?" *CFL, 3rd Ser.,* 31 (1925) 143-144.

L[eander] S. Keyser, "The Claims of Some Scientists," *CFL, 3rd Ser.,* 31 (1925) 197-201.

Henry W. Bromley, "A Personal Letter on Evolution Addressed to the Dean of a Methodist University," *CFL, 3rd Ser.,* 31 (1925) 201-207.

Leander S. Keyser, "A Scientist's Analysis Analyzed," *CFL, 3rd Ser.,* 31 (1925) 297-303.

H. Gracey, "Evolution and the Honey Bee," *CFL, 3rd Ser.,* 31 (1925) 442-444.

Leander S. Keyser, "'The Case Against Evolution'," *CFL, 3rd Ser.,* 31 (1925) 451-456.

P[hilip] M[auro], "'Evidences for Evolution'," *CFL, 3rd Ser.,* 31 (1925) 457-459.

P[hilip] M[auro], "'The Bee's Knees'," *CFL, 3rd Ser.,* 31 (1925) 467-469.

P[hilip] M[auro], "Evolution as a Religious Dogma," *CFL, 3rd Ser.,* 31 (1925) 470-472.

Leander S. Keyser, "The Reasoning of an Evolutionist—Is It Valid and Convincing?" *CFL, 3rd Ser.,* 31 (1925) 482-486.

Arthur I. Brown, "Evolution and Blood Tests," *CFL, 3rd Ser.,* 31 (1925) 533-541.

P[hilip] M[auro], "Evidences as to Evolution," *CFL, 3rd Ser.,* 31 (1925) 584-586.

William B. Riley, "Resolved, That the Earth and all Life in it are the Result of Evolution," *CFL, 3rd Ser.,* 31 (1925) 598-605.

Arthur I. Brown, "The Recapitulation Theory," *CFL, 3rd Ser.,* 31 (1925) 606-615.

George McCready Price, "Revelation and Evolution: Can They be Harmonized?"*JTVI* 57 (1925) 167-182, 187-189. (Discussion and Communications, pp. 183-187)

George McCready Price, "Modern Botany and the Theory of Organic Evolution," *PTR* 23 (1925) 51-65.

David S. Clark, "Theology and Evolution," *PTR* 23 (1925) 193-212. [I. Evolution and God; II. Evolution and Creation; III. Evolution and Man; IV. Evolution and Sin; V. Evolution and the Scriptures; VI. Evolution and Christ; VII. Evolution and Salvation]

I. O. Nothstein, "'The Phantom of Organic Evolution'," *AugQ* 5 (1926) 49-57.

George M'Cready Price, "On Being a Good Scientific Sport," *BS* 83 (1926) 298-311.

P[hilip] M[auro], "Does Science Oppose the Bible?" *CFL, 3rd Ser.,* 32 (1926) 1-3.

L[eander] S. K[eyser], "Unbelief and Evolution," *CFL, 3rd Ser.,* 32 (1926) 5-6.

Ernest Andrew Timmons, "Evolution, Nature, and the Bible," *CFL, 3rd Ser.,* 32 (1926) 18-19.

L[eander] S. Keyser, "A Scientific Definition," *CFL, 3rd Ser.,* 32 (1926) 19-21.

L[eander] S. K[eyser], "Dr. McCosh and Evolution," *CFL, 3rd Ser.,* 32 (1926) 241-242.

Arthur I. Brown, "Geology, Fossils and Evolution," *CFL, 3rd Ser.,* 32 (1926) 269-273, 326-329.

Henry Frey Lutz, "Evolution and Scholarship: The Limitations of Scholarship," *CFL, 3rd Ser.,* 32 (1926) 273-277.

*Byron C. Nelson, "The Distribution of Plants and Animals in the Light of the Bible," *CFL, 3rd Ser.,* 32 (1926) 329-333.

D[udley] J[oseph] Whitney, "Fruit-Flies and Evolution," *CFL, 3rd Ser.,* 32 (1926) 361-362.

L[eander] S. K[eyser], "The Time Element in Evolution," *CFL, 3rd Ser.,* 32 (1926) 381-383.

Edwin Deacon, "Moses and the Scientists," *CFL, 3rd Ser.,* 32 (1926) 442-444.

Arthur I. Brown, "What Makes Evolution Unbelievable," *CFL, 3rd Ser.,* 32 (1926) 449-451.

Arthur I. Brown, "The Law of Mendel versus the Theory of Evolution," *CFL, 3rd Ser.,* 32 (1926) 517-521.

Michael Browne, "Modern Theories of Evolution," *IER, 5th Ser.,* 27 (1926) 561-570; 28 (1926) 35-43, 124-132, 561-582.

W. R. Siegart, "Some Reflections on Evolution," *LQ* 56 (1926) 153-158.

Floyd E. Hamilton, "Modern Aspects of the Theory of Evolution," *PTR* 24 (1926) 396-448.

Fulton J. Sheen, "God in Evolution," *TFUQ* 1 (1926-27) 575-587.

P[aul] M[auro], "The Amazing Credulity of the Evolutionist, *CFL, 3rd Ser.,* 33 (1927) 65-66.

Oliver L. Ross, "The Evolution Problem," *CFL, 3rd Ser.,* 33 (1927) 158-159.

L[eander] S. K[eyser], "Were Plants and Animals evolved from a Common Stock?" *CFL, 3rd Ser.,* 33 (1927) 191-192.

George Boddis, "Are all Scientists Evolutionists?" *CFL, 3rd Ser.,* 33 (1927) 202-206.

*Frank R. Buckalew, "The Science of the Bible," *CFL, 3rd Ser.,* 33 (1927) 278-280.

G. H. Richardson, "Fossils and Fundamentalists," *ACM* 21 (1927) 222-227.

Leander S. Keyser, "The Clear and Definite meaning of Evolution," *CFL, 3rd Ser.,* 33 (1927) 234-236.

George McCready Price, "Some Evolutionary Falsehoods Exposed," *CFL, 3rd Ser.,* 33 (1927) 270-272.

William B. Riley, "Whence Life and Species?" *CFL, 3rd Ser.,* 33 (1927) 272-273.

George Boddis, "Do the Evidences Prove Evolution?" *CFL, 3rd Ser.,* 33 (1927) 348-352.

*D[udley] J[oseph] Whitney, "Evolution and Early Man," *CFL, 3rd Ser.,* 33 (1927) 468-469.

D[avid] S. K[ennedy], "Evolution and Religion," *CFL, 3rd Ser.,* 33 (1927) 489-490.

L[eander] S. K[eyser], "Some Random Thoughts on Evolution," *CFL, 3rd Ser.,* 33 (1927) 612-614.

J. A. O. Stub, Sterling P. King, J. M. Stanfield, Theodore Graebner, Victor I. Masters, William E. Biederwolf, Arthur I. Brown, Byron C. Nelson, Alvin S. Zerbe, and R. A. Meek, "A Symposium on Evolution," *CFL, 3rd Ser.,* 33 (1927) 637-642.

Alexander MacDonald, "The Bee and Evolution," *TFUQ* 2 (1927-28) 464-475.

George McC[ready] Price, James M. Gray, John A. Huffman, W. A. Williams, William B. Riley, S. James Bole, T. C. Horton, Reginald Cock, William Schoeler, G. T. Lee, H. W. Magoun, Ort A. Keyser, Alexander Hardie, Floyd E. Hamilton, Charles B. McMullen, William Hallock Johnson, John F. Herget, A. F. Finn, Thomas Carey Johnson, Chester K. Lehman, William James Robinson, Glenn Gates Cole, L. M. Davies, and Charles H. Coates, "A Symposium on Evolution," *CFL, 3rd Ser.,* 34 (1928) 25-31, 89-93, 157-158.

Frank E. Allen, "Sir Arthur Keith versus the Bible," *CFL, 3rd Ser.,* 34 (1928) 34-37.

[Leander S. Keyser(?)], "Random Thoughts on Evolution," *CFL, 3rd Ser.,* 34 (1928) 54-55.

George Boddis, "Does Theism Explain the Origin of the Universe?" *CFL, 3rd Ser.,* 34 (1928) 79-83.

Z. T. Osborn, "Possible Causes of the Arrested Evolution of Reptiles," *CFL, 3rd Ser.,* 34 (1928) 201-204.

W. Maslin Frysinger, "The Miracles of Evolution," *CFL, 3rd Ser.,* 34 (1928) 213-214.

A. Fleischmann, "Twelve Counts Against the Theory," *CFL, 3rd Ser.,* 34 (1928) 215-216. *(Trans. by H. O. Schneider)*

Parl F. Mellenbruch, "Evolution Weighed in the Balance of Psychology and Found Wanting," *CFL, 3rd Ser.,* 34 (1928) 269-270.

Dudley Joseph Whitney, "No Naturalistic Origin for the Earth," *CFL, 3rd Ser.,* 34 (1928) 275-277.

L[eander] S. K[eyser], "Defining Evolution Once More," *CFL, 3rd Ser.,* 34 (1928) 301-302. *(Editorial)*

P[hilip] M[auro], "A Rock on Which Evolution Goes to Pieces," *CFL, 3rd Ser.,* 34 (1928) 312-313. *(Editorial)*

Dwight L. Chapin, "What I Think of the Theory," *CFL, 3rd Ser.,* 34 (1928) 388-389.

C. William Anderson, "What Darwin Actually Said," *CFL, 3rd Ser.,* 34 (1928) 391.

D[udley] J[oseph] Whitney, "The Geologist's Dilemma," *CFL, 3rd Ser.,* 34 (1928) 393.

L[eander] S. K[eyser], "How the Theorists Treat the Bible, with an Added Thought on Creation," *CFL, 3rd Ser.,* 34 (1928) 413-415. *(Editorial)*

J. Newton Parker, "The Scientific Status of Evolution," *CFL, 3rd Ser.,* 34 (1928) 422-429.

W. Henry Thompson, "The Primal Fire Mist and Other Primal Matters," *CFL, 3rd Ser.,* 34 (1928) 430-440.

W. B. Riley, "Evolution vs. Creation Or, Darwin vs. The Divine Word," *CFL, 3rd Ser.,* 34 (1928) 446-448.

W. Maslin Frysinger, "Evolution Self-Contradictory," *CFL, 3rd Ser.,* 34 (1928) 450-451.

George Boddis, "Evolution: Is it True or False?" *CFL, 3rd Ser.,* 34 (1928) 543-546, 600-604, 652-657.

Dudley Joseph Whitney, "What Theory of Earth History shall we Adopt?" *CFL, 3rd Ser.,* 34 (1928) 616-618.

Dudley Joseph Whitney, "Creation, Evolution or Xenogenesis," *CFL, 3rd Ser.,* 34 (1928) 670-671.

Frederick Tracey, "Evolution and the Higher Life of Man," *CQ* 5 (1928) 131-139.

Arthur Keith, "The Evolution of the Human Races. *The Huxley Memorial Lecture for* 1928," *JRAI* 58 (1928) 305-321.

Ambrose J. Wilson, "What Charles Darwin Really Found," *PTR* 26 (1928) 515-530.

Joseph Ratner, "Fundamentalism and the Doctrine of Evolution," *OC* 42 (1928) 348-362.

J. V. Nash, "The Religious Evolution of Darwin," *OC* 42 (1928) 449-463.

E. O. James, "Evolution and Faith," *Theo* 16 (1928) 2-9.

W. Exon, "Darwinism and What it Implies," *HJ* 27 (1928-29) 666-675.

George Boddis, "Evolution: Is it True or False?" *CFL, 3rd Ser.,* 35 (1929) 18-24. [A Review of the Evidences. Embryology and Blood Tests]

C. H. Buchanan, "Orthodox Evolution," *CFL, 3rd Ser.,* 35 (1929) 247-249, 357-362, 416-420.

Dudley Joseph Whitney, "The Miracles of Evolution," *CFL, 3rd Ser.,* 35 (1929) 250-252.

Frank E. Allen, "Dr. Clark Arouses a Furor Among Evolutionists," *CFL, 3rd Ser.,* 35 (1929) 309-312.

D. L. Chapin, "Creation and Evolution Compared," *CFL, 3rd Ser.*, 35 (1929) 423-424.

George McCready Price, "A Solution of the Evolution Riddle," *CFL, 3rd Ser.*, 35 (1929) 468-474.

Dudley Joseph Whitney, "The Origin of Species," *CFL, 3rd Ser.*, 35 (1929) 475-479.

Dudley Joseph Whitney, "The Confusion about Darwin," *CFL, 3rd Ser.*, 35 (1929) 479-482.

L[eander] S. K[eyser], "Professor Clark on Evolution and Creation," *CFL, 3rd Ser.*, 35 (1929) 483-485. [Letter from Austin H. Clark, p. 483]

George Boddis, "Evolution: Is it True or False? Review of the Evidences, Geology and History," *CFL, 3rd Ser.*, 35 (1929) 522-529.

C. H. Buchanan, "Orthodox Evolution—Its Philosophy," *CFL, 3rd Ser.*, 35 (1929) 534-537.

Byron C. Nelson, "More about the Origin of Species," *CFL, 3rd Ser.*, 35 (1929) 539-540.

George Boddis, "Evolution: Is it True or False? Can the Bible and Science be Harmonized?" *CFL, 3rd Ser.*, 35 (1929) 600-604.

G. W. Dunham, "A Layman's Reply to Dr. Clark," *CFL, 3rd Ser.*, 35 (1929) 641-644.

Joseph Dudley Whitney, "The Heart of Organic Evolution," *CFL, 3rd Ser.*, 35 (1929) 644-647.

C. H. Buchanan, "Orthodox Evolution—Its Wrecking Tendency," *CFL, 3rd Ser.*, 35 (1929) 647-650.

*Alan Stuart, "Genesis and Geology," *EQ* 1 (1929) 345-360.

Arthur John Hubbard, "Evolution and the Modernist: 'Is it Peace?'," *Theo* 18 (1929) 122-127.

Leonard Darwin, "Darwinism. A Reply to the Bishop of Exeter," *HJ* 28 (1929-30) 273-281.

Antoine Grange, "Have Men Animal Ancestors?" *TFUQ* 4 (1929-30) 440-465.

H. W. Magoun, "Some Neglected Factors in the Evolution Problem," *CFL, 3rd Ser.*, 36 (1930) 23-26.

C. H. Buchanan, "Orthodox Evolution—A Close-Up View," *CFL, 3rd Ser.*, 36 (1930) 32-34.

Dudley Joseph Whitney, "The First Living Thing," *CFL, 3rd Ser.*, 36 (1930) 35-37.

P[aul] M[auro], "Supposed Fossil Evidences for Evolution Repudiated by Higher Scientific Authority," *CFL, 3rd Ser.*, 36 (1930) 64-65.

George McCready Price, "What are the Big Questions at Issue?" *CFL, 3rd Ser.*, 36 (1930) 139-141.

Dudley Joseph Whitney, "The Problems of Organic Evolution," *CFL, 3rd Ser.*, 36 (1930) 197-199.

H. W. Magoun, "More About the Evolution Problem," *CFL, 3rd Ser.*, 36 (1930) 305-308.

W. G. Bennett, "Another Theory of Evolution," *CFL, 3rd Ser.*, 36 (1930) 380-382.

Dudley Joseph Whitney, "Deluge Geology and Evolution," *CFL, 3rd Ser.*, 36 (1930) 425-428.

George Boddis, "Evolution Cross Examined By Facts," *CFL, 3rd Ser.*, 36 (1930) 527-537.

Dudley Joseph Whitney, "The Arguments for Evolution," *CFL, 3rd Ser.*, 36 (1930) 553-556.

G. L. Young, "The Tendency of Evolution," *CFL, 3rd Ser.*, 36 (1930) 547-551, 580-585, 645-648.

L[eander] S. K[eyser], "Do the Evolutionists Reason Well?" *CFL, 3rd Ser.*, 36 (1930) 569-571.

Byron C. Nelson, "What Concession, if any, must we in Interest of Truth make to the Evolutionists?" *TF* 2 (1930) 1-13.

G. F. Scott-Elliot, "What Darwinism Does Not Imply," *HJ* 29 (1930-31) 342-352.

W. Bell Dawson, "Science and the Divine Revelation," *BR* 16 (1931) 77-96.

*Herbert W. Magoun, "Are Geological Ages Irreconcilable with Genesis?" *BS* 88 (1931) 347-357.

George McCready Price, "Apologia Pro Fide Mea," *BS* 88 (1931) 392-405.

George McCready Price, "Some Facts about the Geological 'Ages'," *CFL, 3rd Ser.*, 37 (1931) 29-31.

*Elmer Ellsworth Helms, "Is the Bible Unscientific?" *CFL, 3rd Ser.*, 37 (1931) 92-95.

Dudley Joseph Whitney, "Can Evolution be Theistic?" *CFL, 3rd Ser.*, 37 (1931) 131-133.

F. P. Dunnington, "Is Evolution Science?" *CFL, 3rd Ser.*, 37 (1931) 465-468.

P. E. Kretzmann, "Has Our Church a Quarrel with Science?" *CTM* 2 (1931) 833-838.

Edward O. Sisson, "Religious Implications of Evolution," *OC* 45 (1931) 458-473.

Carl J. Nolstad, "What Is True About Evolution?" *TF* 3 (1931) 267-274.

*John Lowell Butler, "Astronomical Solution of Ancient and Modern Climates," *BS* 89 (1932) 68-86.

George Lindley Young, "Origin and Destiny," *BS* 89 (1932) 453-469.

George McCready Price, "How Old is the Earth?" *CFL, 3rd Ser.*, 38 (1932) 20-23.

L[eander] S. K[eyser], "Quotations from Harry Rimmer," *CFL, 3rd Ser.* 38 (1932) 272-273.

*George McCready Price, "Some Scientific Aspects of Apologetics," *EQ* 4 (1932) 234-243.

Henry R. Kindersley, "The Bible and Evolution: The Evidence of History and Science," *JTVI* 64 (1932) 191-202, 207-208. [(Discussion, pp. 202-206) (Communication by A. G. Short, pp. 206-207)]

James Knight, "The Evolution Theory To-day," *EQ* 5 (1933) 3-12.

Albertus Pieters, "Science and the Bible," *EQ* 5 (1933) 257-270.

W. Bell Dawson, "The Bible and Science," *CFL, 3rd Ser.*, 40 (1934) 35-39.

George McCready Price, "The Fallacy about the Time-Values of the Fossils," *CFL, 3rd Ser.*, 40 (1934) 134-138.

Arthur Stevens Phelps, "What is Theistic Evolution?" *CQ* 11 (1934) 335-340.

Edward Scribner Ames, "Christianity and Scientific Thinking," *JR* 14 (1934) 4-12.

John M. Cooper, "The Scientific Evidence Bearing Upon Human Evolution," *AQW* 8 (1935) #1/2, 1-56.

George McCready Price, "Guarding the Sacred Cow," *CFL, 3rd Ser.*, 41 (1935) 124-130.

[Harry] Rimmer, "The Alphabet of Science and the Word of God," *CFL, 3rd Ser.*, 41 (1935) 187-192, 239-243; 42 (1936) 15-17, 120-131, 199-207.

G. Louis Tufts, "Evolution Tested by Geology," *CFL, 3rd Ser.*, 41 (1935) 284-294.

George McCready Price, "New Proofs of an Original Creation," *CTM* 6 (1935) 931-936.

*Ambrose Fleming, "Modern Anthropology *versus* Biblical Statements on Human Origin," *JTVI* 67 (1935) 15-40, 42. (Discussion, pp. 40-42)

C. T. Schwarze, "The Bible and the Science of Astronomy," *BS* 93 (1936) 204-213.

James R. Randolph, "When Worlds Collide," *CFL, 3rd Ser.*, 42 (1936) 55-59.

H. S. Harrison, "Presidental Address. Concerning Human Progress," *JRAI* 66 (1936) 1-17.

John Ashton, "Why Be Evolutionists?" *TFUQ* 11 (1936-37) 238-251.

J. Newton Parker, "Facts About Evolution," *CFL, 3rd Ser.*, 43 (1937) 152-154.

James R. Randolph, "Do Mendel's Laws Disprove Evolution?" *CFL, 3rd Ser.*, 43 (1937) 155-157.

H[arry] R[immer], "The Collapse of the Theory of Evolution," *CFL, 3rd Ser.*, 43 (1937) 241-248.

*W[illiam] B. R[iley], "Are the Scriptures Scientific?" *CFL, 3rd Ser.*, 43 (1937) 255-262.

W. Bell Dawson, "Evolution and Its Danger," *CFL, 3rd Ser.*, 43 (1937) 306-307.

H. J. Fleure, "Racial Evolution and Archæology. (*Huxley Memorial Lecture*, 1937)," *JRAI* 67 (1937) 205-229.

Alan Stuart, "Science and the Interpretation of Scripture," *JTVI* 69 (1937) 90-108, 124-132. [(Discussion, pp. 108-114) (Communications by Ambrose Fleming, pp. 114-118; L. M. Davies, pp. 118-120; E. Cecil Curwen, p. 120; J. Barcroft Anderson, pp. 120-121; P. W. O'Gorman, pp. 121-124; W. Bell Dawson, p. 124)]

Henry R. Kindersley, "Organic Evolution," *CFL, 3rd Ser.*, 44 (1938) 229-230.

( ) A. "Evolution Opposed," *CTM* 9 (1938) 528-529.

Gustave Mie, "Natural Science and Faith in God," *LCQ* 11 (1938) 405-413.

H. D. Koehne, "'The Assured Results of Geology'," *AusTR* 10 (1939) 70-80, 97-106.

Arthur Custance, "Modern Geology and the Bible," *BS* 96 (1939) 164-182.

Anonymous, "Did This Fish Live Too Long?" *CTM* 10 (1939) 774.

J. H. Morrison, "Some Changes in the Scientific Mind," *ET* 51 (1939-40) 57-61.

Anonymous, "The Bible and Evolution," *CTM* 11 (1940) 300-301.

*Hugh Miller, James D. Dana, J. William Dawson, and Harold Jeffries, "The Relation of Geology to the Days of Creation and the Sabbath Rest," *JTVI* 72 (1940) 202-211. *(Compiled by William Bell Dawson)*

Anonymous, "Evolution, Science and Faith," *CTM* 12 (1941) 859-861.

Hans Dressel, "The Bearing of Evolution on the Teachings of the Bible," *KZ* 65 (1941) 399-412.

Douglas Dewar, "Dr. Julian Huxley on Evolution," *EQ* 15 (1943) 199-205.

H. G. Wells, "Memorandum on Biological Survival," *HJ* 42 (1943-44) 97-106.

L. Richmond Wheeler, "Survival: Biological and Human," *HJ* 42 (1943-44) 204-212.

P. E. Kretzmann, "The Ghost Is Not Yet Laid," *CTM* 15 (1944) 339-340.

Arthur I. Brown, "Fade-Out of Evolution," *CTM* 15 (1944) 764-766.

Douglas Dewar, "Current Theories of the Origin of Living Organisms," *JTVI* 76 (1944) 53-75, 85-93. (Communications by L. R. Wheeler, pp. 75-78; L. M. Davies, pp. 78-79; O. R. Barclay, pp. 79-80; Philip G. Fothergill, pp. 80-83; A. Morly Davies, pp. 83-85)

*Oscar E. Olson, "The Book of Genesis and Modern Science," *CovQ* 5 (1945) #3, 131-137.

*Russell L. Mixter, "Genesis and Geology," *CO* 3 (1945-46) 119-121.

*Julian O. Krusling, "Evolution and Man," *SS* 15 (June, 1946) 38-47.

Joseph L. Blau, "An American-Jewish View of the Evolution Controversy," *HUCA* 20 (1947) 617-634.

R[ussell L.] Mixter, "The Science of Heredity and the Source of Species," *JASA* 1 (1949) #3, 1-6. (Discussion, pp. 6-9)

Bernard Ramm, "The Scientifico-Logical Structure of the Theory of Evolution," *JASA* 1 (1949) #3, 10-15. (Discussion, p.15)

E. Y. Monsma, "Some Presuppositions in Evolutionary Thinking," *JASA* 1 (1949) #3, 15-19. (Discussion, pp. 19-30)

*Frederick Moriarty and William G. Guindon, "Genesis and Scientific Studies on the Origin of the World," *CBQ* 12 (1950) 428-438.

J. Lawrence Kulp, "Deluge Geology," *JASA* 2 (1950) #1, 1-15.

Anonymous, "Comment on the 'Deluge Geology'," *JASA* 2 (1950) #2, 2.

J. Franklin Ewing, "Précis on Evolution," *TFUQ* 25 (1950) 53-78.

Michael J. Gruenthaner, "Evolution and the Scriptures," *CBQ* 13 (1951) 21-27.

*M. T. Brackbill, "Modern Physcial Science in the Bible," *JASA* 3 (1951) #1, 23-27.

S. Zuckerman, "*An* Ape or *The* Ape," *JRAI* 81 (1951) 57-60.

H. Francis Davis, "Organic Evolution," *ClR* 37 (1952) 478-489.

P. G. Fothergill, "Why Attack Evolution?" *DR* 226 (1952) 58-64.

Wilbur L. Bullock, "The 'Kind of Genesis and the Species' of Biology," *JASA* 4 (1952) #2, 5-7.

W. R. Thompson, "The Status of Evolutionary Theory," *LTP* 8 (1952) 196-202.

William Robinson, "Christian Belief in a Scientific Age," *ET* 64 (1952-53) 268-273.

J. Lever, "Evolution and creationism in biology," *FUQ* 2 (1952-53) 141-155.

John F. Devane, "The Age of the Earth," *MH* 9 (Winter, 1953) 10-14.

Bermudo Melendez, "Teleogenesis: A New *Finalistic* Theory of Evolution," *TD* 1 (1953) 123-127.

Bernard Ramm, "The Catholic Appoach to Bible and Science," *BS* 111 (1954) 204-212.

August C. Renhwaldt, "Some Scriptural Aspects of Processes in Nature," *CTM* 25 (1954) 433-448.

Carl S. Wise, "The Bible and Physical Research," *JASA* 6 (1954) #1, 21-23.

Chester K. Lehman, "Biblicism and Science," *JASA* 6 (1954) #4, 3-7.

Milton Millhauser, "The Scriptural geologists: An Episode in the History of Opinion," *Osiris* 11 (1954) 65-86.

Carl Tabb Bahner, "Science and God's Creation," *R&E* 51 (1954) 324-328. *[Article ends abruptly in the middle of a word—never continued or rectified!]*

H. R. Woltjer, "The age of the earth," *FUQ* 3 (1954-55) 188-204.

Thomas H. Leith, "The Scientist and the Universe," *GR* 1 (1955) 13-18.

Walter R. Hearn, "Biochemical Complexity and Its Significance In Evolution," *JASA* 7 (1955) #2, 8-12.

J. Oliver Buswell Jr., "Scientific Facts and Theology," *JASA* 7 (1955) #3, 32-37.

Herbert Freely, "The Impact of Geological Dating Upon the Interpretation of Biblical Chronology," *JASA* 7 (1955) #3, 46-49.

William Etkin, "Science and Creation," *Jud* 4 (1955) 132-141.

Dom Bruno Webb, "Evolution From a Theological Viewpoint," *DownsR* 74 (1955-56) 302-328.

W. David Stacey, "The Christian View of Nature," *ET* 67 (1955-56) 364-367.

Philip E. Hughes, "Evolutionary Dogma and Christian Theology," *WTJ* 18 (1955-56) 34-48.

*Edmund W. Sinnott, "Biology and Spiritual Values," *JR* 36 (1956) 177-189.

*P. Ronflette, "Biological Finality and God's Existence," *TD* 4 (1956) 13-16.

G. C. Berkouwer, "Christian Faith and Science," *FUQ* 4 (1956-57) 3-10.

I. A. Diepenhorts, "Science, its nature, its possibilites and its limitations," *FUQ* 4 (1956-57) 11-37.

C. C. Jonker, "The limits of physics," *FUQ* 4 (1956-57) 56-65.

Thomas H. Leith, "Radiocarbon Dating," *GR* 3 (1957) 3-8, 60-67.

George K. Schweitzer, "The Origin of the Universe," *R&E* 54 (1957) 178-194.

J. S. MacArthur, "The Church and Science," *SJT* 10 (1957) 35-44.

Sven Behrens, "The Biblical Belief About Creation and Modern Natural Science," *RefmR* 5 (1957-58) 147-150.

Gordon E. Barnes, "The Concepts of Randomness and Progress in Evolution," *F&T* 90 (1958) 183-204; 91 (1959-60) 120, 123-124. (Communications by W. G. Clarke, *F&T* 91 (1959-60) p. 65; Julian Huxley, pp. 120-121; C. W. Hume, pp. 121-123)

Walter R. Hearn, "The Creation of Life," *GR* 4 (1958) 156-165.

Heinrich D. Holland, "The Conflict Between Science and Religion," *GR* 4 (1958) 192-197.

R. Laird Harris, "Theological Aspects of Mechanists' Views of the Origin of Life," *JASA* 10 (1958) #1, 5-8.

Wayne Frair, "What Are the Scientific Possibilites For Original Kinds?" *JASA* 10 (1958) #1, 12-16.

J. Barton Payne, "The Concept of 'Kinds' in Scripture," *JASA* 10 (1958) #2, 17-19.

Janet Traver, "Enzymology and its Relation to the Genesis of Life," *JASA* 10 (1958) #3, 12-14.

Wilfred LeGros Clark, "Bones of Contention. *The Huxley Memorial Lecture, 1958,*" *JRAI* 88 (1958) 131-145.

Gavin de Beer, "Charles Darwin," *PBA* 44 (1958) 163-183.

J. A. Friend, "Theology and the Darwin Centenary," *RTR* 17 (1958) 43-53.

Ely E. Pilchik, "Of Adam and Darwin," *CCARJ* #27 (1959) 37-39.

James O. Buswell III, "Is There an Alternative to Organic Evolution," *GR* 5 (1959) 2-13.

Wilbur L. Bullock, "Evolution Versus Creation—in Retrospect and Prospect," *GR* 5 (1959) 74-79.

Allen H. Miller, "Classroom Treatments of Difficulties in Biblical Interpretation. An Approach to the Teaching of Evolution," *JCE* 2 (1959) 97-103.

F. Howarth, "Evolution or Special Creation," *LQHR* 184 (1959) 306-309.

J. O'Neill, "The Bible and Evolution," *Scrip* 11 (1959) 6-22.

J. O'Neill, "The Bible and Evolution—II," *Scrip* 11 (1959) 42-51.

Gordon E. Barnes, "Some Reflections on the Evolution Controversy," *F&T* 91 (1959-60) 158-176. [A. Introduction; B. Philosophical and Theological Conflicts, *Evolution and the Concept of Creation, Evolution and Genesis, Evolution and the Nature of Man, Evolution and the Character of God, Evolution and Natural Theology, Evolution and Ethics, Evolution and Vitalism, Evolution and Mysticism, Evolution and Humanism;* C. Some Consequences of the Controversy; D. The Christian's Attitude to Evolutionary Theories]

Julian S. Huxley, "Darwin and the Idea of Evolution," *HJ* 58 (1959-60) 1-12.

Anonymous, "Gamaliel," *LofS* 14 (1959-60) 175-178. *[Question and Answer on Genesis Creation and Evolution]*

Uuras Saarnivaara, "The Authority of the Bible and the Theory of Evolution," *RefmR* 7 (1959-60) 7-18.

Alexander Wolsky, "A Hundred Years of Darwinism in Biology," *TFUQ* 34 (1959-60) 165-184.

James Collins, "Darwin's Impact on Philosophy," *TFUQ* 34 (1959-60) 185-248.

Robert W. Gleason, "A Note on Theology and Evolution," *TFUQ* 34 (1959-60) 249-258.

G. Bosio, "Reflections on Darwinism," *AER* 143 (1960) 1-17.

*B. Škerlj, "Human Evolution and the Neanderthal Man," *Antiq* 54 (1960) 90-99.

W. R. Thompson, "'A Critique of Evolution'," *JASA* 12 (1960) #1, 2-9.

J. Frank Cassel, "Species Concepts and Definitions," *JASA* 12 (1960) #2, 2-3, 5.

Frank L. Marsh, "The Genesis Kinds in Our Modern World," *JASA* 12 (1960) #2, 4-8, 11, 13.

Rousas John Rushdoony, "The Concept of Evolution as a Cultural Myth," *IRB* #5 (1960) 6-13.

*Andres Ibanez Arana, "The age of man and biblical genealogies," *TD* 8 (1960) 149-153.

Lawrence A. Block, "Dialogues with Darwinism," *CCARJ* 8 (1960-61) #1, 34-41, 72.

John F. Hayward, "Evolution as a Theological Symbol," *HJ* 59 (1960-61) 331-342.

Uuras Saarnivaara, "The Kingdom of Heaven and the Theory of Evolution," *RefmR* 8 (1960-61) 159-169.

James D. Bales, "The Relevance of Scriptural Interpretation to Scientific Thought," *BETS* 4 (1961) 121-128.

Anonymous, "Creation and Evolution. Questions for Study," *IRB* #7 (1961) 13-20.

J. R. Huizenga, "Origin of the Universe," *JASA* 13 (1961) 34-37.

Walter R. Hearn, "Origin of Life," *JASA* 13 (1961) 38-39.

J. Frank Cassel, "Comments on the Origin of Species," *JASA* 13 (1961) 42-45.

J. Frank Cassel, "Christian Thought Today—On Origin of Species," *JASA* 13 (1961) 45-47.

James D. Bales, "The Relevance of Scriptural Interpretation to Scientific Thought," *JASA* 13 (1961) 77-82.

G. M. Balding, "Teaching Biology: The Theory of Evolution," *JCE* 4 (1961) 82-93.

Robert O. Johann, "The Logic of Evolution," *TFUQ* 36 (1961) 595-612.

R. E. D. Clark, "The Design Argument and the Limits of Science (A Comment on the Paper of Mr. G. E. Barnes—Some Reflections on the Evolution Controversy)," *F&T* 92 (1961-62) 105-111.

G. J. Sizoo, "Physical knowledge and creation," *FUQ* 8 (1961-62) 99-107.

J. V. Peach, "The Age of the Universe," *HeyJ* 3 (1962) 111-125.

Eric C. Rust, "Creation and Evolution," *R&E* 59 (1962) 181-199.

William J. Schmitt, "Spontaneous Generation and Creation," *TFUQ* 37 (1962) 269-287.

Francis Grech, "Creation and Science," *BC* 3 (1962-64) 183-189.

Bernard Ramm, "Theological Reaction to the Theory of Evolution," *JASA* 15 (1963) 71-77.

J. D. Conway, "A Roman Catholic Statement on Evolution," *JASA* 15 79-82.

John W. Klotz, "Theistic Evolution: Some Theological Implications," *JASA* 15 (1963) 82-86.

Charles K. Robinson, "Biblical Theism and Modern Science," *JR* 43 (1963) 118-138.

Kirtley F. Mather, "Creation and Evolution," *LTSB* 43 (1963) #3, 13-20.

P. Groen, "Faith and Physics," *FUQ* 9 (1963-65) 148-159.

Lawrence A. Kratz, "Notes on the Scientific Accuracy of the Bible," *SR* 9 (1963-64) 33-37.

Henry M. Morris, "The Bible *Is* a Textbook of Science," *BS* 121 (1964) 341-350; 122 (1965) 63-69.

Henry M. Morris, "The Spirit of Compromise," *GJ* 5 (1964) #1, 3-12. *[Creation or Evolution]*

Donald R. Burrill, "Science, Theology, and the Interpretation of Evidence," *JASA* 16 (1964) 68-72.

Alwyn Harry, "A Commentary on Evolution," *MH* 10 (Spring, 1964) 46-57.

Henry M. Morris, "Biblical Creationism and Philosophical Evolutionism," *LSQ* 5 (1964-65) #1, 6-14.

*J. Barton Payne, "Theistic Evolution and the Hebrew of Genesis 1-2," *BETS* 8 (1965) 85-90.

Allan A. MacRae, "Abraham and the Stars," *BETS* 8 (1965) 97-100.

Henry M. Morris, "Seven Reasons for Opposing Evolution," *BS* 122 (1965) 254-269.

Gilbert B. Weaver, "A 'Systematic Theology' of a 'Religion Based on Science'," *GJ* 6 (1965) #3, 30-42.

*George F. Howe, "Miracles and the Study of Origins," *JASA* 17 (1965) 93-96.

William F. Tanner, "Chronology of the Ice Ages," *JASA* 17 (1965) 112-116.

Jack T. Kent, "The Origin of the Solar System, Galaxy, and the Universe," *JASA* 17 (1965) 104-108, 117.

J. Nathaniel Deely, "Evolution: Concept and Content," *Listen* 0 (1965) #0, 27-50; 1 (1966) #1, 38-66.

Vincent Parkin, "Ends and Means in Evolution," *PQL* 2 (1965) 263-267.

*Pierre Smulders, "Evolution and original sin," *TD* 13 (1965) 172-176.

Raymond J. Nogar, "The wisdom of evolution," *TD* 13 (1965) 269-280.

A. Van der Ziel, "Science and Beginning," *JASA* 18 (1966) 15-18.

Harold T. Wiebe, "What Can be Learned from the Evolutionist Who Takes a Hard Look at His Own Theory," *JASA* 18 (1966) 112-116.

*John H. Giltner, "Genesis and Geology: The Stuart—Silliman—Hitchcock Debate," *JRT* 23 (1966-67) 3-13.

*F. H. Cleobury, "God, Creation and Evolution," *MC, N.S.,* 10 (1966-67) 7-18.

Charles C. Ryrie, "The Bible and Evolution," *BS* 124 (1967) 66-80.

Hillyer H. Straton, "John Roach Straton: The Great Evolution Debate," *Found* 10 (1967) 137-149.

George B. Murray, "Teilhard and Orthogenetic Evolution," *HTR* 60 (1967) 281-295.

Henry [M.] Morris, "The Bible and Modern Science," *SR* 14 (1967-68) #1, 3-14.

Henry M. Morris, "Biblical Creation and Modern Science," *BS* 125 (1968) 20-28.

Henry M. Morris, "Biblical Catastrophism and Modern Science," *BS* 125 (1968) 107-115.

Lewis S. Ford, "Is Process Theism Compatible with Relativity Theory?" *JR* 48 (1968) 124-135.

Dunstan Jones, "Biological Possibility and Christian Doctrine," *Theo* 71 (1968) 291-297, 342-348.

Gerald Holton, Michael Polanyi, Ernest Nagel, John R. Platt, and Barry Commoner, "Do Life Processes Transcend Physics and Chemistry," Z 3 (1968) 442-472. *[Symposium]*

*Bernard Ramm, "The Relationship of Science, Factual Statements and the Doctrine of Biblical Inerrancy," *JASA* 21 (1969) 98-104.

Jerry D. Albert, Marie H. Berg, Richard H. Bube, Wilbur L. Bullock, Stephen W. Calhoon Jr., Gary R. Collins, Roger J. Cuffey, Russell H. Heddendorf, George R. Horner, Irving W. Knobloch, T. H. Leith, Gordon R. Lewthwaite, Russell Maatman, George I. Mavrodes, John A. McKintyre, John Warwick Montgomery, W. Jim Neidhardt, James A. Oakland, C. Eugene Walker, and Robert Lake Wilson, "Symposium: The Relationship Between the Bible and Science," *JASA* 21 (1969) 104-123. (Summary, p. 124)

Robert B. Smith, "Orthogenesis and God-Omega," *HTR* 62 (1969) 411-427.

*Michael Negus, "Man, Creation and the Fossil Record," *SCR* 3 (1969) 49-55.

§170 *2.5.6.1 Studies in Anthropology in Relation to the Ancient Near East [See also: Studies in the Doctrine of Man →]*

*†J. Robinson, "Migration of Man, after the Flood," *MMBR* 30 (1810-11) 6-8.

†Anonymous, "Researches into the Physical History of Mankind," *BCQTR, 4th Ser.*, 4 (1828) 33-61. *(Review)*

†Anonymous, "Characteristics," *ERCJ* 54 (1831) 351-383. *(Review) [Anthropology]*

Philip Lindsley, "The Primitive State of Mankind. *An attempt to prove that the original or most ancient condition of the human family was* civilized *not* savage," *BRCR, N.S.*, 4 (1840) 277-298, 6 (1841) 1-27.

Jos. Von Szabó, "On the Descent of the Magyar from the Ancient Persians," *TPS* (1842-44) 127-129.

Samuel Forry, "The Mosaic Account of the Unity of the Human Race, confirmed by the Natural History of the American Aborigines," *BRCR, N.S.*, 10 (1843) 29-80.

†[George W.] Bethune, "Remarks on Ethnology (Ethnography)," *PAPS* 4 (1843-47) 358-360.

†Anonymous, "Pritchard's Natural History of Man," *ERL* 1 (1844) 271-304. *(Review)*

J. B., "Thoughts on the Primeval Condition of Man," *MQR* 2 (1848) 21-51.

†Anonymous, "Ethnology—The Unity of Mankind," *BQRL* 10 (1849) 408-440. *(Review)*

†Anonymous, "The Pre-Adamite Earth, and Man Primeval," *CRB* 14 (1849) 402-412. *(Review)*

†[Henry Holland], "Natural History of Man," *QRL* 86 (1849-50) 1-40. *(Review)*

Anonymous, "The Unity of the Race," *SPR* 3 (1849-50) 124-166. *(Review)*

Anonymous, "Ethnography," *SPR* 3 (1849-50) 233-258. *(Review)*

Anonymous, “Two Lectures on the Connection between the Biblical and Physical History of Man,” *SPR* 3 (1849-50) 426-490. *(Review)*

†Anonymous, “Man Primeval,” *BQRL* 11 (1850) 135-154. *(Review)*

L. A., “The Diversity of the Origin of the Human Races,” *CE* 49 (1850) 110-145.

Anonymous, “The Races of Man, and Their Geographical Distribution,” *CTPR, 3rd Ser.*, 6 (1850) 48-59. *(Review)*

Anonymous, “The Natural History of the Varieties of Man,” *CTRP, 3rd Ser.*, 6 (1850) 449-458. *(Review)*

M. Jacobs, “Unity of Origin of the Human Race,” *ER* 2 (1850-51) 451-488.

Anonymous, “The Unity of the Human Race,” *SPR* 4 (1850-51) 357-381. *(Review)*

†Anonymous, “Professor Agassiz’s Theory of the Origin of the Human Race,” *TLJ* 3 (1850-51) 424-445. *(Review)*

[George I. Chace], “Origin of the Human Race,” *CRB* 16 (1851) 226-244.

Anonymous, “The Unity of the Human Race,” *SPR* 5 (1851-52) 572-601.

Robert Turnbull, “Unity of the Race in Its Higher Relations,” *CRB* 17 (1852) 68-85.

S. R., “Mr Gliddon’s Biblical Criticisms,” *CE* 57 (1854) 340-364. *(Review)*

†Anonymous, “American School of Ethnology,” *LQHR* 3 (1854-55) 68-93.

*†Anonymous, “Types of Mankind—Ethnology and Revelation,” *BQRL* 22 (1855) 1-45. *(Review) [Authenticity]*

W. N. Pendelton, “The Parentage of Mankind,” *MQR* 9 (1855) 321-345.

Anonymous, “Types of Mankind,” *WR* 65 (1856) 356-386. *(Review)*

†Anonymous, “Bachman on the unity of the human race,” *ER* 7 (1855-56) 400-412. *(Review)*

Anonymous, “Types of Mankind,” *SPR* 9 (1855-56) 250-299. *(Review)*

W. N. Pendelton, “The Antiquity of Our Race,” *MQR* 12 (1858) 1-18.

*John Hogg, "On the Supposed Antiquity of the Alluvium of the Nile and Man's Existence," *JSL, 3rd Ser.*, 9 (1859) 386-388.

†[R. C. Ketchum], "The Testimony of Modern Science to the Unity of Mankind," *SPR* 12 (1859-60) 115-131. *(Review)*

†Anonymous, "Ethnological Varieties," *BQRL* 31 (1860) 144-172. *(Review)*

Joseph P. Thompson, "Quatrefages and Gordon in Reply to Agassiz on the Origin and Distribution of Mankind," *BS* 19 (1862) 607-632.

Henry Crossley, "Notes on Excavated Prisons; and the Scriptural Doctrine of the Origin of Mankind," *JSL, 4th Ser.*, 2 (1862-63) 431-434.

†Anonymous, "Antiquity of Man—Sir Charles Lyell," *BQRL* 37 410-441. *(Review)*

†Anonymous, "Modern Anthropology," *BQRL* 38 (1863) 466-498. *(Review)*

†Anonymous, "Lyell on the Antiquity of Man," *LQHR* 20 (1863) 271-304. *(Review)*

†Anonymous, "Antiquity of Man," *QRL* 114 (1863) 368-417. *(Review)*

Anonymous, "The Antiquity of Man," *CE* 77 (1864) 339-351. *(Review)*

Anonymous, "The Antiquity of Man," *CongR* 4 (1864) 50-65. *(Review)*

Anonymous, "The Alleged Geological Evidences of the Antiquity of Man," *ThE* 1 (1864) 29-64.

Anonymous, "The Origin of Man," *CE* 80 (1866) 60-77. *(Review)*

†R. Weiser, "Pre-Adamite Man," *ER* 17 (1866) 222-236. *(Review)*

James Reddie, "On the Various Theories of Man's Past and Present Condition," *JTVI* 1 (1866-67) 174-198. [(Discussion, pp. 198-213) (Note, pp. 214-220)]

Robinson Thorton, "On Comparative Philology with Reference to the Theories of Man's Origin," *JTVI* 1 (1866-67) 148-162. (Discussion, pp. 162-173)

J. K. E., "The Alleged Antiquity of Man," *ERG, 4th Ser.*, 2 (1867-68) 89-104.

C. J. D'Oyly, "Man in Creation," *ContR* 8 (1868) 550-568.*(Review)*

Anonymous, "The Antiquity of Man," *PRev* 40 (1868) 574-608.

Worthington Hooker, "Man an Original Creation, not a Development, as Taught by Darwin and Huxley," *ThE* 5 (1868) 62-81.

Anonymous, "Recent Speculations on Primeval Man," *ThE* 5 (1868) 578-599.

Anonymous, "The Antiquity of Man," *BFER* 18 (1869) 288-316.

Anonymous, "Glimpses of Pre-Historic Humanity," *DUM* 74 (1869) 584-600.

*W. MacDonald, "On Man's Place in Creation; Geologically, Chronologically, Zoologically, Ethnologically, and Historically Considered," *JTVI* 4 (1869-70) 199-214, 230. (Discussion, pp. 214-229)

E. H. Capen, "Primeval Man," *UQGR, N.S.,* 7 (1870) 26-34. *(Review)*

*William Taylor, "The Variation of Languages and Species," *BFER* 20 (1871) 695-719.

E. Nisbet, "The Antiquity of Man," *BQ* 5 (1871) 460-477.

Anonymous, "Mr. Darwin and the Origin of Man," *BQRL* 54 (1871) 460-485. *(Review)*

†Anonymous, "Darwin *on the Descent of Man,*" *ERCJ* 134 (1871) 195-235.

Henry W. Crosskey, "The Early History of Mankind," *TR* 8 (1871) 111-130. *(Review)*

C. Staniland Wake, "The Adamites," *JRAI* 1 (1871-72) 363-374. (Discussion, pp. 375-376)

†Anonymous, "Flints and their Evidence," *LQHR* 37 (1871-72) 150-175. *(Review)*

Malcolm White, "Does Scripture settle the Antiquity of Man?" *BFER* 21 (1872) 128-137.

J. Gould Avery, "Racial Characteristics, as related to Civilisation," *JRAI* 2 (1872-73) 63-64. (Discussion, pp. 63-67) *[Abstract]*

C. Staniland Wake, "Man and the Ape," *JRAI* 2 (1872-73) 315-318. (Discussion, pp. 328-330)

*J. H. Titcomb, "Ethnic Testimonies to the Pentateuch," *JTVI* 6 (1872-73) 234-258. [(Paper by P. H. Gosse, pp. 258-259) (Discussion, pp. 259-271)]

George Harris, "Theories regarding Intellect and Instinct; with an attempt to deduce a satisfactory conclusion therefrom," *JRAI* 3 (1873-74) 73-84. (Discussion, pp. 84-85)

Anonymous, "The Antiquity of Man," *BQRL* 59 (1874) 342-367. *(Review)*

†Anonymous, "Primitive Man: Tylor and Lubbock," *QRL* 137 (1874) 40-77. *(Review)*

George Darwin, "Note upon the Article 'Primitive Man—Tylor and Lubbock', in No. 273.," *QRL* 137 (1874) 587-588. (Reply by Editor (?), pp. 588-589)

Dunbar Isidore Heath, "On the Origin and Development of the Mental Function of Man," *JRAI* 4 (1874-75) 66-77. (Discussion, pp. 77-78)

( ) Owen, "Contributions of the Ethnology of Egypt," *JRAI* 4 (1874-75) 223-254. (Discussion, p. 254)

*J. W. Dawson, "Primitive Man and Revelation," *JTVI* 8 (1874-75) 59-63.

Enoch Pond, "Origin of the Human Race," *BQ* 9 (1875) 102-116.

*A. H. Sayce, "Language and Race," *JRAI* 5 (1875-76) 212-216. (Discussion, pp. 216-220)

Herbert Spencer, "The Comparative Psychology of Man," *JRAI* 5 (1875-76) 301-315. (Discussion, pp. 315-316)

W. D. Wilson, "The Origin of Man and of his Civilization," *DTQ* 2 (1876) 120-132.

F. Jeffery Bell, "Note on the name 'Mediterranean', as applied to part of the Human Race; together with the Proposal of a New Term in its Place," *JRAI* 6 (1876-77) 271-278.

Joseph P. Thompson, "Implements of the Stone Age a Primitive Demarcation between Man and other Animals," *BS* 34 (1877) 70-78.

Anonymous, "The Recent Origin of Man," *SPR* 28 (1877) 102-128. *(Review)*

Anonymous, "Ethics of Evolution:—The Nature of Evil and the Genesis of Conscience," *BQRL* 68 (1878) 30-62.

John T. Duffield, "Evolutionism Respecting Man, and the Bible," *PRev* 54 (1878) Part 1, 150-177.

*R. F. Burton, "Stones and Bones from Egypt and Midian," *JRAI* 8 (1878-79) 290-319. [Part III. The Bones, pp. 318-319]

C. Carter Blake, "Notes on the Skulls brought by Captain R. F. Burton from the East," *JRAI* 8 (1878-79) 319-321.

G. Busk, "Notes on a Skull termed 'Nabatæan'," *JRAI* 8 (1878-79) 321-323.

( ) Owen, "Observations on the Collection of Skulls sent by Capt. Burton, F.R.G.S., &c., to the British Museum, September 1878," *JRAI* 8 (1878-79) 323-324 [Palmyra Skulls; Egyptian Skulls]

*H. E. D[ennehy], "Revelation, Geology, the Antiquity of Man," *IER, 3rd Ser.,* 1 (1880) 185-193, 260-272.

Francis Bowen, "The Human and the Brute Mind," *PRev* 56 (1880) Part 1, 321-343.

J. W. Dawson, "Haeckel on 'The Evolution of Man'," *PRev* 56 (1880) Part 1, 444-464.

Alexander MacWhorter, "The Edenic Period of Man," *PRev* 56 (1880) Part 2, 62-91.

J. W. Dawson, "The Antiquity of Man and the Origin of the Species," *PRev* 56 (1880) Part 2, 383-398.

E. Nesbet, "The Antiquity of Man—Its Present Phase," *BQR* 3 (1881) 18-29.

*St. George Mivart, "Intellect and Evolution," *BQRL* 74 (1881) 298-332.

C. W. Miller, "Pre-Adamites," *MQR, 2nd Ser.,* 3 (1881) 1-29.

J. T. Sunderland, "Dr. Winchell's 'Preadamites'," *URRM* 15 (1881) 204-224. *(Review)*

Stephen Alexander, "Origin and Primitive State of Man," *JCP* 1 (1881-82) #2, Article 2, 1-12.

W. H. Flower, "Address to the Department of Anthropology of the British Association, delivered at the York Meeting, September 1st, 1881," *JRAI* 11 (1881-82) 184-194.

George Rawlinson, "The Antiquity of Man Historically Considered," *JCP* 2 (1882-83) 339-364.

*S. R. Pattison, "The Age of Man Geologically Considered," *JCP* 2 (1882-83) 471-486.

†Anonymous, "The Antiquity of Man," *LQHR* 60 (1883) 107-135. *(Review)*

Joseph S. Van Dyke, "Is Man's Moral Nature an Evolution from the Instinct of Animals?" *JCP* 3 (1883-84) 266-277.

W. H. Flower, "On the Aims and Prospects of the Study of Anthropology," *JRAI* 13 (1883-84) 488-501.

John W. Bardsley, "The Origin of Man," *JTVI* 17 (1883-84) 254-274. (Discussion, pp. 274-281)

[Samuel Martin] Deutsch, "The Respective 'Ages' of the Semitic and Indo-Germanic Families," *ONTS* 3 (1883-84) 204-205.

John B. Kieffer, "On the Testimony of Language to the Unity of the Human Race," *RChR* 31 (1884) 460-486.

*A. H. Keane, "Ethnology of Egyptian Sudan," *JRAI* 14 (1884-85) 91-113. [I. The Bantus, p. 92; II. The Negroes, pp. 93-95; The Semites, pp. 95-97; The Hamites, pp. 97-101; The Nubas, pp. 101-106]

W. H. Flower, "Address delivered at the Anniversary Meeting of the Anthropological Institute of Great Britain and Ireland, January 27th, 1885, on the Classification of the Varieties of the Human Species," *JRAI* 14 (1884-85) 378-395.

*John B. Wood, "The Antiquity of Man," *CR* 46 (1885) 159-170.

George D. Armstrong, "Primeval Man," *CT* 3 (1885-86) 97-121. [I. What can Geology tell us respecting the age of primeval man? II. What can Anthropology tell us respecting primeval man? III. What can archaeologists tell us respecting primeval man? IV. Turn we now to the testimony of history, written and monumental; V. Traditional testimony; VI. The claims of Manetho, Berosus, and Moses examined; VII. Testimony of the Pentateuch]

A. Neubauer, "Notes on the Race-Types of the Jews," *JRAI* 15 (1885-86) 17-23.

Joseph Jacobs, "On the Racial Characteristics of Modern Jews," *JRAI* 15 (1885-86) 23-56. [Discussion pp. 56-62. (Note by F. Galton, p. 62)]

James Dallas, "On the Primary Divisions and Geographical Distribution of Mankind," *JRAI* 15 (1885-86) 304-330.

*J. Hassell, "Was Primeval Man a Savage?" *JTVI* 19 (1885-86) 193-208. (Discussion, pp. 208-211)

*S. R. Pattison, "The Age of Man Geologically Considered," *ColTM* 6 (1886) 302-320.

Reginald Stuart Poole, "The Egyptian Classification of the Races of Man," *JRAI* 16 (1886-87) 370-377. (Discussion, pp. 377-379)

‡Terrien de Lacouperie, "The races of Man in the Egyptian Documents. [A Bibliographical Notice]," *BOR* 2 (1887-88) 133-134.

W. M. Flinders Petrie, "Ethnographic Casts from Egypt," *BOR* 2 (1887-88) 134-137.

C[laude] R. Conder, "Hittite Ethnology," *JRAI* 17 (1887-88) 137-155. (Discussion, pp. 155-158)

Claude R. Conder, "Early Racial Types," *PEFQS* 20 (1888) 160-165. (Corr. p. 249)

G. Bertin, "The Races of the Babylonian Empire," *JRAI* 18 (1888-89) 104-118. (Discussion, pp. 118-120)

Henry George Tomkins, "Remarks on Mr. Flinders Petrie's Collection of Ethnographic Types from the Monuments of Egypt," *JRAI* 18 (1888-89) 206-238. (Discussion, pp. 238-239)

John S. Vaughan, "Man or Monkey?" *IER, 3rd Ser.,* 10 (1889) 1-11.

C[laude] R. Conder, "The Early Race Types of Western Asia," *JRAI* 19 (1889-90) 30-49. (Discussion, pp. 49-51)

D. G. W. Ellis, "The Unity of the Human Race," *MQR, 3rd Ser.,* 7 (1889-90) 309-317.

Charles H. Hitchcock, "Wright's 'Ice Age in North America and its Bearing on the Antiquity of Man'," *BS* 47 (1890) 99-121. *(Review)*

*R. Abbey, "The Three Theories of Human Origin," *CT* 8 (1890-91) [Garden of Eden Theory; Evolution; God Created Man]

Thomas Scott Bacon, "Primitive Man," *CT* 8 (1890-91) 415-436.

Rudolph Virchow, "The Origin of Man," *JTVI* 24 (1890-91) 255-266.

T. G. Pinches, "Upon the Types of the Early Inhabitants of Mesopotamia," *JRAI* 21 (1891-92) 86-97. (Discussion, pp. 97-99)

Francis R. Beattie, "Primeval Man.—I.," *USR* 3 (1891-92) 122-130.

Francis R. Beattie, "Primeval Man. II.," *USR* 3 (1891-92) 224-233.

Francis R. Beattie, "Primeval Man. III.," *USR* 3 (1891-92) 293-303.

G. Frederick Wright, "Recent Discoveries Bearing on the Antiquity of Man," *BS* 48 (1891) 298-309.

*Frank Cramer, "The Theological and Scientific Theories of the Origin of Man," *BS* 48 (1891) 510-516.

Edward M. Deems, "The Common Origin of Man," *CT* 9 (1891-92) 378-386.

T. G. Pinches, "Upon the Types of the Early Inhabitants of Mesopotamia," *JRAI* 21 (1891-92) 86-97 (Discussion, pp. 97-99)

Warren Upham, "Geologic Time Ratios, and Estimates of the Earth's Age and of Man's Antiquity," *BS* 50 (1893) 131-149.

*J. A. Zahm, "The Age of the Human Race according to Modern Science and Biblical Chronology," *ACQR* 18 (1893) 225-248; 19 (1894) 260-272.

William Hayes Ward, "Light on Scriptural Texts from Recent Discoveries. Beginning of the Human Race," *HR* 28 (1894) 413-415.

Francis R. Beattie, "Primeval Man," *PQ* 9 (1895) 351-371.

*Karl Blind, "Ale Drinking in Old Egypt and the Thrako-Germanic Race," *SRL* 25 (1895) 23-41.

Anonymous, "The Early Ages of the Human Race," *LQHR* 86 (1896) 205-233. *(Review)*

C. M. Mead, "The Age of Man as Indicated by the Natural Increase of Population," *BS* 55 (1898) 356-359.

Anonymous, "Probable Rapidity of Man's Early Development," *BS* 55 359-360.

Ernst Haeckel, "On Our Present Knowledge of the Origin of Man," *SIR* (1898) 461-480.

David MacIver, "Recent Anthropometrical Work in Egypt," *JRAI* 30 (1900) 95-103.

A. H. Sayce, "The Antiquity of Civilized Man," *AJT* 5 (1901) 692-702.

W. M. Flinders Petrie, "The Races of Early Egypt," *JRAI* 31 (1901) 248-255.

Warren Upham, "Primitive Man in the Ice Age," *BS* 59 (1902) 730-743.

William H. Holmes, "Classification and Arrangement of the Exhibits of an Anthropological of an Anthropological Museum," *JRAI* 32 (1902) 353-372.

Thomas E. Converse, "The Original Capacities of Man as Deduced from Recent Explorations," *PQ* 16 (1902-03) 365-372.

P. A. Peter, "Was the First Man a Savage?" *ColTM* 23 (1903) 298-303.

J. K. Richardson, "The Antiquity of Man," *HR* 45 (1903) 218-223.

[A. C. Haddon], "President's Address. Anthropology, Its Position and Needs," *JRAI* 33 (1903) 11-23.

Karl Pearson, "On the Inheritance of the Mental and Moral Characters in Man, and its Comparision with the Inheritance of Physical Characters. *The Huxley Lecture for* 1903," *JRAI* 33 (1903) 179-237.

*P. Molesworth Sykes, "Anthropological Notes on South Persia," *JRAI* 32 (1903) 339-352.

Hiram King, "The Evolution of Man," *RChR, 4th Ser.,* 7 (1903) 69-83.

T. M. Fothergill, "Higher Criticism and the Antiquity of Man," *CFL, 3rd Ser.,* 1 (1904) 571-573.

H. Balfour, "President's Address. The Relationship of Museums to the Study of Anthropology," *JRAI* 34 (1904) 10-19.

Charles S. Myers, "Contributions to Egyptian Anthropometry. II. The Comparative Anthropology of the Most Ancient and Modern Inhabitants," *JRAI* 35 (1905) 80-91.

Arthur Thomson, "Note on Dr. A. Keith's review of 'The Ancient Races of Thebaïd'," *Man* 5 (1905) #58.

Karl Pearson, "Note on Dr. Keith's review of 'The Ancient Races of Thebaïd'," *Man* 5 (1905) #65.

Henry Proctor, "Hebrew Anthropology," *AAOJ* 28 (1906) 11-13.

Henry Proctor, "Giant Races in Arabia Petra," *AAOJ* 28 (1906) 108-109.

*W. M. Flinders Petrie, "Migrations. (*The Huxley Lecture for* 1906)," *JRAI* 36 (1906) 189-232.

Charles S. Myers, "Contribution to Egyptian Anthropology," *JRAI* 36 (1906) 237-271. [III. The Anthropometry of the Modern Mohammedans, pp. 237-263; IV. The Comparison of the Mohammedans with the Copts and with the "Mixed" Group, pp. 261-271]

D. Gath Whitley, "What was the Primitive Condition of Man?" *PTR* 4 (1906) 513-534.

*(Mrs.) Harriet Boyd Hawes, "Minoans and Mycenaeans: A Working Hypothesis for the Solution of Certain Problems of Early Mediterranean Race and Culture," *AJA* 11 (1907) 57-58.

*N. McConaughy, "Scripture Chronology—How Old is Man?" *CFL, 3rd Ser.,* 6 (1907) 122-128. [I. Comparative Claims of the Chronology of the Hebrew Scriptures and the Septuagint]

N. McConaughy, "Scripture Chronology—How Old is Man?" *CFL, 3rd Ser.,* 7 (1907) 27-31. [II. The Test by Astronomical Data]

Charles S. Myers, "Contribution to Egyptian Anthropology," *JRAS* 38 (1908) 99-147. [V. General Conclusions]

*W. M. Flinders Petrie, "The Peoples of the Persian Empire," *Man* 8 (1908) #71.

A. A. W. Hubrecht, "Darwin and the Descent of Man," *Janus* 14 (1909) 862-875.

William Ridgeway, "Presidental Address: The Relation of Anthropology to Classical Studies," *JRAI* 39 (1909) 10-25.

D. Gath Whitley, "The High Intellectual Character of Primeval Man," *RP* 8 (1909) 39-56.

Anonymous, "Resemblances and Differences Between the Italiots and the Etruscans," *RP* 8 (1909) 63-64.

C. Staniland Wake, "Unity or Plurality of Humankind?" *AAOJ* 32 (1910) 65-76.

Charles Hallock, "How Old is Man?" *AAOJ* 32 (1910) 190-194.

H. B. Hastings, "'The Age of Man'—According to Some Geologists," *CFL, 3rd Ser.*, 13 (1910) 181-182.

*Charles Gelderd, "Prehistoric Man: His Civilization and Religion," *IER, 4th Ser.*, 27 (1910) 337-357.

William Ridgeway, "Presidental Address: The Influence of Enviroment on Man," *JRAI* 40 (1910) 10-22.

Anonymous, "Thumb Marks in Babylonia," *RP* 9 (1910) 120.

*Charles H. Hawes, "Cretan Anthropometry," *AJA* 15 (1912) 65-67.

Anonymous, "Prehistoric Man," *ERCJ* 215 (1912) 358-382.

*Clark Wissler, "The Doctrine of Evolution and Anthropology," *AJRPE* 6 (1913) 223-237.

Warren Upham, "Origin and Antiquity of Man," *BS* 70 (1913) 28-39.

B. C. A. Windle, "Early Man," *DR* 152 (1913) 311-325. *(Review)*

C. G. Seligmann, "Some Aspects of the Hamitic Problem in Anglo-Egyptian Sudan," *JRAI* 43 (1913) 593-705.

*N. de G. Davies, "A Foreign Type from a Theban Tomb," *AAA* 6 (1913-14) 84-86.

*L[uther] T. Townsend, "The First Man. How Man Did Not Originate," *CFL, 3rd Ser.,* 18 (1914) 195-199; 19 (1915) 56-61.

*L[uther] T. Townsend, "The First Man, According to Evolution," *CFL, 3rd Ser.,* 20 (1915) 154-157.

G. Elliot Smith, "Primitive Man," *PBA* 7 (1915-16) 454-504.

*Boyd Dawkins, "The Antiquity of Man and the Dawn of Art in Europe," *ERCJ* 224 (1916) 80-98.

William Hollinshed, "The Antiquity of Man," *HR* 71 (1916) 253.

George W. Gilmore, "Man's Antiquity Tested by Geology, Archaeology, and Anatomy," *HR* 71 (1916) 284-285. *(Review)*

Dyson Hauge, "The Antiquity of Man," *HR* 72 (1916) 167-168.

*Harold Peake, "Racial Elements Concerned in the First Siege of Troy," *JRAI* 46 (1916) 154-172.

Louis D. Covitt, "The Anthropology of the Jew," *Monist* 26 (1916) 366-396.

Th. Graebner, "'How Old is Man?'," *TQ* 20 (1916) 129-136, 231-250.

W. M. F[linders] P[etrie], "Racial Types at Abu Simbel," *AEE* 4 (1917) 57-61. [Extract of a Letter by W. Golénicheff, p. 57 *(French Text)*]

L[uther] T. Townsend, "Scientific Opinion As to the Age of the Human Race," *CFL, 3rd Ser.,* 23 (1917) 300-304.

Anonymous, "The Antiquity of Man," *HR* 73 (1917) 57.

Joseph E. Parsons, "The Antiquity of Man," *IER, 5th Ser.,* 9 (1917) 378-390.

*L[uther] T. Townsend, "Historical Geology, Historical Anthropology, and the Theory of Evolution," *CFL, 3rd Ser.,* 24 (1918) 251-253, 294-296.

Luther T. Townsend, "Prehistoric People in Europe and America; Their Bearing upon the Theory of Evolution," *CFL, 3rd Ser.*, 24 (1918) 377-380.

L[uther] T. Townsend, "Prehistoric Peoples; Their Bearing on the Theory of Evolution," *CFL, 3rd Ser.*, 24 (1918) 421-424.

L[uther] T. Townsend, "Prehistoric Peoples of the Western Continent; Their Bearing on the Theory of Evolution," *CFL, 3rd Ser.*, 24 (1918) 469-472.

*L[uther] T. Townsend, "Prehistoric Egypt—Its Bearing on the Theory of Evolution," *CFL, 3rd Ser.*, 25 (1919) 1-7.

L[uther] T. Townsend, "Prehistoric Babylon, Nineveh and the Hittite Empire; their Bearing on the Theory of Evolution," *CFL, 3rd Ser.*, 25 (1919) 45-49.

*L[uther] T. Townsend, "Cretans and other Prehistoric Peoples: Their Bearing on the Theory of Evolution," *CFL, 3rd Ser.*, 25 (1919) 89-93.

L[uther] T. Townsend, "Unity of the Human Race; its Bearing on the Theory of Evolution," *CFL, 3rd Ser.*, 25 (1919) 144-149.

Luther T. Townsend, "The Ice Age as Related to the Origin of Man and its Bearing on the Theory of Evolution," *CFL, 3rd Ser.*, 25 (1919) 177-182.

*Luther T. Townsend, "Origin of the First Man; through Chance or by Jehovah—Which?" *CFL, 3rd Ser.*, 25 (1919) 221-225, 265-269.

*Luther T. Townsend, "The Origin of the First Man; his Creation by Jehovah," *CFL, 3rd Ser.*, 25 (1919) 354-359, 397-403.

*Luther T. Townsend, "The Origin of the First Man; Christ the Creator," *CFL, 3rd Ser.*, 25 (1919) 440-445, 499-504; 26 (1920) 4-8.

Wallace N. Stearns, "Notes on the Troglodytes in Palestine," *BS* 77 (1920) 14-22.

John Knox Miller, "Man Created, not Evolved—An Explanation," *CFL, 3rd Ser.*, 27 (1921) 204-205.

Hermann Junker, "The First Appearance of the Negroes in History," *JEA* 7 (1921) 121-132.

G[eorge] W. Gilmore, "When Did the Negro Enter History," *HR* 83 (1922) 478-479.

S. F. MacLennan, "Religion and Anthropology," *JR* 2 (1922) 600-615.

H. l'Abbé Breuil*[sic]*, "Palæolithic Man at Gibraltar: New and Old Facts," *JRAI* 52 (1922) 46-54.

Leander S. Keyser, "The Dawn Man of Evolution: Was he a Real or an Imaginary Being?" *CFL, 3rd Ser.*, 29 (1923) 548-554.

H. W. Seton-Karr, "Prehistoric Man in the Sinai Peninsula," *Man* 23 (1923) #123.

C. G. Seligman, "Presidential Address. Anthropology and Psychology: A Study of some Points of Contact,"*JRAI* 54 (1924) 13-46.(erratum, p. iv)

Ernest Jones, "Psycho-Analysis and Anthropology," *JRAI* 54 (1924) 47-66.

P. E. Newberry, "Egypt as a field for anthropological research," *SIR* (1924) 435-459.

W. M. Flinders Petrie, "Early Man in Egypt," *Man* 25 (1925) #78.

*G. W. B. Huntingford, "On the Connection Between Egypt and the Masai-Nandi Group of East Africa," *AEE* 11 (1926) 10-11.

Arthur I. Brown, "Hailing Another Missing Link: A Study of the African Ape-Child," *CFL, 3rd Ser.*, 32 (1926) 22-25.

D[udley] J[oseph] Whitney, "The Origin of the Races," *CFL, 3rd Ser.*, 32 (1926) 33-35.

George McCready Price, "In whose Image was Man made, God's or Ape's?" *CFL, 3rd Ser.*, 32 (1926) 335-338.

[W. M.] Flinders Petrie, "Early Man in Egypt," *OOR* 1 (1926) #1, 19.

E. A. Hooton, "Where did Man originate?" *Antiq* 1 (1927) 133-150.

D[udley] J[oseph] Whitney, "The Nature of Early Men," *CFL, 3rd Ser.*, 33 (1927) 276-278.

*D[udley] J[oseph] Whitney, "Evolution and Early Man," *CFL, 3rd Ser.*, 33 (1927) 468-469.

Aleš Ardlička, "The Neanderthal Phase of Man. *The Huxley Memorial Lecture for* 1927," *JRAI* 57 (1927) 249-274.

Henry Fairfield Osborn, "Recent Discoveries Relating to the Origin and Antiquity of Man," *PAPS* 66 (1927) 373-389.

William K. Gregory, "The Origin of Man from an Anthropoid Stem—When and Where?" *PAPS* 66 (1927) 439-463.

George Wilson Brent, "Race Origin in the Bible: An Explanation," *CFL, 3rd Ser.,* 34 (1928) 41-42.

Henry Fairfield Osborn, "Present Status of the Problem of Human Ancestry," *PAPS* 67 (1928) 151-155.

Anonymous, "Notes and Comments. How Old is Man?" *A&A* 27 (1929) 281.

Dudley Joseph Whitney, "That Nordic-Like Cro-Magnon Man," *CFL, 3rd Ser.,* 35 (1929) 79.

George Wilson Brent, "Dr. Brent Replies to Mr. Whitney," *CFL, 3rd Ser.,* 35 (1929) 652-653.

*K[enneth] S. Sandford and A. J. Arkell, "The Relation of Palæolithic Man to the History and Geology of the Nile Valley in Egypt," *Man* 29 (1929) #50.

Dudley Joseph Whitney, "Mr. Whitney Replies Briefly," *CFL, 3rd Ser.,* 36 (1930) 201.

C. H. Buchanan, "Darwin's Monkey Origin of Man," *CFL, 3rd Ser.,* 36 (1930) 436-439.

*G. P. G. Sobhy, "Miscellanea," *JEA* 16 (1930) 3-5. [1. The Persistence of Ancient Facial Types Amongst Modern Egyptians, p. 3]

*A. H. Sayce, "The Antiquity of Civilized Man. *The Huxley Memorial Lecture for* 1930," *JRAI* 60 (1930) 269-282.

L. B. Ellis, "The Unity of Man (Part 2)," *AEE* 16 (1931) 45-50. *[Part 1 not published until 1933! - see below]*

L. B. Ellis, "The Unity of Man, Part 3," *AEE* 16 (1931) 101-108.

L[eander] S. K[eyser], "Is Man an Accident? So Says a British Evolutionist," *CFL, 3rd Ser.,* 37 (1931) 62-64.

Kenneth S. Sandford, "Recent Developments in the Study of Paleolithic Man in Egypt," *AJSL* 48 (1931-32) 170-183.

*E[phraim] A. Speiser, "The Bearing of the Excavations at Tell Billa and at Tepe Gawra upon the Ethnic Problems of Ancient Mesopotamia," *AJA* 36 (1932) 29-35.

*Walton Brooks McDaniel, "A Fresco Picturing Pygmies," *AJA* 36 (1932) 260-271.

Henry Field, "The Cradle of Homo Sapiens," *AJA* 36 (1932) 426-430.

(Miss) Caroline Ryley, "The Antiquity of Man," *Antiq* 6 (1932) 87-88.

H. J. Fleure, "An Early Chapter of the Story of *Homo Sapiens,*" *BJRL* 16 (1932) 413-427.

L. B. Ellis, "The Unity of Man," *AEE* 18 (1933) 49-53. *[Part I; Parts II & III published in 1931! - see above]*

H. J. Fleure, "An Early Chapter of the Story of *Homo Sapiens,*" *BJRL* 16 (1932) 413-427.

E. Paget Thurstan, "Early Races of Mankind," *EQ* 5 (1933) 246-256, 344-356.

*George G. MacCurdy, "Prehistoric Research in the Near East," *PAPS* 72 (1933) 121-135.

*W. W. Tarn, "Alexander the Great and the Unity of Mankind," *PBA* 19 (1933) 123-166.

Anonymous, "More Prehistoric Men," *CFL, 3rd Ser.,* 40 (1934) 108-109.

*N. de G. Davies, "Foreigners in the Tomb of Amenemḥab (No. 85)," *JEA* 20 (1934) 189-192.

G. R. Gair, "The Cradle of Mankind," *JTVI* 66 (1934) 90-106, 109. (Discussion, pp. 106-109)

John K. Lipman, "The Age of Man. I. Pithecanthropus to Neanderthal," *TFUQ* 9 (1934-35) 108-122.

John K. Lipman, "The Age of Man. II. Post-Neanderthal Races," *TFUQ* 9 (1934-35) 206-221.

James B. Johnston, "The Antiquity and Development of Man," *ContR* 148 (1935) 721-730.

*Ambrose Fleming, "Modern Anthropology *versus* Biblical Statements on Human Origin," *JTVI* 67 (1935) 15-40, 42. (Discussion, pp. 40-42)

K. B. Aikman, "Race Mixture with Some Reference to Bible History," *JTVI* 67 (1935) 43-57, 62-64. (Discussion, pp. 57-62)

M. T. W., "'The Origin of Mankind'," *AusTR* 7 (1936) 56-57. *(Review)*

*G. R. Gair, "'Syro-Mesopotamian Ethnology: As Outlined in a Biblical Document'," *EQ* 8 (1936) 225-232.

*G. R. Gair, "The Races and Peoples of the Early Hebrew World," *JTVI* 68 (1936) 194-209, 212. (Discussion, pp. 209-212)

J. M. Stanfield, "Is Man 50,000 Years Old?" *CFL, 3rd Ser.,* 43 (1937) 304-305.

G. E[rnest] Wright, "Troglodytes and Giants in Palestine," *JBL* 56 (1937) iv.

G. Ernest Wright, "The Troglodytes of Gezer," *PEQ* 69 (1937) 67-78.

*Hazel D. Hansen, "The Racial Continuity of Prehistoric Thessaly," *AJA* 42 (1938) 122.

*R. Engelbach, "Some remarks on *Ka*-statues of abnormal men in the Old Kingdom," *ASAE* 38 (1938) 285-296. (Addendum, p. 399)

Warren R. Dawson, "Pygmies and Dwarfs in Ancient Egypt," *JEA* 24 (1938) 185-189.

G. E[rnest] Wright, "Troglodytes and Giants in Palstine," *JBL* 57 (1938) 305-310.

‡Harold J. E. Peake, "The Study of Prehistoric Times. *The Huxley Memorial Lecture for* 1940," *JRAI* 70 (1940) 103-146. [Bibliography, pp. 136-146]

[J.] Lawrence Angel, "Physical Types of Ancient Corinth," *AJA* 45 (1941) 88.

Cornelius J. Connolly, "Palestinian Anthropology. The Paleolithic People of Palestine," *CBQ* 5 (1943) 191-198.

H. J. Braunholtz, "Anthropology in Theory and Practice. *Presidental Address,*" *JRAI* 73 (1943) 1-8.

F. C. Bartlett, "Anthropology in Reconstruction," *JRAI* 73 (1943) 9-16.

M. D. W. Jeffreys, "Primitive Man—Where is He to be Found?" *HJ* 42 (1943-44) 359-366.

Raymond W. Murray, "New Knowledge About Prehistoric Man," *ACSR* 5 (1944) 169-176.

*Dom Ralph Russell, "The Bible and Human Origins," *DownsR* 62 (1944) 77-83.

J. Philip Hyatt, "'Adam' in Palestine," *JAAR* 12 (1944) 232-236.

J. Lawrence Angel, "Neolithic Ancestors of the Greeks," *AJA* 49 (1945) 252-260.

A. L. Kroeber, "The Ancient Okoumené as an Historic Culture Aggregate. *Presidental Address,*" *JRAI* 75 (1945) 9-20.

Abbé Henri Breuil, "The Discovery of the Antiquity of Man: Some of the Evidence. *Huxley Memorial Lecture for* 1941," *JRAI* 75 (1945) 21-31.

*A. Batrawi, "The Racial History of Egypt and Nubia. Part I. The Craniology of Lower Nubia from Predynastic Times to the Sixth Century A.D.," *JRAI* 75 (1945) 81-101.

*William Young, "What the Bible Teaches About the Origin of Races and Languages," *CO* 3 (1945-46) 3-7.

*A. Batrawi, "The Racial History of Egypt and Nubia. Part II. The Racial Relationships of the Ancient and Modern Populations of Egypt and Nubia," *JRAI* 76 (1946) 131-156.

M. Stekelis, "Prehistoric Man in Palestine," *Kobez* 4 (1945) XXII-XXIII.

*J. Lawrence Angel, "Some Interrelationships of Classical Archaeology with Anthropology," *AJA* 50 (1946) 401.

William J. Conner, "The Unity of the Human Race," *SS* 15 (June, 1946) 48-56.

A. H. Armstrong, "Studies in Traditional Anthropology I—Plato," *DownsR* 65 (1947) 237-245, 363-373; 66 (1948) 148-164.

Robert J. Braidwood, "Asiatic Prehistory and the Origin of Man: A Review Article," *JNES* 6 (1947) 30-42. *(Review)*

V. G. C., "Palaeolithic Man in Greece," *Antiq* 22 (1948) 210.

A. H. Armstrong, "Studies in Traditional Anthropology II—Plotinus," *DownsR* 66 (1948) 405-418; 67 (1949) 123-133, 406-419.

†Cuthbert Lattey, "The Encyclical *Humani Generis* and the Origins of the Human Race," *Scrip* 4 (1949-51) 278-279.

Humphrey J. T. Johnson, "The Unity of the Human Race," *DownsR* 68 (1950) 324-340.

F. J. Cole, "Aristotle's Lantern," *Cent* 1 (1950-51) 377. *[The eye(?)]*

Sylvester A. Sieber, "The Problem of Man's Physical Origins," *ACSR* 12 (1951) 217-232.

Humphrey Humphreys, "Dental Evidence in Archaeology," *Antiq* 25 (1951) 16-18.

Cyril Vollert, "Evolution of the Human Body: Scientific *Status Quo* and Theological Implications," *CTSP* 6 (1951) 122-145.

Albert L. Schulitzer, "The Position of Modern Theology on the Evolution of Man," *LTP* 8 (1952) 208-229.

*Kathleen M. Kenyon, "Neolithic Portrait-Skulls from Jericho," *Antiq* 27 (1953) 105-107.

*Dorothy Kent Hill, "A Bronze Statuette of a Negro," *AJA* 57 (1953) 265-267.

*E[phraim] A. Speiser, "On the Alleged *namru* 'fair(-skinned)'," *Or, N.S.,* 23 (1954) 235-236.

Vittorio Marcozzi, "The Origin of Man According to Science," *TD* 2 (1954) 43-47.

*H. Hamann, "Some Neo-Orthodox Voices on Anthropology," *AusTR* 26 (1955) 69-85.

Humphrey J. T. Johnson, "The Origin of Man. Scientific Considerations," *ClR* 41 (1956) 395-406, 477-485.

C. A. Wilson, "The Date of Man's Appearance on the Earth," *AT* 1 (1956-57) #4, 10-13.

*E. Badian, "Alexander the Great and the Unity of Mankind," *HJAH* 7 (1958) 425-444.

Conor Reilly, "Adam and Primitive Man," *ITQ* 26 (1959) 331-345.

Walter J. Beasley, "Ancient Man and the Bible: Guessing at Man's Antiquity," *AT* 4 (1959-60) #2, 11-17.

*W[alter] J. Beasley, "That Noah Story: How did the various races of Mankind originate?" *AT* 4 (1959-60) #4, 6-9.

*B. Íkerlj, "Human Evolution and the Neanderthal Man," *Antiq* 34 (1960) 90-99.

J. Frank Casel, "The Origin of Man and the Bible," *JASA* 12 (1960) #2, 13-16, 28.

James O. Buswell III, "The Origins of Man, and the Bio-cultural Gap," *JASA* 13 (1961) 47-55.

*A. E. Mourant, "Evolution, Genetics and Anthropology. *The Huxley Memorial Lecture, 1961*," *JRAI* 91 (1961) 151-165.

*Avraham Biran, "Archaeological Activities in Israel, 1961/62," *CNI* 13 (1962) #1, 16-22. [Part I: Neanderthal Man, pp. 16-17]

M. G. Smith, "History and Social Anthropology," *JRAI* 92 (1962) 73-85.

I. Schapera, "Should Anthropologists be Historians? *Presidental Address*," *JRAI* 92 (1962) 143-156.

G. T. Emery, "Dental Pathology and Archaeology," *Antiq* 37 (1963) 274-281.

*Henry G. Fischer, "Varia Aegyptiaca," *JARCE* 2 (1963) 17-51. [1. Yellow-skinned Representation of Men in the Old Kingdom, pp. 17-22; 5. A Nubian (or Puntite) of the Archaic Period, pp. 34-39]

*Robert H. Dyson Jr., "Ninth Century Men in Western Iran," *Arch* 17 (1964) 3-11.

*William C. Hayes, "Most Ancient Egypt," *JNES* 23 (1964) 73-114, 145-192, 207-274. [Chapter II. Paleolithic Man in Egypt, pp. 145-192]

G. H. R. Koenigswald, "Early Man: Facts and Fantasy. *The Huxley Memorial Lecture 1964,*" *JRAI* 94 (1964) 67-79.

*R. L. Fleischer, P. B. Price and R. M. Walker, "Applications of Fission Tracks and Fission Track Dating to Anthropology," *AJA* 69 (1965) 167-168.

James M. Murk, "Evidence for a Late Pleistocene Creation of Man," *JASA* 17 (1965) 37-49.

James O. Buswell III, "Homo Habilis: Implications for the Creationist," *JASA* 17 (1965) 74-78.

Brian V. Hill, "The Origin of Man: Pointers for Teachers and Counsellors," *JCE* 8 (1965) 22-30.

*W. Shanklin and M. Ghantus, "A preliminary report on the anthropology of the Phoenicians," *BMB* 19 (1966) 91-94.

M. W. Prausnitz, "A Study in Terminology: The Kebaran, the Natufian and the Tahunian," *IEJ* 16 (1966) 220-230.

[Paul H. Seely], "Letters to the Editor. The Antiquity of Warfield's Paper on the Antiquity of Man," *JASA* 18 (1966) 28-31.

James O. Buswell III, "Warfield and Creationist Anthropology. A Rejoinder to Paul A. Seely (*Journal of Am. Sci. Affil. March* 1966)," *JASA* 18 (1966) 117-120.

*David B. Richardson, "Linear History and the Unity of Mankind," *Person* 47 (1966) 5-15.

George R. Horner, "The Bible and Human Evolution: Problems in the Classification and Change in Man," *JASA* 19 (1967) 105-110.

A. Caroline Berry, R. J. Berry, and Peter J. Ucko, "Genetical change in ancient Egypt," *Man, N.S.,* 2 (1967) 551-568.

Tamar Yizraeli, "Mesolithic Hunters' Industries at Ramat Matred (The Wilderness of Zin)," *PEQ* 99 (1967) 78-85.

Anonymous, "The Date of Man's First Appearance on the Earth," *BH* 5 (1969) 26-30.

*C. D. Darlington, "The Genetics of Society," *P&P* #43 (1969) 3-33.

Elizabeth C. Evans, "Physiognomics in the Ancient World," *TAPS, N.S.*, 59 (1969) Part 5, 3-101.

§171 *2.5.6.2 Studies Regarding Specific Remains*

S. G. Morton, "On the Form of the Head, and other Ethnographic Characters of the Ancient Egyptians," *PAPS* 2 (1841-43) 239-241.

C. Carter Blake, "Notes on Human Remains from Palmyra," *JRAI* 1 (1871-72) 312-319. (Discussion, pp. 319-320)

†C. Carter Blake, "Notes on Human Remains from the Holy Land," *JRAI* 2 (1872-73) 53-62. [1. Description of Remains from Siloam; 2. Description of Skull obtained by M. Clermont-Ganneau from Deir-es-Sinné, near Siloam, from one of the graves in the necropolis termed Mághára 'Isá ("Tomb of Jesus"); 3. Description of Human and Animal Remains from Marad Syria; 4. Description of Remains from Bassus's Tower at Shakkah; 5. Description of Remains from Yabrúd. Part I. Captain Burton's Collection; Description of Remains from Yabrúd.—Part II. Mr. Tyrwhitt Drake's Collection] (Discussion, pp. 62-63)]

*C. F. Tyrwitt Drake, "Note on Collection of Flints and Skulls brought from Palestine," *JRAI* 4 (1874-75) 14-15 [Remarks by A. W. Franks, pp. 15-17. (Discussion, p. 18)]

Geo. Busk, "Notes on Some Skulls from Palmyra, present to the Institute by the late Mr. Cotesworth," *JRAI* 4 (1874-75) 366-368.

Joseph Bonomi, "Some Observations on the Skeleton of an Egyptian Mummy," *SBAT* 4 (1875) 251-252.

*E. A. Wallis Budge, "The Mummy and Coffin of Nes-Ames, Prophet of Ames and Chonsu," *SBAP* 8 (1885-86) 106-108.

J. William Dawson, "Prehistoric Man in Egypt and the Lebanon," *JTVI* 18 (1884-85) 287-299, 313. [(Report of W. Boyd Dawkins on the Teeth, Bones, and Flint Implements found, pp. 300-301) (Discussion, pp. 301-312)]

Eugene Dubois, "On Pithecanthropus Erectus: a Transitional Form betwen Man and the Apes," *JRAI* 25 (1895-96) 240-248. (Discussion, pp. 248-255) *[Abstract]*

(Mrs.) Cornelius Stevenson, "On the Remains of Foreigners Discovered in Egypt by Mr. Flinders-Petrie, 1895, now in the Museum of the University of Pennsylvania," *PAPS* 35 (1896) 56-64.

W. L. H. Duckworth, "Note on a Skull from Syria," *JRAI* 29 (1899) 145-151.

E. T. Newton, "Note on Bones Brought from Eastern Hauran, Syria, by Mr. Mark Sykes," *PEFQS* 31 (1899) 56.

G. Sergi, "Notes on the Skulls of Erganos," *AJA* 5 (1901) 315-318.

G. Frederick Wright, "The Lansing Skull and the Early History of Mankind," *BS* 60 (1903) 28-32.

Luella A. Owen, "More Concerning the Lansing Skeleton," *BS* 60 (1903) 572-578.

A. Macalister, "Report on the Human Remains Found at Gezer, 1902-03," *PEFQS* 35 (1903) 322-332.

Arthur Thomson, "Composite Photographs of Early Egyptian Skulls," *Man* 5 (1905) #38.

*G. Elliot Smith, "An Account of the Mummy of a Priestess of Amen, supposed to be Ta-usert-em-suten-pa (With which is incorporated a detailed account of the wrappings by M. A. C. Mace and some archæological notes by M. Georges Daressy)," *ASAE* 7 (1906) 155-182.

A[rthur] Thomson and D. Randall-MacIver, "Egyptian Craniology," *Man* 6 (1906) #36.

*G. Elliot Smith, "Report of the Unwrapping of the Mummy of Menephtah," *ASAE* 8 (1907) 108-112.

Anonymous, "Mummy of Priestess of Amen Ra," *RP* 7 (1908) 122.

A. M. Paterson and W. Broad, "Human Skulls from Sisma in Asia Minor," *AAA* 2 (1909) 94-96.

*Anonymous, "Mummy of Ra-Nafer," *RP* 9 (1910) 226.

Anonymous, "Female Skeleton from Saqkara," *RP* 11 (1912) 281.

Arthur Keith, "Presidental Address. The Reconstruction of Fossil Human Remains," *JRAI* 44 (1914) 12-31.

G. Elliot Smith, "Note on the Skull of Kerma 1065 A.," *ZÄS* 52 (1914) 39.

Walter Amsden, "Skulls of the XIIth Dynasty," *AEE* 2 (1915) 53-55. [Note by W. M. F. Petrie, p. 55]

*Arthur Weigall, "The Mummy of Akhenaton," *JEA* 8 (1922) 193-200.

G. W. Murray and D. E. Derry, "Physical Anthropology: A Pre-dynastic Burial on the Red Sea Coast of Egypt," *Man* 23 (1923) #81.

T. Crouther Gordon, "The Finding of the Galilee Skull," *GUOST* 5 (1923-28) 37-39.

Warren R. Dawson, "A Mummy from Torres Straits," *AAA* 11 (1924) 87-94.

*Arthur Keith, "Neanderthal Man in Malta. *with an account of the survey of Dalam Cave (Ghar Dalam)* by Mr. George Sinclair," *JRAI* 54 (1924) 251-275. ["Ghar Dalam and the Eurafrican Land Bridge," by George Sinclair with some additions by Arthur Keith, pp. 261-275]

*F. T[urville]-P[etrie], "Excavations of Two Palaeolithic Caves in Galilee," *BSAJB* #7 (1925) 99-101. [Addendum: Note on the Galilee Skull, by Arthur Keith, p. 102]

Warren R. Dawson, "A Mummy of the Persian Period," *JEA* 11 (1925) 76-77.

Anonymous, "Notes and Comments. Galilee Cave Skull in Jerusalem Museum," *A&A* 24 (1927) 94.

Warren R. Dawson, "On Two Mummies formerly belonging to the Duke of Sutherland," *JEA* 13 (1927) 155-160. (Supplementary Note by M. L. Tildesley, pp. 160-161)

*H. J. Orr-Ewing, "The Lion and the Cavern of Bones at Petra," *PEFQS* 59 (1927) 155-156.

*Dorothy A. E. Garrod, L. H. Dudley Buxton, G. Elliot Smith, and Dorothea M. A. Bate, "Excavation of a Mourterian Rock-Shelter at Devil's Tower, Gibraltar," *JRAI* 58 (1928) 33-113. [II.—Human Remans, by L. H. Dudley Buxton, pp. 57-85; III.—The Endocranial Cast, by G. Elliot Smith, pp. 86-91]

M. R. Drennan, "An Australaid Skull from the Cape Flats," *JRAI* 59 (1929) 417-427.

*Douglas E. Derry, "Note on the Skeleton hitherto believed to be that of King Akhenaten," *ASAE* 31 (1931) 115-119. *[Smenkhkerê]*

L. H. Dudley Buxton and D. Talbot Rice, "Report on the Human Remains found at Kish," *JRAI* 61 (1931) 57-119.

Douglas E. Derry, "Report on four skulls of the XIIth Dynasty, Dashûr," *ASAE* 32 (1932) 174-176.

LaRue VanHook, "On the Lacedaemonians Buried in the Kerameikos," *AJA* 36 (1932) 290-292.

[W. M.] Flinders Petrie, "The Peoples of Palestine," *A&A* 34 (1933) 71-74, 106. *[Skeletal Remains at Gaza]*

Edith M. Guest, "A Note on an Alleged Resemblance between Deformed Skulls of the Caucasus Region and the Heads of El Amarna," *AEE* 18 (1933) 113-114.

*Douglas E. Derry, "An X-Ray examination of the mummy of King Amenophis I," *ASAE* 34 (1934) 47-48.

D[ouglas] E. Derry, "Report on human remains from the granite sarcophagus chamber in the Pyramid of Zoser," *ASAE* 35 (1935) 28-30.

W. B. Kennedy Shaw, "Two Burials from the South Libyan Desert," *JEA* 22 (1936) 47-50.

Henry Field, "Human Remains from Jemdet Nasr, Mesopotamia," *JRAS* (1932) 967-970.

George Grant MacCurdy, "Prehistoric Man in Palestine," *PAPS* 76 (1936) 523-541.

*J. W. Jack, "The Trephined Skulls from Lachish," *PEQ* 69 (1937) 62-66.

*R. Engelbach, "Notes on the coffin and 'mummy' of Princess Sit-Amûn," *ASAE* 39 (1939) 405-407.

*D[ouglas] E. Derry, "The 'Mummy' of Sit-Amûn," *ASAE* 39 (1939) 411-416.

*D[ouglas] E. Derry, "Note on the remains of Shashanq," *ASAE* 39 (1939) 549-551.

Robert W. Ehrich, "Preliminary Notes on Tarsus Crania," *AJA* 44 (1940) 87-92.

*D[ouglas] E. Derry, "An examination of the Bones of King Psusennes I," *ASAE* 40 (1940-41) 969-970.

*Arthur Keith, "The Men of Lachish," *PEQ* 72 (1940) 7-12.

*Muzaffer Süleyman Şenyürek, "A Craniological Study of the Copper Age and Hittite Populations of Anatolia," *TTKB* 5 (1941) 237-253.

*D[ouglas] E. Derry, "Report on the skeleton of king Amenemōpet," *ASAE* 41 (1942) 149.

D[ouglas] E. Derry, "Ḥar Nakht," *ASAE* 41 (1942) 150.

W. E. Le Gros Clark, "Pithecanthropus in Peking," *Antiq* 19 (1945) 1-5.

*P. Ghalioungui, "A medical study of Akhenaten," *ASAE* 47 (1947) 29-46.

A. Batrawi, "The Pyramid Studies. Anatomical reports," *ASAE* 47 (1947) 97-111.

*Guy Brunton, "The Burial of Prince Ptah-Shepses at Saqqara," *ASAE* 47 (1947) 125-133.

*[Douglas] E. Derry, "The bones of Prince Ptah-Shepses," *ASAE* 47 (1947) 139-140.

A. Batrawi, "Report on the anatomical remains recovered from the tombs of Akhet-Hetep and Ptah-Iron-Ka, and a comment on the statues of Akhet-Hetep," *ASAE* 48 (1948) 487-497.

A. Batrawi, "The Pyramid Studies. A small mummy from the Pyramid of Dahshur," *ASAE* 48 (1948) 585-598.

Carleton S. Coon, "The Eridu Crania. A Preliminary Report," *Sumer* 5 (1949) 103-106.

Muzaffer Süleyman Şenyürek, "Study of the Skulls from Karahöyük, Excavated under the Auspices of the Turkish Historical Society," *TTKB* 13 (1949) 11-20.

Muzaffer Süleyman Şenyürek, "The Occurrence of Taurodontism in the Ancient Inhabitants of Anatolia. A Preliminary Report," *TTKB* 13 (1949) 222-227.

Muzaffer Süleyman Şenyürek, "The Attrition of Molars in the Ancient Inhabitants of Anatolia. A Preliminary Report," *TTKB* 13 (1949) 237-244.

Wilton Marion Krogman, "Ancient Cranial Types at Chatal Hüyük and Tell al-Judaidah, Syria, from the Late Fifth Millennium B.C. to the Mid-Seventh Century, A.D.," *TTKB* 13 (1949) 407-477.

Muzaffer Süleyman Şenyürek, "A Short Preliminary Report of the Two Fossil Teeth from the Cave of Karain, Excavated under the Auspices of the Turkish Historical Society," *TTKB* 13 (1949) 835-836.

J. Lawrence Angel, "Skeletons," *Arch* 3 (1950) 233-241.

*A. Batrawi, "Remains of the Ka-Nefer family, a scribe of Ptah's temple at Memphis during the XXVIth Dynasty," *ASAE* 50 (1950) 477-491.

Carleton S. Coon, "Three Skulls from Hassuna," *Sumer* 6 (1950) 93-96.

Muzaffer Süleyman Şenyürek, "A note on three Skulls from Alaca-Höyük," *TTKB* 14 (1950) 71-84.

A. Batrawi, "The skeletal remains from the Northern Pyramid of Sneferu," *ASAE* 51 (1951) 435-440.

*Muzaffer Süleyman Şenyürek, "Two cases of premature suture closure among the ancient inhabitants of Anatolia," *TTKB* 15 (1951) 247-262.

Muzaffer Süleyman Şenyürek and Seniha Tunakan, "The Skeletons from Şeyh Höyük," *TTKB* 15 (1951) 439-445.

Muzaffer Süleyman Şenyürek, "Fluctuation of the Cranial Index in Anatolia, from the Fourth Millennium B.C. to 1200 B.C.," *TTKB* 15 (1951) 593-616.

J. Lawrence Angel, "The Human Skeletal Remains from the Hotu Cave, Iran," *PAPS* 96 (1952) 258-269.

Muzaffer Süleyman Şenyürek, "A Study of the Dentition of the Ancient Inhabitants of Alaca Höyük," *TTKB* 16 (1952) 153-224.

Muzaffer Süleyman Şenyürek, "A Study of the Human Skeletons from Kültepe, Excavated under the Auspices of the Turkish Historical Society," *TTKB* 16 (1952) 323-343.

W. M. Shanklin and A. J. Dark, "Two Skulls from Jordan," *ADAJ* 2 (1953) 57-61.

*Kathleen M. Kenyon, "Neolithic Portrait-Skulls from Jericho," *Antiq* 27 (1953) 105-107.

*Ralph S. Solecki, "The Shanidar Cave Sounding, 1953 Season with Notes Concerning the Discovery of the First Paleolithic Skull in Iraq," *Sumer* 9 (1953) 229-232.

O. G. S. C[rawford], "The Fate of the Chinese Skulls," *Anitq* 28 (1954) 226-227.

Anonymous, "Palaeolithic Child Found in Iraq," *Arch* 7 (1954) 21.

Henri V. Vallois, "Neandertals[sic] and Praesapians. *The Huxley Memorial Lecture, 1954,*" *JRAI* 84 (1954) 111-130.

Santiago Genovés, "The Problem of the Sex of Certain Fossil Hominids, with Special Reference to the Neandertals[sic] Skeletons from Spy," *JRAI* 84 (1954) 131-144.

Muzaffer Süleyman Şenyürek, "A note on the Skulls of Chalcolithic Age from Yümüktepe," *TTKB* 18 (1954) 1-25.

Muzaffer Süleyman Şenyürek, "A Note on the Long Bones of Chalcolithic Age from Yümüktepe," *TTKB* 18 (1954) 519-522.

J. Lawrence Angel, "Newly Excavated Human Bones from Greece," *AJA* 59 (1955) 169.

Ralph Solecki, "The Shanidar Child: A Palaeolithic Find in Iraq," *Arch* 8 (1955) 169-175.

Muzaffer [Süleyman] Şenyürek, "A note on the long bones of Chalcolithic Age from Şeyh Höyük," *TTKB* 19 (1955) 247-270.

Muzaffer [Süleyman] Şenyürek, "Order of Eruption of the Permanent Teeth in the Chalcolithic and Copper Age Inhabitants of Anatolia," *TTKB* 20 (1956) 1-28.

Muzaffer [Süleyman] Şenyürek, "The time of eruption of the third molars in the Chalcolithic and copper age inhabitants of Anatolia," *TTKB* 20 (1956) 207-212.

Muzaffer Şenyürek, "The skeleton of the fossil infant in Shanidar cave, Northern Iraq—Preliminary Report—," *A(A)* 2 (1957) 49-56.

Muzaffer Şenyürek, "A further note on the Palaeolithic Shanidar infant," *A(A)* 2 (1957) 111-112.

J. Lawrence Angel, "Kings and Commoners," *AJA* 61 (1957) 181.

Ralph S. Solecki, "Two Neanderthal Skeletons from Shanidar Cave," *Sumer* 13 (1957) 59-60.

J. Lawrence Angel, "The People of Lerna," *AJA* 62 (1958) 221.

Henry W. Seaford Jr., "Near-Man of South Africa," *GR* 4 (1958) 165-192.

T. D. Stewart, "The Restored Shanidar I Skull," *SIR* (1958) 473-480.

T. D. Stewart, "First Views of the Restored Shanidar I skull," *Sumer* 14 (1958) 90-96.

Muzaffer [Süleyman] Şenyürek, "A Study of a Human Skeleton Found in Öküzini in the Province of Antalya," *TTKB* 22 (1958) 491-516.

Ralph S. Solecki, "Three Adult Neanderthal Skeletons From Shanidar Cave, Northern Iraq," *SIR* (1959) 603-635.

Muzaffer Şenyürek, "The Relative size of the Permanent Incisors in the Suborder Anthropoidea," *A(A)* 5 (1960) 47-85.

H. Nathan, "The Skeletal Material from Naḥar Ḥever. Cave No. 8—the 'Cave of Horror'," *'Atiqot* 3 (1961) 165-175.

T. D. Stewart, "The Skull of Shanidar II," *SIR* (1961) 521-533.

Ralph S. Solecki, "Three Adult Neanderthal Skeletons From Shanidar Cave, Northern Iraq," *Sumer* 17 (1961) 71-96.

T. D. Stewart, "The Skull of Shanidar II," *Sumer* 17 (1961) 97-106.

*Henry Field, "Fauna and Human Crania from Near Haditha," *Sumer* 17 (1961) 121-123.

H. Nathan, "The Skeletons of the Nahal Mishmar Caves," *IEJ* 11 (1961) 70-72.

Dorothy [A. E.] Garrod, "The Middle Palaeolithic of the Near East and the Problem of the Carmel Man. *The Huxley Memorial Lecture, 1962*," *JRAI* 92 (1962) 232-251.

N. Haas, "Human Skeletal Remains in Two Burial Caves," *IEJ* 13 (1963) 93-96.

T. D. Stewart, "Shanidar Skeletons IV and VI," *Sumer* 19 (1963) 8-26.

Anonymous, "Recent Acquisitions by the Institute. An Egyptian Mummy of a Graeco-Roman Period. About 100 B.C—A. D. 100," *BH* 2 (1965) #2, 4-9.

*H. Watanabe, "Amud Cave," *IEJ* 15 (1965) 246. [Note on Human Bones, pp. 246-247]

George J. Armelagos, George H. Ewing, David L. Greene, and Kathleen K. Greene, "Report of the Physical Anthropology Section, University of Colorado Nubian Expedition," *Kush* 13 (1965) 24-27.

J. Lawrence Angel, "Human Skeletal Remains at Karataş (Excavations at Karataş-Semayük in Lycia, 1965: Appendix," *AJA* 70 (1966) 255-257.

Filce F. Leek, "Observations on the Dental Pathology seen in Ancient Egyptian Skulls," *JEA* 52 (1966) 59-64.

*R. G. Harrison, "An Anatomical Examinaton of the Pharaonic Remains Purported to be Akhenaten," *JEA* 52 (1966) 95-119.

Mohammad Hasan Abdul Aziz and Jaroslav Slípka, "Twins from Tell Hassuna," *Sumer* 22 (1966) 45-50.

P. H. K. Gray, "Two Mummies of Ancient Egyptians in the Hancock Museum, Newcastle," *JEA* 53 (1967) 75-78.

E. Anati and N. Haas, "A Palaeolithic Site with Pithecanthropian Remains in the Plain of Esdraelon," *IEJ* 17 (1967) 114-118.

Enver Bostancı, "Morphological and Biometrical Examination of Some Skulls from the Sardis Excavations," *TTKB* 31 (1967) 1-48.

*N. Haas and H. Nathan, "Anthropological Survey on the Human Skeletal Remains in Qumran," *RdQ* 6 (1967-69) 345-352.

*Michael H. Jameson, "Halieis—Poroto Cheli, 1968," *AJA* 73 (1969) 238.

J. Lawrence Angel, "Appendix: Human Remains at Karataş," *AJA* 72 (1968) 260-263.

Ali M. Dinçol, Koray Dinçol and Âdil Öner, "Paleoserolojik Araştirmalar," *AAI* 3 (1969) 141-159. [English Summary pp. 156-157]

Ali M. Dinçol, Koray Dinçol and Pernur Öner, "Paleobiyokimyasal Araştirmalar," *AAI* 3 (1969) 161-166. [English Summary p. 165]

*Robert M. Little, "An Anthropological Preliminary Note on the First Season at *Tell Ḥesbân,*" *AUSS* 7 (1969) 232-239.

M. E. L. Mallowan and Hilda Linford, "Rediscovered Skulls from Arpachiyah," *Iraq* 31 (1969) 49-58. [1. Introductory Discussion, by M. E. L. Mallowan, pp. 49-55; Notes by M. E. L. Mallowan and Hilda Linford, pp. 55-56; 2. Examination of the Skeletal Remains, by Hilda Linford, pp. 56-58]

John R. Baker, "The Cro-Magnon discovery," *Man, N.S.,* 4 (1969) 135-136.

§172 ***2.5.6.3 Natural History - General Studies***

†Anonymous, "Harris's Natural History of the Bible," *BCQTR, 3rd Ser.,* 3 (1826) 128-143. *(Review)*

Anonymous, "Natural History of the Bible," *PRev* 7 (1835) 559-573. *(Review)*

†Anonymous, "Natural History of the Bible," *QRL* 114 (1863) 43-76. *(Review)*

G. W. Samson, "New Readings of Familiar Texts. No. III. Rediscovered Plants and Animals," *HR* 8 (1883-84) 766-769.

*Byron C. Nelson, "The Distribution of Plants and Animals in the Light of the Bible," *CFL, 3rd Ser.,* 32 (1926) 329-333.

§173 ***2.5.6.3.1 Animals - General Studies***

†Anonymous, "Aristotle's *History of Animals,*" *QRL* 117 (1865) 28-57. *(Review)*

*George Harris, "The Comparative Longevity of Animals of Different Species, and of Man; and the Probable Causes which mainly conduce to promote this Difference," *JRAI* 2 (1872-73) 69-78.

*(Miss) A. W. Buckwald, "Mythological Birds Ethnologically Considered," *JRAI* 4 (1874-75) 277-292.

*William Houghton, "On the Mammalia of the Assyrian Sculptures," *SBAT* 5 (1876-77) 33-64, 319-383.

†Anonymous, "Aristotle's History of Animals," *ERCJ* 160 (1884) 460-489.

Julius Sachs, "Notes on Homeric Zoölogy," *PAPA* 18 (1886) xiv.

Julius Sachs, "Notes on Homeric Zoölogy," *TAPA* 17 (1886) 17-23.

Selah Merrill, "Birds and Animals New to Palestine," *PEFQS* 22 (1890) 40-44.

T[errien] de L[acouperie], "Centaurs and Hippocentaurs of Western and Eastern Asia," *BOR* 6 (1892-93) 167-168.

*George A. Barton, "Tiamat," *JAOS* 15 (1893) 1-27, xiii-xv. *[Assy. = Heb. תְּהוֹם]*

*H. Colley March, "The Mythology of Wise Birds," *JRAI* 27 (1897-98) 209-232.

E. Martinengo Cesaresco, "The Hebrew Conception of Animals," *OC* 15 (1901) 110-114.

*W. Boyd-Dawkins, "Remains of Animals found in the Dictæan Cave in 1901," *Man* 2 (1902) #114.

*Anonymous, "The Entomology of the Scarab," *RP* 3 (1904) 375.

Sherwood Owen Dickerman, "Some Stock Illustrations of Animal Intelligence in Greek Psychology," *TAPA* 42 (1911) 123-130.

*Ira Maurice Prince, "The Animal DUN in the Sumerian Inscriptions," *JAOS* 33 (1913) 402-404.

*Alan Ball, "The Comic Beast in Roman Art," *A&A* 3 (1916) 99-105.

*Alan Ball, "The Comic Beast in Roman Art (Concluded)," *A&A* 3 (1916) 153-163.

*Felix von Oefele, "The Assyrian Veterinary Physician," *JAOS* 37 (1917) 331-332.

H. Northcote, "The Animal World in the Bible," *ICMM* 14 (1917-18) 145-151.

George Jennison, "The Animals of Ancient Rome," *ERCJ* 234 (1921) 100-110.

*Joseph Offord, "Archaeological Notes on Jewish Antiquities. XV. *Propagation of Plague by Insects and Rodents in the Old Testament and Monumental Records*," *PEFQS* 48 (1916) 141-143.

C. Ryder Smith, "The Bible and Animals," *ET* 35 (1923-24) 89-91.

*S. R. K. Glanville, "A Note on Herodotus II, 93," *JEA* 12 (1926) 75-76. *[Animal Behavior]*

*Dorothy A. E. Garrod, L. H. Dudley Buxton, G. Elliot Smith, and Dorothea M. A. Bate, "Excavation of a Mourterian Rock-Shelter at Devil's Tower, Gibraltar," *JRAI* 58 (1928) 33-113. [The Animal Remains, by Dorothea M. A. Bate, pp. 92-110; Appendix B: Note on Fossil Voles, by Martin A. C. Hinton, pp. 110-111; Appendix C: Fossil Mollusca, by Paul Fischer, pp. 111-113]

*Dorothea M. A. Bate, "A Note on the Fauna of the Athlit Caves," *JRAI* 62 (1932) 277-279.

*Warren R. Dawson, "Studies in the Egyptian Medical Texts—IV," *JEA* 20 (1934) 185-188. [The animal , p. 19]

E. Douglas Van Buren, "Mesopotamian Fauna in the Light of the Monuments. Archaeological Remarks upon Landsberger's 'Fauna des alten Mesopotamien'," *AfO* 11 (1936-37) 1-37.

Dorothea M. A. Bate, "Vertebrate remains from Wadi Dhobai," *JPOS* 18 (1938) 254-277.

I.*[sic]* Aharoni, "On Some animals mentioned in the Bible," *Osiris* 5 (1938) 461-478.

*Steven T. Byington, "Hebrew Marginalia III," *JBL* 64 (1945) 339-355. [3. Some Hebrew Zoology: Ps. 58:5; Jer. 8:17; Isa. 59:5; Ezek. 28:12ff.; Job 39:20; pp. 344-347]

*Steven T. Byington, "Zoological Hebrew," *ET* 57 (1945-46) 81-82.

Hugh Pope, "A Day at the Zoo with St. Jerome," *ClR* 27 (1947) 1-15. *[Animals in the O.T.]*

Margaret Morse Nice, "Incubation Periods Throughout the Ages," *Cent* 3 (1953-54) 311-359. [The Old World, Aristotle and Pliny, pp. 311-316]

*I. Jakobovits, "The Medical Treatment of Animals in Jewish Law," *JJS* 7 (1956) 207-220.

*Sylvia Benton, "Birds on the cup of Arkesilas," *Arch* 12 (1959) 178-182.

S. Angress, "Mammal Remains from Ḥorvat Beter (Beersheba)," *'Atiqot* 2 (1959) 53-71.

R. H. Dyson, "A Note on Queen Shub-ad's 'Onagers'," *Iraq* 22 (1960) 102-104.

Dexter Perkins Jr., "The Faunal Remains of Shanidar Cave and Zawi Chemi Shanidar: 1960 Season," *Sumer* 16 (1960) 77-78.

*Henry Field, "Fauna and Human Crania from Near Haditha," *Sumer* 17 (1961) 121-123.

D. A. Hooijer, "Middle Pleistocene mammals from Latamne, Orontes Valley, Syria," *AAAS* 12&13 (1961-62) 117-132.

*Sabri Doğuer (and staff), "Osteological Investigations of the Animal Remains Recovered from the Excavations of Ancient Sardis," *A(A)* 8 (1964) 49-56.

*K. L. McKay, "Animals in War and *ἰσονομία*," *AJP* 85 (1964) 124-135.

Y. Shauki Moustafa, "The domesticated animals of the *Sekhem-Khet* Step-Pyramid," *ASAE* 58 (1964) 255-265.

*P. R. Smythe, "Our Duty to Animals," *MC, N.S.,* 8 (1964-65) 263-268. [O.T. refs., p. 265]

D. A. Hooijer, "Additional notes on the pleistocene mammalian fauna of the Orontes valley," *AAAS* 15 (1965) #2, 101-104.

[D.] A. Hooijer, "Report on an antler of Dama mesopotamica*[sic]* (Brooke) from Tell Kazel," *AAAS* 15 (1965) #2, 105-106.

*Raymond E. Chaplin, "Animals in Archaeology," *Antiq* 39 (1965) 204-211.

*H. Watanabe, "Amud Cave," *IEJ* 15 (1965) 246. [Note on Animal Bones, p. 247]

Dexter Perkins Jr., "Three Faunal Assemblages from Sudanese Nubia," *Kush* 13 (1965) 56-61.

*Frank W. Wilson, "Thoughts on the Theology of Animal Welfare," *PQL* 11 (1965) 222-228. [I. The Old Testament, pp. 223-225]

D. A. Hooijer, "Preliminary notes on the animal remains found at Bouqras and Ramad in 1965," *AAAS* 16 (1966) #2, 193-195.

*Kent V. Flannery and Henry T. Wright, "Faunal Remains from 'Hut Sounding' at Eridu, Iraq," *Sumer* 22 (1966) 61-63.

*E. Danelius and H. Steinitz, "The Fishes and other Aquatic Animals on the Punt-Reliefs at Deir El-Baḥri," *JEA* 43 (1967) 15-24.

Kent V. Flannery and Jane C. Wheeler, "Animal Bones from Tell as-Sawwan Level III (Samarran Period)," *Sumer* 23 (1967) 179-182.

Dexter Perkins Jr., "The Pleistocene Fauna from the Yabroud Rockshelters," *AAAS* 18 (1968) 123-130.

Grover S. Krantz, "A New Method of Counting Mammal Bones," *AJA* 72 (1968) 286-288.

Frank N. Egerton III, "Ancient Sources for Animal Demography," *Isis* 59 (1968) 175-189.

*P. Ghalioungui, "The *'smr'* Animal of the Ebers Papyrus," *BIFAO* 68 (1969) 39-40.

§174 ***2.5.6.3.2 Alphabetical Listing of Animals***

A

A. Lowy, "Notice in Ancient Jewish Writings on the Sagacity and Habits of Ants," *SBAP* 3 (1880-81) 68-70.

*S. R. K. Glanville, "Some Notes on Material for the Reign of Amenophis III," *JEA* 15 (1929) 2-8. [III. Seated figure of an ape in crystalline standstone, p. 6]

William Coffman McDermott, "The Ape in Greek Literature," *TAPA* 66 (1935) 165-176.

William Coffman McDermott, "The Ape in Roman Literature," *TAPA* 67 (1936) 148-167.

B

*Manfred Cassirer, "An early faience statuette of a baboon," *JEA* 39 (1953) 108-109.

*Nina M. Davies, "Birds and Bats at Beni Ḥasan," *JEA* 35 (1949) 13-20.

*R. Campbell Thompson, "Assyrian *Garidu* = 'Beaver'," *JRAS* (1927) 723.

*A. H. Sayce, "Notes," *RAAO* 22 (1925) 93. [LAL-KI, a bee hive]

Grahame Clark, "Bees in Antiquity," *Antiq* 16 (1942) 208-215.

*C. de W. Brower, "The Beetle that Influenced a Nation," *RP* 3 (1904) 73-79. *[Scarab]*

*Warren R. Dawson, "Studies in the Egyptian Medical Texts—IV," *JEA* 20 (1934) 185-188. [18. The Beetle in medicine, p. 187]

(   ) Tristram, "List of Birds Collected for the Palestine Exploration Fund by the Survey Party in Palestine," *PEFQS* 8 (1876) 200-204.

*†W[illiam] Houghton, "On the Birds of the Assyrian Records and Monuments," *SBAP* 4 (1881-82) 57-60.

*William Houghton, "The Birds of the Assyrian Monuments and Records," *SBAT* 8 (1883-84) 42-142.

*†Theo. G. Pinches, "Assyriological Notes," *SBAP* 8 (1885-86) 240-245. [Assyrian Bird-Names, pp. 244-245]

*Charles Whymper, "Birds in Ancient Egyptian Art," *AEE* 2 (1915) 1-5.

*S[tephen] Langdon, "Philological Note," *RAAO* 29 (1932) 121-122. [*The Bird* URINNU (not SISINNU) p. 122]

P. E. Kretzmann, "Birds of Jerusalem and Vicinity," *CTM* 4 (1933) 693-694.

*James Hornell, "The Role of Birds in Early Navigation," *Antiq* 20 (1946) 142-149.

*Nina M. Davies, "Birds and Bats at Beni Ḥasan," *JEA* 35 (1949) 13-20.

G. R. Driver, "Birds in the Old Testament. I. Birds in Law," *PEQ* 87 (1955) 5-20.

G. R. Driver, "Birds in the Old Testament. II. Birds in Life," *PEQ* 87 (1955) 129-140.

G. R. Driver, "Once Again: Birds in the Bible," *PEQ* 90 (1958) 56-58.

*Paul Haupt, "Pelican and Bittern," *JBL* 39 (1920) 158-161. [Addenda, p. 171]

*Donald P. Hansen, "An Archaic Bronze Boar from Sardis," *BASOR* #168 (1962) 27-36.

Paul Haupt, "The Mountain-Bull," *JBL* 36 (1917) 249-253.

*G. D. Hornblower, "An Humped Bull of Ivory," *JEA* 13 (1927) 222-225.

C

W. Houghton, "Was the Camel known to the Ancient Egyptians?" *SBAP* 12 (1889-90) 81-84.

*W. L. Nash, "An Egyptian Representation of the Camel," *SBAP* 24 (1902) 309.

*W. M. Flinders Petrie, "The Ten Temples of Abydos," *AAOJ* 26 (1904) 273-280. [The Camel in Egyptian History, pp. 277-278]

G. Caton-Thompson, "The Camel in Dynastic Egypt," *Man* 34 (1934) #24.

*Joseph P. Free, "Abraham's Camels," *JNES* 3 (1944) 187-193.

B. S. J. Isserlin, "On Some Possible Early Occurrences of the Camel in Palestine," *PEQ* 82 (1950) 50-53.

W[illiam] F[oxwell] Albright, "Zur Zähmung des Kamels," *ZAW* 62 (1950) 315. *[Camels - English Text]*

*Henry Field, "Camel Brands and Graffiti from Iraq, Syria, Jordan, Iran, and Arabia," *JAOSS* #15 (1952) i-vi, 1-41.

*F. E. Zeuner, "The Identity of the Camel on the Khurab Pick," *Iraq* 17 (1955) 162-163.

W. G. Lambert, "The Domesticated Camel in the Second Millennium—Evidence Alalakh and Ugarit," *BASOR* #160 (1960) 42-43.

*Shnayer Z. Leiman, "The Camel in the Patriarchal Narrative," *YR* 6 (1967) 16-26.

Anonymous, "Your Questions Answered. The Camels are Coming, They are, They are!" *BH* 5 (1969) 119-121. *[Camels in the Old Testament]*

*( ) Placzek, "The Weasel and Cat in Ancient Times," *SBAP* 7 (1884-85) 97-98. *(Trans. by A. Lowy)*

( ) Placzec[sic]*, "The Weasel and the Cat in Ancient Times," *SBAT* 9 (1886-93) 155-156.*(Trans. by A. Lowy)*

*R. Campbell Thompson, "(1) On *KUR.GI.ḪU, kurkû* = the Crane; (2) *šikkû* = Cat; (3) *kamunu* = Red Worms," *JRAS* (1929) 339-343.

*Neville Langton, "Notes on Some Small Egyptian Figures of Cats," *JEA* 22 (1936) 115-120.

*N[eville] Langton, "Further Notes on Some Egyptian Figures of Cats," *JEA* 24 (1938) 54-58.

*G. D. Hornblower, "The Divine Cat and the Snake in Egypt," *Man* 43 (1943) #65.

*Sidney S. Schipper, "Cat or Marten?" *Arch* 5 (1952) 25-29.

*F. E. Zeuner, "Dog and Cat in the Neolithic of Jericho," *PEQ* 90 (1958) 52-55.

*A. J. Arkell, "An early pet cat," *JEA* 48 (1962) 158.

*G. J. Verwers, Hans-Åke Nordström, H. T. B. Hall, "Archaeological Survey of the West Bank of the Nile," *Kush* 10 (1962) 10-75. [A Note on the Cattle Skulls Excavated at Faras, pp. 58-61]

*S[tephen] Langdon, "Four Assyriological Notes," *JRAS* (1919) 37-42. [2. *Apsasû,* a Kind of Wild Cattle, pp. 41-42]

*John P. Peters, "The Cock," *JAOS* 33 (1913) 363-396.

*John P. Peters, "The Cock in the Old Testament," *JBL* 33 (1914) 152-156.

*Julius J. Price, "Kapporoth," *OC* 37 (1923) 176-180; 38 (1924) 499-503. *[The cock in Jewish religion]*

*Howard Carter, "An Ostracon depicting a Red Jungle-Fowl. (The earliest known drawing of the domestic cock.)," *JEA* 9 (1923) 1-4.

G. R. Crotch, "The Coleoptera of Palestine," *PEFQS* 1 (1869) 141-143. *[Insects]*

*R. Campbell Thompson, "(1) On *KUR.GI.ḪU, kurkû* = the Crane; (2) *šikkû* = Cat; (3) *kamunu* = Red Worms," *JRAS* (1929) 339-343.

*W. A. Oldfather, "Turkeys or Cranes on a Laconian Hydria," *AJA* 43 (1939) 104-105.

Claude R. Conder, "The Crocodiles in the Nahr ez Zerka," *PEFQS* 20 (1888) 166.

George Buchanan Gray, "Crocodiles in Palestine," *PEFQS* 52 (1920) 167-176.

E. W. G. Masterman, "Crocodiles in Palestine," *PEFQS* 53 (1921) 19-22.

Anonymous, "Crocodiles in Palestine," *PEFQS* 55 (1923) 102.

Gilbert Bagnani, "The Great Egyptian Crocodile Mystery," *Arch* 5 (1952) 76-78.

D

*W[illiam] F[oxwell] Albright, "An Incised Representation of a Stag from Tell el-ʿOreimeh," *JPOS* 6 (1926) 167-168. *[Deer]*

*Jean De. Mot, "The Devil Fish in Ancient Art," *RP* 9 (1910) 276-278.

A[ug.] C. Merriam, "The Dogs of Æsculapius," *AAOJ* 7 (1885) 285-289.

*P. Hippolyte-Boussac, "The Typhonic Dog," *A&A* 25 (1928) 181-185.

Max Hilzheimer, "Dogs," *Antiq* 6 (1932) 411-419. (Corrigenda, *Antiq* 7 (1933) p. 228) *(Trans. by Roland G. Austin)*

*F. E. Zeuner, "Dog and Cat in the Neolithic of Jericho," *PEQ* 90 (1958) 52-55.

*Nelson Glueck, "Nabataean Dolphins," *EI* 7 (1964) 40*-43*. *[Sculptures]*

David Flusser, "Tales About Dolphins in the Greek World," *Sefunim* 2 (1967-68) 17-27.

*Paul Haupt, "Sumerian, *tu,* dove, and *nam,* swallow," *JSOR* 1 (1917) 3-9.

Eliezer D. Oren, "The 'Herodian Doves' in the Light of Recent Archaeological Discoveries," *PEQ* 100 (1968) 56-61.

†Anonymous, "On the Dragon of the Ancients," *MMBR* 2 (1796) 779-780.

E

C. Ryder Smith, "The Eagle and Her Young," *ET* 36 (1914-15) 237.

*Anonymous, "The Use of Elephants in War," *DUM* 21 (1843) 117-120. *(Review)*

*Percy E. Newberry, "Extracts from my Note-Books. V.," *SBAP* 24 (1902) 244-252. [37. A Prehistoric Figure of an Elephant, p. 251]

*George Henslow, "The Carob and the Elephant," *ET* 15 (1903-04) 429.

Anonymous, "Elephants in the Euphrates Valley," *RP* 7 (1908) 210.

Bayard Dodge, "Elephants in the Bible Lands," *BA* 18 (1955) 17-20.

C. E. Stevens, "Julius Caesar's Elephant," *HT* 9 (1959) 626-627.

John Dayton, "The Lost Elephants of Arabia," *Antiq* 42 (1968) 42-45.

F

†Theo. G. Pinches, "Notes on the use of the Falcon in Ancient Assyria," *SBAP* 6 (1883-84) 57-59.

P[aul] Haupt, "The Peregrine Falcon," *JBL* 38 (1919) 152-156.

*Edward Hull, "On the Physical Conditions of the Mediterranean Basin, which have Given Rise to a Community of Some Species of Fresh-Water Fishes in the Nile and the Jordan Basins," *JTVI* 31 (1897-98) 111-120. (Discussion, p. 121)

*Walter L. Nash, "Egyptian Models of Fish," *SBAP* 21 (1899) 311-312. (Note by A. H. Sayce, *SBAP* 22 (1900) p. 86)

*Walter L. Nash, "Ancient Egyptian Models of Fish," *SBAP* 22 (1900) 163-165.

*R. Engelbach, "Notes on the Fish of Mendes," *ASAE* 24 (1924) 161-168.

*F. A. Wood, "Greek Fish-Names," *AJP* 48 (1927) 197-325.

*F. A. Wood, "Greek Fish-Names. Part II," *AJP* 49 (1928) 36-56.

*F. A. Wood, "Greek Fish-Names. Part III," *AJP* 49 (1928) 167-187.

*D'Arcy Wenthworth Thompson, "On Egyptian Fish-names used by Greek Writers," *JEA* 14 (1928) 22-23.

*Warren R. Dawson, "Studies in the Egyptian Medical Texts—II," *JEA* 19 (1933) 133-137. [8. The fish [hieroglyphs] p. 137]

Henry Field, "Fish in Mesopotamian 'Flood' Deposits," *Man* 36 (1936) #75.

Alfred C. Andrews, "Greek and Latin Mouse-fishes and Pig-fishes," *TAPA* 79 (1948) 232-253.

*Daniel Sperber, "Some Observations of Fish and Fisheries in Roman Palestine," *ZDMG* 118 (1968) 265-269.

*C[laude] R. Conder, "Notes on 'Across the Jordan'," *PEFQS* 18 (1886) 83-88. [Foxes, p. 88] *(Review)*

*G. Schumacher, "Across the Jordan. A Reply to C. R. C's Notes thereon," *PEFQS* 18 (1886) 167-171. [10. Foxes, p. 170]

*Rachel Wischnitzer-Bernstein, "The Messianic Fox," *RR* 5 (1940-41) 257-263.

*Paul Romanoff, "The Fox in Jewish Tradition," *RR* 6 (1941-42) 184-187.

*Rachel Wischnitzer-Bernstein, "A Reply to Dr. Romanoff," *RR* 6 (1941-42) 187-190. *[Fox in Jewish Tradition]*

*Clive H. Carruthers, "Some Hittite Etymologies," *Lang* 6 (1930) 159-163. [2. *akuwakuwaš* 'frog, toad', p. 160]

G

James Francis, "The Giraffe," *ET* 29 (1917-18) 139.

*S. R. K. Glanville, "Some Notes on Material for the Reign of Amenophis III," *JEA* 15 (1929) 2-8. [IV. Wooden head of a goat, pp. 6-7]

*S[tephen] Langdon, "Notes on Sumerian Etymology and Syntax," *JRAS* (1933) 857-866. [IV. [sìg-úz = šarti enzi "fleece of a she goat" also šartu "hair of humans"] , pp. 859-860]

Wolfgang Amschler, "Goats from Ur and Kish," *Antiq* 11 (1937) 226-228.

O. G. S. C[rawford], "The Kish Goat, Bulgaria," *Antiq* 12 (1938) 81-82.

F. E. Zeuner, "The Goats of Early Jericho," *PEQ* 87 (1955) 70-86.

*S[tephen] Langdon, "Critical Notes," *AJSL* 31 (1914-15) 282-286. [III. Kusarikku, "goat-fish", pp. 283-285]

*F. A. Walker, "Locusts and Grasshoppers, with Special Reference to Biblical Species," *JTVI* 34 (1902) 197-211. (Discussion, pp. 211-215)

*J. L. Benson, "The Griffin in the Minoan-Mycenaean World," *AJA* 63 (1959) 186.

*Tariq Madhloum, "More Notes on the Near Eastern Griffin," *Sumer* 20 (1964) 57-62.

H

*W. Wright, "The Arabic Term for *Hare*," *JSL, 4th Ser.*, 10 (1866-67) 180-182.

William Gillespie, "The Hare," *JSL, 4th Ser.*, 10 (1866-67) 475.

*R. D. Barrett, "The Hawk in Phoenicia," *Iraq* 6 (1939) 100.

*Steven T. Byington, "Hebrew Marginalia I," *JBL* 60 (1941) 279-288. [Two Species of Hawk, pp. 283-284]

*Machteld J. Mellink, "A Votive Bird from Anatolia," *Exped* 6 (1963-64) #2, 28-32. *[Hawk]*

Mahmoud effendi Roushdy, "Some notes on the hedgehog," *ASAE* 11 (1911) 281-282.

*W. M. Crompton, "Two Glazed Hippopotamus Figures Hitherto Unpublished," *AEE* 16 (1931) 21-27.

Georg Haas, "On the Occurrence of Hippopotamus in the Iron Age of the Coastal Area of Israel (Tell Qasîleh)," *BASOR* #132 (1953) 30-34.

*Anonymous, "Sesostris, the Hornet of Exod. 23:28, Deut. 7:20; Josh. 24:12," *QCS, 3rd Ser.,* 10 (1838) 281-285.

John Campbell, "The Hornets of Scripture, as connected with Jewish and Egyptian history," *PQPR* 4 (1875) 677-692.

Ross G. Murison, "The Hornet," *ET* 16 (1904-05) 239.

*P. le Page Renouf, "The Horse in the Book of the Dead," *SBAP* 7 (1884-85) 41-42.

William Hayes Ward, "Oriental Antiquities. 1. The Horse in Ancient Babylonia," *AJA* 2 (1898) 159-162.

*Claude R. Conder, "Notes on New Discoveries," *PEFQS* 41 (1909) 266-275. [Horses, pp. 270-271]

*Paul Haupt, "Critical Notes," *AJSL* 33 (1916-17) 45-48. [I. Assyr. *mûr-nisqi,* "War-Horse", pp. 45-47]

H. Northcote, "The Horse in the Bible," *ICMM* 20 (1923-24) 300-305.

J. E. Quibell and A. Olver, "An ancient Egyptian Horse," *ASAE* 26 (1926) 172-176.

*Philip J. Baldensperger, "The Immovable East. *Horses,*" *PEFQS* 61 (1929) 183-189.

*Max Hilzheimer, "The Evolution of the Domestic Horse," *Antiq* 9 (1935) 133-139.

*O. R. Gurney, "Hittite *Paras* = Horse?" *PEQ* 69 (1937) 194-195.

*Grahame Clark, "Horses and Battle-axes," *Antiq* 15 (1941) 50-70.

*V. Gordon Childe, "Horses, Chariots, and Battle-axes," *Antiq* 15 (1941) 196-199.

*Harold A. Liebowitz, "Horses in New Kingdom Art and the Date of an Ivory from Megiddo," *JARCE* 6 (1967) 129-134.

*Mary B. Moore, "Horses by Exekias," *AJA* 72 (1968) 357-368.

*Nina M. Davies, "Amenemḥab encountering a Hyena. *From the tomb of Amenemḥab at Thebes* (no. 85)," *JEA* 26 (1940) 82.

I

*Dorothy Kent Hill, "An Ancient Persian Ibex," *Arch* 2 (1949) 193.

*A. Lucas, "Notes on some of the objects from the tomb of Tut-Ankhamun," *ASAE* 41 (1942) 135-147; 45 (1947) 133-134. [Insects, p. 143]

K

*G. Levi Della Vida, "On Kirmiz," *JAOS* 61 (1941) 287-288. *[Insect]*

L

*John D. Davis, "The Symbolism of the Lamb," *CFL, N.S.,* 1 (1900) 71-72.

W[illiam] M. Ramsay, "Specimens of Anatolian Words," *OOR* 1 (1926) #2, 1-7. [III. Korud: The Lark, p. 2]

*Joseph Bourke, "'Leviathan Which Yahweh Made to Laugh At'," *LofS* 13 (1958-59) 122-129.

*Cyrus H. Gordon, "Leviathan: Symbol of Evil," *LIST* 3 (1966) 1-9.

*Karl J. Grimm, "The Polychrome Lion recently found in Babylon," *JAOS* 22 (1901) 27-34.

A. B. Meyer, "The Antiquity of the Lion in Greece," *SIR* (1903) 661-667.

*Anonymous, "The Lion in Ancient Art," *RP* 8 (1909) 57.

P. Hippolyte-Boussac, "The Persian Lion," *A&A* 28 (1929) 74-83.

*Cyril G. E. Bunt, "The Lion and the Unicorn," *Antiq* 4 (1930) 425-437.

*(Mrs.) C. N. Deedes, "The Lion and the Unicorn," *Antiq* 6 (1932) 341-342.

*Oscar Broneer, "The Lion at Amphipolis," *AJA* 42 (1938) 128-129.

*Herbert Hoffmann, "Lion at Didyma," *Arch* 6 (1953) 103.

*Robert H. Dyson, "A Babylonian Lion in Toledo," *Exped* 5 (1962-63) #2, 14-15.

*Gölül Öney, "Lion Figures in Anatolian Seljuk Architecture," *A(A)* 13 (1969) 43-67.

Anonymous, "Ravages of Locusts," *MR* 11 (1828) 219-220.

*F. A. Walker, "Locusts and Grasshoppers, with Special Reference to Biblical Species," *JTVI* 34 (1902) 197-211. (Discussion, pp. 211-215)

*T. K. Cheyne, "The Carob and the Locust. I.," *ET* 15 (1903-04) 335.

*George Farmer, "The Carob and the Locust. II.," *ET* 15 (1903-04) 336.

*George Henslow, "The Carob and the Locust," *ET* 15 (1903-04) 285-286.

*George Farmer, "'Locusts,' or 'Carob Beans'," *ET* 16 (1904-05) 382.

Eugene Parsons, "Locusts in Palestine," *HR* 71 (1916) 21-23.

F. S. Bodenheimer, "Note on Invasions of Palestine by Rare Locusts," *IEJ* 1 (1950-51) 146-148.

M

*Sidney S. Schipper, "Cat or Marten?" *Arch* 5 (1952) 25-29.

*Thomas Oldfield, "Remarks on Facsimile of a Metal Mouse in the Collection of Baron Ustinoff at Jaffa," *PEFQS* 26 (1894) 189-190.

*J. Campbell Gibson, "Was it Bubonic Plague?" *ET* 12 (1900-01) 378-380. *[Mice and Emerods]*

*Geo. J. Dann, "'Mice' and 'Emerods'," *ET* 15 (1903-04) 476-478.

*Felix von Oefele, “A Babylonian representation of a jumping mouse,” *JAOS* 38 (1918) 140.

*Warren R. Dawson, “The Mouse in Egyptian and Later Medicine,” *JEA* 10 (1924) 83-86.

*†Edward Sachau, “The Cappadocian Cuneiform Inscription,” *SBAP* 4 (1881-82) 117. *[Kutin = mule //* Aramaic כּוּדְנָיָא or כּוּדְנָא*]*

O

*A. H. Godbey, “SISINNU = ‘Horsebird’ = Ostrich,” *AJSL* 20 (1903-04) 257-258.

*Paul Haupt, “Critical Notes. II. The Hebrew Names for ‘Ostrich’,” *AJSL* 32 (1915-16) 142-143.

*Berthold Laufer, “Ostrich Egg-Shell Cups from Mesopotamia. The Ostrich in Ancient Times,” *OC* 40 (1926) 257-268.

*Helene J. Kantor, “Oriental Institute Museum Notes. A Predynastic Ostrich Egg with Incised Decoration,” *JNES* 7 (1948) 46-51. [#5]

*G. D. Hornblower, “The Barndoor Fowl in Egyptian Art,” *AEE* 20 (1935) 82.

Percy E. Newberry, “The Owls in Ancient Egypt,” *JEA* 37 (1951) 72-74.

*P. S. Ronzevalle, “Some Examples of the Hunchbacked Ox in Syrian Art,” *RP* 10 (1911) 317-321. *(Trans. by Helen M. Wright)*

*G. W. Murray, “Graves of Oxen in the Eastern Desert of Egypt,” *JEA* 12 (1926) 248-249.

P

*W[illiam] M. Ramsay, “Specimens of Anatolian Words,” *OOR* 1 (1926) #2, 1-7. [II. The Peacock: Name imported into Anatolia, pp. 1-2]

*Paul Haupt, “Pelican and Bittern,” *JBL* 39 (1920) 158-161. [Addenda, p. 171]

*Warren R. Dawson, "The Pig in Ancient Egypt: A Commentary on Two Passages of Herodotus," *JRAS* (1928) 597-608. [I The Pig in Agriculture, pp. 597-599; II The Pig in Medicine, Magic and Mythology, pp. 599-608]

*P[ercy] E. Newberry, "The Pig and the Cult-Animal of Set," *JEA* 14 (1928) 211-225.

*S[tephen] Langdon, "Philological Note," *RAAO* 29 (1932) 121-122. [*adudîlu* = Mantis religiosa, p. 121] *[Praying Mantis]*

R

Y. Z., "The Rats of Herodotus," *MMBR* 58 (1824-25) 406.

George A. Barton, "Traces of the Rhinoceros in Ancient Babylonia," *JSOR* 10 (1926) 92-95.

D. A. Hooijer, "The Dicerorhmus Hemitoechus (falconer) at Yabroud," *AAAS* 16 (1966) #2, 155-156. *[Rhinoceros]*

Claude R. Conder, "The Roebuck," *PEFQS* 8 (1876) 152-153.

George E. Post, "The Roebuck in Palestine," *PEFQS* 22 (1890) 171-172.

C[laude] R. Conder, "The Roebuck," *PEFQS* 22 (1890) 173.

S

*S[tephen] Langdon, "Assyriological Notes," *RAAO* 30 (1933) 105-110. [I. *Anduḫallatu, imduḫallatu,* gecko, salamander, pp. 105-106]

*Alfred C. Andrews, "Greek and Latin Terms for Salmon and Trout," *TAPA* 86 (1955) 308-318.

*E. Douglas Van Buren, "The Scorpion in Mesoptamian Art and Religion," *AfO* 12 (1937-39) 1-28.

Marcus N. Tod, "The Scorpion in Graeco-Roman Egypt," *JEA* 25 (1939) 55-61.

*C. J. Gadd, "Two Assyrian Observations," *Iraq* 10 (1948) 19-25. [(b) The 'River-Man' from Egypt and the Broken Obelisk, pp. 21-25] *[Seal]*

*Ross G. Murison, "The Serpent in the Old Testament," *AJSL* 21 (1904-05) 115-130.

*[Julian] Morganstern, "On Gilgames-Epic XI, 274-320. A Contribution to the Study of the Role of the Serpent in Semitic Mythology," *ZA* 29 (1914-15) 284-300.

*H. L. Parker, "'Fiery Serpents'," *PEFQS* 61 (1929) 58.

Max Hilzheimer, "Sheep," *Antiq* 10 (1936) 195-206. *(Trans. by Roland G. Austin)*

*H. Wittmann, "A Note on the Linguistic Form of Hittite 'sheep'," *RHA* 22 (1964) 117-118.

*P. Ghalioungui, "The *'smr'* Animal of the Ebers Papyrus," *BIFAO* 68 (1969) 39-40.

*Stuart A. Harris, "On the land snails of Iraq and their potential use in determining past climatic conditions," *Sumer* 17 (1961) 107-113.

*G. D. Hornblower, "The Divine Cat and the Snake in Egypt," *Man* 43 (1943) #65.

*S[tephen] Langdon, "Assyriological Notes," *RAAO* 30 (1933) 105-110. [II. B) ZARAḪ, stork, pp. 106-107]

(Mrs.) E. A. Finn, "Sun-Birds," *PEFQS* 22 (1890) 194. (Note by C. R. Conder, p. 330)

*Paul Haupt, "Sumerian, *tu,* dove, and *nam,* swallow," *JSOR* 1 (1917) 3-9.

*I. M. Price, "Swine in Old Testament Taboo," *JBL* 44 (1925) 154-157.

T

*Clive H. Carruthers, "Some Hittite Etymologies," *Lang* 6 (1930) 159-163. [2. *akuwakuwaš* 'frog, toad', p. 160]

*Rudolf Anthes, "Memphis (Mit Rahineh) in 1956," *UMB* 21 (1957) #2, 3-34. (Fig. 12. Toad, p. 34) *[Figurine]*

Eb. Nestle, "Tortoise in the Bible," *ET* 14 (1902-03) 189.

J. D. Crace, "Tortoises," *ET* 14 (1902-03) 286.

*Alfred C. Andrews, "Greek and Latin Terms for Salmon and Trout," *TAPA* 86 (1955) 308-318.

*W. A. Oldfather, "Turkeys or Cranes on a Laconian Hydria," *AJA* 43 (1939) 104-105.

U

I. J., "The Unicorn of the Sacred Scriptures," *CongML* 26 (1843) 399-404.

*Anonymous, "The Unicorn," *CRB* 21 (1856) 34-45. [רְאֵם]

*Cyril G. E. Bunt, "The Lion and the Unicorn," *Antiq* 4 (1930) 425-437.

*(Mrs.) C. N. Deedes, "The Lion and the Unicorn," *Antiq* 6 (1932) 341-342.

Allen H. Godbey, "The Unicorn in the Old Testament," *AJSL* 56 (1939) 256-296.

W. H. Riddell, "Concerning Unicorns," *Antiq* 19 (1945) 194-202.

W. H. Riddell, "Further note on the Unicorn," *Antiq* 20 (1946) 100-102.

Rachel Wischnitzer [-Bernstein], "The Unicorn in Christian and Jewish Art," *HJud* 13 (1951) 141-156.

Humphrey Humphreys, "The Horn of the Unicorn," *Antiq* 27 (1953) 15-19.

Elmer G. Suhr, "An Interpretation of the Unicorn," *Folk* 75 (1964) 91-109.

V

J.*[sic]* Aharoni, "The Bearded Vulture," *BIES* 6 (1938-39) #2, III.

*M. Zeidel, "Leḥayath—a vulture," *BIES* 6 (1938-39) #3, IV.

W

*(   ) Placzek, "The Weasel and Cat in Ancient Times," *SBAP* 7 (1884-85) 97-98. *(Trans. by A. Lowy)*

(   ) Placzec[sic]*, "The Weasel and the Cat in Ancient Times," *SBAT* 9 (1886-93) 155-156.*(Trans. by A. Lowy)*

*R. Campbell Thompson, "(1) On *KUR.GI.ḪU, kurkû* = the Crane; (2) *šikkû* = Cat; (3) *kamunu* = Red Worms," *JRAS* (1929) 339-343.

§175 *2.5.6.3.3 Botanical Studies - General*

H. M., "Biblical Botany," *TE* 2 (1865) 81-115.

Leo H. Grindon, "The Flowers of the Bible," *DUM* 90 (1877) 84-91.

*John R. Jackson, "Notes on Vegetable Remains from the Egyptian Tombs," *SBAP* 1 (1878-79) 36-37. (Remarks by Alexander Taylor, W. Harry Rylands, and W. F. Birch, p. 37; by George Murray, pp. 37-38.) *[Note: pp. 34-35 duplicated in error]*

E. Bonavia, "The Cone-Fruit of the Assyrian Monuments," *BOR* 2 (1887-88) 138-142, 170-172, 173-178.

*E. Bonavia, "Sacred Trees of the Assyrian Monuments," *BOR* 3 (1888-89) 7-12, 35-40, 56-61.

G. E. Post, "On the Botanical Geography of Syria and Palestine," *JTVI* 22 (1888-89) 253-298. [(Discussion, pp. 299-307) (Notes by F. A. Walker, pp. 308-311)]

*W. St. C[had] Boscawen, "Notes on the Assyrian Sacred Trees," *BOR* 4 (1889-90) 95-96.

*W. Houghton, "The Tree Fruit represented by the *Tappūakh* (תַּפּוּחַ) of the Hebrew Scriptures," *SBAP* 12 (1889-90) 42-48.

*A[ngus] C[rawford], "Notes—Archæological, Etc.," *PER* 13 (1899-1900) 48-50. *[Dried flowers in mummy wrappings]*

E. Bonavia, "Some un-noticed Plants on the Assyrian Monuments (British Museum)," *BOR* 5 (1891) 196-200.

*George E. Post, "Narrative of a Second Journey to Palmyra. List of Plants Collected During the Journey," *PEFQS* 25 (1893) 152-162.

George E. Post, "Narrative of an Expedition to Lebanon, Anti-Lebanon and Damascus. List of Plants Collected in Northern Lebanon, Anti-Lebanon and Damascus, " *PEFQS* 25 (1893) 235-239.

*Theo. G. Pinches, "Names of Plants and Things made therefrom in Babylonia," *SBAP* 16 (1893-94) 308-311.

[Henry Baker] Tristram, "Flora of Syria, Palestine, and Sinai," *PEFQS* 29 (1897) 151-153. *(Review)*

F. A. Walker, "Herodotus. II.—As a Botanist. (Viewed in the Light of Recent Travel and Investigation of Plants and Trees in Egypt," *JTVI* 31 (1897-98) 73-108. (Discussion, pp. 108-110)

E. W. G. Masterman, "The Trees and Shrubs of the Holy Land," *PEFQS* 39 (1907) 66-67.

W. T. Thiselton-Dyer, "On some ancient plant-names," *JP* 33 (1913) 195-207.

W. T. Thiselton-Dyer, "On some ancient plant-names II.," *JP* 34 (1915-18) 78-96.

W. T. Thiselton-Dyer, "On some ancient plant-names III.," *JP* 34 (1915-18) 290-312.

Anonymous, "Bible Renderings," *HR* 78 (1919) 387. *[Plants]*

Alfred B. Rendle, "Plants of the Bible," *JTVI* 51 (1919) 100-110. (Discussion, pp. 110-114)

Ethel Mary Greeves, "Currents Notes and News. Plant-lore in Olden Times," *A&A* 13 (1922) 145.

*Paul Haupt, "Philological Studies," *AJP* 45 (1924) 47-63. [1. Ambrosian Mangers, pp. 47-48] *[Sweet-scented grasses or herbs]*

*Allan Chester Johnson, "Ancient Forests and Navies," *TAPA* 58 (1927) 199-209.

*A. E. Watkins, "The Origin of Cultivated Plants," *Antiq* 7 (1933) 73-80.

*Warren R. Dawson, "Studies in the Egyptian Medical Texts—III," *JEA* 20 (1934) 41-46. [9. The herb ; 10. The plant ; 11. The plant ; 12. The plant ; 13. The herb ; 14. The plant]

*Warren R. Dawson, "Studies in the Egyptian Medical Texts—IV," *JEA* 20 (1934) 185-188. [16. The plant p. 186; 17. The plant ; p. 186]

*Warren R. Dawson, "Studies in the Egyptian Medical Texts—V," *JEA* 21 (1935) 37-40. [21. The plant , pp. 37-38; 22. The Plant , pp. 38-39]

*A. Lucas, "Notes on some of the objects from the tomb of Tut-Ankhamun," *ASAE* 41 (1942) 135-147; 45 (1947) 133-134. [Botany, pp. 144-146]

Jiří Neustupný, "Alliaceous Plants in Prehistory and History," *ArOr* 20 (1952) 356-385.

D. V. Zaitschek, "Remains of Cultivated Plants from 'Afula," *'Atiqot* 1 (1955) 71-74.

M. Negbi, "The Botanical Finds at Tell Abu Matar, near Beersheba," *IEJ* 5 (1955) 257-258.

*B. S. J. Isserlin, "Ancient Forests in Palestine: Some Archaeological Indications," *PEQ* 87 (1955) 87-88.

D. V. Zaitschek, "Remains of Cultivated Plants from Ḥorvat Beter (Beersheba). Preliminary Notes," *'Atiqot* 2 (1959) 48-52.

D. V. Zaitschek, "The Expedition to the Judean Desert, 1961. Remains of Plants from the Cave of the Pool," *IEJ* 12 (1962) 184-185.

John C. Trever, "The Flora of the the Bible and Biblical Scholarship," *JAAR* 27 (1959) 45-49.

A. C. Western, "The Identity of Some Trees Mentioned in the Bible," *PEQ* 93 (1961) 89-100.

*R. K. Harrison, "Healing Herbs of the Bible," *Janus* 40 (1961-63) 9-54.

Jane Gray and Watson Smith, "Fossil Pollen and Archaeology," *Arch* 15 (1962) 16-26. [Assyrian plant fertilization, p. 17 ¶2]

A. Fahn, N. Wachs, and C. Ginzburg, "Dendrochronological studies in the Negev," *IEJ* 13 (1963) 291-300.

W[illem] van Zeist and S. Bottema, "Paleobotanical investigations at Ramad," *AAAS* 16 (1966) #2, 179-180.

Willem van Zeist, "A First Impression of the Plant Remains from Selenkahiye," *AAAS* 18 (1968) 35-36.

Hans G. Güterbock, "Oil Plants in Hittite Anatolia," *JAOS* 88 (1968) 66-71.

*M. E. Weichselfish, "The Plants באשה and אנא, איזמא," *Lĕš* 34 (1969-70) #4, n.p.n.

§176 *2.5.6.3.4 Alphabetical Listing of Plants*

A

Ross G. Murison, "The Almond," *ET* 16 (1904-05) 334-335.

T. K. Cheyne, "Almug Trees, with a Study of the Passages Referring to Them," *ET* 9 (1897-98) 470-473.

*Fritz Hommel, "Miscellanea," *ET* 9 (1897-98) 524-526. [3. *(Almug Trees)* pp. 525-526]

*Claude R. Conder, "Notes on New Discoveries," *PEFQS* 41 (1909) 266-275. [Almug or Algum trees (1 Kgs. 10:11; 2 Chron. 9:10) p. 274]

George Henslow, "Almug or Algum," *ET* 18 (1906-07) 527.

James Hope Moulton, "Almug," *ET* 18 (1906-07) 567.

Wilfred H. Schoff, "Aloes," *JAOS* 42 (1922) 171-185.

B

*David Yellin, "Emek ha-bakha: Bekhaim," *JPOS* 3 (1923) 191-192. *[Bakha tree]*

*E. Bonavia, "Bananas and Melons as Dessert Fruits of Assyrian Monarchs and Courtiers," *BOR* 4 (1889-90) 169-175.

T[errien] de L[acouperie], "On Eastern Names of the Banana," *BOR* 4 (1889-90) 176.

*Philip Keep Reynolds, "Earliest Evidence of Banana Culture," *JAOSS* #12 (1951) 1-28. *[Graeco-Roman References, pp. 9-11]*

*L[udwig] Keimer, " 'Falcon-face'," *AEE* 14 (1929) 47-48. *[Beans]*

*Paul Haupt, "Philological Studies," *AJP* 45 (1924) 47-63. [3. Shady Broom-plants, pp. 50-51]

C

*Terrien de Lacouperie, "The Calendar Plant of China, the Cosmic Tree, and the Date-Palm of Babylonia," *BOR* 4 (1889-90) 217-231, 246-251.

Wilfred H. Schoff, "Camphor," *JAOS* 42 (1922) 355-370.

*T. K. Cheyne, "The Carob and the Locust. I.," *ET* 15 (1903-04) 335.

*George Farmer, "The Carob and the Locust. II.," *ET* 15 (1903-04) 336.

*George Henslow, "The Carob and the Locust," *ET* 15 (1903-04) 285-286.

*George Henslow, "The Carob and the Elephant," *ET* 15 (1903-04) 429.

*George Farmer, "'Locusts,' or 'Carob Beans'," *ET* 16 (1904-05) 382.

*Winfred H. Schoff, "Cinnamon, Cassia and Somaliland," *JAOS* 40 (1920) 260-270.

S[imeon] H. Calhoun, "The Cedars of Lebanon," *BS* 14 (1857) 200-202.

[Simeon H.] Calhoun, "On the Cedars of Lebanon," *JAOS* 9 (1871) x-xi.

E. R. Shaw, "A Visit to the Cedars of Lebanon," *PEFQS* 36 (1904) 137-141.

George Frederick Wright, "The Cedars of Lebanon," *RP* 5 (1906) 195-204.

*Joseph Offord, "Archaeological Notes on Jewish Antiquities. LIII. *How Cedars were Transported,* " *PEFQS* 50 (1918) 181-183.

Paul Haupt, "Heb. ärz, cedar < Ass. irêšu, balsamic juice," *JAOS* 45 (1925) 322-323.

J. D. U. Ward, "The Cedar of Lebanon," *QRL* 287 (1949) 471-482.

*Wilfred H. Schoff, "Cinnamon, Cassia and Somaliland," *JAOS* 40 (1920) 260-270.

E. Bonavia, "On the Antiquity of the Citron-tree in Egypt," *BOR* 6 (1892-93) 203-208.

*Percy E. Newberry, "Extracts from my Notebooks (III).," *SBAP* 22 (1900) 142-154. [14. The Cornflower in Egyptian Art, pp. 141-144]

*L. W. King, "An Early mention of Cotton: the Cultivation of *Gossypium Arboreum,* or Tree-Cotton, in Assyria in the Seventh Century, B.C.," *SBAP* 31 (1909) 339-343.

*Percy E. Newberry, "Extracts from my Notebooks (III).," *SBAP* 22 (1900) 142-154. [16. The *Nefu,* "Root of the *Cyperus esculentus,* L.", pp. 146-148]

D

*Percy E. Newberry, "Extracts from my Notebooks VII," *SBAP* 25 (1903) 357-362. [56. The Daisy in Egyptian Art, p. 361]

E. Bonavia, "Did the Assyrians know the Sexes of the Date Palms? No.," *BOR* 4 (1889-90) 64-69, 89-95, 116-117.

T[errien] de L[acouperie], "Stray notes on Ancient Date Palms in Anterior Asia," *BOR* 4 (1889-90) 117-118.

*Terrien de Lacouperie, "The Calendar Plant of China, the Cosmic Tree, and the Date-Palm of Babylonia," *BOR* 4 (1889-90) 217-231, 246-251.

*Paul Popenoe, "The Propagation of the Date Palm: Materials for a Lexicographical Study in Arabic," *JAOS* 35 (1915) 207-212.

*Stephen [H.] Langdon, "Lexigraphical Notes," *SBAP* 38 (1916) 37-40, 55-59. [II. *Našbaṭu,* "Branch of the Male Date-Palm", pp. 38-39]

*A. H. Pruessner, "Date Culture in Ancient Babylonia," *AJSL* 36 (1919-20) 213-232.

*George Sarton, "The artificial fertilization of date-palms in the time of Ashur-nasir-pal B.C. 885-860," *Isis* 21 (1934) 8-13.

*Solomon Gandz, "Artifical fertilization of date-palms in Palestine and Arabia," *Isis* 23 (1935) 245-250.

*George Sarton, "Additional note on date culture in ancient Babylonia," *Isis* 23 (1935) 251-252.

*George Sarton, "Third note on date culture in ancient Babylonia," *Isis* 26 (1936) 95-98.

E

*George Henslow, "Two Unrecognized Plants Indirectly Alluded to in the Bible," *ET* 9 (1897-98) 381. *[Madder; Everlasting]*

F

*Percy E. Newberry, Extracts from my Notebooks (III).," *SBAP* 22 (1900) 142-154. [17. The *ṭab arḳ* (?) 'string of dried figs,' in ancient lists of offerings, p. 148]

Gustaf Dalman, "Under the Fig-Tree," *ET* 32 (1920-21) 252-253.

J. W. Wenham, "The Fig Tree in the Old Testament," *JTS, N.S.*, 5 (1954) 206-207.

*Gus W. Van Beek, "Frankincense and Myrrh in Ancient South Arabia," *JAOS* 78 (1958) 141-152.

*Gus W. Van Beek, "Frankincense and Myrrh," *BA* 23 (1960) 70-95.

*Hiroshi Ogino, "Frankincense and Myrrh of Ancient South Arabia," *Orient* 3 (1967) 21-39.

F. Nigel Hepper, "Arabian and African Frankincense Trees," *JEA* 55 (1969) 66-72.

G

*Joseph Offord, "Notes and Queries. (1) *Garlic*," *PEFQS* 40 (1908) 338-339.

*A. H. Sayce, "Assyriological Notes," *SBAP* 39 (1917) 207-212. [Gopher-wood, p. 210]

C. C. R. Murphy, "What is Gopher Wood?" *IAQR* 42 (1946) 79-81.

*David I. Macht, "A Pharmacological Study of Biblical 'Gourds'," *JQR, N.S.*, 10 (1919-20) 185-197.

*[H. Rood], "The Grapes of Eshcol," *BJ* 1 (1842) 94-99.

*Battiscombe Gunn, "Miszellen. The writings of the word 'grapes'," *ZÄS* 59 (1924) 71-72.

H

Warren R. Dawson, “The Plant called ‘Hairs of the Earth’,” *JEA* 12 (1926) 240-241.

J. Forbes Royle, “On the Hyssop of Scripture,” *JRAS* (1846) 193-212.

J. Forbes Royle, “On the Hyssop of Scripture,” *JSL, 1st Ser.,* 4 (1849) 257-276.

(Mrs.) G. M. Crowfoot and (Miss) L. Baldensperger, “Hyssop,” *PEFQS* 63 (1931) 89-98.

R. K. Harrison, “The Biblical Problem of Hyssop,” *EQ* 26 (1954) 218-224.

I

D. M. Dixon, “The Transplantation of Punt Incense Trees in Egypt,” *JEA* 55 (1969) 55-65.

*R. Campbell Thompson, “$^{\acute{u}}$*Kurangu* and $^{\acute{u}}$*Lal(l)angu* as possibly ‘Rice’ and ‘Indigo’ in Cuneiform,” *Iraq* 6 (1939) 180-183.

J

Henry Ludwig Fr. Lutz, “The Name of the Jujube Tree in Babylonia,” *JAOS* 70 (1950) 108-109.

K

*Henry Lobdell, “Correspondence,” *BS* 12 (1855) 396-398. [Remarks by C. E. Stowe, pp. 398-401. (“Kikaion—Wonder-tree” translated from Rosenmüller’s *Alterthumskunde,* pp. 399-401)]

L

*†Anonymous, “Lemons,” *MMBR* 29 (1810) 250. *[Misnumbered as p. 242]*

W. D. Spanton, “The Water Lilies of Ancient Egypt,” *AEE* 4 (1917) 1-20.

M

*George Henslow, "Two Unrecognized Plants Indirectly Alluded to in the Bible," *ET* 9 (1897-98) 381. *[Madder; Everlasting]*

*R. Campbell Thompson, "On Mandrake and Tragacanth in Cuneiform," *JRAS* (1926) 100-103.

*Percy E. Newberry, "Note on the Sculptured Slab No. 15000 in the Berlin Museum," *JEA* 14 (1928) 117. *[Mandrakes]*

R. K. Harrison, "The Mandrake and the Ancient World," *EQ* 28 (1956) 87-92.

Raymond J. Clark, "A Note on Medea's Plant and the Mandrake," *Folk* 79 (1968) 227-231.

*Alfred C. Andrews, "Melons and Watermelons in the Classical Era," *Osiris* 12 (1956) 368-375.

*Alfred C. Andrews, "The Mints of the Greeks and Romans and Their Condimentary Use," *Osiris* 13 (1958) 127-149.

Jerry Stannard, "The Plant called Moly," *Osiris* 14 (1962) 254-307.

*David Yellin, "Emek ha-bakha: Bekhaim," *JPOS* 3 (1923) 191-192. *[Mulberry Tree]*

*S[tephen] Langdon, "Critical Notes," *AJSL* 31 (1914-15) 282-286. [IV. KID-ni-e = siḫ-li-e, "Mustard"(?), pp. 285-286]

*A. Lucas, "Notes on Myrrh and Stacte," *JEA* 23 (1937) 27-33.

*Gus W. Van Beek, "Frankincense and Myrrh in Ancient South Arabia," *JAOS* 78 (1958) 141-152.

*Gus W. Van Beek, "Frankincense and Myrrh," *BA* 23 (1960) 70-95.

*Hiroshi Ogino, "Frankincense and Myrrh of Ancient South Arabia," *Orient* 3 (1967) 21-39.

N

Vivi Laurent-Täckholm, "The plant of Naqada," *ASAE* 51 (1951) 299-312.

Hjalmar Larsen, "On a detail of the Naqada plant," *ASAE* 54 (1956-57) 239-244.

O

Conrad Schick, "Reports by Dr. Conrad Schick. V. *Abraham's Oak at Hebron,*" *PEFQS* 31 (1899) 39-40.

*Albrecht Goetze, "Contributions to Hittite Lexicography," *JCS* 1 (1947) 307-320. [(4) *šuppi-wašhar* - "onion", pp. 318-320]

P

Anonymous, "Papyrus on the Upper Nile," *RP* 13 (1914) 117-118.

Joseph Offord, "The Disappearance of the Papyrus Plant in Egypt," *PEFQS* 47 (1915) 38-39.

*F. N. Hepper and T. Reynolds, "Papyrus and the adhesive properties of its cell sap in relation to paper-making," *JEA* 53 (1967) 156-157.

*Percy E. Newberry, "Extracts from my Notebook (I).," *SBAP* 21 (1899) 303-308. [2. The Persea Tree in Ancient Egypt, pp. 303-305]

Terrien de Lacouperie, "The Pomegranate from Parthia to China, 116 B.C.," *BOR* 6 (1892-93) 239-240.

*Percy E. Newberry, "The Tree of the Herakleopolite Nome," *ZÄS* 50 (1912) 78-79. *[Pomegranate]*

W[illiam] M. Ramsay, "Specimens of Anatolian Words," *OOR* 1 (1926) #2, 1-7. [I. Sbida: Pomegranate, p. 1]

*Percy E. Newberry, "Extracts from my Notebooks (III).," *SBAP* 22 (1900) 142-154. [15. The Poppy in Egyptian Art, pp. 144-146]

Q

Terrein de Lacouperie, "On Quinces from Media to Ancient China (660 B.C.)," *BOR* 6 (1892-93) 265-271.

R

*R. Campbell Thompson, "[ú]*Kurangu* and [ú]*Lal(l)angu* as possibly 'Rice' and 'Indigo' in Cuneiform," *Iraq* 6 (1939) 180-183.

C. Rabin, "Rice in the Bible," *JSS* 11 (1966) 2-9.

*Claude R. Conder, "The Rose of Sharon. (Cant. ii. 1; Isaiah xxxv. 1)," *PEFQS* 10 (1878) 46.

(Mrs.) E. A. Finn, "The Rose of Sharon," *PEFQS* 10 (1878) 51.

*Conrad Schick, "Reports by Dr. Conrad Schick. II. The Rose of Jericho," *PEFQS* 32 (1900) 63-65.

W. L. Carter, "Roses in Antiquity," *Antiq* 14 (1940) 250-256.

S

*Samuel Krauss, "Service Tree in Bible and Talmud and in Modern Palestine," *HUCA* 1 (1924) 179-217.

*Albrecht Goetze, "Contributions to Hittite Lexicography," *JCS* 1 (1947) 307-320. [(3) *ḫašuwai* - "soda plant", pp. 315-318]

*E. Naville, "Hebraeo-Aegyptiaca. I. The Shittim Wood," *SBAP* 34 (1912) 180-190. [Note, p. 256]

*Fritz Hommel, "Assyriological Notes. *(Continuation),*" *SBAP* 21 (1899) 115-139. [§48. *lardu* = spikenard, Hebrew נֵרְדְּ, *νάρδος*, p. 136]

Wilfred H. Schoff, "Nard," *JAOS* 43 (1923) 216-228. *[Spikenard]*

*A. Lucas, "Notes on Myrrh and Stacte," *JEA* 23 (1937) 27-33.

Robert O. Steuer, "Stactē in Egyptian Antiquity," *JAOS* 63 (1943) 279-284.

George Henslow, "The Sycamore Fig and Sycophant," *ET* 19 (1907-08) 566.

T

*J. Martin Plumley, "Notes on אֶשֶׁל the Tamarisk Tree," *JMUEOS* #23 (1942) 15-18.

*H. B. Hackett, "Scripture Facts and Illustrations Collected During a Journey in Palestine," *CRB* 18 (1853) 404-424, 517-537. [Thorns, pp. 531-532]

*Alfred C. Andrews, "Thyme as a Condiment in the Graeco-Roman Era," *Osiris* 13 (1958) 150-156.

*R. Campbell Thompson, "On Mandrake and Tragacanth in Cuneiform," *JRAS* (1926) 100-103.

*W. R. Hutton, "Tumbleweed," *ET* 61 (1949-50) 59-60.

U

*C. J. Ball, "Note on the Wood called *Ukarina,*" *SBAP* 11 (1888-89) 143-144.

W

*Alfred C. Andrews, "Melons and Watermelons in the Classical Era," *Osiris* 12 (1956) 368-375.

Terrien de Lacouperie, "Wheat carried from Mesopotamia to Early China," *BOR* 2 (1887-88) 184-192.

Alph. de Candolle, "The Wheat Indigenous in Mesopotamia (A Letter)," *BOR* 2 (1887-88) 266.

R. A. S. Macalister, "Notes and Queries. (5.) *Wild Wheat in Palestine,*" *PEFQS* 40 (1908) 343.

W. M. F[linders] P[etrie], "For Reconsideration. Mummy Wheat," *AEE* 1 (1914) 78-79.

Anonymous, "Mummy Wheat," *Antiq* 5 (1931) 364-365.

*T. Burton Brown, "Early Bread Wheat," *Antiq* 24 (1950) 40.

*Jack R. Harlan, "A Wild Wheat Harvest in Turkey," *Arch* 19 (1966) 197-201.

§177 ***2.5.6.4 Disease, Medical Practices, and Hygiene***

Anonymous, "Ancient Physic and Physicians," *DUM* 47 (1856) 405-414.

*G. S. Drew, "On the Social and Sanitary Laws of Moses," *ContR* 2 (1866) 514-534.

*S[amuel] Birch, "Medical Papyrus with the name of Cheops," *ZÄS* 9 (1871) 61-64.

*P. le Page Renouf, "Notes on the Medical Papyrus of Berlin," *ZÄS* 11 (1873) 123-125.

Benjamin Ward Richardson, "The Mosaic Sanitary Code," *CM* 12 (1881) 129-138, 240-250.

Anonymous, "The Medical Art Among the Hebrews," *ONTS* 1 (1882) 53. *[From the British Medical Journal]*

*A. H. Sayce, "An ancient Babylonian Work on Medicine," *ZK* 2 (1885) 1-14, 205-216.

E. Bonavia, "Physiology among the ancient Assyrians," *BOR* 2 (1887-88) 255-256.

*F. L. Griffith, "The Metrology of the Medical Papyrus Ebers," *SBAP* 13 (1890-91) 392-406, 526-538.

*A. Eisenlohr, "Extract from a Letter," *SBAP* 13 (1890-91) 596-598. *[Ref. Medical Papyrus Ebers]*

*J. Snowman, "Medicine in the Talmud," *EN* 4 (1892) 184-185.

Marcus N. Adler, "The Health Laws of the Bible, and Their Influence upon the Life-Condition of the Jews," *IAQR, 2nd Ser.*, 3 (1892) 136-146.

J. H. McCormick, "The Psychological Development of Medicine," *AAOJ* 18 (1896) 211-227. *[Near Eastern References, p. 218]*

*J. F. Hewitt, "History of the Physicians and the Sun-God as the Great Physician," *WR* 145 (1896) 357-387.

*J. Campbell Gibson, "Was it Bubonic Plague?" *ET* 12 (1900-01) 378-380. *[Mice and Emerods]*

*William R. Harper, "Constructive Studies in the Priestly Element in the Old Testament. X: The Laws and Usages Concerning Clean and Unclean Considered Comparatively," *BW* 18 (1901) 368-379.

Thomas Chaplin, "On Some Diseases Mentioned in the Bible," *JTVI* 34 (1902) 255-269. [(Discussion, pp. 269-275) (Communications by E. W. Gurney Masterman, pp. 276-280; W. Jervis, pp. 280-284)]

*Edgar J. Goodspeed, "A Medical Papyrus Fragment," *AJP* 24 (1903) 327-329.

Anonymous, "Medicine in Ancient Egypt," *RP* 3 (1904) 255.

*Geo. J. Dann, "'Mice' and 'Emerods'," *ET* 15 (1903-04) 476-478.

*John C. Rolfe, "Some References to Seasickness in Greek and Latin Writers," *AJP* 25 (1904) 192-200.

*S. M. Zwemer, "The Bubonic Plague at Ashdod," *HR* 47 (1904) 281-282.

Edward M. Merrins, "Biblical Epidemics of Bubonic Plague," *BS* 61 (1904) 292-304.

Anonymous, "Egyptian Medicine," *RP* 6 (1907) 93.

*Edward M. Merrins, "The Patience of Job," *BS* 64 (1907) 224-249. *[Discussion of Job's Affliction]*

W. H. S. Jones, "Disease and History," *Janus* 12 (1907) 686-689.

W. H. S. Jones, "Malaria in Ancient Greece and Rome, by Jones, Ross and Ellett. Addenda et Corrigenda," *Janus* 12 (1907) 690-693.

*Edward M. Merrins, "The Plagues of Egypt," *BS* 65 (1908) 401-429, 611-635.

Anonymous, "Appendicitis and Other Maladies of Ancient Egypt," *RP* 7 (1908) 260-261.

*R. Campbell Thompson, "An Assyrian Incantation against Rheumatism," *SBAP* 30 (1908) 73-69, 145-152, 245-251.

*Campbell Bonner, "Notes on a Certain Use of the Reed, with Special Reference to Some Doubtful Passages," *TAPA* 39 (1908) 35-48.

W. H. S. Jones, "Disease and History," *AAA* 2 (1909) 33-45.

[Paul Carus], "Healing by Conjuration in Ancient Babylon," *OC* 23 (1909) 65-74.

Anonymous, "Medical Papyrus," *RP* 11 (1912) 105.

Anonymous, "Ancient Assyrian Medicine," *RP* 12 (1913) 182.

J. D. Rolleston, "The Medical Aspects of the Greek Anthology," *Janus* 19 (1914) 35-45, 105-131.

Richard J. Cyriax, "A Short History of Mechano-Therapeutics in Europe until the Time of Ling," *Janus* 19 (1914) 178-240. [Ancient Greece, pp. 178-188; The Roman Empire until the Seventh Century A.D., pp. 189-201]

Edward Chauncey Baldwin, "A Neglected Aspect of Our Modern Debt to Israel," *HR* 69 (1915) 196-199. *[Hygiene]*

*Joseph Offord, "Archaeological Notes on Jewish Antiquities. XV. *Propagation of Plague by Insects and Rodents in the Old Testament and Monumental Records,* " *PEFQS* 48 (1916) 141-143.

*Felix von Oefele, "Babylonian Title of Medical Textbooks," *JAOS* 37 (1917) 252.

*Felix von Oefele, "The Assyrian Veterinary Physician," *JAOS* 37 (1917) 331-332.

*Paul Haupt, "The Disease of King Teumman of Elam," *JSOR* 1 (1917) 88-91.

*Charles Newton Smiley, "Epidaurus and Greek and Roman Medicine," *A&A* 7 (1918) 121-130.

E. W. G. Masterman, "Hygiene and Disease in Palestine in Modern and in Biblical Times," *PEFQS* 50 (1918) 13-20, 56-71, 112-119; 51 (1919) 27-36.

Felix von Oefele, "*Ascalabotes fascicularis* in old Babylonian medicine," *JAOS* 39 (1919) 284-285.

H. F. Lutz, "A Contribution to the Knowledge of Assyrio-Babylonian Medicine," *AJSL* 36 (1919-20) 67-83.

*Lawrence Parmly Brown, "The Cosmic Leprosy and Dropsy," *OC* 34 (1920) 15-33.

S[tephen] Langdon, "Note. *Ur-^{d}Lugal-edin-n the Physician,*" *RAAO* 17 (1920) 51. *[Seal]*

M. A. Murray, "The Ceremony of Anba Tarabo," *AEE* 6 (1921) 110-114. *[Ceremony performed over a person bitten by a dog]*

H. Lamar Crosby, "Lucian and the Art of Medicine," *PAPA* 54 (1923) xv-xvi.

*Warren R. Dawson, "The Mouse in Egyptian and Later Medicine," *JEA* 10 (1924) 83-86.

Bruno Meinecke, "Medicine and Health in Horace," *PAPA* 58 (1927) xxii.

*Warren R. Dawson, "Three Anatomical Terms," *ZÄS* 62 (1927) 20-23. [I. *mnd.t,* "Cheeks"; II. *wdd,* "gall, gall-bladder"; III. *kns,* "pubes, hypogastric region"]

Anonymous, "Notes and Comments. A Record of Egyptian Anatomical Knowledge," *A&A* 26 (1928) 99.

*Warren R. Dawson, "The Pig in Ancient Egypt: A Commentary on Two Passages of Herodotus," *JRAS* (1928) 597-608. [II The Pig in Medicine, Magic and Mythology, pp. 599-608]

*George S. Duncan, "Prehistoric Disease, Medicine and Surgery," *AJA* 34 (1930) 53-54.

*Warren R. Dawson, "Studies in the Egyptian medical texts," *JEA* 18 (1932) 150-154. [1. The words and ; 2.The bird; 3. The Lettuce as an Aphrodisiac; 4. The word]

*E[dith] M. Guest, "Pathology and Art at El Amarna," *AEE* 18 (1933) 81-88.

*Warren R. Dawson, "Studies in the Egyptian Medical Texts—II," *JEA* 19 (1933) 133-137. [5. The herb ; 6. The drug ; 7. The word (dets. , ,); 8. The fish ; Additional Note on]

*Clive H. Carruthers, "More Hittite Words," *Lang* 9 (1933) 151-161. [7. *irmas, irmalas, irmalanza,* 'ill', 'illness' *irmal(l)iya* 'be ill', pp. 159-160]

Don Clawson, "Phoenician Dental Art," *Bery* 1 (1934) 23-31.

*Warren R. Dawson, "Studies in the Egyptian Medical Texts—III," *JEA* 20 (1934) 41-46. [9. The herb ; 10. The plant ; 11. The plant ; 12. The plant ; 13. The herb ; 14. The plant]

*Warren R. Dawson, "Studies in the Egyptian Medical Texts—IV," *JEA* 20 (1934) 185-188. [15. The affection called ; 16. The plant ; 17. The plant ; 18. The Beetle in medicine; 19. The animal ; 20. The mineral]

Herbert Newell Couch, "The Hippocratean Patient and His Physician," *TAPA* 65 (1934) 138-162.

*Warren R. Dawson, "Studies in the Egyptian Medical Texts—V," *JEA* 21 (1935) 37-40. [21. The plant ; 22. The Plant ; 23. The Mineral ; 24. The affection called]

Herbert Newell Couch, "The Medical Equipment of the Hippocratean Physician," *TAPA* 67 (1936) 191-207.

Jul. Wiberg, "The Medical Science of Ancient Greece: The Doctrine of the Heart," *Janus* 41 (1937) 225-254.

*J. W. Jack, "The Trephined Skulls from Lachish," *PEQ* 69 (1937) 62-66.

*B. R. Townend, "An Assyrian Dental Diagnosis," *Iraq* 5 (1938) 82-84. [K. 1102]

Arthur Stanley Pease, "Some Remarks on the Diagnosis and Treatment of Tuberculosis in Antiquity," *Isis* 31 (1939) 380-393.

A. Rendle Short, "The Old Testament and Modern Medical Knowledge," *EQ* 13 (1941) 39-45.

Maurice Bear Gordon, "Medicine Among the Ancient Hebrews," *Isis* 33 (1941) 454-485.

*W. H. S. Jones, "'Hippocrates' and the *Corpus Hippocraticum*," *PBA* 31 (1945) 103-125.

*George G. Cameron, "The Babylonian Scientist and His Hebrew Colleague," *BA* 7 (1944) 21-29, 32-40. [Diseases and their Remedy, pp. 28-29, 32-34]

*Steven T. Byington, "Some Bits of Hebrew. II. Medical and Physiological Hebrew," *ET* 57 (1945-46) 52.

*J. L[awrence] Angel, "Health and Society in Greece," *AJA* 52 (1948) 373.

*M. I. Hussey, "Anatomical Nomenclature in an Akkadian Omen Text," *JCS* 2 (1948) 21-32.

W. H. Gispen, "The Distinction between Clean and Unclean," *OTS* 5 (1948) 190-196.

*Gregory Vlastos, "Religion and Medicine in the Cult of Asclepius: A Review Article," *RR* 13 (1948-49) 269-290. *(Review)*

George P. G. Sobhy Bey, "Studies in Ancient Egyptian Medicine. Comparison of the medical treatment of intestinal worms in ancient Egypt with the present day folklore and domestic medicines in Egypt," *ArOr* 20 (1952) 626-628.

R. K. Harrison, "Disease, Bible and Spade," *BA* 16 (1953) 88-92.

Owsei Temkin, "Greek Medicine as Science and Craft," *Isis* 44 (1953) 213-225.

*G. R. Driver, "Some Hebrew Medical Expressions," *ZAW* 65 (1953-54) 255-262.

I. E. Darbkin, "Remarks on Ancient Psychopathology," *Isis* 46 (1955) 223-234.

*J. V. Wilson Kinnier, "Two Medical Texts from Nimrud," *Iraq* 18 (1956) 130-146; 19 (1957) 40-49. [ND 4358; 4368]

*I. Jakobovits, "The Medical Treatment of Animals in Jewish Law," *JJS* 7 (1956) 207-220.

Muzaffer Şenyürek, "A case of trepanation among the inhabitants of the Assyrian trading Colony at Kültepe," *A(A)* 3 (1958) 51-52.

Aryeh Feigenbaum, "Archaeological Evidence of the Occurrence of Regular Seasonal Ophthalmias in Ancient Egypt," *Janus* 46 (1957) 165-172.

*Ernest Kennaway, "Some Biological Aspects of Jewish Ritual," *Man* 57 (1957) #83. *[Naddah]*

*Wilder Penfield, "The Asclepiad Physicians of Cnidus and Cos with a Note on the Probable Site of the Triopion Temple of Apollo," *PAPS* 101 (1957) 393-400.

*Erica Reiner, "KÙ.GI in medical texts," *AfO* 18 (1957-58) 394.

*Z. M. Rabinowitz, "Yannay's *Qerova* to Lev. 15, 1 (Sources and Interpretation)," *Tarbiz* 28 (1958-59) #3/4, VII.

H. W. M. De Jong, "Medical Prognostication in Babylon," *Janus* 48 (1959) 252-257.

Gerald T. Kennedy, "Medicine and the Bible," *AER* 142 (1960) 87-95.

J. Lawrence Angel, "Civilization and Dental Disease," *AJA* 64 (1960) 182.

*R. K. Harrison, "Healing Herbs of the Bible," *Janus* 50 (1961-63) 9-54.

A. L. Oppenheim, "On the Observation of the Pulse in Mesopotamian Medicine," *Or, N.S.*, 31 (1962) 27-33.

*Paul Ghalioungui, "Some body swellings illustrated in two tombs of the ancient Empire and their possible Relation to *âaâ*," *ZÄS* 87 (1962) 108-114.

S. D. Goitein, "The Medical Profession in the Light of the Cairo Geniza Documents," *HUCA* 34 (1963) 177-194.

J. Z. Baruch, "The Social Position of the Physician in Ancient Israel," *Janus* 51 (1964) 161-168.

*J. Z. Baruch, "The Relation between Sin and Disease in the Old Testament," *Janus* 51 (1964) 295-302.

S. Levin, "Bacteriology in the Bible," *ET* 76 (1964-65) 154-157.

Peter R. Ackroyd, "Bacteriology in the Bible," *ET* 76 (1964-65) 230.

C. Sandulescu, "*Primum non nocere:* Philological Commentaries on a Medical Aphorism," *AAASH* 13 (1965) 359-368.

V. Møller-Christensen and D. R. Hughes, "An early case of leprosy from Nubia," *Man, N.S.*, 1 (1967) 242-243.

J. G. W. Gispen, "'Measuring' the Patient in Ancient Egyptian Medical Texts," *Janus* 54 (1967) 224-227.

F. Filce Leek, "The Practice of Dentistry in Ancient Egypt," *JEA* 53 (1967) 51-58.

‡J. V. Kinnier Wilson, "Gleanings from the Iraq Medical Journals," *JNES* 27 (1968) 243-247

*Gerald D. Hart, "The Diagnosis of Disease from Ancient Coins," *AJA* 73 (1969) 236.

*W. G. Lambert, "A Middle Assyrian Medical Text," *Iraq* 31 (1969) 28-39.

Donald Broadribb, "Ancient Concepts of Health and Disease," *Mwa-M* #9 (1969) 51-58.

*Menachem M. Brayer, "Psychosomatics, Hermetic Medicine, and Dream Interpretation in the Qumran Literature," *JQR, N.S.*, 60 (1969-70) 112-127, 213-230.

§178 *2.5.6.4.1 Drug Use and Abuse*

A. W. Buckland, "Ethnological Hints afforded by the Stimulants in use among Savages and among the Ancients," *JRAI* 8 (1878-79) 239-253. (Disucssion, p. 254)

*J. A. Stokes Little, "Was Saul a Hachish-Eater?" *ET* 15 (1903-04) 239.

*George Henslow, "Did Jonathan taste Hachish?" *ET* 15 (1903-04) 336.

*Benj. W. Bacon, "Was Saul a Hachish-Eater?" *ET* 15 (1903-04) 380.

C. Creighton, "On Indications of the Hachish-Vice in the Old Testament," *Janus* 8 (1903) 241-246, 297-303.

R. Campbell Thompson, "Assyrian Prescriptions for Diseases of the Head," *AJSL* 24 (1907-08) 1-6, 323-353.

*David I. Macht, "A Pharmacological Study of Biblical 'Gourds'," *JQR, N.S.*, 10 (1919-20) 185-197.

*Paul Haupt, "Philological and Archaeological Studies," *AJP* 45 (1924) 238-259. [3. Mercury in Roman Medicine, pp. 244-245]

C. J. S. Thompson, "The Dawn of Medication: A Chapter in the History of Pharmacy from Earliest Times to the Tenth Century," *Janus* 28 (1924) 425-450.

*Paul Haupt, "Arab. *samm,* poison = Sum. *šem, ἄρωμα,*" *BAVSS* 10 (1927) Heft 2, 84-95

Warren R. Dawson, "Studies in Medical History: (*a*) The Origin of the Herbal. (*b*) Castor- oil in Antiquity," *Aeg* 10 (1929) 47-72.

R. Campbell Thompson, "Assyrian Medical Prescriptions for Diseases of the Stomach," *RAAO* 26 (1929) 47-92.

R. Campbell Thompson, "Assyrian Medical Prescriptions against *šimmatu* 'poison'," *RAAO* 27 (1930) 127-136.

R. Campbell Thompson, "Assyrian Prescriptions for Treating Bruises or Swellings," *AJSL* 47 (1930-31) Number 1, Part 1, 1-25.

R. C[ampbell] Thompson, "Assyrian Prescriptions for Ulcers or similar Affections," *JSOR* 15 (1931) 53-59.

*Warren R. Dawson, "Studies in the Egyptian Medical Texts—II," *JEA* 19 (1933) 133-137. [6. The drug pp. 135-136]

R. Campbell Thompson, "Assyrian Prescriptions for Diseases of the Chest and Lungs," *RAAO* 31 (1934) 1-29.

R. Campbell Thompson, "Assyrian Prescriptions for Diseases of the Urine, etc.," *Baby* 14 (1934) 57-151.

R. Campbell Thompson, "An Assyrian Chemist's Vade-mecum," *JRAS* (1934) 771-785.

R. Campbell Thompson, "Assyrian Prescriptions for Stone in the Kidneys, for the 'middle', and for Pneumonia," *AfO* 11 (1936-37) 336-340.

R. Campbell Thompson, "Assyrian Prescriptions for the Head," *AJSL* 53 (1936-37) 217-238.

R. Campbell Thompson, "Assyrian Prescriptions for the Head—*Concluded*," *AJSL* 54 (1937) 12-40.

R. Campbell Thompson, "Assyrian Prescriptions for Diseases of the Ears," *JRAS* (1937) 1-25.

R. Campbell Thompson, "Assyrian Prescriptions for Diseases of the Feet," *JRAS* (1937) 265-286, 413-432.

A. Lucas, "Poisons in Ancient Egypt," *JEA* 24 (1938) 198-199.

*L[eon] L[egrain], "Nippur Old Drugstore," *UMB* 8 (1939-40) #1, 25-27. [C.B.S. 14221]

Harold W. Miller, "*On Ancient Medicine* and the Origin of Medicine," *TAPA* 80 (1949) 187-202.

*Erik Sjöqvist, "Morgantina: Hellenisitic Medicine Bottles," *AJA* 64 (1960) 78-83.

P. Ghalioungui, "Ancient Egyptian Remedies and Mediaeval Arabic Writers," *BIFAO* 68 (1969) 41-46.

§179 ***2.5.6.4.2 Leprosy***

[D. M. Graham], "Leprosy in Israel," *FBQ* 6 (1858) 273-287.

W. St. Chad Boscawen, "Babylonian Medicine.—I. Leprosy," *BOR* 3 (1888-89) 204-210.

T. Wytton Davies, "Bible Leprosy," *ONTS* 11 (1890) 134-141.

Anonymous, "Leprosy," *CFL, O.S.*, 1 (1897) 47-48.

Jay F. Schamberg, "The Nature of Leprosy of the Bible. From a Medical and Biblical Point of View," *BW* 13 (1899) 162-169.

Anonymous, "Biblical Research and Discovery," *CFL, O.S.*, 2 (1898) 192. *[Leprosy]*

Ernest L. McEwen, "The Leprosy of the Bible in Its Medical Aspect," *BW* 38 (1911) 194-202.

*J. Denley Prince, "Note on Leprosy in the Old Testament," *JBL* 38 (1919) 30-34.

*Lawrence Parmly Brown, "The Cosmic Leprosy and Dropsy," *OC* 34 (1920) 15-33.

Lee S. Huizenga, "Leprosy—A Study," *BS* 83 (1926) 29-46, 202-212.

Lee S. Huizenga, "Bible Leprosy the Same as that of Today," *BS* 86 (1929) 432-435.

Lee S. Huizenga, "Bible Leprosy the Same as that of Today," *TF* 2 (1930) 312-315.

John Todd, "Leprosy, Biblical and Mediaeval," *MC* 34 (1944-45) 129-137.

Lucan Freppert, "Leprosy: Biblical and Modern," *Scotist* 7 (1948) 11-19.

Harold M. Spinka, "Leprosy in Ancient Hebraic Times," *JASA* 11 (1959) #1, 17-20.

K. P. C. A. Gramberg, "'Leprosy' and the Bible," *BTr* 11 (1960) 10-23.

*Eugene A. Nida, "The Translation of 'Leprosy', a brief contribution to the discussion," *BTr* 11 (1960) 80-81.

D. H. Wallington, "'Leprosy' and the Bible—Conclusion," *BTr* 12 (1961) 75-79.

R. G. Cochrane, "Biblical Leprosy," *BTr* 12 (1961) 202-203.

J. V. Kinnier Wilson, "Leprosy in Ancient Mesopotamia," *RAAO* 60 (1966) 47-58.

J. V. Kinnier Wilson, "Notes Breves, 6.," *RAAO* 61 (1967) 189-190. *[Leprosy]*

§180 *2.5.6.4.3 Ancient Surgery*

*Herman Heager, "Army surgeons in ancient Greek warfare," *JP* 8 (1879) 14-17.

*(Miss) A. W. Buckland, "Surgery and Superstition in Neolithic Times," *JRAI* 11 (1881-82) 7-20 (Discussion, pp. 20-21)

Anonymous, "Markings on Neolithic Crania," *RP* 3 (1904) 315.

*Anonymous, "Surgical Treatment of the Eye and Hammurabi's Code," *ICMM* 1 (1905) 163.

Anonymous, "Surgical Instruments in Greek and Roman Times," *RP* 6 (1907) 343.

Anonymous, "Archaeological Notes and Comments. Egyptians Had Find Surgeons in 1700 B.C.," *A&A* 14 (1922) 164.

*George S. Duncan, "Prehistoric Disease, Medicine and Surgery," *AJA* 34 (1930) 53-54.

*J. W. Jack, "The Trephined Skulls from Lachish," *PEQ* 69 (1937) 62-66.

*Muzaffer Süleyman Şenyürek, "Two cases of premature suture closure among the ancient inhabitants of Anatolia," *TTKB* 15 (1951) 247-262.

K. P. Oakley, (Miss) Winifred M. A. Brooke, A. Roger Akester, and D. R. Brothwell, "Contributions on Terpanning or Trephination in Ancient and Modern Times," *Man* 59 (1959) #133.

Jeffrey Boss, "Cæsarean Section with Maternal Survival among the Jews in the Roman Period," *Man* 61 (1961) #6.

§181 2.5.7 Archaeological Expeditions and Societies - General Studies [See also: §167 and §168 Alphabetical Listing of Specific Places ←]

†(   ) W., "Introduction to the Study of Archeology," *MMBR* 17 (1804) 135-138, 224-226, 331-335, 531-534; 18 (1804) 113-117, 289-293.

John Pickering, "Address," *JAOS* 1 (1849) 1-60. *[Address at the First Meeting of the American Oriental Society]*

†Anonymous, "Oriental Discovery: its Progress and Results," *LQHR* 1 (1853) 297-327. *(Review)*

*[Joseph P. Thompson(?)], "Egyptology, Oriental Archaeology and Travel," *BS* 19 (1862) 881-890. *(Review)*

*Joseph P. Thompson, "Egyptology, Oriental Archaeology and Travel," *BS* 20 (1863) 650-660 *(Review)*, 879-884; 22 (1865) 684-689.

H. B. Hackett, "Explorations in Palestine," *BS* 27 (1870) 570-574.

Charles Warren, "Our Summer in the Lebanon. 1869," *PEFQS* 2 (1870) 215-244.

Charles Warren, "Expedition to East of Jordan, July and August, 1867," *PEFQS* 2 (1870) 284-306.

*C. Clermont-Ganneau, "Notes on Certain New Discoveries at Jerusalem," *PEFQS* 3 (1871) 103-107. [1. Hebrew inscription in Phoenician characters; 2. Roman inscription; 3. Fragment of a vase with Hebrew Phoenician characters; 4. Greek inscriptions in the so-called Tomb of the Prophets; 5. Ancient Jewish sarcophagus; 6. The tomb of Absalom cleared out; 7. Stone of Bohan; 8. Pool of Strouthion; 9. Bahurim]

Jos. P. Thompson, "American Explorers in Palestine," *PEFQS* 3 (1871) 170-172.

Hyde Clarke, "On the Relations of Canaanite Exploration to Pre-Historic Classic Archaeology," *PEFQS* 3 (1871) 176-196.

A. E. Northey, "Expedition to the East of Jordan," *PEFQS* 4 (1872) 57-72.

G. F. Wright, "Recent Works on Prehistoric Archaeology," *BS* 30 (1873) 381-384.

*Hyde Clarke, "Researches in Prehistoric and Protohistoric Comparative Philology, Mythology, and Archæology in Connection with the Origin of Culture in America, and its Propagation by the Sumerian or Akkad Families," *JRAI* 4 (1874-75) 148-212. (Discussion, pp. 212-231)

Howard Crosby, "The Progress and Prospects of Oriental Discovery," *PQPR* 4 (1875) 476-493.

John Evans, "Note on a Proposed International Code of Symbols for use on Archæological Maps," *JRAI* 5 (1875-76) 427-435. (Discussion, pp. 435-436)

Selah Merrill, "Letter from Rev. Selah Merrill," *PEFQS* 8 (1876) 177-181. *[Expeditions]*

J. P. Mahaffy, "Modern Excavations," *ContR* 29 (1876-77) 888-900.

Selah Merrill, "The American Explorers in Palestine," *PEFQS* 9 (1877) 150-154.

J. D. Baldwin, "A Problem in Archaeology," *JAOS* 10 (1880) xi-xii.

*Justin A. Smith, "Studies in Archaeology and Comparative Religion," *ONTS* 3 (1883-84) 295-304, 340-346, 381-387; 4 (1884-85) 19-25, 59-66, 105-113, 162-169, 213-221.

John Phelps Taylor, "Archaeological Notes," *AR* 1 (1884) 95-101, 560-569; 3 (1885) 61-67; 4 (1885) 266-272; 6 (1886) 548-557; 9 (1888) 308-319; 11 (1889) 193-202; 13 (1890) 219-228; 14 (1890) 185-191; 15 (1891) 311-320; 18 (1892) 297-305; 19 (1893) 338-348, 717-727.

*Selah Merrill, "On Palestinian Archaeology," *JAOS* 11 (1885) xxiii-xxv.

*Justin A. Smith, "Studies in Archaeology and Comparative Religion: IX. The Literature of Paganism," *ONTS* 5 (1885-86) 16-24.

*Justin A. Smith, "Studies in Archaeology and Comparative Religion: Pagan Literature in Relation to Pagan Faith," *ONTS* 5 (1885-86) 75-82.

*Justin A. Smith, "Studies in Archaeology and Comparative Religion: XI. The Idea of Evil, as to Origin," *ONTS* 5 (1884-85) 128-135.

*Justin A. Smith, "Studies in Archaeology and Comparative Religion: XII. The Idea of Evil, as to its Nature," *ONTS* 5 (1884-85) 171-177.

*Justin A. Smith, "Studies in Archaeology and Comparative Religion: XIII. The Idea of Redemption," *ONTS* 5 (1884-85) 228-233, 267-273.

Albrecht Socin, "The Survey of Western Palestine. A Critical Estimate of the Work of the Palestine Restoration Fund," *Exp, 3rd Ser.*, 2 (1885) 241-262.

C[laude] R. Conder, "The English Explorations in Palestine. A Reply to Professor Socin," *Exp, 3rd Ser.*, 3 (1886) 321-335.

Laurence Oliphant, "New Discoveries," *PEFQS* 18 (1886) 73-83.

Claude R. Conder, "Notes by Captain Conder. II. 'Twenty-one Years' Work'," *PEFQS* 18 (1886) 166-167.

G. Schumacher, "Researches in Southern Palestine," *PEFQS* 18 (1886) 171-197.

J. W. McGarvey, "Palestine Exploration: What Remains to be Done," *ONTS* 6 (1886-87) 69-70.

E. C. Michell, "American Explorers in Palestine," *ONTS* 6 (1886-87) 213-219, 273-277.

A. H. Sayce, "The Latest Results of Oriental Archæology," *ContR* 58 (1890) 907-912.

George H. Schodde, "Recent Researches in Bible Lands," *HR* 20 (1890) 107-112.

Charles H. H. Wright, "The Encouragement of Oriental Research at the Universities," *IAQR, 2nd Ser.*, 2 (1891) 407-412.

Frederick Jones Bliss, "Excavating from its Picturesque Side," *PEFQS* 23 (1891) 291-298.

Robert Francis Harper, "The Expedition of the Babylonian Exploration Fund," *ONTS* 14 (1892) 160-165, 213-217; 15 (1892) 12-16. [A. New York to Aleppo; B. Aleppo to Baghdad]

W. St. Chad Boscawen, "Archæological Notes," *BOR* 7 (1892-93) 109-113.

*W. W. Moore, "Recent Discoveries in Palestine," *USR* 4 (1892-93) 177-192. [The Siloam Inscription; The Pool of Bethesda; Teh Gezer Inscription; The Temple Tablet; The Latest Discovery (the Lachish Letters)]

Charles F. Kent, "The Present Possiblities of Excavations in Palestine," *BW* 1 (1893) 220-225.

George H. Schodde, "Recent Research in Bible Lands," *LQ* 23 (1893) 1-9.

H. M. Mackenzie, "Abstract of Lectures on Oriental Archæology at the British Museum," *BOR* 7 (1893-94) 164-168.

Henry W. Haynes, "Some Unwarranted Assumptions in Archæology," *AJA, O.S.,* 9 (1894) 26-31.

*Andrew Harper, "Archæology and Criticism," *Exp, 4th Ser.,* 10 (1894) 372-385.

*Alex. Macalister, "The Higher Criticism and the Verdict of the Monuments," *Exp, 4th Ser.,* 9 (1894) 401-416. *(Review)*

A. A. Berle, "Professor Sayce on Archaeology," *BS* 53 (1896) 159-161.

Anonymous, "Report of the Palestine Exploration Fund," *MR* 78 (1896) 802.

Thomas Wilson, "A Canon in Pre-Historic Archæology," *AAOJ* 19 (1897) 125-135.

‡Harold N. Fowler, "Bibliography of Current Archaeological Literature 1897," *AJA* 1 (1897) 525-580. [Egyptian Archaeology, pp. 528-531; Oriental Archaeology, pp. 531-535]

‡Harold N. Fowler, "Bibliography of Current Archaeological Literature 1898 January - June," *AJA* 2 (1898) 403-464. [Egyptian Archaeology, pp. 410-413; Oriental Archaeology, pp. 413-417]

‡Harold N. Fowler, "Bibliography of Current Archaeological Literature 1898 July - December," *AJA* 3 (1899) 433-506. [Egyptian Archaeology, pp. 442-447; Oriental Archaeology, pp. 447-453]

J. F. McCurdy, "Method in the Bible Study of the Monuments," *HR* 38 (1899) 397-403.

*W. M. Flinders Petrie, "Sequences in Prehistoric Remains," *JRAI* 29 (1899) 295-301.

Mark Sykes, "Narrative of a Journey East of Jabel ed-Druse," *PEFQS* 31 (1899) 47-56.

Anonymous, "'Authority and Archaeology'," *CQR* 49 (1899-1900) 167-190. *(Review)*

A. H. Sayce, "Literary and Archaeology Notes," *ET* 11 (1899-1900) 430.

C. W. Wilson, "Address Delivered at the Annual Meeting of the Fund," *PEFQS* 31 (1899) 304-316. (Notes by C. Clermont-Ganneau, *PEFQS* 32 (1900) p. 78)

‡Harold N. Fowler, "Bibliography of Archaeological Books," *AJA* 4 (1900) 387-414. [Egyptian Archaeology, pp. 392-393; Oriental Archaeology, pp. 394-395]

Lewis B. Paton, "Archæology in the Nineteenth Century," *HSR* 11 (1900-01) 77-81.

‡Harold N. Fowler, "Bibliography of Archaeological Books 1900," *AJA* 5 (1901) 201-223. [Egyptian Archaeology, pp. 206-207; Oriental Archaeology, pp. 207-208]

James B. Nies, "The Opportunity of the American School of Archaeology in Palestine," *JBL* 20 (1901) 31-37.

M. J. Lagrange, "Ten Years in Palestine," *AER* 26 (1902) 544-559.

‡Harold N. Fowler, "Bibliography of Archaeological Books 1901," *AJA* 6 (1902) 237-258. [Egyptian Archaeology, p. 241; Oriental Archaeology, pp. 241-242]

*F[rederick] J[ones] Bliss, "Summer in Palestine and Syria," *BW* 20 (1902) 89-98.

[Stephen D. Peet], "Recent Discoveries in the East," *AAOJ* 25 (1903) 263-278. *(Editorial)*

*George F. Barton, "Some Archaeological Notes on Asia Minor and Syria," *AJA* 7 (1903) 82-83.

‡Harold N. Fowler, "Bibliography of Archaeological Books 1902," *AJA* 7 (1903) 209-228. [Egyptian Archaeology, pp. 212-213; Oriental Archaeology, p. 213]

*George A. Barton, "Researches of the American School in Palestine," *JBL* 22 (1903) 164-186. [1. The Tombs of the Judges, and a Neighboring Tomb Hitherto Unexplored; 2. Investigations near the Damascus Gate of Jerusalem; 3. The Inner Harbor of Joppa]

A. H. Sayce, "Recent Biblical and Oriental Archaeology. A New Exploration Society," *ET* 15 (1903-04) 369.

*Thomas D. Seymour, "The Homeric Poems as a Source of Archaeological Knowledge," *AJA* 8 (1904) 87.

‡James M. Paton, "Bibliography of Archaeological Books 1903," *AJA* 8 (1904) 239-261. [Egyptian Archaeology, p. 243; Oriental Archaeology, pp. 243-244]

Ira Maurice Price, "Exploration and Discovery: The French in the Orient," *BW* 23 (1904) 229-230.

M. G. Kyle, "'Unscientific Handling of the Facts of Archaeology'," *CFL, 3rd Ser.,* 1 (1904) 360-364.

James Orr, "The Contributions of Archaeology to Faith," *HR* 47 (1904) 10-14.

*Anonymous, "Excavations in Palestine," *MR* 86 (1904) 976-979.

‡Harold N. Fowler, "Bibliography of Archaeological Books 1904," *AJA* 9 (1905) 242-262. [Egyptian Archaeology, pp. 245-246; Oriental Archaeology, p. 246]

*Hugh Pope, "Recent Excavations of Biblical Sites in Palestine," *DR* 136 (1905) 27-47.

Anonymous, "Notes and Comments. Archaeology," *ICMM* 1 (1905) 197-199.

‡Harold N. Fowler, "Bibliography of Archaeological Books 1905," *AJA* 10 (1906) 221-250. [Egyptian Archaeology, pp. 226-227; Oriental Archaeology, pp. 227-228]

‡James M. Paton, "Bibliography of Archaeological Books 1906," *AJA* 11 (1907) 252-278. [Egyptian Archaeology, pp. 258-259; Oriental Archaeology, p. 259]

Fayette L. Thompson, "The Romance of the Excavator's Spade," *CFL, 3rd Ser.,* 6 (1907) 269-273.

*Anonymous, "Excavations in Palestine," *MR* 89 (1907) 979-982.

Robert W. Rogers, "Why I Became an Archeologist," *BRec* 4 (1907) 275-276.

*David G. Lyon, "Recent Excavations in Palestine," *HTR* 1 (1908) 70-96.

R. A. Stewart Macalister, "Gleanings from the Minute-Books of the Jerusalem Literary Society," *PEFQS* 40 (1908) 52-60, 116-125; 41 (1909) 42-49, 258-265; 42 (1910) 27-31, 116-126; 43 (1911) 28-33, 83-90.

Aug. Koester, "Objects and Methods of Archaeological Excavators," *RP* 7 (1908) 3-14.

‡James M. Paton, "Bibliography of Archaeological Books 1907," *AJA* 12 (1908) 263-286. [Egyptian Archaeology, pp. 267-268; Oriental Archaeology, pp. 268-269]

*Anonymous, "Methods of Work at Karnak," *RP* 7 (1908) 258. *[Archaeological Methodology]*

‡William N. Bates, "Bibliography of Archaeological Books 1908," *AJA* 13 (1909) 249-270. [Egyptian Archaeology, pp. 251-252; Oriental Archaeology, pp. 252-253]

‡William N. Bates, "Bibliography of Archaeological Books 1909," *AJA* 14 (1910) 266-289. [Egyptian Archaeology, pp. 267-268; Oriental Archaeology, pp. 268-269]

‡William N. Bates, "Bibliography of Archaeological Books 1910," *AJA* 15 (1911) 267-292. [Egyptian Archaeology, pp. 269-270; Oriental Archaeology, p. 270]

D. D. Luckenbill, "The Excavations in Palestine," *BW* 35 (1910) 21-32, 97-106.

A. H. Sayce, "Recent Oriental Archaeology," *ET* 22 (1910-11) 39-41. *(Review)*

David G. Lyon, "On the Archaeological Exploration of Palestine," *JBL* 30 (1911) 1-17.

Anonymous, "Proposed Research in Asia Minor and Syria," *MR* 93 (1911) 796-799.

Duncan Mackenzie, "Reports from Dr. Duncan Mackenzie," *PEFQS* 43 (1911) 8-11. [1. Amman; 2. Madeba; 3. Diban; 4. Rabbath Moab; 5. The Kerak Region; 6. Petra]

‡William N. Bates, "Bibliography of Archaeological Books 1911," *AJA* 16 (1912) 318-342. [Egyptian Archaeology, p. 320; Oriental Archaeology, p. 321]

*T. H. Weir, "A Survey of Recent Archaeology in Relation to Palestine," *RTP* 8 (1912-13) 1-13.

‡William N. Bates, "Bibliography of Archaeological Books 1912," *AJA* 17 (1913) 326-352. [Egyptian Archaeology, pp. 329-330; Oriental Archaeology, pp. 330-331]

Melvin Grove Kyle, "Archaeology, The Science of Antiquities," *CFL, 3rd Ser.,* 16 (1913) 80-82.

James Orr, "Oriental Archaeology," *CFL, 3rd Ser.,* 16 (1913) 82-83.

Camden M. Cobern, "Daily Life in an Excavator's Camp," *HR* 66 (1913) 438-443.

Anonymous, "The Morality of Excavation," *MR* 95 (1913) 138-141.

A. S. Anspacher, "Archeological Research in Bible Lands," *YCCAR* 23 (1913) 363-382.

*W. M. F[linders] P[etrie], "The New Law in the Antiquities of Egypt," *AEE* 1 (1914) 128-129.

‡William N. Bates, "Bibliography of Archaeological Books 1913," *AJA* 18 (1914) 259-283. [Egyptian Archaeology, pp. 262-263; Oriental Archaeology, pp. 263-264]

*Camden M. Cobern, "Most Recent Excavations in Palestine," *HR* 67 (1914) 94-100.

W. M. Flinders Petrie, "The British School of Archaeology in Egypt," *JEA* 1 (1914) 43-44, 185-186.

H. G. Lyons, "The Law relating to Antiquities in Egypt," *JEA* 1 (1914) 45-46.

‡William N. Bates, "Bibliography of Archaeological Books 1914," *AJA* 19 (1915) 215-235. [Egyptian Archaeology, pp. 218-219; Oriental Archaeology, p. 220]

G. Haughton Porter, "Archaeology," *CFL, 3rd Ser.,* 19 (1915) 111-113.

Joseph Offord, "Archaeological Notes," *PEFQS* 47 (1915) 198-205; 48 (1916) 38-44, 94-97.

‡William N. Bates, "Bibliography of Archaeological Books 1915," *AJA* 20 (1916) 267-281. [Egyptian Archaeology, pp. 269-271; Oriental Archaeology, pp. 271-272]

*Anonymous, "Excavations in Palestine, 1907-1914," *HR* 71 (1916) 403.

Stephen Bleecker Luce Jr., "The Year's Work in Oriental Archaeology," *JAOS* 36 (1916) 348-354.

Anonymous, "The Palestine Exploration Fund," *MR* 98 (1916) 133-138.

Estelle Blyth, "Lord Kitchener's Work in Palestine," *PEFQS* 48 (1916) 178-190; 49 (1917) 40-50.

John D. Davis, "Suggestions of the Survey Party Regarding Biblical Sites," *PTR* 14 (1916) 417-447.

Joseph Offord, "Archaeological Notes on Jewish Antiquities," *PEFQS* 48 (1916) 138-148, 191-196; 49 (1917) 94-103, 137-143, 179-184; 50 (1918) 35-39, 88-92, 132-139, 180-185; 51 (1919) 37-38, 86-87, 138-139, 182-186; 52 (1920) 41-42, 77-78.

‡William N. Bates, "Bibliography of Archaeological Books 1916," *AJA* 21 (1917) 241-254. [Egyptian Archaeology, Oriental Archaeology, pp. 243-244]

Anonymous, "The Latest in Archæology," *MR* 99 (1917) 465-470.

C. M. Watson, "Bonaparte's Expedition to Palestine in 1799," *PEFQS* 49 (1917) 17-35.

*(Miss) Gisela M. A. Richter, "What an Archaeologist can Learn at a Modern Pottery School," *AJA* 22 (1918) 65.

‡William N. Bates, "Bibliography of Archaeological Books 1917," *AJA* 22 (1918) 241-250. [Egyptian Archaeology, Oriental Archaeology, pp. 243-244]

‡William N. Bates, "Bibliography of Archaeological Books 1918," *AJA* 23 (1919) 207-218. [Egyptian Archaeology, Oriental Archaeology, pp. 210-212]

George W. Gilmore, "A Turning Point in Archaeological Work," *HR* 78 (1919) 133-134.

F. Legge, "The Society of Biblical Archaeology," *JRAS* (1919) 25-36.

‡William N. Bates, "Bibliography of Archaeological Books 1919," *AJA* 24 (1920) 275-290. [Egyptian Archaeology, Oriental Archaeology, pp. 276-279]

James H. Breasted, "The First Expedition of the Oriental Institute of the University of Chicago," *JAOS* 40 (1920) 282-285.

Anonymous, "The Outlook in Archæology," *MR* 103 (1920) 128-133.

Frederick J. Bliss, "The Hopes for Palestine Exploration," *PEFQS* 52 (1920) 127-132.

‡Sidney N. Deane, "Bibliography of Archaeological Books 1920," *AJA* 25 (1921) 207-221. [Egyptian Archaeology, Oriental Archaeology, pp. 211-212]

R. A. S. Macalister, "Thirty Years of Palestine Exploration," *ET* 33 (1921-22) 87-92.

W. J. Phythian-Adams, "The Future of Excavation in the Holy Land," *IAQR* 17 (1921) 333-338.

J. P. Peters, "The Present Archaeological Outlook in Palestine," *JBL* 40 (1921) 1-22.

*Guido Calza, "Art and Archaeology in Italy in 1921," *A&A* 13 (1922) 217-230.

‡Sidney N. Deane, "Bibliography of Archaeological Books 1921," *AJA* 26 (1922) 237-259. [Egyptian Archaeology, Oriental Archaeology, pp. 241-245]

*John Garstang, Louis Vincent, W. F. Albright, and W. J. Phythian-Adams, "A New Chronological Classification of Palestinian Archaeology," *BASOR* #7 (1922) 9.

W[illiam] F[oxwell] Albright, "Archaeological Discovery in the Holy Land," *BS* 79 (1922) 401-417.

Anonymous, "Excavations in Palestine," *IAQR* 18 (1922) 345-346.

*T. Eric Peet, "The Antiquity of Egyptian Civilization being a plea for some attempt to formulate the laws which form the basis of archaeological argument," *JEA* 8 (1922) 5-12.

R. A. S. Macalister, "Thirty Years of Palestine Exploration," *PEFQS* 54 (1922) 79-86.

Stanley A. Cook, "Notes on Discoveries and Excavations," *PEFQS* 54 (1922) 157-160.

B. L. Ullman, "Archaeology and Moving Pictures," *A&A* 15 (1923) 177-183.

B. L. Ullman, "Archaeology and Moving Pictures," *AJA* 27 (1923) 58.

William H. Buckler, "Historical and Archaeological Opportunities in the Near East," *AJA* 27 (1923) 62.

*William J. Hinke, "Recent Excavations in Palestine," *AJA* 27 (1923) 66-67.

R. A. MacLean, "The Aeroplane and Archaeology," *AJA* 27 (1923) 68-69.

‡Sidney N. Deane, "Bibliography of Archaeological Books 1922," *AJA* 27 (1923) 235-263. [Egyptian Archaeology, pp. 239-240; Oriental Archaeology, pp. 240-242]

*W[illiam] F[oxwell] Albright, "Some Archaeological and Topographical Results of a Trip through Palestine," *BASOR* #11 (1923) 3-14. [The Home of Joshua, Zeredah, Jeroboam's Home, A Philistine Military Base, The Nations of Gilgal, The Coasts of Dor, Some Ancient Mounds, From Tabor to the Jordan, A New Royal Canaanite City]

Bruce Byran, "Movie Realism and Archaeological Fact," *A&A* 18 (1924) 131-144.

*W[illiam] F[oxwell] Albright, "The Archaeological Results of an Expedition to Moab and the Dead Sea," *BASOR* #14 (1924) 2-12. [Archaeological Survey of the Southern Ghor, The Early Sanctuary of Bab ed Draʿ, The Cities of the Plain, Shihan and Ader, The Moabite Capital]

*W[illiam] F[oxwell] Albright, "Researches of the School in Western Judaea," *BASOR* #15 (1924) 2-11.

‡Sidney N. Deane, "Bibliography of Archaeological Books 1923," *AJA* 28 (1924) 209-238. [Egyptian Archaeology, pp. 214-216; Oriental Archaeology, pp. 216-217]

*W[illiam] F[oxwell] Albright, "The Fall Trip of the School in Jerusalem: From Jerusalem to Gaza and Back," *BASOR* #17 (1925) 4-9.

*W[illiam] F[oxwell] Albright, "To Engedi and Masada," *BASOR* #18 (1925) 11-15.

*W[illiam] F[oxwell] Albright, "Bronze Age Mounds of Northern Palestine: The Spring Trip of the School in Jerusalem," *BASOR* #19 (1925) 5-19. [From Jerusalem to Samaria by the Western Hills, The Ancient Cities of Esdraelon, Northeastern Galilee, Argob and Bashan, The Bronze Age Mounds of the Jordan Valley]

‡Edward H. Heffner, "Bibliography of Archaeological Books 1924," *AJA* 29 (1925) 223-238. [Egyptian Archaeology, pp. 225-226; Oriental Archaeology, pp. 226-227]

W. C. Taylor, "The Romance of Archaeology—The Story Retold," *CQ* 2 (1925) 437-447.

*T. Crouther Gordon, "Theology and Archaeology," *ET* 37 (1925-26) 425-428.

*Stanley A. Cook, "Recent Excavations in Palestine," *ET* 37 (1925-26) 487-492.

E. Douglas Van Buren, "Archaeologists in Antiquity," *Folk* 36 (1925) 69-81.

Anonymous, "Glossary," *A&A* 21 (1926) 301; 22 (1926) 53, 101, 150, 197, 244; 23 (1927) 44-92, 142, 190, 237, 286; 24 (1927) 48, 96, 144, 192, *[A ←] [B & C →]* 242; 25 (1928) 109, 158-205, 260, 309; 26 (1928) 54, 100, 149, 197, 251. *[Glossary of Archaeological Terms-incomplete]*

‡Edward H. Heffner, "Bibliography of Archaeological Books 1925," *AJA* 30 (1926) 231-247. [Egyptian Archaeology, pp. 239-241; Oriental Archaeology, pp. 241-243]

*W[illiam] F[oxwell] Albright and R. P. Dougherty, "From Jerusalem to Bagdad down the Euphrates I. From Jerusalem to Aleppo," *BASOR* #21 (1926) 1-10. [Present Excavation in Northern Palestine, Archaeological Remains in Southern Phoenicia, The Irrigation Culture of Northern Phoenicia, Kades on the Orontes and Mishreifeh, Early Bronze age Mounds near Aleppo]

*W[illiam] F[oxwell] Albright and R. P. Dougherty, "From Jerusalem to Bagdad down the Euphrates II. From Aleppo to Baghdad," *BASOR* #21 (1926) 11-21. [The Mounds of the Balîkah, The Search for Ancient Mari, Among the Mounds of Khana, The Land of the Shuhites]

Stanley A. Cook, "Notes on Excavations," *PEFQS* 58 (1926) 90-91; 206-214.

William Ransted Berry, "The Archaeologist in the Field," *A&A* 23 (1927) 170-174.

‡Edward H. Heffner, "Bibliography of Archaeological Books 1926," *AJA* 31 (1927) 226-267. [Egyptian Archaeology, pp. 237-238; Oriental Archaeology, pp. 239-241]

*Anonymous, "Sir Flinders Petrie's Excavations in Palestine," *Antiq* 1 (1927) 348-351.

John-Baptist Reeves, "The Resurrection of Adam," *NB* 8 (1927) 75-81. *[Criticism of Archaeology]*

Kevin Clark, "The Resurrection of Archæology," *NB* 8 (1927) 180-182. [Reply by John-Baptist Reeves, pp. 182-184]

*Joseph Pijoan, "Art and Archaeology in the Movies," *A&A* 25 (1928) 267-275.

[W. M.] Flinders Petrie, "Cares of Archaeological Discovery," *AEE* 13 (1928) 67.

‡Edward H. Heffner, "Bibliography of Archaeological Books 1927," *AJA* 32 (1928) 221-277. [Egyptian Archaeology, pp. 233-235; Oriental Archaeology, pp. 235-237]

W[illiam] F[oxwell] Albright, "Progress in Palestinian Archaeology During the Year 1928," *BASOR* #33 (1929) 1-10.

Samuel A. B. Mercer, "Excavations in Palestine Since the Great War," *CJRT* 5 (1928) 185-194.

Stanley A. Cook, "Notes on Recent Excavations," *PEFQS* 60 (1928) 52-54; 61 (1929) 111-118.

‡Edward H. Heffner, "Bibliography of Archaeological Books 1928," *AJA* 33 (1929) 265-333. [Egyptian Archaeology, pp. 279-282; Oriental Archaeology, pp. 282-285]

*W[illiam] F[oxwell] Albright, "New Israelite and Pre-Israelite Sites: The Spring Trip of 1929," *BASOR* #35 (1929) 1-14. [The Occupation of Ephraim in the Second Millennium B.C., Bronze Age Mounds in Northwestern Samaria, Explorations in Galilee, The Fourteenth Chapter of Genesis, Some Other Bronze and Iron Age Sites in Eastern Palestine]

Samuel A. B. Mercer, "The Archaeological Year of 1928 in Palestine," *CJRT* 6 (1929) 194-196.

John L. Myers, "British School of Archaeology in Jerusalem. Work of the Season 1928-9," *PEFQS* 61 (1929) 95-97.

[W. M.] Flinders Petrie, "Fifty Years' Experience of Digging," *AEE* 15 (1930) 1-7.

‡Edward H. Heffner, "Bibliography of Archaeological Books 1929," *AJA* 34 (1930) 223-259. [Egyptian, pp. 230-231; Oriental Archaeology, pp. 231-232]

Chester C. McCown, "Palestinian Archaeology in 1929," *BASOR* #37 (1930) 2-20. [Tell el-Fâriʿ; Megiddo; Tell en-Nashbeh; 'Ain Shems; Seilûn; Jerash; Beth Alpha; Monastic Research; Prehistory—Mughâret el Wâd, Varia]

Melvin Grove Kyle, "Excavations and Explorations in Bible Lands," *BS* 87 (1930) 382-404.

J. A. Huffman, "Christianity's Debt to Archaeology," *CFL, 3rd Ser.,* 36 (1930) 594-595.

Anonymous, "Dr. Kyle's Explorations," *CFL, 3rd Ser.,* 36 (1930) 603.

‡Edward H. Heffner, "Bibliography of Archaeological Books 1930," *AJA* 35 (1931) 203-236. [Egyptian, pp. 208-209; Oriental Archaeology, pp. 209-211]

*Chester C. McCown, "Palestinian Archaeology in 1930," *BASOR* #41 (1931) 2-18. [Tell el-Fâr'ah and Tell el-'Ajjûl; Tell Beit Mirsim; 'Ain Shems; Megiddo; Beisân; Jericho; Transjordan; Petra; 'Ammân; Jerash; Teleilât el-Ghassûl; Prehistory; Mughâret et-Wâd; El-'Adeimeh; The Kerâzeh Dolmen Field; Mediaeval Castles; Vaira]

William R. Dawson, "Archæology in the Near East: Some Recent Publications," *IAQR* 27 (1931) 164-168. *(Review)*

Anonymous, "The Interest in Archeology Continues," *TF* 3 (1931) 318-320.

*Millar Burrows, "Palestinian and Syrian Archaeology in 1931," *AJA* 36 (1932) 64-73. [I. Palestine, pp. 64-70; II. Transjordan, pp. 70-71; III. Syria, pp. 71-73]

‡Edward H. Heffner, "Bibliography of Archaeological Books 1931," *AJA* 36 (1932) 219-248. [Egyptian, pp. 228-230; Oriental Archaeology, pp. 230-234]

I. G. Matthews, "On the Trail of the Archaeologist," *CQ* 9 (1932) 52-61.

*‡L. A. Mayer and M. Avi-Yonah, "Concise Bibliography of Excavations in Palestine," *QDAP*1 (1932) 86-94, 139-149, 163-199.

*Nelson Glueck, "Palestinian and Syrian Archaeology in 1932," *AJA* 37 (1933) 160-172. [Teleilât el-Gaassûl; Masada; 'Athlît; Tell el-'Ajjûl; Tell Beit Mirsim; Jewish Tombs; Jericho; Tell en-Nasbeh; Seilûn; Sebaṣṭiyeh; Beisân; Meggido; 'Ein eṭ-Ṭâbighah; Khirbet Minyeh; Tell el-'Oreimeh; El-Hammah; Mînet el-Beiḍa and Râs eš-Šamrah; Present and Future Excavations]

‡David M. Robinson, "Bibliography of Archaeological Books, 1932," *AJA* 37 (1933) 363-375. [Egyptian, pp. 364-365; Oriental, pp. 365-367]

*Millar Burrows, "Palestinian and Syrian Archaeology in 1931," *BASOR* #45 (1932) 20-32. [I. Palestine, pp. 20-28; II. Transjordan, pp. 28-29; III. Syria, pp. 29-32]

D. Randall-MacIver, "Archaeology as a Science," *Antiq* 7 (1933) 5-20.

*Nelson Glueck, "Archaeological Work in Palestine and Syria During 1932," *BASOR* #49 (1933) 15-19.

*W[illiam] F[oxwell] Albright, "Archaeological and Topographical Explorations in Palestine and Syria," *BASOR* #49 (1933) 23-31. [The Sites of Tirzah and Tappuah, Soundings at Deir Ghassâneh (Zeredah?), Explorations in Transjordan, Explorations in Syria]

*Nelson Glueck, "From Dr. Glueck's Report on His Explorations in Eastern Palestine," *BASOR* #50 (1933) 8-11.

*Nelson Glueck, "Further Explorations in Eastern Palestine," *BASOR* #51 (1933) 9-18.

W[illiam] F[oxwell] Albright, "How to Study the Archaeology of Palestine," *BASOR* #52 (1933) 12-15.

*E[phraim] A. S[peiser], "First Steps in Mesopotamian Archaeology," *BASOR* #52 (1933) 15-18.

*W. A. Maier, "Archaeology—The Nemesis," *CTM* 4 (1933) 95-102, 176-183, 264-274.

Millar Burrows, "Archaeological Discoveries in Palestine," *JAAR* 1 (1933) #1, 17-18.

*George Grant MacCurdy, "Prehistoric Research in the Near East," *PAPS* 72 (1933) 121-135.

George G. Cameron, "The Oriental Institute Archeological Report on the Near East," *AJSL* 50 (1933-34) 251-272.

*W[illiam] F[oxwell] Albright, "Archaeology in Palestine and Syria During 1933," *BASOR* #53 (1934) 22-25.

*G. I. Bell, "Archaeology and Architecture," *Iraq* 1 (1934) 1.

*Nelson Glueck, "Explorations in Eastern Palestine and the Negeb," *BASOR* #55 (1934) 3-21.

James L. Kelso, "Some Recent Archaeological Discoveries," *BS* 91 (1934) 177-179.

*Anonymous, "Archaeological Expedition to the Near East and Asia, Season, 1935-6," *AEE* 20 (1935) 92-96.

‡David M. Robinson, "Bibliography of Archaeological Books 1933 and 1934," *AJA* 39 (1935) 284-292. [Egyptian, pp. 285-286; Oriental, pp. 286-287]

Waldo H. Dubberstein, "The Oriental Institute Archaeological Report on the Near East," *AJSL* 51 (1934-35) 50-71. (Prepared with the cooperation of James H. Breasted)

Walter G. Williams, "The Oriental Institute Archaeological Report on the Near East," *AJSL* 51 (1934-35) 132-144. (Prepared with the cooperation of James H. Breasted)

Neilson C. Debevoise, "The Oriental Institute Archaeological Report on the Near East," *AJSL* 51 (1934-35) 195-216. (Prepared in cooperation with James H. Breasted)

Robert M. Engberg, "The Oriental Institute Archaeological Report on the Near East," *AJSL* 51 (1934-35) 252-277. (Prepared with the cooperation of James H. Breasted)

[W. M.] Flinders Petrie, "The Future of Archaeology," *AEE* 20 (1935) 97-99.

*‡Anonymous, "Excavations in Palestine, 1933-4," *QDAP* 4 (1935) 194-213. [Bibliography, pp. 211-213]

Waldo H. Dubberstein, "The Oriental Institute Archaeological Report on the Near East," *AJSL* 52 (1935-36) 49-72.

George R. Hughes, "The Oriental Institute Archaeological Report on the Near East," *AJSL* 52 (1935-36) 123-142.

Robert S. Hardy, "The Oriental Institute Archaeological Report on the Near East," *AJSL* 52 (1935-36) 257-276.

‡David M. Robinson, "Bibliography of Archaeological Books—1935," *AJA* 40 (1936) 296-300. [Egyptian, pp. 296-297; Oriental, pp. 297-298]

*‡Anonymous, "Excavations in Palestine, 1934-5," *QDAP* 5 (1936) 194-212. [Bibliography, pp. 211-212]

*Nelson Glueck, "Archaeological Exploration and Excavation in Palestine, Transjordan, and Syria during 1937," *AJA* 42 (1938) 165-176.

*‡Anonymous, "Excavations in Palestine, 1935-6," *QDAP* 6 (1938) 212-219. [Bibliography, pp. 227-229]

Richard A. Parker, "The Oriental Institute Archaeological Report on the Near East," *AJSL* 53 (1936-37) 52-72.

Raymond A. Bowman, "The Oriental Institute Archaeological Report on the Near East," *AJSL* 53 (1936-37) 100-125.

George R. Hughes, Robert M. Engberg, Waldo H. Dubberstein, "The Oriental Institute Archaeological Report on the Near East," *AJSL* 53 (1936-37) 256-277.

Nelson Glueck, "Explorations in Palestine III," *BASOR* #64 (1936) 9-10.

*Erwin R. Goodenough, "Archaeology and Jewish History," *JBL* 55 (1936) 211-220.

C. C. McCown, "Recent Palestinian Archaeology," *RL* 5 (1936) 552-563.

‡David M. Robinson, "Bibliography of Archaeological Books—1936," *AJA* 41 (1937) 354-359. [Oriental, pp. 354-355; Egyptian p. 355]

‡[Stephen B. Luce], "Bibliography of Archaeological Books—1937," *AJA* 42 (1938) 324-329. [Near East, pp. 324-325; Egypt, pp. 325-326]

Peter de Hemmer Gudme, "Arabic Excavation Terminology in Iraq and Syria," *AO* 16 (1937-38) 105-130.

Nelson Glueck, "Explorations in Eastern Palestine III (continued)," *BASOR* #65 (1937) 8-29.

‡George R. Hughes, Robert Engberg, Waldo H. Dubberstein, "The Oriental Institute Archaeological Report on the Near East," *AJSL* 55 (1938) 97-112, 209-224, 319-336, 426-442.

A. T. Olmstead, "A Year of Research in the Near East," *BASOR* #69 (1938) 21-25.

James L. Kelso, "The Work Behind an Archaeological Expedition," *BS* 95 (1938) 40-44.

C. J. Gadd, "A Visiting Artist at Nineveh in 1850," *Iraq* 5 (1938) 118-122.

*‡Anonymous, "Bibliography of Excavations in Palestine and Trans-Jordan, 1936-7," *QDAP* 7 (1938) 61-62.

‡David M. Robinson, "Bibliography of Archaeological Books—1938," *AJA* 43 (1939) 371-377. [Near East, pp. 371-372, Egypt, pp. 372-373]

‡George R. Hughes, A. Douglas Tushingham, and Waldo H. Dubberstein, "The Oriental Institute Archaeological Report on the Near East," *AJSL* 56 (1939) 95-112, 162-174, 310-324, 423-442.

Edward A. Cerny, "Archaeological Corner," *CBQ* 1 (1939) 82-85.

William F. Stinespring, "Edward Robinson in Jerusalem," *DDSR* 4 (1939) 10-16.

*William Bell Dinsmoor, "Archæology and Astronomy," *PAPS* 80 (1939) 95-173.

Kathleen M. Kenyon, "Excavation Methods in Palestine," *PEQ* 71 (1939) 29-43.

*‡Anonymous, "Bibliography of Excavations in Palestine and Trans-Jordan, 1937-8," *QDAP* 8 (1939) 177-178.

W. A. Heurtley, "Presidential Address," *JPOS* 19 (1939-40) 129-135. [The Palaeolithic and Mesolithic Ages; The Neolithic and Chalcolithic Ages; Early Bronze Age; Middle Bronze Age; Late Bronze Age; Iron Age I and II; Persian and Hellenic Periods; Roman Imperial Period; Byzantine and Early Islamic Periods through Crusader's Periods]

*A Löhnberg, "The Application of Geophysical Measurements to Archaeological Excavations," *JPOS* 19 (1939-40) 245-252.

Nelson Glueck, "Archaeological Exploration and Excavation in Palestine and Transjordan during 1939,"*AJA* 44 (1940) 139-144.

‡David M. Robinson, "Bibliography of Archaeological Books—1939," *AJA* 44 (1940) 286-292. [Near East, p. 287; Egypt, 287-288]

‡George R. Hughes, Robert S. Hardy, Waldo H. Dubberstein, Henry Field, and Eugene Prostov, "The Oriental Institute Archaeological Report on the Near East," *AJSL* 57 (1940) 102-112, 188-196, 321-329.

*W[illiam] F[oxwell] Albright, "New Light on the History of Western Asia in the Second Millennium, B.C.," *BASOR* #77 (1940) 20-32. [Recent Excavations at Mari; Alalakh and Ugarit; Excavations at Mari, 1936-1939; Excavations at Alalakh, 1936-39; Excavations at Ugarit, 1936-1939; The Chronology of Western Asia before 1500 B.C.; The West and Northwest in the Mari Archives (cir. 1775 B.C.)]

J[ames] L. Kelso, "A Resume of Recent Archaeological Research," *BS* 97 (1940) 476-481.

Nelson Glueck, "Excavations in Palestine and Transjordan in 1940," *AJA* 45 (1941) 116-117.

‡David M. Robinson, "Bibliography of Archaeological Books—1940," *AJA* 45 (1941) 329-332. [Near East, pp. 329-330; Egypt, p. 330]

‡George R. Hughes, George G. Cameron, and Waldo H. Dubberstein, "The Oriental Institute Archaeological Report on the Near East," *AJSL* 58 (1941) 104-112.

‡George R. Hughes, George G. Cameron, and Waldo H. Dubberstein, "The Oriental Institute Archaeological Report on the Near East, 1941," *AJSL* 58 (1941) 405-416.

Edward A. Cerny, "Archaeological Corner. Prehistory, Protohistory, History," *CBQ* 3 (1941) 179-181.

*Nelson Glueck, "How Archaeology Has Contributied to Our Knowledge of the Bible and the Jew," *YCCAR* 51 (1941) 299-327. {Discussion by: [Samuel B.] Freehof, p. 327; Nelson Glueck, pp. 327-330; [Joshua] Trachtenburg, p. 327; [Israel] Harburg, p. 328; [Ephraim] Frisch, p. 328; [David] Philipson, p. 328; Max Raisin, p. 329; Leo Shubow, p. 329; Clifton Herby Levy, p. 330; [Ahron] Opher, p. 330; W. Gunther Plaut, p. 330}

‡David M. Robinson, "Bibliography of Archaeological Books—1941," *AJA* 46 (1942) 314-316. [Near East, p. 314; Egypt, p. 314]

*Nelson Glueck, "Further Explorations in Eastern Palestine," *BASOR* #86 (1942) 14-24.

E. L. Sukenik, "Extracts from a Report of Archaeological Progress in Palestine by Professor E. L. Sukenik," *BASOR* #88 (1942) 36-38.

John A. Wilson, "Archaeology as a Tool in Humanistic and Social Studies," *JNES* 1 (1942) 3-9.

*O. Püttrich-Reignard, Gordon Loud, B[enjamin] Maisler, Nelson Glueck, P. P. Köppel, Wolfgang Darsow, and Frau Dr. Püttrich, "Excavations in Palestine and Trans-Jordan, 1938-9," *QDAP* 9 (1942) 207-216.

*‡Anonymous, "Bibliography of Excavations in Palestine and Trans-Jordan, 1938-9," *QDAP* 9 (1942) 216-218.

Nelson Glueck, "Archaeological Activity in Palestine and Transjordan in 1941-1942," *AJA* 47 (1943) 125-131.

‡David M. Robinson, "Bibliography of Archaeological Books—1942," *AJA* 47 (1943) 261-263. [Near East, p. 261; Egypt, p. 261]

T. A. Rickard, "The Nomenclature of Archaeology," *AJA* 48 (1944) 10-16.

‡David M. Robinson, "Bibliography of Archaeological Books—1943," *AJA* 48 (1944) 226-228. [Near East, p. 226; Egypt, pp. 226-227]

V. Gordon Childe, "Archæological Ages and Technological Stages," *JRAI* 74 (1944) 7-24.

V. Gordon Childe, "The Future of Archæology," *Man* 44 (1944) #7.

William B. Dinsmoor, "Early American Studies of Mediterranean Archaeology," *PAPS* 87 (1944) 70-104.

M. E. Kirk, "Short History of Palestinian Excavation," *PEQ* 76 (1944) 131-144.

*‡Anonymous, "Bibliography of Excavations in Palestine and Trans-Jordan, 1939-40," *QDAP* 10 (1944) 208-209.

‡David M. Robinson, "Bibliography of Archaeological Books—1944," *AJA* 49 (1945) 205-208. [Near East, pp. 205-206; Egypt, p. 206]

‡[Ernest DeWald and Saul S. Weinberg], "Bibliographies of Books Published Since the Outbreak of the War," *AJA* 49 (1945) 209-220.

S. Yeiven, "New Problems in the Archaeology of the Ancient Near East," *Kobez* 4 (1945) VI-VIII.

*‡Anonymous, "Bibliography of Excavations in Palestine and Trans-Jordan, 1940-2," *QDAP* 11 (1945) 119-120.

‡David M. Robinson, "Bibliography of Archaeological Books—1945," *AJA* 50 (1946) 335-340. [Near East, pp. 335-336; Egypt, p. 336]

*J. Lawrence Angel, "Some Interrelationships of Classical Archaeology with Anthropology," *AJA* 50 (1946) 401.

Stephen L. Caiger, "Archaeological Fact and Fancy," *BA* 9 (1946) 62-67.

John A. Wilson, "The Near East in 1946," *BA* 9 (1946) 70-73.

G. E. Kirk, "Archaeological Activities in Palestine and Transjordan since 1939," *PEQ* 78 (1946) 92-102.

Ann Perkins and Robert J. Braidwood, (eds.), "Archaeological News: *The Near East,* " *AJA* 51 (1947) 191-202, 419-431.

‡David M. Robinson, "Bibliography of Archaeological Books—1946," *AJA* 51 (1947) 211-217. [Near East, pp. 211-212; Egypt, pp. 212-213]

‡David M. Robinson, "Bibliography of Archaeological Books—1947," *AJA* 52 (1948) 534-544. [Near East, pp. 535-537; Egypt, p. 537]

*James L. Kelso, "Implements of Interpretation V. *Archaeology,*" *Interp* 2 (1948) 66-73.

*C. N. Johns, "Discoveries in Palestine Since 1939," *PEQ* 80 (1948) 81-101. [Prehistoric (to Early Bronze); Canaanite (Middle to Late Bronze Age); Phoenician and Israelite, Jewish; Roman; Christian and Moslem; Discoveries at St. John's, 'Ein Karim, 1941-2; Moslem]

*G. Lankester Harding, "Recent Discoveries in Trans-Jordan," *PEQ* 80 (1948) 118-120.

*P. R[oland] de Vaux, "Excavations in Palestine, 1943-6," *QDAP* 13 (1948) 166-171. ['Ein el Ma'mudiya and Khirbat ed Deir; Tell el Far'a; Kh. Karak; The Citadel, Jerusalem]

*‡Anonymous, "Bibliography of Excavations in Palestine and Trans-Jordan, 1945-6," *QDAP* 13 (1948) 172.

Ann L. Perkins, "Archaeological News. *The Near East,*" *AJA* 53 (1949) 36-57.

‡Sterling Dow, "Archaeological Indexes. A Review Article," *AJA* 54 (1950) 41-57.

Ann L. Perkins, "Archaeological News. *The Near East,*" *AJA* 54 (1950) 58-72. [Egypt, p. 58; Israel and Arab Palestine, pp. 58-61; Syria and Lebanon, p. 61; Turkey, pp. 61-64; Iran, pp. 64-67; Afghanistan, p. 67; Caucasus and Central Asia, pp. 67-72]

‡C. Bradford Welles, "Archaeological Bibliography," *AJA* 54 (1950) 75-80, 135-141, 227-235, 386-393. [Israel and Jordan, pp. 388-389; Egypt, p. 389]

*Kathleen M. Kenyon, "Palestinian Excavations," *Antiq* 24 (1950) 196-200.

*B. S. J. Isserlin, "Some Archaeological News from Israel," *PEQ* 82 (1950) 92-101.

*J. A. Thompson, "Thirty Years of Palestinian Archaeology," *ABR* 1 (1951) 88-111.

‡C. Bradford Welles and Ann Perkins, "Archaeological Bibliography," *AJA* 55 (1951) 71-80, 196-207, 245-254. [Egypt, pp. 75-76, 200-201; Syria, Lebanon, Israel, Jordan, Arabia, p. 75, 199-200, 247]

Ann Perkins, "Archaeological News, Near East," *AJA* 55 (1951) 81-100.

‡C. B[radford] Welles, "Archaeological Bibliography," *AJA* 55 (1951) 387-398. [The Ancient Near East, pp. 388-390]

James Muilenburg, "The Importance of Archaeology for the Minister," *USQR* 7 (1951-52) #3, 15-18.

William Stevenson Smith, "Archaeological News, *Near East, 1950-1951,*" *AJA* 56 (1952) 39-50.

‡C. Bradford Welles, "Archaeological Bibliography of Current Periodical Literature," *AJA* 56 (1952) 69-82. [The Ancient Near East, pp. 70-82]

Mortimer Wheeler, "Archaeology and the Transmission of Ideas," *Antiq* 26 (1952) 180-192.

B[enjamin] Maisler, "Archaeology in the State of Israel," *BA* 15 (1952) 18-24.

Carl H. Kraeling, "Archaeological Notes on the Near East," *BA* 15 (1952) 67-68.

*B. S. J. Isserlin, "Some Recent Archaeological News from Israel," *PEQ* 84 (1952) 42-47.

*G. Lankester Harding and William L. Reed, "Archaeological News from Jordan," *BA* 16 (1953) 2-17. [The Museums; East Jordan, Tombs and Isolated Objects, Early Arab Inscriptions, Ancient Dibon (Dhiban); West Jordan, Khirbet Qumran, Murabba'at Caves, Qumran Caves, Bethany, Tell el-Far'ah, New Jericho (Tulul Abu el-'Alayiq), Early Jericho (Tell es-Sultan), Conclusion]

Naji al-Asil, "Landmarks In Archaeological Progress," *Sumer* 9 (1953) 3-6.

*Frank M. Cross Jr., "Notes on Recent Research in Palestine," *McQ* 7 (1953-54) #8, 11-14.

James Muilenburg, "A Letter from Palestine," *USQR* 9 (1953-54) #2, 22-25.

*Frank M. Cross Jr., "A Footnote to Biblical History," *McQ* 9 (1955-56) #2, 7-10. *[Unsolved problems of Biblical History and Archaeology]*

Margaret Wheeler, "The Lighter Side of Dig Life," *PEQ* 87 (1955) 184-185.

Oliver H. Myers, "Scientific Archaeology in the Near East," *Kush* 4 (1956) 62-65.

*G. Ernest Wright, "Palestinian Excavation, 1956," *McQ* 10 (1956-57) #3, 3-6.

*H. C. Kee and L[awrence] E. Toombs, "The Second Season of Excavation at Shechem," *BA* 20 (1957) 82-105. [Part I. What Goes On At A Dig? pp. 82-92]

J. A. Home, "History from the Earth," *AT* 2 (1957-58) #1, 3-5.

*Anonymous, "Ten Years of Archaeology in Israel," *IEJ* 8 (1958) 52-65.

V. Gordon Childe, "Valediction," *ULBIA* 1 (1958) 1-8.

*Lester J. Kuyper, "Report from Palestine," *RefR* 12 (1958-58) #3, 1-10.

William F[oxwell] Albright, "Archaeology and Religion," *CC* 9 (1959) 107-124. [I. The Scientific Study of Archaeology; II. The Scientific Study of Religion; III. Judaeo-Christianity in the Light of Archaeology; IV. Archaeology, History, and Religion; V. Theism and Religious Humanism in the Light of History]

H. Neil Richardson, "A Decade of Archaeology in Palestine," *JAAR* 27 (1959) 91-101.

Jacquetta Hawkes, "Archaeology and the Concept of Progress," *HT* 10 (1960) 73-82.

Charles T. Fritsch and Immanuel Ben-Dor, "The Link Expedition to Israel, 1960," *BA* 24 (1961) 50-59.

Margaret Murray, "First Steps in Archaeology," *Anitq* 35 (1961) 8-13.

G. R. H. Wright, "Reconstructing Archaeological Remains," *BA* 24 (1961) 25-31.

*W[illiam] F[oxwell] Albright, "Reports of Excavations in the Near East and Middle East (Outside of Palestine and Syria Proper)," *BASOR* #161 (1961) 55, #163 (1961) 54-55.

*Lawrence E. Toombs, "Archaeology and Theological Studies," *DG* 32 (1961-62) 26-34.

*James F. Ross, "What We Do When We Dig," *DG* 32 (1961-62) 149-155.

G. Ernest Wright, "Archaeological Fills and Strata," *BA* 25 (1962) 34-40.

*‡W. C. Heiser, "Theology Digest magazine list," *TD* 10 (1962) 152-170. [VI. a. Biblical Archaeology, pp. 159-160]

*Sadiq al-Hasani, "Projects and Accomplishments of the Department of Antiquities in Iraq," *Sumer* 20 (1964) 105-109.

Frances James, "A Milestone in Palestinian Archaeology," *Exped* 7 (1964-65) #4, 34-38. *[Centenary of the Palestine Exploration Fund]*

*Raymond E. Chaplin, "Animals in Archaeology," *Antiq* 39 (1965) 204-211.

Thomas Aquinas Collins, "The Great Archaeologists," *BibT* #16 (1965) 1028-1034.

‡Howard M. Jamieson Jr., "Biblical Studies. Archaeology," *PP* 7 (1965) #3, 21. *[Bibliography]*

*Mahboub al-Chalabi, "Applications of Geo-electrical Methods in Archaeology," *Sumer* 21 (1965) 119-135.

*K. de B. Codrington, "Art for Archaeologists," *BJRL* 48 (1965-66) 98-117.

Harry S. May, "Why Do They Dig?" *RL* 35 (1965-66) 603-607.

Olga Tufnell, "Excavator's Progress. Letters of F. J. Bliss, 1889-1900," *PEQ* 97 (1965) 112-127.

*Henry O. Thompson, "Science and Archaeology," *BA* 39 (1966) 114-125.

Olfret Voss, "Problems of documentation in archaeology," *Kuml* (1966) 122-133.

Henrik Thrane, "New trends in archaeological publications," *Kuml* (1966) 143-144.

Homer A. Thompson, "Archaeology: Horizons New and Old. Classic Lands," *PAPS* 110 (1966) 100-104.

Robert McC. Adams, "Archaeology: Horizons New and Old. Trend and Tradition in Near Eastern Archaeology," *PAPS* 110 (1966) 105-110.

G. R. H. Wright, "A Method of Excavation Common in Palestine," *ZDPV* 82 (1966) 113-124.

Bruce G. Trigger, "Major concepts of archaeology in historical perspective," *Man, N.S.,* 3 (1968) 527-541.

John Piet, "Now in Archaeology: The Underground Revealed," *JANES* 1 (1968-69) #1, 11-18.

Karen Rubinson, "Now in Archaeology: Some Comments," *JANES* 1 (1968-69) #2, 62-65.

G. Ernest Wright, "Archaeological Method in Palestine—An American Interpretation," *EI* 9 (1969) 120-133. *[Non-Hebrew Section]*

David Noel Freedman, "Archaeology in the Promised Land—1968," *A/R* 2 (1969) #2, 8-10.

Bahadır Alkım, "Önsöz," *AAI* 3 (1969) 1-8. [Foreword in English, pp. 5-7]

Ali M. Dinçol and Sönmez Kantman, "Tanitma ve Arkeolojik Araştirma Metodunun Kritiği," *AAI* 3 (1969) 9-13. [English Summary, pp. 12-13]

Sönmez Kantman, "Prehistorik Arkeolojide Kavramyapim," *AAI* 3 (1969) 47-62. [English Summary, pp. 59-60]

Sönmez Kantman, "Deneyse Katki Gözlemcilik ve Fonksiyonalizmin Arkeolojik Tipbilimde Önemi," *AAI* 3 (1969) 63-80. [English Summary, pp. 78-79]

Robert Drake, "Scientific Method and Archaeology," *SR* 15 (1969-70) 11-25.

§182 *2.5.7.1 Modern Travels in the Ancient Near East*

†Anonymous, "Sonnini's Travels in Upper and Lower Egypt," *BCQTR* 15 (1800) 270-271, 524-530.

†Anonymous, "Olivier's Travels in the Ottoman Empire, Egypt, and Persia," *ERCJ* 1 (1802-03) 44-95. *(Review)*

†Anonymous, "Denon's Travels in Egypt," *ERCJ* 1 (1802-03) 330-345. *(Review)*

†Anonymous, "Various Translations of Denon's Egypt," *BCQTR* 21 (1803) 618-623; 22 (1803) 18-25. *(Review)*

†Anonymous, "Wittman's Travels in Turkey, Asia Minor, Syria, &c. and into Egypt," *ERCJ* 2 (1803) 330-337. *(Review)*

†Anonymous, "Morier's Embassy to Persia," *MMBR* 34 (1812-13) 575-613.

Anonymous, "In Greece, Palestine, Egypt, and Barbary. During the Years 1806 and 1807. by F. A. de Chateaubriand," *MMBR* 32 (1811-12) 627-670. *(Translated from the French)*

†Anonymous, "Kinnier and Morier on Persia," *QRL* 9 (1813) 57-89. *(Review)*

Anonymous, "A Journey through Albania, and other Provinces of Turkey, in Europe and Asia, to Constantinople, during the years 1809 and 1810," *QRL* 10 (1813-14) 175-203. *(Review)*

†Anonymous, "Eustace's *Tour through Italy,*" *QRL* 10 (1813-14) 222-250. *(Review)*

†Anonymous, "Clarke's Travels in Europe, Asia, and Africa, Greece, Egypt, and the Holy Land," *MMBR* 37 (1814) 611-636.

Anonymous, "Narrative of a Journey in Egypt, and the Country beyond the Cataracts. By Thomas Legh, Esq. M. P.," *ERCJ* 27 (1816) 422-444. *(Review)*

Anonymous, "Travels of Ali Bey, in Morocco, Tripoli, Cyprus, Egypt, Syria, and Turkey, between the years 1803 and 1807," *QRL* 15 (1816) 299-345. *(Review)*

†Anonymous, "Legh's *Journey in Egypt and Nubia,*" *QRL* 16 (1816-17) 1-27. *(Review)*

†Anonymous, "Legh's Travels in Egypt," *BCQTR, N.S.,* 7 (1817) 271-285. *(Review)*

*†Anonymous, "Morier's Second Journey through Persia to Constantinople," *MMBR* 45 (1818) 607-626. *(Review)*

Anonymous, "Travels in Egypt, Nubia, Holy Land, Mount Libanon,*[sic]* and Cyprus, in the Year 1814," *QRL* 19 (1818) 178-204. (Addendum, pp. 280-281)*(Review)*

†Anonymous, "Dodwell's Tour through Greece," *BCQTR, N.S.,* 11 (1819) 225-242. *(Review)*

†Anonymous, "Kotzebue's Journey into Persia," *BCQTR, N.S.,* 12 (1819) 308-319. *(Review)*

*Anonymous, "Account of Newly-discovered Antiquities in Arabia Petræa, derived from the Personal Inspection of a recent British Traveler," *MMBR* 47 (1819) 481-485.

†Anonymous, "Sir William Ouseley's Travels in the East," *BCQTR, N.S.,* 14 (1820) 337-355. *(Review)*

Anonymous, "Travels in Nubia. By the Late John Lewis Burckhardt," *ERCJ* 36 (1820) 109-121. *(Review)*

†Anonymous, "Tancorgne's Journey into Persia," *BCQTR, N.S.,* 15 (1821) 279-285.

†Anonymous, "Laurent's Travels in Greece," *BCQTR, N.S.,* 16 (1821) 405-411. *(Review)*

†Anonymous, "Ker Porter—*Travels in Georgia, Persia, &c.,*" *QRL* 26 (1821-22) 437-454. *(Review)*

†Anonymous, "Waddington's Visit to Ethiopia," *BCQTR, N.S.,* 18 (1822) 57-72. *(Review)*

†Anonymous, "Burckhardt's Travels in Syria and the Holy Land," *BCQTR, N.S.,* 18 (1822) 243-267. *(Review)*

*†Anonymous, "Sir R. Ker Porter's Travels in Georgia, Persia, Armenia, &c.," *MMBR* 53 (1822) 577-612. *(Review)*

†Anonymous, "Waddington's Visit to Ethiopia," *QRL* 27 (1822) 215-239. *(Review)*

†Anonymous, "Egypt, Nubia, Berber, and Sennaar," *QRL* 28 (1822-23) 60-97. *(Review)*

†Anonymous, "Edmonstone's Journey in Upper Egypt," *BCQTR, N.S.*, 19 (1823) 254-259. *(Review)*

Anonymous, "Travels in Egypt and the Holy Land. By William Rae Wilson, Esq.," *ERCJ* 38 (1823) 398-413. *(Review)*

†Anonymous, "Buckingham's Travels," *BCQTR, 3rd Ser.*, 1 (1825-26) 452-480. *(Review)*

†Anonymous, "Travels in the East," *BCQTR, 4th Ser.*, 3 (1828) 132-163. *(Review)*

[Ernst Fredric Karl] Rosemüller, "A review of Travels to the East; from 'Rosemüller's Alterthumskunde'," *BibR* 4 (1828) 492.

Anonymous, "Turkey, Constantinople, Egypt, Nubia and Palestine," *MMBR, N.S.*, 8 (1829) 157-172. *(Review)*

†Anonymous, "Pilgrimages to Mekka*[sic]* and Medina," *QRL* 42 (1830) 18-49. *(Review)*

[Edward Robinson], "Sketches of Idumea and its Present Inhabitants. From the Travels of Burckhardt and Legh. *With an Historical Introduction*," *BRCR* 3 (1833) 247-287, 393-444, 613-652.

†Anonymous, "Travels in the Valley of the Nile," *ERCJ* 59 (1834) 404-425. *(Review)*

†Anonymous, "Hoskins's *Travels in Ethiopia*," *ERCJ* 62 (1835-36) 45-72. *(Review)*

*†Anonymous, "Journey through Arabia Petræa to Mount Sinai and the Excavated City of Petra, the Edom of the Prophecies," *BCQTR, 4th Ser.*, 20 (1836) 446-474. *(Review)*

Anonymous, "Outlines of a Journey through Arabia Petræa, to Mount Sinai and the Excavated City of Petra—the Edom of the Prophecies," *DR* 1 (1836) 174-200.

†Anonymous, "Dr. Hogg's *Visit to Jerusalem*," *WR* 24 (1836) 31-47. *(Review)*

†Anonymous, "Monro's Ramble in Syria," *WR* 25 (1836) 103-137. *(Review)*

[James D. Knowles], "Jones' Visit to Egypt and Jerusalem," *CRB* 2 (1837) 10-20. *(Review)*

†Anonymous, "Modern Egypt and the Modern Egyptians," *ERCJ* 65 (1837) #132, 146-173. [Additional Notes, p. 283] *(Review)*

†Anonymous, "Pashley's Travels in Crete," *BCQTR, 4th Ser.,* 23 (1838) 225-247. *(Review)*

H. W. Jr., "Incidents of Travel in Egypt, Arabia Petræa, and the Holy Land. By an American," *CE* 24 (1838) 31-47. *(Review)*

Anonymous, "Lord Lindsay's Letters from the East—Egyptian Magic," *DUM* 12 (1838) 568-592. *(Review)*

†Anonymous, "Wellsted's *Travels in Arabia, &c.*," *QRL* 61 (1838) 301-326. *(Review)*

Edward Robinson, "A Brief Report of Travels in Palestine and the adjacent Regions in 1838; undertaken for the illustration of Biblical Geography, by the Rev. Prof. E. Robinson and Rev. E. Smith. Prepared and read before the Geographical Society of Berlin, Dec. 8, 1838, and Jan. 6, 1839," *BRCR, N.S.,* 1 (1839) 400-430.

Anonymous, "Dr. Burton's Journey to Jerusalem," *DUM* 14 (1839) 59-68. *(Review)*

Anonymous, "Letters on Egypt, Edom, and the Holy Land," *QRL* 63 (1839) 166-192. *(Review)*

Anonymous, "Travels in Koordistan and Mesopotamia," *DR* 8 (1840) 414-448. *(Review)*

†Anonymous, "Fellowes' Excursion in Asia Minor," *ERCJ* 71 (1840) 396-410. *(Review)*

G. E. E., "Biblical Researches in Palestine, Mount Sinai, and Arabia Petræa, a Journal of Travels in the year 1838. By E. Robinson and E. Smith. Undertaken in reference to Biblical Geography. Drawn up from the original Diaries, with historical Illustrations. By Edward Robinson, D. D.," *CE* 31 (1841-42) 222-252. *(Review)*

†Anonymous, "Robinson's Travels in Palestine," *QRL* 69 (1841-42) 150-185. *(Review)*

†Anonymous, "Mure's *Tour of Greece,*" *QRL* 70 (1842) 129-157. *(Review)*

†Anonymous, "Travels and Researches in Asia Minor," *ERCJ* 77 (1843) 443-470. *(Review)*

H. A. Homes, "Review of Boré's Travels in Turkey and Persia," *BRCR, N.S.,* 11 (1844) 28-65. *(Review)*

*Anonymous, "The Highlands of Ethiopia," *CRB* 9 (1844) 396-415.

†Anonymous, "Eōthen, or Traces of Travel brought Home from the East," *QRL* 75 (1845) 54-76. *(Review)*

†Anonymous, "The Lands of the Bible," *BQRL* 6 (1847) 459-489. *(Review)*

*E. Robinson, "Notes on Biblical Geography," *BS* 4 (1847) 403-409. [II. Antiquities on the route from Ba'albek to Hamath and Aleppo, pp. 403-408.

S. G. B., "Millard's Travels," *CE* 43 (1847) 199-203. *(Review)*

†Anonymous, "Travels in Lycia, Milyas, and the Cibyratis, in Company with the late Rev. E. T. Daniell," *DR* 22 (1847) 158-190. *(Review)*

†Anonymous, "Lands of the Bible," *NBR* 8 (1847-48) 107-129. *(Review)*

W[illiam] M. Thomson, "Tour from Beirut to Aleppo in 1845," *BS* 5 (1848) 1-23, 243-262.

William M. Thomson, "Travels in Northern Syria. Description of Seleucia, Antioch, Aleppo, etc.," *BS* 5 (1848) 447-480.

William M. Thomson, "Journey from Aleppo to Mount Lebanon by Jeble el-Aala, Apamia, Ribla, etc.," *BS* 5 (1848) 663-700.

Anonymous, "The Lands of the Bible," *DUM* 31 (1848) 266-284. *(Review)*

†Anonymous, "Spratt and Forbes's Travels in Lycia, Milyas, and the Cibyratis," *TLJ* 1 (1848-49) 488-503.

Anonymous, "A Few More Random Records of a Ramble in the East," *DUM* 35 (1850) 169-181, 309-327, 615-633.

*Justin Perkins, "Journal of a Tour from Oroomiah to Mosul, through the Koordish Mountains, and a Visit to the Ruins of Nineveh," *JAOS* 2 (1851) 69-119.

Henry A. DeForest, "Notes on a Tour in Mount Lebanon, and to the eastern side of Lake Hûleh," *JAOS* 2 (1851) 235-247.

†Anonymous, "Patterson's Tour in Egypt, Palestine, Syria, and Greece," *DR* 32 (1852) 407-435. *(Review)*

( ) Z., "Recent Travels in Palestine," *JSL, 2nd Ser.,* 2 (1852) 143-175. *(Review)*

E[dward] Robinson, "Outlines of a Journey in Palestine in 1852 by E. Robinson, E. Smith, and others," *BS* 10 (1853) 113-151.

A[dolph] L. Kœppen, "A Visit to the Desert and the Dead Sea," *RChR* 5 (1853) 521-554.

E[dward] Robinson, "Robinson's Journal in Palestine. Outlines of a Journey in Palestine in 1852 by E. Robinson, E. Smith and others," *JSL, 2nd Ser.,* 5 (1853-54) 9-44.

J. L. Porter, "Excursion to the Lakes East of Damascus," *BS* 11 (1854) 329-344. *[Excursion to Kesweh, from p. 342 on]*

J. L. Porter, "Excursion from Damascus to Yabrud, etc.," *BS* 11 (1854) 433-455.

J. L. Porter, "Notes on a Tour from Damascus to Ba'albek and Hums," *BS* 11 (1854) 649-693.

Anonymous, "Notes of a Week in Palestine," *CRB* 19 (1854) 343-361.

†Anonymous, "Recent Works on Palestine," *BFER* 3 (1854) 413-442. *(Review)*

S. C. M., "Three Months in the Holy Land," *JSL, 2nd Ser.,* 7 (1854-55) 310-331; *3rd Ser.,* 1 (1855) 245-267; 2 (1855-56) 15-48, 326-350; 3 (1856) 77-114; 4 (1856-57) 17-35; 6 (1857-58) 273-294.

Adolph L. Kœppen, "Sketches of a Traveler from Greece, Constantinople, Asia Minor, Syria, and Palestine," *RChR* 7 (1855) 1-20, 163-194, 337-361; 8 (1856) 40-79, 350-383; 9 (1857) 208-250, 402-434.

†Anonymous, "Travels in Arabia and Palestine, Early and Recent," *NBR* 27 (1857) 513-555. *(Review)*

†Anonymous, "Persia," *QRL* 101 (1857) 501-541. *(Review)*

†Anonymous, "Suez and Euphrates Routes," *QRL* 102 (1857) 354-397. *(Review)*

O. S., "Some Strictures upon that Portion of Stanley's Sinai and Palestine, which Treats of the Latter Country; by a Recent Traveler there," *JSL, 3rd Ser.,* 6 (1857-58) 117-147.

†Anonymous, "The Land of Promise," *TLJ* 11 (1858-59) 147-167. *(Review)*

Horatio B. Hackett, "A Journey to Neapolis and Philippi," *BS* 17 (1860) 866-898.

*[Joseph P. Thompson(?)], "Notices of New Publications," *BS* 19 (1862) 671-684. [Recent Works on Egyptology, Oriental Travel and Geography, pp. 671-678] *(Review)*

*[Joseph P. Thompson(?)], "Egyptology, Oriental Archaeology and Travel," *BS* 19 (1862) 881-890. *(Review)*

Anonymous, "The Strongholds of Syria," *DUM* 59 (1862) 699-704.

*Joseph P. Thompson, "Egyptology, Oriental Archaeology and Travel," *BS* 20 (1863) 650-660*(Review)*, 879-884; 22 (1865) 684-689.

Anonymous, "From Jaffa to Jerusalem," *DUM* 61 (1863) 477-481.

*Joseph P. Thompson, "Egyptology, Oriental Travel and Discovery," *BS* 21 (1864) 425-435, 666-669. *(Review)*

Anonymous, "Rambles in the Deserts of Syria," *NBR* 40 (1864) 471-497. *(Review)*

William Gifford Palgrave, "Narrative of a Year's Journey through Central and Eastern Arabia," *BQR* 42 (1865) 297-330.

H. W. C., "Tristram's Land of Israel," *TRL* 2 (1865) 678-696. *(Review)*

H. A., "The Peninsula of Sinai: Notes on Travel therein," *BQRL* 43 (1866) 86-125.

Anonymous, "Palgrave's Central Arabia," *NBR* 44 (1866) 1-35. *(Review)*

†Anonymous, "Palgrave's *Arabia*," *QRL* 119 (1866) 182-215. *(Review)*

Anonymous, "Travel in the Desert and the Holy Land," *ERG, 4th Ser.*, 2 (1867-68) 192-204. *(Review)*

Wm. T. Savage, "A Month in Egypt," *CongR* 8 (1868) 140-154.

Wm. T. Savage, "The Arabian Desert.—Part I.," *CongR* 8 (1868) 274-285.

Wm. T. Savage, "The Arabian Desert.—Part II.," *CongR* 8 (1868) 371-382.

Wm. T. Savage, "Gaza and Jerusalem," *CongR* 9 (1869) 164-175.

Charles Warren, "Remarks on a Visit to 'Ain Jidy and the Southern Shores of the Dead Sea in Mid-Summer 1867," *PEFQS* 1 (1869) 143-150.

†Anonymous, "Rassam's *Abyssinia*," *QRL* 126 (1869) 299-327. *(Review)*

†Anonymous, "Travels in Greece," *QRL* 126 (1869) 479-499. *(Review)*

Henry M. Canfield, "Notes on a Surveying Trip from the Phenician[sic]* Coast to the Euphrates River," *JAOS* 9 (1871) lxv.

E. H. Palmer, "Notes on a Tour in the Lebanon," *PEFQS* 3 (1871) 107-118.

†Anonymous, "The Shah of Persia," *QRL* 135 (1873) 241-265. *(Review)*

†Anonymous, "The Land of Moab," *QRL* 135 (1873) 481-509. *(Review)*

†Anonymous, "Provincial Turkey," *QRL* 137 (1874) 313-354. *(Review)*

†Anonymous, "The Revival of Turkey," *QRL* 146 (1878) 549-594. *(Review)*

*F. W. Holland, "A Journey on Foot Through Arabias Petraea," *PEFQS* 11 (1879) 59-72.

Greville J. Chester, "A Journey to the Biblical Sites in Lower Egypt, etc.," *PEFQS* 12 (1880) 133-158. [Heliopolis; Tel-el-Yahoudeh; Tel-Basta; Tel-Fakus; San; From San to el Arish]

John N. Dalton, "The Prince's Journey Through the Holy Land," *PEFQS* 14 (1882) 193-195.

Claude Reignier Conder, "Report on the Visit of Their Royal Highnesses Princes Albert Victor and George of Wales to the Hebron Haram, on 5th April, 1882," *PEFQS* 14 (1882) 197-213. (Note by C. W. Wilson, pp. 213-214)

C[laude] R. Conder, "Tour of Their Royal Highnesses Princes Albert Victor and George of Wales in Palestine," *PEFQS* 14 (1882) 214-234.

W[illia]m Hayes Ward, "Extract from a Private Letter of Dr. Ward from Babylon," *AJA., O.S.,* 1 (1885) 182-183.

William Summers, "A Trip to the East," *CongRL* 2 (1888) 541-550, 623-631, 825-832, 1020-1026.

†Anonymous, "Layard's Early Adventures," *QRL* 166 (1888) 87-111. *(Review)*

†Anonymous, "The Early Adventures of Sir Henry Layard," *ERCJ* 167 (1888) 519-553. *(Review)*

F. L. Griffith, "Notes on a Tour in Upper Egypt," *SBAP* 11 (1888-89) 228-234.

F. L. Griffith, "Notes on a Tour to Upper Egypt," *SBAP* 12 (1889-90) 89-113.

Robert Francis Harper, "Down the Euphrates Valley," *ONTS* 10 (1890) 55-57, 118-119, 367-368.

W. M. Flinders Petrie, "Journals of Mr. W. M. Flinders Petrie," *PEFQS* 22 (1890) 219-246. [Note by C. R. Conder, *PEFQS* 23 (1891) p. 73]

George E. Post, "Narrative of a Trip to Palmyra in April, 1890," *PEFQS* 23 (1891) 20-49.

George E. Post, "Narrative of a Second Journey to Palmyra," *PEFQS* 24 (1892) 154-167, 252-262, 322-328; 25 (1893) 36-43, 147-164.

George E. Post, "Narrative of an Expedition to Lebanon, Anti-Lebanon and Damascus," *PEFQS* 25 (1893) 219-239.

John P. Peters, "Notes on Eastern Travel," *AJA, O.S.*, 8 (1893) 325-334.

†Anonymous, "Persia and the Persia Question," *QRL* 176 (1893) 166-197. *(Review)*

F[rederick] J. Bliss, "The Recent Pilgrimage to Jersualem," *PEFQS* 26 (1894) 101-108. (Note by C. R. Conder, p. 207)

W. Ewing, "A Journey in the Hauran," *PEFQS* 27 (1895) 60-67, 161-184, 281-294, 355-368.

Frederick Jones Bliss, "Narrative of an Expedition to Moab and Gilead in March, 1895," *PEFQS* 27 (1895) 203-235. (Notes by C. R. Conder, p. 332)

Gray Hill, "A Journey East of the Jordan and the Dead Sea, 1895," *PEFQS* 28 (1896) 24-46.

A. F. Spender, "Impressions of the Holy Land," *DR* 122 (1898) 74-92. [I. Jerusalem; II. Bethlehem, Jordan, and the Dead Sea; III. Samaria, Nazareth, and the Lake of Galilee]

†Anonymous, "Dongola," *ERCJ* 187 (1898) 67-100. *(Review) [Travel in Nubia]*

Angus Crawford, "East of the Jordan," *PER* 12 (1898-99) 340-346.

Edgar J. Goodspeed, "From Ḥaifa to Nazareth," *BW* 16 (1900) 407-413.

*James B. Nies, "Excavations in Palestine and what may be expected from them, and some observations made in 1899, during a series of journeys which covered the greater part of Eastern and Western Palestine," *AJA* 5 (1901) 7-8.

*F. J. Bliss, "Summer in Palestine and Syria," *BW* 20 (1902) 89-98.

George L. Robinson, "The Ancient 'Circuit of Argob'," *BW* 20 (1902) 248-259.

*George Adam Smith, "Notes on a Journey Through Hauran, with Inscriptions Found by the Way," *PEFQS* 33 (1901) 340-361. [Note by R. A. S. Macalister, *PEFQS* 34 (1902) p. 79]

James B. Nies, "Notes on a Cross Jordan Trip made October 23rd to November 7th, 1899," *PEFQS* 33 (1901) 362-368.

E. W. G. Masterman, "Miscellaneous Notes Made During a Journey East and West of Jordan," *PEFQS* 34 (1902) 299-301.

Anonymous, "Turkey and Armenia," *QRL* 195 (1902) 590-616. *(Review)*

E. T. Wellford, "A Pastor's Visit to Bible Lands," *PQ* 16 (1902-03) 402-406.

William Watson Goodwin, "A Recent Visit to Greek Lands," *AJA* 7 (1903) 91-92.

Herbert Rix, "Notes Taken on a Tour in Palestine in the Spring of 1901," *PEFQS* 35 (1903) 159-162. [1. Bethlehem of Galilee; 2. A Spring near 'Ain et-Tabigha; 3. Bethabara]

John P. Peters, "Dr. John P. Peters' Account of His Visit to and Explorations in Palestine," *RP* 2 (1903) 31-32.

A. V. Williams Jackson, "Notes of a Journey to Persia, I," *JAOS* 25 (1904) 176-184. *[No "Part II"!]*

J[ohn] P. Peters, "Visit to Kefr Shiyan, Janieh, and Neighbourhood," *PEFQS* 36 (1904) 377-386.

Rufus B. Richardson, "Mountain Climbing in Greece," *AJA* 8 (1905) 72-73.

George Anderson, "Some Impressions of a Visit to the Holy Land, March and April, 1910," *GUOST* 3 (1907-12) 40-42.

J. Renwick Metheny, "Road Notes from Cilicia and North Syria," *JAOS* 28 (1907) 155-163.

R. A. Stewart Macalister, "Diary of a Visit to Safed," *PEFQS* 39 (1907) 91-130. [With Travel-notes of the Journey from Nablus to Safed, viá Beisân, by E. W. G. Masterman]

John Garstang, "Notes on a Journey through Asia Minor," *AAA* 1 (1908) 1-12.

E. W. G. Masterman, "Notes of a Visit to Engedy, Masada, and Jebel Usdum," *PEFQS* 40 (1908) 229-244.

W. M. Calder, "A Journey round the Proseilemmene," *Klio* 10 (1910) 232-242.

R. Campbell Thompson, "A Journey by some Unmapped Routes in the Western Hittite Country between Angora and Eregii," *SBAP* 32 (1910) 181-191, 237-242, 289-295; 33 (1911) 8-14.

*Arthur W. Sutton, "From Suez to Sinai," *JTVI* 45 (1913) 249-264.

*Edgar J. Banks, "To the Summit of Mount Ararat," *OC* 27 (1913) 398-410.

Elizabeth Hazelton Haight, "A Visit to Horace's Sabine Farm," *A&A* 1 (1914-15) 177-186.

*Lewis R. Freedman, "A Day at Babylon," *ContR* 110 (1916) 779-788.

Edwina Stanton Babcock, "Reading into Tempe," *A&A* 6 (1917) 203-214.

J. C. Roome, "A Ride Through Persia and Mesopotamia," *IAQR* 8 (1917) 58-62.

H. H. Kitchener, "Our Ride from Gaza to Jerusalem, with a Description of the Greek Holy Fire," *PEFQS* 49 (1917) 66-72.

Anonymous, "The Director in Egypt," *MJ* 10 (1919) 188-209.

Anonymous, "A Tour on Foot Through Samaria and Galilee," *BASOR* #4 (1921) 7-13.

Albert T. Clay, "Dr. Clay's Story of His Oriental Journey," *BASOR* #13 (1924) 5-10.

Edward Chiera, "Travel Notes of an Excavator," *CQ* 3 (1926) 339-350, 465-473.

Henry Rushton Fairclough, "The Italian Virginian Cruse," *A&A* 31 (1931) 261-267, 288.

Erich Schmidt, "From Iraq to Persia: An Archaeological Interlude," *A&A* 32 (1932) 59-69.

Gordon Cumming, "First Impressions of Palestine," *BTSAB* 7 (1932-33) #2, 3, 5-6, 8.

Mary I. Hussey, "From Palestine to Mesopotamia," *BASOR* #49 (1933) 19-22.

Edward Mack, "Impressions of Present Day Palestine," *USR* 45 (1933-34) 122-135.

(Miss) Christabell Draper, "Early Women Travellers in Arabia," *IAQR* 27 (1931) 563-569.

P[atrick] P. M'Kenna, "From Jerusalem to Jericho," *IER, 5th Ser.,* 50 (1937) 25-34.

A. R. Adair, "A Journey Through Syria," *IAQR* 34 (1938) 729-733.

Nelson Glueck, "On the Occasion of the Centenary of Edward Robinson's First Journey to Palestine in 1838," *BASOR* #74 (1939) 2-4.

P[atrick] P. M'Kenna, "Some Interesting Places of Pilgrimage in Northern Palestine," *IER, 5th Ser.,* 54 (1939) 76-87.

P[atrick] P. M'Kenna, "Places of Pilgrimage Near Jerusalem," *IER, 5th Ser.,* 54 (1939) 502-514.

Willis A. Chamberlin, "On Horseback Through Palestine: Journal of a Tour of the Holy Land by William Arnold Stevens in 1883," *CRDSB* 15 (1942-43) 24-36.

†Anonymous, "A Pilgrimage to the Temples and Tombs of Egypt, Nubia, and Palestine, in 1845-6," *DR* 21 (1946-47) 401-418. *(Review)*

*Yehuda Karmon, "Geographical Influences on the Historical Routes in the Sharon Plain," *PEQ* 93 (1961) 43-60.

H. J. Richards, "Bible Lands by Jeep—I," *Scrip* 13 (1961) 88-92.

H. J. Richards, "Bible Lands by Jeep—II," *Scrip* 13 (1961) 117-124.

H. J. Richards, "Bible Lands by Jeep—III," *Scrip* 14 (1962) 12-25.

Hilda Pendlebury, "A Journey in Crete," *Arch* 17 (1964) 162-168.

Edward W. Bodnar, "Cyriacus of Ancona's Visit to Delos, April, 1445," *AJA* 70 (1966) 183.

Pierre A. MacKay, "A Turkish Traveler in Northern Greece," *AJA* 73 (1969) 242-243. *[17th Century]*

§183 *2.5.7.2 Archaeological Societies, Oriental Congresses, Conferences, Meetings, etc.*

D. C. Gilman, "On the Work of the Palestine Exploration Fund," *JAOS* 10 (1880) xii-xiii.

Henry W. Hulbert, "A Proposed School of Biblical Archaeology and Philology in the East," *PR* 8 (1887) 71-84.

Lewis B. Paton, "The Old Testament Society in Berlin," *ONTS* 12 (1891) 339-340.

A. R. S. Kennedy, "Notes from the Oriental Congress," *ET* 4 (1892-93) 59-62.

Tony André, "The Geneva Oriental Congress," *IAQR, 2nd Ser.,* 8 (1894) 377-389.

R. N. Cust, "The International Congress of Orientalists," *IAQR, 3rd Ser.,* 4 (1897) 79-98. (Remarks by Henri Cordier, p. 98)

Joseph Offord, "Notes on the Congress of Orientalists held at Paris, 1897," *SBAP* 19 (1897) 305-311.

A. H. Sayce, "Oriental Archaeology at the Congress of Orientalists," *ET* 9 (1897-98) 57-59.

F. Legge, "Report on the XIIth Congress of Orientalists held at Rome, October 3-15," *SBAP* 21 (1899) 261-268. [(1) Biblical; (2) Egyptological; (3) Assyriological]

E[dward] Montet, "The Congress of Orientalists at Rome," *IAQR, 3rd Ser.,* 9 (1900) 113-117. [Semitic Section, pp. 114-115]

Anonymous, "American School of Research in Palestine," *MR* 82 (1900) 812.

Agnes Smith Lewis, "What I Saw at the Orientalist Congress," *ET* 14 (1902-03) 93-96.

Theophilus G. Pinches, "Report on the Congress of Orientalists held at Hamburg in September, 1902," *JTVI* 35 (1903) 228-236.

Anonymous, "Berlin and Archaeology," *MR* 85 (1903) 979-982.

Ira Maurine Price, "The Oriental Exploration Fund," *BW* 23 (1904) 7-15.

Halil Hilio, "Oriental Studies in England and on the Continent," *IAQR, 3rd Ser.,* 18 (1904) 341-351.

E. E. Braithwaite, "The Semitic Museum of Harvard," *RP* 5 (1904) 243-251. [The First Floor; The Assyrian Room; The Oldest Material; Biblical Material; Miscellaneous Contents (of the Assyrian Room); East India House Inscription; Palestine Room; Papyrus Manuscript of Rom. 1:1-7; Antique Lamps and Various Models]

(Miss) Isabel Frances Dodd, "The Archaeological Congress at Athens," *RP* 4 (1905) 199-202.

James A. Montgomery, "The American School of Oriental Research in Jerusalem," *A&A* 7 (1918) 173-179.

James Henry Breasted, "The Oriental Institute of the University of Chicago," *AJSL* 35 (1918-19) 196-204.

Anonymous, "The British Society for Biblical Archaeology," *HR* 77 (1919) 110.

W. M. Flinders Petrie, "The British School of Archaeology in Egypt," *IAQR* 15 (1919) 631-634.

Anonymous, "The Palestine Oriental Society," *HR* 79 (1920) 216.

J. Garstang, "The Organisation of Archaeological Research in Palestine," *AAA* 8 (1921) 61-62.

James Henry Breasted, "The Oriental Institute of the University of Chicago—A Beginning and a Program," *AJSL* 38 (1921-22) 233-328.

*Harold North Fowler, "The American School of Classical Studies at Athens," *A&A* 14 (1922) 171-260. [Foundation; Organization, and Work of the School, pp. 171-183; Publications of the School, pp. 246-250]

George T. Allen, "The Oriental Institute of the University of Chicago," *A&A* 16 (1923) 241-246.

Nathaniel Schmidt, "Early Oriental Studies in Europe and the Work of the American Oriental Society, 1842-1922," *JAOS* 43 (1923) 1-14.

George Grant MacCurdy, "The International Archaeological Congress in Syria and Palestine," *A&A* 22 (1926) 36-38.

Anonymous, "Notes and Comments. Archaeological Congresses Have a Lighter Side," *A&A* 23 (1927) 42.

W[illiam] F[oxwell] Albright, "The Archaeology of Western Asia at the Leyden Congress," *BASOR* #43 (1931) 21-23.

George Foucart, "An Open Letter to the Egypt Exploration Society on the occasion of its Jubilee," *JEA* 19 (1933) 8-15.

W[illiam] F[oxwell] Albright, "The Ancient Near East at the Congress of Orientalists in Rome," *BASOR* #60 (1935) 2-9.

Norman W. Porteous, "Second International Congress of Old Testament Scholars at Göttingen, September 4-10," *ET* 47 (1935-36) 84-88.

Francis O. Allen, "The Oriental Institute Archaeological Report on the Near East," *AJSL* 52 (1935-36) 201-214.

Charles F. Nims, "The Oriental Institute Archaeological Report on the Near East," *AJSL* 53 (1936-37) 199-216.

Theophile J. Meek, "The Challenge of Oriental Studies to American Scholarship," *JAOS* 63 (1943) 83-93.

T. George Allen, "Publication Problems of the Orientalist," *JNES* 5 (1946) 115-127.

N[orman] W. Porteous, "International Meeting of the Society for Old Testament Study at Cardiff, September 9-13, 1946," *ET* 58 (1946-47) 106-109.

E[phraim] A. Speiser, "Near Eastern Studies in America, 1939-45," *ArOr* 16 (1947-49) 76-88.

C. R. North, "The International Congress of Old Testament Scholars, Leiden, 1950," *ET* 62 (1950-51) 48-50.

H. H. Rowley, "The Copenhagen Old Testament Congress," *ET* 65 (1953-54) 50-52.

H. H. Rowley, "The Strasbourg Old Testament Congress," *ET* 68 (1956-57) 71-73.

I. M. Diakonoff, "Ancient Near East in Soviet Research," *ArOr* 27 (1959) 143-148.

Edith Porada, "Orientalists Meet in Moscow," *Arch* 13 (1960) 279-286.

*Emmett L. Bennett Jr., "Third International Colloquium for Mycenaean Studies," *KZFE* 1 (1962) 79-81.

*Froelich Rainey, "The Applied Science Center for Archaeology," *AJA* 67 (1963) 294-295. *[Radioactive Carbon Dating]*

Peter R. Ackroyd, "The Fourth Congress of the International Organisation for the Study of the Old Testament, Bonn, 1962," *ET* 75 (1963-64) 19-20.

M. E. L. Mallowan, "Department of Western Asiatic Archaeology 1947-62: Retrospect," *ULBIA* 4 (1964) 157-164.

Dermont Ryan, "Fifth International Congress for Old Testament Study," *ITQ* 32 (1965) 352-361.

*Emmett L. Bennett [Jr.], "Fourth International Colloquium of Mycenaean Studies," *KZFE* 4 (1965) 169-170.

*Roland F. Willetts, "The Second International Cretological Congress," *KZFE* 5 (1966) 162-163.

*A. Bartoněk, "The Mycenaean Symposium of Brno 13th-14th April 1966," *KZFE* 5 (1966) 163-165.

*W[illiam] C. Brice, "The Fourth Edinburgh Minoan-Mycenaean Symposium," *KZFE* 5 (1966) 166-168.

F. F. Bruce, "The Society for Old Testament Study, 1917-1967," *ET* 78 (1966-67) 147-148.

*William C. Brice, "The First Conference of the British Association for Mycenaean Studies," *KZFE* 7 (1968) 178-179.

G. W. Anderson, "The Sixth International Congress for the Study of the Old Testament," *ET* 80 (1968-69) 8-11.

*Heinz Geiss, "The First International Congress of Cypriot Studies," *KZFE* 8 (1969) 162-164.

Takahito Mikasa, "Near Eastern Studies in Japan," *Orient* 5 (1969) 1-6.

§184 *2.5.7.3 Marine and Underwater Archaeology*

Byron Khun de Prorok, “The Sunken Treasure Galley of Mahdia Tunisia,” *A&A* 17 (1924) 54-57.

A. Merlin, “Submarine discoveries in the Mediterranean,” *Antiq* 4 (1930) 405-414.

S. Casson, “Submarine Research in Greece,” *Antiq* 13 (1939) 80-86.

Lionel S. Casson, “Sea-Digging,” *Arch* 6 (1953) 221-228.

Lionel [S.] Casson, “More Sea-Digging,” *Arch* 10 (1957) 248-257.

*G. Roger Edwards, “Hellenistic Pottery from the Antikythera Wreck,” *AJA* 64 (1960) 183-184.

George F. Bass, “A Bronze Age Shipwreck,” *Exped* 3 (1960-61) #2, 2-11.

George F. Bass, “Underwater Excavations at Cape Gelidonya (Turkey): A Bronze-Age Shipwreck,” *AJA* 65 (1961) 186.

Immanuel Ben-Dor, “A Marine Expedition to the Holy Land, Summer 1960,” *AJA* 65 (1961) 186.

George F. Bass, “The Cape Gelidonya Wreck: Preliminary Report,” *AJA* 65 (1961) 267-276.

George F. Bass and Peter Throckmorton, “Excavating a Bronze Age Shipwreck,” *Arch* 14 (1961) 78-87.

*Thomas Beran, Tahsin Özgüç, Hâmit Z. Koşay, G. M. A. Hanfmann, A. H. Detweiler, J. M. Cook, and Miss Joan du Plat Taylor, “Summary of Archaeological Research in Turkey in 1960,” *AS* 11 (1961) 15-27. [Underwater Expedition off Cape Gelidonya, pp. 26-27]

D. Barag, “A Survey of the Vessels Recovered from the Sea off the Coast of Israel,” *BIES* 25 (1961) #4, I.

*George F. Bass, “Report of the Underwater Excavation at Cape of Gelidonya,” *TAD* 11 (1961) #1, 7-9.

Peter Throckmorton and John M. Bullitt, “Underwater Surveys in Greece: 1962,” *Exped* 5 (1962-63) #2, 17-23.

Vladimir D. Blavatsky, "An Underwater Expedition to the Azov and Black Seas," *Arch* 16 (1963) 93-98.

*G. Roger Edwards, P. Neve, Tahsin Özgüç, E. Boehringer, R. Naumann,G. M. A. Hanfmann, U. Bahadır Alkım, and Nimet Özgüç, "Summary ofArchaeological Research in Turkey in 1962," *AS* 13 (1963) 19-28. [Underwater Excavations at Yassi Ada, pp. 26-27]

George F. Bass, "The Promise of Underwater Archaeology," *SIR* (1963) 461-471.

Peter Throckmorton, "Ships Wrecked in the Aegean Sea," *Arch* 17 (1964) 250-256.

*George F. Bass, "Underwater Excavations at Yassi Ada 1962-1963," *TAD* 13 (1964) #1, 41-51.

George F. Bass, "The Asherah: A Submarine for Archaeology," *Arch* 18 (1965) 7-14.

*John B. Ward-Perkins and Peter Throckmorton, "New Light on the Roman Marble Trade: The San Pietro Wreck," *Arch* 18 (1965) 201-209.

*P. Neve, Tahsin Özgüç, Nimet Özgüç, Baki Ögün, U. Bahadır Alkım, Jacques Bordaz, Winfried Orthmann, George Bass, Ian A. Todd, and D. H. French, "Recent Archaeological Research in Turkey," *AS* 15 (1965) 23-39. [Underwater Excavations at Yassi Ada, pp. 33-34]

Gladys D. Weinberg, Virginia G. Grace, G. Roger Edwards, Henry S. Robinson, Peter Throckmorton, and Elizabeth K. Ralph, "The Antikythera Shipwreck Reconsidered," *TAPS, N.S.*, 55 (1965) Part 3, 3-48.

Honor Frost, "The Arwad Plans 1964: A Photogrammetric Survey of Marine Installations," *AAAS* 16 (1966) #1, 13-28.

Anna M. McCann, "Maria SS. di Altomare: An Early Hellenistic Shipwreck near Taranto," *AJA* 70 (1966) 192.

E. T. Hall, "The Use of the Proton Magnetometer in Underwater Archaeology," *Archm* 9 (1966) 32-44.

*P. Neve, Tahsin Özgüç, Nimet Özgüç, Emin Bilgiç, U. Bahadır Alkım, Jacques Bordaz, R. Naumann, R. M. Harrison, Machteld Mellink, Kenan T. Erim, F. K. Dörner, G. M. A. Hanfmann, George F. Bass, Ian A. Todd, and D. H. French, "Recent Archaeological Research in Turkey," *AS* 16 (1966) 25-53. [Underwater Survey, pp. 42-43]

E. S. Ramage and R. L. Scranton, "Corinthian Kenchreai: Exploration and Salvage, 1966," *AJA* 71 (1967) 193.

Joseph W. Shaw, "Shallow-water Excavation at Kenchreai," *AJA* 71 (1967) 223-231.

Alfonso de Franciscis, "Underwater Discoveries Around the Bay of Naples," *Arch* 20 (1967) 209-216.

J. N. Green, E. T. Hall, and M. L. Katzen, "Survey of a Greek Shipwreck off Kyrenia, Cyprus," *Archm* 10 (1967) 47-56.

George F. Bass, "Cape Gelidonya: A Bronze Age Shipwreck," *TAPS, N.S.,* 57 (1967) Part 8, 3-177. [With the collaboration of Peter Throckmorton, Joan du Plat Taylor, J. B. Hennessy, Alan R. Shulman, and Hans-Günter Buchholz]

George F. Bass, "The Turkish Aegean: Proving Ground for Underwater Archaeology," *Exped* 10 (1967-68) #3, 3-10.

Michael Katzev and Susan Womer (Katzev), "The Search Below," *Exped* 10 (1967-68) #3, 11-14.

George F. Bass, "Underwater Operations in Turkey, 1965-1967," *AJA* 72 (1968) 161.

*Frank J. Frost, "Some Underwater Sites in the Peloponnesus," *AJA* 72 (1968) 165.

George F. Bass and Michael L. Katzev, "New Tools for Underwater Archaeology," *Arch* 21 (1968) 164-173.

Peter Throckmorton and Gerhard Kapitän, "An Ancient Shipwreck at Pantano Longarini," *Arch* 21 (1968) 182-187.

Michael L. Katzev, "Excavation of a Greek Shipwreck off Kyrenia, 1968," *AJA* 73 (1969) 238-239.

George F. Bass and Lawrence T. Joline, "Problems of Deep Wreck Identification," *Exped* 11 (1968-69) #1, 9-12.

Michael L. Katzen, "The Kyrenia Shipwreck," *Exped* 11 (1968-69) #2, 55-59.

Michael L. Katzen, "Kyrenia 1969: A Greek Ship is Raised," *Exped* 12 (1969-70) #4, 6-14.

§185 ***2.5.7.4 Preservation of Archaeological Antiquities***

A. Lane Fox, "Society for the Protection of Ancient Buildings," *JRAI* 7 (1877-78) 186.

S[elah] M[errill], "Destruction of Ancient Monuments," *AAOJ* 2 (1879-80) 169-170.

Selah Merrill, "Destruction of Ancient Monuments," *OBJ* 1 (1880) 14.

Robert Francis Harper, "The Destruction of Antiquities in the East," *AJSL* 6 (1889-90) 225-226.

*Lucien C. Warner, "A Recent Discovery in Egypt and the Care of Antiquities," *RP* 3 (1904) 116-117.

*W. M. F[linders] P[etrie], "The New Law in the Antiquties of Egypt," *AEE* 1 (1914) 128-129.

Howard Crosby Butler, "The Future Protection of Historical Monuments of Nearer Asia," *AJA* 23 (1919) 70.

*Anonymous, "Current Notes and News. Saving the Excavations at Corinth," *A&A* 9 (1920) 50-51.

*Warren R. Dawson, "The Necropolis of Ancient Thebes. A Rescue from Oblivion," *IAQR* 17 (1921) 181-184, 339-342.

A. Lucas, "Notes on the cleaning of certain objects in the Cairo Museum," *ASAE* 24 (1924) 15-16.

A. Lucas, "Methods used in cleaning ancient bronze and silver," *ASAE* 24 (1924) 186.

*A. Lucas, "Damage caused by Salt at Karnak," *ASAE* 25 (1925) 47-54.

*Anonymous, "Notes and Comments. Patching Up the Sphinx," *A&A* 22 (1926) 194.

*A. Kenneth Graham, "Scientific Notes on the Finds from Ur," *MJ* 20 (1929) 246-257. [I. Restoration of the Silver; II. Metallurgical Notes; III. The Cosmetics of Queen Shubad (Note by the editor, pp. 255-257)]

Anonymous, "Notes and Comments. Worth-While Restoration," *A&A* 32 (1931) 43-44.

M. R. W., "The Cleaning and Restoration of Ancient Bronzes," *UMB* 4 (1932-33) 110-114.

H. I. Bell, "Note on the Treatment and Preservation of Ostraca from Egypt," *CdÉ* 10 (1935) 133-137.

A. Lucas, "The cleaning of the statue," *ASAE* 39 (1939) 333-334.

*O. H. Myers, "Note on the Treatment of a Bronze Weight," *JEA* 25 (1939) 102-103.

Zaky Iskander Hanna*[sic]*, "Cleaning, preservation and restoration of the silver coffin and cartonnage of Shashanq," *ASAE* 40 (1940-41) 581-588.

Abdel Salam Moḥamed Ḥussein, "The reparation of the Mastaba of Meḥu at Saqqara (1940)," *ASAE* 42 (1943) 417-425.

Mason Hammond, "From Syracuse to Berlin," *AJA* 50 (1946) 290-292.

Ahmed Youssef Moustafa, "Reparation and restoration of antiquities," *ASAE* 47 (1947) 77-95.

Ahmed Youssef, "Reparations of ancient tombs. Descripton of a method of treating a dangerous case at Thebes," *ASAE* 48 (1948) 513-516.

Osman R. Rostem, "The scheme planned by the late Abdel Salam Mohammed Husein for the protection of the monuments of Seti I at Abydos," *ASAE* 50 (1950) 65-71.

Ralph S. Solecki, "A Program For Salvage Archaeology in the Protected Flood Basins of Iraq," *Sumer* 9 (1953) 101-105.

Zaky Iskander, "Description of a method of treating a dangerous case at Thebes," *ASAE* 54 (1956-57) 39-42.

*Ahmed Youssef Moustafa, "Reparation and restoration of antiques. The golden belt of Prince Ptah-Shepses," *ASAE* 54 (1956-57) 149-151.

A. E. A. Werner, "Technical Notes on a New Material in Conservation," *CdÉ* 33 (1958) 273-278. [1. The Desalting of Ostraka; 2. The Reattachment of Flaking Paint]

Jean Vercoutter, "Sudan Archaeology Endangered—an S. O. S.," *Arch* 12 (1959) 206-208.

Froelich Rainey, "Archaeological Salvage in Egypt: An Example of International Cooperation," *Exped* 2 (1959-60) #4, 2-3. *(Editorial)*

H. J. Plenderleith, "Reminiscences from the Laboratories," *Iraq* 22 (1960) 20-22.

*D. Thomas-Goorieckx and R. Lefève, "Examination and Treatment of a Bronze Dagger with Ivory Hilt (± 1800 B.C.); property of the Khartoum Museum no. 1228; length 56 cm (Plates XXXV-XXXVII)," *Kush* 8 (1960) 266-267.

*Žbyněk Žába, "Ancient Nubia Calls for Help," *NOP* 1 (1960) #3, 6-9.

Anonymous, "The Land of the Nile: An Attempt to Save the Treasures of Nubia," *AT* 5 (1960-61) #1, 2-3.

Rhys Carpenter, "On Restoring the Pediment of the Parthenon," *AJA* 66 (1962) 265-268.

Jeffrey Orchard, "Recent Restoration Work in Iraq," *Iraq* 24 (1962) 73-77.

Zaky Iskander, "Bees in the Temple of Edfu and their Control," *ASAE* 58 (1964) 187-196.

F[riedrich] Hinkel, "Report on the Dismantling and Removal of Endangered Monuments in Sudanese Nubia, 1962-63," *Kush* 12 (1964) 111-118.

Seymour Howard, "Pulling Herakles' Leg," *AJA* 69 (1965) 170.

Friedrich Hinkel, "Progress Report on the Dismantling and Removal of Endangered Monuments in Sudanese Nubia from August 1963 to August 1964," *Kush* 13 (1965) 96-101. *(Trans by A. J. Mills)*

Kyle Meredith Phillilps Jr., "Archaeological Flood Damage," *AJA* 71 (1967) 113.

Friedrich Hinkel, "Progress Report on the Removal of Endangered Monuments from Sudanese Nubia," *Kush* 15 (1967-68) 79-83.

Geoffrey Pearce, "The Conservation of Wall Paintings in Tomb 35 at Dra Abu el-Naga," *Exped* 11 (1968-69) #3, 38-43.

*İrem Acaroğlu, "The Keban Project; Salvage Archaeology in Turkey," *Arch* 22 (1969) 319-320.

§186 *2.5.8 Architecture - General Studies (includes building "Hardware") [For "City Planning" see: Urban Studies §75 ←]*

J[oseph] H[ager], "General Observations on the Persepolitan Characters, with a Description and Representation of some bricks lately sent to Europe from the Site of Antient[sic]* Babylon," *MMBR* 12 (1801) 2-6.

†Anonymous, "Restoration of the Parthenon," *ERCJ* 38 (1823) 126-144. *(Review)*

†Anonymous, "Grecian, Gothic, and Egyptian Architecture," *WR* 8 (1827) 31-70. *(Review)*

*Anonymous, "Art and Architecture," *DUM* 33 (1849) 151-168.

†Anonymous, "Athenian Architecture," *ERCJ* 95 (1852) 359-405. *(Review)*

P. S., "Did the Jews Use Glass-Windows?" *JSL, 3rd Ser.,* 7 (1858) 59-69.

Anonymous, "History of Architecture," *QRL* 120 (1866) 425-461. *(Review)*

Claude R. Conder, "Notes on Masonry," *PEFQS* 8 (1876) 197-199.

Claude R. Conder, "Notes on Architecture in Palestine," *PEFQS* 10 (1878) 29-40. [I. Jewish Architecture, pp. 29-31]

Stephen D. Peet, "Ancient Temple Architecture," *AAOJ* 4 (1881-82) 89-100.

Stephen D. Peet, "The Origin of the Architectural Orders: Comparison between the Historic and Prehistoric Works of the Eastern and Western Hemispheres," *AAOJ* 4 (1881-82) 303-322.

*Thomas W. Ludlow, "The Athenian Naval Arsenal of Philon," *AJP* 3 (1882) 317-328.

C[laude] R. Conder, "Mason's Marks," *PEFQS* 15 (1883) 130-133.

*S[amuel] Birch, "On a Tablet in the British Museum relating to two Architects," *SBAT* 8 (1883-84) 143-163.

†Anonymous, "Mr. Furgusson's *Parthenon and Temple of Diana,*" *QRL* 158 (1884) 184-211. *(Review)*

Arthur Richmond Marsh, "Ancient crude-brick construction and its influence on the Doric Style," *AJA, O.S.,* 1 (1885) 46-53.

A. C. Merriam, "Ancient Tunnels," *PAPA* 17 (1885) li. *[Published in full in the* School of Mines Quarterly, *New York, 1885]*

Joseph T. Clarke, "A proto-Ionic capital from the site of Neandreia," *AJA, O.S.,* 2 (1886) 1-20, 136-148.

Joseph T. Clarke, "A Doric shaft and base found at Assos," *AJA, O.S.,* 2 (1886) 267-285.

*J. Leslie Porter, "On the Connexion Between Jewish, Phoenician, and Early Greek Art and Architecture," *JTVI* 21 (1886-87) 23-41, 51-52. (Discussion, pp. 41-50)

William Simpson, "Stone Doors I," *PEFQS* 18 (1886) 142-144.

A. G. Weld, "II. The Stone Doors of Tiberias," *PEFQS* 18 (1886) 144.

*J. Leslie Porter, "On the Connexion Between Jewish, Phoenician, and Early Greek Art and Architecture," *JTVI* 21 (1886-87) 23-41, 51-52. (Discussion, pp. 41-50)

*A. L. Frothingham Jr., "A Proto-Ionic Capital, and Bird Worship, Represented on an Oriental Seal," *AJA, O.S.,* 3 (1887) 57-61.

W[illiam] H. Goodyear, "Egyptian Origin of the Ionic Capital and of the Anthemion," *AJA, O.S.,* 3 (1887) 271-302.

S. B. P. Trowbridge, "Archaic Ionic Capitals Found on the Akropolis," *AJA, O.S.,* 4 (1888) 22-27.

Allan Marquand, "Early Athenian Ionic Capitals Found on the Akropolis," *AJA, O.S.,* 4 (1888) 42-44.

*Carl D. Buck, "Discoveries in the Deme of Ikaria, 1888," *AJA, O.S.,* 5 (1889) 135-181. [VI. Architectural Remains, pp. 165-181]

Allan Marquand, "Reminiscences of Egypt in Doric Architecture," *AJA, O.S.*, 6 (1890) 47-58.

*George B. Hussey, "Greek Sculptures Crowns and Crown Inscriptions," *AJA, O.S.*, 6 (1890) 69-95.

*John C. Rolfe, "Discoveries at Anthedon in 1889," *AJA, O.S.*, 6 (1890) 96-107. [III. Architectural Discoveies at Anthedon, pp. 101-104]

Allan Marquand, "Reminiscences of Egypt in Doric architecture," *JAOS* 14 (1890) cxlvii-cxlviii.

C[laude] R. Conder, "Notes on the *Quarterly Statement*, July, 1890. *Drafted Masonry*," *PEFQS* 22 (1890) 329.

*J. William Dawson, "Notes on Useful and Ornamental Stones of Ancient Egypt," *JTVI* 26 (1892-93) 265-282. (Discussion, pp. 282-288) [1. Granitic, Dioritic, and Gneissic Rocks; 2 Basalt with Olivine; 3. The Nubian Sandstone; 4. Limestone, &c.; 5. Miocene Quartzite of Jebel Ahmar, &c.; 6. Various Stones and Gems; 7. Flint Flakes, Knives, Saws, &c.]

*C[onrad] Schick, "Letters from Baurath C. Schick," *PEFQS* 24 (1892) 24-25. [Chisel Marks in the Cotton Grotto at Jerusalem, pp. 24-25]

*W. M. Flinders Petrie, "Note on the Chisel Marks on Rock Described by Herr Schick," *PEFQS* 24 (1892) 26-27.

*J. Norman Lockyer, "The Early Temple and Pyramid Builders," *SIR* (1893) 95-105.

*Rufus B. Richardson, "Papers of the American School of Classical Studies at Athens. Stamped Tiles from the Argive Heræum," *AJA, O.S.*, 9 (1894) 340-350.

*Allan Marquand, "A Study of Greek Architectural Proportions. The Temples of Selinous," *AJA, O.S.*, 9 (1894) 521-532.

*W[illia]m Henry Goodyear, "A Discovery of Horizontal Curves in the Roman Temple Called 'Maison Carrée' at Nimes," *AJA, O.S.*, 10 (1895) 1-12.

John P. Peters, "University of Pennsylvania Excavations at Nippur. II. The Nippur Arch," *AJA, O.S.*, 10 (1895) 347-351.

*Anna Louis Perry, "Papers of the American School of Classical Studies at Athens. The Dimensions of the Athena Parthenos," *AJA, O.S.,* 11 (1896) 335-346. [Note by Alfred Emerson, pp. 346-349]

*Rufus B. Richardson, "Notes. Notes from Corinth," *AJA, O.S.,*11 (1896) 371-372. [Statuary and Architectural Members, p. 372]

John Bellows, "Chisel-Drafted Stones at Jerusalem," *PEFQS* 28 (1896) 219-223.

*C[onrad] Schick, "Reports and Papers by Dr. Conrad Schick," *PEFQS* 29 (1897) 103-122. (Notes by C. R. Conder, p. 211) [V. The Stone "Hat-Toîm", pp. 113-114]

Hormuzd Rassam, "Door Lintel discovered by Mr. George Smith at Kouyunjik," *SBAP* 20 (1898) 52.

C[onrad] Schick, "Reports by Dr. Conrad Schick. 1. *A Stone Pillar, partly quarried,*" *PEFQS* 31 (1899) 213.

E. Towry Whyte, "Note on an Egyptian Bolt," *SBAP* 21 (1899) 286.

Harold North Fowler, "The Connexion of Phidias with Pericles and his Buildings," *AJA* 5 (1901) 9.

A. L. Frothingham Jr., "Did the Triumphal Arch originate with the Romans or the Greeks?" *AJA* 5 (1901) 27-28.

*Howard Crosby Butler, "The Roman Aqueducts as Monuments of Architecture," *AJA* 5 (1901) 175-200.

Luigi Savignoni, "Fragments of Cretan Pithoi," *AJA* 5 (1901) 404-417.

T. W. Heermance, "The Reciprocal Influence of the Doric and Ionic Styles in Greek Architecture," *AJA* 6 (1902) 25.

Stephen D. Peet, "Architectural Styles in the Old and the New World," *AAOJ* 25 (1903) 343-359.

Joseph Offord, "Caryatide Architectural Figures," *AAOJ* 25 (1903) 359-361.

Chalres H. Weller, "The Pre-Periclean Propylon of the Acropolis at Athens," *AJA* 7 (1903) 93-94.

Edward L. Tilton, "A Greek Door of Stone at the Argive Heraeum," *AJA* 7 (1903) 94-95.

Clarence S. Fisher, "The Architecture of Nippur," *RP* 2 (1903) 99-118.

Robert Francis Harper, "The Evolution of the Babylonian Brick," *BW* 24 (1904) 218-223.

R. Sewell, "Tiles from Mycenae, with the Cartouche of Amenhetep III," *SBAP* 26 (1904) 258-259.

F. B. Tarbell, "Notes on the Ceiling of the Greek Temple-Cella," *AJA* 9 (1905) 87.

Allan Marquand, "The Facade of the Temple of Apollo, Near Miletus," *RP* 4 (1905) 1-15.

*G. Legrain, "The King Samou or Seshemou and the Enclosures of El-Kab," *SBAP* 27 (1905) 106-111.

William H. Goodyear, "The Discovery, by Professor Gustavo Giovannnoi, of Curves in the Plan, Concave to the Exterior, in the Façade of the Temple at Cori," *AJA* 11 (1907) 52-54.

*James H. Breasted, "The Temple of Soleb, A New Form of Egyptian Architecture," *AJA* 13 (1909) 53-54.

Anonymous, "Origin of the Ionic Capital," *RP* 8 (1909) 59.

Anonymous, "Origin of the Ionic Frieze," *RP* 8 (1909) 215.

John L. Myres, "Herodotus and the Egyptian Labyrinth," *AAA* 3 (1910) 134-136.

*F. B. Tarbell, "Architecture on Attic Vases," *AJA* 14 (1910) 428-433.

Anonymous, "Ancient Roman Concrete," *RP* 9 (1910) 58.

*Christopher Johnston, "Assyrian Lexicographical Notes," *AJSL* 27 (1910-11) 187-189. [*d*) tikpu 'row, course of stone, or brick,' pp. 188-189]

*P. P. Flournoy, "Ahab's Palace and Jezebel's Table," *USR* 23 (1911-12) 130-134.

*William Bell Dinsmoor, "Attic Building Accounts," *AJA* 17 (1913) 53-80, 242-265, 371-398; 25 (1921) 118-129, 233-247.

Archibald C. Dickie, "The Jews as Builders," *JMUEOS* #3 (1913-14) 57-65.

Eugene P. Andrews, "Archaeological Notes," *AJA* 18 (1914) 76. *[Blocks and pins]*

Margaret C. Waites, "The Etruscan and Roman House," *AJA* 18 (1914) 77-78.

John Shapley, "The Human Figure as an Architectural Support," *A&A* 2 (1915) 1-9.

C. G. Seligman, "An Undescribed Type of Building in the Eastern Province of the Anglo-Egyptian Sudan," *JEA* 2 (1915) 178-183.

*Howard Carter and Alan H. Gardiner, "The Tomb of Ramesses IV and the Turin Plan of a Royal Tomb," *JEA* 4 (1916) 130-158.

N. de Garis Davies, "An Architect's Plan from Thebes," *JEA* 4 (1916) 194-199.

N. de Garis Davies, "An Architectural Sketch at Sheikh Said," *AEE* 4 (1917) 21-25.

Leichester B. Holland, "The Origin of the Doric Entablature," *AJA* 21 (1917) 117-158.

Stephen Bleecker Luce Jr.*[sic]* and Leicester Bodine Holland, "An Etruscan Openwork Grill in the University Museum, Philadelphia," *AJA* 21 (1917) 296-307.

Albert W. Barker, "The Subjective Factor in Greek Architecture," *AJA* 22 (1918) 1-24.

Stephen B[leecker] Luce, "A Group of Etruscan Antefixes from Cerverti," *AJA* 22 (1918) 65.

W. R. Lethaby, "Note on Bases in the Form of an Ionic Capital," *AJA* 22 (1918) 340.

Stephen Bleecker Luce and Leicester Bodine Holland, "Terracotta Revetments from Etruria in the University Museum, Philadelphia," *AJA* 22 (1918) 319-339.

Oliver M. Washburn, "Iphigenia Taurica 113 as a Document in the History of Architecture," *AJA* 22 (1918) 434-437.

Oliver M. Washburn, "The Origin of the Triglyph Frieze," *AJA* 23 (1919) 33-49.

E. Douglas Van Buren, "Terracotta Revetments from Etruria," *AJA* 23 (1919) 157-160.

Stephen Bleecker Luce, "Note on Etruscan Architectural Terracottas," *AJA* 23 (1919) 161-162.

H. F. Lutz, "The oldest monumental evidence of a dome-structure," *JAOS* 39 (1919) 122.

Joseph Offord, "Plan of a Migdol," *PEFQS* 51 (1919) 175-177.

Stephen Bleecker Luce, "Archaic Antefixes from Cerverti in the University Museum, Philadelphia, Pa.," *AJA* 24 (1920) 27-36.

Leicester B. Holland, "Primitive Aegean Roofs," *AJA* 24 (1920) 323-341.

Stephen Bleecker Luce, "Etruscan Shell-Antefixes in the University Museum, Philadelphia," *AJA* 24 (1920) 352-369.

David M. Robinson, "Etruscan and Later Terra-cotta Antefixes at John Hopkins University," *AJA* 25 (1921) 79-80.

Charles Heald Weller, "The Original Plan of the Erechtheum," *AJA* 25 (1921) 130-141.

*Stephen Bleecker Luce, "A Group of Terra-cottas from Corneto," *AJA* 25 (1921) 266-278.

*Ernest Mackay, "The Cutting and Preparation of Tomb-Chapels in the Theban Necropolis," *JEA* 7 (1921) 154-168.

William Bell Dinsmoor, "Structural Iron in Greek Architecture," *AJA* 26 (1922) 148-158.

Dudley S. Corett, "The Magic Art of Egypt," *A&A* 15 (1923) 155-166.

William Bell Dinsmoor, "A Note on the New Bases at Athens," *AJA* 27 (1923) 23-24.

R. Engelbach, "The Supports of the Pylon Flagstaves," *AEE* 8 (1923) 71-74.

David M. Robinson, "Etruscan-Campanian Antefixes and Other Terra-cottas from Italy at the Johns Hopkins University," *AJA* 27 (1923) 1-22.

William Bell Dinsmoor, "The Aeolic Capitals of Delphi," *AJA* 27 (1923) 164-173.

*W[alter] R. Agard, "The Date of the Metopes of the Athenian Treasury at Delphi," *AJA* 27 (1923) 174-183.

*Walter R. Agard, "The Metopes of the Athenian Treasury as Works of Art," *AJA* 27 (1923) 322-333.

David M. Robinson, "An Addendum to the Article on Antefixes and Other Terra-cottas, A.J.A. XXVII, 1923, pp. 1ff.," *AJA* 27 (1923) 340.

George A. Barton, "The Form and Nature of E-PA at Lagash," *JAOS* 43 (1923) 92-95.

*Theophile James Meek, "Babyloniaca," *JAOS* 43 (1923) 353-357. [Names of Parts of the Doorway, pp. 354-357]

*R. Engelbach, "Origin of the Great Hypostyle Hall at Karnak," *AEE* 9 (1924) 65-71.

*G. A. Wainwright, "Wooden door and stool from Kom Washim," *ASAE* 25 (1925) 105-111.

Harriet Boyd Hawes, "The Parthenon Pediments *and* The Original Plan of the Erechtheum," *AJA* 28 (1924) 74-75.

Leon Legrain, "Two Door Sockets of the Kings of Ur," *MJ* 15 (1924) 77-79.

Anonymous, "The Builders' Art at Ur," *MJ* 16 (1925) 217-306.

*J. Walter Johnshoy, "Studies in Biblical Archaeology," *TTM* 9 (1925-26) 116-135. [*Cities and Houses,* pp. 130-135]

*[W. M.] Flinders Petrie, "Egyptian Working Papyrus," *AEE* 11 (1926) 24-27. *[Blueprint]*

*R. W. Sloley, "An Ancient Surveying Instrument," *AEE* 11 (1926) 65-67.

*Andrew Fossum, "Harmony in the Theatre at Epidauros," *AJA* 30 (1926) 70-75.

William Bell Dinsmoor, "The Sculptured Parapet of Athena Nike," *AJA* 30 (1926) 1-31.

Rhys Carpenter, "Vitruvius and the Ionic Order," *AJA* 30 (1926) 259-269.

*Battiscombe Gunn, "Inscriptions from the Step Pyramid site," *ASAE* 26 (1926) 177-202. [II. An Architect's Diagram of the Third Dynasty, pp. 107-202]

*William Hovgaard, "The Arsenal in Piraeus and the Ancient Building Rules," *Isis* 8 (1926) 12-20.

Raymond P. Dougherty, "Survivals of Sumerian Types of Architecture," *AJA* 31 (1927) 153-159.

R. Engelbach, "An Architect's project from Thebes," *ASAE* 27 (1927) 72-75.

Karl P. Harrington, "Occident and Orient in Architectural Ornament," *AJA* 32 (1928) 58.

*R. Engelbach, "An experiment on the accuracy of shaping of a monolithic column of circular section of the Vth dynasty from Abusîr," *ASAE* 28 (1928) 144-152.

Campbell Bonner, "A Dionysiac Miracle at Corinth," *AJA* 33 (1929) 368-375.

*Rhys Carpenter, "The Sculptural Composition of the Nike Parapet," *AJA* 33 (1929) 467-483.

J.-P. Lauer, "The Discovery in Egypt of a New Architecture," *A&A* 30 (1930) 177.

O. E. Ravn, "Some Disputed Points in Babylonian Sacred Architecture," *AA* 1 (1930) 87-97.

*[W. M.] Flinders Petrie, "The Building of a Pyramid," *AEE* 15 (1930) 33-39.

Philip H. Davis, "The Foundations of the Philonian Portico at Eleusis," *AJA* 34 (1930) 1-19.

S. R. K. Glanville, "Working Plan for a Shrine," *JEA* 16 (1930) 237-239.

*R. Engelbach, "Recent Acquisitions in the Cairo Museum," *ASAE* 31 (1931) 126-131. [IV. Four Models of Græco-Roman Buildings, pp. 129-131]

J. Garrow Duncan, "The Painted Houses at Teleilat Ghassul," *AEE* 17 (1932) 65-67.

Anonymous, "A Model of a Roman Town House," *UMB* 4 (1932-33) 139-140.

*Alfred Westholm, "The Paphian Temple of Aphrodite and its Relation to Oriental Architecture," *AA* 4 (1933) 201-236.

Naphtali Lewis, "New Light on the Greek House from the Zenon Papyri," *AJA* 37 (1933) 397-399.

William Bell Dinsmoor, "The Nike Parapet Once More," *AJA* 34 (1933) 281-295.

Seton Lloyd, "Model of a Tell el-ʿAmarnah House," *JEA* 19 (1933) 1-7.

*S[tephen] Langdon, "Notes on Sumerian Etymology and Syntax," *JRAS* (1933) 857-866. [II. É-SAL *(áma, ame, âm)* = mašaku *(chamber, room sanctuary)*, pp. 857-585]

P. J. Riis, "The Etruscan City Gates in Perugia," *AA* 5 (1934) 65-98.

*L. B. Holland and Philip Davis, "The Porch-Ceiling of the Temple of Apollo on Delos," *AJA* 38 (1934) 71-80.

William B. Dinsmoor, "The Repair of the Athena Parthenos: A Story of Five Dowels," *AJA* 38 (1934) 93-106.

Leicester B. Holland, "Uncoffered Ceilings," *AJA* 38 (1934) 190.

Gorham P. Stevens, "Concerning the Curvature of the Steps of the Parthenon," *AJA* 38 (1934) 533-542.

*C. H. Kraeling, "The Earliest Synagogue Architecture," *BASOR* #54 (1934) 18-20.

E[phraim] A. Speiser, "A Rare Brick of Sennacherib," *BASOR* #55 (1934) 22-23.

R. Campbell Thompson, "The Buildings on Quyunjiq, the Larger Mound of Nineveh," *Iraq* 1 (1934) 95-104.

Axel Boëthius, "Remarks on the Developments of Domestic Architecture in Rome," *AJA* 38 (1934) 158-170.

*G. I. Bell, "Archaeology and Architecture," *Iraq* 1 (1934) 1.

S. Yeivin, "The Masonry of the Early Bronze People," *PEFQS* 66 (1934) 189-191.

B[attiscombe] G[unn], "An Early Egyptian Door-Socket," *UMB* 5 (1934-35) 9-13.

Anonymous, "Houses of the Past," *UMB* 5 (1934-35) #6, 84-85. *[House of an Egyptian Nobleman of 1400 B.C.]*

Ernst Diez, "The African Root of Roman Building," *AJA* 39 (1935) 112.

*George W. Elderkin, "Architectural Detail in Antique Sepulchral Art," *AJA* 39 (1935) 518-525.

P. J. Riis, "Greek and Roman Architectural Fragments in the Danish National Museum," *AA* 7 (1936) 229-243.

Leicester B. Holland, "Gongylos Lithos," *AJA* 40 (1936) 120.

*Philip H. Davis, "Delian Building Contracts," *AJA* 40 (1936) 122.

C. C. McCown, "A Rock Cutting from Beit Ras in Transjordan," *BASOR* #64 (1936) 21-23.

S. A. S. Husseini, "An Unfinished Monolith Column in Maḥneh Yehūdah Quarter, Jerusalem," *QDAP* 5 (1936) 1-2.

*Gordon Loud, "An Architectural Formula for Assyrian Planning Based on the Results of Excavations at Khorsabad," *RAAO* 33 (1936) 153-160.

Valentin Müller, "Studies in Oriental Archaeology. I. Plano-convex Bricks," *JAOS* 57 (1937) 84-87.

*W. F. J. Knight, "The Sumerian Provenience of Greek Defensive Sanctity," *PAPA* 68 (1937) xxxiv-xxxv.

J. Penrose Harland, "Helladic Bothroi," *AJA* 42 (1938) 121.

*Walter B. Emery, "A preliminary report on the architecture of the tomb of Nebetka," *ASAE* 38 (1938) 455-468.

Robert Scranton, "The Walls of the Peiraeus," *AJA* 43 (1939) 301-302.

Philip H. Davis and Leicester B. Holland, "The Coffering of the Erechtheion," *AJA* 43 (1939) 303-304.

Jotham Johnson, "Apotropaic Serpents in Minturnae Temple Decoration," *AJA* 43 (1939) 306.

Axel Boëthius, "Vitruvius and Roman Architecture," *AJA* 43 (1939) 307.

Lucy T. Shoe, "Western Greek Architectural Mouldings," *AJA* 44 (1940) 112.

Inez Scott Ryberg, "The Date of a Terracotta Pediment from the Caelian Hill," *AJA* 44 (1940) 114.

Socrates M. Eliopoulos, "The Ramp of the Temple of Askelpios at Epidauros," *AJA* 44 (1940) 222-224.

Valentin Müller, "Types of Mesopotamian Houses. Studies in Oriental Archaeology III," *JAOS* 60 (1940) 151-180.

*J. W. Jack, "Recent Biblical Archaeology," *ET* 52 (1940-41) 112-115. [Windows, Doors, Locks, pp. 112-113]

P. J. Riis, "Notes on Etruscan Architectural Terracottas," *AA* 12 (1941) 66-78.

*Clark Hopkins, "The Architectural Background in the Paintings at Dura-Europos," *AJA* 45 (1941) 18-29.

Neilson C. Debevoise, "The Origin of the Decorative Stucco," *AJA* 45 (1941) 45-61.

Agnes K. Lake, "A Note on the Pediment of the 'Tuscan Temple'," *AJA* 45 (1941) 71-72.

*W[illiam] F[oxwell] Albright, "Two Unpublished Phoenician 'Thymiateria' and the Temple of Solomon," *AJA* 45 (1941) 87.

*J. Penrose Harland, "Helladika," *AJA* 45 (1941) 91. *[Roof]*

Alva Elford, "Helladic Terracotta Roof Tiles," *AJA* 45 (1941) 95.

Isabelle Kelly, "The Ionic Treatment of Some Early Doric Capitals," *AJA* 45 (1941) 95-96.

William Bell Dinsmoor, "An Archaeological Earthquake at Olympia," *AJA* 45 (1941) 399-427.

H[enri] Frankfort, "The Origin of Monumental Arichitecture in Egypt," *AJSL* 58 (1941) 329-358.

Sidney Smith, "Timber and Brick or Masonry Construction," *PEQ* 73 (1941) 5-13. [Note Additionalle (French Text, pp 11-13) (Addendum by C. F.-A. Schaeffer, pp. 13-17)]

E. Baldwin Smith, "The Megaron and Its Roof," *AJA* 46 (1942) 99-118.

Bluma L. Trell, "Contribution to Anatolian Temple Architecture," *AJA* 46 (1942) 120.

William Bell Dinsmoor, "Notes on Megaron Roofs," *AJA* 46 (1942) 370-372.

*Donald F. Brown, "The Arcuated Lintel and Its Symbolic Interpretation in Late Antique Art," *AJA* 46 (1942) 389-399.

A. H. Detweiler, "Some Early Jewish Architectural Vestiges from Jerash," *BASOR* #87 (1942) 10-17.

*F. P. Johnson, "Three Notes on Bassai," *AJA* 47 (1943) 15-18.

*William Bell Dinsmoor, "A Further Note on Bassai," *AJA* 47 (1943) 19-21.

*George M. A. Hanfmann, "The Evidence of Architecture and Sculpture," *AJA* 47 (1943) 94-100. *[Etruscan]*

*Leroy Waterman, "The Damaged 'Blueprints' of the Temple of Solomon," *JNES* 2 (1943) 284-294.

P. J. Riis, "Three Aeginetan Fragments in the Danish National Museum," *AA* 15 (1944) 98-99.

Valentin Müller, "Development of the 'Megaron' in Prehistoric Greece," *AJA* 48 (1944) 342-348.

Carl W. Blegen, "The Roof of the Mycenaean Megaron," *AJA* 49 (1945) 35-44.

C. C. McCown, "The Long-Room House at Tell en-Naṣbeh," *BASOR* #98 (1945) 2-15.

Robert L. Scranton, "Interior Design of Greek Temples," *AJA* 50 (1946) 39-51 [Erratum, p. 283]

M. Kon, "The Stone Capitals from Ramat Rahel," *BIES* 13 (1946-47) #3/4, II.

Roar Hauglid, "The Greek Acanthus. Problems of Origin," *AA* 18 (1947) 93-116.

*N. Avigad, "Architectural Observations on some Rock-cut Tombs," *PEQ* 79 (1947) 112-122.

William A. McDonald, "Types of Greek Civic Architecture—The Prytaneion," *AJA* 52 (1948) 374-375.

*Alex Boëthius, "Ancient Town Architecture and the New Material from Olynthus," *AJP* 69 (1948) 396-407.

*L. R. Palmer, "The Homeric and the Indo-European House," *TPS* (1948) 92-120.

Lucy T. Shoe, "Architectural mouldings of Dura-Europos," *Bery* 9 (1948-49) 1-40.

Franklin P. Johnson, "A Note on Egyptian Masonry," *AJA* 53 (1949) 34-35.

Oscar Broneer, "Measurements and Refinements of the South Stoa at Corinth," *AJA* 53 (1949) 146-147.

*A. Leo Oppenheim, "Akk. *arad ekalli* = 'Builder'," *ArOr* 17 (1949), Part 2, 227-235.

Osman R. Rostem, "Observations on the architecture of the Pyramid age," *ASAE* 49 (1949) 223-231.

I. E. S. Edwards, "Some Early Dynastic Contributions to Egyptian Architecture," *JEA* 35 (1949) 123-128.

*Louise Adams Holland, "Forerunners and Rivals of the Primitive Roman Bridge," *TAPA* 80 (1949) 281-319.

William Tongue, "The Brick-Stamps of Cosa," *AJA* 54 (1950) 263.

Leicester B. Holland, "The Katastegasma of the Walls of Athens," *AJA* 54 (1950) 337-356.

*Charles F. Nims, "Bricks Without Straw?" *BA* 13 (1950) 22-28.

*Robert L. Scranton, "Greek Arts in Greek Defense," *Arch* 3 (1950) 4-11.

*Francis W. Schehl, "The Date of Hermogenes the Architect," *AJA* 55 (1951) 152.

Oscar Broneer, "Odeion and Skene," *AJA* 56 (1952) 172.

L. T. Shoe, "Etruscan and Republican Roman Architectural Mouldings," *AJA* 56 (1952) 177.

*S. S. Weinberg, "Kourion-Bamboula: The Late Bronze Age Architecture," *AJA* 56 (1952) 178.

*E. Douglas Van Buren, "The Building of a Temple-tower," *RAAO* 46 (1952) 65-74.

B. Sapir, "Door-Panel with a Menorah from 'Ibellin in Galilee," *BIES* 17 (1952-53) #3/4, VII.

Kristian Jeppesen, "The Pedimental Compositions of the Parthenon. A Critical Survey," *AA* 24 (1953) 103-125.

Carla Gottlieb, "The East Wall in Temple A at Prinias," *AJA* 57 (1953) 106-107.

J. Walter Graham, "Comments on the 'House of Many Colors' at Olynthus," *AJA* 57 (1953) 107.

*R. D. Barnett, "The Phrygian Rock Façades and the Hittite Monuments," *BO* 10 (1953) 72-82.

*Elizabeth Thomas, "Air channels in the Great Pyramid," *JEA* 39 (1953) 113.

H. G. Quaritch Wales, "The Sacred Mountain of the Old Asiatic Religion," *JRAS* (1953) 23-30. [Mesopotamian Ziggurats, pp. 23-25]

Emeline Hill Richardson, "Some Observations on Roman Fortifications and Architecture in Spain," *AJA* 58 (1954) 148.

Oscar Broneer, "An Ancient Monument of World Unity: The South Stoa at Corinth," *Arch* 7 (1954) 74-81.

Homer A. Thompson, "Rebuilding the Stoa of Attalos *Progress Report: Spring 1954,*" *Arch* 7 (1954) 180-182.

Kr[istian] Jeppesen, "The Architect in Antiquity," *Kuml* (1954) 90-91.

*J. Gwyn Griffiths, "Three notes on Herodotus, Book II," *ASAE* 53 (1955) 139-152. [3. The Tools of the Pyramid-Builders, pp. 149-152]

John H. Young, "Ancient Towers on the Island of Siphnos," *AJA* 60 (1956) 51-55.

J. W. Graham, "The Phaistos 'Piano Nobile'," *AJA* 60 (1956) 151-157.

*Carla Bottlieb, "Restoration of the Epistyle from the Nereid Monument now in the British Museum," *AJA* 60 (1956) 177-178.

A. Rabitschek, "The Gates in the Agora," *AJA* 60 (1956) 279-282.

J. L. Benson, "Spirally Fluted Columns in Cyprus," *AJA* 60 (1956) 385-387.

Oscar Broneer, "An Archaeological Enigma," *Arch* 9 (1956) 134-137.

*Dows Dunham, "Building an Egyptian Pyramid," *Arch* 9 (1956) 157-165.

Oscar Broneer, "The Enigma Explained," *Arch* 9 (1956) 268-272.

Alexander Badawy, "The Ideology of the Superstructure of the Mastaba-Tomb in Egypt," *JNES* 15 (1956) 180-183.

Alexandre[sic]* Badawy, "Philological evidence about methods of construction in ancient Egypt," *ASAE* 54 (1956-57) 51-74.

Rhys Carpenter, "Houses Built of Salt," *AJA* 61 (1957) 176-177.

Carla Gottlieb, "Further to the 'Nereid' Monument," *AJA* 61 (1957) 183.

Machteld Mellink, "Gordion 1956: Lydian Architecture on the Lesser Mound," *AJA* 61 (1957) 184.

Jean-Phillippe Lauer, "Rebuilding Imhotep's Masterpiece," *Arch* 10 (1957) 274-279.

A. Trevor Hodge, "Slot Ceilings," *AJA* 62 (1958) 223.

Gus W. Van Beek, "Marginally Drafted, Pecked Masonry in the Ancient Near East," *AJA* 62 (1958) 227.

Ruth B. K. Amiran and I. Dunayevsky, "The Assyrian Open-Court Building and its Palestinian Derivatives," *BASOR* #149 (1958) 25-32.

W[illiam] F[oxwell] Albright, "The Assyrian Open-Court Building and the West Building of Tell Beit Mirsim," *BASOR* #149 (1958) 32.

Alexander Badawy, "Architectural Provision Against Heat in the Orient," *JNES* 17 (1958) 122-128.

A. Trevor Hodge, "Western Greek Building Techniques," *AJA* 63 (1959) 189.

Gus W. Van Beek, "A New Interpretation of the So-Called South Arabian House Model," *AJA* 63 (1959) 269-273.

*James Mellaart, "Notes on the Architectural Remains of Troy I and II," *AS* 9 (1959) 131-162.

Phllip Gillon, "Biblical Architecture," *AT* 4 (1959-60) #1, 7-10.

Rodney S. Young, "Gordion: Phrygian Construction and Architecture," *Exped* 2 (1959-60) #2, 2-9.

A. Trevor Hodge, "Trusses in Sicily?" *AJA* 64 (1960) 185-186.

Erwin Riefler, "Historical Metrology and the Riddle of Proportions in the Temple of Olympian Zeus at Athens. A Simple Solution," *AJA* 64 (1960) 188.

J. Walter Graham, "Windows, Recesses and the Piano Nobile in the Minoan Palaces," *AJA* 64 (1960) 329-333.

*J. Walter Graham, "The Minoan Unit of Length and Minoan Palace Planning," *AJA* 64 (1960) 335-341.

J. Walter Graham, "Mycenaean Architecture," *Arch* 13 (1960) 46-54.

*C. A. Burney and G. R. J. Lawson, "Measured Plans of Urartian Fortresses," *AS* 10 (1960) 177-196.

*P. Delougaz, "Architectural Representations on Steatite Vases," *Iraq* 22 (1960) 90-95.

*W. K. Simpson, "The Nature of the brick-work calculations in *Kah. Pap.* XXIII, 24-40," *JEA* 46 (1960) 106-107.

J. Walter Graham, "The Minoan Banquet Hall. A Study of the Blocks north of the Central Court at Phaistos and Mallia," *AJA* 65 (1961) 165-172.

J. Walter Graham, "Bathrooms or Lustral Chambers?" *AJA* 65 (1961) 189.

*Alan Rowe, "Studies in the Archaeology of the Near East: II. Some Facts Concerning the Great Pyramids of el-Giza and Their Royal Constructors," *BJRL* 44 (1961-62) 100-118.

Rodney S. Young, "Gordion: Phrygian Construction and Architecture. II," *Exped* 4 (1961-62) #4, 2-12.

Alexander Badawy, "The Harmonic System of Architectural Design in Ancient Egypt," *MIO* 8 (1961-63) 1-14.

Lucy T. Shoe, "The Architectural Ornament of the Theater at Morgantina," *AJA* 66 (1962) 199.

Axel Boëthius, "Of Tuscan Columns," *AJA* 66 (1962) 249-254.

Osman Rifki Rostom, "Modern Granaries as relics of an ancient Building," *ASAE* 57 (1962) 99-105.

*Abd El-Hamid Zayed, "Miscellaneous Notes," *ASAE* 57 (1962) 115-124. [II. Notes on the Building of the Temple Sety I at Abydos, pp. 119-124]

A[lexander] Badawy, "Special Problems of Egyptian Architecture," *OA* 1 (1962) 185-195.

Helle Salskov Roberts, "Some Bronze Plaques with Repoussé Decoration in the Danish National Museum. An Investigation into an Early Etruscan Style of Decoration," *AA* 34 (1963) 135-184.

*Emily Vermeule, "The Fall of Knossos and the Palace Style," *AJA* 67 (1963) 195-199.

*Bernard Goldman, "The Oriental Gate of Heaven," *AJA* 67 (1963) 211.

Clark Hopkins, "A Review of the Throne Room at Cnossos," *AJA* 67 (1963) 416-419.

*Alexander Badawy, "The Architectural Symbolism of the Massisi-Chapels in Egypt," *CdÉ* 38 (1963) 78-90.

Seton Lloyd, "Bronze Age Architecture of Anatolia," *PBA* 49 (1963) 153-176.

*Tahsin Özgüç, "The Art and Architecture of Ancient Kanish," *A(A)* 8 (1964) 27-48.

Elizabeth R. Gebhard, "The Greek Orchestra: Form and Evolution," *AJA* 68 (1964) 194.

A. Trevor Hodge, "Beveled Joints in Greek Architecture," *AJA* 68 (1964) 195.

*Anonymous, "Villas and Victuals," *BH* 1 (1964) #1, 3-7. *[A Typical Jewish House]*

A. Negev, "Stonedressers' Marks from a Nabataean Sanctuary at 'Avdat," *EI* 7 (1964) 167*.

*Virginia Trimble, "Astronomical Investigation Concerning the So-called Air-Shafts of Cheops' Pyramid," *MIO* 10 (1964) 183-187.

*Alexander Badawy, "The Stella Destiny of Pharaoh and the So-Called Air-Shafts of Cheops' Pyramid," *MIO* 10 (1964) 189-206.

Beatrice Playne, "Suggestions on the Origin of the 'False Doors' of the Axumite Stalae," *AE* 6 (1965) 79-80.

Michael Cheilik, "Roman Stucco Decoration," *AJA* 69 (1965) 166.

James E. Packer, "Architectural Structure and Decoration in Roman Ostia," *AJA* 69 (1965) 172.

*A. D. Mavrikios, "Aesthetic Analysis Concerning the Curvature of the Parthenon," *AJA* 69 (1965) 264-268.

Gisela M. A. Richter, "The Furnishings of Ancient Greek Houses," *Arch* 18 (1965) 26-33.

Anonymous, "A Mud and Straw Brick from Egypt," *BH* 2 (1965) #3, 19-24.

Anonymous, "Glazed Bricks from Babylon. The significance of the coloured and embossed bricks from Nebuchadnezzar's magnificent city of Babylon," *BH* 2 (1965) #4, 4-10.

A. Negev, "Stonedresser's*[sic]* Marks from a Nabatean Sanctuary at 'Avdat," *IEJ* 15 (1965) 185-194.

G. R. H. Wright, "Fluted Columns in the Bronze Age Temple of Baal-Berith at Shechem," *PEQ* 97 (1965) 66-84.

*F. E. Winter, "Notes on Military Architecture in the Termessos Region," *AJA* 70 (1966) 127-137.

Colin N. Edmonson and William F. Wyatt, "The Ceiling of the Hephaisteion," *AJA* 70 (1966) 188.

*Phyllis W. Lehmann, "The Meander Door: A Labyrinthine Symbol," *AJA* 70 (1966) 192.

Carol LaBranche, "The Greek Figural Capital," *Bery* 16 (1966) 71-96.

*C. Nylander, "Clamps and Chronology (Achaemenian Problems II)," *IA* 6 (1966) 130-146.

*Susan Handler, "The Architecture of Alexandria in Egypt as seen on the Bronze Alexandrian Coinage of the Roman Imperial Period," *AJA* 71 (1967) 188.

Donald A. Preziosi, "Minoan Palace Planning and its Origins," *AJA* 71 (1967) 193.

J. Walter Graham, "A Banquet Hall at Mycenaean Pylos," *AJA* 71 (1967) 353-360.

N. W. Alcock, "Two Door Latches from the Konya Plain," *AS* 16 (1967) 179-180.

*R. Ross Holloway, "Panhellenism in the Sculptures of the Zeus Temple at Olympia," *GRBS* 8 (1967) 93-101.

Robert Scranton, "The Architecture of the Sanctuary of Apollo at Kourion," *TAPS, N.S.,* 57 (1967) Part 5, 3-85.

*G. R. H. Wright, "Recent Discoveries in the Sanctuary of the Qsar Bint Far'un at Petra. II. Some Aspects Concerning the Architecture and Sculpture," *ADAJ* 12&13 (1967-68) 20-29.

Richard E. M. Moore, "A Newly Observed Stratum in Roman Floor Mosaics," *AJA* 72 (1968) 57-68.

James [R.] Wiseman, "An Unfinished Colossus on Mt. Pendeli," *AJA* 72 (1968) 75-76.

Susan B. Downey, "Antefixes from the Regia," *AJA* 72 (1968) 164.

William L. MacDonald, "Severan Design at Lepcis Magna and Cuicul (Djemila)," *AJA* 72 (1968) 168.

Ned Nabers, "The Architectural Variations of the Macellum," *AJA* 72 (1968) 169.

Donald A. Preziosi, "The Harmonic System of Minoan Architectural Design," *AJA* 72 (1968) 171.

Rhys Carpenter, "The Unfinished Colossus of Mt. Pendeli," *AJA* 72 (1968) 279-280.

Karl Schefold, "The Architecture of Eretria," *Arch* 21 (1968) 272-281.

H. Keith Beebe, "Ancient Palestinian Dwellings," *BA* 31 (1968) 38-58.

Kazimierz Michalowski, "The Labyrinth Enigma: Archaeologiocal Suggestions," *JEA* 54 (1968) 219-222.

*Maurits van Loon, "The Oriental Institute Excavations at Mureybiṭ, Syria: Preliminary Report on the 1965 Campaign, Part I: Architecture and General Finds," *JNES* 27 (1968) 265-281.

*G. R. H. Wright, "Tell el-Yehūdīyah and the Glacis," *ZDPV* 84 (1968) 1-17.

Peter J. Parr, "The Origin of the Rampart Fortifications of Middle Bronze Age Palestine and Syria," *ZDPV* 84 (1968) 18-45.

*Gölül Öney, "Lion Figures in Anatolian Seljuk Architecture," *A(A)* 13 (1969) 43-67.

Otto Brendel, "Ganymede Group from Cosa," *AJA* 73 (1969) 232.

*Vincent J. Bruno, "Fragments of a Temple Decoration from the Arx at Coas," *AJA* 73 (1969) 232.

A. Trevor Hodge, "Deliberate Carelessness in Classical Greek Architecture," *AJA* 73 (1969) 237.

*Bluma L. Trell, "Architectura Numismatica Orientalis," *AJA* 73 (1969) 246.

*Edith Porada, "Iranian Art and Archaeology: A Report on the Fifth International Congress, 1968," *Arch* 22 (1969) 54-65. [Achaemenid Architecture, pp. 64-65]

David Ussishkin, "The Date of the Neo-Hittite Enclosure in Karatepe," *AS* 19 (1969) 121-137.

H. Kalayan, "The engraved drawing on the Trilithon and the related problems about the constructional history of Baalbeck Temples," *BMB* 22 (1969) 151-155.

T. Cuyler Young Jr., "Thoughts on the architecture of Hasanlu IV," *IA* 6 (1969) 48-71.

Jadwiga Lipińska, "The architectural design of the temple of Tuthmosis III at Deir el-Bahari," *MDIÄA* 25 (1969) 85-89.

G. R. H. Wright, "Another Fluted Column Fragment from Bronze Age Shechem," *PEQ* 101 (1969) 34-36.

Henry O. Thompson, "Apsidal Construction in the Ancient Near East," *PEQ* 101 (1969) 69-86.

G. R. H. Wright, "Iran and the Glacis," *ZDPV* 85 (1969) 24-34.

Dominique Collon, "Mesopotamian Columns," *JANES* 2 (1969-70) 1-18.

§187 *2.5.8.1 Buildings, Structures, and Related Edifices (includes Foundation Deposits) - General Studies*

M. L. Lortet, "A Station of the Age of Stone near Tyre," *PEFQS* 12 (1880) 198-200.

A. Lowy, "Underground Structures in Biblical Lands," *SBAP* 5 (1882-83) 140-146.

*Frank C. Roberts, "The Bridges of Ancient Rome," *AAOJ* 6 (1884) 145-155.

A. M. Wilcock, "Mr. Doerpfeld's restoration of the Propylaia," *AJA, O.S.,* 1 (1885) 157-159.

A. A. Caruana, "Remains of an Ancient Greek Building Discovered in Malta," *AJA, O.S.,* 4 (1888) 450-454.

(Mrs.) E. A. Finn, "The Stone Mounds on the Rephaim Plains," *PEFQS* 22 (1890) 195.

†Anonymous, "The Acropolis at Athens," *QRL* 171 (1890) 122-149. *(Review)*

Claude R. Conder, "Notes by Major Conder. IV. The Lachish Pillar," *PEFQS* 23 (1891) 71.

*C[onrad] Schick, "Reports from Jerusalem. Letters from Herr Schick. Discoveries in 'Solomon's Stables'," *PEFQS* 23 (1891) 198-199.

*C[onrad] Schick, "Letters from Baurath C. Schick," *PEFQS* 24 (1892) 9-25. [Buildings South of the "Double Gate", pp. 19-24]

*N. E. Crosby, "Notes. The topography of Sparta and the building of Epimenides," *AJA, O.S.,* 9 (1894) 212-213.

A. L. Frothingham Jr., "Notes. A primitive dome with pendentives at Vetulonia," *AJA, O.S.,* 9 (1894) 213-216.

Charles Waldstein, "Correspondence. The circular bulding at Sparta," *AJA, O.S.,* 9 (1894) 545-546.

Rufus B. Richardson, "Papers of the American School of Classical Studies at Athens. The Gymnasium at Eretria," *AJA, O.S.,* 11 (1896) 152-165.

*Anna Louis Perry, "Papers of the American School of Classical Studies at Athens. The Dimensions of the Athena Parthenos," *AJA, O.S.,* 11 (1896) 335-346. [Note by Alfred Emerson, pp. 346-349]

John P. Peters, "University of Pennsylvania Expedition to Babylon III. The Court of Columns at Nippur," *AJA, O.S.,* 10 (1895) 439-468.

Theodore F. Wright, "King David's Stairs," *AAOJ* 18 (1896) 324-325.

*E. P. Andrews, "Color on the Parthenon and the Elgin Marbles, recently Discovered Facts and Resultant Theories," *AJA* 5 (1901) 21-22.

George A. Barton, "On the Partheon of Tyre," *JAOS* 22 (1901) 115-117.

J. E. Hanauer and E. W. Gurney Masterman, "The Ruin at Khurbet Beit Sawir," *PEFQS* 33 (1901) 305-307.

Gray Hill, "The Ruin at Khurbet Beit Sawir," *PEFQS* 33 (1901) 407.

R. A. Stewart Macalister, "Reports by R. A. Stewart Macalister, M.A., F.S.A. III. The Ancient Necropolis at Kerm esh-Sheikh," *PEFQS* 34 (1902) 120.

Martin L. D'Ooge, "New Points in the History of the Acropolis at Athens," *AJA* 7 (1903) 81-82.

*Percy E. Newberry, "Extracts from my Notebooks. VII," *SBAP* 25 (1903) 357-362. [57. Some Miscellaneous Antiquities, pp. 361-362 (*Limestone Lintel, p. 362*)]

*Anonymous, "Asia:—Babylonia," *RP* 2 (1903) 347. *[Excavation of a school house]*

Samuel Ball Planter, "The Rostra," *AJA* 9 (1905) 83.

John P. Peters, "The Palace at Nippur Babylonian not Parthian," *AJA* 9 (1905) 450-452.

*Anonymous, "Notes and Comments. Egyptian Foundation Deposits," *ICMM* 1 (1905) 371-372.

*John P. Peters, "The Nippur Library," *JAOS* 26 (1905) 145-164.

*Theodore F. Wright, "The Siloam and Simplon Tunnels," *BW* 27 (1906) 468-472.

*Anonymous, "The Excavations of Two Large Banking Houses," *MQR, 3rd Ser.*, 32 (1906) 184.

*Lewis Bayles Paton, "Jerusalem in Bible Times: VII. Solomon's Buildings," *BW* 30 (1907) 7-17.

*W. A. Harper, "Roman Bridges of the Tiber," *AAOJ* 30 (1908) 193-209.

Anonymous, "Restoration of Pylon at Karnak," *RP* 9 (1910) 58.

Anonymous, "The Size of the Earlier Parthenon," *RP* 9 (1910) 226-227.

B. H. Hill, "Parthenon Studies," *AJA* 15 (1911) 75.

J. Grafton Milne, "The Sanatorium of Dêr-el-Baḥri," *JEA* 1 (1914) 96-98.

T. E. Peet, "Primitive Stone Buildings in Sinai," *Man* 15 (1915) #87.

H. E. Winlock, "The Theban Necropolis in the Middle Kingdom," *AJSL* 32 (1915-16) 1-37.

Anna Spaulding Jenkins, "The Auditorium of Maecenas," *A&A* 3 (1916) 223-227.

*James Henry Breasted, "Studio of an Egyptian Portrait Sculptor in the Fourteenth Century B.C.," *A&A* 4 (1916) 233-242.

Edgar James Banks, "The Seven Wonders of the Ancient World. VII—The Seventh Wonder: The Lighthouse of Alexandria," *A&A* 6 (1917) 77-81.

*Joseph Offord, "Archaeological Notes on Jewish Antiquities XLIX. *The Alexandrian Jewish Alabarches of Josephus,* " *PEFQS* 50 (1918) 136-137.

E. J. H. Mackay, "Observations on a Megalithic Building at Bet Sawir (Palestine)," *JPOS* 1 (1920-21) 95-102.

Guido Calza, "The Memorials of Rome in the Italian Colonies," *A&A* 11 (1921) 131-144.

Fritz Hommel, "The Oldest Dome-Structure in the World," *JAOS* 41 (1921) 230-234.

Leicester B. Holland, "Erechtheum Papers," *AJA* 28 (1924) 1-23. [I. The Remains of the Pre-Erechtheum]

Leicester B. Holland, "Erechtheum Papers II. The Strong House of Erechtheus," *AJA* 28 (1924) 142-169.

Leicester B. Holland, "Erechtheum Papers," *AJA* 28 (1924) 402-434. [III. The Post-Persian Revision, pp. 402-425; IV. "The Building Called the Erechtheum", pp. 425-434]

Franklin P. Johnson, "The 'Dragon-Houses' of Southern Euboea," *AJA* 29 (1925) 398-412.

*Jean Capart, "Some Remarks on the Sheikh el-Beled," *JEA* 6 (1926) 225-233.

Richard Stillwell, "Upper Peirene on Acrocorinth," *AJA* 31 (1927) 94-95.

*R. Engelbach, "An experiment on the accuracy of shaping of a monolithic column of circular section of the Vth dynasty from Abusîr," *ASAE* 28 (1928) 144-152.

Anonymous, "The Acropolis," *Antiq* 3 (1929) 348-350.

Anonymous, "Notes and Comments. A Foundation-Box from Tell Abu-Maria in Iraq," *A&A* 30 (1930) 190-191.

*F. Ll. Griffith, "Four Granite Stands at Philæ," *BIFAO* 30 (1931) 127-130.

William Bell Dinsmoor, "The Burning of the Opisthodomos at Athens, I. The Date," *AJA* 36 (1932) 143-172.

William Bell Dinsmoor, "The Burning of the Opisthodomos at Athens, II. The Site," *AJA* 36 (1932) 307-326.

Leicester B. Holland, "The Mantic Mechanism at Delphi," *AJA* 37 (1933) 201-214.

*Kathleen Kenyon, "Excavations at Samaria. The Forecourt of the Augusteum," *PEFQS* 65 (1933) 74-87.

William B. Dinsmoor, "The Date of the Older Parthenon," *AJA* 38 (1934) 408-448.

William B. Dinsmoor, "The Older Parthenon: Additional Notes," *AJA* 39 (1935) 508-509.

G. E. Kirk, "Gymnasium or Khan? A Hellenistic Building at Babylon," *Iraq* 2 (1935) 223-231.

E[phraim] A. S[peiser], "The Oldest Acropolis," *UMB* 6 (1935-37) #6 20-24. *[Tepe Gawra]*

E. L. Sukenik, "A Chalcolithic Necropolis at Ḫererah," *JPOS* 17 (1937) 15-30.

Leicester B. Holland, "The Hall of the Athenian Kings," *AJA* 42 (1938) 122-123; 43 (1939) 289-298.

Donald N. Wilber, "The Parthian Structures at Takht-i-Sulayman," *Antiq* 12 (1938) 389-410.

Donald F. Brown, "The Hexagonal Court at Baalbek," *AJA* 43 (1939) 285-288.

*G. W. Murray, "The Archaic Hut in Wādi Umm Sidrah," *JEA* 25 (1939) 38-39.

Stuart M. Shaw, "Excavations of the Arsinoeion of Samothrace," *AJA* 44 (1940) 107-108.

Robert Scranton, "Buildings on the West Terrace of the Agora at Corinth," *AJA* 45 (1941) 88-89.

William Bell Dinsmoor, "The Athenian Treasury as Date in Its Ornament," *AJA* 50 (1946) 86-121.

*M. F. Laming Macadam, "Gleanings from the Bankes MSS," *JEA* 32 (1946) 57-64. *[Egyptian Buildings]*

A. S. Kirkbride, "Desert 'Kites'," *JPOS* 20 (1946) 1-5.

*William Bell Dinsmoor, "The Hekatompedon on the Athenian Acropolis," *AJA* 51 (1947) 109-151.

Alexander Badawy, "A collection of Foundation-Deposits of Thutmosis III," *ASAE* 47 (1947) 145-156.

Zaki Iskandar, "Foundation deposits of Thutmosis IIIrd (M. A. Mansour)," *ASAE* 47 (1947) 157.

Emil Kunze and Hans Weber, "The Olympian Stadium, The Echo Colonnade and an 'Archaeological Earthquake'," *AJA* 52 (1948) 490-496.

Helen E. Searls and William B. Dinsmoor, "The Date of the Olympia Heraeum," *AJA* 49 (1945) 62-80.

[G.] Lankester Harding, "Recent Work on the Jerash Forum," *PEQ* 81 (1949) 12-20.

Lucy Talcott, "Athens: A Mycenaean Necropolis under the Agora Floor," *Arch* 4 (1951) 223-225.

H. T. Norris, "Arslan Tash (Rock of the Lion)," *PEQ* 83 (1951) 168-174.

*Elinor N. Husselman, "The Granaries of Karanis," *TAPA* 83 (1952) 56-73.

*G. Lankester Harding, "The Cairn of Hani'," *ADAJ* 2 (1953) 8-56.

Alison Frantz, "The Hephaisteion Revisited," *Arch* 7 (1954) 244-248.

J. Walter Graham, "Where Was the Cretan Bull-Ring?" *AJA* 59 (1955) 171.

J. Walter Graham, "The Central court as the Minoan Bull-Ring," *AJA* 61 (1957) 255-262.

John L. Heller, "A Labyrinth from Pylos?" *AJA* 64 (1960) 185; 65 (1961) 57-62.

Evelyn B. Harrison, "The Date of the Kikai from the Stoa of Zeus in Athens," *AJA* 65 (1961) 190.

*Nicholas M. Verdelis, "A Private House Discovered at Mycenae," *Arch* 14 (1961) 12-17.

James B. Pritchard, "A Bronze Age Necropolis at Gibeon," *BA* 24 (1961) 19-24.

Sadik Nur, "The Circular Brick Building of Wad Ban Naga," *CdÉ* 37 (1962) 76.

G. R. H. Wright, "Structure of the Qasr Bint Far'un. A Preliminary Report," *PEQ* 93 (1961) 8-37.

Gorham P. Stevens, "Concerning the Impressiveness of the Parthenon," *AJA* 66 (1962) 337-338.

L. Richardson Jr., "The Form and Location of the Rostra of the Forum Romanum," *AJA* 67 (1963) 216.

*James B. Pritchard, "Two Tombs and a Tunnel in the Jordan Valley: Discoveries at the Biblical Zarethan," *Exped* 6 (1963-64) #4, 2-9.

Phyllis Williams Lehmann, "The Reconstruction and History of the Hieron in Samothrace," *AJA* 68 (1964) 196-197.

Lucy T. Shoe, "The Stoa Poikile in the Athenian Agroa," *AJA* 68 (1964) 200.

*R. E. Wycherley, "The Olympieion at Athens," *GRBS* 5 (1964) 161-179.

*J. A. Bundgård, "Caesar's Bridges of the Rhine," *AA* 36 (1965) 87-103.

*A. D. Mavrikios, "Aesthetic Analysis Concerning the Curvature of the Parthenon," *AJA* 69 (1965) 264-268.

Peter J. Parr, "The Date of the Qasr Bint Far'un at Petra," *JEOL* #19 (1965-66) 550-557.

David Ussishkin, "The Date of the Neo-Hittite Enclosure at Sakçagözü," *BASOR* #181 (1966) 15-23.

*Donald White, "The Post-Classical Cult of Malophoros at Selinus," *AJA* 71 (1967) 335-352.

Phyllis Williams Lehmann, "Letter to the Editor," *AJA* 71 (1967) 429-432. *[A Building at Samothrace]*

*Margarete Bieber, "The Aqua Marcia in Coins and in Ruins," *Arch* 20 (1967) 194-196.

James Parker, "The Casa di Via Giulio Romano," *AJA* 72 (1968) 170.

*Barbara Switalski Lesko, "Royal Mortuary Suites of the Egyptian New Kingdom," *AJA* 73 (1969) 453-458.

Robert G. Boiling, "Bronze Age Buildings at the Shechem High Place: *ASOR* Excavations at Tananir," *BASOR* 32 (1969) 81-103.

§188 ***2.5.8.2 Arches, Fortifications, Gates, Towers and Walls***

(   ) D., "On the Ruins of the Tower of Babel," *CongML* 1 (1818) 35-49.

J. B. Lightfoot, "On the Long Walls of Athens," *JCSP* 4 (1857-60) 294-302.

*W. Simpson, "Robinson's Arch," *PEFQS* 1 (1869) 46-48.

Theophilus G. Pinches, "Upon the Bronze gates of Shalmaneser II., discovered by Mr. Rassam, at Balawat. Part I," *SBAP* 1 (1878-79) 3-6.

*W. F. Birch, "Nehemiah's Wall and David's Tomb," *PEFQS* 11 (1879) 176-179.

J. N. Seep, "The Stone Hat-toim on Ecce-homo Arch," *PEFQS* 11 (1879) 195-197.

*C. W. Wilson, "The Masonry of the Haram Wall," *PEFQS* 12 (1880) 9-65, 195-196.

*Claude R. Conder, "Notes on Colonel Wilson's Paper on the Masonry of the Haram Wall," *PEFQS* 12 (1880) 91-97.

*Charles Warren, "Notes on Colonel Wilson's Paper on the Masonry of the Haram Wall," *PEFQS* 12 (1880) 159-166.

Theo. G. Pinches, "The Bronze Gates discovered by Mr. Rassam at Balawat," *SBAT* 7 (1880-82) 83-118.

C[laude] R. Conder, "The Fortress of Canaan," *PEFQS* 15 (1883) 175-176.

R. F. Hutchinson, "The Tower of Edar," *PEFQS* 19 (1887) 167-169.

*George St. Clair, "Nehemiah's South Wall, and the Locality of the Royal Sepulchres," *PEFQS* 21 (1889) 90-102.

*Charles Waldstein, H. S. Washington, and W. Irving Hunt, "Discoveries in Plataia in 1890," *AJA, O.S.*, 6 (1890) 445-475. [III. Description of the Site and Walls of Plataia, by H. S. Washington, pp. 452-462]

*George St. Clair, "Nehemiah's Wall and the Sepulchres of the Kings," *PEFQS* 22 (1890) 212.

John P. Peters, "University of Pennsylvania Excavations at Nippur. II. The Nippur Arch," *AJA, O.S.*, 10 (1895) 352-368.

A. L. Frothingham Jr., "Did the Triumphal Arch originate with the Romans or the Greeks?" *AJA* 5 (1901) 27-28.

Joseph Offord, "The Migdol Towers of Egypt and Palestine," *AAOJ* 25 (1903) 112-114.

Gorham P. Stevens, "The East Wall of the Erechtheum," *AJA* 10 (1906) 47-71, 83.

Anonymous, "Wall of Themistocles," *RP* 7 (1908) 211. *[Athens]*

A. H. Sayce, "The Figure of an Amazon at the East Gate of the Hittite Capital at Boghaz Keui," *SBAP* 32 (1910) 25-26.

*Somers Clarke, "Ancient Egyptian Frontier Fortresses," *JEA* 3 (1915) 155-179.

R. Douglas Wells, "A Note of the Fortress of Gazîrat el-Malik," *JEA* 3 (1915) 180-181.

Edgar James Banks, "Seven Wonders of the Ancient World. II—The Second Wonder: The Walls of Babylon," *A&A* 3 (1916) 131-136.

Warren J. Moulton, "The Citadel of Jerusalem," *A&A* 7 (1918) 163-172.

Tenney Frank, "Notes on the Servian Wall," *AJA* 22 (1918) 175-188.

Joseph Offord, "Some Migdols of Palestine and Egypt," *PEFQS* 52 (1920) 23-29.

J. P. Droop, "A Greek Tower in Naxos," *AAA* 10 (1923) 41-45.

*Leon Legrain, "King Nabonidus and the Great Walls of Babylon," *MJ* 14 (1923) 282-287.

Leicester B. Holland, "The Chariot at the Gates of the Acropolis," *AJA* 28 (1924) 77.

I. O. Nothstein, "Hittite Citadel," *AugQ* 7 (1928) 267-268.

*John Day, "Phalerum and the Phaleric Wall," *TAPA* 59 (1928) 164-178.

Anonymous, "The Round Towers of Moab," *Antiq* 3 (1929) 342-343.

Anonymous, "Megalithic Complexes, Transjordan," *Antiq* 12 (1938) 93-94.

Glanville Downey, "The Gate of the Cherubim at Antioch," *JQR, N.S.*, 29 (1938-39) 167-177.

Louis E. Lord, "Watchtowers and Fortresses in Argolis," *AJA* 43 (1939) 78-84.

*Henry S. Robinson, "The Tower of Winds and the Roman Market-place," *AJA* 46 (1942) 123-124; 47 (1943) 291-305.

*William Bell Dinsmoor, "The Temple of Ares and the Roman Agora," *AJA* 47 (1943) 383-384. *[Tower of Winds]*

Leicester Bodine Holland, "The Foundations of the Arch of Augustus," *AJA* 57 (1953) 1-4.

F. E. Winter, "Philo of Byzantion and the Study of Hellenistic Fortifications," *AJA* 57 (1953) 112.

*Alan Rowe, "A Contribution to the Archaeology of the Western Desert: III (The Temple-Tombs of Alexander the Great and His Palace in Rhacotis: The Great Wall of the Libyan Desert)," *BJRL* 38 (1955-56) 139-165.

M. Avi-Yonah, "The Missing Fortress of Flavius Josephus," *IEJ* 3 (1953) 94-98.

*Yigael Yadin, "Hyksos Fortifications and the Battering-ram," *BASOR* #137 (1955) 23-32.

Frederick E. Winter, "The Fortifications on the Side of Pamphylia," *AJA* 62 (1958) 227-228.

*T. Wheildon Brown, "The Discovery of a Line of Ancient Fortifications on a Ridge to the East of Rania Plain, Sulaimaniya Liwa," *Sumer* 14 (1958) 122-124.

Yohanah Aharoni, "The Date of Casemate Walls in Judah and Israel and Their Purpose," *BASOR* #154 (1959) 35-39.

*S. Yeivin, "The Western Tower at Tell Beit Mirsim," *BIES* 23 (1959) #1/2, I.

David Oates, "Fort Shalmaneser—An Interim Report," *Iraq* 21 (1959) 98-129.

Anonymous, "Egyptian Fortress Found in Sudan," *AT* 4 (1959-60) #2, 9-10.

James R. McCredie and Arthur Steinberg, "A Ptolemaic Fort in Attica," *AJA* 65 (1961) 191.

James R. Wiseman, "The University of Chicago Isthmian Excavations: Another Trans-Isthmian Wall," *AJA* 65 (1961) 193.

S. Bulow and R. A. Mitchell, "An Iron Age II Fortress on Tel Nagila," *IEJ* 11 (1961) 101-110.

*G. R. H. Wright, "Petra—The Arched Gate," *PEQ* 93 (1961) 124-135.

S. Applebaum, "The Initial Date of the Limes Palaestinae," *Zion* 27 (1962) #1/2, I.

F. E. Winter, "The Chronology of the Euryalos Fortress at Syracuse," *AJA* 67 (1963) 363-387.

*Barry J. Kemp, "Excavations at Hierakonpolis Fort, 1905: A Preliminary Note," *JEA* 49 (1963) 24-28.

William F. Stinespring, "Wilson's Arch Revisited," *BA* 29 (1966) 27-36.

James A. Dengate, "Observations on the Sounion Fortifications," *AJA* 71 (1967) 185-186.

William F. Stinespring, "Wilson's Arch and the Masonic Hall," *BA* 30 (1967) 27-31.

*Y[ohanan] Aharoni, "Forerunners of the Limes: Iron Age Fortresses in the Negev," *IEJ* 17 (1967) 1-17.

*M Gihon, "Idumean and the Herodian Limes," *IEJ* 17 (1967) 27-45.

*E. Dabrowska and P. Gartkiewicz, "Preliminary Report Concerning Restoration of the Wall of the 3rd Terrace of the Hatshepsut Temple at Deir el-Bahari during the Season 1965-1966," *ASAE* 60 (1968) 213-219.

*L. B. Kreitner, "Archaeological Notes. A Greek Arch and Parmenides' Head: *A Report on Velia-Elea*," *HT* 18 (1968) 129, 131.

Perrie A. MacKay, "A Turkish Description of the Tower of the Winds," *AJA* 73 (1969) 468-469.

V. A. Lekvinadze, "The Pontic 'limes'," *VDI* (1969) #2, 93.

§189 ***2.5.8.3 Houses***

C[onrad] Schick, "Reports from Herr Baurath von Schick. 2. Herod's House," *PEFQS* 28 (1896) 215-217.

W. Pleyte, "Dwelling-houses in Egypt," *SBAP* 24 (1902) 146.

Aylward M. Blackman, "The *Ka*-House and the Serdab," *JEA* 3 (1915) 250-254.

L[eon] Legrain, "The Boudoir of Queen Shubad," *MJ* 20 (1929) 211-245.

David M. Robinson, "The Villa of Good Fortune at Olynthos," *AJA* 38 (1934) 501-510.

C[harles] B[ache], "The Round House at Gawra," *UMB* 6 (1935-37) #4, 111-117. [Note by E. A. Speiser, p. 117]

Jerome Sperling, "Houses of Troy I," *AJA* 41 (1937) 110.

Agnes K. Lake, "The Origin of the Roman House," *AJA* 41 (1937) 598-601.

John L. Caskey, "The Pillar House of Troy VI," *AJA* 43 (1939) 299.

*Valentin Müller, "Types of Mesopotamian Houses. (Studies in Oriental Archaeology III)," *JAOS* 60 (1940) 151-180.

*Bernard M. Boyle, "The Ancient Italian Town-house Reconsidered," *AJA* 73 (1969) 231-232.

§190 ***2.5.8.4 Monuments (uninscribed) and Obelisks (includes Fountains and Sphinxes) - General Studies***

†Anonymous, "Egyptian Monuments in the British Museum," *MMBR* 15 (1803) 16-18.

P. Rainier, "Account of the Avenue of Sphinxes, discovered by Capt. Rainier, C. B., R.N., at Ben-i-Hassan, in January 1829," *TRAS* 3 (1835) 268-270.

Charles Pickering, "On the Egyptian Monuments of El-Amarna," *PAOS* (May, 1858) 7.

Hyde Clark, "On the Assyro-Pseudo-Serostris," *JAOS* 8 (1866) lxxxiv.

Ferdinand Piper, "The Study of Monuments," *BS* 24 (1867) 276-296. *(Trans. from the German by Charles M. Mead)*

*H. J. Van Lennep, "On the Niobe of Mt. Sipylus," *JAOS* 9 (1871) xvi.

*Hyde Clarke, "On the Niobe of Magnesia ad Siphylum; and, On the newly discovered Lydo-Assyrian Monument of Smyrna," *JAOS* 9 (1871) ix-x.

[Theodore D.] Woolsey, "On two recently discovered monuments," *JAOS* 9 (1871) xci-xcii.

Selah Merrill, "Assyrian and Babylonian Monuments in America," *BS* 32 (1875) 320-349.

S[elah] M[errill], "A Monument of Cyrus the Great," *AAOJ* 2 (1879-80) 168-169.

Anonymous, "Cleopatra's Needles," *AAOJ* 2 (1879-80) 296-297.

*Samuel Birch, "Monuments of the Reign of Tirhaka," *SBAP* 2 (1879-80) 60.

Selah Merrill, "On the Assyrian and Babylonian Monuments in America," *JAOS* 10 (1880) xcix-c.

Selah Merrill, "A Monument of Cyrus the Great," *OBJ* 1 (1880) 13-14.

A. H. Sayce, "The Monuments of the Hittites," *SBAT* 7 (1880-82) 248-293.

Augustus C. Merriam, "An arrangement of Hair on the Sphinxes at Eujuk," *AJA, O.S.,* 1 (1885) 159-160.

Selah Merrill, "On the Assyrian Monuments in the Museum of Fine Arts at Boston," *JAOS* 11 (1885) lxx.

†E. A. Wallis Budge, "On an Egyptian Stele in the Museum at Bath," *SBAP* 8 (1885-86) 213-214.

Anonymous, "The Sphinx," *JTVI* 20 (1886-87) 328.

Augustus C. Merriam, "Painted Sepulchral Stelai[sic]* from Alexandria," *AJA, O.S.,* 3 (1887) 261-268.

*Carl D. Buck, "Discoveries in the Attic deme of Ikaria, 1888. II. Stele of a Warrior," *AJA, O.S.,* 5 (1889) 9-17.

Camden M. Cobern, "Egyptology.—No. II.—The Riddle of the Sphinx," *HR* 18 (1889) 116-120.

Claude R. Conder, "Notes by Major Conder, R.E. II. The so-called Hittite Monuments of Kaller," *PEFQS* 21 (1889) 85-87.

Claude R. Conder, "Notes by Major Conder, R.E. III. The Tell es Salahiyah Monument," *PEFQS* 21 (1889) 87-88.

Claude R. Conder, "Notes by Major Conder, D.C.L., R.E. III. Hittite Monuments," *PEFQS* 21 (1889) 145.

A. G. Weld and Selah Merrill, "The Tell es Salahiyah Monument," *PEFQS* 21 (1889) 152.

C. W. Wilson, "The Tell es-Salahiyeh Monument," *PEFQS* 21 (1889) 210.

*S. Y. Stevenson, "Two Egyptian Monuments from the Site of Herakleopolis," *AJA, O.S.,* 7 (1891) 449-453. *[Statue of Rameses the Great]*

Claude R. Conder, "Rude Stone Monuments in Syria," *SRL* 17 (1891) 33-59.

Ira M. Price, "A New Find in Chaldæa," *BW* 2 (1893) 132-133. *[Stele of the Vultures (from Tello)]*

William Simpson, "A Hittite Monument," *PEFQS* 26 (1894) 199-200.

H. P. Laird, "The Egyptian Monuments," *RChR* 41 (1894) 504-517.

R. B. Richardson, "An Ancient Fountain in the Agora of Corinth," *AJA* 6 (1902) 29-30.

*Percy E. Newberry, "Extracts from my Notebooks. VI.," *SBAP* 25 (1903) 130-138. [45. A Monument of Kah-ankh-ra Sebekhetep, pp. 136-137]

Joseph Offord, "Monuments of Primitive Pharaohs," *AAOJ* 26 (1904) 240-242.

Paul Carus, "Naram-Sin's Stele," *OC* 18 (1904) 563-567.

Max W. Müller, "The Egyptian Monument of Tell esh-Shihâb," *PEFQS* 36 (1904) 78-80.

A. H. Sayce, "Notes and Queries. 5. *Paran on the Egyptian Monuments,*" *PEFQS* 37 (1905) 169.

*C. W. H. Johns, "Ancient Monuments in the British Museum: Illustrative of Biblical History," *BW* 27 (1906) 7-22.

Arthur E. P. Weigall, "A Report on some Objects recently found at Sebakh, and other Diggings," *ASAE* 8 (1907) 39-50. [Stele of Psammetikh II from Shellal, pp. 39-42]

Joseph Offord, "A Photographic Collection of Ancient Egyptian Monuments," *AAOJ* 29 (1907) 205-209.

*Ira Maurice Price, "Ancient Monuments in the Louvre Museum Illustrative of Biblical History," *BW* 30 (1907) 429-437.

W. Attmore Robinson, "A Monuments of Tshok-Göz-Köprüköe," *SBAP* 30 (1908) 25-27.

Guillaume de Jerphanion, "Two New Hittite Monuments from the Cappadocian Taurus," *SBAP* 30 (1908) 42-44.

Anonymous, "Removal of Obelisk to Cairo," *RP* 8 (1909) 214. *[Obelisk of Rameses the Great]*

Joseph Offord, "The Antiquity of the Great Sphinx," *AAOJ* 32 (1910) 27-28.

P. S. Ronzevalle, "Hittite Monuments of Arslân-tépé," *RP* 9 (1910) 69-73. *(Trans. by Helen M. Wright)*

Guillaume de Jerphanion, "Hittite Monuments of Cappadocia," *SBAP* 32 (1910) 168-174.

Anonymous, "A Find of Egyptian Stelæ," *RP* 10 (1911) 238.

A. Wiedemann, "Notes on Some Egyptian Monuments. I," *SBAP* 33 (1911) 162-170.

A. Wiedemann, "Notes on Some Egyptian Monuments. II," *SBAP* 33 (1911) 197-203.

John Garstang, "A New Royal Hittite Monument from Marash in Northern Syria," *AAA* 4 (1911-12) 126-127.

Felix J. Koch, "The Greatest Collection of Egyptian Monuments in the World," *AAOJ* 34 (1912) 219-223.

J. Dyneley Prince, "An Akkadian Cruciform Monument," *AJSL* 29 (1912-13) 95-110.

L. W. King, "The cruciform monument of Manishtusu," *RAAO* 9 (1912) 91-105.

A. Wiedemann, "Notes on Some Egyptian Monuments. III," *SBAP* 34 (1912) 298-307.

[Paul Carus], "The Sphinx," *OC* 27 (1913) 169-176.

P. S. Ronzevalle, "Phoenician Monuments in the Museum at Constantinople," *RP* 12 (1913) 59-64. *(Trans. by Helen M. Wright)*

George A. Reisner, "An Absurd Sphinx Story Denied," *RP* 12 (1913) 103-104.

A. Wiedemann, "Notes on Some Egyptian Monuments. IV," *SBAP* 35 (1913) 252-260.

*Percy E. Newberry, "Egyptian Historical Notes. II," *SBAP* 36 (1914) 35-39. [6. The Stela of King Zer, p. 35]

A. Wiedemann, "Notes on Some Egyptian Monuments. V," *SBAP* 36 (1914) 48-63.

A. Wiedemann, "Notes on Some Egyptian Monuments. VI," *SBAP* 36 (1914) 107-119.

A. Wiedemann, "Notes on Some Egyptian Monuments. VII," *SBAP* 36 (1914) 199-211.

Alan H. Gardiner, "An Archaic Funerary Stele," *JEA* 4 (1916) 256-260.

W. M. F[linders] Petrie, "The Sphinxes of Tanis," *AEE* 5 (1920) 105.

W. M. Dinsmoor, "The Monument of Agrippa at Athens," *AJA* 24 (1920) 83.

R. Engelbach, "Was the Constantinople Obelisk Part of the 108-Cubit Obelisk of Hatshapsôwet?" *AEE* 7 (1922) 100-102. {Note by [W. M.] F[linders] P[etrie], p. 102. (Correction *AEE* 8 (1923) p. 62)}

*Pere Alois Mallon, "Flint Implements and Megalithic Monuments," *BS* 81 (1924) 271-275. *(Trans. by W. F. Albright)*

George W. Gilmore, "The Problem of the Obelisks," *HR* 87 (1924) 444-446. *(Review)*

F. Ll. Griffith, "Stela in Honour of Amenophis III and Taya, from Tell el-'Amarnah," *JEA* 12 (1926) 1-2.

Anonymous, "Notes and Comments," *A&A* 24 (1927) 44. *[The Sphinx]*

*Anonymous, "Notes and Comments. A Queen's Sphinxes," *A&A* 26 (1928) 53.

R. Engelbach, "The so-called Hyksos Monuments," *ASAE* 28 (1928) 13-28. [Postscript, p. 80]

*G. A. Wainwright, "The aniconic Form of Amon in the New Kingdom," *ASAE* 28 (1928) 175-189.

*L[eon] L[egrain], "Old Sumerian Art," *MJ* 19 (1928) 221-247. [The Inlay Stela, pp. 225-235]

*J. M. Unvala, "Ancient Sites in Susiana," *RAAO* 25 (1928) 83-93. [Two monuments of the Partho-Roman period recently discovered at Susa, pp. 88-90]

Gorham P. Stevens, "The Fountain of Peirence in the time of Herodes Atticus," *AJA* 38 (1934) 55-58. (Corrigendia, p. 279)

Stephen Bleecker Luce, "An Attic Grave Stele in Providence," *AJA* 38 (1934) 43-44.

Guy Brunton, "Ramesside Stelae from the Eastern Desert," *ASAE* 36 (1936) 201.

Francis Henry Taylor, "A Fifth Century Stele in the Worcester Art Museum," *AJA* 41 (1937) 6-7.

*Ahmed Fakury, "Miscellanea," *ASAE* 37 (1937) 25-38. [1. Two New Stelae of Tiberius from Luxor Temple, pp. 25-27; 3. A Note on the Zernikh Stele, pp. 30-33]

Jane E. Brownlow, "The Attic Grave Stele in the Rhode Island School of Design," *AJA* 43 (1939) 309.

*A. E. Raubitschek, "Two Monuments Erected after the Victory of Marathon," *AJA* 44 (1940) 53-59.

Hetty Goldman, "The Sandon Monument of Tarsus," *JAOS* 60 (1940) 544-553.

Labib Habachi, "The monument of Biyahmû," *ASAE* 40 (1940-41) 721-732.

*W[illiam] F[oxwell] Albright, "A Votive Stele Erected by Ben-Hadad I of Damascus to the God Melcarth," *BASOR* #87 (1942) 23-29.

*Labib Ḥabachi, "Sais and its monuments," *ASAE* 42 (1943) 369-407.

*G. Levi Della Vida, "Some Notes on the Stele of Ben-Hadad," *BASOR* #90 (1943) 30-32.

*W[illiam] F[oxwell] Albright, "Reply to 'Some Notes on the Stele of Ben-Hadad', by G. Levi Della Vida," *BASOR* #90 (1943) 32-34.

I. J. Gelb, "The Date of the Cruciform Monument of Maništušu," *JNES* 8 (1949) 346-348.

George E. Mylonas, "Mycenaean Stelae," *AJA* 54 (1950) 255-256.

Ahmed Fakhry, "The Excavation of Snefru's Monuments at Dahshur. Second Preliminary Report," *ASAE* 52 (1952-54) 363-594.

J. B. Segal, "Pagan Syriac Monuments in the Vilayet of Urfa," *AS* 3 (1953) 97-119.

*R. D. Barnett, "The Phrygian Rock Façades and the Hittite Monuments," *BO* 10 (1953) 72-82.

William E. N. Kensdale, "The Red Granite Stela of Maʿīn," *JNES* 12 (1953) 194-196. *[Southern Arabian]*

Faraj Basmachi, "An Akkadian Stela," *Sumer* 10 (1954) 116-119.

J. R. Harris, "The date of the 'Hyksos' sphinxes," *JEA* 41 (1955) 123.

Labib Habachi, "A Strange Monument of the Ptolemaic Period from Crocodilopolis," *JEA* 41 (1955) 106-111.

Hans G. Güterbock, "Notes on Some Hittite Monuments," *AS* 6 (1956) 53-56.

William K. Simpson, "The Single-Dated Monuments of Sesostris I: An Aspect of the Institution of Congruency in the Twelfth Dynasty," *JNES* 15 (1956) 214-219.

Anonymous, "Akkadian Stele," *Sumer* 13 (1957) 222.

M. Katherine Donaldson, "Early Travelers' Interpretations of Three Athenian Monuments," *AJA* 62 (1958) 222-223.

K. Jartiz, "The Problem of the 'Broken Obelisk'," *JSS* 4 (1959) 204-215. *[Assyrian]*

*George G. Cameron, "The Monument of King Darius at Bisitun," *Arch* 13 (1960) 162-171.

*R. D. Barnett, "Two Chance Finds from Ur," *Iraq* 22 (1960) 172-173. *[Stela fragment of a Cymbal Player]*

Faraj Basmachi, "The Stele of Ur-Nanshe," *Sumer* 16 (1960) 45-47.

James Mellaart, "The Late Bronze Age Monuments of Eflatun Pinar and Fasillar near Beyşehir," *AS* 12 (1962) 111-117.

Herbert Bloch, "A Monument of the *Lares Augusti* in the Forum of Ostia," *HTR* 55 (1962) 211-223.

Bengt Julius Peterson, "A Stela of the Viceroy Hori I," *AO* 27 (1963) 3-9.

Dorothy Kent Hill, "The Animal Fountain of 'Araq el-Emir," *BASOR* #171 (1963) 45-55.

*Henry G. Fischer, "Varia Aegyptiaca," *JARCE* 2 (1963) 17-51. [7. The Stelae of Den and Other Rulers of the Archaic Period, pp 41-43]

John D. Cooney, "Fragments of a Great Saite Monument," *JARCE* 3 (1964) 79-87.

C. J. Edmonds, "Some Ancient Monuments on the Iraqi-Persian Boundary," *Iraq* 28 (1966) 159-163.

*Labib Habachi, "Three Monuments of the Unknown King Sehetepibre Pedubastis," *ZÄS* 93 (1966) 69-74.

David Ussishkin, "Observations on Some Monuments from Carchemish," *JNES* 26 (1967) 87-92.

Miroslav Verner, "Ancient Egyptian Monuments as seen by A Bohemian Missionary V. R. Prutky in the 18th Century," *ArOr* 36 (1968) 371-380.

Henry G. Fischer, "Monuments of the Old Kingdom in the Cairo Museum," *CdÉ* 43 (1968) 305-312.

Gus W. Van Beek, "Monuments of Axum in the Light of South Arabian Archaeology," *JAOS* 87 (1967) 113-122.

Kenneth A. Kitchen, "Two Donation Stelae in The Brooklyn Museum," *JARCE* 8 (1969-70) 59-67.

§191 *2.5.8.5 Palaces*

( ) S., "Ancient Oriental Palaces," *JSL, 2nd Ser.,* 1 (1851-52) 422-433.

Anonymous, "A Buried Temple and Palace," *AAOJ* 2 (1879-80) 297-298. *[At Nineveh]*

William Copley Winslow, "The Palace of Minos in Crete," *AAOJ* 23 (1901) 54-57.

Arthur J. Evans, "The Palace of Minos," *SIR* (1901) 425-437.

Anonymous, "Exploration and Discovery: The Unearthing of the Throne-Room of Nebuchadnezzer," *BW* 19 (1902) 209.

Thomas B. Lindsay, "The Basilica Aemilia," *AJA* 7 (1903) 88.

*P. C. V. Baur, "The Palace of Thetis on the François Vase," *AJA* 8 (1904) 88.

Clarence S. Fisher, "The Mycenaean Palace at Nippur," *AJA* 8 (1904) 403-432.

D. G. Hogarth, "The Palace of Knossos," *QRL* 200 (1904) 374-395. *(Review)*

Allan Marquand, "The Palace at Nippur not Mycenæan but Hellenistic," *AAOJ* 27 (1905) 163-165.

Allan Marquand, "The Palace at Nippur not Mycenaean but Hellenistic," *AJA* 9 (1905) 7-10.

Anonymous, "Palace at Cnossus, Crete," *RP* 5 (1906) 158-159.

E. G. Hermer, "Belshazzar's Hall—Nebuchadnezzar's Palace Laid Bare," *CFL, 3rd Ser.,* 12 (1910) 381-383.

Anonymous, "Persian Palace of Ukheithar," *RP* 9 (1910) 62.

*P. P. Flournoy, "Ahab's Palace and Jezebel's Table," *USR* 23 (1911-12) 130-134.

Anonymous, "A Palace of Darius I," *OC* 29 (1915) 507-511.

Samuel E. Bassett, "The Palace of Odysseus," *AJA* 23 (1919) 288-311.

Samuel E. Bassett, "The Palace of Odysseus, *A.J.A.* XXIII, pp. 288-311," *AJA* 23 (1919) 413.

Clarence S. Fisher, "The Throne Room of Merenptah," *MJ* 12 (1921) 30-34.

Clarence S. Fisher, "Merenptah's Throne Room," *MJ* 15 (1924) 93-100.

Walton Brooks McDaniels, "Basilica Aemilia," *AJA* 32 (1928) 155-178.

J. M. Unvala, "The Palace of Darius the Great and the Apadana of Artaxerxes II in Susa," *BSOAS* 5 (1928-30) 229-232.

Arthur Evans, "'The Palace of Minos'," *Antiq* 4 (1930) 96-97.

R. Campbell Thompson and R. W. Hutchinson, "The Site of the Palace of Ashurnasirpal at Nineveh, excavated in 1929-30 on behalf of the British Museum," *AAA* 18 (1931) 79-112.

Percy Gardner, "The Palace of Minos," *Antiq* 5 (1931) 315-321.

[W. M.] Flinders Petrie, "The Palaces of Ancient Gaza. Tell el Ajjūl," *AEE* 17 (1932) 1-9.

Valentin Müller, "The Palace of Vouni in Cyprus," *AJA* 36 (1932) 408-417.

Einar Gjerstad, "Further Remarks on the Palace of Vouni," *AJA* 37 (1933) 589-598.

Valentin Müller, "A Reply," *AJA* 37 (1933) 599-601.

Einar Gjerstad, "Final Reply on Vouni," *AJA* 37 (1933) 658-659.

Anonymous, "The Palace of Darius at Persepolis," *Antiq* 7 (1933) 219-220.

R. G. Kent, "The Record of Darius's Palace at Susa," *JAOS* 53 (1933) 1-23. (Addendum, p. 166)

W. A. Heurtley, "The Site of the Palace of Odysseus," *Antiq* 9 (1935) 410-417.

*C. C. McCown, "Two Year's Achievements in Palestinian Archaeology," *RL* 8 (1939) 97-108. [Umaiyad Palaces, pp. 103-104]

Edward A. Cerny, "Archaeological Corner. Jerusalem: Palace of Herod the Great," *CBQ* 4 (1942) 258-261.

Carl W. Blegen, "The Palace of King Nestor," *Arch* 5 (1952) 130-135.

H[enri] Frankfort, "The Origin of the Bît Halani," *Iraq* 14 (1952) 120-131. *[Palace]*

Carl W. Blegen, "King Nestor's Palace: New Discoveries," *Arch* 6 (1953) 203-207.

Carl W. Blegen, "The Palace of Nestor: Excavations of 1954," *AJA* 59 (1955) 31-37.

John L. Caskey, "A Palace of the Early Bronze Age at Lerna," *AJA* 59 (1955) 171.

Oscar Broneer, "The Temple of Poseidon at the Isthmia," *AJA* 59 (1955) 170.

Carl W. Blegen, "The Palace of Nestor Excavations of 1955," *AJA* 60 (1956) 95-101.

*Alan Rowe, "A Contribution to the Archaeology of the Western Desert: III (The Temple-Tombs of Alexander the Great and His Palace in Rhacotis: The Great Wall of the Libyan Desert)," *BJRL* 38 (1955-56) 139-165.

*David Oates and J. H. Reid, "The Burnt Palace and the Nabu Temple; Nimrud, 1955," *Iraq* 18 (1956) 22-39.

Carl W. Blegen, "The Palace of Nestor Excavations of 1956," *AJA* 61 (1957) 129-135.

C[arl] W. Blegen, "The Palace of Nestor Excavations of 1957: Part I," *AJA* 62 (1958) 175-181.

Mabel Lang, "The Palace of Nestor Excavations: Part II," *AJA* 62 (1958) 181-191.

Joan Gorell, "Babylon: Nebuchadnezzer's Palace," *AT* 3 (1958-59) #2, 3-5.

Joan Gorell, "Babylon: Nebuchadnezzar's Palace. Part 2," *AT* 3 (1958-59) #3, 17-19.

J. Walter Graham, "The Residential Quarter of the Minoan Palace," *AJA* 63 (1959) 47-52.

*Carl W. Blegen, "The Palace of Nestor Excavations of 1958: Part I," *AJA* 63 (1959) 121-127.

Carl W. Blegen and Mabel Lang, "The Palace of Nestor Excavations of 1959," *AJA* 64 (1960) 153-164. *[Parts I & II]*

George M. A. Hanfmann, "On the Date of the Late Hittite Palace at Sakçegözü," *BASOR* #160 (1960) 43-45.

Carl W. Blegen and Mabel Lang, "The Palace of Nestor Excavations of 1960," *AJA* 65 (1961) 153-163. *[Parts I & II]*

Hans G. Güterbock, "When Was the Late Hittite Palace at Sakçagözü Built?" *BASOR* #162 (1961) 49-50.

Carl W. Blegen and Mabel Lang, "The Palace of Nestor Excavations of 1961," *AJA* 66 (1962) 145-152. *[Parts I & II]*

*Carl W. Blegen and Mabel Lang, "The Palace of Nestor Excavations of 1962," *AJA* 67 (1963) 151-162.

T. Leslie Shear Jr., "New Exploration of the Palace of Mycenae," *AJA* 67 (1963) 217.

Nicholas Platon, "A New Minoan Palace," *Arch* 16 (1963) 269-275.

Behman Abu es-Soof, "Further Investigations in Assur-Nasir-Pal's Palace," *Sumer* 19 (1963) 66-68.

*Carl W. Blegen and Mabel Lang, "The Palace of Nestor Excavations of 1963," *AJA* 68 (1964) 95-105.

Leon Pomerance, "Kato Zakro: The Fourth Great Cretan Palace," *AJA* 68 (1964) 198.

M. R. Popham, "The Palace at Knossos: A Matter of Definition and a Question of Fact," *AJA* 68 (1964) 349-354.

*Edouard B.Ghazouli, "The palace and magazines attached to the Temple of Sety I at Abydos and the facade of this Temple,"*ASAE* 58(1964) 99-186.

P. R. S. Moorey, "The 'Plano-Convex Building' at Kish and Early Mesopotamian Palaces," *Iraq* 26 (1964) 83-98.

Carl W. Blegen, "The Palace of Nestor Excavations of 1965," *AJA* 70 (1966) 101-103.

*M[ervyn] R. Popham, "The Destruction of the Palace of Knossos and its Pottery," *Antiq* 40 (1966) 24-28.

D[avid] Ussishkin, "King Solomon's Palace and Building 1723 in Megiddo," *IEJ* 16 (1966) 174-186.

*Mervyn R. Popham, "The Palace of Knossos: its destruction and reoccupation reconsidered," *KZFE* 5 (1966) 17-24.

Geoffrey Turner, "The Palace and Bâtiment aux Ivories at Arslan Tash: A Reappraisal," *Iraq* 30 (1968) 62-68.

J. E. Reade, "The Palace of Tiglath-pileser III," *Iraq* 30 (1968) 69-73.

§192 ***2.5.8.6 Pyramids***

Joseph Hager, "Observations on the Name and Origin of the Pyramids of Egypt," *MMBR* 12 (1801) 185-189.

†Anonymous, "Gabb's Disquisitions on the Great Pyramid," *BCQTR* 29 (1807) 610-618. *(Review)*

T. Squire, "Section of the Second Pyramid of Gheza, in Egypt," *MMBR* 48 (1819-20) 1-2.

†Anonymous, "The Pyramids and their Builders," *ERL* 5 (1846) 87-119. *(Review)*

*G. Seyffarth, "Three Lectures on Egyptian Antiquities, &c., delivered at the Stuyvesant Institute, New York, May 1856," *ER* 8 (1856-57) 34-104. [XVIII. The Pyramid of Cheops, pp. 90-91]

Anonymous, "The Great Pyramid," *NBR* 47 (1867) 149-188. *(Review)*

Anonymous, "Piazzi Smith and the Great Pyramid," *CE* 84 (1868) 62-71. *(Review)*

Geo. W. Anderson, "The Great Pyramid of Gizeh," *BQ* 3 (1869) 193-209.

Anonymous, "Jeeseh, The Great Pyramid: Its Age, Design and Origin," *CR* 21 (1869-70) 53-72.

*S. M. Drach, "Note on Universal Type-Numbers, and Pyramid Casing Stone," *SBAT* 1 (1872) 385.

S. M. Drach, "Observations on Base-Length of Great Pyramid, and Royal Coffer's Dimensions," *SBAT* 1 (1872) 335-338.

Richard A. Proctor, "The Problem of the Great Pyramid," *ContR* 36 (1879) 93-119.

†Anonymous, "The Great Pyramid and its Interpreters," *LQHR* 55 (1880-81) 265-313. *(Review)*

Samuel Birch, "The Pyramid of Sakkara recently opened," *SBAP* 3 (1880-81) 93.

*†Samuel Birch, "A Description of the Pyramid of King Pepi, and the position of the Inscriptions and Sarcophagus," *SBAP* 3 (1880-81) 93-96.

†Samuel Birch, "Notes on the Recently discovered Pyramid of Pepi (VIth Dynasty) at Sakkara," *SBAP* 3 (1880-81) 111-116.

*Theo. G. Pinches, "The name Ben-Hadad," *SBAP* 5 (1882-83) 71-74. [Remarks by George Bertin, pp. 75-76] *[Pyramids]*

R. Meade Bache, "The Latest Phase of the Great Pyramid Discussion," *ACQR* 10 (1885) 457-477.

W. F. Adeney, "Up the Great Pyramid and Inside It," *CongL* 14 (1885) 388-395.

*J. Norman Lockyer, "The Early Temple and Pyramid Builders," *SIR* (1893) 95-105.

*Alfred C. Bryant, "The Great Pyramid and the Book of the Dead," *BOR* 7 (1893-94) 134-144.

W. Marsham Adams, "The Great Pyramid," *BOR* 7 (1893-94) 153-155.

Anonymous, "The Great Pyramids of Gizeh," *MQR, 3rd Ser.*, 31 (1905) 389.

Anonymous, "The Origin of the Pyramids," *AAOJ* 31 (1909) 94-95.

Walter Woodburn Hyde, "A Visit to the Pyramids of Gizeh. Part I," *RP* 9 (1910) 247-265.

Walter Woodburn Hyde, "A Visit to the Pyramids of Gizeh. Part II," *RP* 9 (1910) 312-327.

Lee H. McCoy, "The Riddle of the Pyramid," *AAOJ* 33 (1911) 123-134.

W. M. F[linders] P[etrie], "British School of Archaeology in Egypt. The Treasure of Lahun," *AEE* 1 (1914) 97-100. *[Pyramid of Senusert II at Lahun]*

Anonymous, "Archaeology—The Mystery of a Plunder Pyramid," *HR* 68 (1914) 281-283. *[Pyramid of Senusert II]*

Albert M. Lythgoe, "Excavations at the South Pyramid of Lisht in 1914. Report from the Metropolitan Museum, New York," *AEE* 2 (1915) 145-153.

Edgar J. Banks, "Seven Wonders of the Ancient World. I—The First Wonder: The Pyramid of Cheops," *A&A* 3 (1916) 27-33.

*G. W. Gilmore, "Astronomy and Egyptian Pyramids and Temples," *HR* 83 (1922) 479.

J. Tarrell, "The Great Pyramid Courses," *AEE* 10 (1925) 36-39. *(Trans. by W. M. Flinders Petrie]*

*Cecil M. Firth, "Excavations of the Department of Antiquities at the Step Pyramid, Saqqara (1924-1925)," *ASAE* 25 (1925) 149-159.

R. Engelbach, "Précis of the Survey of Egypt Paper No. 39, by J. H. Cole, on the size and orientation of the Great Pyramid," *ASAE* 25 (1925) 167-173.

C. M. Firth, "The Step Pyramid, Saqqara," *Antiq* 2 (1928) 461-463.

*[W. M.] Flinders Petrie, "The Building of a Pyramid," *AEE* 15 (1930) 33-39.

*Kurt Vogel, "The Truncated Pyramid in Egyptian Mathematics," *JEA* 16 (1930) 242-249.

Noel F. Wheeler, "Pyramids and their Purpose," *Antiq* 9 (1935) 5-21.

Noel F. Wheeler, "Pyramids and their Purpose. II. The Pyramid of Khufu," *Antiq* 9 (1935) 161-189.

Noel F. Wheeler, "Pyramids and their Purpose. III. Pyramid Mysticism and Mystification," *Antiq* 9 (1935) 292-304.

P. E. K[retzmann], "Pyramids and Their Purpose," *CTM* 6 (1935) 615.

*F. Blaess, "'The Altar to the Lord' and the Great Pyramid. Isaiah 19:18-20," *AusTR* 8 (1937) 70-84, 97-103.

Louis E. Lord, "The Pyramids of Argolis," *AJA* 42 (1938) 123.

A. Lucas, "Were the Giza Pyramids painted?" *Antiq* 12 (1938) 26-30.

J. W. Crowfoot, "The Giza Necropolis," *Antiq* 20 (1946) 186-190.

*R. Engelbach, "An essay on the advent of the dynastic race in Egypt and its consequences," *ASAE* 42 (1943) 193-221.

J. E. G. Harris, "A Suggestion regarding the Construction of the Pyramids," *JEA* 30 (1944) 74.

Ahmed Fakhry, "The southern pyramid of Snefru," *ASAE* 51 (1951) 509-522.

Hassan Mustapha, "The Surveying of the Bent Pyramid at Dahshur," *ASAE* 52 (1952-54) 595-602.

*Dows Dunham, "From Tumulus to Pyramid—and Back," *Arch* 6 (1953) 87-94.

*H[enri] Frankfort, "Pyramid Temples and the Religion of the Old Kingdom," *BO* 10 (1953) 157-162.

*Elizabeth Thomas, "Air channels in the Great Pyramid," *JEA* 39 (1953) 113.

*J. Gwyn Griffiths, "Three notes on Herodotus, Book II," *ASAE* 53 (1955) 139-152. [3. The Tools of the Pyramid-Builders, pp. 149-152]

*Dows Dunham, "Building an Egyptian Pyramid," *Arch* 9 (1956) 157-165.

*Alan Rowe, "Studies in the Archaeology of the Near East: II. Some Facts Concerning the Great Pyramids of el-Giza and Their Royal Constructiors," *BJRL* 44 (1961-62) 100-118.

*Virginia Trimble, "Astronomical Investigation Concerning the So-called Air-Shafts of Cheops' Pyramid," *MIO* 10 (1964) 183-187.

*Alexander Badawy, "The Stella Destiny of Pharaoh and the So-Called Air-Shafts of Cheops' Pyramid," *MIO* 10 (1964) 189-206.

*John Bennett, "Pyramid names," *JEA* 52 (1966) 174-176.

Norman Neuerburg, "Greek and Roman Pyramids," *AJA* 71 (1967) 192.

*Hubert Paulsen, "The Cubit—Remen Applied to the Geometry of the Cheops Pyramid," *AA* 40 (1969) 185-200.

Norman Neuerburg, "Greek and Roman Pyramids," *Arch* 22 (1969) 106-115.

*John Bennett, "The names of the pyramids of the Twelfth Dynasty," *JEA* 55 (1969) 216.

Wiesław Koziński, "The Investment Process of the Cheops Pyramid (Some Problems)," *ZÄS* 96 (1969-70) 115-124.

§193 ***2.5.8.7 Sanctuaries, Shrines, Temples, and Ziggurats***

Anonymous, "Account of the Subterranean Temple of Ipsambul, lately discovered in Egypt by Belzoni and Beechey, and described by Lieutenant-Colonel Stratton, in a paper read before the Royal Society of Edinburgh," *MMBR* 50 (1820-21) 27-29.

Eli Smith, "An Ancient Temple on Mount Lebanon," *BS* (1843) 557-563. [Note by Edward Robinson, pp. 562-563]

Anonymous, "The Temples of Jupiter Panhellenius at Ægina and of Apollo Epicurius at Bassœ, near Phigaleia in Arcadia," *DR* 50 (1861) 302-312. *(Review)*

Henry C. Rawlinson, "On the Birs Nimrud, or the Great Temple of Borsippa," *JRAS* (1861) 1-34.

C. W. Goodwin, "On the age of the Temple of Denderah," *ZÄS* 5 (1867) 49-52.

Charles Warren, "The Temples of Coele-Syria," *PEFQS* 2 (1870) 183-210.

O. D. Miller, "A Pyramidal Temple," *AAOJ* 3 (1880-81) 105-114.

Isaac H. Hall, "A Temple of Zeus Labranios in Cyprus," *JAOS* 11 (1885) clxvi-clxx.

*William Simpson, "The Tower of Babel and the Birs-Nimroud—Suggestions as to the Origin of Mesopotamian Tower Temples," *SBAP* 8 (1885-86) 83-86.

William Simpson, "The Tower of Babel, and the Birs-Nimroud. *Suggestions as to the origin of Mesopotamian Tower-Temples*," *SBAT* 9 (1886-93) 307-332.

George B. Hussey, "The Distribution of Hellenic Temples," *AJA, O.S.*, 6 (1890) 59-64.

*John C. Rolfe, "Discoveries at Anthedon in 1889," *AJA, O.S.*, 6 (1890) 96-107. [A Small Temple at Anthedon, p. 104]

Henry S. Washington, "Excavations by the American School at Plataia in 1891. Discovery of a Temple of Archaic Plan," *AJA, O.S.*, 7 (1891) 390-405. (Comment by Charles Waldstein, p. 390)

Harold N. Fowler, "The Temple of the Acropolis Burnt by the Persians," *AJA, O.S.*, 8 (1893) 1-17.

Walter Miller, "A History of the Akropolis of Athens," *AJA, O.S.*, 8 (1893) 473-556.

*Allan Marquand, "A Study of Greek Architectural Proportions. The Temples of Selinous," *AJA, O.S.*, 9 (1894) 521-532.

Herman V. Hilprecht, "Exploration of the Temple of Bel," *AAOJ* 17 (1895) 334-337.

*W[illia]m Henry Goodyear, "A Discovery of Horizontal Curves in the Roman Temple Called 'Maison Carrée' at Nimes," *AJA, O.S.*, 10 (1895) 1-12.

Rufus R. Richardson, "Papers of the American School of Classical Studies at Athens. A Temple in Eretria," *AJA, O.S.*, 10 (1895) 326-337.

Ludwig Borchardt, "Exploration and Discovery. The Discovery of a New Temple on Philae," *BW* 7 (1896) 218.

Wm. C. Winslow, "The Temple of Queen Hatasu at Thebes," *AAOJ* 19 (1897) 32-34.

Joseph A. Seiss, "The Great Temples of Baalbec—Who Built Them?" *LCR* 17 (1898) 217-293.

*Theo. G. Pinches, "The Temples of Ancient Babylonia. Part I.," *SBAP* 22 (1900) 358-371. *[Part II never published]*

A. E. P. R. Dowling, "The Greek Temples in Sicily," *ACQR* 26 (1901) 694-714.

W. N. Bates, "The Old Temple of Athena on the Acropolis," *AJA* 5 (1901) 3.

Samuel Hudson Chapman, "The Discovery of a Doric Temple at Locri, Italy," *AJA* 5 (1901) 18.

William K. Prentice, "The Sanctuary of Zeus Madbachos on the Djebel Shêkh Berekât in Syria," *AJA* 6 (1902) 27-28.

Edward L. Tilton, "Concerning the Two Temples of Hera at Agros," *AJA* 6 (1902) 32.

Charles C. Torrey, "(1) A recently discovered Phoenician Temple Ruin," *AJA* 6 (1902) 33.

*A. H. Sayce, "Notes from Egypt," *SBAP* 24 (1902) 86. [Temple of Seti II, at Eshmunen]

*Howard Carter, "Report of Work done in Upper Egypt," *ASAE* 4 (1903) 171-180. [I. Edfou Temple, pp. 171-172]

*W. M. Flinders Petrie, "The Ten Temples of Abydos," *AAOJ* 26 (1904) 273-280.

Anonymous, "The Temple of Abu Simbel," *AAOJ* 27 (1905) 295-296.

Ettore Pais, "The Topography of the Temple of the Sirens on the Sorrentine Peninsula," *AJA* 9 (1905) 71-72.

Allan Marquand, "The Temple of the Didymaean Apollo near Miletus," *AJA* 9 (1905) 79-80.

H. R. Hall, "The Excavation of the XI dynasty Temple at Deir el-Bahari, Thebes," *Man* 5 (1905) #66.

J. D. Crace, "The Trilithon and Great Temple at Baalbek," *PEFQS* 37 (1905) 262-265.

Percy E. Newberry, "The Temple of Erment as it was in 1850," *SBAP* 27 (1905) 100.

H. R. Hall, "The XIth Dynasty Temple at Deir el-Bahari," *SBAP* 27 (1905) 173-183.

Edgar James Banks, "The Bismya Temple," *AJSL* 22 (1905-06) 29-34.

Arthur E. P. Weigall, "A Report on the Excavation of the funeral Temple of Thoutmôsis III at Gurneh," *ASAE* 7 (1906) 121-141.

Benjamin W. Bacon, "Among the Sun-Temples of Coele-Syria," *RP* 5 (1906) 67-83.

Anonymous, "Temple at Deir el-Bahari," *RP* 5 (1906) 154.

Edgar James Banks, "The Bismya Temple," *RP* 5 (1906) 227-236.

Anonymous, "Sun-Temple at Abusir," *RP* 5 (1906) 352.

James H. Breasted, "Oriental Exploration Fund of the University of Chicago. First Preliminary Report of the Egyptian Expedition," *AJSL* 23 (1906-07) 1-64. *[The Temples of Lower Nubia]*

Albert W. Van Buren, "The Temples at Astia," *AJA* 11 (1907) 55-56.

Arthur E. P. Weigall, "Report on the Discovery of part of a Temple at Asfun," *ASAE* 8 (1907) 106-107.

Arthur E. P. Weigall, "Report on Work done in the Temple of Luxor, in 1905-1906," *ASAE* 8 (1907) 113-115.

Arthur E. P. Weigall, "Note Additionnelle," *ASAE* 8 (1907) 286. *[Plan of the Mortuary Temple of Thoutmose III]*

Anonymous, "The Old Temple in Egypt," *MQR, 3rd Ser.*, 33 (1907) 196-197.

Anonymous, "Ancient Temple at Thebes," *RP* 6 (1907) 93-94.

Anonymous, "Greek Temple at Prinias in Crete," *RP* 6 (1907) 339.

Anonymous, "Temple of Mentuhetep at Deir El-Bahari," *RP* 6 (1907) 342.

*P. Scott-Moncrieff, "Some Notes on the XVIIth Dynasty Temple at Wady Ḥalfa," *SBAP* 29 (1907) 39-46.

D. D. Luckenbill, "The Temples of Babylonia and Assyria," *AJSL* 24 (1907-08) 291-322.

Arthur E. P. Weigall, "A Report of the so-called Temple of Redesiyeh," *ASAE* 9 (1908) 71-84.

R. C. Bosanquet, "Greek Temples and Early Religion," *QRL* 208 (1908) 252-279. *(Review)*

Anonymous, "Origin of the Greek Temple," *RP* 7 (1908) 61.

Anonymous, "Temple of Jupiter Stator," *RP* 7 (1908) 172.

Anonymous, "Temple at the Shire of Artemis Orthia," *RP* 7 (1908) 210.

*James H. Breasted, "The Temple of Soleb, A New Form of Egyptian Architecture," *AJA* 13 (1909) 53-54.

Arthur E. Henderson, "The Croesus (VIth Century B.C.) Temple of Artemis (Diana) at Ephesus," *RP* 8 (1909) 195-206.

*A. H. Sayce, "A Greek Inscription of a King (?) of Axum Found at Meroë. Meroitic Inscriptions," *SBAP* 31 (1909) 189-203. [The Temple of Basa, p. 200]

Anonymous, "Temples in Ancient Egypt," *AAOJ* 32 (1910) 31-34.

Anonymous, "Sun Temple on Site of Meroe," *RP* 9 (1910) 284-285.

*C. C. Edgar, "Notes from the Delta," *ASAE* 11 (1911) 87-96. [II. The Temple of Samanoud, pp. 90-96]

Anonymous, "Temple of Abu Simbel," *RP* 11 (1912) 106.

T. G. Pinches, "The Bird of Temple 'Z' at Babylon," *SBAP* 34 (1912) 144-145.

Anonymous, "Foundations of a Temple of Minerva at Syracuse," *RP* 12 (1913) 99.

*G. Elliot Smith, "Oriental Tombs and Temples," *JMUEOS* #4 (1914-15) 55-60.

C. C. Edgar, "A Building of Merenptah of Mit Rahineh," *ASAE* 15 (1915) 97-104.

*G. Elliot Smith, "Oriental Tombs and Temples," *JMUEOS* #4 (1914-15) 55-60.

Anonymous, "A Great Temple Discovered in Ancient Memphis," *A&A* 2 (1915) 59.

H. G. Lyons, "The Temple at Mirgisse," *JEA* 3 (1915) 182-183.

Garrett Chatfield Pier, "The Great Temple of Amora at Karnak *(Illustrated with Original Photographs by the Writer),*" *A&A* 4 (1916) 91-100.

M. A. Murray, "The Temple of Ramses II at Abydos," *AEE* 3 (1916) 121-138.

George A. Reisner, "The Barkal Temples in 1916," *JEA* 4 (1916) 213-227.

George A. Reisner , "The Barkal Temples in 1916 (*continued from Vol. IV, p.* 227)," *JEA* 5 (1918) 99-112.

George A. Reisner, "The Barkal Temples in 1916 (*continued from Vol. V, p.* 112)," *JEA* 4 (1920) 247-264.

Edgar James Banks, "Seven Wonders of the Ancient World. IV—The Fourth Wonder: The Temple of Diana at Ephesus," *A&A* 5 (1917) 13-19.

*Otto H. Boström, "The Babylonian Temple and its Place in the Ancient Community," *TTKF* 19 (1917) 28-36.

C. Leonard Woolley, "The Egyptian Temple at Byblos," *JEA* 7 (1921) 200-201.

A. V. D. Hort, "Archæological Notes on the 'Neolithic' Temples of Malta," *Man* 21 (1921) #99.

*Somers Clarke, "El-Kâb and its Temples," *JEA* 8 (1922) 16-40.

Anonymous, "Archaeological Notes and Comments. Bare Ancient Temple in Ur of Chaldeans," *A&A* 15 (1923) 193.

*R. Engelbach, "Origin of the Great Hypostyle Hall at Karnak," *AEE* 9 (1924) 65-71.

C. M. Firth, "Two mastaba chapels of the IIIrd dynasty at Sakkara," *ASAE* 24 (1924) 122-127.

C. L[eonard] Woolley, "The Ziggurat of Ur. From the Report of the Joint Expedition of the British Museum University to Mesopotamia," *MJ* 15 (1924) 107-114.

Byron Khun deProrok, "The Excavations of the Sanctuary of Tanit at Carthage," *A&A* 19 (1925) 37-44.

Benjamin T. Kurtz, "Abu Simbel, Greatest of Egyptian Temples," *A&A* 19 (1925) 135-145.

*Horace W. Wright, "The Janus Shrine at the Forum," *AJA* 29 (1925) 79-81.

William Nickerson Bates, "The E of the Temple at Delphi," *AJA* 29 (1925) 239-246.

Anonymous, "Tomb-Chapel 525 at Tell El-ʿAmarna," *JEA* 11 (1925) 36.

C. Leonard Woolley, "A Great Temple of Babylonia," *MJ* 16 (1925) 57-59.

Alan Rowe, "Discovery of the Temple of Ashtaroth. Report of the Expedition to Palestine," *MJ* 16 (1925) 307-313.

Anonymous, "Notes and Comments. A Hidden Temple of Demeter in Sicily," *A&A* 21 (1926) 47.

Alan Rowe, "The Temples of Dagon and Ashtoreth at Beth-Shan," *MJ* 17 (1926) 295-304.

W[illiam] F[oxwell] Albright, "The date of the foundation of the early Egyptian temple of Byblos," *ZÄS* 62 (1927) 62-63.

I. O. Nothstein, "The Temple of Dagon at Beth-Shan," *AugQ* 7 (1928) 44-45.

*Rowe Alan, "Excavations at Beisan During the 1927 Season. Two Temples of Thothmes III, etc.," *PEFQS* 60 (1928) 73-90.

Anonymous, "Notes and Comments. Greek Shrines Near Girgenti," *A&A* 27 (1929) 281.

*George P. Hedley, "The 'Temple of Dagon' at Beth-Shan," *AJA* 33 (1929) 34-36.

Jotham Johnson, "Hera in Xypete," *AJA* 33 (1929) 400-401. *[Temple]*

Anonymous, "The Temples of Philae," *Antiq* 3 (1929) 227-228.

Clark Hopkins, "Further Discoveries in the Temple of the Palmyrene Gods at Doura," *PAPA* 60 (1929) xvi-xvii.

Anonymous, "Notes and Comments. Himera's Doric Temple Excavated," *A&A* 30 (1930) 95-96.

Anonymous, "Notes and Comments. Nebuchadnezzer's Shrine of 2,500 Years Ago," *A&A* 30 (1930) 97.

*Anonymous, "Notes and Comments. Hellenistic Theatre and Temple in Cos," *A&A* 29 (1930) 233.

Frederick Joseph de Waele, "The Greek Stoa North of the Temple of Corinth," *AJA* 35 (1931) 394-434.

Alan Rowe, and Pere Vincent, "New Light on the Evolution of Canaanite Temples," *PEFQS* 63 (1931) 12-22.

*R. Campbell Thompson and R. W. Hamilton, "The British Museum Excavations of the Temple of Ishtar at Nineveh, 1930-31," *AAA* 19 (1932) 55-116.

*Silva New, "The Serabit Expedition of 1930: III. The Temple of Hathor," *HTR* 25 (1932) 122-129.

*Alfred Westholm, "The Paphian Temple of Aphrodite and its Relation to Oriental Architecture," *AA* 4 (1933) 201-236.

Ferdinand Joseph de Waele, "The Sanctuary at Asklepios and Hygieia at Corinth," *AJA* 37 (1933) 417-451.

E. Barrtow Muller and Charles Bahe, "The Prehistoric Temple of Stratum IX at Tepe Gawra," *BASOR* #54 (1934) 13-18.

(Miss) E. W. Gardner, "Notes on a Temple at 'Ain Amur in the Libyan Desert," *AEE* 20 (1935) 108-109.

*J. Prip-Møller, "On the Wall of the Jupiter Temple, Capitol," *AA* 7 (1936) 75-80.

Franklin P. Johnson, "The Kardaki Temple," *AJA* 40 (1936) 46-54.

William Bell Dinsmoor, "Additional Note on the Temple at Kardaki," *AJA* 40 (1936) 55-56.

Harriet Boyd Hawes, "The Ancient Temple of the Goddess on the Acropolis," *AJA* 40 (1936) 120-121.

John L. Caskey, "A Basilica of Troy VI," *AJA* 40 (1936) 122.

George E. Mylonas, "Eleusiniaka," *AJA* 40 (1936) 122. *[Temple]*

*Paolo Zancani [Montuoro] and Umberto Zantotti-Bianco, "Archaeological Notes. The Discovery of the Heraion of Lucania," *AJA* 40 (1936) 185-187. *[Sanctuary]*

*Philip H. Davis, "The Accounts of the Theatre on Delos," *AJA* 41 (1937) 109.

Nelson Glueck, "A Newly Discovered Nabatean Temple of Atargatis and Hadad at Khirbet et-Tannûr, Transjordania," *AJA* 41 (1937) 361-376.

*Ahmed Fakury, "Miscellanea," *ASAE* 37 (1937) 25-38. [2. The Funerary Temple of Tuthmosis III, pp. 27-30]

Nelson Glueck, "The Nabataean Temple of Khirbet et-Tannûr," *BASOR* #67 (1937) 6-16.

Donald F. Brown, "The Temples of Juiper Ultor and Sol Invictus," *AJA* 42 (1938) 129.

Nelson Glueck, "The Early History of a Nabataean Temple (Khirbet et-Tannûr)," *BASOR* #69 (1938) 7-18.

P. Delougaz, "A Short Investigation of a Temple at Al-ʿUbaid," *Iraq* 5 (1938) 1-9.

St John Ervine, "John Tuttle Wood, discoverer of the Artemision 1869," *Isis* 28 (1938) 376-384. *[Temple of Diana]*

William Bell Dinsmoor, "The Temple of Ares in the Agora," *AJA* 43 (1939) 303.

Nelson Glueck, "The Nabataean Temple of Qasr Rabbah," *AJA* 43 (1939) 381-387.

*Ahmed Fakhry, "Baḥria and Farafra Oases. Second Preliminary Report," *ASAE* 39 (1939) 627-642. *[Temples]*

*Ahmed Fakhry, "A new speos from the reign of Hatshepsut and Tuthomsis III at Beni-Ḥasan," *ASAE* 39 (1939) 709-723.

G[eorge] H. McF[ayden], "Sanctuary of Apollo at Kourion," *UMB* 8 (1939-40) #4, 22-28.

Frederick R. Grace, "The Late Mycenaean Sanctuary at Amyclae," *AJA* 44 (1940) 105.

William A. Oldfather, "An Ancient Rock Altar near Thronion in East Locris," *AJA* 44 (1940) 108.

Ahmed Fakhry, "A Roman Temple between Kharga and Dakhla," *ASAE* 40 (1940-41) 761-768.

Ahmed Fakhry, "A Temple of Alexander the Great at Baḥria Oasis," *ASAE* 40 (1940-41) 823-828.

*Jaroslav Černý, "'The Temple', 𓏏𓄿𓉗𓏏𓉐, as an Abbreviated Name for the Temple of Medīnet Habu," *JEA* 26 (1940) 127-130.

*Frederick Poulsen, "Nemi Studies," *AA* 12 (1941) 1-52. [I The Temple of Diana, pp. 1-12; III The Votive Chamber at Nemi, pp. 20-52]

*Frank E. Brown, "The Temple of Zeus Olympios at Dura and the Religious Policy of the Seleucids," *AJA* 45 (1941) 94.

Robert J. Braidwood, "The Date of the Byblos Temples. Buildings II, VIII, and XL," *AJA* 58 (1941) 254-258.

J. W. Crowfoot, "A Temple of Adonis?" *Antiq* 15 (1941) 45-49.

George E. Mylonas, "The Temple of Demeter at Eleusis," *AJA* 46 (1942) 120.

Clark Hopkins, "The Parthian Temple," *Bery* 7 (1942) 1-18.

*William Bell Dinsmoor, "The Temple of Ares and the Roman Agora," *AJA* 47 (1943) 383-384.

G. Ernest Wright, "The Significance of the Temple in the Ancient Near East," *BA* 7 (1944) 41-44.

*Harold H. Nelson, "I. The Egyptian Temple with particular reference to the Theban Temples of the Empire Period," *BA* 7 (1944) 44-53. [The Symbolism of the Egyptian Temple; Deity and the Temple in Egypt; Temple and Community in Egypt]

*Leo A. Oppenheim, "II. The Mesopotamian Temple," *BA* 7 (1944) 54-63. [The Typical Mesopotamian Temple; Temple and Community in Mesopotamia]

Edith Porada, "An Unknown Representation of a Ziggurat," *BASOR* #99 (1945) 18-20.

Margaret Crosby, "The Peribolos of the Twelve Gods in Athens," *AJA* 50 (1946) 403-404.

Jasper Y. Brinton, "Restoration of the Temple of Abusir," *Arch* 1 (1948) 186-187.

M. V. Seton Williams, "Palestinian Temples," *Iraq* 11 (1949) 77-89.

I. Ben-Dor, "A Middle Bronze-Age Temple at Nahariya," *QDAP* 14 (1950) 1-41.

B[enjamin] Maisler, "The Chronology of the Beth-Shean Temples," *BIES* 16 (1951) #3/4, II-IV.

Frank P. Albright, "The Excavation of the Temple of the Moon at Mârib (Yemen)," *BASOR* #128 (1952) 25-38.

*W[illiam] F[oxwell] Albright, "Notes on the Temple 'Awwâm and the Archaic Bronze Statue," *BASOR* #128 (1952) 38-39.

Carla Gottlieb, "The Date of the Temple of Poseidon at Paestum," *AJA* 56 (1952) 173; 57 (1953) 95-101.

P. V. Glob, "Temples at Barbar," *Kuml* (1954) 149-153.

*Oscar Broneer,"The Isthmian Sanctuary of Poseidon,"*Arch* 8 (1955) 56-62.

R. Ghirshman, "The Ziggurat of Choaga-Zanbil," *Arch* 8 (1955) 260-263.

*Nina de G. Davies, "Two Pictures of Temples," *JEA* 41 (1955) 80-82.

*Alan Rowe, "A Contribution to the Archaeology of the Western Desert: III (The Temple-Tombs of Alexander the Great and His Palace in Rhocotis: The Great Wall of the Libyan Desert)," *BJRL* 38 (1955-56) 139-165.

Harald Andersen, "The Building by the Barbar Temple," *Kuml* (1956) 186-188.

Peder Mortensen, "The Temple Oval at Barbar," *Kuml* (1956) 195-198.

*David Oates and J. H. Reid, "The Burnt Palace and the Nabu Temple; Nimrud, 1955," *Iraq* 18 (1956) 22-39.

*Alexander Badawy, "Maru-Aten: Pleasure Resort or Temple?" *JEA* 42 (1956) 58-64.

P. M. Fraser, "A Temple of Ḥatḥōr at Kusae," *JEA* 42 (1956) 97-98.

*Carla Gottlieb, "The Pediment Sculpture and Acroteria from the Hephaisteion and the Temple of Ares in the Agora at Athens,"*AJA* 61 (1957) 161-165.

Oscar Broneer, "Excavation of the Isthmian Scanctuary," *AJA* 61 (1957) 182.

*Seton Lloyd and James Mallaart, "An Early Bronze Age Shrine at Beycesultan," *AS* 7 (1957) 27-36.

Donald Nicol, "The Parthenon," *HT* 7 (1957) 515-524.

David Oates, "Ezida: The Temple of Nabu," *Iraq* 19 (1957) 26-39.

H. L. Lenzen, "The Ningišzida Temple built by Marduk-apla-iddina II at Uruk (Warka)," *Iraq* 19 (1957) 146-150.

Alexander Badawy, "A Sepulchral Chapel of Greco-Roman Times at Kom Abu Billo (Western Delta)," *JNES* 16 (1957) 52-54.

*Wilder Penfield, "The Asclepiad Physicians of Cnidus and Cos with a Note on the Probable Site of the Triopion Temple of Apollo," *PAPS* 101 (1957) 393-400.

Fuad Safar, "The Temple of Sibitti at Khorsabad," *Sumer* 13 (1957) 219-221.

*David Oates, "The Assyrian Building South of the Nabu Temple," *Iraq* 20 (1958) 109-113.

Joan Gorell, "*Babylon:* The Temples," *AT* 3 (1958-59) #1, 14-16.

*R. E. Wycherley, "Two Athenian Shrines," *AJA* 63 (1959) 67-72. [1. Herakleion in Melite; 2. Olympion]

*Yigael Yadin, "The Fourth Season of Excavations at Hazor," *BA* 22 (1959) 2-20. [Area H - Four Canaanite Temples, pp. 3-8]

François Salviat and Nicole Weill, "The Sanctuary of Artemis in Thasos," *Arch* 13 (1960) 97-104.

*Kristian Jeppesen, "A Royal Message to Ikaros: The Hellenistic Temples of Failaka," *Kuml* (1960) 187-193. [Appendix: The Ikaros Inscripton, pp. 194-198]

Jozef M. A. Janssen, "A Brief Description of the Decoration of Room II of the Temple of Soleb," *Kush* 9 (1961) 198-209.

Robert J. Bull, "The Excavation of the Temples at Shechem," *DG* 32 (1961-62) 156-165.

Peter J. Parr, "Nabataean Sanctuary Near Petra: A Preliminary Note," *ADAJ* 6&7 (1962) 21-23.

*Arthur Darby Nock, "Sapor I and the Apollo of Bryaxis," *AJA* 66 (1962) 307-310.

*C. Bradford Welles, "The Discovery of Sarapis and the Foundation of Alexandria," *HJAH* 11 (1962) 271-298.

*C. Bradford Welles, "Sarapis and Alexandria, an Addendum," *HJAH* 12 (1963) 512.

Donald P. Hansen, "Recent Excavatons in the Temple of Inanna at Nippur," *AJA* 66 (1962) 197.

Homer A. Thompson, "Itinerant Temples of Attica," *AJA* 66 (1962) 200.

*Homer A. Thompson, "The Sculptural Adornment of the Hephaisteion," *AJA* 66 (1962) 339-347.

D. H. Trump, "The Origin of the Maltese Temples," *Antiq* 36 (1962) 59-60.

Donald P. Hansen and George F. Dales, "The Temple of Inanna, Queen of Heaven, at Nippur," *Arch* 15 (1962) 75-84.

A. Bellens and P. Vermeir, "The Belgian Photogrammetric Mission to the Temple of Buhen," *Kush* 10 (1962) 150-151.

Alexander Badawy, "The Symbolism of the Temples at 'Amarna," *ZÄS* 87 (1962) 79-95.

A. Trevor Hodge, "Notes on Three Western Greek Temples," *AJA* 68 (1964) 179-184.

T. Leslie Shear Jr., "The Demolished Temple at Eleusis," *AJA* 68 (1964) 200.

Ronald Stroud, "The Sanctuary of Demeter on Acrocorinth," *AJA* 68 (1964) 201.

Leszek Dabrowski, "Preliminary report on the Reconstruction work of the Hatshepsut Temple at Deir El Bahari during the 1961-1962 Season," *ASAE* 58 (1964) 37-60.

*Edouard B. Ghazouli, "The palace and magazines attached to the Temple of Sety I at Abydos and the facade of this Temple," *ASAE* 58 (1964) 99-186.

Homer A. Thompson, "The Sanctuary of Theseus in Athens," *AJA* 69 (1965) 177.

Donald White, "The Hera Temple at Olympia: Some Questions concerning its Wooden Construction," *AJA* 69 (1965) 178.

*Anonymous, "Some Archaeological Notes," *BH* 2 (1965) #3, 16-18. [Shechem—Mt. Gerizim Temple, pp. 17-18]

Robert J. Bull and G. Ernest Wright, "Newly Discovered Temples on Mt. Gerizim in Jordan," *HTR* 58 (1965) 234-237.

*Bernard Goldman, "Persian Fire Temples or Tombs?" *JNES* 24 (1965) 305-308.

Anonymous, "Archaeological News. Amman—Excavation of a Late Bronze Temple," *ADAJ* 11 (1966) 105-106.

Frederick A. Cooper, "The Temple of Apollo at Bassae: New Observations on Its Plan and Orientation," *AJA* 70 (1966) 185-186; 72 (1968) 103-111.

T. Leslie Shear Jr., "A Classical Sanctuary Near Mycenae," *AJA* 70 (1966) 195.

*Giovanni Colonna, "The Sanctuary at Pyrgi In Etruria," *Arch* 19 (1966) 11-23. *(Trans. by Lionel Casson)*

*M. Abdul-Qader Muhammed, "Recent finds," *ASAE* 59 (1966) 143-155. [The Temple of Amenophis III, p. 154]

*David Ussishkin, "Building IV in Hamath and the Temples of Solomon and Tell Tayanat," *IEJ* 16 (1966) 104-110.

*K. Branigan, "The Four-Room Buildings of Tell En-Naṣbeh," *IEJ* 16 (1966) 206-208.

J. B. Hennessy, "Excavation of a Bronze Age Temple at Amman," *PEQ* 98 (1966) 155-162.

G. R. H. Wright, "The Bronze Temple at Amman," *ZAW* 78 (1966) 351-357. [Supplementary Note by J. B. Hennessy, pp. 357-359]

James E. Packer, "The *Domus* of Cupid and Psyche in Ancient Ostia," *AJA* 71 (1967) 123-131.

Michael C. J. Putnam, "The Shrine of Vortumnus," *AJA* 71 (1967) 177-179.

Robert J. Bull, "A Preliminary Excavation of an Hadrianic Temple at Tell er Ras on Mount Gerizim," *AJA* 71 (1967) 387-393.

Jadwiga Lipińska, "Names and History of the Sanctuaries Built by Tuthmosis III at Deir el-Baḥri," *JEA* 53 (1967) 25-33.

David Stronach, "Urartian and Achaemenian Tower Temples," *JNES* 26 (1967) 278-288.

*Hassan S. K. Bakry, "Was there a Temple of Horus at Heliopolis?" *MDIÄA* 22 (1967) 53-59.

Ramadan M. Saad, "New Light on Akhenaten's Temple at Thebes," *MDIÄA* 22 (1967) 64-67.

P[eter] J. Parr, "Recent Discoveries in the Sanctuary of the Qasr Bint Far'un at Petra. I. Account of the Recent Excavations," *ADAJ* 12&13 (1967-68) 5-19.

Ray Winfield Smith, "The Akhenaten Temple Project," *Exped* 10 (1967-68) #1, 24-32.

Gerald V. Lalonde, "A Triangular Sanctuary in the Athenian Agora," *AJA* 72 (1968) 167.

Leszek Dabrowski, "Preliminary Report on the Reconstruction Works of Hatshepsut's Temple at Deir el-Bahari during the 1962-63 and 1963-64 Seasons," *ASAE* 60 (1968) 131-137.

Jadwiga Lipinska, "Preliminary Report on the Reconstruction Works of the Temple of Hatshepsutat Deir el-Bahari during the Season 1964-1965," *ASAE* 60 (1968) 139-152.

*E. Dabrowska and P. Gartkiewicz, "Preliminary Report Concerning Restoration of the Wall of the 3rd Terrace of the Hatshepsut Temple at Deir el-Bahari during the Season 1965-1966," *ASAE* 60 (1968) 213-219.

[M.] Abdel-Qader Muhammad*[sic]*, "Preliminary Report on the Excavations Carried out in the Temple of Luxor, Seasons 1958-1959 and 1959-1960," *ASAE* 60 (1968) 227-279.

Barry J. Kemp, "The Osiris Temple at Abydos," *MDIÄA* 23 (1968) 138-155.

A. Trevor Hodge and R. A. Tomlinson, "Some Notes on the Temple of Nemesis at Rhamnous," *AJA* 73 (1969) 185-192.

Alfred Frazer, "The Propylon of Ptolemy II and the Sanctuary of the Great Gods at Samothrace," *AJA* 73 (1969) 235.

Henry S. Robinson, "The Archaic Temples at Corinth," *AJA* 73 (1969) 244.

Russell T. Scott, "Arx of Cosa 1965-1968," *AJA* 73 (1969) 245.

*Edward F. Campbell Jr. and G. Ernest Wright, "Tribal League Shrines in Amman and Shechem," *BA* 32 (1969) 104-116.

*H. Jacquet-Gordon, C. Bonnet, and J. Jacquet, "Pnubs and the Temple of Tabo on Agro Island," *JEA* 55 (1969) 103-111.

§194 ***2.5.8.8 Synagogues [See also: Synagogue worship→]***

C. W. Wilson, "Notes on Jewish Synagogues in Galilee," *PEFQS* 1 (1869) 37-42.

Claude R. Conder, "The Synagogue of Umm el Amud," *PEFQS* 8 (1876) 22-23.

Edward Atkinson, "Note on the Ancient Synagogue at Meiron," *PEFQS* 10 (1878) 24-27.

H. H. Kitchener, "Synagogues of Galilee," *PEFQS* 10 (1878) 123-129.

*Richard J. H. Gottheil, "An Eleventh-Century Document Concerning a Cairo Synagogue," *JQR* 19 (1906-07) 467-539.

Anonymous, "Synagogue Ruins at Tel-Hun," *RP* 6 (1907) 118.

E. W. G. Masterman, "The Ancient Jewish Synagogues," *BW* 32 (1908) 87-102.

*Stanley A. Cook, "The Synagogue of Theodotos at Jerusalem," *PEFQS* 53 (1921) 22-23.

*A. Marmorstein, "The Inscription of Theodotos," *PEFQS* 53 (1921) 23-28.

Gerald M. FitzGerald, "Notes on Recent Discoveries. II. *Remains of an Ancient Synagogue at Yafa in Galilee*," *PEFQS* 53 (1921) 182-183.

Robert H. Pfeiffer, "The 'Synagogue of the Libertines'," *MR* 104 (1921) 971-972.

R. D. Middleton, "The Synagogue at Tell Ḥum," *PEFQS* 53 (1926) 104.

Harry J. Leon, "The Synagogue of the Herodians," *JAOS* 49 (1929) 318-321.

J. W. Crowfoot and R. W. Hamilton, "The Discovery of a Synagogue at Jerash," *PEFQS* 61 (1929) 211-219.

*A. Marmorstein, "Some Notes on Recent Works on Palestinian Epigraphy," *PEFQS* 62 (1930) 154-157. [(B.) The Cathedra of Moses in the Ancient Synagogues, pp, 155-156]

*I. Ben-Zevil, "Discoveries at Pekiin," *PEFQS* 62 (1930) 210-213. [(1) The Seven-branched Candelabrum; (2) The Door Tablet; (3) The Cluster of Grapes]

E. L. Sukenik, "Designs of the Torah Shrine in Ancient Synagogues in Palestine," *PEFQS* 63 (1931) 22-25.

E. L. Sukenik, "Discovery of an Ancient Synagogue," *A&A* 32 (1932) 207-212. *[Beth-Alpha]*

E. L. Sukenik, "Designs of a Lectern (*ἀνλογεῖον*) in Ancient Synagogues in Palestine," *JPOS* 13 (1933) 221-225.

*C. H. Kraeling, "The Earliest Synagogue Architecture," *BASOR* #54 (1934) 18-20.

E. L. Sukenik, "The Ancient Synagogue of el-Ḥammeh," *JPOS* 15 (1935) 101-180.

A. Marmorstein, "The Synagogue of Claudius Tiberius Polycharmus in Stobi," *JQR, N.S.,* 27 (1936-37) 373-384.

*E. L. Sukenik, "The Ezekiel Panel in the Wall Decoration of the Synagogue of Dura-Europos," *JPOS* 18 (1938) 57-62.

L. A. Mayer and A. Reifenberg, "The Synagogue of Eshtemo‘a. Preliminary Report," *JPOS* 19 (1939-40) 314-326.

*Emil G. Kraeling, "The Meaning of the Ezekiel Panel in the Synagogue at Dura," *BASOR* #78 (1940) 12-18.

*Rachel Wischnitzer-Bernstein, "The Samuel Cycle in the Wall Decoration of the Synagogue at Dura-Europos," *PAAJR* 11 (1941) 85-103.

Charles C. Torrey, "A Synagogue at Elath?" *BASOR* #84 (1941) 4-5.

*Helen Rosenau, "The Synagogue and Protestant Church Architecture," *JWCI* 4 (1941) 80-84.

*Rachel Wischnitzer-Bernstein, "The Samuel Cycle in the Wall Decoration of the Synagogue at Dura-Europos," *PAAJR* 11 (1941) 85-103.

*M. H. Ben-Shammai, "The Legends of the Destruction of the Temple among the Paintings of the Dura Synagogue," *BIES* 9 (1941-42) #4, I.

L. A. Mayer and A. Reifenberg, "The Synagogue of Eshtemo'a," *BIES* 9 (1941-42) #2/3, I; 10 (1942-43) #1, I-II.

E. L. Sukenik, "Did the Synagogue of Capernaum Have a Fixed Torah-Shrine?" *KSJA* 1 (1942) XI.

*Gisela M. A. Richter, "Polychromy in Greek Sculpture with Special Reference to the Archaic Attic Gravestones in the Metropolitan Museum," *AJA* 48 (1944) 321-333.

*Herbert Gordon May, "Synagogues in Palestine," *BA* 7 (1944) 1-20. [Synagogue Origins; The Earliest Synagogues Unearthed; Roman Period Synagogues in Palestine; The Synagogue at Dura-Europos; Byzantine Period Synagogues; The Synagogue Facade; Porch and Courts; Separation of Women in Worship; Locations of Synagogues; The Ark, or Shrine for the Law; Candlesticks, Seating Arrangements; The Priest; Synagogue Inscriptions; Pictures and Figures in the Synagogue]

Rachel Wischnitzer-Bernstein, "A New Aspect of the Iconography of Synagogue Paintings of Dura-Europos," *JBL* 64 (1945) vii.

E. L. Sukenik, "Study of Ancient Synagogues," *Kobez* 4 (1945) XI.

E. L. Sukenik, "The Ancient Synagogue of Eshtemo'a," *KSJA* 2 (1945) VII.

E. L. S[ukenik] and M. Schwabe, "The Ancient Synagogue of Apameia Syriae," *KSJA* 2 (1945) VII.

M. Avi-Yonah, "Remains of an Ancient Synagogue at Fahma Village," *BIES* 13 (1946-47) #3/4, VIII.

E. L. Sukenik, "The Present State of Ancient Synagogue Studies," *RFEASB* 1 (1949) 8-23.

*Harald Riesenfeld, "The Resurrection in Ezekiel XXXVII and in the Dura-Europos Paintings," *UUÅ* (1948) #11, 1-40.

E. L. Sukenik, "The Samaritan Synagogue at Salbit: Preliminary Report," *RFEASB* 1 (1949) 26-30.

E. L. Sukenik, "The Ancient Synagogue at Yafa Near Nazareth: Preliminary Report," *RFEASB* 2 (1951) 6-24.

E. L. S[ukenik], "A New Discovery at Beth Alpha," *RFEASB* 2 (1951) 26. *[Synagogue]*

E. L. S[ukenik], "More About the Ancient Synagogue of Caesarea," *RFEASB* 2 (1951) 28-30.

*I. Sonne, "The Zodiac Panel in the Beth-Alpha Synagogue," *JBL* 72 vi.

Sylvester Saller, "A catalogue of the Ancient Synagogues of the Holy Land," *SBFLA* 4 (1953-54) 219-246.

Anonymous, "Ancient Synagogue Excavated at Nirim (5th Century A.D.)," *AT* 2 (1957-58) #2, 12.

*Eugene Mihaly, "Jewish Prayer and Synagogue Architecture," *Jud* 7 (1958) 309-319.

H. Stern, "The Orpheus in the Synagogue of Dura-Europos," *JWCI* 21 (1958) 1-6.

Martin H. Scharlemann, "The Theology of Synagog Architecture (As Reflected in the Excavations Reports," *CTM* 30 (1959) 902-914.

Erwin R. Goodenough, "The Orpheus in the Synagogue of Dura-Europos: A Correction," *JWCI* 22 (1959) 372.

M. Avi-Yonah, "The Mosaic Pavement on the Maon (Nirim) Synagogue," *EI* 6 (1960) 29*.

S. Levy, "The Ancient Synagogue at Maon (Nirim)," *EI* 6 (1960) 29*.

*L. Y. Rahmani, "The Maon Synagogue (The Small Finds and Coins)," *EI* 6 (1960) 29*.

S. Levy, "The Ancient Synagogue of Ma'on (Nirim). A. Excavation Report," *RFEASB* 3 (1960) 6-13.

*L. Y. Rahmani, "The Ancient Synagogue of Ma'on (Nirim). B. The Small Finds and Coins," *RFEASB* 3 (1960) 14-18.

A. S. Hiram, "The Ancient Synagogue of Ma'on (Nirim). C. Reconstruction (I)," *RFEASB* 3 (1960) 19-21.

I. Dunayevsky, "The Ancient Synagogue of Ma'on (Nirim). D. Reconstruction (II)," *RFEASB* 3 (1960) 22-24.

M. Avi-Yonah, "The Ancient Synagogue of Ma'on (Nirim). E. The Mosaic Pavement," *RFEASB* 3 (1960) 25-35.

*S. Yeivin, "The Ancient Synagogue of Ma'on (Nirim). F. The Inscription," *RFEASB* 3 (1960) 36-40.

M. Avi-Yonah, "The Synagogue of Caesarea: *Preliminary Report*," *RFEASB* 3 (1960) 44-48.

N. Avigad, "A Dated Lintel-Inscription from the Ancient Synagogue of Nabratein," *RFEASB* 3 (1960) 49-56.

M. Avi-Yonah, "Various Synagogual Remains: Ḥuldah," *RFEASB* 3 (1960) 57-60.

M. Avi-Yonah, "Various Synagogual Remains: Ascalon," *RFEASB* 3 (1960) 61.

*N. Avigad, "Synagogue Inscriptions: An Aramaic Inscription from the Synagogue at Umm el-'Amed in Galilee," *RFEASB* 3 (1960) 62-64.

M. Avi-Yonah, "A New Fragment of the Ashdod Chancel Screen," *RFEASB* 3 (1960) 69.

M. Dothan, "Hammath—Tiberias," *IEJ* 12 (1962) 153-154. *[Synagogue]*

David Gordon Mitten, "The Synagogue at Sardis," *AJA* 67 (1963) 215.

Anonymous, "Archaeology and Early Synagogues," *BH* 1 (1964) #4, 18-24.

Joseph A. Grassi, "The Resurrection and the Ezechiel[sic]* Panel of the Dura-Europa Synagogue," *BibT* #11 (1964) 721-726.

S. D. Goitein, "The Synagogue Building and Its Furnishings According to the Records of the Cairo Geniza," *EI* 7 (1964) 169*-172*.

David Gordon Mitten, "The Synagogue and the 'Byzantine Shops'," *BASOR* #177 (1965) 17-37. *(Part of the article on "The Seventh Campaign at Sardis") [A. D. 400]*

Moshe Dothan, "New Light on Ancient Synagogues: Excavations at Hamath-Tiberias on the Sea of Galilee," *AJA* 70 (1966) 186-187.

*George M. A. Hanfmann, "The Eighth Campaign at Sardis (1965)," *BASOR* #182 (1966) 2-8. [Special report by D. G. Mitten, "The Synagogue and Vicinity," pp. 34-45]

*George M. A. Hanfmann, "The Ninth Campaign at Sardis (1966)," *BASOR* #187 (1967) 9-62. [Special report by L. J. Majewski, "Evidence for the Interior Decoration of the Synagogue", pp. 32-62.]

*Erwin R. Goodenough, "The Greek Garments of Jewish Heroes in the Dura Synagogue," *LIST* 2 (1966) 221-237.

N. Zori, "The Ancient Synagogue at Beth-Shean," *EI* 8 (1967) 73*.

Elizabeth R. Gebhard, "Skenika Problemata," *AJA* 73 (1969) 235-236.

*Floyd V. Filson, "Ancient Greek Synagogue Inscriptions," *BA* 32 (1969) 41-46.

A. Ovasdiah, "Excavation in the Area of the Ancient Synagogue at Gaza. (Preliminary Report)," *IEJ* 19 (1969) 193-198.

§195 ***2.5.8.9 Theaters***

C[onrad] Schick, "Herod's Amphitheatre," *PEFQS* 19 (1887) 161-166. [Remarks by Claude R. Conder, pp. 166-167]

*W. J. McMurtry and M. L. Earle, "Papers of the American School of Classical Studies at Athens. Excavations at the Theatre of Sikyon," *AJA, O.S.,* 5 (1889) 286-292. [I. General Report of the Excavations;II. Supplementary Report of the Excavations]

*Charles Waldestein, Rufus B. Richardson, Andrew Fossum, and Carleton L. Brownson, "Papers of the American School of Classical Studies at Athens. Excavations by the American School at Eretria, 1891," *AJA, O.S.,* 7 (1891) 233-280. [III. Excavations in the Theatre of Eretria, pp. 253-257; IV. The State-Building of the Theatre at Eretria, pp. 257-266; V. The Theatre at Eretria, Orchestra and Cavea, pp. 266-280]

Mortimer Lamson Earle, "Papers of the American School of Classical Studies at Athens. Supplementary Excavations at the Theatre of Sikyon, in 1891," *AJA, O.S.,* 7 (1891) 281-282.

Mortimer L. Earle, "Papers of the American School of Classical Studies at Athens. Excavations in the Theatre at Sicyon in 1891," *AJA, O.S.,* 8 (1893) 388-396.

Carleton L. Brownson and Clarence H. Young, "Papers of the American School of Classical Studies at Athens. Further Excavations at the Theatre of Sicyon in 1891," *AJA, O.S.,* 8 (1893) 397-409.

*Edward Capps, "Papers of the American School of Classical Studies at Athens. The Chorus in the later Greek Drama with reference to the stage question," *AJA, O.S.*, 10 (1895) 287-325.

Edward Capps, "Papers of the American School of Classical Studies at Athens. Excavations in the Eretrian Theatre in 1894," *AJA, O.S.*, 10 (1895) 338-346.

T. W. Heermance, "Papers of the American School of Classical Studies at Athens. Excavation of the Theatre at Eretria in 1895," *AJA, O.S.*, 11 (1896) 317-331.

Rufus B. Richardson, "Notes. Notes from Corinth," *AJA, O.S.*, 11 (1896) 371-372. [Discovery of a Theatre, p. 371]

Charles Knopp, "The Roman Theater," *A&A* 1 (1914-15) 137-152.

Charles Knopp, "The Roman Theater (concluded)," *A&A* 1 (1914-15) 187-204.

Charles H. Weller, "The Destruction of the Parthenon," *A&A* 4 (1916) 7-9.

*Andrew Fossum, "Harmony in the Theatre at Epidauros," *AJA* 30 (1926) 70-75.

Richard Stillwell, "The Theatre at Corinth," *AJA* 33 (1929) 77-97.

*Anonymous, "Notes and Comments. Hellenistic Theatre and Temple in Cos," *A&A* 29 (1930) 233.

George Allen, "Some Peculiarities of Theaters in Gaul," *AJA* 41 (1937) 113.

James T. Allen, "The Odeum of Pericles and the Periclean Reconstruction of the Theater," *AJA* 44 (1940) 110.

Richard Stillwell, "The Greek Theatre at Corinth," *AJA* 53 (1949) 147.

H. J. Lenzen, "The Greek Theatre in Babylon," *Sumer* 15 (1959) 39.

*A. E. Raubitschek, "The Marble Prohedria in the Theater of Dionysus," *AJA* 67 (1963) 216.

Elizabeth R. Gebhard, "The Theater at Isthmia," *AJA* 66 (1962) 196.

§196 *2.5.8.10 Tombs, Cromlechs, Dolmens, Graves, Sarchophagi, Tumuli, etc. [For "Cemeteries" see specific cities or places in §167 or §168 ←]*

†Œdipus, "Sarcophagus of Alexander," *MMBR* 17 (1804) 1-4.

†Œdipus, "Alexander's Tomb," *MMBR* 18 (1804) 5-8.

†Anonymous, "Clarke *on the Alexandrian Sarcophagus*," *ERCJ* 7 (1805-06) 480-502. *(Review)*

*†Anonymous, "Sir R. Ker Porter's Travels in Georgia, Persia, Armenia, &c.," *MMBR* 53 (1822) 577-162. *(Review)* [Tomb of Esther, pp. 584-585]

†Anonymous, "Mrs. Hamilton Gray *on Etruscan Tombs*," *QRL* 67 (1840-41) 375-394. *(Review)*

*E. Robinson, "Notes on Biblical Geography," *BS* 1 (1844) 598-604. [II. Rachel's Sepulchre. Ramah of Samuel, pp. 602-604]

*D. K., "Ramathïm Zophim and Rachel's Sepulchre," *JSL, 1st Ser.*, 6 (1850) 403-410.

*John Hogg, "Sidonian Sarcophagus and Inscription," *JSL, 3rd Ser.*, 2 (1855-56) 425-434.

*G. Seyffarth, "Three Lectures on Egyptian Antiquities, &c., delivered at the Stuyvesant Institute, New York, May 1856," *ER* 8 (1856-57) 34-104. [XI. The Sarcophagus of Osimandya, pp. 79-80]

Anonymous, "The Tomb of Cyrus," *MQR* 10 (1856) 445-449.

C. W. Wilson, "Remains of Tombs in Palestine," *PEFQS* 1 (1869) 66-71.

Ch. Sandreczki, "The Rock Tombs of El Medyeh," *PEFQS* 2 (1870) 245-251.

Anonymous, "The Rock Tombs of El Medyeh," *PEFQS* 2 (1870) 390.

*C. Clermont-Ganneau, "Notes on Certain New Discoveries at Jerusalem," *PEFQS* 3 (1871) 103-107. [5. Ancient Jewish Sarcophagus; 6. The tomb of Absalom cleared out]

T. L. Donaldson, "Joseph's Tomb in Sechem," *SBAT* 2 (1873) 80-82.

Charles Warren, "The Tomb of David," *PEFQS* 7 (1875) 102-103.

Titus Tobler, "Letter No. III. from Dr. Tobler," *PEFQS* 8 (1876) 103-104. *[Graves]*

Titus Tobler, "Ancient Jewish Graves. Letter from Dr. Titus Tobler," *PEFQS* 7 (1875) 177-180.

H. H. Kitchener, "Tombs of the Maccabees," *PEFQS* 10 (1878) 74.

*John R. Jackson, "Notes on Vegetable Remains from the Egyptian Tombs," *SBAP* 1 (1878-79) 36-37. [Remarks by W. Harry Rylands, and W. F. Birch, p. 37; George Murray, 37-38] *[Pages 34-35 duplicated in error]*

W. F. Birch, "The Sepulchres of David and the Kings of Judah," *PEFQS* 9 (1877) 195-204.

Claude R. Conder, "Joshua's Tomb," *PEFQS* 10 (1878) 22-23.

Claude R. Conder, "Masonry Tombs," *PEFQS* 8 (1876) 151-152.

W. F. Birch, "The Tomb of David," *PEFQS* 11 (1879) 172-176.

*W. F. Birch, "Nehemiah's Wall and David's Tomb," *PEFQS* 11 (1879) 176-179.

Ign. Goldziher, "Mohammedan Traditions Respecting Joshua's Place of Sepulchre," *PEFQS* 11 (1879) 193-195.

*Claude R. Conder, "Notes on Jerusalem," *PEFQS* 12 (1880) 101-103. [Tombs of the Kings, pp. 101-102]

*W. F. Birch, "The Tomb of David, Zion, and Josephus," *PEFQS* 12 (1880) 167-170.

Claude R. Conder, "Notes on Disputed Points," *PEFQS* 12 (1880) 228-230. *[Tombs of the Kings]*

W. F. Birch, "Rachel's Sepulchre," *PEFQS* 12 (1880) 241.

*†Samuel Birch, "A Description of the Pyramid of King Pepi, and the position of the Inscriptions and Sarcophagus," *SBAP* 3 (1880-81) 93-96.

*W. F. Birch, "The City and Tomb of David," *PEFQS* 13 (1881) 94-97.

W. F. Birch, "It is required to find the Entrance to the Tomb of David," *PEFQS* 13 (1881) 97-100.

Claude R. Conder, "Note on Pre-Historic Remains in Western Palestine," *PEFQS* 14 (1882) 121. *[dolmen]*

(Mrs.) E. A. Finn, "Cromlechs on the East of Jordan," *PEFQS* 14 (1882) 134-135.

Claude R. Conder, "Jewish Traditions in Jerusalem," *PEFQS* 14 (1882) 142-145. *[Tombs]*

H. B. S. W., "The Sepulchres of the Kings. Who were buried in them?" *PEFQS* 14 (1882) 266-269.

G. W. Phillips, "The Cromlechs of Cornwall and Moab," *PEFQS* 14 (1882) 270-271.

Claude R. Conder, "Notes. *Rachel's Tomb*," *PEFQS* 15 (1883) 139.

Claude R. Conder, "Notes. *Tomb of the Patriarchs*," *PEFQS* 15 (1883) 139.

W. F. Birch, "The Tomb of David in the City of David," *PEFQS* 15 (1883) 150-154.

W. F. Birch, "The Entrance to the Tomb of David," *PEFQS* 15 (1883) 155.

Henry A. Harper, "Welsh Cromlechs near Barmouth," *PEFQS* 15 (1883) 159-160.

Alfred Emerson, "Notice of 'Discovery of a Tomb-Cave at Ghain Sielem, Gozo'," *AJA, O.S.*, 1 (1885)

*E. A. Wallis Budge, "The Mummy and Coffin of Nes-Ames, Prophet of Ames and Chonsu," *SBAP* 8 (1885-86) 106-108.

†E. A. Wallis Budge, "Sepulchral Boxes from Echmim," *SBAP* 8 (1885-86) 120-122.

A. Wiedemann, "Tombs of the Nineteenth Dynasty at Der El-Medinet (Thebes)," *SBAP* 8 (1885-86) 225-232.

A. Wiedemann, "A Sarcophagus of the Saitic Period," *SBAP* 8 (1885-86) 232-239.

Claude R. Conder, "Notes. *Phoenician Tombs*," *PEFQS* 18 (1886) 17.

*W. F. Birch, "Notes by Rev. W. F. Birch," *PEFQS* 18 (1886) 26-34. [Tomb of Rachel, p. 31]

*G. Schumacher, "Across the Jordan. A Reply to C. R. C.'s Notes thereon," *PEFQS* 18 (1886) 168-171. [8. *Dolmens,* pp. 169-170]

Anonymous, "The Sepulchral Chambers and the Sarcophagi of Sidon," *JTVI* 21 (1886-87) 53-54.

E. A. Wallis Budge, "Description of the Tombs of Mechu, Ben, and Se-Renpu, discovered by Major-General Sir F. Grenfell," *SBAP* 9 (1886-87) 78-82.

W. K. Eddy, "Letter from Sidon, Phœnicia," *AJA, O.S.,* 3 (1887) 97-101. *[Tombs and Sarcophagi]*

Conrad Schick, "Notes. II. Newly discovered Rock-hewn Tomb at Kolenieh," *PEFQS* 19 (1887) 51-55. [Note by C. R. Conder, p. 105]

C[onrad] Schick, "A Remarkable Tomb," *PEFQS* 19 (1887) 112-115.

A. D. Philps, "The Rock Tombs of Thebes, and the Sepulchre of Moses," *CongRL* 1 (1887-88) 49-56.

George St. Clair, "Boat-Shaped Graves in Syria," *PEFQS* 19 (1887) 236-238. [Note by C. R. Conder, *PEFQS* 20 (1888) 40]

T. Hayter Lewis, "The Sidon Sarcophagi," *PEFQS* 20 (1888) 5-8.

Bey Hamdi, "Account of a Royal Necropolis Discovered at Saida by Hamdi Bey*[sic]*," *PEFQS* 20 (1888) 9-15.

George St. Clair, "Sepulchres of the Kings," *PEFQS* 20 (1888) 48-50.

G. Schumacher, "Recent Discoveries. *Haifa,*" *PEFQS* 20 (1888) 104. *[Jewish Sarcophagi]*

George St. Clair, "Boat-Shaped Graves in Syria," *PEFQS* 20 (1888) 107.

*George St. Clair, "Nehemiah's South Wall, and the Locality of the Royal Sepulchres," *PEFQS* 21 (1889) 90-102.

G. Schumacher, "Notes from Galilee. *Shefa 'Amr,*" *PEFQS* 22 (1890) 24. *[Tomb]*

Claude R. Conder, "The Date of Eshmunazar's Coffin," *PEFQS* 22 (1890) 38-39.

W. M. Flinders Petrie, "Notes on Places Visited in Jerusalem. *Absalom's Tomb,*" *PEFQS* 22 (1890) 157.

W. M. Flinders Petrie, "Notes on Places Visited in Jerusalem. *Rock Tombs,*" *PEFQS* 22 (1890) 158-159.

*George St. Clair, "Nehemiah's Wall and the Sepulchres of the Kings," *PEFQS* 22 (1890) 212.

C[onrad] Schick, "Herr Schick's Reports from Jerusalem," *PEFQS* 22 (1890) 246-259. [III. A newly-discovered Rock-cut Tomb at Aceldama, pp. 248-249; IV. Newly-discovered Rock-cut Tomb near Bethany, pp. 249-252]

Claude R. Conder, "Notes on the *Quarterly Statement,* July, 1890. *Isaiah's Chapel,*" *PEFQS* 22 (1890) 329.

*A. H. Sayce, "Gleanings from the land of Egypt," *RTR* 13 (1890) 62-67, 181-191. [§III. The Tomb of [illegible] at Bersheh, pp. 187-191]

*Daniel Z. Noorian, "Notes from Syria," *AJA, O.S.,* 7 (1891) 444-445. [I. Hittite Ruins, p. 444] *[Gravestone]*

Claude R. Conder, "Note on the Lachish Cornice," *PEFQS* 23 (1891) 185. *[Tombs]*

*C[onrad] Schick, "Letters from Baurath C. Schick," *PEFQS* 24 (1892) 9-25. [Remarkable Rock-Cut Tomb in "Wady el Joz", pp. 13-16]

D. S. Schaff, "The Graves of Egypt," *HR* 26 (1893) 108-116.

*C[onrad] Schick, "Letters from Baurath C. Schick. II. The Tombs of the Prophets," *PEFQS* 25 (1893) 128-132.

*C[onrad] Schick, "Letters from Herr Baurath von Schick. IV. Baron Ustinoff's Collection of Antiquties at Jaffa. 6," *PEFQS* 25 (1893) 296. *[Tomb Stone]*

C. G. Curtis, "The Sidon Sarcophagi," *PEFQS* 26 (1894) 120-126.

*C[onrad] Schick, "Jerusalem Notes," *PEFQS* 26 (1894) 261-266. [9. Tombs of the Judges, p. 265]

T. D. G[oodell], "Papers of the American School of Classical Studies at Athens. Grave-Monuments from Athens," *AJA, O.S.*, 10 (1895) 469-479. *[Part I]*

T. W. Heermance, "Papers of the American School of Classical Studies at Athens. II. Grave Monuments from Athens," *AJA, O.S.*, 10 (1895) 479-484.

W. F. Birch, "The Sepulchres of David on Ophel," *PEFQS* 27 (1895) 261-263. [Note by C. R. Conder, p. 332]

Archibald C. Dickie, "Report on Tomb Discovered Near 'Tombs of the Kings'," *PEFQS* 28 (1896) 305-310.

*C[onrad] Schick, "Reports and Papers by Dr. Conrad Schick," *PEFQS* 29 (1897) 103-122. (Notes by C. R. Conder, p. 211) [II. Newly-discovered Rock Block with Tombs, pp. 105-107]

*Geo. H. Schodde, "Biblical Research Notes," *ColTM* 17 (1897) 371-384. [Tombs of Jewish Kings, pp. 376-377]

Conrad Schick, "The (So-Called) Tombs of the Kings at Jerusalem," *PEFQS* 29 (1897) 182-188.

*Ch. Clermont-Ganneau, "Notes on the Seal Found on Ophel, the Greek Inscriptions from Nazareth and Kefr esh Shems, the Siloam Text, and the Tombs of the Kings," *PEFQS* 29 (1897) 304-307. [(5) Tombs of the Kings, p. 307]

Anonymous, "Recent Discoveries in Egypt," *MR* 80 (1898) 640-643. [The Tomb of Osiris; The Tomb of Menes]

J. E. Hanauer, "Notes by Rev. J. E. Hanauer. III," *PEFQS* 30 (1898) 27-28. *[Sarcophagus]*

*C[onrad] Schick, "Reports by Dr. Conrad Schick," *PEFQS* 30 (1898) 79-85. [V. Another Rock-cut Tomb, pp. 82-83]

*W. F. Birch, "David's Tomb and the Siloam Tunnel," *PEFQS* 30 (1898) 161-167. [Note by C. Clermont-Ganneau, pp. 250-251]

[Stephen D. Peet], "Prehistoric Egyptian Tombs," *AAOJ* 21 (1899) 192-195. *(Editoral)*

W. M. McPheeters, "Biblical Research and Discovery. The Tombs of Esther and Mordecai," *CFL, O.S.,* 3 (1899) 308-309.

W. F. Birch, "Scheme for Finding the Sepulchres of David," *PEFQS* 31 (1899) 273-276. [Note by C. Clermont-Ganneau, p. 355]

(Miss) M. Brodrick and Miss A. Anderson Morton, "The Tomb of Pepi Ankh (Khua) near Sharona," *SBAP* 21 (1899) 26-33.

J. W. Fraser, "The Tomb of Pepi-ankh χhua," *SBAP* 21 (1899) 143.

*A[ngus] C[rawford], "Notes—Archæological, Etc.," *PER* 13 (1899-1900) 48-50. [Tomb of Esther and Mordecai, p. 50]

C. A. Honstein, "Newly-Discovered Tomb on Mount Scopus," *PEFQS* 32 (1900) 75-76.

*H. Porter, "A Cuneiform Tablet, Sarcophagus, and Cippus with Inscription, in the Museum at Beirut," *PEFQS* 32 (1900) 123-124.

C. M. Watson, "The Coffer of the Great Pyramid," *PEFQS* 32 (1900) 151-156.

R. A. Stewart Macalister, "A Dolmen Near Beit Jibrin," *PEFQS* 32 (1900) 222-224.

*J. E. Hanauer, "Notes by the Rev. J. E. Hanauer," *PEFQS* 32 (1900) 250-251. [Terra-cotta Coffins, p. 250]

R. A. Stewart Macalister, "The Rock-Cut Tombs in Wady er-Rababi, Jerusalem," *PEFQS* 32 (1900) 376-377.

*James Henry Breasted, "King Harmhab and his Sakkara tomb," *ZÄS* 38 (1900) 47-50.

William C. Winslow, "The Tomb at Abydos," *AAOJ* 23 (1901) 141-144.

A. L. Frothingham Jr., "Some Contents of Early Etruscan Tombs and their Connection with Greece and the Orient," *AJA* 5 (1901) 17-18.

F. Halbherr, "Three Cretan Necropoleis:*[sic]* Report on the Researches at Erganos, Panaghia, and Courtes," *AJA* 5 (1901) 259-293.

J. E. Quibell, "A Tomb at Hawaret el Gurob," *ASAE* 2 (1901) 141-143.

Howard Carter, "Report on Tomb-Pit opened on the 26th of January 1901, in the Valley of the Tombs of the Kings, between n° 4 and n° 28," *ASAE* 2 (1901) 144-145.

Howard Carter, "Report upon the Tomb of Sen-Nefer found near that of Thotmes III, n° 34," *ASAE* 2 (1901) 196-200.

Howard Carter, "Report on the Tomb of Mentuhotep I at Deir el-Bahari, known as Bab el-Hôçan," *ASAE* 2 (1901) 201-205.

R. A. Stewart Macalister, "The Rock-Cut Tombs in Wady er-Rababi, Jerusalem," *PEFQS* 33 (1901) 145-158, 215-232.

*R. A. Stewart Macalister, "Reports and Notes by R. A. Stewart Macalister, Esq. III. A Note on West Palestinian Dolmens," *PEFQS* 33 (1901) 394.

Walter L. Nash, "The Tomb of Mentuhetap I(?) at Dêri . el . Baḥri, Thebes," *SBAP* 23 (1901) 291-293.

W. L. Nash, "The Tomb of Pa-shedu," *SBAP* 23 (1901) 360-361.

George Fraser, "The early tombs at Tehneh," *ASAE* 3 (1902) 67-76, 121-130.

Howard Carter, "Report on the robbery of the tomb of Amenothes II, Biban el Moluk," *ASAE* 3 (1902) 115-120.

J. E. Quibell, "Notes on a tomb found at Tell er Robâ," *ASAE* 3 (1902) 245-249.

A. Forder, "The Tombs of the Ancients," *BW* 20 (1902) 350-360.

R. A. Stewart Macalister, "Reports by R. A. Stewart Macalister, M.A., F.S.A. II. A Tomb near Edh-Dhaheriyeh," *PEFQS* 34 (1902) 237.

R. A. Stewart Macalister, "Reports by R. A. Stewart Macalister, M.A., F.S.A. III. Rock-cut Tomb near Bethlehem," *PEFQS* 34 (1902) 237-240.

R. A. Stewart Macalister, "Reports by R. A. Stewart Macalister, M.A., F.S.A. IX. A Peculiar Rock-Cutting in the Kedron Valley," *PEFQS* 34 (1902) 247-248.

A. H. Sayce, "Discovery of the Tomb of Thothmes IV," *ET* 14 (1902-03) 333-334.

*Arthur Fairbanks, “A Comparison of the Scenes on White Lecythi and on Grave Stelae,” *AJA* 7 (1903) 84.

John P. Peters, “Two Tombs from the Necropolis of Marissa,” *AJA* 7 (1903) 89-91.

Percy E. Newberry, “A Sixth Dynasty Tomb at Thebes,” *ASAE* 4 (1903) 97-100.

A. H. Sayce, “Inter Alia,” *ET* 15 (1903-04) 406. *[Tomb of Nefert-ari]*

Alex. Macalister, “The Bodies in the Second Burial Cave,” *PEFQS* 35 (1903) 50-51. *[Gezer]*

Anonymous, “Asia Minor,” *RP* 1 (1903) 223. *[Rock Tombs]*

Anonymous, “Egypt,” *RP* 2 (1903) 254. *[Tomb of Thothmes IV]*

Percy E. Newberry, “Discovery of the Tomb of Thothmes IV,” *SBAP* 25 (1903) 111-112.

A. H. Sayce, “Inter Alia,” *ET* 15 (1903-04) 406. *[Tomb of Nefert-ari]*

A. S. Cooley, “Discovery of the Macedonian Tomb at Chaeronea,” *AJA* 8 (1904) 81-82.

Anonymous, “The Tomb of a Great Egyptian Queen,” *MQR, 3rd Ser.*, 30 (1904) 794-795. *[Hatshepsu]*

R. A. Stewart Macalister, “Reports by R. A. Stewart Macalister, M.A., F. S. A. V. The ‘Egyptian Tomb’ at Silwan,” *PEFQS* 34 (1904) 121.

R. A. Stewart Macalister, “The Sculptured Cave at Saris,” *PEFQS* 34 (1904) 125-129.

*Arthur Stoddard Cooley, “The Macedonian Tomb and the Battlefield of Chaironeia,” RP 3 (1904) 131-143.

*Howard Carter and G. Legrain, “Report of Work done in Upper Egypt (1903-1904),” *ASAE* 6 (1905) 112-129. [I. Tomb of Seti I; II. Tomb of Merenptah; III. Tomb of Queen Hatshepsu; IV. Tomb of Set II; *[V" missing]* ; VI. Tomb of the Queens]

*H. W. Seaton-Karr, “How the Tomb Galleries at Thebes were cut and limestone quarried at the Prehistoric flint-mines of the E. Desert,” *ASAE* 6 (1905) 176-184.

Anonymous, "Notes and Comments. The Recent Discovery in Egypt," *ICMM* 1 (1905) 289-290. *[Tomb of Yua and Thua]*

Anonymous, "Relics Discovered in the Tomb of Thuthmes IV," *MQR, 3rd Ser.*, 31 (1905) 385-386.

Anonymous, "A Wonderful Egyptian Tomb," *MQR, 3rd Ser.*, 31 (1905) 598-600. *[Amon-sit]*

Charles De Wolfe Brower, "An American's Recent Discoveries in Egypt," *RP* 4 (1905) 141-144. *[Tombs of Rameses IV and Rameses XII]*

Theodore F. Wright, "The Tombs of Gezer," *RP* 4 (1905) 79-82.

John P. Peters, "The Painted Tombs at Marissa," *RP* 4 (1905) 291-307.

*Percy E. Newberry, "An unpublished Scene from the Tomb of Thy at Sakkara, representing the Manufacture of Seals," *SBAP* 27 (1905) 286.

C. C. Edgar, "Tombs at Abou Billou," *ASAE* 7 (1906) 143-144.

Anonymous, "Tombs at Marissa," *MQR, 3rd Ser.*, 32 (106) 380-381.

Anonymous, "Relics in the Tomb of Thothmes IV," *MQR, 3rd Ser.*, 32 (1906) 610.

Anonymous, "The Tomb of Queen Tyi*[sic]*," *MR* 89 (1906) 641-644.

Anonymous, "Another Tomb in the Valley of the Kings," *RP* 5 (1906) 156-157.

Edward R. Ayrton, "Discovery of the Tomb of Si-ptah in the Bibân el Molûk, Thebes," *SBAP* 28 (1906) 96.

Oliver S. Tonks, "An Interpretation of the so-called Harpy Tomb," *AJA* 11 (1907) 60-61, 321-338.

C. C. Edgar, "The Sarcophagus of an unknown Queen," *ASAE* 8 (1907) 276-277.

J. L. Myres, "The 'Philistine' Graves Found at Gezer," *PEFQS* 39 (1907) 240-243.

Anonymous, "Tomb of Queen Meie at Thebes," *RP* 6 (1907) 119.

Anonymous, "A Phœnician Tomb," *RP* 6 (1907) 190.

E. R. Ayron, "The Tomb of Thyï," *SBAP* 29 (1907) 85-86, 277-281.

A. Burton Buckley, "Note on an Egyptian tomb in Baharia Oasis," *ASAE* 9 (1908) 259-266.

Anonymous, "Queen Tyr's*[sic]* Tomb?" *MR* 90 (1908) 976.

Anonymous, "Tomb of Queen Thyi," *RP* 7 (1908) 170.

Anonymous, "'Tombs of the Giants' in Sardinia," *RP* 7 (1908) 171.

*Margaret A. Murray, "The Coffin of Ta-āath in the Brassey Institute at Hastings," *SBAP* 30 (1908) 20-24.

Anonymous, "Tombs at Gezer," *MR* 91 (1909) 138-141.

Anonymous, "Tombs Near Abydos," *RP* 8 (1909) 265.

Anonymous, "Persian Tomb at Susa," *RP* 8 (1909) 325-326.

*J. L. Myers, "A Tomb of the Early Iron Age, from Kition in Cyprus, containing Bronze Examples of the 'Sigynna' or Cypriot Javelin," *AAA* 3 (1910) 107-117.

Joseph Offord, "New Discoveries by an American Explorer in Egypt.—Mr. Theodore M. Davis, and the Tombs of the Kings," *AAOJ* 32 (1910) 205-208.

*(Miss) Harriet A. Boyd, "Houses and Tombs of the Geometric Period at Kavusi, Crete," *AJA* 5 (1910) 14-15.

W. M. Flinders Petrie, "The Earliest Stone Tombs," *Man* 10 (1910) #79.

Emil G. Knesevich, "An Old Sarcophagus at Gaza," *PEFQS* 42 (1910) 294-296.

*Alan H. Gardiner, "The tomb of Amenemhet, high-priest of Amon," *ZÄS* 47 (1910) 87-99.

*Arthur E. P. Weigall, "Miscellaneous Notes," *ASAE* 11 (1911) 170-176. [12. The tomb of Amenhotep Ist, pp. 174-175]

J. E. Quibell, "Attempts made on the tomb of Bocchoris at Sakkarah," *ASAE* 11 (1911) 275-276.

R. W. Moss, "The Tombs of the Kings," *LQHR* 115 (1911) 326-328.

N. Tagliaferro, "Prehistoric Burials in a Cave at Bur-meghez, near Mkabba, Malta," *Man* 11 (1911) #92.

*W. F. Birch, "Gibeah of Saul and Zela. The Site of Jonathan's Home and Tomb," *PEFQS* 43 (1911) 101-109.

*W. F. Birch, "The City and Tomb of David on Ophel (so called)," *PEFQS* 43 (1911) 187-189.

Anonymous, "Coffin from Beni-Hanan," *RP* 10 (1911) 238.

P. J. O. Minos, "The Tombs of the Kings at Jerusalem," *SBAP* 33 (1911) 19-25.

*E. J. Pilcher, "The Assuan Papyri and the Grave-Goods of Gezer," *PEFQS* 44 (1912) 30-35.

*R. A. Stewart Macalister, "The Topography of Rachel's Tomb," *PEFQS* 44 (1912) 74-82.

A. B. Grimaldi, "Cenotaphs of the Hebrew Patriarchs at the Cave of Machpelah," *PEFQS* 44 (1912) 145-150.

Anonymous, "Etruscan Sarcophagus," *RP* 11 (1912) 239.

*L. W. King, "The Prehistoric Cemetery at Shamiramalti near Van in Armenia," *SBAP* 34 (1912) 198-204. *[Tombs]*

G. Elliot Smith, "The Origin and Meaning of the Dolmen," *JMUEOS* #2 (1912-13) 76.

Joseph Offord, "A United States Explorer at Thebes—Mr. Theodore Davis' Discovery of the Tombs of Harmhabi and Touatakhamanou," *AAOJ* 35 (1913) 92-94.

H. C. Tolman, "The Grave Relief of King Darius," *AJA* 17 (1913) 85-86.

W. M. Flinders Petrie, "The Earliest Perfect Tombs," *Man* 13 (1913) #85.

Camden M. Cobern, "Recently Discovered Painted Rock-cut Tomb at Beit Jibrin," *RP* 12 (1913) 123-124.

N. de G. Davis, "The Tomb of Senman, Brother of Senmut," *SBAP* 35 (1913) 282-285.

W. M. F[linders] P[etrie], "The Tomb of Menna," *AEE* 1 (1914) 95-96.

Anonymous, "Archaeology—The Mystery of a Plundered Pyramid," *HR* 68 (1914) 281-283. *[Pyramid of Senusert II]*

*Edouard Naville, "Excavations at Abydos: The Great Pool and Tomb of Osiris," *JEA* 1 (1914) 159-167.

G. Elliot Smith, "The Origin of the Dolmen," *RP* 13 (1914) 40-43.

*Percy E. Newberry, "Egyptian Historical Notes. II," *SBAP* 36 (1914) 35-39. [8. Two Wooden Coffins from El-Bersheh, p. 36]

Oric Bates, "Archaic Burials at Marsa Maṭrûḥ," *AEE* 2 (1915) 158-165. (Note by W. M. F[linders] P[etrie], pp. 165-166)

Warren J. Moulton, "An Inscribed Tomb at Beit Jibrin," *AJA* 19 (1915) 63-70.

Ernest Mackay, "Note on a New Tomb (No. 260) at Drah Abu'l Naga, Thebes," *JEA* 3 (1915) 125-126.

Howard Carter, "Report on the Tomb of Zeser-ka-ra Amenhetep I, discovered by the Earl of Carnarvon in 1914," *JEA* 3 (1915) 147-154.

L. W. King, "Royal Tombs in Mesopotamia and Egypt: A Comparison suggested by Some Recent Discoveries," *JEA* 2 (1915) 168-172.

*G. Elliot Smith, "Oriental Tombs and Temples," *JMUEOS* #4 (1914-15) 55-60.

C. Leonard Woolley, "A North Syrian Cemetery of the Persian Period," *AAA* 7 (1914-16) 115-129.

Howard Carter, "A tomb prepared for queen Hatshepsuit discovered by the Earl of Carnarvon (October 1916)," *ASAE* 16 (1916) 179-182.

W. M. F[linders] Petrie, "A Cemetery Portal," *AEE* 3 (1916) 174-180.

*Alan H. Gardiner, "The Tomb of a much travelled Theban Offical," *JEA* 4 (1916) 28-38.

*Howard Carter, "A Tomb prepared for Queen Hatshepsuit and other Recent Discoveries at Thebes," *JEA* 4 (1916) 107-118.

Howard Carter and Alan H. Gardiner, "The Tomb of Ramesses IV and the Turin Plan of a Royal Tomb," *JEA* 4 (1916) 130-158.

Edgar J[ames] Banks, "The Seven Wonders of the Ancient World. V—The Fifth Wonder: The Mausoleum at Halicarnassus," *A&A* 5 (1917) 137-141.

Edoardo Galli, "The Etruscan Sarcophagus of Torre San Severo in Orvieto," *A&A* 6 (1917) 229-234.

*Joseph Offord, "Archaeological Notes on Jewish Antiquities. XXX. *A Jewish Sarcophagus,*" *PEFQS* 49 (1917) 99-100.

John P. Peters, "Painted Tombs of Palestine," *A&A* 7 (1918) 181-195.

Francis W. Kelsey, "The Tomb of Virgil," *A&A* 7 (1918) 265-271.

L. G. Eldridge, "A Third Century Etruscan Tomb," *AJA* 22 (1918) 251-294.

*George A. Reisner, "The Tomb of Hepzefa, Nomarch of Siûṭ," *JEA* 5 (1918) 79-98.

C. C. Edgar, "Tomb-stones from Tell el Yahoudieh," *ASAE* 19 (1919) 216-244.

*Ernest Mackay, "On the Use of Beeswax and Resin as Varnishes in Theban Tombs," *AEE* 5 (1920) 35-38. (Note by [W. M.] F[linders] P[etrie], p. 38)

Warren R. Dawson, "The Royal Tombs of Thebes," *IAQR* 16 (1920) 127-128.

*Anonymous, "Tombs of Beit Jibrin," *BASOR* #4 (1921) 5.

Ernest Mackay, "Note on a New Tomb (No. 260) at Drah Abu'l Naga, Thebes," *JEA* 3 (1915) 125-126.

George W. Gilmore, "The Story of A Great Find," *HR* 82 (1921) 3-7. *[The Tomb of* m h n w t f*]*

Jean Capart, "The Memphite Tomb of King Ḥaremḥab," *JEA* 7 (1921) 31-35.

*Ernest Mackay, "The Cutting and Preparation of Tomb-Chapels in the Theban Necropolis," *JEA* 7 (1921) 154-168.

*R. Engelbach, "The Sarcophagus of Pa-Ramessu from Gurob. Was He the Heir of Seti I?" *AEE* 7 (1922) 9-13. (Note by [W. M.] F[linders] P[etrie], p. 13)

William Bell Dinsmoor, "A New Type of Archaic Attic Grave Stele," *AJA* 26 (1922) 261-277.

W. M. Flinders Petrie, "Burials of the First Dynasty," *Man* 22 (1922) #74.

Anonymous, "Archaeological Notes and Comments. Discovery of Royal Tomb of Tutonkhamen*[sic]* in Egypt," *A&A* 15 (1923) 100.

Anonymous, "Archaeological Notes and Comments. Reopening the Tomb of Tutankhamen," *A&A* 16 (1923) 265; 17 (1924) 71.

W. B. Emery, "Two Nubian Graves of the Middle Kingdom at Abydos," *AAA* 10 (1923) 33-35.

F. Ll. Griffith, "The tomb of Tutankhamon," *AEE* 4 (1923) 26-28.

W. M. Flinders Petrie, "The Tomb at Byblos," *AEE* 8 (1923) 33-37.

George W. Gilmore, "An Unprecedented Discovery in Egypt," *HR* 85 (1923) 220-222. *[Tomb of Tutankhamen]*

*George W. Gilmore, "The Archaeological World," *HR* 85 (1923) 393-394. [Tutankhamen's Tomb]

Warren R. Dawson, "The Tombs of the Kings at Thebes: A Chapter from Their Ancient History," *IAQR* 19 (1923) 319-329.

G. W. Murray and D. E. Derry, "Physical Anthropology: A Pre-dynastic Burial on the Red Sea Coast of Egypt," *Man* 23 (1923) #81.

James Henry Breasted, "Some Experiences in the Tomb of Tutenkhamon," *A&A* 17 (1924) 3-17.

A. Lucas, "Note on the temperature and humidity of the several tombs in the Valley of the Tombs of the Kings at Thebes," *ASAE* 24 (1924) 12-14.

Hakim effendi Abou-Seif, "Two granite sarcophagi from Samannûd (Lower Egypt)," *ASAE* 24 (1924) 91-96.

R. Engelbach, "Saite tomb discovered at Beni Hasan," *ASAE* 24 (1924) 159-160.

Anonymous, "Note on a Sculptured Marble Sarcophagus from Caesarea," *BSAJB* #5 (1924) 55-56.

*L. A. Mayer, "A Tomb in the Kedron Valley Containing Ossuaries with Hebrew Graffiti Names," *BSAJB* #5 (1924) 56-60.

G. F. H., "Note on the Roman Tomb Called Taba Bûr, Near Amman," *BSAJB* #6 (1924) 73-74.

Anonymous, "Pharaoh's Magnificence in Death," *HR* 87 (1924) 395-397. *[Tomb of Tutankhamen] (Review)*

H. E. Winlock, "The Tomb of the Kings of the Seventeenth Dynasty at Thebes," *JEA* 10 (1924) 217-277.

Clarence S. Fisher, "A Group of Theban Tombs. Work of the Eckley B. Coxe Jr. Expedition to Egypt," *MJ* 15 (1924) 28-49.

J. Donald Young, "Note on a Sarcophagus at Corinth," *AJA* 29 (1925) 82-83.

*N. de Garis Davis, "The Tomb of Tetaky at Thebes (No. 15)," *JEA* 11 (1925) 10-18.

J. Garrow Duncan, "A Leaden Ossuary," *PEFQS* 57 (1925) 65-67.

Axel Persson, "The Royal Grave at Dendrá," *A&A* 22 (1926) 231-240. *(Trans. by Luise Olson)*

*Battiscombe Gunn, "The inscribed Sarcophagi in the Serapeum," *ASAE* 26 (1926) 82-91.

G. A. Wainwright, "A subsidiary Burial in Ḥap-Zefi's tomb at Assint," *ASAE* 26 (1926) 160-166.

*G. W. Murray, "Graves of Oxen in the Eastern Desert of Egypt," *JEA* 12 (1926) 248-249.

S. Tolkowsky, "Canaanite Tombs Near Jaffa," *JPOS* 6 (1926) 70-74.

Alma Reed, "The Lost Tombs of Canosa," *A&A* 23 (1927) 63-67. (Correction, p. 190)

N. Ashover, "Painted Sarcophagi from Clazomenæ in the Constantinople Museum," *A&A* 23 (1927) 68-75.

[George H. Reisner], "The Archaeological Significance of the Tomb of Hetep-heres," *A&A* 24 (1927) 89-93.

Anonymous, "Archaeological Notes and Comments. Carter Lifts the Lid of the Tutankhamen Sarcophagus and Quits," *A&A* 17 (1924) 139.

*Robert Mondand Walter B. Emery, "Excavations at Sheikh Abd el Gureh 1925-26," *AAA* 14 (1927) 13-34. *[Tombs]*

Harry J. Leon, "The Jewish Catacombs of Rome," *AJA* 31 (1927) 83-84.

Anonymous, "The Tomb of Queen Hetepheres," *Antiq* 1 (1927) 216-218.

Cornelia H. Dam, "The Tomb of Ra-Ka-Pou a Court Offical of 2650 B.C.," *MJ* 18 (1927) 189-200.

L[eon] Legrain, "Discovery of Royal Tombs at Ur of the Chaldees," *MJ* 18 (1927) 442-444.

Anonymous, "Notes and Comments. Has the Tomb of Cyrus been Found?" *A&A* 26 (1928) 250.

*M[argaret] A. Murray, "Egyptian Objects Found in Malta," *AEE* 13 (1928) 45-51. *[Tombs]*

C. Leonard Woolley, "The Royal Tombs of Ur," *Anitq* 2 (1928) 7-17.

E. L. Sukenik, "A Jewish Hypogeum Near Jerusalem," *JPOS* 8 (1928) 113-121.

C. Leonard Woolley, "The Royal Tombs of Ur of the Chaldees," *MJ* 19 (1928) 5-34.

Edith H. Dohan, "Three Greek Grave Monuments," *MJ* 19 (1928) 249-260.

Robert Mond and Walter B. Emery, "The Burial Shaft of the Tomb of Amenemhāt," *AAA* 16 (1929) 49-74.

*H. E. Winlock, "Notes on the Reburial of Tuthmosis I," *JEA* 15 (1929) 56-68.

C. Leonard Woolley, "Ur of the Chaldees: More Royal Tombs," *MJ* 20 (1929) 7-35.

C. Leonard Woolley, "Ur of the Chaldees: more royal tombs," *SIR* (1929) 437-449.

Frederick S. Dunn, "Vergil's*[sic]* Vanishing Tomb," *A&A* 29 (1930) 23-31.

William F. Badè, "A Tell En-Nasheh Tomb from the Time of Herod Archelaus," *AJA* 34 (1930) 49.

Dows Dunham, "Some Problems in the Excavation of the Tomb of Queen Hetep-Heres," *AJA* 34 (1930) 55.

*Chester C. McCown, "Palestinian Archaeology in 1930," *BASOR* #41 2-18. [The Kerâzeh Dolmen Field, p. 17]

*Alan W. Shorter, "The Tomb of Aaḥmose, Supervisor of the Mysteries in the House of the Morning," *JEA* 16 (1930) 54-62.

Anonymous, "The False Door of Ptah-Arit," *UMB* 2 (1930-31) 58-59.

Francis D. Platner, "Tomb Excavations at Corinth 1930: I," *A&A* 31 (1931) 153-160.

Francis D. Platner, "Tomb Excavations at Corinth 1930: II," *A&A* 31 (1931) 225-234.

J. Penrose Harland, "The Shaft Graves and Tholos Tombs at Mykenai," *AJA* 35 (1931) 62-63.

*R. Engelbach, "The so-called Coffin of Akhenaten," *ASAE* 31 (1931) 98-114.

J. D. S. Pendlebury, "Report of the clearance of the Royal Tomb at El-'Amârna," *ASAE* 31 (1931) 123-125.

*Julian Obermann, "The Sepulchre of Maccabean Martyrs," *JBL* 50 (1931) 250-265.

H. E. Winlock, "The Tomb of Queen Inhapi. An Open Letter to the Editor," *JEA* 17 (1931) 107-110.

Dorothy A. E. Garrod, "Mesolithic Burials from Caves in Palestine," *Man* 31 (1931) #159.

*F. Turville Petre, "Dolmen Necropolis near Kerazeh, Galilee. Excavations of the British School of Archaeology in Jerusalem, 1930," *PEFQS* 63 (1931) 155-166.

W[illiam] F[oxwell] Albright, "An Anthropoid Clay Coffin from Saḥâb in Transjordan," *AJA* 36 (1932) 295-306.

Foad Boghdady, "An archaic tomb at Old Cairo," *ASAE* 32 (1932) 153-160.

E. L. Sukenik, "Two Jewish Hypogea," *JPOS* 12 (1932) 22-31.

*E. T. Richmond, "'Loop Pattern' Decorating Lead Sarcophagi," *QDAP* 1 (1932) 36.

D. C. Baramki, "A Tomb Chamber in the Syrian Orphanage, Jerusalem," *QDAP* 1 (1932) 101-102.

Anonymous, "A Reconstruction of a Burial from Persia," *UMB* 4 (1932-33) 114-115.

*Nelson Glueck, "Palestinian and Syrian Archaeology in 1932," *AJA* 37 (1933) 160-172. [Jewish Tombs, pp. 163-165]

George Horsfield, "Dolem-field in Transjordan," *Antiq* 7 (1933) 471-473.

Rosalind Moss, "An Unpublished Rock-tomb at Asyûṭ," *JEA* 19 (1933) 33.

*W. Stevenson Smith, "The Coffin of Prince Min-khar," *JEA* 19 (1933) 150-159.

Champlin Burrage, "A King and Queen of the Mycenaean Age at Midea and their Daughter," *AJA* 38 (1934) 184-185. *[Tombs]*

Ahmed Fakhry, "The tomb of Userḥēt (No. 235) at Qurnet Mura'i at Thebes," *ASAE* 34 (1934) 135-140.

C. J. Edmonds, "A Tomb in Kurdistan," *Iraq* 1 (1934) 183-192.

*N. de G. Davies, "Foreigners in the Tomb of Amenem˙ab (No. 85)," *JEA* 20 (1934) 189-192.

Edith Hall Dohan, "A Ziro Burial from Chiusi," *AJA* 39 (1935) 198-209.

*George W. Elderkin, "Architectural Detail in Antique Sepulchral Art," *AJA* 39 (1935) 518-525.

D. Randall-MacIver, "Etruscan Tombs," *Antiq* 9 (1935) 57-61.

*A. Hamada, "A Sarcophagus from Mit-Rahîna," *ASAE* 35 (1935) 122-131.

D. C. Baramki, "An Early Iron Age Tomb at eẓ Ẓahiriyye," *QDAP* 4 (1935) 109-110.

D. C. Baramki, "An Ancient Tomb Chamber at Waʿr Abu eṣ Ṣafa near Jerusalem," *QDAP* 4 (1935) 168-169.

Inez Scott Rybeg, "The Esquiline Necropolis in the Fifth Century B.C.," *AJA* 40 (1936) 127.

Ahmed Fakhry, "Three unnumbered Tombs at Thebes," *ASAE* 36 (1936) 124-130.

John Franklin Daniel, "Two Late Cypriote II Tombs from Kourion," *AJA* 41 (1937) 56-85.

*Ahmed Fakury, "Miscellanea," *ASAE* 37 (1937) 25-38. [6. Two Granite Fragments from a Sarcophagus, pp. 36-37; 7. Finding of Two Granite Sarcophagi in a Ramasside Tomb, 37-38]

A. Hamada, "The clearance of a tomb found at al-Fostat, 1936," *ASAE* 37 (1937) 58-70.

A. Hamada, "Tomb of Pawen-Ḥatef at al-Fosṭâṭ," *ASAE* 37 (1937) 135-142.

Mary S. Shaw, "Royal Sarcophagi of the XVIIIth Dynasty," *JMUEOS* #21 (1937) 51-57.

E. L. Sukenik, "A Jewish Tomb in the Kedron Valley," *PEQ* 69 (1937) 126-130.

*Moharram Kamal, "An unpublished Middle Empire Coffin in the Egyptian Museum," *ASAE* 38 (1938) 29-34.

*Walter B. Emery, "A preliminary report on the architecture of the tomb of Nebetka," *ASAE* 38 (1938) 455-468.

C. N. Johns, "Excavations at Pilgrims' Castle ('Atlīt). Cremated Burials of Phoenician Origin," *QDAP* 6 (1938) 121-152.

Edith Hall Dohan, "The Chronology of the Etruscan Tombs," *AJA* 43 (1939) 305-306.

Ahmed Fakhry, "The tombs of El-A'reg Oasis in the Libyan Desert," *ASAE* 39 (1939) 609-619.

Ahmed Fakhry, "A new speos from the reign of Hatshepsut and Tuthmosis III at Beni-Ḥasan," *ASAE* 39 (1939) 709-723.

R. Bernheimer, "A Literary Description of the Most Primitive Type of Vault," *JAOS* 59 (1939) 109-110.

A. Westholm, "Some Late Cypriote Tombs at Milia," *QDAP* 8 (1939) 1-20.

Hjalmar Larsen, "Tomb Six at Maassara. An Egyptian Second Dynasty Tomb," *AA* 11 (1940) 103-124.

Hjalmar Larsen, "Three Shaft Tombs with Chambers at Maassara, Egypt," *AA* 11 (1940) 161-206.

Virginia Grace, "A Cypriote Tomb and Minoan Evidence for Its Date," *AJA* 44 (1940) 10-52.

Dorothy K[ent] Hill, "The Etruscan Remains at the Castellaccio of Castel Campanile," *AJA* 44 (1940) 113-114.

Nina M. Davies and N. de G. Davies, "The Tomb of Amenmosĕ (No 89) at Thebes," *JEA* 26 (1940) 131-136.

Edwin C. Broome Jr., "The Dolmens of Palestine and Transjordania," *JBL* 59 (1940) 479-497.

*Ahmed Fakhry, "Baḥria and Farafra Oases. Third Preliminary report on the new discoveries," *ASAE* 40 (1940-41) 855-871. *[Tombs]*

Dorothy Kent Hill, "Some Early Comic Figures from Latium and Etruria," *AJA* 45 (1941) 93-94. *[Cists]*

*J. W. Jack, "Recent Archaeology," *ET* 53 (1941-42) 276-280. [Canaanite Tomb at *Yazur,* (Azor); Ancient Catacombs in Palestine; pp. 279-280]

Robert M. Engberg, "Tombs of the Early Second Millennium from Bāghuz on the Middle Euphrates," *BASOR* #87 (1942) 17-23.

B[enjamin] Maisler, "An EB Age Tomb Found at Kinnereth (Preliminary Report)," *BIES* 10 (1942-44) #1, I.

E. L. Sukenik, "Jewish Tombs in the Kedron Valley," *KSJA* 1 (1942) VIII.

N. Avigad, "Mugharet Umm El-'Amad," *KSJA* 1 (1942) X.

G. M. Fitzgerald, "The Date Assigned to a Tomb at Sardis," *PEQ* 74 (1942) 54-57.

*Ruth B. Kallner, "Khirbet Kerak Ware and its Relation to the EB Tomb Discovered at Kinneret," *BIES* 10 (1942-44) #2/3, III.

Edith Hall Dohan, "Early Etruscan Tomb Groups," *AJA* 47 (1943) 94.

Guy Brunton, "The inner sarcophagus of prince Ramessu from Medinet Habu," *ASAE* 43 (1943) 133-148.

Osman R. Rostem, "Note on the Method of lowering the lid of the sarcophagus at a Saïte tomb," *ASAE* 43 (1943) 351-356.

Aḥmed Fakry, "Tomb of Hebamun, captain of the troops (No. 145 at Thebes)," *ASAE* 43 (1943) 369-379.

Aḥmed Fakry, "Tomb of Paser (No. 367 at Thebes)," *ASAE* 43 (1943) 389-414.

Aḥmed Fakry, "A note on the tomb of Kheruef at Thebes," *ASAE* 43 (1943) 447-508.

Egil Lindsten, "The Runnel Stone from the Tomb of Arteus," *AA* 15 (1944) 193-200.

J. Ory, "A Late Bronze Age Tomb at Tell Jerishe," *QDAP* 10 (1944) 55-57.

J. Ory, "A Bronze Age Tomb near Yazur," *QDAP* 10 (1944) 59-61.

*Gisela M. A. Richter, "Peisistratos' Law Regarding Tombs," *AJA* 49 (1945) 152.

*J. D. Beazley, "The Brygos Tomb at Capua," *AJA* 49 (1945) 153-158.

*Carlo Verdiani, "Original Hellenistic Paintings in a Thracian Tomb (Preliminary Report) *Excerpted from the Italian by Rhys Carpenter*," *AJA* 49 (1945) 402-405.

E. L. Sukenik, "A Jewish Tomb in the Vicinity of 'Isawiyeh," *KSJA* 2 (1945) VI.

[G.] Lankester Harding, "Two Iron Age Tombs from 'Amman," *QDAP* 11 (1945) 67-74.

*Arthur Darby Nock, "Sarcophagi and Symbolism," *AJA* 50 (1946) 140-170. [Note by J. E. Beazley, p. 170]

*Sara A. Immerwahr, "The Latest Elements in the Enkomi Tombs," *AJA* 50 (1946) 402.

J. Ory, "A Middle Bronze Age Tomb at el-Jisr," *QDAP* 12 (1946) 31-42.

J. Ory, "A Chalcolithic Necropolis at Benei Beraq," *QDAP* 12 (1946) 43-57.

G. L[ankester] Harding, "A Nabataean Tomb at 'Amman," *QDAP* 12 (1946) 58-62.

*Guy Brunton, "The Burial of Prince Ptah-Shepses at Saqqara," *ASAE* 47 (1947) 125-133.

*M. Avi-Yonah, "Two Remains of our Ancient Art," *BIES* 12 (1946) I. *[Decorated limestone coffin]*

*N. Avigad, "Architectural Observations on some Rock-cut Tombs," *PEQ* 79 (1947) 112-122.

M[oshe] Stekelis, "A Bronze-Age Tumulus in Eastern Palestine," *BIES* 14 (1947-48) #1/2, I.

Rodney S. Young, "Burials within the Walls of Athens," *AJA* 52 (1948) 378.

S. Yeivin, "The Sepulchers of the Kings of the House of David," *JNES* 7 (1948) 30-45.

G. L[ankester] Harding, "An Iron Age Tomb at Sahab," *QDAP* 13 (1948) 92-102.

G. Bakalakis, "An Anthemion from Thasos," *AJA* 53 (1949) 359-362.

J. Kaplan, "Ancient Jewish Tomb-Caves near Tel-Aviv," *BIES* 15 (1949-50) #3/4, I- II.

*William C. Hayes, "The Sarcophagus of Sennemūt," *JEA* 36 (1950) 19-23.

G. L[ankester] Harding, "An Iron Age Tomb at Meqabelein," *QDAP* 14 (1950) 44-48.

Sylvester Saller, "Ancient rock-cut burial-chambers at Bethany," *SBFLA* 1 (1950-51) 191-226.

G. Lankester Harding, "A Roman Tomb in Amman," *ADAJ* 1 (1951) 30-33.

G. Lankester Harding, "Two Iron-Age Tombs in Amman," *ADAJ* 1 (1951) 37-40.

*Auni Dajani, "Excavations in Jordan, 1949-1950," *ADAJ* 1 (1951) 44-48. [Discoveries in Western Jordan: A Rock Cut Tomb, As-Samu Village, Hebron District, p. 47; An Iron-Age Tomb at al-Jib, p. 48]

J. Kaplan, "An EB Tomb at Tel-Aviv," *BIES* 16 (1951) #3/4, VI.

Theresa Goell, "Nimrud Dagh: *The Tomb of Antiochus I, King of Commagene,*" *Arch* 5 (1952) 136-144.

George E. Mylonas and John K. Papademetriou, "The New Shaft Graves of Mycenae," *Arch* 5 (1952) 194-200.

Julius Jotham-Rothschild, "The Tombs of Sanhedria," *PEQ* 84 (1952) 23-38.

Aşkidil Akaraca, "A Hellenistic tomb in Mylasa," *TTKB* 16 (1952) 399-405.

*G. R. Driver, "Seals and Tombstones," *ADAJ* 2 (1953) 62-65.

Awni Dajani, "An Iron Age Tomb at Al Jib," *ADAJ* 2 (1953) 66-74.

Awni Dajani, "A Hyksos Tomb at Kalandia," *ADAJ* 2 (1953) 75-77.

Awni Dajani, "An Herodian Tomb at Wadi el Badan," *ADAJ* 2 (1953) 78-81.

Gilbert Bagnani, "The Tomb of Patro," *AJA* 57 (1953) 104.

George E. Mylonas, "The New Shaft Graves at Mycenae," *AJA* 57 (1953) 109-110.

*Dows Dunham, "From Tumulus to Pyramid—and Back," *Arch* 6 (1953) 87-94.

*Alan [H.] Gardiner, "The Memphite Tomb of General Ḥaremḥab," *JEA* 39 (1953) 3-12

George H. McFadden, "A Late Cypriote III Tomb from Kourion, Kaloriziki No. 40," *AJA* 58 (1954) 131-142.

Erik Sjöqvist, "Post Scriptum to 'A Late Cypriote III Tomb from Kourion' by G. H. McFadden," *AJA* 58 (1954) 142.

Ruth Amiran, "The Excavation of the Tumuli West of Jerusalem. (Preliminary Report of the Two Seasons 1953)," *BIES* 18 (1954) #1/2, V-VI.

H. Z. Hirschberg, "The Tombs of David and Solomon in Moslem Tradition," *EI* 3 (1954) XIII-XIV.

*Henry G. Fischer, "Four Provincial Administrators at the Memphite Cemeteries," *JAOS* 74 (1954) 26-34. [1. The tomb of *Nfr-m ꜣʿ.t,* at Dahshur; 2. The false door and the statues of *ggi* from Saqqara; 3. The false-mastaba of *Ḫwi-b ꜣ.w,* at Saqqara; 4. The Tomb of *Ḫwi-b ꜣ.w,* at Saqqara; 5. Other nomarchs and officials of the Thinite nome]

Briggs Buchanan, "The Date of the So-Called Second Dynasty Graves of the Royal Cemetery at Ur," *JAOS* 74 (1954) 147-153.

Alan [H.] Gardiner, "The Tomb of Queen Twosre," *JEA* 40 (1954) 40-44.

*P. V. Glob, "Bahrain—Island of the Hundred Thousand Burial-Mounds," *Kuml* (1954) 100-105.

T. G. Bibby, "Five among Bahrain's Hundred Thousand Grave-mounds," *Kuml* (1954) 132-141.

Julius Jotham-Rothschild, "The Tombs of Sanhedria—II," *PEQ* 86 (1954) 16-22.

M. Haran, "The Reliefs on the Sides of the Sarcophagus of Ahiram King of Byblos," *BIES* 19 (1954-55) #1/2, II-III.

S. Charitonides, "A Geometric Grave at Clenia in Corinthia," *AJA* 59 (1955) 125-128.

*Immanuel Ben-Dor, "Some Mediterranean Relations in the 8th Century B.C.—The Excavations of a Phoenician Cemetery in Palestine," *AJA* 59 (1955) 170.

*George E. Mylonas, "The Cemetery of Eleusis and the New Grave Circle of Mycenae," *AJA* 59 (1955) 172-173.

Walter B. Emery, "Royal Tombs at Sakkara," *Arch* 8 (1955) 2-9.

George E. Mylonas and John K. Papademetriou, "The New Grave Circle of Mycenae," *Arch* 8 (1955) 43-50.

John Dimick, "Lifting the Lid from the Cheops Boat Grave," *Arch* 8 (1955) 93-95.

F. E. Zeuner, "Notes on the Bronze Age Tombs of Jericho. I," *PEQ* 87 (1955) 118-128.

Ruth Amiran, "Two Tombs in Jerusalem from the Period of the Kings of Judah," *BIES* 20 (1955-56) #3/4, III-IV.

*Alan Rowe, "A Contribution to the Archaeology of the Western Desert: III (The Temple-Tombs of Alexander the Great and His Palace in Rhacotis: The Great Wall of the Libyan Desert)," *BJRL* 38 (1955-56) 139-165.

K[athleen] M. Kenyon, "Tombs of the Intermediate Early Bronze- Middle Bronze Age at Tell Ajjul," *ADAJ* 3 (1956) 41-55.

J. L. Benson, "A Tomb of the Early Classical Period at Bamboula," *AJA* 60 (1956) 43-50.

Doro Levi, "The Sarcophagus of Hagia Triada Restored," *Arch* 9 (1956) 192-199.

Anonymous, "Progress on the Funerary Boat of Cheops," *Arch* 9 (1956) 206-209.

*R. D. Barnett, "The Treasure of Ziwiyeh," *Iraq* 18 (1956) 111-116. *[Coffin]*

Anonymous, "Excavated Tomb from Jericho, in Melbourne," *AT* 1 (1956-57) #3, 14.

D. C. Baramki, "A Late Bronze Age Tomb at Sarafend, Ancient Sarepta," *Bery* 12 (1956-58) 129-142.

Hjalmar Larsen, "A Second Dynasty Grave at Wardan, Northern Egypt," *OrS* 5 (1956) 3-11.

Theresa Goell, "Report of the Preliminary Survey of the Tomb of Antiochus I King of Commagene conducted by the American Schools of Oriental Research in 1953," *TAD* 6 (1956) #1, 62-65.

*A. M. Habermann, "The Tomb of Rachel and the term נפש," *Tarbiz* 25 (1956-57) #4, I-II.

L. Y. Rahmani, "A Jewish Tomb on the Western Slope of Shahin Hill, Jerusalem," *BIES* 21 (1957) #3/4, III.

Alan [H.] Gardiner, "The So-called Tomb of Queen Tiye," *JEA* 43 (1957) 10-25.

John B. Ward Perkins, "Four Roman Garland Sarcophagi in America," *Arch* 11 (1958) 98-104.

Labib Habachi, "Clearance of the tomb of Kheruef at Thebes (1957-1958)," *ASAE* 55 (1958) 325-350.

M. Naor, "'On the way to Ephrat'," *BIES* 22 (1958) #1/2, VI- VII. *[Rachel's Tomb]*

M. Haran, "The Bas-Reliefs on the Sarcophagus of Ahiram King of Byblos in the Light of Archaeolgoical and Literary Parallels from the Ancient Near East," *IEJ* 8 (1958) 15-25.

L. Y. Rahmani, "A Jewish Tomb on Shahin Hill Jerusalem," *IEJ* 8 (1958) 101-105.

Jean Yoyotte, "The Tomb of a Prince Ramesses in the Valley of the Queens (No. 53)," *JEA* 44 (1958) 26-30.

Rodney S. Young, "The Gordion Tomb," *Exped* 1 (1958-59) #1, 3-13.

Charlotte R. Long, "Shrines in Sepulchres? A Re-examination of Three Middle to Late Minoan Tombs," *AJA* 63 (1959) 59-65.

Pellegrino Claudio Sestieri, "A New Painted Tomb at Paestum," *Arch* 12 (1959) 33-37. (Correction p. 138)

*L. Y. Rahmani, "Transformation of an Ornament," *'Atiqot* 2 (1959) 188-189. *[Ossuary]*

*G. Ernest Wright, "Philistine Coffins and Mercenaries," *BA* 22 (1959) 54-66.

*R. Giveon, "King or God on the Sarcophagus of Ahiram," *IEJ* 9 (1959) 57-59.

Eva Brann, "A Pithos Burial from Aigaleos," *AJA* 64 (1960) 71.

M. F. S. Hood, "*Tholos* Tombs of the Aegean," *Antiq* 34 (1960) 166-176.

John L. Caskey, "Royal Shaft Graves at Lerna," *Arch* 13 (1960) 130-133.

Charles K. Wilkinson, "More Details on Ziwiye," *Iraq* 22 (1960) 213-220. *[Coffin]*

J. Pinkerfeld, "'David's Tomb': Notes on the History of the Building: *Preliminary Report," RFEASB* 3 (1960) 41-43.

Ruth Amiran, "Tombs of the Middle Bronze Age I at Ma'ayan Barukh," *'Atiqot* 3 (1961) 84-92.

L. Y. Rahmani, "Jewish Rock-Cut Tombs in Jerusalem," *'Atiqot* 3 (1961) 93-120.

Elizabeth Thomas, "The Plan of Tomb 55 in the Valley of the Kings," *JEA* 47 (1961) 24.

*Cyril Aldred, "The Tomb of Akhenaten at Thebes," *JEA* 47 (1961) 41-59. [Appendix by A. T. Sandison, pp. 60-65]

Charles K. Williams, "The Wood Tomb Chamber of the Large Grave Mound at Gordion," *AJA* 66 (1962) 201.

N. Avigad, "A Depository of Inscribed Ossuaries in the Kidron Valley," *IEJ* 12 (1962) 1-12.

H. Case and J. C. Payne, "Tomb 100: The Decorated Tomb at Hierakonpolis," *JEA* 48 (1962) 5-18.

Knud Thorvildsen, "Burial Cairns on Umm an-Nar," *Kuml* (1962) 208-219.

Joseph A. Callaway, "The Gezer Crematorium Re-Examined," *PEQ* 94 (1962) 104-117.

George F. Bass, "Mycenaean and Protogeometric Tombs in Caria," *AJA* 67 (1963) 208.

Anne Laidlaw, "A New Roman Tomb Near Lucus Feroniae, Painted in the Second Style," *AJA* 67 (1963) 213-214.

R. Ross Holloway, "A Tomb Group of the Fourth Century B.C. from the Area of Morgantina," *AJA* 67 (1963) 289-291.

George F. Bass, "Mycenaean and Protogeometic Tombs in the Halicarnassus Peninsula," *AJA* 67 (1963) 353-361.

Cyril Aldred, "Valley Tomb no. 56 at Thebes," *JEA* 49 (1963) 176-178.

Jean Leclant, "Le Sarcophage de Ouabset de la Nécropole de Soleb," *Kush* 11 (1963) 141-153. [English Summary-The Sarcophagus from Wabset from the Cemetery at Soleb, pp. 154-158]

Torgny Säve-Söderberg, "The Tomb of the Prince of Teh-Khet, Amenemhet," *Kush* 11 (1963) 159-174.

*James B. Pritchard, "Two Tombs and a Tunnel in the Jordan Valley: Discoveries at the Biblical Zarethan," *Exped* 6 (1963-64) #4, 2-9.

Yusef Saʿad, "A Bronze Age Tomb Group from Hablet el Amud, Silwan Village Lands," *ADAJ* 8&9 (1964) 77-80.

Rafiq Wafa Dajani, "Iron Age Tombs from Irbed," *ADAJ* 8&9 (1964) 99-101.

Donald W. Bradeen, "The Funeral Monument for Koroneia," *AJA* 68 (1964) 192.

Anne Laidlaw, "The Tomb of Montefiore: A New Roman Tomb Painted in the Second Style," *Arch* 17 (1964) 33-42.

Ora Negbi, "Tombs near Manahat South-West of Jerusalem," *IEJ* 14 (1964) 114.

James W. Swauger, "1962 Survey of Three Dolmen Sites in Jordan," *ADAJ* 10 (1965) 5-36.

John E. Coleman, "Middle Bronze Age Burials of Ceos," *AJA* 69 (1965) 167.

Evelyn Lord Smithson, "Dorians on the Acropolis?" *AJA* 69 (1965) 176. *[Tombs]*

*Bernard Goldman, "Persian Fire Temples or Tombs?" *JNES* 24 (1965) 305-308.

B. A. Mastin, "Chalcolithic Ossuaries and Houses for the Dead," *PEQ* 97 (1965) 153-160.

Sylvester Saller, "Iron Age Tombs at Nebo, Jordan," *SBFLA* 16 (1965-66) 165-298.

R. M. Cook, "Painted Sarcophagi from Pitane," *A(A)* 10 (1966) 185-192.

J. B. Hennesy, "An Early Bronze Age Tomb Group from Beit Sahur," *ADAJ* 11 (1966) 19-40.

Rafik Wafa Dajani, "An Iron Age Tomb from Amman (Jabal El-Jofeh Al-Sharqi)," *ADAJ* 11 (1966) 41-47.

Rafik Wafa Dajani, "Jabal Nuzah Tomb at Amman," *ADAJ* 11 (1966) 48-52.

Rafik Wafa Dajani, "Four Iron Age Tombs from Irbed," *ADAJ* 11 (1966) 88-101.

Anonymous, "Archaeological News. Discovery of an Iron Age Burial in Dolmens," *ADAJ* 11 (1966) 102-103.

R. Ross Holloway, "The Tomb of Augustus and the Princess of Troy," *AJA* 70 (1966) 171-173.

Brian F. Cook, "An Alexandrian Tomb-Group Reexamined," *AJA* 70 (1966) 185.

Brian F. Cook, "An Alexandrian Tomb-group Re-examined," *AJA* 70 (1966) 325-330.

Jane C. Waldbaum, "Philistine Tombs at Tell Fara and their Aegean Prototypes," *AJA* 70 (1966) 331-340.

Mounir Basta, "Clearance of some Tombs of the late period near the Serapeum at Saqqara," *ASAE* 59 (1966) 15-22.

*M. Abdul-Qader Muhammed, "Recent finds," *ASAE* 59 (1966) 143-155. [The Tomb of Kheruef, pp. 154-155]

M. Abdul-Qader Muhammed, "Two Theban Tombs Kyky and Bak-En-Amun," *ASAE* 59 (1966) 157-184.

James L. Swauger, "Dolmen Studies in Palestine," *BA* 29 (1966) 106-114.

*Barry J. Kemp, "Abydos and the Royal Tombs of the First Dynasty," *JEA* 52 (1966) 13-22.

N. Avigad, "Jewish Rock-cut Tombs in Jerusalem and in the Judean Hill-Country," *EI* 8 (1967) 72*.

L. Y. Rahmani, "Jason's Tomb," *IEJ* 17 (1967) 61-100.

*Elizabeth Thomas, "Was Queen Mutnedjemet the owner of Tomb 33 in the Valley of the Queens?" *JEA* 53 (1967) 161-163.

Rafik W[afa] Dajani, "Excavations in Dolmens," *ADAJ* 12&13 (1967-68) 56-64.

Rafik W[afa] Dajani, "An (EB-MB) Burial from Amman," *ADAJ* 12&13 (1967-68) 68-69.

Yusuf Boysal, "A Report on the 1969[sic]* Turgut Excavations," *A(A)* 12 (1968) 81-93. [Date of the Tombs pp. 90-91; A General Look at the Tombs, pp. 91-93]

Charlotte R. Long, "The Obsequies of a Prince at Aghia Triadha," *AJA* 72 (1968) 167-168.

*William S. Woodard, "The Later History of Grave Circle A at Mycenae," *AJA* 72 (1968) 174-175.

Paul W. Lapp, "Bâb edh-Dhrâʿ Tomb A 76 and Early Bronze I in Palestine," *BASOR* #189 (1968) 12-41.

Elżbieta Dąbrowska Smektala, "Coffins found in the Area of the Temple of Tutmosis III at Deir el-Bahari," *BIFAO* 66 (1968) 171-181.

*V. Tzaferis, "A Middle Bronze Age I Cemetery in Tiberias," *IEJ* 18 (1968) 15-19.

L. Y. Rahmani, "Jerusalem's Tomb Monuments on Jewish Ossuaries," *IEJ* 18 (1968) 220-225.

W. B. Emery, "Tomb 3070 at Saqqâra," *JEA* 54 (1968) 11-13.

Silvio Curto and M. Mancini, "News of Khaʿ and Meryt," *JEA* 54 (1968) 77-79. *[Tombs]*

*Labib Habachi, "The Owner of Tomb no. 282 in the Theban Necropolis," *JEA* 54 (1968) 107-113.

Stanislao Loffreda, "Typological Sequence of Iron Age Rock-cut Tombs in Palestine," *SBFLA* 18 (1968) 244-287.

Christoph W. Clairmont, "An Exceptional Attic Gravestone of the Mid-fourth Century B.C.," *AJA* 73 (1969) 233.

*Barbara Switalski Lesko, "Royal Mortuary Suites of the Egyptian New Kingdom," *AJA* 73 (1969) 453-458.

Evelyn Lord Smithson, "The Grave of an Early Athenian Aristocrat," *Arch* 22 (1969) 18-25.

A. Biran and R. Gophna, "An Iron Age Burial Cave at Tel Ḥalif," *EI* 9 (1969) 135. *[English Summary]*

*A. Negev, "Seal-Impressions from Tomb 107 at Kurnub (Mampsis)," *IEJ* 19 (1969) 89-106.

*R. Gophna, "A Middle Bronze Age I Tomb with Fenestrated Axe at Ma'abarot," *IEJ* 19 (1969) 174-177.

Bruce R. Trigger, "The Royal Tombs at Qusṭul and Ballâna and their Meroïtic Antecedents," *JEA* 55 (1969) 117-128.

D. Webley, "A Note on the Dolmen Field at Tell El-Adeimeh and Teleilat Ghassul," *PEQ* 101 (1969) 42-43.

Machteld J. Mellink, "Excavation of a Lycian Painted Tomb near Elmali, Kizilbel," *TAD* 18 (1969) #2, 141-144.

§197 *2.5.9 Artifacts - General Studies*

J[oseph] H[ager], "General Observations on the Persepolitan Characters, with a Description and Representation of some bricks lately sent to Europe from the Site of Antient[sic]* Babylon," *MMBR* 12 (1801) 2-6.

*J. P. Lesley, "A Classified Catalogue of Antiquities Collected by Mr. Harris, and now in his Museum in Alexandria Egypt," *PAPS* 10 (1865-69) 561-582.

Richard F. Burton, "On Anthropological Collections from the Holy Land," *JRAI* 1 (1871-72) 300-312.

*R[ichard] F. Burton, "On Anthropological Collections from the Holy Land. No. II," *JRAI* 1 (1871-72) 321-342. [Note on the Implements from Bethlehem by John Evans, pp. 342-344 (Discussion, pp. 344-345)]

*Claude R. Conder, "The Collection of M. Péretié," *PEFQS* 13 (1881) 214-218.

*†W. [M.] Flinders Petrie, "Pottery and Implements collected at Giseh and the neighbourhood, from December 1880 to June 1881," *SBAP* 4 (1881-82) 76.

F. G. Hilton Price, "Notes on the Antiquities from Bubastis, in the Collection of F. G. Hilton Price, F.S.A.," *SBAP* 7 (1884-85) 75-79. *[Egyptian Antiquities]*

†F. G. Hilton Price, "Notes on some Egyptian Antiquities in his Collection," *SBAP* 8 (1885-86) 149-154.

Claude R. Conder, "Notes. *Phoenician Antiquities,*" *PEFQS* 18 (1886) 15-17.

F. G. Hilton Price, "Notes on the Antiquities from Bubastis (Tel Basta). In the collection of F. G. Hilton Price, F.S.A.," *SBAT* 9 (1886-93) 44-73.

William Hayes Ward, "On certain Babylonian objects," *JAOS* 13 (1889) ccxxxii-ccxxxiii.

August Eisenlohr, "Egyptian Antiquities at Brussels," *SBAP* 11 (1888-89) 254-266.

Cyrus Adler, "On a study-collection of casts of Assyrian and Babylonian antiquities in the National Museum at Washington," *JAOS* 13 (1889) ccxxxiv.

Cyrus Adler, "Note on the Collection of Oriental Antiquities in the National Museum at Washington, D. C.," *JAOS* 13 (1889) ccci-cccii.

*J. William Dawson, "Notes on Useful and Ornamental Stones of Ancient Egypt," *JTVI* 26 (1892-93) 265-282. (Discussion, pp. 282-288) [1. Granitic, Dioritic, and Gneissic Rocks, 2. Basalt with Olivine, 3. The Nubian Sandstone, 4. Limestone, &c., 5. Miocene Quartzite of Jebel Ahmar, &c., 6. Various Stones and Gems, 7. Flint Flakes, Knives, Saws, &c.]

*C[onrad] Schick, "Letters from Herr Baurath von Schick. IV. Baron Ustinoff's Collection of Antiquities at Jaffa," *PEFQS* 25 (1893) 294-297.

*Theo. G. Pinches, "Names of Plants and Things made therefrom in Babylonia," *SBAP* 16 (1893-94) 308-311.

James Henry Breasted, "The New-Found Treasure of the Twelfth Dynasty," *BW* 3 (1894) 362-364.

F. J. Bliss, "Marble Fragment from Jebail," *PEFQS* 26 (1894) 118-120. (Note by C. R. Conder, p. 207)

D. Lee Pitcairn, "Note on the Marble Fragment from Jebail," *PEFQS* 26 (1894) 200-201.

A. H. Sayce, "Note on the Objects Discovered by Dr. Bliss at Tell Zakariya," *PEFQS* 31 (1899) 210-212. [(Note by L. Gautier, p. 356) (C. Clermont-Ganneau, *PEFQS* 32 (1900) p. 79)]

*(Mrs.) Sara Y. Stevenson, "Notes on Some Important Objects in the Egyptian Collection of the University of Pennsylvania," *AJA* 5 (1901) 34-35.

Christopher Johnston, "The Narburg Collection of Cypriote Antiquities," *JAOS* 22 (1901) 18-19.

Arthur E. Weigall, "Egyptian Notes," *SBAP* 23 (1901) 10-15. [Antiquities in the Museum of the Société Jersiaise, pp. 12-13]

*Percy E. Newberry, "Extracts from my Notebooks (IV)," *SBAP* 23 (1901) 218-224. [24. Some Egyptian Antiquities in the Dattari Collection, pp. 220-222]

I. M. Casanowicz, "The Collection of Oriental Antiquities at the United States National Museum," *JAOS* 23 (1902) 44-47.

H. B. Walters, "Note on Certain Antiquities from Cyprus in the British Museum," *Man* 2 (1902) #66.

E. Towry Whyte, "Ancient Egyptian Objects in Wood and Bone," *SBAP* 24 (1902) 84-85.

W. M. Flinders Petrie, "Notes on Objects from Gezer," *PEFQS* 36 (1904) 244-245.

Anonymous, "Two Exhibitions of Egyptian Antiquities," *RP* 3 (1904) 287-288.

Edgar James Banks, "Spurious Antiquities in Bagdad," *AJSL* 21 (1904-05) 60-62.

M[elvin] G[rove] Kyle, "Egyptian Antiquities in the Free Museum of Science and Art of the University of Pennsylvania," *RP* 4 (1905) 259-266.

W. L. Nash, "Himyaritic Objects from the Lower Yafi Valley. Belonging to Major Merewether, *R.E.*," *SBAP* 27 (1905) 184.

George Frederick Wright, "The Archaeological Museum of Florence, Italy," *RP* 5 (1906) 59-63. *[Artifacts]*

Anonymous, "Egyptian Relics at John Hopkins University," *RP* 6 (1907) 94-95.

W. L. Nash, "Notes on some Egyptian Antiquities," *SBAP* 29 (1907) 175-176.

W. L. Nash, "Notes on some Egyptian Antiquities. II," *SBAP* 29 (1907) 297-298.

Jean Capart, "Some Egyptian Antiquities in the Soane Museum," *SBAP* 29 (1907) 311-314.

E. R. Ayrton, "Recent Discoveries in the Baban el-Moluk at Thebes," *SBAP* 30 (1908) 116-117. *[Artifacts]*

W. L. Nash, "Notes on some Egyptian Antiquities. III," *SBAP* 30 (1908) 153-154.

W. L. Nash, "Notes on some Egyptian Antiquities. IV," *SBAP* 30 (1908) 292-293.

Tewfik effendi Boulos, "A Report on some Antiquities found in the Inspectorate of Miniéh," *ASAE* 10 (1909) 114-115.

R. A. S[tewart] Macalister, "Notes and Queries. (6.) *Archaeological discoveries at Nablus,*" *PEFQS* 41 (1909) 74. *[Artifacts]*

W. L. Nash, "Notes on Some Egyptian Antiquities. V," *SBAP* 31 (1909) 255.

W. L. Nash, "Notes on some Egyptian Antiquities. VI.," *SBAP* 32 (1910) 37-38.

W. L. Nash, "Notes on some Egyptian Antiquities. VII.," *SBAP* 32 (1910) 124-125.

W. L. Nash, "Notes on Some Egyptian Antiquities. VIII.," *SBAP* 32 (1910) 193-194.

L. Earle Rowe, "Notes on the Recent Egyptian Acquisitions from Gizeh in the Boston Museum of Fine Arts," *AJA* 15 (1911) 72.

W. L. Nash, "Notes on Some Egyptian Antiquities. IX," *SBAP* 33 (1911) 34-39.

W. L. Nash, "Notes on Some Egyptian Antiquities. X," *SBAP* 33 (1911) 104-109.

W. L. Nash, "Notes on Some Egyptian Antiquities. XI," *SBAP* 33 (1911) 135-136.

W. L. Nash, "Notes on Some Egyptian Antiquities. XII," *SBAP* 34 (1912) 35-38.

W. L. Nash, "Notes on Some Egyptian Antiquities. XIII," *SBAP* 34 (1912) 213-214.

Max Kellner, "A Day with the Neoliths," *PEFQS* 45 (1913) 184-190.

W. L. Nash, "Notes on Some Egyptian Antiquities. XIV," *SBAP* 35 (1913) 196-197.

W. L. Nash, "Notes on Some Egyptian Antiquities. XV," *SBAP* 36 (1914) 249-252.

W. L. Nash, "Notes on Some Egyptian Antiquities. XVI," *SBAP* 37 (1915) 145-148.

F. Ll. Griffith, "A Tourist's Collection of Fifty Years Ago," *JEA* 3 (1916) 193-198.

W. L. Nash, "Notes on Some Egyptian Antiquities. XVII," *SBAP* 38 (1916) 35-37.

*Aylward M. Blackman, "The Nugent and Haggard Collections of Ancient Egyptian Antiquities," *JEA* 4 (1917) 39-46.

Caroline Ransom Williams, "The Egyptian Collection in the Museum of Art at Cleveland, Ohio," *JEA* 5 (1918) 166-178, 272-285.

*M. Rostovtzeff, "The Sumerian Treasure of Astrabad," *JEA* 6 (1920) 4-27.

Gordon Forsayeth, "A Few Antiquities from Macedonia," *Man* 20 (1920) #30.

Stephen Bleecker Luce, "Recent Classical Accessions of the Rhode Island School of Design," *AJA* 28 (1924) 73.

G. A. Wainwright, "Antiquities from Middle Egypt and the Fayûm," *ASAE* 25 (1925) 144-148.

[W. M.] Flinders Petrie, "Small Objects from Naqadeh," *AEE* 12 (1927) 14-15.

H. R. Hall "Objects of Tut'ankhamūn in the British Museum," *JEA* 14 (1928) 74-77.

*E[phraim] A. Speiser, "Traces of the oldest cultures of Babylon and Assyria," *AfO* 5 (1928-29) 162-164.

*E[phraim] A. Speiser, "Some Prehistoric Antiquities from Mesopotamia," *JQR, N.S.,* 19 (1928-29) 345-354.

Josephine Platner, "Out of the Tombs at Corinth: I," *A&A* 29 (1930) 195-202.

Josephine Platner, "Out of the Tombs at Corinth: II," *A&A* 29 (1930) 257-265.

Dorothy A. E. Garrod, "Note on Three Objects of Mesolithic Age from a Cave in Palestine," *Man* 30 (1930) #63.

Anonymous, "The New Ur Collections," *UMB* 1 (1930) #3, 5-6.

H[elen] E. F[ernald], "The Maikop Treasure," *UMB* 2 (1930-31) 6-11. *[Scythian Artifacts]*

Anonymous, "Notes and Comments. The Pliny Relics Located," *A&A* 31 (1931) 186-187.

D. A. Allan, "Hittite and Ægean Material in the Liverpool Public Museum," *AAA* 18 (1931) 50.

H. R. Hall, "Objects belonging to the Memphite High-Priest Ptaḥmase," *JEA* 17 (1931) 48-49.

*Anonymous, "Objects from Beth Shemesh," *UMB* 3 (1931-32) 121-122.

*Anonymous, "A Collection from Tell Bella and Tepe Gawra," *UMB* 4 (1932-33) 17-20.

Gustavus A. Eisen, "A Minoan Gold Treasure," *A&A* 35 (1934) 135-139.

[W. M.] Flinders Petrie, "Treasures of Ancient Gaza," *AEE* 19 (1934) 1-6.

Anonymous, "Objects from Ur," *UMB* 5 (1934-35) #5, 33-34.

L. D. Casey, "Recent Acquisitions of the Museum of Fine Arts, Boston," *AJA* 40 (1936) 306-313.

W. D. van Wijngaarden, "Objects of Tut'ankhamūn in the Rijksmuseum of Antiquities at Leiden," *JEA* 22 (1936) 1-2.

Dorothy Kent Hill, "Source Materials for Archaeological Study at the Walters Art Gallery," *AJA* 41 (1937) 111-112.

*E[phraim] A. Speiser, "Mesopotamian Miscellanea," *BASOR* #68 (1937) 7-13. [III. Hurrian Material from Khafâjeh, pp. 12-13]

Simone Corbiau, "New Finds in the Indus Valley," *Iraq* 4 (1937) 1-10.

Lankester Harding, "Some Objects from Trans-jordan," *PEQ* 69 (1937) 253-255.

Moharram Kamal, "Gift of His Majesty King Farouk 1st (1937) to the Egyptian Museum," *ASAE* 38 (1938) 1-22.

Alan Rowe, "New light on objects belonging to the generals Potasimto and Amasis in the Egyptian Museum," *ASAE* 38 (1938) 157-196.

William F. Stinespring, "Haverford Collection of Palestinian Artifacts," *DDSR* 5 (1940-41) 97-98.

Gisela M. A. Richter, "Recent Acquisitions of the Metropolitan Museum of Art," *AJA* 44 (1940) 181-186.

*A. Lucas, "Notes on some of the objects from the tomb of Tut-Ankhamun," *ASAE* 41 (1942) 135-147; 45 (1947) 133-134. [I.-Description of the Collection; II.-Were Those Tools Intended for Practical or Votive Purposes? III.-To Which Monument were Those Tools Dedicated?]

Seton Lloyd, "Some Recent Additions to the Iraq Museum," *Sumer* 2 (1946) #1, 1-9.

Leon Legrain, "The Babylonian Collections of the University Museum," *UMB* 10 (1943-44) #3/4, 1-75.

T. Sulimirski, "Scythian Antiquities in Central Europe," *AJ* 25 (1945) 1-11.

R. Engelbach, "A list of the royal names on the objects in the 'King Fouad I Gift' collection with some remarks on its arrangement," *ASAE* 41 (1942) 219-232.

G. Roger Edwards, "The Classical Collection of the Bowdoin College Museum of Fine Arts," *AJA* 44 (1940) 111-112.

Guy Brunton, "Objects from fifth Dynasty Burials at Gebelein," *ASAE* 40 (1940-41) 521-527.

*Niels Breistenstein, "Analacta Acragantina," *AA* 16 (1945) 113-153. *[Artifacts]*

*Robert J. Braidwood, Linda S. Braidwood, Edna Tulane, and Ann L. Perkins, "New Chalcolithic Material of Samarran Type and its Implications. A Report on Chalcolithic Material of the Samarran Type Found at Baghouz on the Euphrates, and a Reconsideration of the Samarran Material in General (Especially the Painted Pottery) in the Light of this New Material," *JNES* 3 (1944) 47-72. [III. Description of the Flint Artifacts of the Baghouz Occurrence, pp. 54-57]

Zaki Iskandar, "Foundation deposits of Thothmes IIIrd (M. A. Mansour)," *ASAE* 47 (1947) 157.

Marie-Louise Buhl, "Recently acquired Iranian Antiquities in the Danish National Museum," *AA* 21 (1950) 183-210.

*Labib Habachi, "Clearance of the area to the east of Luxor Temple and discovery of some objects," *ASAE* 51 (1951) 447-468.

*Louis B. Dupree, "The Pleistocene Artifacts of Hotu Cave, Iran," *PAPS* 96 (1952) 250-257.

*Marie-Louise Buhl, "Antiquities from Djerabis in Syria," *AA* 23 (1952) 155-167.

*P. V. Glob, "The Flint Sites of the Bahrain Desert," *Kuml* (1954) 112-115. *[Artifacts]*

Rodney S. Young, "Grave Robbers' Leavings," *Arch* 8 (1955) 191-197.

P. J. Riis, "A Collection of Oriental and Classical Antiquities in Jutland," *Kuml* (1952) 107.

*R. D. Barnett, "The Treasure of Ziwiyeh," *Iraq* 18 (1956) 111-116.

*S. Applebaum, "A Lamp and Other Remains of the Jewish Community of Cyrene," *IEJ* 7 (1957) 154-162.

Tahsin Özgüç and Mahmut Akok, "Objects from Horoztepe," *TTKB* 21 (1957) 201-219.

C. K. Wilkinson, "More Details of Ziwiye," *Iraq* 22 (1960) 213-220.

Kate Bosse-Griffiths, "Finds from 'The Tomb of Queen Tiye' in the Swansea Museum," *JEA* 47 (1961) 66-70.

*Viggo Nielsen, "The Al Wusail Mesolithic Flint Sites at Qatar," *Kuml* (1961) 181-184.

*Hans Jørgen Madsen, "A Flint Site in Qatar," *Kuml* (1961) 197-201.

Massimo Pallottino, "The Etruscan Lion," *Antiq* 36 (1962) 201-205.

Abd El-Hamid Zayed, "Some miscellaneous objects found in the neighbourhood of el Kharga Oasis," *ASAE* 57 (1962) 125-130.

Abd El-Hamid Zayed, "Some Antiquities Found at El Minchah in 1959," *ASAE* 57 (1962) 131-136.

Cyril Aldred, "The Harold Jones Collection," *JEA* 48 (1962) 160-162.

Edward L. B. Terrance, "Some Recent Finds from Northwest Persia," *Syria* 39 (1962) 212-224.

*C. A. Key, "Note on the Trace-Element Content of the Artifacts of the Kfar Monash Hoard," *IEJ* 13 (1963) 289-290.

Khalil Messiha and Hishmet Messiha, "A new concept about the implements found in the Excavations at Giza," *ASAE* 58 (1964) 209-225.

Ezat O. Negahban, "Notes on Some Objects from Marlik," *JNES* 24 (1965) 309-327.

Charles K. Wilkinson, "The Achaemenian Remains at Qaṣr-i-Abu Naṣr," *JNES* 24 (1965) 341-345.

Jadwiga Lipinska, "List of objects found at Deir El-Bahari Temple of Tuthmosis III, Season 1961/1962," *ASAE* 59 (1966) 63-98.

Bengt Julius Peterson, "Some Objects from the Time of Akhenaten," *JEOL* #20 (1967-68) 21-26.

*Curt W. Beck, "The Provenience of Mycenaean Amber Artifacts," *AJA* 72 (1968) 161.

*Elizabieta Dabrowska-Smektala, "List of Objects Found at Der el-Bahari in the Area of the Tuthmosis III's Temple Seasons 1962-63 and 1963-64," *ASAE* 60 (1968) 95-130.

Jadwiga Lipinska, "A List of Objects Found at Deir el-Bahari in the Area of the Temple of Thuthmosis III," *ASAE* 60 (1968) 153-204.

Jadwiga Lipinska, "List of Objects Found at Deir el-Bahari in the Temple of Tuthmosis III," *ASAE* 60 (1968) 205-212.

Sönmez Kantman, "Cilâli Taş Aletlerde Mikroanalitik Metodla Fonksiyon Tayini," *AAI* 3 (1969) 81-101. [English Summary, p. 89]

Siegfried H. Horn, "Objects from Shechem excavated in 1913 and 1914," *JEOL* #20 (1967-68) 71-90.

John A. Kroll, "Bronze Allotment Plates from Aeolis," *AJA* 73 (1969) 239.

§198 ***2.5.9.1 Agricultural Implements***

Selah Merrill, "Large Millstone on the Shittim Plain," *PEFQS* 15 (1883) 236-238.

*R. A. Stewart Macalister, "The Rock-Cuttings of Tell Es-Sâfi," *PEFQS* 32 (1900) 29-39. *[Winepress]*

*A. T. Clay, "Babylonian Section. An Ancient Plow," *MJ* 1 (1910) 4-6.

*(Miss) Marie N. Buckman, "The Mystery of the Predynastic Egyptian Furnace Solved," *HR* 66 (1913) 114-115. *[Ovens for Grain Preparation]*

*Aylward M. Blackman, "A Painted Pottery Model of a Granary in the Collection of the late Jeremiah James Colman, Esq., of Carrow House, Norwich," *JEA* 6 (1920) 206-218.

*E[phraim] A. Speiser, "Some Prehistoric Antiquities from Mesopotamia," *JQR, N.S.,* 19 (1928-29) 345-354. *[Bronze Sickle]*

*Noble Foster Hoggson, "Oil Jars of Sicily," *A&A* 28 (1929) 89-94.

*E. A. Marples, "Ancient Reaping Hooks," *Man* 29 (1929) #37.

*Cecil E. Curwen, "Agriculture and the Flint Sickle in Palestine," *Antiq* 9 (1935) 62-66.

*L. P. Kirwan, "An Inscribed Block At ʿAṭbara, Sudan," *JEA* 26 (1940) 83. *[Grindstone]*

*Carl O. Sauer, "Jericho and Composite Sickles," *Antiq* 32 (1958) 187-189.

Donald White, "Millstones from Morgantina," *AJA* 66 (1962) 201.

Donald White, "A Survey of Millstones from Morgantina," *AJA* 67 (1963) 199-206.

Gus W. Van Beek and James P. Mandaville Jr., "A Pre-Islamic Hoe from North-Eastern Arabia," *Antiq* 37 (1963) 138-139.

§199 *2.5.9.1.1 Basketry and Related Articles*

*Theo. G. Pinches, "Names of Plants and Things made therefrom in Babylonia," *SBAP* 16 (1893-94) 308-311.

John L. Myres, "Textile Impressions on an Early Clay Vessel from Amorgos," *JRAI* 27 (1897-98) 178-180.

Anonymous, "The Antiquity of Rope," *AAOJ* 26 (1904) 306.

G. A. Wainwright, "Basketry, cordage, etc., from the Fayum," *ASAE* 24 (1924) 108-116.

*G[race] M. Crowfoot, "Mat Impressions of Pot Bases," *AAA* 25 (1938) 3-11.

*H. A. Thompson, "The Influence of Basketry on Attic Geometric Pottery," *AJA* 46 (1950) 286.

§200 *2.5.9.2 Clothing, Textiles, and Weaving Implements*
[See also: §93 Weaving, Dyeing and Clothing Production; & §94 Wearing Apparel and Style ←]

H. Ling Roth, "Studies in Primitive Looms," *JRAI* 46 (1916) 284-308; 47 (1917) 113-150, 323-366; 47 (1917) 103-104; 48 (1918) 103-145.

Bernice M. Cartland, "Balls of Thread wound on Pieces of Pottery," *JEA* 5 (1918) 139.

H. E. Winlock, "Heddle-Jacks of the Middle Kingdom Looms," *AEE* 7 (1922) 71-74.

A. C. Mace, "Loom Weights in Egypt," *AEE* 7 (1922) 75-76.

Kate McK. Elderkin, "Buttons and their Use on Greek Garments," *AJA* 32 (1928) 333-345.

Grace M. Crowfoot, "A Textile from the Hood Collection of Egyptian Antiquities," *AEE* 18 (1933) 43-45.

*Ahmed Youssef Moustafa, "Reparation and restoration of antiques. The golden belt of Prince Ptah-Shepses," *ASAE* 54 (1956-57) 149-151.

*N. Tsori, "A Spindle Whorl with Hebrew Inscription," *IEJ* 9 (1959) 191-192.

John Boardman, "Ionian Bronze Belts," *A(A)* 6 (1961-62) 179-189.

Hans Helbaek, "Textiles from Catal Huyuk," *Arch* 16 (1963) 39-46.

*Abd el-Mohsen el-Khachab, "Some Recent Acquisitions of the Cairo Museum," *JEA* 50 (1964) 144-146. [1. A golden girdle from Ptolemaic Egypt, pp. 144-145]

Arvid Andrén, "An Italic Iron Age Belt Plate," *MB* #4 (1964) 38-41.

§201 ***2.5.9.2.1 Fibulae***

J. L. Myres, "A Type of Fibula of the Early Iron Age, apparently peculiar to Cyprus," *AAA* 3 (1910) 138-144.

J. L. Myres, "A Cypriote Fibula of the Early Iron Age now in the Ashmolean Museum," *AAA* 5 (1912-13) 129-131.

J. L. Myres, "A Fibula of Cypriote Type from Rhodes," *AAA* 8 (1921) 19.

David Stronach, "The Development of the Fibula in the Near East," *Iraq* 21 (1959) 180-206.

Judy Birmingham, "The Development of the Fibula in Cyprus and Levant," *PEQ* 95 (1963) 80-112.

Oscar W[hite] Muscarella, "Ancient Safety Pins: Their Function and Significance," *Exped* 6 (1963-64) #2, 34-40.

John Alexander, "The Spectacle Fibulae of Southern Europe," *AJA* 69 (1965) 7-23.

Oscar White Muscarella, "A Fibula from Hasanlu," *AJA* 69 (1965) 233-240.

*Oscar White Muscarella, "Fibulae Represented on Sculpture," *JNES* 26 (1967) 81-86.

*Ruth Amiran, "Two Luristan fibulae and an Urartian ladle from old excavations in Palestine," *IA* 6 (1969) 88-91.

§202 ***2.5.9.3 Cultic and Funerary Articles***

*S[amuel] Birch, "On sepulchral figures," *ZÄS* 2 (1864) 89-96, 103-105; 3 (1865) 4-8, 20-22.

*Paul Pierret, "Libation Vase of Osor-ur, preserved in the Museum of the Louvre (No. 908)," *SBAP* 2 (1879-80) 57-60.

*Selah Merrill, "A Cinerary Urn," *OBJ* 1 (1880) 81-82. *[Egyptian]*

*Samuel Birch, "Observations on Canopic Vases from Tel-Basta, exhibited by F. G. Hilton-Price," *SBAP* 5 (1882-83) 98-100.

*Selah Merrill, "A Cinerary Urn," *AAOJ* 2 (1879-80) 285-287.

Allan Marquand, "A Silver Patera from Kourion," *AJA, O.S.,* 3 (1887) 322-337.

*William Hayes Ward, "Notes on Oriental Antiquities," *AJA, O.S.,* 3 (1887) 338-343. [IV.*[sic]* The Eye of Nabu, pp. 338-339]

William Hayes Ward, "Notes. I. Assyro-Babylonian Forgery," *AJA, O.S.,* 3 (1887) 383-384. *[Altar(?)]*

*W. M. Flinders Petrie, "Egyptian Funereal Cones," *BOR* 2 (1887-88) 64-65.

Allan Marquand, "An Archaic Patera from Kourion," *AJA, O.S.,* 4 (1888) 169-171.

[William Hayes] Ward, "A Babylonian Cylindrical Object," *JAOS* 14 (1890) lxxxviii-lxxxix.

W. L. Nash, "Ushabti-box of Nes-pa-ched, a Priest of Mentu," *SBAP* 20 (1898) 186.

George Reisner, "The Dated Canopic Jars of the Gizeh Musuem," *ZÄS* 37 (1899) 61-72.

Percy E. Newberry, "Extracts from my Note Books (II).," *SBAP* 22 (1900) 59-66. [11. An Ushabti Figure of Paser, Mayor of Thebes, pp. 64-65]

*Arthur E. Weigall, "Egyptian Notes," *SBAP* 23 (1901) 10-15.[A Small Porcelain Naos of Bast, p. 15]

A. Wiedemann, "Bronze Circles and Purification Vessels in Egyptian Temples," *SBAP* 23 (1901) 263-274.

William H. Ward, "The Hittite Lituus," *AJA* 6 (1902) 41-42.

George F. Moore, "Baetylia and Other Holy Stones," *AJA* 7 (1903) 82.

Anonymous, "Ancient Egyptian Burial Relics," *MQR, 3rd Ser.,* 31 (1905) 180-181.

*Anonymous, "Little Figures from Egyptian Tombs," *RP* 4 (1905) 128.

*Percy E. Newberry, "Extracts from my Notebooks. VIII," *SBAP* 27 (1905) 101-105. [63. Some Small Inscribed Objects, pp. 103-105 (*Shawabti figure, p. 105; Altar, p. 105*)]

*Margaret A. Murray, "The Astrological Character of the Egyptian Magical Wands," *SBAP* 28 (1906) 33-43.

*Arthur E. P. Weigall, "Report on Some Objects recently found in Sebakh and other Diggings," *ASAE* 8 (1907) 40-50. [Shauabti figure of Amoses, a priest at [hieroglyphs], from Thebes, p. 42]

*J[ames] A. Montgomery, "Babylonian Section: A Love Charm on an Incantation Bowl," *MJ* 1 (1910) 48-49.

*S[tephen] Langdon, "A Babylonian Narû," *SBAP* 32 (1910) 255-256.

*Arthur E. P. Weigall, "Miscellaneous Notes," *ASAE* 11 (1911) 170-176. [8. An Inscribed Amulet of Dynasty XIX, pp. 172-173]

J. A. Montgomery, "Babylonian Section. A Magical Skull," *MJ* 2 (1911) 58-60.

*Paul Pierret, "The Ushabti Figures," *SBAP* 34 (1912) 247.

R. Gottheil, "Two Forged Antiques," *JAOS* 33 (1913) 306-312. [A. A Remarkable Gold Amulet, pp. 306-308]

George H. Richardson, "Egyptian Ushabtiu. The Quaint Solution of an Old Problem," *OC* 27 (1913) 497-507.

*Percy E. Newberry, "List of Vases with Cult-Signs," *AAA* 5 (1912-13) 137-142. *[Egyptian]*

*[Hans Henry] Spoer, "An Inscribed Jewish Ossuary," *PEFQS* 46 (1914) 200-201. (Note by G. Buchanan Gray, p. 201)

*Percy E. Newberry, "Egyptian Historical Notes. II," *SBAP* 36 (1914) 35-39. [8. Two Wooden Coffins from El-Bersheh, p. 36; 9. Some Small Historical Antiquities, pp. 36-39 (*Shawabti figure, p. 36*)]

Karl P. Harrington, "The Votive Deposit at Ponte di Nona," *AJA* 19 (1915) 76.

*T. Eric Peet, "A Remarkable Burial Custom of the Old Kingdom," *JEA* 2 (1915) 8-9 *[Mud Balls]*

Winifred M. Crompton, "Two Clay Balls in the Manchester Museum," *JEA* 3 (1916) 128.

*S[tephen] Langdon, "Assyrian Lexicographical Notes," *JRAS* (1921) 573-582. [III. A Bead-Shaped Amulet, p. 574]

Walton Brooks McDaniel, "The Holiness of the Dischi Sacri," *AJA* 28 (1924) 24-46.

*A. M. Tallgren, "The Copper Idols from Galich and Their Relatives," *SO* 1 (1925) 312-341.

*Battiscombe Gunn, "A *shawabti*-figure of Puyamrēʿ from Saqqara," *ASAE* 26 (1926) 157-159.

S. R. K. Glanville, "Egyptian Theriomorphic Vessels in the British Museum," *JEA* 12 (1926) 52-69.

*D. B. Harden, "Punic Cinerary Urns from the Precinct of Tanit at Carthage," *AJA* 31 (1927) 95.

*D. B. Harden, "Punic Urns from the Precinct of Tanit at Carthage," *AJA* 31 (1927) 297-310.

H. R. Hall, "Theriomorphic Canopic Jar-Heads of the Middle Kingdom(?)" *AAA* 16 (1929) 47-48.

H. E. Winlock, "A late Dynastic Embalmer's Table," *ASAE* 30 (1930) 102-104.

Alan W. Shorter, "A Phallic Figure in the British Musuem," *JEA* 16 (1930) 236.

Anonymous, "The New Ur Collections," *UMB* 1 (1930) #3, 5-6.

*R. Engelbach, "An alleged winged Sun-disk of the first Dynasty," *ZÄS* 65 (1930) 115-116.

D. A. Allan, "Hittite and Ægean Material in the Liverpool Public Museum," *AAA* 18 (1931) 50.

*A. Lucas, "The canopic Vases from the 'Tomb of Queen Tîyi'," *ASAE* 31 (1931) 120-122.

*R. Engelbach, "Recent Acquisitions in the Cairo Museum," *ASAE* 31 (1931) 126-131. [III. Sphinx of a Queen, pp. 128-129]

Mary Hamilton Sindler, "A Terracotta Altar in Corinth," *AJA* 36 (1932) 512-520.

A. J. T[obler], "Two Incense-burners from Beth-shan," *UMB* 4 (1932-33) 75-78.

Gustavus A. Eisen, "A Minoan Gold Treasure," *A&A* 35 (1934) 135-139.

*Helen Rees Clifford, "Two Etruscan Funerary Urns in the New York University Archaeological Museum," *AJA* 40 (1936) 118-119; 41 (1937) 300-314.

L. D. Casey, "Recent Acquisitions of the Museum of Fine Arts, Boston," *AJA* 40 (1936) 306-313.

*Ahmed Fakry, "Miscellanea," *ASAE* 37 (1937) 25-38. [5. Six Funerary Cones, pp. 33-35]

Simone Carbiau, "New Finds in the Indus Valley," *Iraq* 4 (1937) 1-10.

Georg Steindorff, "The So-called Omphalos of Napata," *JEA* 24 (1938) 147-150.

*Moharram Kamal, "Some fragments from *Shawabti*-figures of Akhenaten in the Egyptian Museum," *ASAE* 39 (1939) 381-382.

*Gisela M. A. Richter, "Four Notable Acquisitions of the Metropolitan Museum of Art," *AJA* 44 (1940) 428-442. [2. A Bronze Cinerary Urn, pp. 431-434]

Grace W. Nelson, "A Greek Votive Iynx-Wheel in Boston," *AJA* 44 (1940) 443-456.

*Julian Obermann, "Two Magic Bowls: New Incantation Texts from Mesopotamia," *AJSL* 58 (1940) 1-31.

Hetty Goldman, "The Origin of the Greek Herm," *AJA* 45 (1941) 89; 46 (1942) 58-68.

*Elisabeth Jastrow, "The Great Goddess of Nature in Funeral Art of Magna Graecia," *AJA* 46 (1942) 119. *[Arulae]*

M. Hamza, "The alabaster canopic box of Akhenaton and the royal alabaster canopic boxes of the XVIIIth Dynasty," *ASAE* 40 (1940-41) 537-543.

Axel Boëthius, "On the Ancestral Masks of the Romans," *AA* 13 (1942) 226-235.

Inez Scott Ryberg, "A Praenestine Cista in the Vassar College Classical Museum," *AJA* 47 (1943) 217-226.

G. A. Wainwright, "Amûn's sacred object at Thebes," *ASAE* 42 (1943) 185-185. *[Meteroite?]*

Mogens Gjødesen, "Bronze Paterae with Anthropomorphous Handles," *AA* 15 (1944) 101-187.

*J. H. Iliffe, "A Model Shrine of Phoenician Style," *QDAP* 11 (1945) 91-92.

Zaki Iskandar, "Foundation deposits of Thothmes IIIrd (M. A. Mansour)," *ASAE* 47 (1947) 157.

Guy Brunton, "The oracle of Kôm el-Wist," *ASAE* 47 (1947) 293-297.

*Faraj Basmachi, "The Votive Vase from Warka," *Sumer* 3 (1947) 118-127.

*L. J. Krušina-Černý, "Three New Circular Alabaster Idols from Kültepe," *ArOr* 20 (1952) 601-606.

*Ruth Amiran, "Note on the 'Double bowl' found in an EB Tomb at Tel-Aviv," *BIES* 17 (1952-53) #3/4, VII.

*M. Dothan, "Libation cup or lamp?" *BIES* 17 (1952-53) #3/4, VII.

Jaroslav Černý, "A Note on the Recently Discovered Boat of Cheops," *JEA* 41 (1955) 75-79.

Manfred Cassirer, "Two Canopic jars of the Eighteenth Dynasty," *JEA* 41 (1955) 124-125.

Cyril Aldred, "The 'Funerary Cones' of Ramesses III," *JEA* 43 (1957) 113.

*Nimet Özgüç, "Marble Idols and Statuettes from the Excavations at Kültepe," *TTKB* 21 (1957) 71-80.

*Henry G. Fischer, "Varia Aegyptiaca," *JARCE* 2 (1963) 17-51. [4. The Evolution of the Armlike Censer, pp. 28-37]

*Cyrus H. Gordon, "Incantation Bowls from Knossos and Nippur," *AJA* 68 (1964) 194-195.

Helen von Raits, "The Pinakes from Penteskouphia," *AJA* 68 (1964) 198.

*B. Landsberger and H. Tadmor, "Fragments of Clay Liver Models from Hazor," *IEJ* 14 (1964) 201-218.

Arvid Andrén, "An Italic Iron Age Hut Urn," *MB* #4 (1964) 30-37.

*Sterling Dow and David H. Gill, "The Greek Cult Table," *AJA* 69 (1965) 103-114.

*Dawson Kiang, "The Mazarita Altar, A Hellenistic Relief from Egypt," *AJA* 70 (1966) 191.

Susan Downey, "Cult Banks from Hatra," *Bery* 16 (1966) 97-109.

*John Ruffle, "Four Egyptian Pieces from the Birmingham City Museum," *JEA* 53 (1967) 39-46. [1. Part of a New-kingdom funerary group (69'96), pp. 39-41; II. A new kingdom funerary stela (70'96), pp. 41-44]

*Labib Habachi, "An Embalming Bed of Amenhotep, Steward of Memphis under Amenophis III," *MDIÄA* 22 (1967) 42-47.

Richard S. Ellis, "'Papsukkal' figures beneath the daises of Mesopotamian temples," *RAAO* 61 (1967) 51-61.

*William R. Biers, "An Archaic Votive Deposit from Phlius," *AJA* 72 (1968) 162.

*Emeline Hill Richardson, "A Series of Votive Bronzes from Arezzo," *AJA* 72 (1968) 171.

B. J. Kemp, "Canopic Jars in the Lady Lever Art Gallery," *Or, N.S.,* 37 (1968) 63-74.

Steven Diamant and Jeremy Rutter, "Horned Objects in Anatolia and the Near East and Possible Connexions with the Minoan 'Horns of Consecration'," *AS* 19 (1969) 147-177.

T. C. Mitchell, "A South Arabian Tripod Offering Saucer Said to be Ur," *Iraq* 31 (1969) 112-114.

Arvid Andrén, "An Etruscan Terracotta Ash Urn," *MB* #5 (1969) 39-43.

*M. E. L. Mallowan, "Alabaster eye-idols from Tell Brak, North Syria," *MUSJ* 45 (1969) 391-396.

§203 ***2.5.9.3.1 Amulets***

*S[amuel] Birch, "The Amulet of Tie," *ZÄS* 9 (1871) 13-15.

*Greville John Chester, "More Notes on Phoenician Gems and Amulets," *PEFQS* 18 (1886) 43-50.

*Oldfield Thomas, "Remarks on Facsimile of a Metal Mouse in the Collection of Baron Ustinoff at Jaffa," *PEFQS* 26 (1894) 189-190.

*Percy E. Newberry, "Extracts from my Note-Books. V.," *SBAP* 24 (1902) 244-252. [36. Two Prehistoric Slate Amulets, p. 251]

*Hans H. Spoer, "Notes on Jewish Amulets," *JBL* 23 (1904) 97-105.

*A[lice] Grenfell, "Amuletic Scarabs, etc., for the deceased," *RTR* 30 (1908) 105-120.

*Arthur E. P. Weigall, "Miscellaneous Notes," *ASAE* 11 (1911) 170-176. [8. An inscribed amulet of dynasty XIX, pp. 172-173]

*R. Gottheil, "Two Forged Antiques," *JAOS* 33 (1913) 306-312. [A. A Remarkable Gold Amulet, pp. 306-308]

M. A. Murray, "Some Pendant Amulets," *AEE* 4 (1917) 49-56.

Samuel Raffaeli, "A Recently Discovered Samaritan Charm," *JPOS* 1 (1920-21) 143-144.

[W. M.] Flinders Petrie, "Note on Inscribed Amulets in Egypt," *AEE* 20 (1935) 58.

Guy Brunton, "'Pesesh-kef' amulets," *ASAE* 35 (1935) 213-217.

*Alan W. Shorter, "Notes on some Funerary Amulets," *JEA* 21 (1935) 171-176.

*Neville Langton, "Notes on Some Small Egyptian Figures of Cats," *JEA* 22 (1936) 115-120.

*Guy Brunton, "Three seal-amulets," *ASAE* 42 (1943) 79-82.

*H[enri] Frankfort, "A Note on the Lady of Birth," *JNES* 3 (1944) 198-200.

E. Douglas Van Buren, "Amulets in Mesopotamia," *Or, N.S.,* 14 (1945) 18-23.

Campbell Bonner, "Notes on an Amulet in Vienna," *AJA* 53 (1949) 270-272.

E. Douglas Van Buren, "A Pictographic Amulet," *Or, N.S.,* 18 (1949) 419-422.

L. J. Krušina-Černy, "Three New Amulets of Lamashtu," *ArOr* 18 (1950), Part 3, 297-303.

*E. Douglas Van Buren, "Amulets, Symbols or Idols?" *Iraq* 12 (1950) 139-146.

*Beatrice L. Goff, "The Rôle of Amulets in Mesopotamian Ritual Texts," *JWCI* 19 (1956) 1-39.

M. Cassirer, "Two amulets of cats," *JEA* 44 (1958) 117-118.

Anit Hamburger, "A Greco-Samaritan Amulet from Caesarea," *IEJ* 9 (1959) 43-45.

*H. W. F. Saggs, "Pazuzu," *AfO* 19 (1959-60) 123-127.

J. Kaplan, "Two Samaritan Amulets," *IEJ* 17 (1967) 158-162.

§204 *2.5.9.4 Furniture*

E. Towry Whyte, "Egyptian Models of Fish; Egyptian Camp Stool," *SBAP* 22 (1900) 116-117.

John L. Myres, "An Archaic Bronze Tripod from South Persia," *Man* 3 (1903) #20.

*Caroline L. Ransom, "Chronological Survey of the Forms of Egyptian Stools, Chairs, and Couches," *AJA* 10 (1906) 81-82.

George H. Chase, "Three Bronze Tripods," *AJA* 12 (1908) 287-323.

*P. P. Flournoy, "Ahab's Palace and Jezebel's Table," *USR* 23 (1911-12) 130-134.

*G. A. Wainwright, "Wooden door and stool from Kom Washim," *ASAE* 25 (1925) 105-111.

Mary I. Hussey, "Babylonian and Assyrian Chairs," *A&A* 21 (1926) 129-132.

Anonymous, "Notes and Comments. Tutankhamen's Golden Bed," *A&A* 27 (1929) 237.

G. M. FitzGerald, "A Find of Stone Seats at Nablus," *PEFQS* 61 (1929) 104-110.

George H. Reisner, "The Bed Canopy of the Mother of Cheops," *A&A* 33 (1932) 317-322.

*Lily Ross Taylor, "Seats and Peplos on the Parthenon Frieze," *AJA* 40 (1936)121.

*N.Makhouly,"El Ḥamme. *Discovery of Stone Seats,"QDAP* 6(1938)59-62.

Dows Dunham, "An Experiment in Reconstruction at the Museum of Fine Arts, Boston," *JEA* 26 (1940) 137. *[Bed]*

Dorothy Kent Hill, "Young Bacchus, Tables and Tripods," *AJA* 56 (1952) 173-174.

Gisela M. A. Richter, "The Marble Throne on the Akropolis and its Replicas," *AJA* 58 (1954) 271-276.

*Herbert Hoffmann, "A Bronze Fulcrum in Providence," *AJA* 61 (1957) 167-168.

*Dorothy Kent Hill, "Chairs and Tables of the Ancient Egyptians," *Arch* 11 (1958) 276-280.

Alexander Cambitoglou, "Two Fragments of a Geometric Stand in Toronto and Athens," *AJA* 64 (1960) 366-367.

*A. E. Raubitschek, "The Marble Prohedria in the Theater of Dionysus," *AJA* 67 (1963) 216.

Joseph Ternbach, "The Restoration of an Etruscan Bronze Tripod," *Arch* 17 (1964) 18-25.

Dietrich von Bothmer, "Two Red-figured Stands: An Attic Footnote on the Chalcidian Question," *AJA* 70 (1966) 184.

Vassos Karageorghis, "Note on a Footstool from Salamis," *KZFE* 6 (1967) 98-99.

*Labib Habachi, "An Embalming Bed of Amenhotep, Steward of Memphis under Amenophis III," *MDIÄA* 22 (1967) 42-47.

§205 ***2.5.9.5 Glass, Glassware (includes Mirrors, Metal and Glass)***

*A. Lowy, "Notices concerning Glass in Ancient Jewish Records," *SBAP* 4 (1881-82) 84-86.

W[illia]m H. Goodyear, "The Charvet collection of Ancient Glass in the Metropolitan Museum of Art, New York," *AJA, O.S.*, 1 (1885) 163-173.

Richard Norton, "Papers of the American School of Classical Studies at Athens. A Silver 'Mirror Case,' Inlaid with Gold, in the National Museum of Athens," *AJA, O.S.*, 9 (1894) 495-503.

Anonymous, "Ancient Glass Mirrors," *RP* 6 (1907) 270.

John C. Rolfe, "Two Etruscan Mirrors," *AJA* 13 (1909) 3-18.

Anonymous, "Glass in Ancient Egypt," *RP* 8 (1909) 57.

E[dith] H. H[all], "A Collection of Antique Glass," *MJ* 4 (1913) 119-141.

Gustavus A. Eisen, "Stratified Glass. A Hitherto Unidentified Type of Mosaic Glass," *A&A* 6 (1917) 69-76.

L. G. Eldridge, "Six Etruscan Mirrors," *AJA* 21 (1917) 365-386.

Eleanor F. Rambo, "The John Thompson Morris Collection of Ancient Glass," *MJ* 10 (1919) 156-165.

Pere Ronzevalle, "Some Alleged Palestinian Pyxes," *PEFQS* 53 (1921) 172-174.

Warren E. Blake and James E. Dunlap, "The Michigan 'Rosetta' Mirror," *A&A* 27 (1929) 195-200.

Anonymous, "Notes and Comments. Illustrations for 'The Mystery of Ancient Glassware'," *A&A* 29 (1930) 41-43. (Correction p. 43)

D. B. Harden, "Ancient Glass," *Antiq* 7 (1933) 419-428.

A. Lucas, "Ancient Glass," *Antiq* 8 (1934) 94-95.

Louis A. Lord, "The Judgment of Paris on Etruscan Mirrors," *AJA* 41 (1937) 602-606.

D. E. Derry, "An Egyptian Mirror Handle in fossil bone," *Man* 37 (1937) #134.

Gisela M. A. Richter, "An Archaic Greek Mirror," *AJA* 42 (1938) 337-344.

Gisela M. A. Richter, "Archaeological Notes. Another Archaic Greek Mirror," *AJA* 46 (1942) 319-324.

Giacinto Matteucig, "An Etruscan Mirror in Berkeley," *AJA* 50 (1946) 60-66.

Gisela M. A. Richter and Christine Alexander, "A Greek Mirror—Ancient or Modern?" *AJA* 51 (1947) 221-226.

Thomas S. Buechner, "Ancient Glass in the Corning Museum," *Arch* 5 (1952) 216-219.

Mario A. Del Chiaro, "Two Etruscan Mirrors in San Francisco," *AJA* 59 (1955) 277-286.

P. P. Kahane, "Some aspects of Ancient Glass in Israel," *A&S* 2 (1957) #2/3, 208-224.

A. J. Arkell, "Ancient Red Glass at University College, London," *JEA* 43 (1957) 110.

W. E. S. Turner, "Ancient Sealing-wax Red Glasses," *JEA* 43 (1957) 110-112.

Axel von Saldern, "Recent Glass Finds at Gordion," *AJA* 63 (1959) 190.

D. Barag, "The Expedition to the Judean Desert, 1961, Glass Vessels from the Cave of Horror," *IEJ* 12 (1962) 208-214.

Thea Elisabeth Haevernick, "Mycenaean Glass," *Arch* 16 (1963) 190-193.

*Olof Vessberg, "A New Variant of the Helena Myth," *MB* #4 (1964) 54-62. *[Etruscan Bronze Mirror]*

David Crownover, "Some Frit from Northern Mesopotamia," *Exped* 7 (1964-65) #1, 43-44.

R. D. Barnett, "An Urartean Mirror," *AAI* 2 (1965) 51-54.

Herbert Hoffmann, "Graeco-Scythian Mirrors," *AJA* 69 (1965) 65-66.

Lenore O. K. Congdon, "Two Bronze Mirror Caryatids in the National Museum in Warsaw," *AJA* 70 (1966) 161-165.

Andrew Oliver Jr., "A Group of Anatolian Bronze Mirrors," *AJA* 72 (1968) 169.

M. S. Nagaraja Rao, "A bronze mirror handle from the Barhar temple, Bahrain: a further link in the Kulli culture—south Baluchistan," *Kuml* (1969) 219-220.

§206 ***2.5.9.6 Harnesses, Chariots, and Related Transportation Artifacts***

W[illiam] N[ickerson] Bates, "Etruscan Horseshoes from Corneto," *AJA* 6 (1902) 53-54.

William Nickerson Bates, "Etruscan Horseshoes from Corneto," *AJA* 6 (1902) 387-397.

*R. A. S[tewart] Macalister, "Notes and Queries. (3.) *A Bronze Object from Nablus,*" *PEFQS* 40 (1908) 340-341. *[Chariot]*

*E. J. Pilcher, "Notes and Queries. (3.) *Bronze Object from Nablus,*" *PEFQS* 41 (1909) 73-74. *[Chariot or wheeled "car" (?)]*

E[dith] H. H[all], "A Pair of Bits from Corneto," *MJ* 5 (1914) 213-217.

*Edith H. Hall, "Notes on Two Vases in the University Museum," *AJA* 19 (1915) 77-78. *[snaffle bit]*

*William F. Edgerton, "An Ancient Egyptian Steering Gear," *AJA* 30 (1926) 82-83.

H. R. Hall, "A 'Mascot' Rein-Ring from Boghàz Kyöi," *AAA* 17 (1930) 3.

M. E. L. Mallowan, "A Copper Rein-Ring from Southern Iraq," *Iraq* 10 (1948) 51-55.

Clark Hopkins, "A Snaffle Bit from the Early Villanovan Period," *AJA* 54 (1950) 258.

*Marie Matoušová, "The Rein in 'Cappadocian' Seals," *ArOr* 27 (1959) 396-399.

D. H. Trump, "Pottery 'Anchors'," *Antiq* 34 (1960) 295.

M[argaret] A. Murray, "Pottery Anchors," *Antiq* 35 (1961) 59-60.

Pierto Nicola Gargallo, "Anchors of Antiquity," *Arch* 14 (1961) 31-35. *(Translated and adapted by Evelyn Prebesen)*

Ellen Kohler, "Ivory Horse-Trappings from Gordion—1961," *AJA* 66 (1962) 198.

*R. W. Hamilton, "The Decorated Bronze Strip from Gushchi," *AS* 15 (1965) 41-51. *[Chariot Rim](?)*

K. Nikolaou and H. W. Catling, "Composite Anchors in Late Bronze Age Cyprus," *Antiq* 42 (1968) 225-229.

*(Mrs.) Mary Aiken Littauer, "Bits and Pieces," *Antiq* 43 (1969) 289-300. *[Horse Bits]*

Honor Frost, "The stone-anchors of Byblos," *MUSJ* 45 (1969) 423-442.

§207 ***2.5.9.7 Household Articles and Utensils***

*H. B. Hackett, "Scripture Facts and Illustrations Collected During a Journey in Palestine," *CRB* 18 (1853) 404-424, 517-537. [Skin and Leather Bottles, pp. 421-422]

C[onrad] Shick, "Reports by Dr. Conrad Schick. 5. *A Curious Stone Basin,*" *PEFQS* 31 (1899) 214.

C. C. Edgar, "A Thesaurus in the Museum of Cairo," *ZÄS* 40 (1902-03) 140-141. *[Money Box]*

*F. G. Hilton-Price, "Upon a Set of Seven Unguent or Perfume Vases," *SBAP* 25 (1903) 326-328.

*Percy E. Newberry, "Extracts from my Notebooks. VII," *SBAP* 25 (1903) 357-362. [57. Some Miscellaneous Antiquities, pp. 361-362 (*Wooden Head Rest, p. 361-362*)]

*David M. Robinson, "Terra-cottas and Ointment Vases found at Corinth in 1902," *AJA* 10 (1906) 83.

Harry L[angford] Wilson, "A New Italic Divinity," *AJP* 28 (1907) 450-455. *[Bronze Strainer]*

*Arthur E. P. Weigall, "Report on Some Objects recently found in Sebakh and other Diggings," *ASAE* 8 (1907) 40-50. [Set of prehistoric Pots from Edfu, p. 43]

Harry L[angford] Wilson, "A New Italic Divinity," *AJA* 12 (1908) 66. *[Bronze Strainer]*

*C. G. Seligman, "An Early Representation of Taurt," *AEE* 3 (1916) 53. *[Comb]*

David M. Robinson, "A Roman Terracotta Savings-Bank at the Johns Hopkins University," *AJA* 24 (1920) 78-79.

*Cornelia G. Harcum, "Roman Cooking Utensils in the Royal Ontario Museum of Archaeology," *AJA* 25 (1921) 37-54.

David M. Robinson, "Some Roman Terra-cotta Savings Banks," *AJA* 28 (1924) 239-250.

G. A. Wainwright, "Household objects from Kom Washim," *ASAE* 24 (1924) 117-121.

Madeleine Frédéricq, "The Ointment Spoons in the Egyptian Section of the British Museum," *JEA* 13 (1927) 7-13.

F. Ll. Griffith, "A Drinking Siphon from Tell el-ʿAmarnah," *JEA* 12 (1926) 22-23.

*R. Engelbach, "Recent Acquisitions in the Cairo Museum," *ASAE* 31 (1931) 126-131. [I. Set of Agate Vases, pp. 126-127]

*G. D. Hornblower, "The Barndoor Fowl in Egyptian Art," *AEE* 20 (1935) 82. *[Wooden Spoon]*

*J. Penrose Harland, "Helladika," *AJA* 45 (1941) 91. *[Pot Support]*

Margaret Crosby, "A Silver Kyathros from Greece," *AJA* 45 (1941) 94. *[Strainer/Ladel]*

*Lucy Talcott, "From a Fifth Century Kitchen," *AJA* 45 (1941) 94.

Margaret Crosby, "A Silver Ladle and Strainer," *AJA* 47 (1943) 209-216.

Marjorie J. Milne, "A Greek Footbath in the Metropolitan Museum of Art," *AJA* 48 (1944) 26-63.

Dorothy Kent Hill, "Two Praenestine Cistae," *AJA* 57 (1953) 107-108.

*Erik Sjöqvist, "Morgantina: Hellenistic Medicine Bottles," *AJA* 64 (1960) 78-83.

*Alan J. B. Wace, "A Mycenaean Mystery," *Arch* 13 (1960) 40-43. *[Pot Support(?)]*

§208 ***2.5.9.7.1 Drinking Vessels and Jugs [See also: §212 Pottery Finds →]***

Charles Ricketts, "Two Faience Chalices at Eton College from the Collection of the late Major W. J. Myers," *JEA* 5 (1918) 145-147.

Percy E. Newberry, "A Glass Chalice of Tuthmosis III," *JEA* 6 (1920) 155-160.

C. Leonard Woolley, "A Drinking-Horn from Asia Minor," *AAA* 10 (1923) 69-72.

*Berthold Laufer, "Ostrich Egg-Shell Cups from Mesopotamia. The Ostrich in Ancient Times," *OC* 40 (1926) 257-268.

Daniel Catton Rich, "A Rhyton in the Brygan Manner," *AJA* 34 (1930) 53.

J. E. Quibell, "Stone vessels from the Step Pyramid," *ASAE* 34 (1934) 70-75; 35 (1935) 76-80.

J. H. Iliffe, "A Tell Fārʿa Tomb Group Reconsidered. Silver Vessels of the Persian Period," *QDAP* 4 (1935) 182-186.

C[harles] B[ache], "Obsidian Vessels from Tepe Gawra," *UMB* 6 (1935-37) #1, 29-31.

Karl Lehmann-Hartleben, "The Two Silver Jugs with Ilian Scenes from Berthouville," *AJA* 40 (1936) 119.

*Poul Fossing, "Drinking Bowls of Glass and Metal from the Achaemenian Time," *Bery* 3 (1937) 121-129.

*Gisela M. A. Richter, "Two Recent Acquisitions by the Metropolitan Museum of Art," *AJA* 43 (1939) 1-9. [(2) A Cup in the Form of a Cow's Hoof, pp. 6-9]

M. Rostovtzeff, "The Parthian Shot," *AJA* 47 (1943) 174-187. *[cup]*

Eugene Vanderpool, "An Unusual Black-Figured Cup," *AJA* 49 (1945) 436-440.

Lucy Talcott, "Note on a Festival Jug," *AJA* 49 (1945) 526-527.

Marjorie J. Milne, "The Prize for Wool-Working," *AJA* 49 (1945) 528-533. *[Greek Pottery Cup]*

Nimet Özgüç, "A Hittite Jar with animal figures," *TTKB* 11 (1947) 330.

*Helene J. Kantor, "Oriental Institute Museum Notes. A Predynastic Ostrich Egg with Incised Decoration," *JNES* 7 (1948) 46-51. [#5]

G. S. Kirk, "The Ship-Rhyton in Boston," *AJA* 55 (1951) 339-342.

*M. Dothan, "High, Loop-Handled Cups and the Early Relations between Mesopotamia, Palestine and Egypt," *PEQ* 85 (1953) 132-137.

Sherman E. Lee, "A Cup by Douris," *AJA* 58 (1954) 230.

Hans Goedicke, "A Provision-Jar of the Time of Asosis," *RÉg* 11 (1957) 61-71.

Martin Robertson, "The Gorgos Cup," *AJA* 62 (1958) 55-66.

William Kelly Simpson, "A Reconstruction of a Silver and Gold Vessel from Bubastis," *AJA* 62 (1958) 226.

*A. M. ApSimon, "Food Vessels," *ULBIA* 1 (1958) 24-36.

Robert H. Dyson Jr., "An Iranian Drinking Vessel," *Exped* 1 (1958-59) #2, 18-19.

Anonymous, "The Silver Cup of Hasanlu," *Arch* 12 (1959) 171.

Herbert Hoffmann, "Rhyta from the Spoils of Plataea," *AJA* 64 (1960) 186.

*M. Dothan, "An Inscribed Jar from Azor," *'Atiqot* 3 (1961) 181-184.

Claire Epstein, "Bichrome Wheel-Made Tankards from Tell El-ʿAjjul," *PEQ* 93 (1961) 137-142.

Dorothy Kent Hill, "The Long-Beaked Bronze Jug in Greek Lands," *AJA* 66 (1962) 57-63.

Saul S. Weinberg, "How Was the Panagyurishte Gold Phiale Made?" *AJA* 66 (1962) 201.

Dietrich von Bothmer, "Five Attic Black-Figured Lip-Cups," *AJA* 66 (1962) 255-258.

*Osamu Sudzuki, "Royal Lion-hunting Scene on the Silver Cup of Solokha," *Orient* 2 (1962) 37-43.

*Henry G. Fischer, "Varia Aegyptiaca," *JARCE* 2 (1963) 17-51. [8. A First Dynasty Wine Jar from the Eastern Delta, pp. 44-47]

G. A. D. Tait, "The Egyptian Relief Chalice," *JEA* 49 (1963) 93-139.

R. D. Barnett, "A South Arabian Ivory Vessel," *EI* 7 (1964) 4*-5*

*Abd el-Mohsen el-Khachab, "Some Recent Acquisitions of the Cairo Museum," *JEA* 50 (1964) 144-146. [5. A circular marble bottle, p. 146]

Wesley E. Thompson, “The Silver Cups in the Parthenon,” *AJA* 69 (1965) 230-231.

H. W. Catling and A. Millett, “A Study of the Inscribed Stirrup-Jars from Thebes,” *Archm* 8 (1965) 3-85.

Ann Harnwell Ashmead and Kyle Meredith Phillips Jr., “An Unpublished Cup by Makron in Philadephia,” *AJA* 70 (1966) 366-368.

*O. Tufnell and W. A. Ward, “Relations between Byblos, Egypt and Mesopotamia at the end of the third Millennium B.C. A Study of the Montet Jar,” *Syria* 43 (1966) 165-241.

Keith Branigan, “A Unique Juglet from Jericho,” *PEQ* 99 (1967) 98-100.

*Edmond Sollberger, “A Tankard for Atta-Ḫušu,” *JCS* 22 (1968) 30-33.

H. W. Catling and A. Millett, “Theban Stirrup-Jars: Questions and Answers,” *Archm* 11 (1969) 3-20.

Paul Åström, “A Red Lustrous Wheel-made Spindle Bottle and its Contents,” *MB* #5 (1969) 16-21.

§209 ***2.5.9.8 Jewelry, Gems, and Crowns [See also: §95 Cosmetics and Jewelry; and §96 Gems and Minerals ←]***

*William Hayes Ward, “Notes on Oriental Antiquities,” *AJA, O.S.,* 3 (1887) 338-343. [V. A Babylonian Bronze Pendant, pp. 339-341]

*J. William Dawson, “Notes on Useful and Ornamental Stones of Ancient Egypt,” *JTVI* 26 (1892-93) 265-282. (Discussion, pp. 282-288) [6. Various Stones and Gems, pp. 278-279]

*Percy E. Newberry, “Extracts from my Note-Books. V.,” *SBAP* 24 (1902) 244-252. [32. Some inscribed Pendants, Beads, etc., pp. 248-249]

*W. L. Nash, “A Ring with the Cartouche of Nefer-ti-ti,” *SBAP* 24 (1902) 309.

*Percy E. Newberry, “Extracts from my Notebooks. VI.,” *SBAP* 25 (1903) 130-138. [46. Some Small Inscribed Objects, p. 137*[Beads and Box]*]

*Percy E. Newberry, "Extracts from my Notebooks. VII," *SBAP* 25 (1903) 357-362. [57. Some Miscellaneous Antiquities, pp. 361-362 (*Beads, p. 362*)]

*Valdemar Schmidt, "Note on a peculiar Pendant shown on Three Statues of Usertsen III," *SBAP* 28 (1906) 268-269.

*F. Ll. Griffith, "Notes on an Egyptian Signet-Ring," *SBAP* 27 (1905) 38.

*Percy E. Newberry, "Extracts from my Notebooks. VIII," *SBAP* 27 (1905) 101-105. [63. Some Small Inscribed Objects, pp. 103-105 (*Beads, p. 104*)]

William N. Bates, "Note on a Roman Ring," *PAPA* 43 (1911) xvii.

Gustavus Eisen, "The Characteristics of Eye Beads from the Earliest Times to the Present," *AJA* 20 (1916) 1-27.

Gustavus Eisen, "Button Beads—With Special Reference to Those of the Etruscan and Roman Periods," *AJA* 20 (1916) 299-307.

*Walton Brooks McDaniel, "The So-Called Athlete's Ring," *AJA* 22 (1918) 295-303.

S[tephen] B. L[uce], "A Red-Figured Pyxis," *MJ* 7 (1916) 269-276. *[Cosmetic Dish]*

A. C. Mace, "The Lahun Caskets," *AEE* 6 (1921) 4-6. *[Jewelry Boxes]*

T. Zammit, "Phoenician Ring from Malta," *AJ* 5 (1925) 266-267.

A. Zakharov, "A Fragment of a Crown of Osiris from South of Russia," *AEE* 11 (1926) 85.

*S. R. K. Glanville, "Some Notes on Material for the Reign of Amenophis III," *JEA* 15 (1929) 2-8. [Fayence ring of Amenophis III, pp. 7-8]

Horace C. Beck, "Beads from Nineveh," *Antiq* 5 (1931) 427-437.

*Horace C. Beck, "Notes on Glazed Stones," *AEE* 19 (1934) 69-83; 20 (1935) 19-37.

A. Lucas and Guy Brunton, "The Medallion of Dahshûr," *ASAE* 36 (1936) 197-200.

*Gisela M. A. Richter, "Four Notable Acquisitions of the Metropolitan Museum of Art," *AJA* 44 (1940) 428-442. [3. A Set of Etruscan Jewelry, pp. 434-439]

Guy Brunton, "The Bead network of Shashanq Heq-Kheper-Re, Tanis," *ASAE* 42 (1943) 187-191.

Tsoming N. Shiah, "The Date of Certain Egyptian Stratified Eye-Beads of Glass," *AJA* 48 (1944) 269-273.

A. J. Arkell, "A Mother-of-pearl Shell Disk of Sen-wosret III," *JEA* 30 (1944) 74.

Chrysoula P. Cardaras, "Gold Crowns from Mycenae," *AJA* 54 (1950) 260-261.

L. Keimer, "A Gold Pectoral from Napata," *JNES* 10 (1951) 225-227.

Cyril Aldred, "A pearl shell disk of Amenemes II," *JEA* 38 (1952) 130-132.

Dows Dunham, "Notes on a Gold Pectoral from Napata," *JNES* 11 (1952) 111-112. (Critical Note by George T. Allen, pp. 112)

Hazel Palmer, "Persephone's Crown," *Arch* 6 (1953) 36-38.

*Awni K. Dajani, "Some of the Industries of the Middle Bronze Period," *ADAJ* 6&7 (1962) 55-75. [Faience Ointment Vases, pp 69-75]

Oscar Broneer, "The Isthmian Victory Crown," *AJA* 66 (1962) 259-263.

*Abd el-Mohsen el-Khachab, "Some Recent Acquisitions of the Cairo Museum," *JEA* 50 (1964) 144-146. [3. A terracotta medallion, p. 145]

*George F. Bass, "Troy and Ur: Gold Links Between Two Ancient Capitals," *Exped* 8 (1965-66) #4, 26-39.

Edith Porada, "Further Notes on the Cylinders from Thebes," *AJA* 70 (1966) 194.

*Emily Vermeule, "A Mycenaean Dipinto and Graffito," *KZFE* 5 (1966) 142-146. [2. Graffito on a steatite jewelry mold from Mycenae, pp. 144-146]

Edith Porada, "Of deer, bells, and pomegranates," *IA* 7 (1967) 99-120.

Anit Hamburger, "Gems from Caesarea Maritima," *'Atiqot* 8 (1968) 1-37.

Joan Crowfoot Payne, "Lapis Lazuli in Early Egypt," *Iraq* 30 (1968) 58-61.

Bruce G. Trigger, "The Social Significance of the Diadems in the Royal Tombs at Ballana," *JNES* 28 (1969) 255-261.

§210 *2.5.9.9 Lamps, Lighting Fixtures, and Related Artifacts*

H. A. Harper, "Jewish Lamps," *PEFQS* 22 (1890) 45-46.

G. R. Lees, "Letter from Mr. G. R. Lees on Lamps, &c.," *PEFQS* 24 (1892) 124-126.

Charles Burton Gulick, "Notes on Greek Lampstands," *AJA* 7 (1903) 79-80.

Edward W. Clark, "Roman Terra-cotta Lamps," *RP* 5 (1906) 170-186.

Anonymous, "Use of Ancient Lamps," *RP* 8 (1909) 215.

Alan S. Hawkesworth, "Greek Lamps," *OC* 25 (1911) 319.

Anonymous, "Purpose of 'Kolhons' from Bœotia," *RP* 12 (1913) 131. *[Lamps]*

R. E. Plimpton and Grace T. Hadley, "Lights of Yesterday and Today," *A&A* 5 (1917) 270-274.

N. de Garis Davies, "A Peculiar Form of New Kingdom Lamp," *JEA* 10 (1924) 9-14.

J. P. T. Burchell, "A Note on Two Objects from among the Tombs of the Old Kingdom at El Kab," *Man* 24 (1924) #28. *[Candlesticks(?)]*

Oscar Broneer, "A Late Type of Wheel-Made Lamps from Corinth," *AJA* 31 (1927) 329-337.

L. A. Mayer and A. Reifenberg, "A Samaritan Lamp," *JPOS* 16 (1936) 44-45.

R. H. Howland, "Early Greek Lamps from Agora," *AJA* 43 (1939) 303.

G. Ernest Wright, "Lamps, Politics, and Jewish Religion," *BA* 2 (1939) 22-24.

F. W. Robins, "Graeco-Roman Lamps from Egypt," *JEA* 25 (1939) 48-51.

F. W. Robins, "The Lamps of Ancient Egypt," *JEA* 25 (1939) 184-187.

Louise A. Shier, "Lamps of the Roman Period from University of Michigan Excavations in Egypt," *AJA* 46 (1942) 125.

*Niels Breitenstein, "Analacta Acragantina," *AA* 16 (1945) 113-153. *[Lamps]*

James C. Rubright, "Lamps in the Robinson Collection," *AJA* 54 (1950) 263-264.

Miriam Schaar Schloessinger, "Five Lamps with Fish Reliefs: From Israel and Other Mediterranean Countries," *IEJ* 1 (1950-51) 84-95.

Hazel Palmer, "Ancient Greek Candles," *Arch* 5 (1952) 118.

Louise A. Shier, "Roman Lamps and Lamp Makers of Egypt," *AJA* 57 (1953) 110-111.

*M. Dothan, "Libation cup or lamp?" *BIES* 17 (1952-53) #3/4, VII.

Miriam Schaar Schloessinger, "Another Lamp With Fish Reliefs," *IEJ* 6 (1956) 51-53.

Philip C. Hammond Jr., "Nabataean New Year Lamps from Petra," *BASOR* #146 (1957) 10-13.

*S. Applebaum, "A Lamp and Other Remains of the Jewish Community of Cyrene," *IEJ* 7 (1957) 154-162.

D. Cracknell, "Lamps Through the Ages," *AT* 5 (1960-61) #4, 17-20.

*I. Ben-Zvi, "A Lamp with a Samaritan Inscription: *'There is none like unto the God of Jeshurun'*," *IEJ* 11 (1961) 139-142.

Robert Houston Smith, "The 'Herodian' Lamp of Palestine: Types and Dates," *Bery* 14 (1961-63) 53-65.

Charles A. Kennedy, "The Development of the Lamp in Palestine," *Bery* 14 (1961-63) 67-115.

Robert Houston Smith, "The Household Lamps of Palestine in Old Testament Times," *BA* 27 (1964) 2-31.

Robert Houston Smith, "The Household Lamps of Palestine in Intertestamental Times," *BA* 27 (1964) 101-124.

J. Brand, "Indications of Jewish Vessels in the Mishnaic Period," *EI* 9 (1969) 135. *[English Summary]*

§211 ***2.5.9.10 Metal Articles - General Studies*** ***[See also: §99 Metallurgy ←]***

Claude R. Conder, "Notes by Captin Conder. I. Bronze Vase from Nablus," *PEFQS* 18 (1886) 165.

A. L. Frothingham Jr., "Early Bronzes Recently Discovered on Mount Ida in Krete," *AJA, O.S.,* 4 (1888) 431-449.

*A. L. Frothingham Jr., "Early Bronzes Discovered in the Cave of Zeus on Mount Ida in Krete," *AJA, O.S.,* 5 (1889) 48.

*J. H. Gladstone, "On Copper and Bronze of Ancient Egypt and Assyria," *SBAP* 12 (1889-90) 227-234.

*John C. Rolfe, "Discoveries at Anthedon in 1889," *AJA, O.S.,* 6 (1890) 96-107. [IV. Bronze Implements found at Anthedon, pp. 104-107]

*Oldfield Thomas, "Remarks on Facsimile of a Metal Mouse in the Collection of Baron Ustinoff at Jaffa," *PEFQS* 26 (1894) 189-190.

*F. G. Hilton Price, "Two Objects from prehistoric tombs," *ZÄS* 37 (1899) 47. *[Gold Artifact]*

Fr. W. v[on] Bissing, "Two Silversmith's Models from Egypt," *AEE* 1 (1914) 112-114.

Kurt Sethe, "Hitherto unnoticed evidence regarding copper works of art of the oldest period of Egyptian history," *JEA* 1 (1914) 233-236.

*G. W. Elderkin, "Archaeological Studies," *AJA* 21 (1917) 397-408. [I. The Design of the Reliefs on the Vaphio Cups, pp. 397-400]

G. A. Wainwright, "A hoard of silver from Menshah, Girga, Mudiriah," *ASAE* 25 (1925) 120-134.

*Anonymous, "Objects from Ur," *UMB* 2 (1930-31) 178-182. *[Copper Bowl]*

Anonymous, "A Collection of Bronzes from Luristan," *UMB* 2 (1930-31) 194-195, 198-202.

Anonymous, "Notes and Comments. The Luristan Bronzes," *A&A* 31 (1931) 187.

*Alexander David Fraser, "The Panoply of the Ethiopian Warrior," *PAPA* 63 (1932) lix.

L. P. Kirwan, "Some græco-roman bronzes in the Cairo Museum," *BIFAO* 34 (1934) 43-62.

*A. D. Fraser, "The Panoply of the Ethiopian Warrior," *AJA* 39 (1935) 35-45.

Gisela M. A. Richter, "A Greek Bronze Hydria in the Metropolitan Museum," *AJA* 41 (1937) 532-538.

*Poul Fossing, "Drinking Bowls of Glass and Metal from the Achaemenian Time," *Bery* 3 (1937) 121-129.

Walter B. Emery, "A preliminary report on the first dynasty copper treasure from north Saqqarah," *ASAE* 39 (1939) 427-437.

*Gisela M. A. Richter, "A Greek Silver Phiale in the Metropolitan Museum And the Light It Throws On Greek Embossed Metalwork (*Toreutice*) of the Fifth Century B.C. and on the 'Calene' Phialai Mesomphaloi of the Hellenistic Period," *AJA* 45 (1941) 363-389.

David M. Robinson, "New Greek Bronze Vases. A Commentary on Pindar," *AJA* 46 (1942) 172-197.

Otto Brendel, "Three Archaic Bronze Disks from Italy," *AJA* 47 (1943) 194-208.

*Gisela M. A. Richter, "Five Bronzes Recently Acquired by the Metropolitan Museum," *AJA* 48 (1944) 1-9.

David M. Robinson, "New Greek Bronze Vases from the Peloponnesus—A Commentary on Pindar," *AJA* 44 (1940) 109.

*Gisela M. A. Richter, "Four Notable Acquisitions of the Metropolitan Museum of Art," *AJA* 44 (1940) 428-442. [2. A Bronze Cinerary Urn, pp. 431-434]

John Myres, "Fragments of an Engraved Metal Bowl from Cyprus," *Man* 45 (1945) #106.

Gisela M. A. Richter, "A Fourth-century Bronze Hydra in New York," *AJA* 50 (1946) 361-367.

*H[enri] Frankfort, "Oriental Institute Museum Notes, Two Acquisitions for the Simkhovitch Collection," *JNES* 5 (1946) 153-156. [2. An Assyrian Bronze Bowl, pp. 155-156]

*Dorothy Kent Hill, "The Technique of Greek Metal Vases and Its Bearing on Vase Form in Metal and Pottery," *AJA* 51 (1947) 248-256.

D. A. Amyz, "Geometric Platform Bronzes," *AJA* 53 (1949) 147-148.

*Gisela M. A. Richter, "Greek Fifth-Century Silverware and Later Imitations," *AJA* 54 (1950) 357-370. *[Phiale]*

*M. W. Lightner, "Analyses of Iron Implements from Tel Beit Mirsim," *BASOR* #119 (1950) 22-24.

E. S. G. Robinson, "A 'Silversmith's Hoard' from Mesopotamia," *Iraq* 12 (1950) 44-51.

R. D. Barnett and N. Gökce, "The Find of Urartian Bronzes at Altin Tepe, Near Erzincan," *AS* 3 (1953) 121-129.

K. R. Maxwell-Hyslop, "Urartian Bronzes in Etruscan Tombs," *Iraq* 18 (1956) 150-167.

Hugh Hencken, "Horse Tripods of Etruria," *AJA* 61 (1957) 1-4. *[Caldron]*

*Herbert Hoffmann, "A Bronze Fulcrum in Providence," *AJA* 61 (1957) 167-168.

Helene J. Kantor, "Oriental Institute Museum Notes, No. 9: A "Syro- Hittite' Treasure in the Oriental Institute Museum," *JNES* 16 (1957) 145-162. *[Gold Disk]*

R. D. Barnett, "A Syrian Silver Vase," *Syria* 34 (1957) 243-248.

Rodney S. Young, "Bronzes from Gordion's Royal Tomb," *Arch* 11 (1958) 227-231. *[Situlae]*

David Stronach, "Metal Objects from the 1957 Excavations at Nimrud," *Iraq* 20 (1958) 169-181.

*Gisela M. A. Richter, "Calenian Pottery and Classical Metalware," *AJA* 63 (1959) 241-249.

*Hazel Palmer and Cornelius Vermeule, "Ancient Gold and Silver in the Museum of Fine Arts, Boston," *Arch* 12 (1959) 2-7.

Clark Hopkins, "The Origin of the Etruscan-Samian Griffon Cauldrons," *AJA* 64 (1960) 186, 368-370.

*Ann Konrad Knudsen, "Bronze Vessels from Gordion, and Evidence for Phrygian Metal-Working Techniques," *AJA* 64 (1960) 187.

Charles K. Wilkinson, "More Details on Ziwiye," *Iraq* 22 (1960) 213-220.

Robert H. Dyson Jr., "An Iran Gold Piece," *Exped* 3 (1960-61) #3, 34-36.

*Ann Konrad Knudsen, "The Relation between the Pottery and Metal Vessel Industries of Gordion in the Eighth Century B.C.," *AJA* 65 (1961) 191.

A. D. H. Bivar, "A Rosette *Phialē* Inscribed in Aramaic," *BSOAS* 24 (1961) 189-199.

*W. Culican, "The Hasanlu Bowl," *Mwa-M* #1 (1961) 63-73.

Dietrich von Bothmer, "Greek Gold Phialai," *AJA* 67 (1963) 108.

Judy Birmingham, "Iranian Bronzes in the Nicholson Museum, University of Sydney," *Iran* 1 (1963) 71-82.

*Ezat O. Negahban, "The Treasures of Marlik," *Arch* 18 (1965) 109-112. *[Bronze Articles; Gold Bowls]*

Guitty Azarpay, "Some New Evidence in the Dating of the Luristan Bronzes," *AJA* 69 (1965) 164.

Dietrich von Bothmer, "Four Bronze Hydriai in the Metropolitan Museum of Art," *AJA* 69 (1965) 165.

R. W. Hamilton, "A Silver Bowl in the Ashmolean Museum," *Iraq* 28 (1966) 1-17.

Brian F. Cook, "A Class of Etruscan Bronze Omphalos-Bowls," *AJA* 71 (1967) 185.

*J. T. Hooker, "The Mycenae Siege Rhyton and the Question of Egyptian Influence," *AJA* 71 (1967) 269-281.

J. M. Munn-Rankin, "Luristan Bronzes in the Fitzwilliam Museum, Cambridge," *Iraq* 29 (1967) 1-2.

Rodney S. Young, "A Bronze Bowl in Philadelphia," *JNES* 26 (1967) 145-154.

John D. Cooney, "Experiences with Bronzes," *AJA* 72 (1968) 163-164.

Brian F. Cook, "A Class of Etruscan Bronze Omphalos-bowls," *AJA* 72 (1968) 337-344.

*David Gordon Mitten and Suzannah Doeringer, "Master Bronzes from the Classical World," *Arch* 21 (1968) 6-13.

Ibrahim Kamel, "A Bronze Hoard at Athribis," *ASAE* 60 (1968) 65-71.

*W. G. Lambert, "Three Inscribed Luristran Bronzes," *AfO* 22 (1968-69) 9-11.

*Ali M. Dinçol and Yusuf Tekiz, "Maden Eserlerin İcelemeinde Radyoloijk Metodlar," *AAI* 3 (1969) 119-139. [English Summary, p. 126] *[Toggle Pins]*

§212 ***2.5.9.11 Pottery Finds [See also: §97 Pottery Manufacture ←; and §215 Jar Handles and Stamps → (For Canopic Jars see: §202 Cultic and Funerary Articles) ←]***

†Anonymous, "Birch's *History of Ancient Pottery,*" *ERCJ* 108 (1858) 377-407. *(Review)*

*C. Clermont-Ganneau, "Notes on Certain New Discoveries at Jerusalem," *PEFQS* 3 (1871) 103-107. [3. Fragment of a vase with Hebrew Phoenician characters, p. 104]

Greville J. Chester, "Note on Vases Found at the Birket Israel," *PEFQS* 4 (1872) 122.

*Dunbar I. Heath, "The Moabite Jars, with a Translation," *JRAI* 2 (1872-73) 331-341. (Discussion, p. 341)

J. M. Rodwell, "Remarks on a Terra-Cotta (Assyrian) Vase," *SBAT* 2 (1873) 114-118.

*Paul Pierret, "Libation Vase of Osor-ur, preserved in the Museum of the Louvre (No. 908)," *SBAP* 2 (1879-80) 57-60.

*Selah Merrill, "A Cinerary Urn," *OBJ* 1 (1880) 81-82. *[Egyptian]*

*†W. [M.] Flinders Petrie, "Pottery and Implements collected at Giseh and the neighbourhood, from December 1880 to June 1881," *SBAP* 4 (1881-82) 76.

*W. H. Rylands, "An Inscribed Stone Bowl," *SBAP* 7 (1884-85) 154-155.

*Augustus C. Merriam, "Inscribed sepulchral vases from Alexandria," *AJA, O.S.,* 1 (1885) 18-33.

John Henry Wright, "Unpublished White Lekythoi from Attika," *AJA, O.S.,* 2 (1886) 385-407.

W. St. Chad Boscawen, "Notes on Pottery from Egypt," *BOR* 3 (1888-89) 259-264.

Isaac H. Hall, "On a Rhodian jar in the Boston Museum of Fine Arts," *JAOS* 13 (1889) cclxxxv.

Allan Marquand, “A Phœnician Bowl in the Metropolitan Museum, New York,” *AJA, O.S.*, 7 (1891) 19-24.

G. Robinson Lees, “Notes by G. Robinson Lees, F. R. G. S. 1. *Pottery from the Saris Cave,*” *PEFQS* 24 (1892) 196-197.

Joseph Clark Hoppin, “A Kylix by the Artist Psaix,” *AJA, O.S.*, 10 (1895) 485-493.

T. W. Heermance, “Papers of the American School of Classical Studies at Athens. Fragment of a Dated Panathenaic Amphora from the Gymnasium at Eretria,” *AJA, O.S.*, 11 (1896) 331-334.

*Rufus B. Richardson, “Notes. Notes from Corinth,” *AJA, O.S.*,11 (1896) 371-372. [Greek Vases, p. 372]

*Percy E. Newberry, “Extracts from my Notebook (I).,” *SBAP* 21 (1899) 303-308. [3. A Stone Vase of Ptahmes, High Priest at Memphis under Amenhetep III, pp. 305-306]

T. W. Heermance, “A New Class of Greek Geometric Pottery,” *AJA* 4 (1900) 152.

F. B. Tarbell, “A Signed Cylix by Duris inWashington, D.C.,” *AJA* 4 (1900) 161.

Joseph Clark Hoppin, “The Death of Argos on a Red-figure Hydra,” *AJA* 4 (1900) 162-163.

(Miss) May Louise Nichols, “Geometric Vases from Corinth,” *AJA* 4 (1900) 163.

L. Mariani, “The Vases of Erganos and Courtes,” *AJA* 5 (1901) 302-314.

*Henry Balfour, “Guilloche Pattern on an Etruscan Portsherd,” *Man* 1 (1901) #4.

J[ohn] L. Myers, “Prehistoric Pottery in the Valletta Museum in Malta,” *Man* 1 (1901) #71.

*John L. Myers, “Note on the Use of the Words ‘Glaze’ and ‘Varnish’ in the Description of Painted Pottery,” *Man* 1 (1901) #78.

*Percy E. Newberry, “Extracts from my Notebooks (IV),” *SBAP* 23 (1901) 218-224. [24. Some Egyptian Antiquities in the Dattari Collection, pp. 220-222 (*Ring Stand for a Vase*)]

Joseph Clark Hoppin, "A Cylix in the Style of Duris," *AJA* 6 (1902) 24.

(Miss) May Louise Nichols, "The Origin of the Red-figured Technique in Attic Vases," *AJA* 6 (1902) 39-40.

(Miss) Blanche E. Wheeler, "The Pottery at Gournia," *AJA* 6 (1902) 49. *[Crete]*

*John Garstang, "A Pre-dynastic Pot-Kiln, recently discovered at Mahâsna, in Egypt," *Man* 2 (1902) #29.

W. M. Flinders Petrie, "Prehistoric Egyptian Pottery," *Man* 2 (1902) #83.

J. L. Myres, "Note on Ægean Vase in the Salford Museum," *Man* 2 (1902) #96.

*Arthur Fairbanks, "A Comparison of the Scenes on White Lecythi and on Grave Stelae," *AJA* 7 (1903) 84.

George H. Chase, "An Amphora with a New *καλός*-Name, in the Boston Museum of Fine Arts," *AJA* 7 (1903) 96-97.

John L. Myers, "Early Pot-Fabrics of Asia Minor," *JRAI* 33 (1903) 367-400.

William N. Bates, "A Signed Amphora of Meno," *AJA* 9 (1905) 68.

(Mrs.) Blanche E. Wheeler Williams, "The Pottery from Gournia, Crete," *AJA* 9 (1905) 77.

*Percy E. Newberry, "Extracts from my Notebooks. VIII," *SBAP* 27 (1905) 101-105. [63. Some Small Inscribed Objects, pp. 103-105 (*Vase, p. 104, 105*)]

Edgar James Banks, "Plain Stone Vases from Bismya," *AJSL* 22 (1905-06) 35-40.

Edgar James Banks, "Terra-Cotta Vases from Bismya," *AJSL* 22 (1905-06) 139-143.

Joseph C[lark] Hoppin, "A Panathenaic Amphora with the Name of the Archon Theophrastus," *AJA* 10 (1906) 74-75.

Alice Walton, "An Unpublished Amphora and Eye Cylix, signed by Amasis, in the Boston Museum," *AJA* 10 (1906) 75-76.

(Miss) Edith H. Hall, "The Designs of Cretan Bronze-Age Vases," *AJA* 10 (1906) 83-84.

*Anonymous, "Egyptian Images and Vases," *MQR, 3rd Ser.*, 32 (1906) 386.

*A. H. Sayce, "The Oldest Book in the World," *AAOJ* 29 (1907) 303-315. [Ancient Phoenician Bowls, pp. 304-305]

William N. Bates, "Notes on Greek Vases at the University of Pennsylvania," *AJA* 11 (1907) 57.

*Stanley A. Cook, "Notes and Queries. (4) *Inscribed Objects from Gezer,*" *PEFQS* 39 (1907) 319-320. *[Jar Handle]*

Anonymous, "Proto-Corinthian Vase from Roman Forum," *RP* 6 (1907) 267.

George H. Chase, "Notes on Arretine Pottery," *AJA* 12 (1908) 64-65. *[Roman]*

Rudolf Pagenstecher, "Dated Sepulchral Vases from Alexandria," *AJA* 13 (1909) 387-416.

Anonymous, "Character of Black Glaze Found on Greek Vases," *RP* 8 (1909) 61-62.

James R. Wheeler, "Notes on a Scyphus in Boston," *AJA* 14 (1910) 87. *[Greek vase]*

*F. B. Tarbell, "Architecture on Attic Vases," *AJA* 14 (1910) 428-433.

A[lbert] T. Clay, "A Vase of Xerxes," *MJ* 1 (1910) 6-7.

*J[ames] A. Montgomery, "Babylonian Section: A Love Charm on an Incantation Bowl," *MJ* 1 (1910) 48-49.

W. L. Nash, "Fragment of an Alabaster Jar inscribed with the name of Nebuchadnezzar," *SBAP* 32 (1910) 180.

T. Eric Peet, "Prehistoric Painted Pottery in Malta," *AAA* 4 (1911-12) 121-125.

Oliver S. Tonks, "A Marble Roman Bowl from Bagdad," *AJA* 15 (1911) 62.

James A. Montgomery, "Some Incantation Bowls from Nippur," *AJA* 15 (1911) 67-68.

T. Whittemore, "Stone Vases of the Bishârîn," *Man* 12 (1912) #65.

E[dith] H. Hall, "Two Black-Figured Amphoræ with Scenes Portraying the Birth of Athena," *MJ* 3 (1912) 68-75.

Anonymous, "Trojan Vases," *RP* 11 (1912) 280.

John Garstang, "Note on a Vase of Minoan Fabric from Abydos (Egypt)," *AAA* 5 (1912-13) 107-111.

*Percy E. Newberry, "List of Vases with Cult-Signs," *AAA* 5 (1912-13) 137-142. *[Egyptian]*

E[dith] H. Hall, "Attic Vases from Orvieto," *MJ* 4 (1913) 147-161.

E[dith] H. Hall, "A Red-Figured Kylix," *MJ* 4 (1913) 162-163.

*H. R. Hall, "Yuia the Syrian," *SBAP* 35 (1913) 63-65. *[Pottery]*

A. H. Sayce, "The Sumerian Vase," *SBAP* 35 (1913) 191.

A. H. Sayce, "The Biscuit or Egg-shell Ware of the Sudan and China," *AEE* 1 (1914) 145-147.

Paul V. C. Baur, "The Stoddard Collection of Greek Vases at Yale University," *AJA* 18 (1914) 79.

J. Grafton Milne, "Antony and Cleopatra?" *JEA* 1 (1914) 99. *[Jar]*

E[dith] H. H[all], "A Red-Figured Amphora Signed by the Potter Meno," *MJ* 5 (1914) 31-37.

E[dith] H. H[all], "A Red-Figured Stamnos of the Periklean Period," *MJ* 5 (1914) 38-42.

E[dith] H. H[all], "Some Greek and Italian Vases in the Museum," *MJ* 5 (1914) 218-230.

*Percy E. Newberry, "Egyptian Historical Notes. II," *SBAP* 36 (1914) 35-39. [7. A Blue Glazed Vase of the Chancellor Amenhetep, pp. 35-36]

Herbert E. Clark and R. A. S[tewart] Macalister, "Some Interesting Pottery Remains," *PEFQS* 47 (1915) 35-37.

E[dith] H. D[ohan], "Four Covered Bowls from Orvieto," *MJ* 6 (1915) 173-179.

*Edith H. Hall, "Notes on Two Vases in the University Museum," *AJA* 19 (1915) 77-78.

E[dith] H. H[all], "Two Black-Figured Amphoræ from Orvieto," *MJ* 6 (1915) 85-93.

S[tephen] B. L[uce], "An Attic Black-Figured Panel-Amphora in the University Museum," *MJ* 6 (1915) 169-172.

A[lbert] T. Clay, "A Vase of Xerxes," *A&A* 4 (1916) 59-60.

H. Rushton Fairclough, "Some Greek Vases in the Stanford Museum," *AJA* 20 (1916) 73-74.

*Eugen von Merclin, "New Representations of Chariots on Attic Geometric Vases," *AJA* 20 (1916) 397-406.

Joseph Offord, "Archaeological Notes on Jewish Antiquities. XX. *A New Jewish Incantation Bowl from Mesopotamia*," *PEFQS* 48 (1916) 191.

Gisela M. A. Richter, "Two Vases Signed by Hieron in the Metropolitan Museum of Art," *AJA* 21 (1917) 1-7.

L. G. Eldridge, "An Unpublished Calpis," *AJA* 21 (1917) 38-54.

David M. Robinson, "Some Greek Vases at the Johns Hopkins University," *AJA* 21 (1917) 86-87.

Stephen Bleecker Luce, "Some Lost Vases Found," *AJA* 21 (1917) 409-416.

Stephen B. Luce Jr. *[sic]*, "A Group of Greek Vases," *MJ* 8 (1917) 15-28.

Stephen B. Luce Jr. *[sic]*, "The Exploits of Herakles, on Greek Vases in the University Museum," *MJ* 8 (1917) 145-155.

Stephen B. Luce Jr. *[sic]*, "A Loan of Three Greek Vases," *MJ* 8 (1917) 188-196.

H. C. R., "Current Notes and News. A Treat for the Lover of Greek Vases," *A&A* 5 (1917) 303.

J[oseph] C[lark] Hoppin, "Some Unpublished Greek Vases in an American Collection," *AJA* 22 (1918) 69.

Oliver M. Washburn, "The Vivenzio Vase and the Tyrannicides," *AJA* 22 (1918) 146-153.

Stephen Bleecker Luce, "The Diphilos-Dromippos Lecythi and Their Relation to Mr. Beazley's 'Achilles Master.'," *AJA* 23 (1919) 19-32.

Paul V. C. Baur, "Some Black-Figured Vases in the Stoddard Collection," *AJA* 23 (1919) 66-67.

(Miss) Gisela M. A. Richter, "Notes on the Technique of Greek Vases," *AJA* 23 (1919) 67.

*(Miss) Ida C. Thallon, "Some Balkan and Danubian Connections of Troy," *AJA* 23 (1919) 67-68.

Eleanor F. Rambo, "On the Design of Greek Vases," *MJ* 10 (1919) 8-14.

Eleanor F. Rambo, "An Attic Black-Figured Skyhos," *MJ* 10 (1919) 15-19.

Stephen B. Luce, "Early Vases from Apulia," *MJ* 10 (1919) 217-225.

Stephen Bleecker Luce, "Notes on 'Lost' Vases," *AJA* 24 (1920) 271-272.

Stephen B. Luce, "Attic Vases from Orvieto," *MJ* 11 (1920) 56-67.

*Stephen B. Luce, "An Early Potter's Wheel," *MJ* 11 (1920) 245-250.

David M. Robinson, "A Cylix in the Style of Duris," *AJA* 25 (1921) 1-17.

*Rhys Carpenter, "Dynamic Symmetry: A Criticism," *AJA* 25 (1921) 18-36.

George H. Chase, "Two Vases from Sardis," *AJA* 25 (1921) 111-117.

J. D. Beazley, "An Askos by Macron," *AJA* 25 (1921) 325-336.

*Randall MacIver, "On the Manufacture of Etruscan and other Ancient Black Wares," *Man* 21 (1921) #51.

David M. Robinson, "An Amphora of Nicosthenes in Baltimore," *AJA* 26 (1922) 54-58.

*Gisela M. A. Richter , "Dynamic Symmetry from the Designer's Point of View," *AJA* 26 (1922) 59-73. [Professor Carpenter's Reply, pp. 74-76; Rejoinder, by Gisela M. A. Richter, p. 76]

E. T. Leeds, "Alabaster Vases of the New Kingdom from Sinai," *JEA* 8 (1922) 1-4.

*H. R. Hall, "The Discoveries at Tell el 'Obeid in Southern Babylonia and Some Egyptian Comparisons," *JEA* 8 (1922) 241-257. *[Pottery]*

Eleanor F. Rambo, "Stories on Some Greek Vases. Notes on some Vases in the University Museum," *MJ* 13 (1922) 79-86.

C. L. Woolley, "Early Pottery from Jebeil," *AAA* 10 (1923) 36-40.

Stephen Bleecker Luce, "Notes on 'Lost' Vases: II," *AJA* 27 (1923) 184-187.

Gisela M. A. Richter, "Red-Figured Athenian Vases Recently Acquired by the Metropolitan Museum of Art," *AJA* 27 (1923) 265-285.

Stephen Bleecker Luce, "Heracles and Achelous on a Cylix in Boston," *AJA* 27 (1923) 425-437.

Anonymous, "El Harbaj: Notes on Pottery Found at el Harbaj, Summer, 1923," *BSAJB* #4 (1924) 45-46.

*G. A. Wainwright, "The Red Crown in Early Prehistoric Times," *JEA* 9 (1923) 26-33.

R. W. Hutchinson, "A Macedonian Vase," *AAA* 14 (1924) 117-118.

Mary H. Swindler, "Greek Vases in the Gallatin Collection," *AJA* 28 (1924) 278-289.

E. S. Thomas, "Note on a fragment of stone vessel from an ancient mining site," *ASAE* 24 (1924) 10-11.

Gerald M. FitzGerald, "The So-called Maccabaean Pottery," *PEFQS* 57 (1925) 189-192.

J. P. Droop, "The Pottery from Arcadia, Crete," *AAA* 12 (1925) 11-14.

*J. Penrose Harland, "An Inscribed Hydra in Aegina," *AJA* 29 (1925) 76-78.

Stephen Bleecker Luce, "Notes on 'Lost' Vases: III," *AJA* 29 (1925) 188-190.

G. M. F. G., "Excavations at Tanturah, 1924," *BSAJB* #7 (1925) 80-98. [V.—The Pottery, pp. 80-81]

*G. Caton-Thompson, "Preliminary Report on Neolithic Pottery and Bone Implements from the Northern Fayum Desert, Egypt," *Man* 25 (1925) #96.

J. Garrow Duncan, "'Maccabaean' Ware," *PEFQS* 58 (1926) 33-40.

G. M. Fitzgerald, "'Maccabaean Pottery': A Rejoinder," *PEFQS* 58 (1926) 84-90.

Gisela M. A. Richter, "'Attributed' Vases Recently Acquired by the Metropolitan Museum of Art," *AJA* 30 (1926) 32-43.

Albert Gallatin, "The Origin of the Form of the 'Nikosthenes Amphora'," *AJA* 30 (1926) 76-78.

H. R. W. Smith, "The Skyphos of Klitomenes," *AJA* 30 (1926) 432-441.

W[illiam] F[oxwell] Albright, "Proto-Mesopotamian Painted Ware from the Balîkh Valley," *Man* 26 (1926) #25.

W. A. Heurtley, "Early Iron Age Pottery from Macedonia," *AJ* 7 (1927) 44-59.

Stephen Bleecker Luce, "Notes on 'Lost' Vases: IV," *AJA* 31 (1927) 177-179.

G. Canton-Thompson, "Neolithic Pottery from the Northern Fayûm," *AEE* 13 (1928) 70-89.

Edith H. Dohan, "Recent Additions to the Collection of Greek Vases," *MJ* 19 (1928) 72-84.

David M. Robinson, "Four Unpublished Vases in the Style of the Brygos Painter," *AJA* 32 (1928) 33-55.

H. R. W. Smith, "Newly Identified Fragments of Chalcidian Pottery in the Museum of the University of Pennsylvania," *AJA* 32 (1928) 63-64.

Stephen B. Luce, "Two Kylikes at Providence," *AJA* 32 (1928) 435-446.

J. M. Unvala, "The Ceramic Art of Susa," *BSOAS* 5 (1928-30) 1-14.

Alexander Scharff, "Some Prehistoric Vases in the British Museum and Remarks on Egyptian Prehistory," *JEA* 14 (1928) 261-276.

H[enri] Frankfort, "Some Notes on Pottery from Ur," *AJ* 9 (1929) 344-348.

Charles F. Binns and A. D. Fraser, "The Genesis of the Greek Black Glaze," *AJA* 33 (1929) 1-9.

A. Lucas, "The Nature of the Colour of Pottery, with Special reference to that of Ancient Egypt," *JRAI* 59 (1929) 113-129.

John Mauchline, "The Jericho Pottery (1931 Collection) in the Hunterian Museum," *GUOST* 6 (1929-33) 47-50.

Frances Lance Ferrero, "That Amphora and the Death of Pliny the Elder," *A&A* 29 (1930) 51-55, 75.

Daniel Cotton Rich, "Five Red-Figured Vases in the Art Institute of Chicago," *AJA* 34 (1930) 153-176.

David M. Robinson, "The Lasso on a Pyxis in the Style of the Penthesilea Painter," *AJA* 34 (1930) 177-181.

Stephen Bleecker Luce, "Attic Red-Figured Vases and Fragments from Corinth," *AJA* 34 (1930) 334-343.

David M. Robinson, "An Illustration of Hesiod on a Black-Figured Plate by the Strife Painter," *AJA* 34 (1930) 353-359.

A. A. Zakharov, "Cappadocian Pottery," *ArOr* 2 (1930) 255-261.

*G. D. Hornblower, "Funerary Designs on Predynastic Jars," *JEA* 16 (1930) 10-18.

A. Lucas, "Egyptian Predynastic Stone Vessels," *JEA* 16 (1930) 200-212.

Anonymous, "A Red-Figured Loutrophoros," *UMB* 1 (1930) #2, 15-18.

E[dith] H. D[ohan], "Four New Geometric Vases," *UMB* 2 (1930-31) 11-14.

E[dith] H. D[ohan], "An Amphora from the Hope Collection," *UMB* 2 (1930-31) 90-91, 94.

E[dith] H. D[ohan], "Two Plastic Vases," *UMB* 2 (1930-31) 123-127.

Agnes Newhall, "The Corinthian Kerameikos," *AJA* 35 (1931) 1-30.

B. H. Hill, "Note on *A.J.A.* XXXIV, pp. 334-43," *AJA* 35 (1931) 51-53.

*David M. Robinson, "Bouzyges and the First Plough on a Krater by the Painter of the Naples Hephaistos," *AJA* 35 (1931) 152-160.

Stephen Bleecker Luce, "Four Red-Figured Vases in Providence," *AJA* 35 (1931) 298-303.

G[eorge] A. Reisner, "Stone Vessels found at Crete and Babylonia," *Antiq* 5 (1931) 200-212.

Anonymous, "Potsherds from the Transjordan Desert," *Antiq* 5 (1931) 363.

*A. Lucas, "The canopic Vases from the 'Tomb of Queen Tîyi'," *ASAE* 31 (1931) 120-122.

Pehr Lugh, "A 'Beaker' Pot in the Stockholm Egyptian Museum," *JEA* 17 (1931) 22.

E[dith] H. D[ohan], "A Greek Cup by the 'Foundry Painter'," *UMB* 3 (1931-32) 23, 26.

E[dith] H. D[ohan], "An Amphora by the 'Berlin Painter'," *UMB* 3 (1931-32) 53-54.

*Anonymous, "Objects from Beth Shemesh," *UMB* 3 (1931-32) 121-122.

R. W. Hutchinson, "A Note on Late Mycenaean Vases," *AAA* 19 (1932) 117-120.

J. D. Beazley, "Not in Providence," *AJA* 36 (1932) 139-142. *[Greek Pottery]*

S. Yeivin, "An Egyptian vase from Ancient Parthia," *ASAE* 32 (1932) 151-152.

David Moore Robinson, "Illustrations of Aeschylus' *Choephoroi* and of a Satyr-Play on Hydrias by the Niobid Painter," *AJA* 36 (1932) 401-407.

Gisela M. A. Richter, "An Aryballos by Nearchos," *AJA* 36 (1932) 272-275.

A. Lucas, "Black and black-topped pottery," *ASAE* (1932) 93-96.

*E[phraim] A. Speiser, "The 'Chalice' Ware of Northern Mesopotamia and Its Historical Significance," *BASOR* #48 (1932) 5-10.

J. D. Beazley, "Battle-Loutrophoros," *MJ* 23 (1932) 5-22.

E[dith] H. Dohan, "Four Vases from the Henry C. Lea Collection," *MJ* 23 (1932) 23-44.

E[dith] H. Dohan, "A Late Minoan Pyxis," *MJ* 23 (1932) 55-59.

E[dith] H. Dohan, "A Lydian Imitation of a Laconian Vase," *MJ* 23 (1932) 61-63.

E[dith] H. Dohan, "Two Vases from the Hegeman Collection," *MJ* 23 (1932) 64-74.

E[phraim] A. Speiser, "The Pottery of Tell Billa: A Preliminary Account," *MJ* 23 (1932) 249-308.

Grace M. Crowfoot, "Pots, Ancient and Modern," *PEFQS* 64 (1932) 179-187.

B[enjamin] Maisler, "Cypriote Pottery at a Tomb-Cave in the Vicinity of Jerusalem," *AJSL* 49 (1932-33) 248-253.

E[dith] H. D[ohan], "A Corinthian Amphora," *UMB* 4 (1932-33) 48-49.

V. Gordon Childe, "Notes on Some Indian and East Iranian Pottery," *AEE* 18 (1933) 15-25.

Frederick O. Waagé, "Roman and Byzantine Pottery from the Athenian Agora," *AJA* 37 (1933) 111.

Franklin P. Johnson, "A Vase Painted by Hermonax," *AJA* 37 (1933) 113.

A. M. G. Little, "Hellenistic Influences in Syrian Glazed Pottery," *AJA* 37 (1933) 114-115.

Frederick O. Waagé 3d*[sic]*, "Note on Mottled Vases," *AJA* 37 (1933) 404-406.

*O. H. Myers, "Two Prehistoric Objects," *JEA* 19 (1933) 55. *[Pottery]*

J. H. Iliffe, "Pre-Hellenistic Greek Pottery in Palestine," *QDAP* 2 (1933) 15-26.

D. B. Harden, "Excavations at Kish and Barghuthiat 1933. II, Pottery," *Iraq* 1 (1934) 124-136.

E[phraim] A. Speiser, "The continuance of painted pottery in Northern Mesopotamia," *AfO* 9 (1933-34) 48-50.

Herbert G[ordon] May, "An Inscribed Jar from Megiddo," *AJSL* 50 (1933-34) 10-14.

*Carl W. Blegen, "Inscriptions on Geometric Pottery from Hymettos," *AJA* 38 (1934) 10-28.

Frederick O. Waagé, "The Earliest Red-glazed 'Roman' Pottery," *AJA* 38 (1934) 183-184.

Lucy Talcott, "Some Greek Pottery from the Agora," *AJA* 38 (1934) 185.

David M. Robinson, "Some Unpublished Attic Vases," *AJA* 38 (1934) 188.

L. D. Caskey, "Odysseus and Elpenor on a Pelike in Boston," *AJA* 38 (1934) 339-340.

Edith H. Dohan, "Some Unpublished Vases in the University Museum, Philadelphia," *AJA* 38 (1934) 523-532.

George W. Elderkin, "The Dioscuri on the Early Protocorinthian Aryballos," *AJA* 38 (1934) 543-546.

Guy Brunton, "Some Tasian pottery in the Cairo Museum," *ASAE* 34 (1934) 94-96.

Guy Brunton, "Modern painting on Predynastic pots," *ASAE* 34 (1934) 149-156.

Harold H. Helson, "Fragments of Egyptian Old Kingdom Stone Vases from Byblos," *Bery* 1 (1934) 19-22.

C. Leonard Woolley, "The Prehistoric Pottery of Carchemish," *Iraq* 1 (1934) 146-162.

J. H. Iliffe, "Nabaean Pottery from the Negeb. *Its Distribution in Palestine*," *QDAP* 3 (1934) 132-135.

E[dith] H. D[ohan], "Attic Vases from Memorial Hall," *UMB* 5 (1934-35) #6, 70-73, 76.

M[argaret] A. Murray, "Coptic Painted Pottery," *AEE* 20 (1935) 1-15.

V. I. Avdief, "Geometrical Ornament on Archaic Egyptian Pottery," *AEE* 20 (1935) 37-48.

*D. B. Harden, "Pottery and Beads from near Nehavand, N.W. Persia, in the Ashmolean Museum," *AEE* 20 (1935) 73-81.

A. Orlandos, "The Discovery of Painted Pinakes near Corinth," *AJA* 39 (1935) 5.

*Frederick D. Crane, "Materials and Methods of Early Potters," *AJA* 40 (1936) 116-117.

Henry Field and Richard A. Martin, "Painted Pottery from Jemdet Nasr, Iraq," *AJA* 39 (1935) 310-320.

Edith H. Dohan, "A Recent Acquisition of the University Museum, Philadelphia," *AJA* 39 (1935) 451. *[Greek Vase]*

Neilson C. Debevoise, "The Oriental Amphora," *Bery* 2 (1935) 1-4.

R. W. Hutchinson, "Uruk and Yortan," *Iraq* 2 (1935) 211-222. *[Pottery]*

*S. Yeivin, "Note on the Duweir Ewer," *JPOS* 15 (1935) 98-100. *[Bowl]*

G. M. Fitzgerald, "The Earliest Pottery of Beth-Shan," *MJ* 24 (1935) #1, 5-32.

W. A. Heurtley, "Note on a Palestinian Painted Sherd at Athens," *QDAP* 4 (1935) 179-180.

W. A. Heurtley, "Note on Fragments of Two Thessalian Proto-Geometric Vases found at Tell Abū Hawām," *QDAP* 4 (1935) 181.

E[dith] H. D[ohan], "A Daphnae Situla from Memphis," *UMB* 6 (1935-37) #1, 15-17.

Gisela M. A. Richter, "The Kleophrades Painter," *AJA* 40 (1936) 100-115.

David M. Robinson, "Some Unpublished Greek Vases in Baltimore," *AJA* 40 (1936) 117-118.

George M. A. Hanfmann, "Etruscan Bucchero Bowls," *AJA* 40 (1936) 118.

*Helen Rees Clifford, "Two Etruscan Funerary Urns in the New York University Archaeological Museum," *AJA* 40 (1936) 118-119.

Franklin P. Johnson, "Sherds in Chicago," *AJA* 40 (1936) 119. *[Greek Pottery Fragments]*

M. Money-Coutts, "A Stone Bowl and Lid from Byblos," *Bery* 3 (1936) 129-136.

David Moore Robinson and Sarah Elizabeth Freeman, "The Lewis Painter = Polygnotos II," *AJA* 40 (1936) 215-227.

Grace W. Nelson, "A Faience Rhyton from Abydos," *AJA* 40 (1936) 501-506.

David M. Robinson, "A New Lebes Gamikos with a Possible Representation of Apollo and Daphne," *AJA* 40 (1936) 507-519.

A. Lucas, "Glazed Ware in Egypt, India, and Mesopotamia," *JEA* 22 (1936) 141-164.

*E. L. Sukenik, "Potsherds from Samaria, Inscribed with the Divine Name," *PEFQS* 68 (1936) 34-37.

*W. E. Staples, "A Note on an Inscribed Potsherd," *PEFQS* 68 (1936) 155. *[Hebrew]*

Howard Comfort and F[rederick] O. Waagé, "Selected Pottery from Beth Shan (Roman Date)," *PEFQS* 68 (1936) 221-224.

E. L. Sukenik, "The Late Chalcholithic Pottery from 'Affûleh," *PEFQS* 68 (1936) 250-254.

W. A. Heurtley, "The Relationship between 'Philistine' and Mycenaean Pottery," *QDAP* 5 (1936) 90-110.

J. H. Iliffe, "Pottery from Rās el 'Ain," *QDAP* 5 (1936) 113-126.

M. Rostovtzeff, "Two Homeric Bowls in the Louvre," *AJA* 41 (1937) 86-96.

John L. Caskey, "The Pottery from the 'Basilica' of Troy VI," *AJA* 41 (1937) 110-111.

*Frederick O. Waagé, "Potters' Stamps in Samian and Pergamene Wares," *AJA* 41 (1937) 115-116.

Cedric G. Boulter, "A Pottery-Deposit Near Temple E at Corinth," *AJA* 41 (1937) 217-236.

*Helen Rees Clifford, "Two Etruscan Funerary Urns in the New York University Archaeological Museum," *AJA* 41 (1937) 300-314.

Howard Comfort, "Nine *Terra Sigillata* Bowls from Egypt," *AJA* 41 (1937) 406-410.

D. B. Harden, "The Pottery from the Precinct of Tanit at Salammbo, Carthage," *Iraq* 4 (1937) 59-89.

George E. Mylonas, "A so-called Minoan Vase from Macedonia," *Man* 37 (1937) #87.

Sylvia Benton, "A so-called Minoan Vase from Macedonia," *Man* 37 (1937) #88.

*G[race] M. Crowfoot, "Mat Impressions of Pot Bases," *AAA* 25 (1938) 3-11.

Cedric G. Boulter, "The Pottery of Troy VIII," *AJA* 42 (1938) 121.

George E. Mylonas, "Greek Vases in the Collection of Washington University," *AJA* 42 (1938) 124.

Howard Comfort, "Terra Sigillata from Minturnae," *AJA* 42 (1938) 128.

A. M. G. Little, "The Phlyax Types and Roman Comedy," *AJA* 42 (1938) 129.

Franklin P. Johnson, "Red-Figured Pottery at Chicago," *AJA* 42 (1938) 345-361.

Semni Papaspyridi-Karouzou, "A Proto-Panathenaic Amphora in the National Museum at Athens," *AJA* 42 (1938) 495-505.

Mogens B. Mackeprang, "Late Mycenaean Vases," *AJA* 42 (1938) 537-559.

A. Lucas, "Early Red Faience," *JEA* 24 (1938) 245.

Geoffrey M. Shipton, "The Early Pottery of Meggido, Season 1937-8," *JPOS* 18 (1938) 54-56.

J. H. Iliffe, "Sigillata Wares in the Near East," *QDAP* 6 (1938) 4-53.

*Gisela M. A. Richter, "Two Recent Acquisitions by the Metropolitan Museum of Art," *AJA* 43 (1939) 1-9. [(1) A Pelike by the Meidias Painter, pp. 1-6]

D. A. Amyx, "The Gorgon-Hydria from Eretria," *AJA* 43 (1939) 305.

Dorothy Kent Hill, "The Pottery from Castel Campanile," *AJA* 43 (1939) 306.

J. D. Beazley, "Prometheus Fire-Lighter," *AJA* 43 (1939) 618-639. *[Attic calyx-krater]*

Howard Comfort, "Italian 'China' in Palestinian Homes," *BA* 2 (1939) 9-10.

A. M. Honeyman, "The Pottery Vessels of the Old Testament," *PEQ* 71 (1939) 76-90.

*W. A. Oldfather, "Turkeys or Cranes on a Laconian Hydria," *AJA* 43 (1939) 104-105.

J. R. Stewart, "An Imported Pot from Cyprus," *PEQ* 71 (1939) 162-168.

*W. A. Heurtley, "A Palestinian Vase-Painter of the Sixteenth Century B.C.," *QDAP* 8 (1939) 21-37.

*A. J. B. Wace and C. W. Belgen, "Pottery as Evidence for Trade and Colonisation in the Aegean Bronze Age," *Klio* 32 (1939-40) 131-147.

Frances Follin Jones, "The Hellenistic and Roman Pottery from Gözlü Kule, Tarsus," *AJA* 44 (1940) 108.

Saul S. Weinberg, "Corinthian Protogeometric and Geometric Pottery," *AJA* 44 (1940) 108-109.

George E. Mylonas, "Greek Vases in the Collection of Washington University in St. Louis," *AJA* 44 (1940) 187-211.

J. D. Beazley, "Postscript to Prometheus," *AJA* 44 (1940) 212. *[AJA* 43 (1939) 618-639 *(Bell-krater or calyx-krater)]*

*Gisela M. A. Richter, "Four Notable Acquisitions of the Metropolitan Museum of Art," *AJA* 44 (1940) 428-442. [1. An Athenian White-Ground Pxyis = Kylichnis, pp. 428-431]

A. D. Fraser, "The Geometric Oenochoe with Crossed Tubes from the Athenian Agora," *AJA* 44 (1940) 457-463.

*Julian Obermann, "Two Magic Bowls: New Incantation Texts from Mesopotamia," *AJSL* 57 (1940) 1-31.

E. L. Sukenik, "Note on a Pottery Vessel of the Old Testament," *PEQ* 72 (1940) 59-60.

Grace M. Crowfoot, "Some Censer Types from Palestine," *PEQ* 72 (1940) 150-153.

G. Ernest Wright, "The Syro-Palestinian Jar from Vounous, Cyprus," *PEQ* 72 (1940) 154-157.

Joseph Carson Wampler, "Triangular Impressed Design in Palestinian Pottery," *BASOR* #80 (1940) 13-16.

Saul S. Weinberg, "What is Protocorinthian Geometric Ware?" *AJA* 45 (1941) 30-44.

D. A. Amyx, "The Gorgon-Hydria from Eretria," *AJA* 45 (1941) 64-69.

Henry S. Robinson, "Pottery of the Early Roman Period from the Agora Excavations," *AJA* 45 (1941) 92-93.

George M. A. Hanfmann, "A Group of Polychrome Etruscan Vases," *AJA* 45 (1941) 94.

Gisela M. A. Richter, "A Greek Phiale," *AJA* 45 (1941) 94.

*John Franklin Daniel, "Late Mycenaean Pottery with Pictorial Representations," *AJA* 46 (1942) 121.

P. V. C. Baur, "Megarian Bowls in the Rebecca Darlington Stoddard Collection of Greek and Italian Vases in Yale University," *AJA* 45 (1941) 229-248.

Gisela M. A. Richter, "A Kyathos by Psiax in the Museo Poldi-Pezzoli," *AJA* 45 (1941) 587-592.

Rodney S. Young, "Graves from the Phaleron Cemetery," *AJA* 46 (1942) 23-57. *[Pottery]*

*John Franklin Daniel, "Late Mycenaean Pottery with Pictorial Representations," *AJA* 46 (1942) 121.

Majorie J. Milne, "Three Names on a Corinthian Jar," *AJA* 46 (1942) 217-222.

*Wayne M. Felts, "A Petrographic Examination of Potsherds from Ancient Troy," *AJA* 46 (1942) 237-244.

George E. Mylonas, "A Note on the Painter of the Cerberus Amphora of Washington University. *Addenda to AJA*. XLIV, 1940, pp. 187-211," *AJA* 46 (1942) 368-369.

*Edith Hall Dohan and H. M. Hoenigswald, "Three Inscriptions in the University Museum, Philadelphia," *AJA* 46 (1942) 532-537. *[Strigil]*

J. H. Iliffe, "Sigillata Wares in the Near East II.," *QDAP* 9 (1942) 31-76.

*Ruth B. Kallner, "Khirbet Kerak Ware and its Relation to the EB Tomb Discovered at Kinneret," *BIES* 10 (1942-44) #2/3, III.

Edith Hall Dohan, "An Italiote Krater in the University Museum, Philadelphia," *AJA* 47 (1943) 171-173.

Howard Comfort, "Terra Sigillata from Minturnae," *AJA* 47 (1943) 313-330.

Franklin P. Johnson, "Black-Figure Pottery at Chicago," *AJA* 47 (1943) 385-402.

J. D. Beazley, "Panathenaica," *AJA* 47 (1943) 441-465. *[Pottery]*

Margarete Bieber, "Two Attic Black-Figured Lekythoi in Buffalo," *AJA* 48 (1944) 121-129.

J. M. T. Charlton, "New Black-Figure Vases," *AJA* 48 (1944) 251-259.

J. D. Beazley, "A Paestan Vase," *AJA* 48 (1944) 357-366.

*W[illiam] F[oxwell] Albright, J. L. Kelso, and J. Palin Thorley, "Early-Bronze Pottery from Bâb ed-Drâʿ in Moab," *BASOR* #95 (1944) 3-13. [I. Description and Chronology; II. Ceramic Techniques]

*Robert J. Braidwood, Linda S. Braidwood, Edna Tulane, and Ann L. Perkins, "New Chalcolithic Material of Samarran Type and its Implications. A Report on Chalcolithic Material of the Samarran Type Found at Baghouz on the Euphrates, and a Reconsideration of the Samarran Material in General (Especially the Painted Pottery) in the Light of this New Material," *JNES* 3 (1944) 47-72. [II. The Pottery of the Baghouz Occurrence on the Euphrates, pp. 51-53; IV. A Repertoire of the Samarran Painted Pottery Style, pp. 57-65]

D. C. Baramki, "Pottery from Kh. el Mefjer," *QDAP* 10 (1944) 65-103.

Francis Follin Jones, "Rhosica Vasa," *AJA* 49 (1945) 45-51.

*J. D. Beazley, "The Brygos Tomb at Capua," *AJA* 49 (1945) 153-158. *[Vases]*

H. R. W. Smith, "From Farthest West," *AJA* 49 (1945) 465-479. *[Greek Vases]*

Franklin P. Johnson, "The Late Vases of Hermonax," *AJA* 49 (1945) 491-502.

Sara Anderson Immerwahr, "Three Mycenaean Vases from Cyprus in the Metropolitan Museum of Art," *AJA* 49 (1945) 534-556.

*J. L. Kelso and J. Palin Thorley, "Palestinian Pottery in Bible Times," *BA* 8 (1945) 82-93. [Palestine's Archaeological Periods; Pottery as Artistic Achievement; Decoration of Pottery Vessels; Household Idols in Clay; Other Uses of Pottery]

E. Henschel-Simon, "Note on the Pottery of the 'Amman Tombs," *QDAP* 11 (1945) 75-80.

I[mmanuel] Ben-Dor, "Palestinian Alabaster Vases," *QDAP* 11 (1945) 93-112.

Virginia Grace, "Early Thasian Stamped Amphoras," *AJA* 50 (1946) 31-38.

Franklin P. Johnson, "Pottery in Chicago," *AJA* 50 (1946) 285.

George M. A. Hanfmann, "Geometric Pottery in Sardis," *AJA* 50 (1946) 286.

Nelson Glueck, "Band-Slip Ware in the Jordan Valley and Northern Gilead," *BASOR* #101 (1946) 3-20.

*J. L. Kelso and J. Palin Thorley, "A Ceramic Analysis of Late-Mycenaean and Other Late-Bronze Vases from Jett in Palestine," *BASOR* #104 (1946) 21-25.

*Ruth B. Kallner and J. Vroman, "Petrographical Examination of Pottery," *BIES* 12 (1946) I.

*J. L. Kelso and J. Palin Thorley, "Palestinian Pottery in Bible Times," *SIR* (1946) 361-371.

Hamit Z. Koşay and Mahmut Akok, "The Pottery of Alaca Höyük," *AJA* 51 (1947) 152-157.

*Dorothy Kent Hill, "The Technique of Greek Metal Vases and Its Bearing on Vase Forms in Metal and Pottery," *AJA* 51 (1947) 248-256.

G. Bakalakis, "A Lekythos from Skopelos," *AJA* 51 (1947) 263-266.

Ludwig Budde, "A Nolan Amphora of the Kleophrades Painter," *AJA* 51 (1947) 267-268.

John Garstang and Hetty Goldman, "A Conspectus of Early Cilician Pottery," *AJA* 51 (1947) 370-388.

*Yigael Sukenik, "On the Technique of Khirbet Kerak Ware," *BASOR* #106 (1947) 9-17.

*Faraj Basmachi, "The Votive Vase from Warka," *Sumer* 3 (1947) 118-127.

*Virginia Grace, "Fractional Stamped Containers," *AJA* 52 (1948) 381.

M. V. Seaton Williams, "Neolithic Burnished Wares in the Near East," *Iraq* 10 (1948) 34-50.

*A. J. Arkell, "The Harpoon on Egyptian Pottery," *Man* 48 (1948) #128.

Seton Lloyd, "Uruk Pottery. *A Comparative Study in Relation to Recent Finds at Eridu,*" *Sumer* 4 (1948) 39-51.

Ludwig Budde, "A New Skyphos by the Pisticci Painter," *AJA* 53 (1949) 32-33.

Franklin P. Johnson, "Eight Pieces of Pottery," *AJA* 53 (1949) 241-248.

J. R. T. Pollard, "The Boston Siren Aryballos," *AJA* 53 (1949) 357-359.

L. Keimer, "The Decoration of a New Kingdom Vase," *JNES* 8 (1949) 1-5.

*David M. Robinson, "A Small Hoard of Mycenaean Vases and Statuettes," *AJA* 54 (1950) 1-9.

Gianguido Belloni, "A Fragment of Euphronios in the Musei Civici in Milan," *AJA* 54 (1950) 119-120.

Cedric Boulter, "Sherds from a White-Ground Krater," *AJA* 54 (1950) 120-121.

*H. A. Thompson, "The Influence of Basketry on Attic Geometric Pottery," *AJA* 46 (1950) 286.

Faraj Basmachi, "The Pottery of the Eastern Cave of Hazer Merd," *Sumer* 6 (1950) 104-105.

Fuad Safar, "Pottery from Caves of Baradost," *Sumer* 6 (1950) 118-121.

Faraj Basmachi, "Sculptured Stone Vases in the Iraq Museum," *Sumer* 6 (1950) 165-176.

Hazel D. Hansen, "Protogeometric Vases from Skyros," *AJA* 55 (1951) 149.

J. M. T. Charlton, "A Boeotian Bell-krater in Rochdale," *AJA* 55 (1951) 336-339.

Beatrice de Cardi, "A New Prehistoric Ware from Baluchistan," *Iraq* 13 (1951) 63-75.

*Cyrus H. Gordon, "Two Magic Bowls from Teheran," *Or, N.S.*, 20 (1951) 306-315.

*Marie-Louise Buhl, "Antiquities from Djerabis in Syria," *AA* 23 (1952) 155-167. *[Pottery]*

J. D. Beazley, "The New York 'Phlyax-Vase'," *AJA* 56 (1952) 193-195.

C. N. Bromhead, "What was Murrhine?" *Antiq* 26 (1952) 65-70. *[Vases]*

P. Kahane, "Pottery Types from the Jewish Ossuary-Tombs around Jerusalem: An archaeological contribution to the problem of the Hellenization of Jewry in the Herodian Period,"*IEJ* 2(1952)125-139, 176-182.

John Forsdyke, "Minos of Crete," *JWCI* 15 (1952) 13-19. *[Vessel]*

*Ruth Amiran, "Note on the 'Double bowl' found in an EB Tomb at Tel-Aviv," *BIES* 17 (1952-53) #3/4, VII.

*M. Dothan, "Libation cup or lamp?" *BIES* 17 (1952-53) #3/4, VII.

*Christoph Clairmont, "Studies in Greek Mythology and Vase-Painting," *AJA* 57 (1953) 85-94. (Correction, p. 243)

Cedric Boulter, "Pottery of the Mid-Fifth Century," *AJA* 57 (1953) 105.

Saul S. Weinberg, "Corinthian Relief Ware," *AJA* 57 (1953) 111-112.

A. D. Ure, "Boeotian Vases with Women's Heads," *AJA* 57 (1953) 245-249.

Chrysoula Kardara, "The Arapides Oinochoe," *AJA* 57 (1953) 277-280.

Ruth B. Kallner-Amiran, "Two Notes on the Repertoire of the Chalcolithic Pottery of Palestine," *BASOR* #130 (1953) 11-14.

P. Kahane, "Pottery Types from the Jewish Ossuary Tombs around Jerusalem—III," *IEJ* 3 (1953) 48-54.

M. V. Seton-Williams, "A Painted Pottery of the Second Millennium from Southern Turkey and Northern Syria," *Iraq* 15 (1953) 57-68.

A. J. Arkell, "The Sudan Origin of Predynastic 'Black Incised' Pottery," *JEA* 39 (1953) 76-79.

T. Rönne and P. M. Fraser, "A Hadra-Vase in the Ashmolean Museum," *JEA* 39 (1953) 84-94.

Kristian Jeppesen, "A Greek Pyxis from the age of Homer," *Kuml* (1953) 169.

John L. Myres, "A Painted Graeco-Phoenician Vase from Ormidhia in Cyprus," *AJA* 58 (1954) 39-44.

Seymour Howard and Franklin P. Johnson, "The Saint-Valentin Vases," *AJA* 58 (1954) 191-207.

J. Kaplan, "Two Chalcolithic Vessels," *BIES* 18 (1954) #1/2, VI-VII.

Joan [Oates] Lines, "Late Assyrian Pottery from Nimrud," *Iraq* 16 (1954) 164-167.

P. S. Rawson, "Palace Wares from Nimrud: Technical Observations on Selected Examples," *Iraq* 16 (1954) 168-172.

John Forsdyke, "The 'Harvester' Vase of Hagia Triada," *JWCI* 17 (1954) 1-9.

M. W. Prausnitz, "Abydos and Combed Ware," *PEQ* 86 (1954) 91-96.

J. Kaplan, "Two Chalcolithic Vessels from Palestine," *PEQ* 86 (1954) 97-100.

Christoph Clairmont, "Greek Pottery from the Near East," *Bery* 11 (1954-55) 85-139.

*Cornelius C. Vermeule, "Notes on a New Edition of Michaelis: Ancient Marbles in Great Britain," *AJA* 59 (1955) 129-150.

D. A. Amyx, "The Amphoras of Alcibiades," *AJA* 59 (1955) 169.

Dietrich von Bothmer, "Two Oltos Vases in New York," *AJA* 59 (1955) 157-158.

Christoph Clairmont, "An Imperial Relief Vase from al Mina, Turkey," *AJA* 59 (1955) 171.

David M. Robinson, "Some New Greek Vases in the Robinson Collection," *AJA* 59 (1955) 173-174.

James R. Stewart, "When did Base-ring Ware First Occur in Palestine?" *BASOR* #138 (1955) 47-49.

Ruth B. K. Amiran, "The 'Cream Ware' of Gezer and the Beersheba Late Chalcolithic," *IEJ* 5 (1955) 240-245.

James Mellaart, "Iron age pottery from Southern Anatolia," *TTKB* 19 (1955) 115-136.

David M. Robinson, "Unpublished Greek Vases in the Robinson Collection," *AJA* 60 (1956) 1-25.

*Dorothy Kent Hill, "Other Geometric Objects in Baltimore," *AJA* 60 (1956) 35-42.

V[assos] Karageorghis, "Two Mycenaean Bull-Craters in the G. G. Pierides Collection, Cyprus," *AJA* 60 (1956) 143-149.

B. B. Shefton, "Medea at Marathon," *AJA* 60 (1956) 159-163.

Thalia Phillies Howe, "Sophokles, Mikon and the Argonauts," *AJA* 60 (1956) 178-179.

Jean M. Davison*[sic]*, "Attic Geometric Pottery: The Birdseed Painter," *AJA* 60 (1956) 182-183.

Vassos Karageorghis, "Some Inscribed Iron-Age Vases from Cyprus. I. The Vases," *AJA* 60 (1956) 351-354.

*Cornelius C. Vermeule and D. von Bothmer, "Notes on a New Edition of Michaelis: Ancient Marbles in Great Britain. Part Two," *AJA* 60 (1956) 129-150.

Christoph Clairmont, "Greek Pottery from the Near East II. Black Vases," *Bery* 12 (1956-58) 1-34.

*Yonanan Aharoni, "Galilean Survey: Israelite Settlements and their Pottery," *EI* 4 (1956) VI.

A. J. Arkell, "Stone bowls of Khaʿba (Third Dynasty)," *JEA* 42 (1956) 116.

Tahsin Özgüç, "The Bitik vase," *A(A)* 2 (1957) 57-78.

*Sylvester J. Saller, "Ez-Zahiriyye in the light of Ancient Pottery," *SBFLA* 7 (1956-57) 53-63.

Ruth B. K. Amiran, "The Story of Pottery in Palestine," *A&S* 2 (1957) #2/3, 187-207.

S. Chartonides, "More Geometric from Corinthia," *AJA* 61 (1957) 169-171.

Cedric G. Boulter, "Pottery from Periclean Athens," *Arch* 10 (1957) 191-197.

Ruth B. K. Amiran, "Tell el-Yahudiyeh Ware in Syria," *IEJ* 7 (1957) 93-97.

Marie Farnsworth and Harriet Wisely, "Fifth Century Intentional Red Glaze," *AJA* 62 (1958) 165-173. [Appendix by Dietrich von Bothmer, p. 173]

Frederick R. Matson and Henry S. Robinson, "Amarousion Potters at Work," *AJA* 62 (1958) 224.

*Vassos Karageorghis, "Myth and Epic in Mycenaean Vase Painting," *AJA* 62 (1958) 383-387.

James Mellaart, "Pottery from the Lower Levels of Beycesultan," *AS* 8 (1958) 113-125.

Paul Lapp and Nancy Lapp, "A Comparative Study of the Hellenistic Pottery Group from Beth-Zur," *BASOR* #151 (1958) 16-27.

E. Martin Burgess, "The Reconstruction of the Ḥatḥōr Bowl," *JEA* 44 (1958) 6-11.

A. J. Arkell, "Stone bowls of Khaʿba (Third Dynasty)," *JEA* 44 (1958) 120.

P. V. Glob, "Alabaster Vases from the Bahrain Temples. The Danish Archaeological Bahrain-Expedition's Fifth Excavation Campaign," *Kuml* (1958) 144-145.

James Mellaart, "Second Millennium Pottery from the Konya Plain and Neighbourhood," *TTKB* 22 (1958) 311-345.

*A. M. ApSimon, "Food Vessels," *ULBIA* 1 (1958) 24-36.

Edith Porada, "The Hasanlu Bowl," *Exped* 1 (1958-58) #3, 18-22.

William Kelly Simpson, "The Vessels with Engraved Designs and the Repoussé Bowl from Tell Bastra Treasure," *AJA* 63 (1959) 29-45.

*[Cornelius] C. Vermeule and D. von Bothmer, "Notes on a New Edition of Michaelis: Ancient Marbles in Great Britain. Part Three: 1," *AJA* 63 (1959) 139-166.

Eva Brann, "An Early Protoattic Hydria," *AJA* 63 (1959) 178-179.

Herbert Hoffmann, "An Etruscan Rhyton in Vienna," *AJA* 63 (1959) 180-181.

Dorothy Kent Hill, "Greek Vases Acquired by the Walters Art Gallery," *AJA* 63 (1959) 181-183.

Franklin P. Johnson, "Two Panathenaic Amphoras," *AJA* 63 (1959) 189.

*Gisela M. A. Richter, "Calenian Pottery and Classical Metalware," *AJA* 63 (1959) 241-249.

Howard Comfort, "An Unusual Roman Bowl at Strasbourg," *AJA* 63 (1959) 277-278.

*[Cornelius] C. Vermeule and D. von Bothmer, "Notes on a New Edition of Michaelis: Ancient Marbles in Great Britain. Part Three: 2," *AJA* 63 (1959) 329-348.

*Marie Farnsworth, "Types of Greek Glaze Failure," *Arch* 12 (1959) 242-250.

Ruth Amiran, "A Late Assyrian Stone Bowl from Tell el-Aitaf in the Bet-She'an Valley," *'Atiqot* 2 (1959) 129-132.

J. Kaplan, "The Neolithic Pottery of Palestine," *BASOR* #156 (1959) 15-22.

Joan du Plat Taylor, "The Cypriot and Syrian Pottery from Al Mina, Syria," *Iraq* 21 (1959) 62-92.

Joan Oates, "Late Assyrian Pottery from Fort Shalmaneser," *Iraq* 21 (1959) 130-146.

Awni K. Dajani, "Middle Bronze Age Pottery," *ADAJ* 4&5 (1960) 99-113.

Eva Brann, "An Early Protoattic Amphora," *AJA* 64 (1960) 71-72.

Marie Farnsworth, "Draw Pieces as Aids to Correct Firing," *AJA* 64 (1960) 72-75.

*Andreina Leanza Becker-Colonna, "The Explorations of Mt. Kronion Caves and the Finding of Pre-historical Vases," *AJA* 64 (1960) 182.

*John L. Caskey, "Lerna, the Cyclades, and Crete," *AJA* 64 (1960) 183. *[Pottery]*

*G. Roger Edwards, "Hellenistic Pottery from the Antikythera Wreck," *AJA* 64 (1960) 183-184.

Howard Comfort, "Roman Ceramic-and-Glass Vases at Heidelberg and New York," *AJA* 64 (1960) 273.

V[assos] Karageorghis, "Mycenaean Birds Reunited," *AJA* 64 (1960) 278-280. *[Pottery]*

Maria D. Theocharis, "A Knossian Vase from Attica," *Antiq* 34 (1960) 266-269.

J. Kaplan, "The Relation of the Chalcolithic Pottery of Palestine to Halafian Ware," *BASOR* #159 (1960) 32-36. (Correction, *BASOR* #162 (1961) p. 51)

Howard Comfort, "Some Imported Pottery at Khor Rori (Dhofar)," *BASOR* #160 (1960) 15-20.

Ruth Amiran, "A Late Bronze Age II Pottery Group from a Tomb in Jerusalem," *EI* 6 (1960) 27*.

Ruth Amiran, "The Pottery of the Middle Bronze Age I in Palestine," *IEJ* 10 (1960) 204-225.

*Joan Oates, "Ur and Eridu, the Prehistory," *Iraq* 22 (1960) 32-50. *[Pottery]*

*P. Delougaz, "Architectural Representations on Steatite Vases," *Iraq* 22 (1960) 90-95.

A. J. Arkell, "The origin of black-topped red pottery," *JEA* 46 (1960) 105-106.

Namio Egami, "Figurative Pottery in Prehistoric Iran," *Orient* 1 (1960) 53-58.

J. L. Benson, "A Syrian Krater from Bamboula at Kourion," *PEQ* 92 (1960) 64-69.

Iris Ainley, "A Short Note on Pottery from Iran," *PEQ* 92 (1960) 120-121.

Kathleen M. Kenyon, "Observations on Mrs. Ainley's Note," *PEQ* 92 (1960) 122-123.

*D. A. Amyx, "The Medallion Painter," *AJA* 65 (1961) 1-15.

J. L. Benson, "Pictorial Mycenaean Fragments from Kourion," *AJA* 65 (1961) 53-54. [Errata, p. 219]

Mario A. Del Chiaro, "Caeretan vs. Faliscan: Two Etruscan Red-Figured Hydriae," *AJA* 65 (1961) 56-57.

*Brian F. Cook, "Potters and Painters of Red-Figured Lekythoi," *AJA* 65 (1961) 188.

*Ann Konrad Knudsen, "The Relation between the Pottery and Metal Vessel Industries of Gordion in the Eighth Century B.C.," *AJA* 65 (1961) 191.

D. H. French, "Late Chalcolithic Pottery in North-West Turkey and the Aegean," *AS* 11 (1961) 99-141.

*Henry G. Fischer, "A First Dynasty Bowl Inscribed with the Group Ḥt," *CdÉ* 36 (1961) 19-22.

*W. Culican, "The Hasanlu Bowl," *Mwa-M* #1 (1961) 63-73.

J. L. Benson, "The White Slip Sequence at Bamboula, Kourion," *PEQ* 93 (1961) 61-69. *[Pottery]*

Jean M. Davidson, "Attic Geometric Workshops," *YCS* 16 (1961) i-xi, 1-161.

Maurits N. van Loon, "A Lion Bowl from Hasanlu," *Exped* 4 (1961-62) #2, 14-19.

*Awni K. Dajani, "Some of the Industries of the Middle Bronze Period," *ADAJ* 6&7 (1962) 55-75. [Alabaster, pp. 67-69; Faience Ointment Vases, pp.69-75]

P. Lawrence, "Notes on the Chimaera Group," *AJA* 66 (1962) 185-187. *[Greek Pottery]*

Mariateresa Moevs Marabini*[sic]*, "The Dating of the Italic 'Megarian' Bowls in the Light of the Findings from Cosa," *AJA* 66 (1962) 198.

D. A. Amyx, "Xenokles in Seattle," *AJA* 66 (1962) 229-232. *[Greek Pottery]*

Marjorie J. Milne, "Three Attic Red-Figured Vases in New York," *AJA* 66 (1962) 305-306.

H. R. W. Smith, "A Phlyax Vase in Rio de Janeiro," *AJA* 66 (1962) 323-331.

A. D. Trendall, "A South Italian Fragment in New York," *AJA* 66 (1962) 349-351.

*Alan L. Boegehold, "The Nessos Amphora—A Note on the Inscription," *AJA* 66 (1962) 405-406.

P. O. A. L. Davies, "Red and Black Egyptian Pottery," *JEA* 48 (1962) 19-24.

Ruth Amiran, "The 'Arm-Shaped' Vessel and Its Family," *JNES* 21 (1962) 161-174.

Pär Göran Gierow, "The Latial Iron Age Tomb-Group," *MB* #2 (1962) 32-38. *[Pottery]*

J. L. Benson, "Coarse Ware Stirrup Jars of the Aegean," *Bery* 14 (1962-63) 37-51.

Frances W. James, "The Pottery of the Old Testament," *Exped* 5 (1962-63) #1, 36-41.

T. Cuyler Young, "Dalma Painted Ware," *Exped* 5 (1962-63) #2, 38-39.

Sara A. Immerwahr, "Imitation Metal Vases from Mycenaean Tombs," *AJA* 67 (1963) 212-213.

*Mariateresa Marabini Moevs, "From Campanian Black to Sigillata Red and the Rise of Orange Gloss and Metallic Gloss," *AJA* 67 (1963) 215.

*Marie Farnsworth and Ivor Simmons, "Coloring Agents for Greek Glazes," *AJA* 67 (1963) 389-396.

H. W. Catling, "Minoan and Mycenaean Pottery: Composition and provenance," *Archm* 6 (1963) 1-9.

J. B. Hennessy and A. Millett, "Spectographic Analysis of the Foreign Pottery from the Royal Tombs of Abydos and Early Bronze Age Pottery of Palestine," *Archm* 6 (1963) 10-17.

D. Barag, "A Survey of Pottery Recovered from the Sea off the Coast of Israel," *IEJ* 13 (1963) 13-19.

R. Giveon, "A Ptolemaic Fayence Bowl," *IEJ* 13 (1963) 20-29.

Tullia Rönne-Linders, "A Black-Figured Neck-Amphora of the Leagros Group," *MB* #3 (1963) 54-66.

*Robert North, "Ghassul's New Found Jar-Incision," *ADAJ* 8&9 (1964) 68-74.

Mario A. Del Chiaro, "Classical Vases in the Santa Barbara Museum of Art," *AJA* 68 (1964) 107-112.

J. L. Benson, "Corinthian Vases at Wellesley College," *AJA* 68 (1964) 167-172.

Richard Bronson, "A Re-examination of the Late Attic Geometric Hydria No. 1212 in the Museum of the Villa Giulia,"*AJA* 68 (1964) 174-178.

*Cyrus H. Gordon, "Incantation Bowls from Knossos and Nippur," *AJA* 68 (1964) 194-195.

*Clark Hopkins, "The Seasonal Drama Illustrated in Phoenician Bowls," *AJA* 68 (1964) 196.

Iris C. Love, "Karchesion or Kantharos?" *AJA* 68 (1964) 197. *[Pottery]*

Margaret Thompson, "A Pot Hoard from Gordion," *AJA* 68 (1964) 201.

*Marie Farnsworth, "Greek Pottery: A Mineralogical Study," *AJA* 68 (1964) 221-228.

Philip C. Hammond, "The Physical Nature of Nabataean Pottery," *AJA* 68 (1964) 259-268.

Erik J. Holmberg, "The Appearance of Neolithic Black Burnished Ware in Mainland Greece," *AJA* 68 (1964) 343-348.

Kyle Meredith Phillips Jr., "A New Acropolis Fragment," *AJA* 68 (1964) 401. *[Pottery]*

Arvid Andrén, "An Italic Iron Age Hut Urn," *MB* #4 (1964) 30-37.

D. H. French, "Late Chalcolithic Pottery in North-West Turkey and the Aegean. Additional Notes," *AS* 14 (1964) 134-137.

Nancy R. Lapp, "Pottery from Some Hellenistic Loci at Balâṭah (Shechem)," *BASOR* #175 (1964) 14-26.

Peter J. Parr, "Objects from Thaj in the British Museum," *BASOR* #176 (1964) 20-28. *[Nabataean Pottery]*

Ann Konrad Knudsen, "From a Sardis Tomb: A Lydian Pottery Imitation of a Phrygian Metal Bowl?" *Bery* 14 (1964) 59-69.

Ruth Amiran and A. Eitan, "A Krater of Bichrome Ware from Tel Nagila," *IEJ* 14 (1964) 219-231.

H. J. Franken, "The Stratigraphic Context of the Clay Tablets found at Deir 'Alla," *PEQ* 96 (1964) 73-78. *[Pottery]*

Behnam Abu es-Soof, "Uruk Pottery from Dokan-Shahrazur and the Distribution of Ninevete[sic]* V Pottery in Iraq," *Sumer* 20 (1964) 37-44.

T. B. L. Webster, "Greek Vases in the Stanford Museum," *AJA* 69 (1965) 63-65.

Saul S. Weinberg, "A Note of Correction,"*AJA* 69 (1965) 160-161. *[Ref.* Erik J. Holmberg, *AJA* 68 (1964) 343-348-*Pottery]*

D. A. Amyx, "Ancient Vases in the Seattle Art Museum," *AJA* 69 (1965) 164.

*Patricia Lawrence, "The Protocorinthian and Corinthian Well at Anaploga," *AJA* 69 (1965) 170-171. *[Pottery]*

I. K. Raubitschek, "The Potter Menaidas," *AJA* 69 (1965) 174.

Oscar White Muscarella, "Lion Bowls from Hasanlu," *Arch* 18 (1965) 41-46.

*Ruth Amiran, "Yanik Tepe, Shengavit, and the Khirbet Kerak Ware," *AS* 15 (1965) 165-167.

Claire Epstein, "Bichrome Vessels in the Cross Line Style," *PEQ* 97 (1965) 42-53.

*D. H. French, "Early Pottery Sites from Western Anatolia," *ULBIA* 5 (1965) 15-24.

Takey Dabbagh, "Hassuna Pottery," *Sumer* 21 (1965) 93-111.

Kutlu Emre, "The Pottery from Acemhöyük," *A(A)*10 (1966) 99-153.

Fauzi Zayadin, "Early Hellenistic Pottery from the Theater Excavations at Samaria," *ADAJ* 11 (1966) 53-64.

Emily Vermeule, "The Boston Oresteia Krater," *AJA* 70 (1966) 1-22.

Mario A. Del Chiaro, "The Caeretan Figured Group," *AJA* 70 (1966) 31-36. *[Greek Pottery]*

Vronwy Hankey, "Late Mycenaean Pottery at Beth Shan," *AJA* 70 (1966) 169-171.

Betty Grossman, "'Lost and Found' Kalyx Krater by the Marlay Painter in the Collection of the City Art Museum of St. Louis," *AJA* 70 (1966) 190.

Elizabeth Gummey, "The Vrysoula Classical Deposit," *AJA* 70 (1966) 190.

Elizabeth Milburn, "Pottery of the Late Bronze Age from Ceos," *AJA* 70 (1966) 192-193.

Sevim Buluç, "An Onesimos Fragment in Philadelphia," *AJA* 70 (1966) 369-370. *[Greek Pottery]*

*M[ervyn] R. Popham, "The Destruction of the Palace of Knossos and its Pottery," *Antiq* 40 (1966) 24-28.

Bray Warwick, "Neolithic Painted Ware in the Adriatic," *Antiq* 40 (1966) 100-106.

Mario A. Del Chiaro, "Etruscan Bucchero Pottery," *Arch* 19 (1966) 98-103.

Joseph V. Noble, "The Forming of Attic Vases," *Arch* 19 (1966) 173-181.

R. C. A. Rottländer, "Is Provinicial-Roman Pottery Standardized?" *Archm* 9 (1966) 76-91.

B. Peckham, "An Inscribed Jar from Bat-Yam," *IEJ* 16 (1966) 11-17.

George A. Reisner, "Black-Topped Pottery," *JARCE* 5 (1966) 7-10. *[Egyptian Pottery]*

*Edward L. B. Terrace, "'Blue Marble' Plastic Vessels and Other Figures," *JARCE* 5 (1966) 57-63.

*Joan Crowfoot Payne, "Spectrographic analysis of some Egyptian pottery of the Eighteenth Dynasty," *JEA* 52 (1966) 176-178.

Sinclair Hood, "Date of the 'Reoccupation' Pottery from the Palace of Minos at Knossos," *KZFE* 5 (1966) 121-141.

*Emily Vermeule, "A Mycenaean Dipinto and Graffito," *KZFE* 5 (1966) 142-146. [1. Painted potmark on the base of a sherd from Blypha, pp. 142-144]

M. W. Prausnitz, "A Phoenician Krater from Akhziv," *OA* 5 (1966) 177-188.

Takey Dabbagh, "Halaf Pottery," *Sumer* 22 (1966) 23-43.

William R. Biers, "Six Sherds from Phlius," *AJA* 71 (1967) 79-80.

*R. G. Hood, "A Geometric Oenochoe with Ship Scene in Hobart," *AJA* 71 (1967) 82-87.

R. G. Hood, "A Mycenaean Hydria in Hobart," *AJA* 71 (1967) 87-89.

*John G. Griffith, "*Aegisthus Citharista,*" *AJA* 71 (1967) 176-177. *[Pottery]*

Per A. Ålin, "Early Mycenaean Pottery from Asine and its Implications for Aegean Connections," *AJA* 71 (1967) 183.

Elizabeth MacNeil Boggess, "The Development of the Attic Pithos," *AJA* 71 (1967) 183-184.

John T. Cummings, "A Red-Figure Kylix at Michigan State University," *AJA* 71 (1967) 185.

*Frederick R. Matson, "Could Pottery Have Been Made at Kea?" *AJA* 71 (1967) 191.

Mariateresa Marabini Moevs, "The Iron Age Tradition in Roman Pottery of the Late Republican-Early Imperial Period," *AJA* 71 (1967) 192.

Gustavus F. Swift Jr., "A Late Mycenaean-Protogeometric Horizon at Sardis," *AJA* 71 (1967) 194-195.

*Emily Vermeule, "A Love Scene by 'the Panaitios Painter'," *AJA* 71 (1967) 311-341. *[Pottery]*

R. C. A. Rottländer, "Standardization of Roman Provincial Pottery. II: Function of the Decorative Collar on Form Drag. 38," *Archm* 10 (1967) 35-45.

G. H. Brown, "Prehistoric Pottery from the Antitaurus," *AS* 17 (1967) 123-164.

Nelson Glueck, "Some Edomite Pottery from Tell el-Kheleifeh," *BASOR* #188 (1967) 8-38. [Parts I & II]

M. Prausnitz, "A Krater from Akhziv," *EI* 8 (1967) 71*.

Ruth Amiran, "Khirbet Kerak Ware in Ai," *IEJ* 17 (1967) 185-186.

Keith Branigan, "A Unique Juglet from Jericho," *PEQ* 99 (1967) 98-100.

Nehemia Tsori, "On Two Pithoi from the Beth-Shean Region and the Jordan Valley," *PEQ* 99 (1967) 101-103.

Benham Abu Al-Soof, "A Note on the Question of Painted Jamdat Nasr Pottery," *Sumer* 23 (1967) 210-211.

*H. W. Catling, "A Mycenaean Puzzle from Lefkandi in Euboea," *AJA* 72 (1968) 41-49. *[Pottery]*

*George M. A. Hanfmann and Jane C. Waldbaum, "Two Submycenaean Vases and a Tablet from Stratonikeia in Caria," *AJA* 72 (1968) 51-56.

Ellen Roberts Young, "A Red-figured Oinochoe in the Collection of Mrs. Lyman Spitzer, Jr.," *AJA* 72 (1968) 76.

J. L. Benson, "Corinthian Geometric Workshops," *AJA* 72 (1968) 161-162.

Elizabeth Milburn, "The Late Helladic IIIC Pottery from Lefkandi in Euboea," *AJA* 72 (1968) 169.

J. L. Benson, "A Mycenaean Vase in Toronto," *AJA* 72 91968) 203-209.

Christoph Clairmont, "A Note on the Portland Vase," *AJA* 72 (1968) 280-281.

Elizabeth Finkenstaedt, "A Red-figure Kylix by Oltos at Mount Holyoke College," *AJA* 72 (1968) 383.

Hans E. Wulff, Hildegard S. Wulff, and Leo Koch, "Egyptian Faïence: A Possible Survival in Iran," *Arch* 21 (1968) 98-107.

Anonymous, "Ancient Pots from the Sea Near Israel," *BH* 4 (1968) 62.

Anonymous, "Vessels of Wrath—and Other Vessels," *BH* 4 (1968) 116-118.

Keith Stanley, "An Archaic Cypriote Amphora at Duke University," *GRBS* 9 (1968) 355-358.

D. Ussishkin, "A Chalcolithic Basalt Chalice from Tiberias," *IEJ* 18 (1968) 45-46.

Ruth Amiran, "Two Canaanite Vessels Excavated in Egypt with Egyptian 'Signatures'," *IEJ* 18 (1968) 241-243.

R. Giveon, "An Alexandrine Basin Rim from Ascalon," *IEJ* 18 (1968) 247.

Behnam Abu al-Soof, "Distribution of Uruk, Jamdat Nasr and Ninevite V Pottery as Revealed by Field Survey Work in Iraq," *Iraq* 30 (1968) 74-86.

Edward L. Ochsenschlager, "The *Plemochoe* A Vessel from Thmuis," *JARCE* 7 (1968) 55-71.

Joseph Veach Noble, "Some Trick Greek Vases," *PAPS* 112 (1968) 371-378.

*N. Avigad, "An Inscribed Bowl from Dan," *PEQ* 100 (1968) 42-44.

R. S. Merrillees, "Evidence for the Bichrome Wheel-made Ware in Egypt," *AJBA* 1 (1968-71) #3, 3-27.

Machteld Mellink, "A Four-Spouted Krater from Karataş," *A(A)* 13 (1969) 69-76.

Frances Jones, "Sherds from Kululu," *A(A)* 13 (1969) 97-100.

Mehmet Eskioğlu, "Two Vases from Kayseri Region," *A(A)* 13 (1969) 101.

*J. T. Cummings, "The Michigan State University Kylix and its Painter," *AJA* 73 (1969) 69-71.

*Sartantis Symeonoglou, "Mycenaean Pottery and other Finds from Thebes," *AJA* 73 (1969) 245-246.

Joseph Veach Noble, "The Technique of Egyptian Faïence," *AJA* 73 (1969) 435-439.

*Sheila McNally, "An Attic Geometric Vase in the Collection of Mt. Holyoke College," *AJA* 73 (1969) 459-464.

Cynthia K. King, "Bis Patriae Cecidere Manus," *AJA* 73 (1969) 464-465. *[Vase]*

*Edith Porada, "Iranian Art and Archaeology: A Report on the Fifth International Congress, 1968," *Arch* 22 (1969) 54-65. [Grey Wares and the Problem of Indo-Europeans in Iran, pp. 58-60]

Siegfried H. Horn and Lenel G. Moulds, "Pottery from Shechem: Excavated 1913 and 1914," *AUSS* 7 (1969) 17-46.

Olga Tufnell, "The Pottery from Royal Tombs I-III at Byblos," *Bery* 18 (1969) 5-33.

Nelson Glueck, "Some Ezion-Geber: Elath Iron II Pottery," *EI* 9 (1969) 51-59.

*Ruth Amiram, "Canaanite Jars Depicted on Egyptian First Dynasty Wooden Labels and Ivory Inlays," *EI* 9 (1969) 137. *[English Summary*

M. J. Mellink, "The Hasanlu bowl in Anatolia perspective," *IA* 6 (1969) 72-87.

Kutlu Emre, "The Urartian Pottery from Altintepe," *TTKB* 33 (1969) 292-301.

§213 ***2.5.9.11.1 Pottery Chronology, History and Scientific Study***

C[laude] R. Conder, "Notes by Major Conder. I. Chronology of Pottery," *PEFQS* 23 (1890) 69.

W. M. Flinders Petrie, "Chronology of Pottery," *PEFQS* 23 (1891) 68.

*W. M. Flinders Petrie, "Sequences in Prehistoric Remains," *JRAI* 29 (1899) 295-301.

*F. Legge, "New Light on Sequence-Dating," *SBAP* 35 (1913) 101-113.

William Badè, "Ceramics and History in Palestine," *JBL* 50 (1931) 1-19.

*E[phraim] A. Speiser, "The 'Chalice' Ware of Northern Mesopotamia and Its Historical Significance," *BASOR* #48 (1932) 5-10.

T. Eric Peet, "The Classification of Egyptian Pottery," *JEA* 19 (1933) 62-64.

D. B. Harden, "A Typological Examination of Sumerian Pottery from Jamdat Masr and Kish," *Iraq* 1 (1934) 30-44.

*E[phraim] A. Speiser, "Mesopotamian Miscellanea," *BASOR* #68 (1937) 7-13. [I. A Distinctive Ceramic Family from Gawra XII, pp. 7-10]

*Hazel D. Hansen, "The Racial Continuity of Prehistoric Thessaly," *AJA* 42 (1938) 122. *[Pottery Types]*

*Donald Horton, "Technological Methods in the Study of Pottery from Greece and Italy," *AJA* 42 (1938) 128.

*G. Ernest Wright, "The Chronology of Palestinian Pottery in Middle Bronze I," *BASOR* #71 (1938) 27-34.

John Franklin Daniel, "Cypriote Connections of the Late Geometric Pottery of Greece," *AJA* 43 (1939) 300-301.

V. Gordon Childe, "Ceramic Art in Early Iran," *Antiq* 16 (1942) 353-358. *(Review)*

*W[illiam] F[oxwell] Albright, "Observations on the Date of the Pottery-Bearing Stratum of Mughâret Abū Uṣbaʿ," *BASOR* #86 (1942) 10-14.

*W[illiam] F[oxwell] Albright, J. L. Kelso, and J. Palin Thorley, "Early-Bronze Pottery from Bâb ed-Drâʿ in Moab," *BASOR* #95 (1944) 3-13. [I. Description and Chronology; II. Ceramic Techniques]

Marian Welker, "The Painted Pottery of the Near East in the Second Millennium B.C. and Its Chronological Background," *TAPS, N.S.,* 38 (1948) 185-245.

A. Dönmez and W. C. Brice, "The Distribution of Some Varieties of Early Pottery in South-East Turkey," *Iraq* 11 (1949) 44-58.

W[illiam] F[oxwell] Albright and Einar Gjerstad, "Correspondence with Professor Einar Gjerstand on the Chronology of 'Cypriote' Pottery from Early Iron Levels in Palestine," *BASOR* #130 (1953) 22-26.

Philip C. Hammond Jr., "Pattern Families in Nabataean Painted Ware," *AJA* 63 (1959) 371-382.

Anonymous, "Map Showing Distribution of Mycenaean Pottery before 1200 B.C.," *Arch* 13 (1960) 2-3. *[with Editorial]*

Clotilda Brokaw, "Chronology of Protoattic Style," *AJA* 65 (1961) 187.

G. Rogers Edwards, "The Chronology of Attic Hellenistic Pottery," *AJA* 65 (1961) 188.

*George W. Frey, "Pottery and the Study of the Old Testament,"*UTSB* 56 (1961-62) #2, 28-36.

Philip C. Hammond, "A Classification of Nabataean Fine Ware," *AJA* 66 (1962) 169-180.

Behnam Abu es-Soof, "Uruk Pottery from Dokan-Shahrazur and the Distribution of Ninevete[sic]* V Pottery in Iraq," *Sumer* 20 (1964) 37-44.

T. Cuyler Young Jr., "A Comparative Ceramic Chronology for Western Iran, 1500-500 B.C.," *Iran* 3 (1965) 53-85.

*A. Biran and Ora Negbi, "The Stratigraphical Sequence at Tel Ṣippor," *IEJ* 16 (1966) 160-173.

Ruth Amiran and A. Eitan, "Notes on the Functions of Pottery-Mending in Excavations," *PEQ* 98 (1966) 99-102.

*J. T. Hooker, "The Mycenae Siege Rhyton and the Question of Egyptian Influence," *AJA* 71 (1967) 269-281.

Behnam Abu al-Soof, "The Relevance of the Diyala Sequence to South Mesopotamian Sites," *Iraq* 29 (1967) 133-142.

*Ruth Amiran, "Chronological Problems of the Early Bronze Age; Early Bronze I-II: The City of Arad; Early Bronze III: The Khirbet Kerak Ware," *AJA* 72 (1968) 316-318.

*Behnam Abu al-Soof, "Distribution of Uruk, Jamdat Nasr and Ninevite V Pottery as revealed by Field Survey Work in Iraq,"*Iraq* 30 (1968) 74-86.

Joseph R. Caldwell, "Pottery and Cultural History on the Iranian Plateau," *JNES* 27 (1968) 178-183.

Behnam Abu al-Soof, "A Discussion of Uruk and Related Pottery in Iran, Northern Syria, Anatolia and Egypt in Relation to Mesopotamia," *Mesop* 3&4 (1968-69) 159-178.

*Ali M. Dinçol and Fuat Baykal, "Petrografik Metodlarla Keramik İncelenmesi," *AAI* 3 (1969) 103-117. [English Summary, pp. 112-113]

*T. Cuyler Young, "The Chronology of the Late Third and Second Millennia in Central Western Iran as seen from Godin Tepe," *AJA* 73 (1969) 287-291.

E. J. Peltenburg, "Al Mina Glazed Pottery and its Relations," *L* 1 (1969) 73-96.

Koichiro Goto, "Methodological Reflection on the Pottery Chronology of Tel Zeror, Area A I," *Orient* 5 (1969) 41-53.

§214 ***2.5.9.12 Seals and Signets***

A. H. Sayce, "On an Accadian seal," *JP* 3 (1871) 1-50.

A. H. Sayce, "The Babylonian Cylinders *found by* General di Cesnola *in the Treasury of the Temple at Kurium,*" *SBAT* 5 (1876-77) 441-444.

Isaac H. Hall, "On a Himyaritic Seal found in the Hauran," *SBAT* 5 (1876-77) 445-446.

W. F. Prideaux, "On an Aramaean Seal," *SBAT* 5 (1876-77) 456-458.

*†Henry C. Reichart, "Cylinder with Phoenician Inscription," *SBAP* 6 (1883-84) 16-17. (Remarks by W. H. Rylands, p. 17)

†W. H. Rylands, "Terra Cotta Seals in the possession of M. Schlumberger," *SBAP* 6 (1883-84) 111.

W. H. Rylands, "Terra-Cotta Seals," *SBAT* 8 (1883-84) 422-424.

George T. Stockes, "The Seal of Obadiah," *Exp, 3rd Ser.*, 1 (1885) 475-476.

W[illiam] Hayes Ward, "On Certain Points connected with Chaldean Seals," *JAOS* 11 (1885) xxxix-xli.

W[illia]m Hayes Ward, "Notes on Oriental Antiquities. I. Two Babylonian seal-cylinders," *AJA, O.S.*, 2 (1886) 46-48.

Émile Duval, "A Hittite Cylinder in the Musée Fol at Geneva," *AJA, O.S.*, 2 (1886) 132-135.

*W[illia]m Hayes Ward, "Notes on Oriental Antiquities. II. Two seals with Phoenician inscriptions," *AJA, O.S.*, 2 (1886) 155-156.

J[oachim] Menant, "Oriental cylinders of the Williams Collection," *AJA, O.S.*, 2 (1886) 247-260.

*W[illia]m Hayes Ward, "Notes on Oriental Antiquities. III. A god of Agriculture," *AJA, O.S.*, 2 (1886) 261-266. *[Seal]*

Thomas Tyler, "New Hittite Seal, Found Near Tarsus," *BOR* 1 (1886-87) 150-151.

†E. A. Wallis Budge, "Account of an Haematite Seal found in Asia Minor," *SBAP* 9 (1886-87) 27.

William Hayes Ward, "Notes on Oriental Antiquities. IV. The Rising Sun on Babylonian Cylinders," *AJA, O.S.*, 3 (1887) 50-56.

William Hayes Ward, "Notes. II. The Sun-God on Babylonian Cylinders," *AJA, O.S.*, 3 (1887) 385-386. *[Seals]*

*A. L. Frothingham Jr., "A Proto-Ionic Capital, and Bird Worship, Represented on an Oriental Seal," *AJA, O.S.*, 3 (1887) 57-61.

W. M. Flinders Petrie, "A Royal Egyptian Cylinder with Figures," *BOR* 2 (1887-88) 36-38.

*C. J. Ball, "New readings of the Hieroglyphs from Northern Syria," *SBAP* 10 (1887-88) 437-449. ["Seal(?) of Tarcondemus", pp. 439-442]

Claude R. Conder, "Altaic Cylinders," *PEFQS* 20 (1888) 239-246.

*William Hayes Ward, "Notes on Oriental Antiquities. VIII. 'Human Sacrifices' on Babylonian Cylinders," *AJA, O.S.*, 5 (1889) 34-43.

†W[illiam] Hayes Ward, "Rev. W. Hayes Ward exhibited and described two seals with Phœnician inscriptions of unknown locality, brought by him this year from Western Asia," *JAOS* 13 (1889) xlvii-xlviii.

W[illiam] Hayes Ward, "The rising sun on Babylonian seals," *JAOS* 13 cliv-clv.

*W[illiam] H[ayes] Ward, "On some Babylonian cylinders supposed to represent human sacrifices," *JAOS* 13 (1889) cccii-ccciv.

T[errien] de Lacouperie, "The Genuineness of the Cylinder of Ur-Ban," *BOR* 4 (1889-90) 9-11.

W[illiam] Hayes Ward, "Sir Henry Peek's Oriental Cylinders," *BOR* 4 (1889-90) 241-245.

*William Hayes Ward, "Notes on Oriental Antiquities. X. Tiamat and Other Evil Spirits, as Figured on Oriental Seals," *AJA, O.S.*, 6 (1890) 291-298.

*W[illia]m Hayes Ward, "The Babylonian Caduceus," *JAOS* 14 (1890) lxxxv-lxxxviii.

William Hayes Ward, "On Babylonian-Assyrian cylinder seals," *JAOS* 14 (1890) cxlii-cxliv.

*C[laude] R. Conder, "The Seal of Haggai," *PEFQS* 22 (1890) 121-122.

Morris Jastrow Jr., "A Phoenician Seal," *AJSL* 7 (1890-91) 257-267.

Fr. V. Scheil, "The Iovanoff Seal," *BOR* 5 (1891) 10-13.

Theo. G. Pinches, "Sir Henry Peek's Oriental Cylinders," *BOR* 5 (1891) 30-31.

A. H. Sayce, "Babylonian Cylinders in the Hermitage at St. Petersburg," *ZA* 6 (1891) 161-163.

*I[saac] H. Hall, "On a scarab seal with a Cypriote Inscription in the Metropolitan Museum of Art, New York," *JAOS* 15 (1893) ccviii-ccix.

Anonymous, "Cylinders in the British Museum," *MR* 78 (1896) 799-802.

C[laude] R. Conder, "Seal from Hebron," *PEFQS* 28 (1896) 224.

A. H. Sayce, "Note on the Seal Found on Ophel," *PEFQS* 29 (1897) 181-182.

*Ch. Clermont-Ganneau, "Notes on the Seal Found on Ophel, the Greek Inscriptions from Nazareth and Kefr esh Shems, the Siolam Text, and the Tombs of the Kings," *PEFQS* 29 (1897) 304-307. [(1) Seal of Ophel, pp. 304-306]

William Hayes Ward, "Some Hittite Seals," *AJA, O.S.*, 9 (1894) 361-365.

William Hayes Ward, "On some Hittite seal cylinders," *JAOS* 16 (1894-96) cxxix-cxxxi.

W[illiam] H[ayes] Ward, "A Royal cylinder of Burnaburiash," *JAOS* 16 (1894-96) cxxxi-cxxxii.

A. H. Sayce, "Haematite Cylinder from Cappadocia," *SBAP* 19 (1897) 301.

E. J. Pilcher, "Notes on the Ophel Signet. I.," *PEFQS* 29 (1897) 309.

A. H. Sayce, "Notes on the Ophel Signet. II.," *PEFQS* 29 (1897) 310.

*William Hayes Ward, "Bel and the Dragon," *AJSL* 14 (1897-98) 94-105. *[Seal]*

William Hayes Ward, "Oriental Antiquities. 3. A Hittite Cylinder Seal," *AJA* 2 (1898) 165-168.

*William Hayes Ward, "The Babylonian Representation of the Solar Disk," *AJT* 2 (1898) 115-118.

*Ebenezer Davis, "On the Date of the Siloam Inscription. II.," *PEFQS* 30 (1898) 58-60. *[Ref. - The Seal of Haggai]*

*A[ngus] Crawford, "Palestinian Antiquities," *PER* 12 (1898-99) 392-398. [Seal of Haggai, pp. 392-393; The Ophel Seal, pp. 397-398]

Theophilus G. Pinches, "An Interesting Cylinder-Seal," *SBAP* 21 (1899) 168-169.

Walter L. Nash, "Cylinder of Pepi Ist," *SBAP* 21 (1899) 170.

Percy E. Newberry, "Extracts from my Note Books (II).," *SBAP* 22 (1900) 59-66. [10. A Cylinder of the Vezîr Ankhu, p. 64]

*A. H. Sayce, "(I) Objects from the Tomb of a Pre-dynastic Egyptian King; (II) Some early Egyptian Seal-cylinders," *SBAP* 22 (1900) 278-280.

*John Ward, "A Collection of Historical Scarabs and others, with a few Cylinders," *SBAP* 22 (1900) 305-320, 386-401. *[Egyptian]*

James T. Dennis, "An Early Egyptian Cylinder," *JAOS* 22 (1901) 76-77.

E. J. Pilcher, "A Cylinder-Seal bearing the name of Gehazi," *SBAP* 23 (1901) 362.

*William Hayes Ward, "The Hittite Lituus," *AJA* 6 (1902) 41-42. *[Seal of a rod curved up at the bottom; a serpent]*

Theo. G. Pinches, "Cylinder Seals in the possession of J. Offord, Esq.," *SBAP* 24 (1902) 87-94.

R. A. Stewart Macalister, "Reports by R. A. Stewart Macalister, M.A., F.S.A. V. An Old Hebrew Seal from Deir Aban," *PEFQS* 34 (1902) 242-244.

C. Clermont-Ganneau, "Archaeological and Epigraphic Notes on Palestine. 20. *Three New Archaic Seals*," *PEFQS* 34 (1902) 262-268.

*W. L. Nash, "An Egyptian Representation of the Camel," *SBAP* 24 (1902) 309. *[Seal]*

*William Hayes Ward, "A New Inscription of Ine-Sin, King of Ur," *AJSL* 19 (1902-03) 149-151. *[Seal]*

*Charles C. Torrey, "Semitic Epigraphical Notes," *JAOS* 24 (1903) 205-226. [I. An Old Hebrew Seal, pp. 205-206]

C[laude] R. Conder, "Notes and Queries. *The Name of Jehovah on Seals*," *PEFQS* 35 (1903) 96.

A. H. Sayce, "A Seal-Cylinder," *SBAP* 24 (1903) 62-63.

T[heophilus] G. Pinches, "Cylinder-seals belonging to Mr. Rigg," *SBAP* 25 (1903) 71-74.

*Percy E. Newberry, "Extracts from my Notebooks. VII," *SBAP* 25 (1903) 357-362. [57. Some Miscellaneous Antiquities, pp. 361-362 (*Seal, p. 362*)]

Ira Maurice Price, "Four Babylonian Seal Cylinders," *AJSL* 20 (1903-04) 109-115.

S[tanley] A. Cook, "Notes and Queries. 3. *A newly-discovered Hebrew Seal*," *PEFQS* 36 (1904) 287-291.

W. M. Flinders Petrie, "Notes and Queries. 4. *The Egyptian Cylinder*," *PEFQS* 37 (1905) 88.

*F. Ll. Griffith, "Notes on an Egyptian Signet-Ring," *SBAP* 27 (1905) 38.

*Percy E. Newberry, "Extracts from my Notebooks. VIII," *SBAP* 27 (1905) 101-105. [63. Some Small Inscribed Objects, pp. 103-105 (*Seal, p. 105*)]

*Percy E. Newberry, "An unpublished Scene from the Tomb of Thy at Sakkara, representing the manufacture of Seals," *SBAP* 27 (1905) 286.

*W. Spiegelberg, "Note on the Word *khelemŷ,* 'a Seal-maker'," *SBAP* 27 (1905) 287.

David G. Lyon, "The Seal Impressions on an Early Babylonian Contract (Harvard Semitic Museum, No. 109)," *JAOS* 27 (1906) 135-141.

*George A. Barton, "Three Objects in the Collection of Mr. Herbert Clark, of Jerusalem," *JAOS* 27 (1906) 400-401. [A Hittite(?) seal(?)]

*Anonymous, "The Ring and Seal of Cheops Discovered," *MQR, 3rd Ser.,* 32 (1906) 181-182.

*A. H. Sayce, "The Ivriz Texts. The Ardistama Inscriptions. Some Hittite Seals," *SBAP* 28 (1906) 133-137. [Hittite seals, pp. 136-137]

J. E. Quibell, "Babylonian cylinders from Memphis,"*ASAE* 8 (1907) 60-61.

*Charles C. Torrey, "Epigraphic Notes," *JAOS* 28 (1907) 349-354. [3. A Phoenician Seal, p. 354]

*Hans H. Spoer, "Some Hebrew and Phoenician Inscriptions," *JAOS* 28 (1907) 355-359. [2. A Phoenician Seal, p. 359]

M[argaret] A. Murray, "Ptolemaic clay-sealings," *ZÄS* 44 (1907) 62-70.

Percy E. Newberry, "Impressions of Seals from Abydos," *AAA* 2 (1909) 130.

Joseph Offord, "Three Syrian or Hittite Cylinders," *PEFQS* 41 (1909) 60-63.

*A. H. Sayce, "Notes and Queries. 5. *The Early Jewish Inscriptions on Mr. H. Clarke's Seals,*" *PEFQS* 41 (1909) 155-156. (Note by Stanley A. Cook, p. 232)

Albert T. Clay, "Ancient Oriental Seals," *RP* 8 (1909) 253-257. *(Review)*

*C. H. W. Johns, "The Sissiktu," *SBAP* 31 (1909) 78-80. *[Seals] (Babylonian Word)*

C. H. W. Johns, "Thumb-Prints in Babylonia," *SBAP* 31 (1909) 88. *[Seals]*

Ira Maurice Price, "Some Seals in the Goucher Collection," *AJSL* 26 (1909-10) 169-176.

Stephen Langdon, "Two Babylonian Seals," *Baby* 3 (1909-10) 236-238.

*[Paul Carus], "A Yahveh Picture and What it Teaches," *OC* 24 (1910) 391-404. *[Seal]*

A. H. Sayce, "A Seal-Cylinder from Kara Eyuk," *SBAP* 32 (1910) 177-180.

Alice Grenfell, "A Syrian Seal-Cylinder in the Ashmolean Museum," *SBAP* 32 (1910) 268-271.

*Arthur E. P. Weigall, "Miscellaneous Notes," *ASAE* 11 (1911) 170-176. [2. A royal cylinder of the Middle Kingdom, p. 170]

Anonymous, "The Seal Cylinders of Western Asia," *MR* 93 (1911) 128-132.

T[heophilus] G. Pinches, "Three Cylinder-Seals," *SBAP* 33 (1911) 130-134.

T[heophilus] G. Pinches, "An Interesting Cylinder-Seal," *SBAP* 33 (1911) 213-220.

A. H. Sayce, "Three Seal-Cylinders from Memphis," *SBAP* 33 (1911) 259-260.

S[tephen] Langdon, "A Cylinder Seal of the Hammurabi Period," *SBAP* 34 (1912) 158-159.

E. J. Pilcher, "Old Hebrew Signets from Gezer," *PEFQS* 45 (1913) 143-146.

Anonymous, "The Babylonian Sisiktu," *RP* 12 (1913) 182.

*A. H. Sayce, "A Pictographic Inscription from Babylonia," *SBAP* 36 (1914) 6-7.

*Percy E. Newberry, "Egyptian Historical Notes. II," *SBAP* 36 (1914) 35-39. [9. Some Small Historical Antiquities, pp. 36-39 (*Seal, pp. 37, 39*)]

*Percy E. Newberry, "Egyptian Historical Notes. III," *SBAP* 36 (1914) 168-174. [12. Clay Sealing of [hieroglyphs] *Princess Neitocross,* p. 169; 13. Clay Sealing of *the Chief Steward of the Divine Votress named Pedineit,* p. 169]

S[tephen] Langdon, "A Seal of Nidaba, the Goddess of Vegetation," *SBAP* 36 (1914) 280-281.

E. J. Pilcher, "A Moabite Seal," *PEFQS* 47 (1915) 42.

Duffield Osborne, "Middle Italian Signets of Approximately 350 to 50 B.C.," *AJA* 20 (1916) 28-31.

George Hempl, "Minoan Seals," *AJA* 20 (1916) 93.

E. J. Pilcher, "An Old Hebrew Signet from Jerusalem," *PEFQS* 50 (1918) 93-94.

*E. J. Pilcher, "Signet with Old-Hebrew Inscription," *PEFQS* 51 (1919) 177-181.

*S[tephen] Langdon, "The religious interpretation of babylonian seals and a new prayer of Shamash-sum-ukîn (BM. 78219)," *RAAO* 16 (1919) 49-68.

S[tephen] Langdon, "Inscriptions of Cassite seals," *RAAO* 16 (1919) 69-95.

S[tephen] Langdon, "Note. *Ur-^{d}Lugal-edin-na the Physician,*" *RAAO* 17 (1920) 51. *[Seal]*

Theophilus G. Pinches and Percy E. Newberry, "A Cylinder-Seal inscribed in Hieroglyphic and Cuneiform in the Collection of the Earl of Carnarvon," *JEA* 7 (1921) 196-199.

*S[tephen] Langdon, "Assyrian Lexicographical Notes," *JRAS* (1921) 573-582. [II. A New Cassite Seal, pp. 573-574]

*E. J. Pilcher, "Neo-Babylonian Signet with Phoenican Inscription," *PEFQS* 53 (1921) 16-19.

W. G. Emery, "A New Cylinder Seal," *AAA* 9 (1922) 65-66.

Sidney Smith, "Babylonian Cylinder Seals from Egypt," *JEA* 8 (1922) 207-210.

D. G. Hogarth, "Engraved Hittite Objects," *JEA* 8 (1922) 211-218. *[Seals]*

A. H. Sayce, "A Cappadocian Seal," *JRAS* (1922) 265-266.

G. A. Cooke, "Epigraphical Notes. No. 1. A Persian Seal Cylinder," *JRAS* (1922) 270-271.

*Samuel A. B. Mercer, "Liturgical Elements in Babylonian and Assyrian Seal Cylinders," *JSOR* 6 (1922) 106-116.

Leon Legrain, "Five Royal Seal Cylinders," *MJ* 13 (1922) 60-78. [I. The Oldest Dated Royal Seal. The Seal of Basha Enzu, B.C. 2900; II. Two Royal Seal Cylinders of the First Dynasty of Babylon, Sumuabum and Zabum, B.C. 2050-1996; III. The Oldest Cassite Royal Seal And the Cassite War God *Shaugamuna;* IV. The Seal Cylinder of King Kurigalzu, about B.C. 1390]

Leon Legrain, "Some Seals of the Babylonian Collections," *MJ* 14 (1923) 135-161.

E. J. Pilcher, "Signet of Hananiah," *PEFQS* 55 (1923) 94-97.

( ) Buchler, "Notes and Queries," *PEFQS* 55 (1923) 154. *[Seals]*

V. Struve, "Egyptian Sealings in the Collection of the Academician N. P. Likhatschew," *AEE* 11 (1926) 116-119.

L. A. Waddell, "'Indo-Sumerian Seals'," *JRAS* (1926) 115-116.

*Sidney Smith, "Archaeological Notes," *JRAS* (1926) 433-446. [The Seal before God, pp. 442-446]

C. Ransom Williams, "A Cylinder Seal of a King Userkerē," *ZÄS* 61 (1926) 81-83.

*A. H. Godbey, "Men of a Name," *AJSL* 43 (1926-27) 42-44. *[Use of Seals]*

Alexis Zakharof, "Some Caucasian Seals," *AAA* 14 (1927) 55-56.

Stanley Casson, "Some Greek Seals of the 'Geometric' Period," *AJ* 7 (1927) 38-43.

S[tephen] Langdon, "Six Babylonian and Assyrian Seals," *JRAS* (1927) 43-50.

Marion F. Williams, "The Collection of Western Asiatic Seals in the Haskell Oriental Museum," *AJSL* 44 (1927-28) 232-253.

Percy E. Newberry, "Miscellanea," *JEA* 14 (1928) 109-111. [V. Two Gold Button-Seals, p. 110]

L[eon] Legrain, "Gem Cutters in Ancient Ur," *MJ* 20 (1929) 258-306.

*W. R. Taylor, "Recent Epigraphic Discoveries in Palestine," *JPOS* 10 (1930) 16-22. [Two Seals, pp. 18-19]

*C. Leonard Woolley, "Excavations at Ur, 1929-30," *MJ* 21 (1930) 81-105. [Appendix: Tablets and Seal-Impressions, by E. Burrows, pp. 106-107]

*S[tephen] Langdon, "Adonis in Assyria?" *RAAO* 27 (1930) 23-25. *[Seals]*

*A. H. Sayce, "The hieroglyphic Inscription on the Seal of Subbiluliuma," *AfO* 7 (1931-32) 184-185.

*W. A. Irwin, "An Ancient Biblical Text," *AJSL* 48 (1931-32) 184-193. *[Seal]*

O. E. Ravn, "Seal 8361 of the Collection of Cylinder Seals, Nationalmuseet, Kobenhavn," *AO* 10 (1931-32) 1-8.

Charles C. Torrey, "Pehlevi Seal Inscriptions from Yale Collections," *JAOS* 52 (1932) 201-207.

*W[illiam] F[oxwell] Albright, "The Seal of Eliakim and the Latest Preëxilic History of Judah, with Some Observations on Ezekiel," *JBL* 51 (1932) 77-106.

*Patrick Railton, "Some Remains of the Ancient Near East," *JMUEOS* #18 (1932) 55-59. [A. Mesopotamia, II, p. 58 (Seals)]

C. J. Gadd, "Seals of Ancient Indian Style found at Ur," *PBA* 18 (1932) 191-210.

M. Rostovtzeff, "Seleucid Babylonia: Bullae and Seals of Clay with Greek Inscriptions," *YCS* 3 (1932) 1-114.

M. Sprengling, "An Aramaic Seal Impression from Khorsabad," *AJSL* 49 (1932-33) 46-52.

Anonymous, "A Seal from Tell Billa," *UMB* 4 (1932-33) 37-40.

Anonymous, "Notes and Comments. An Assyrian Adam and Eve?" *A&A* 34 (1933) 54-55. *[Seal]*

Champlin Burrage, "A Study of Three Prehistoric Trojan Seals found by Schliemann at Ilios," *AJA* 37 (1933) 109-110.

P. E. K[retzmann], "Recent Archaeological Discoveries," *CTM* 4 (1933) 371-372. *[Adam and Eve Seal]*

W. F. Bade, "The Seal of Jaazaniah," *ZAW* 51 (1933) 150-156.

G. D. Hornblower, "A Temple Seal and Its Connections," *AEE* 19 (1934) 99-106.

David M. Robinson, "A Bronze State Seal of Larissa Kremaste," *AJA* 38 (1934) 219-222.

E[phraim] A. Speiser, "Impression of a Cylinder Seal from Gawra VI," *BASOR* #55 (1934) 2-3.

*H[enri] Frankfort, "Gods and Myths on Sargonid Seals," *Iraq* 1 (1934) 2-29.

Robert M. Engberg and Geoffrey M. Shipton, "Another Sumerian Seal Impression from Megiddo," *PEFQS* 66 (1934) 90-93.

S. H. Hooke, "An Israelite Seal from Tell Duweir," *PEFQS* 66 (1934) 97-98.

E. Douglas Van Buren, "Seals of the Gods," *SMSDR* 10 (1934) 165-173.

*E. Douglas Van Buren, "A Problem of Early Sumerian Art," *AÌO* 10 (1935) 237-251.

Herbert G[ordon] May, "Seal of Elamar," *AJSL* 52 (1935-36) 197-199.

Simone Corbiau, "An Indo-Sumerian Cylinder," *Iraq* 3 (1936) 100-103.

A. Bergman, "Two Hebrew Seals of the *'Ebed* Class," *JBL* 55 (1936) 221-226.

Alexis A. Zakharov, "Materials for the Corpus Sigillorum Asiae Anterioris Antique III-IV," *ArOr* 9 (1937) 78.

Dorothy Kent Hill, "The Rediscovered Seal of Tarqumuwa, King of Mera," *ArOr* 9 (1937) 307-310.

G. Ernest Wright, "Some Personal Seals of Judean Royal Officials," *BA* 1 (1938) 10-12.

G. Ernest Wright, "Qosanal, Servant of the King," *BA* 1 (1938) 16.

Nelson Glueck, "The First Campaign at Tell el-Kheleifeh (Ezion-geber)," *BASOR* #71 (1938) [Note by W. F. Albright, "The Seal of Quasʿnl," pp. 17-18]

A. Reifenberg, "Some Ancient Hebrew Seals," *PEQ* 70 (1938) 113-116. *[Part I]*

*G. R. Driver, "Old and New Semitic Texts," *PEQ* 70 (1938) 188-192. [III. On Mr. J. L. Starkey's Two Seals from Tel ed-Duweir, pp 190-192]

*Herbert Gordon May, "Three Hebrew Seals and the Status of Exiled Jehoiakin," *AJSL* 56 (1939) 146-148.

O. E. Ravn, "A Kassite Seal from Hama," *Bery* 6 (1939-41) 19-25.

R. D. Barnett, "A Cylinder Seal from Syria," *Iraq* 6 (1939) 1-2.

Cyrus H. Gordon, "Western Asiatic Seals in the Walters Art Gallery," *Iraq* 6 (1939) 5-34.

A. Reifenberg, "II. Some Ancient Hebrew Seals," *PEQ* 71 (1939) 195-198.

Charles C. Torrey, "A Hebrew Seal from the Reign of Ahaz," *BASOR* #79 (1940) 27-28.

Charles C. Torrey, "The Seal from the Reign of Ahaz Again," *BASOR* #82 (1941) 16-17.

E. L. Sukenik, "A Note on the Seal of the Servant of Ahaz," *BASOR* #84 (1941) 17-18. [Postscript by W. F. Albright, pp. 18-19]

*S. Spiegel, "The Seal of Gedaliah (Lachish) and Jeremiah," *JBL* 60 (1941) vi.

E. Douglas Van Buren, "A Collection of Cylinder seals in the Biblioteca Vaticana," *AJA* 46 (1942) 360-365.

*J. A. Thompson, "On Some Stamps and a Seal from Lachish," *BASOR* #86 (1942) 24-27.

*Edith Porada, "The Warrior with Plumed Helmet, a Study of Syro-Cappadocian Cylinder Seals and Bronze Figurines," *Bery* 7 (1942) 57-63.

E. L. Sukenik, "Three Ancient Seals," *KSJA* 1 (1942) VII.

A. Reifenberg, "Ancient Hebrew Seals III," *PEQ* 74 (1942) 109-112.

*Guy Brunton, "Three seal-amulets," *ASAE* 42 (1943) 79-82.

Theophile J. Meek, "Four Syrian Cylinder Seals," *BASOR* #90 (1943) 24-27.

Albrecht Goetze, "Three Achaemenian Tags," *Bery* 8 (1943-44) 97-101. *[Seal impressions]*

*David Diringer, "Note on Some Jar-Stamps and Seals Discovered at Lachish," *PEQ* 75 (1943) 55-56.

Theophile J. Meek, "Ancient Oriental Seals in the Royal Ontario Museum," *Bery* 8 (1943-44) 1-16.

Stuart Piggott, "A Cylinder-seal from South India," *Antiq* 18 (1944) 98-99.

Theophile J. Meek, "Ancient Oriental Seals in the Redpath Library," *BASOR* #93 (1944) 2-13.

J. Kutscher, "Two Hebrew Seals," *KSJA* 2 (1945) VI.

E. L. Sukenik, "A Further Note on Hebrew Seals," *KSJA* 2 (1945) VI.

G. R. Driver, "Brief Notes (I) A New Israelite Seal," *PEQ* 77 (1945) 5.

G. R. Driver, "Seals from "Amman and Petra," *QDAP* 11 (1945) 81-82.

*[Immanuel] Ben-Dor, "A Hebrew Seal in a Gold Ring," *BIES* 12 (1946) III.

A. Reifenberg, "Two Moabite Seals," *BIES* 12 (1946) III.

Edith Porada, "The Origin of Winnirke's Cylinder Seal," *JNES* 5 (1946) 257-259.

N. Avigad, "A Seal of a Slave-Wife (Amah)," *PEQ* 78 (1946) 125-134.

I[mmanuel] Ben-Dor, "A Hebrew Seal from Samaria," *QDAP* 12 (1946) 77-83.

Walter B. Emery, "A Cylinder seal of the Uruk period," *ASAE* 45 (1947) 147-150.

E[dith] Porada, "Suggestions for the Classification of Neo-Babylonian Seals," *Or, N.S.,* 16 (1947) 145-165.

Edith Porada, "The Cylinder Seals of the Late Cypriote Bronze Age," *AJA* 52 (1948) 178-198.

David Diringer, "Royal Seals in Ancient Israel: Archaeological Evidence," *JJS* 1 (1948-49) 161-171.

*I[mmanuel] Ben-Dor, "Two Hebrew Seals," *QDAP* 13 (1948) 64-67. [1. A Hebrew Signet-ring, pp. 64-66]

I[mmanuel] Ben-Dor, "A Hebrew Seal," *QDAP* 13 (1948) 90-91.

Barbara Parker, "Cylinder Seals from Palestine," *Iraq* 11 (1949) 1-43.

E. Douglas Van Buren, "The Cylinder Seals from Brak," *Iraq* 11 (1949) 59-76.

*Martin P. Nilsson, "Oriental Import in Minoan and Mycenaean Greece," *ArOr* 17 (1949), Part 2, 210-212.

D[avid] Diringer, "Three Early Hebrew Seals," *ArOr* 18 (1950), Part 3, 65-69.

*N. Avigad, "Epigraphical Gleanings from Gezer," *PEQ* 82 (1950) 43-49.

R. D. Barnett, "A Group of Seals," *JKF* 1 (1950-51) 100-102.

B. Kirschner, "Remarks on Hebrew Inscriptions," *BIES* 16 (1951) #3/4, VIII. [1. The Seal B ' d ' l = Ben ' Ed(i) ' el?]

E. Douglas Van Buren, "A cylinder seal with a history," *JCS* 5 (1951) 133-134. *[Haematite Cylinder Seal]*

Edith Porada and Faraj Basmachi, "Nergal in the Old Babylonian Period," *Sumer* 7 (1951) 66-68. [IM. 15218 - Seal]

N. Avigad, "An Ammonite Seal," *IEJ* 2 (1952) 163-164.

Sabatino Moscati, "On Ancient Hebrew Seals," *JNES* 11 (1952) 164-168.

*E. Douglas Van Buren, "The Building of a Temple-tower," *RAAO* 46 (1952) 65-74. *[Seals]*

N. Avigad, "Two Ahab Seals," *BIES* 17 (1952-53) #1/2, II.

*G. R. Driver, "Seals and Tombstones," *ADAJ* 2 (1953) 62-65.

*Albrecht Goetze, "A Seal Cylinder with an Early Alphabetic Inscription," *BASOR* #129 (1953) 8-11.

Eckhard Unger, "Two Seals of the Ninth Century B.C. from Shadikanni on the Ḫabur," *BASOR* #130 (1953) 15-21.

A. J. Sachs, "The Late Assyrian Royal Seal Type," *Iraq* 15 (1953) 167-170.

M. Spengling, "Iranica," *JNES* 12 (1953) 189-193. [Seals, New and Old]

C[yrus] H. Gordon, "Near East Seals in Princeton and Philadelphia," *Or, N.S.,* 22 (1953) 242-250.

N. Avigad, "Seven Ancient Hebrew Seals," *BIES* 18 (1953-54) #3/4, IV.

*A. Reifenberg, "Hebrew Seals and Stamps IV," *IEJ* 4 (1954) 139-142.

N. Avigad, "Three Ornamented Hebrew Seals," *IEJ* 4 (1954) 236-238.

John L. Myres, "An Early Ægean Sealstone with Linear Signs," *Man* 54 (1954) #75.

R. F. G. Sweet, "Drawings of Three Sakje-gözü Seals," *MCS* 4 (1954) 22-23.

E. Douglas Van Buren, "Seals of the Second Half of the Layard Collection," *Or, N.S.,* 23 (1954) 97-113.

R. B. Y. Scott, "Another Griffin Seal from Samaira," *PEQ* 86 (1954) 87-90.

Edith Porada, "Greek Influence on a Seal-Cutter from Ur," *AJA* 59 (1955) 173.

M. Prausnitz, "Notes on a Cylinder Seal Impression," *'Atiqot* 1 (1955) 139.

*Yigael Yadin, "The Earliest Record of Egypt's Military Penetration into Asia? Some Aspects of the Narmer Palette, the 'Desert Kites' and Mesopotamian Seal Cylinders," *IEJ* 5 (1955) 1-16.

M. W. Prausnitz, "Earliest Palestinian Seal Impressions," *IEJ* 5 (1955) 190-193.

Barbara Parker, "Excavations at Nimrud 1949-1953: Seals and Seal Impressions," *Iraq* 17 (1955) 93-125.

G[eorge] A. Reisner, "Clay Sealings of Dynasty XIII from Uronarti Fort," *Kush* 3 (1955) 26-69.

Nehemia Zori, "A Cylinder-Seal Impression from Mount Gilboa," *PEQ* 87 (1955) 89-90.

G. R. Driver, "Hebrew Seals," *PEQ* 87 (1955) 183.

*E. Douglas Van Buren, "The Sun-God Rising," *RAAO* 49 (1955) 1-14. *[Seal]*

E. Douglas Van Buren, "A proposed Interpretation of a Seal Found at Ur," *RAAO* 49 (1955) 97-98.

W. J. Hemp, "Seals," *Antiq* 30 (1956) 42.

Ruth B. K. Amiran, "A Seal from Brak; Expressions of Consecutive Movements in Late Minoan Glyptic," *Iraq* 18 (1956) 57-59.

*E. Douglas Van Buren, "A Ritual Sequence," *Or, N.S.,* 25 (1956) 39-41.

*Mebrure Tosun, "The Significance of the Symbols of Gods in the Mesopotamian Cylinder Seals," *TTKB* 20 (1956) 49-59.

Philip C. Hammond, "A Note on a Seal Impression from Tell es-Sulṭûn," *BASOR* #147 (1957) 37-39.

*W[illiam] F[oxwell] Albright, "The Seal Impression from Jericho and the Treasurers of the Second Temple," *BASOR* #148 (1957) 28-30.

Briggs Buchanan, "On the Seal Impressions on Some Old Babylonian Tablets," *JCS* 11 (1957) 45-52.

Briggs Buchanan, "Further Observations on the Syrian Glyptic Style," *JCS* 11 (1957) 74-76. *[Seals]*

Edith Porada, "Syrian Seal Impressions on Tablets Date in the Time of Hammurabi and Samsu-iluna," *JNES* 16 (1957) 192-197.

E. Douglas Van Buren, "The Drill-Worked Jamdat Nasr Seals," *Or, N.S.,* 26 (1957) 289-305.

P. C. Hammond, "A Note on Two Seal Impressions from Tell Es-Sulṭan," *PEQ* 89 (1957) 68-69, 145.

*C. J. Gadd, "Three Roman Parallels," *AfO* 18 (1957-58) 318. [2. The two royal seals of Ugarit]

M. W. Prausnitz, "Cylinder Seal Impressions in the Eastern Mediterranean Area at the End of the Third Millennium B.C.," *EI* 5 (1958) 84*.

N. Avigad, "New Light on the MṢH Seal Impressions," *IEJ* 8 (1958) 113-119.

N. Avigad, "An Early Aramaic Seal," *IEJ* 8 (1958) 228-230.

D. A. Kennedy, "The Inscribed Hittite seals in the Ashmolean Museum," *RHA* 16 (1958) 65-84.

*Kemal Balkan, "Inscribed Bullae from Daskyleion-Ergili," *A(A)* 4 (1959) 123-128.

*Marie Matoušová, "The Rein in 'Cappadocian' Seals," *ArOr* 27 (1959) 396-399.

*Nelson Glueck, "A Seal Weight from Nebi Rubin," *BASOR* #153 (1959) 35-38.

J. M. Munn-Rankin, "Ancient Near Eastern Seals in the Fitzwilliam Museum, Cambridge," *Iraq* 21 (1959) 20-37.

Paul W. Lapp, "Late Royal Seals from Judah," *BASOR* #158 (1960) 11-22.

N. Avigad, "*Yehûd or Haʿîr*?" *BASOR* #158 (1960) 23-27.

Y[igael] Yadin, "A Hebrew Seal from Tell Jemmeh," *EI* 6 (1960) 28*.

S. Yeivin, "The Date of the Seal of 'Shemaʿ Servant of Jeroboam'," *EI* 6 (1960) 28*.

Edith Porada, "Notes on the Sargonid Seal, Ur 364," *Iraq* 22 (1960) 116-123.

S. Yeivin, "The Date of the Seal 'Belonging to Shemaʿ (the) Servant (of) Jeroboam'," *JNES* 19 (1960) 205-212.

W. Culican, "Melqart Representations on Phoenician Seals," *Abr-N* 2 (1960-61) 41-54.

N. Avigad, "The Jotham Seal from Elath," *BASOR* #163 (1961) 18-22.

N. Avigad, "Some Unpublished Ancient Seals," *BIES* 25 (1961) #4, II.

Raphael Giveon, "Two New Hebrew Seals and Their Iconographic Background," *PEQ* 93 (1961) 38-42. [I. A Seal from the Valley of Aijalon; II. A Seal from the Region of Dan]

Alan Millard, "A Seal from Petra," *PEQ* 93 (1961) 136.

Rafiq Wafa Dajani, "Neo-Babylonian Seal from Amman," *ADAJ* 6&7 (1962) 124-125.

G. Ernest Wright, "Selected Seals from the Excavations at Balaṭah (Shechem)," *BASOR* #167 (1962) 5-13.

Frank M. Cross Jr., "An Inscribed Seal from Balaṭah (Shechem)," *BASOR* #167 (1962) 14-15.

Siegfried H. Horn, "An Early Aramaic Seal with an Unusual Design," *BASOR* #167 (1962) 16-18.

Frank Moore Cross Jr., "An Archaic Inscribed Seal from the Valley of Aijalon," *BASOR* #168 (1962) 12-18.

*W. B. Henning, "A Bactrian Seal-Inscription," *BSOAS* 25 (1962) 335.

Barbara Parker, "Seals and Seal Impressions from the Nimrud Excavations, 1955-58," *Iraq* 24 (1962) 26-40.

*Victor E. G. Kenna, "Seals and Script with special reference to ancient Crete," *KZFE* 1 (1962) 1-15.

N. Avigad, "A Seal of 'Manasseh Son of the King'," *IEJ* 13 (1963) 133-136.

N. Avigad, "Two Newly Found Hebrew Seals," *IEJ* 13 (1963) 322-324. [1. The Seal of Achbor; 2. The Seal of Yeshaʿ yahu]

*Victor E. G. Kenna, "Seals and Script II," *KZFE* 2 (1963) 1-6.

Hans Goedicke, "A Cylinder Seal of a Ruler of Byblos of the Third Millennium," *MDIÄA* 19 (1963) 1-6.

*W[illiam] A. Ward, "Cylinders & Scarabs from a Late Bronze Temple at 'Amman," *ADAJ* 8&9 (1964) 47-55.

Victor E. G. Kenna, "Cretan and Mycenaean Seals in North America," *AJA* 68 (1964) 1-12.

L. Y. Rahmani, "Two Syrian Seals," *IEJ* 14 (1964) 180-184.

N. Avigad, "Seals and Sealings," *IEJ* 14 (1964) 190-194.

N. Avigad, "The Seal of Jezebel," *IEJ* 14 (1964) 274-276.

Lamia Al-Gailani, "Akkadian Cylinder Seals in the Iraq Museum," *Sumer* 20 (1964) 53-56.

*Victor E. G. Kenna, "Seals and Script III: Cretan Seal Use and Dating of Linear Script B," *KZFE* 3 (1964) 29-57.

*Wilfred G. Lambert, "The Reading of a Seal Inscription from Thebes," *KZFE* 3 (1964) 182-183.

M. F. Martin, "Six Palestinian Seals," *RDSO* 39 (1964) 203-210.

R. B. Y. Scott, "The Seal of Šmryw," *VT* 14 (1964) 108-110.

I[gnace] J. Gelb, "On some Old and New Hieroglyphic Hittite Seals," *AAI* 2 (1965) 223-226.

E[dith] Porada, "Some Seals from Acemhöyük," *AAI* 2 (1965) 365-370.

Edith Porada, "Cylinder Seals from Thebes; A Preliminary Report," *AJA* 69 (1965) 173.

N. Avigad, "Seals of Exiles," *IEJ* 15 (1965) 222-232.

H. Tadmore, "A Note on the Seal of Mannu-ki-Inurta," *IEJ* 15 (1965) 233-234.

R. Giveon, "A sealing of Khyan from the Shephela of Southern Palestine," *JEA* 51 (1965) 202-204.

A. R. Millard, "The Assyrian Royal Seal Type Again," *Iraq* 27 (1965) 12-16.

V[ictor] E. G. Kenna, "The Chronology of the sealings in the South West Basement of the Palace at Knossos," *KZFE* 4 (1965) 74-78.

Sami Ahmed, "A Note on the Style of the Syrian Glyptic," *ZA* 57 (1965) 173-176.

Nimet Özgüç, "Seals allegedly from the regions of Kayseri, Afyonkarahisar and Malatya," *A(A)* 10 (1966) 167-178.

*William A. Ward, "Scarabs, Seals and Cylinders from two Tombs at Amman," *ADAJ* 11 (1966) 5-18.

V[ictor] E. G. Kenna, "Cretan And Mycenaean Seals," *Arch* 19 (1966) 248-250.

N. Avigad, "A Hebrew Seal with a Family Emblem," *IEJ* 16 (1966) 50-53.

*A[nson] F. Rainey, "Private Seal-Impressions: A Note on Semantics," *IEJ* 16 (1966) 187-190.

N. Avigad, "Two Phoenician Votive Seals," *IEJ* 16 (1966) 243-251.

W. G. Lambert, "Ancient Near Eastern Seals in Birmingham Collections," *Iraq* 28 (1966) 64-83.

Hans Goedicke, "The Cylinder Seal of a Ruler of Byblos Reconsidered," *JARCE* 5 (1966) 19-21.

*Margaret A. V. Gill, "Seals and Sealings: some comments. The Knossos Sealings with Linear B Inscriptions," *KZFE* 5 (1966) 1-16.

John Boardman, "Hittite and related Hieroglyphic Seals from Greece," *KZFE* 5 (1966) 47-48.

M. Matousova, "Running Adad," *Sumer* 22 (1966) 115-119. *[Seal]*

Martha Heath Wiencke, "The Beulah H. Emmet Collection of Minoan Seals," *AJA* 71 (1967) 196.

*Briggs Buchanan, "A Dated Seal Impression Connecting Babylonia and India," *Arch* 20 (1967) 104-107.

Anonymous, "A Lady in Exile: 'Jehovah will Hear'," *BH* 3 (1967) #3, 11-13. *[Seal]*

Yohanan Aharoni, "Seals of Royal Functionaries from Arad," *EI* 8 (1967) 71*.

Barbara Parker, "A Cappadocian Cylinder Seal," *Iraq* 29 (1967) 3-5.

J. B. Segal, "A Syriac Seal Impression," *Iraq* 29 (1967) 6-15.

R. W. Hamilton, "A Sumerian Cylinder Seal with Handle in the Ashmolean Museum," *Iraq* 29 (1967) 34-41.

Briggs Buchanan, "Five Hittite Hieroglyphic Seals," *JCS* 21 (1967) 18-23.

W. A. Ward, "Three Phoenician Seals of the Early First Millennium B.C.," *JEA* 53 (1967) 69-74.

*John H. Betts, "New Light on Minoan Bureaucracy. *A Re-examination of some Cretan Sealings,*" *KZFE* 6 (1967) 15-40.

Raphael Giveon, "Royal Seals of the XIIth Dynasty from Western Asia," *RÉg* 19 (1967) 29-37.

*Abdul Kareem Abdullah, "The Paramount God and the Old Name of Al-Dhiba'i," *Sumer* 23 (1967) 189-192. *[Seal]*

*V. E. G. Kenna, "Ancient Crete and the Use of the Cylinder Seal," *AJA* 72 (1968) 321-336.

Edith Porada, "True or False? Genuine and False Cylinder Seals at Andrews University," *AUSS* 6 (1968) 134-149.

Siegfried H. Horn, "An Inscribed Seal from Jordan," *BASOR* #189 (1968) 41-43.

N. Avigad, "Notes on Some Inscribed Syro-Phoenician Seals," *BASOR* #189 (1968) 44-49.

Richard N. Frye, "Sasanian Clay Sealings in the Collection of Mohsen Foroughi," *IA* 8 (1968) 188-132.

N. Avigad, "The Seal of Abigad," *IEJ* 18 (1968) 52-53.

*Georgina Herrmann, "Lapis-Lazuli: The Early Phases of its Trade," *Iraq* 30 (1968) 21-57. *[Seals]*

William C. Brice, "An inscribed terra-cotta seal from Crete," *KZFE* 7 (1968) 103-104.

*William C. Brice, "Epigraphische Mitteilungen," *KZFE* 7 (1968) 180-181. [Hieroglyphic Script from Mallia, pp. 180-181] *[Seal]*

Antonio Invernizzi, "Bullae from Seleucia," *Mesop* 3&4 (1968-69) 69-124. *[Greek Seals]*

William A. Ward, "The Four-Winged Serpent on Hebrew Seals," *RDSO* 43 (1968) 135-143.

A.D.Tushingham, "The God in a Boat," *AJBA* 1 (1968-71) #4, 23-28. *[Seal]*

W. Culican, "The Iconography of Some Phoenician Seals and Seal Impressions," *AJBA* 1 (1968-71) #1, 50-103. [Seal Impressions of Baal and Astarte Enthroned; Four Seal-Impressions of Lion Slayers; A Seal in the Zeno Pierides Collection; Two Bullae from Akko]

Susan Bodenstein, "Morgan Seal 652," *JANES* 1 (1968-69) #2, 5-13.

Martha H. Wiencke, "The Beulah H. Emmet Collection of Minoan Seals," *AJA* 73 (1969) 33-38.

Richard W. Berry, "Cylinder Seal Mineralogy and Petrology," *AJA* 73 (1969) 67-69.

*Edith Porada, "Cylinder Seals from Enkomi, Cyprus, and a Re-appraisal of Early Glyptic Art in Cyprus," *AJA* 73 (1969) 244.

N. Avigad, "A Group of Hebrew Seals," *EI* 9 (1969) 134. *[English Summary]*

*A. Negev, "Seal-Impressions from Tomb 107 at Kurnub (Mampsis)," *IEJ* 19 (1969) 89-106.

*Briggs Buchanan, "The End of the Assyrian Colonies in Anatolia: The Evidence of the Seals," *JAOS* 89 (1969) 758-762.

Victor E. G. Kenna, "The provenience of seals and sealings with hieroglyphic script," *KZFE* 8 (1969) 103-109.

John Piet, "An Old Babylonian Crystal Seal," *JANES* 2 (1969-70) 30-36.

§215 *2.5.9.12.1 Brick Stamps, Jar Handles, Jar Stamps, and Potters' Marks*

J. Baker Greene, "Some Remarks on the Interpretation of the Impressions on the Vase Handles Found at the Foot of the Temple Wall," *PEFQS* 13 (1881) 304-311.

Isaac H. Hall, "The Greek Stamps on the Handles of Rhodian Amphorae, Found in Cyprus, and now in the Metropolitan Museum of New York," *JAOS* 11 (1882-85) 389-396.

Isaac H. Hall, "The Greek Stamps on the handles of Rhodian Amphoræ, found in Cyprus, and now in the Metropolitan Museum of New York," *JAOS* 13 (1889) xxi.

*E. J. Pilcher, "Herodian Pottery and the Siloam Inscription," *SBAP* 20 (1898) 213-222. [Plate I. Stamps upon Handles of Herodian Pottery, pp. 219-221]

*C. Clermont-Ganneau, "Note on the Inscribed Jar-Handle and Weight Found at Tell Zakariya. 1. The Handle of the Royal Jar of Hebron," *PEFQS* 31 (1899) 204-207.

C[laude] R. Conder, "Notes on the July 'Quarterly Statement.' *Jar-handles,*" *PEFQS* 31 (1899) 353. (Note by C. Clermont-Ganneau, *PEFQS* 32 (1900) p. 79)

*A[ngus] C[rawford], "Notes—Archæological, Etc.," *PER* 13 (1899-1900) 48-50. *[Jar Handle Inscriptions]*

A. H. Sayce, "The Age of the Inscribed Jar-Handles from Palestine," *PEFQS* 32 (1900) 66-69.

A. H. Sayce, "The Jar-Handles Discovered by Dr. Bliss," *PEFQS* 32 (1900) 170.

C. Clermont-Ganneau, "Notes on the October 'Quarterly Statement'. p. 290. *Royal Israelite Jar-handles,*" *PEFQS* 32 (1900) 78.

C. Clermont-Ganneau, "Inscribed Jar-Handles of Palestine," *PEFQS* 32 (1900) 251-253.

F. J. Bliss, "List of Casts and Wax Impressions of Stamped Jar-Handles. Sent to London by Dr. Bliss, April 27th, 1900," *PEFQS* 32 (1900) 298.

Joseph Offord, "Note on the Winged figures on the Jar-Handles Discovered by Dr. Bliss," *PEFQS* 32 (1900) 379-380.

Theodore F. Wright, "Exploration and Discovery: Jar-Handles," *BW* 17 (1901) 135-136.

Theodore F. Wright, "Jar-Handle Inscriptions. I," *PEFQS* 33 (1901) 60-63.

C[laude] R. Conder, "Jar-Handle Inscriptions. II," *PEFQS* 33 (1901) 63.

R. A. Stewart Macalister, "Amphora Handles, with Greek Stamps, from Tell Sandahannah," *PEFQS* 33 (1901) 25-43, 124-144.

Joseph Offord, "Note on the Winged Figures upon the Jar-Handles Discovered by Dr. Bliss," *PEFQS* 33 (1901) 64.

C. Clermont-Ganneau, "Archaeological and Epigraphic Notes on Palestine. 2. *Rhodian, and not Jewish Amphora-handles,*" *PEFQS* 33 (1901) 114-115.

T[heodore] F. Wright, "Jar-Handle Stamp at Cambridge, U.S.," *PEFQS* 33 (1901) 250. (Note by R. A. Stewart Macalister, p. 250)

R. A. Stewart Macalister, "Reports and Notes by R. A. S. Macalister, Esq. IV. Addenda to the List of Rhodian Stamped Jar-Handles from Tell Sandahannah," *PEFQS* 33 (1901) 394-397.

R. A. Stewart Macalister, "Reports by R. A. Stewart Macalister, M.A., F.S.A.," *PEFQS* 34 (1902) 118-124. [IV. Further Jar-Handles with Rhodian Stamps, p. 121]

*R. A. S[tewart] Macalister, "Notes and Queries. 3. *Note on Objects in the Government Museum at Jerusalem,*" *PEFQS* 36 (1904) 402. [1. The Zakariya Jar-handle]

Anonymous, "Jar-Handles from Gezer," *RP* 6 (1907) 92.

E. J. Pilcher, "Notes and Queries. (2.) *Stamped jar-handles from Gezer,*" *PEFQS* 40 (1908) 76.

S[tanley] A. Cook, "Notes and Queries. (3.) *The inscribed Objects from Gezer,*" *PEFQS* 40 (1908) 76-77. *[Jar-stamp]*

Mark Lidzbarski, "Notes and Queries. 3. *The Old Hebrew Jar-Seals from Gezer,*" *PEFQS* 41 (1909) 154.

L. W. King, "A New Brick Stamp of Naram-Sin, King of Akkad. From Tello," *SBAP* 31 (1909) 286-288.

E. J. Pilcher, "The Jewish Royal Pottery-Stamps," *SBAP* 32 (1910) 93-101, 143-152.

F. W. Read, "The Persian and Egyptian Affinities of the Jewish Royal Pottery Stamps," *PEFQS* 42 (1910) 232-234.

G. A. Wainwright, "A New Kingdom Potter's Mark," *AEE* 4 (1917) 97-99.

Winifred M. Crompton, "A Stamp Seal from Egypt," *JMUEOS* #7 (1917-18) 59-64.

V. Struve, "A Stamp of Amenhotep III. From the Collection of N. P. Likhacheff," *AEE* 10 (1925) 74-77.

V. Struve, "A Wood Stamp of the Hermitage Collection," *AEE* 10 (1925) 77-78. *[Egyptian Stamp]*

Stanley A. Cook, "Inscribed Jar-Handles," *PEFQS* 57 (1925) 91-95.

A. H. Sayce, "The Jerusalem Sealings on Jar-handles," *PEFQS* 59 (1927) 216-217.

*H. Comfort, "Arretine Signatures Found in the Excavations in the Theatre District of Corinth," *AJA* 33 (1929) 484-501.

W. F. Bade, "A Jar Handle Stamp from Tell en-Nasben," *ZAW* 50 (1932) 89-92.

E. L. Sukenik, "The 'Jerusalem' and 'The City' Stamps on Jar Handles," *JPOS* 13 (1933) 226-231.

*E. L. Sukenik, "Paralipomena Palestinensia," *JPOS* 14 (1934) 178-184. [II. Stamped Jar-Handles of the Post-Exilic Age, pp. 182-184]

A. Procope-Walter, "Syro-Cappadocian Stamp Seals in the Museum of the Academy of Science, Leningrad," *AEE* 20 (1935)100-107.

Frederick O. Waagé, "Potters' Stamps in Samian and Pergamene Wares,"*AJA* 41 (1937) 115-116.

*S. Klein, "Eliakim, Steward of Joiachin," *BIES* 5 (1937-38) #3, IV. *[Jar Stamp]*

Howard Comfort, "Supplementary Sigillata Signatures in the Near East," *JAOS* 58 (1938) 30-60.

A. Reifenberg, "I. Ancient Jewish Stamps," *PEQ* 71 (1939) 193-194.

*Ruth B. Kallner, "Two Inscribed Sherds," *KSJA* 1 (1942) VII. [2. A Stamped Jar-handle]

*J. A. Thompson, "On Some Stamps and a Seal from Lachish," *BASOR* #86 (1942) 24-27.

E. L. Sukenik, "Note on a Jar Stamp Discovered at Tell Ed-Duweir," *PEQ* 74 (1942) 57.

*David Diringer, "Note on Some Jar-Stamps and Seals Discovered at Lachish," *PEQ* 75 (1943) 55-56.

E. L. Sukenik, "A Stamp of a Jewish Wine-Merchant from the Vicinity of Jerusalem," *KSJA* 2 (1945) V.

*E. L. Sukenik, "The Meaning of the 'Le-Melekh' Inscriptions," *KSJA* 2 (1945) VI. *[Jar Stamps]*

N. Avigad, "A 'Gezer' Stamp," *BIES* 13 (1946-47) #3/4, VI.

*I[mmanuel] Ben-Dor, "Two Hebrew Seals," *QDAP* 13 (1948) 64-67. [2. Two Stamped Jar-handles from Tell Judeida, pp. 66-67]

David Diringer, "The Royal Jar-Handle Stamps of Ancient Judah," *BA* 12 (1949) 70-86. [Jar-Handle Stamps; The First Discoveries; The Impressions; The Four-Winged Symbol; The Two-Winged Symbol; The Reform of Josiah; The Inscriptions; The Script; Interpretation; Royal Potteries; Royal Emblems; Date of the Royal Stamps]

Sylvester J. Saller, "Stamped impressions on the Pottery of Bethany," *SBFLA* 3 (1952-53) 5-39.

James Muilenberg, "A Hyksos Scarab Jar Handle from Bethel," *BASOR* #136 (1954) 20-21.

*A. Reifenberg, "Hebrew Seals and Stamps IV," *IEJ* 4 (1954) 139-142.

N. Avigad, "A New Class of *Yehud* Stamps," *IEJ* 7 (1957) 146-153.

Faraj Basmachi, "Two Stamp Seals," *Sumer* 13 (1957) 58.

James B. Pritchard, "The Inscribed Jar-Handles from Gibeon," *AJA* 62 (1958) 225.

G. W. Van Beek and A. Jamme, "A South-Arabian Clay Stamp from Bethel," *BASOR* #151 (1958) 9-16.

N. Avigad, "A New Class of *Yehud* Stamps," *BIES* 22 (1958) #1/2, I.

Y. H. Landau, "A Stamped Jar-Handle from Jaffa," *'Atiqot* 2 (1959) 186-187.

Howard Comfort, "An Arretine-Type Signature from Lezoux," *AJA* 63 (1959) 179-180.

Y[ohanan] Aharoni, "Some More *YHWD* Stamps," *IEJ* 9 (1959) 55-56.

James B. Pritchard, "More Inscribed Jar Handles from el-Jib," *BASOR* #160 (1960) 2-6.

Philip C. Hammond, "An Ammonite Stamp Seal from 'Amman," *BASOR* #160 (1960) 38-41.

Y[ohanan] Aharoni, "Hebrew Jar-Stamps from Ramat Raḥel," *EI* 6 (1960) 28*.

G. W. Van Beek, "The South-Arabian Clay Stamp from Bethel Again," *BASOR* #163 (1961) 15-18. [Note by A. Jamme, p. 18]

Paul W. Lapp, "Ptolemaic Stamped Handles from Judah," *BASOR* #172 (1963) 22-35.

*A. Millett, J. B. Pritchard and E. K. Ralph, "A Spectrographic Investigation of Jar Handles Bearing the 'Royal' Stamp of Judah," *Archm* 7 (1964) 67-71.

Briggs Buchanan, "The Prehistoric Stamp Seal. A Reconsideration of Some Old Excavations," *JAOS* 87 (1967) 265-279, 525-540.

H. Neil Richardson, "A Stamped Handle from Khirbet Yarmuk," *BASOR* #192 (1968) 12-16.

Yigael Yadin, "An Inscribed South-Arabian Clay Stamp from Bethel?" *BASOR* #196 (1969) 37-45.

Frank Moore Cross Jr., "Judean Stamps," *EI* 9 (1969) 20-27. *[Non-Hebrew Section]*

§216 ***2.5.9.12.2 Scarabs, Engraved Gems, and Cartouches***

*†W. Wright, L.L.D., "On three Gems bearing Phoenician Inscriptions," *SBAP* 4 (1881-82) 54.

†W. Wright, L.L.D, "On Five Phoenician Gems," *SBAP* 5 (1882-83) 100-101. (Remarks by W. Wright, D.D., pp. 102-103)

W. H. Rylands, "Engraved Gem from Nineveh," *SBAP* 6 (1883-84) 228-229.

*Greville John Chester, "More Notes on Phoenician Gems and Amulets," *PEFQS* 18 (1886) 43-50.

*†F. Ll. Griffith, "Scarabs belonging to Mr. John Ward. The Khyan Group of Kings. The Israel Stela. Additional Notes to 'Egyptian Literature'," *SBAP* 19 (1897) 293-300.

†Walter L. Nash, "Scarab of Ahmes," *SBAP* 21 (1899) 80.

G. Willoughby Fraser, "Notes on Scarabs," *SBAP* 21 (1899) 148-157.

John Ward, "Egyptian Scarabs," *SBAP* 22 (1900) 274.

*A. H. Sayce, "(I) Objects from the Tomb of a Pre-dynastic Egyptian King; (II) Some early Egyptian Seal-cylinders," *SBAP* 22 (1900) 278-280.

*John Ward, "A Collection of Historical Scarabs and others, with a few Cylinders," *SBAP* 22 (1900) 305-320, 386-401.

James T. Dennis, "A Rare Royal Cartouche," *JAOS* 22 (1901) 78.

John Ward, "Mr. Ward's Collection of Scarabs," *SBAP* 23 (1901) 19-34, 79-91.

F. Ll. Griffith, "The Faser Scarabs," *SBAP* 23 (1901) 137-139.

A[lice] Grenfell, "Note on Scarab 384, Plate XV in Part 2, Vol. XXIII of the *Proceedings* (Belonging to Mr. John Ward)," *SBAP* 23 (1901) 139-141.

*Alice Grenfell, "The Iconography of Bes, and of Pheonician Bes-Hand Scarabs," *SBAP* 24 (1902) 21-40.

*W. L. Nash, "A Ring with the Cartouche of Nefer-ti-ti," *SBAP* 24 (1902) 309.

*W. [M.] Flinders Petrie, "Description of the Scarabs and Weights," *PEFQS* 34 (1902) 365. *[Weights and Scarabs found at Gezer]*

*Percy E. Newberry, "Extracts from my Notebooks. VII," *SBAP* 25 (1903) 357-362. [57. Some Miscellaneous Antiquities, pp. 361-362 (*Scarab, p. 362*)]

*C. de W. Brower, "The Beetle that Influenced a Nation," *RP* 3 (1904) 73-79. *[Scarab]*

*Anonymous, "The Entomology of the Scarab," *RP* 3 (1904) 375.

Garrett Chatfield Pier, "Typical Middle Kingdom Scarabs," *AJSL* 22 (1905-06) 41-42.

Garrett Chatfield Pier, "Historical Scarab Seals from the Art Institute Collection, Chicago," *AJSL* 23 (1906-07) 75-94.

Anonymous, "Scarab Added to the Boston Museum of Fine Arts," *RP* 6 (1907) 191.

*A[lice] Grenfell, "Amuletic Scarabs, etc., for the deceased," *RTR* 30 (1908) 105-120.

A[lice] Grenfell, "The rarer scarabs of the New Kingdom," *RTR* 32 (1910) 113-136.

*Percy E. Newberry, "Egyptian Historical Notes. II," *SBAP* 36 (1914) 35-39. [9. Some Small Historical Antiquities, pp. 36-39 (*Scarabs, pp. 37-39*)]

*Percy E. Newberry, "Egyptian Historical Notes. III," *SBAP* 36 (1914) 168-174. [17. Some Small Historical Antiquities, pp. 170-174 *[Scarabs]*]

*W. L. Nash, "A Scarab and a Leaden Sling-bolt from Samaria," *SBAP* 36 (1914) 278-279.

Alice Grenfell, "The Scarab Collection of Queen's College, Oxford," *JEA* 2 (1915) 217-228.

*Alice Grenfell, "The Ka on Scarabs," *RTR* 37 (1915) 77-93.

W. M. F[linders] P[etrie], "The Grenfell Collection of Scarabs," *AEE* 3 (1916) 22-31.

Joseph Offord, "Palestinian Scarabs," *PEFQS* 50 (1918) 175-179.

Wm. [M.] Flinders Petrie, "Palestinian Scarabs," *PEFQS* 51 (1919) 46.

Arthur C. Mace, "A Group of hitherto Unpublished Scarabs in the Metropolitan Museum, New York,"*JEA* 7 (1921) 36-38.

A. C. Mace, "A Group of Scarabs found at Lisht," *JEA* 8 (1922) 13-15.

*G. D. Hornblower, "Some Hyksos Plaques and Scarabs," *JEA* 8 (1922) 201-206.

[W. M.] Flinders Petrie, "Types of Early Scarabs," *AEE* 8 (1923) 65-66.

[W. M.] Flinders Petrie, "The Spencer-Churchill Scarabs," *AEE* 11 (1926) 12-14.

Militza Matthieu, "Some Scarabs from South of Russia," *AEE* 11 (1926) 68-69.

W. Spiegelberg, "A Heart Scarab of the Mnevis Bull," *JEA* 14 (1928) 12.

E. L. Sukenik, "An Israelite Gem from Samaria," *PEFQS* 60 (1928) 51.

Alan W. Shorter, "Historical Scarabs of Thuthmosis IV and Amenophis III,"*JEA* 17 (1931) 23-25.

*P. E. Newberry, "Miscellanea," *JEA* 18 (1932) 141-142. *[Scarabs]*

[W. M.] Flinders Petrie, "Rare Scarabs," *AEE* 18 (1933) 37-38.

*Percy E. Newberry, "A Statue and a Scarab," *JEA* 19 (1933) 53-54.

S. H. Hooke, "A Scarab and Sealing from Tell Duweir," *PEFQS* 67 (1935) 195-197.

*F. A. Bannister and H. J. Plenderleith, "Physico-Chemical Examination of a Scarab of Tuthmosis IV bearing the name of the God Aten," *JEA* 22 (1936) 3-6.

S. H. Hooke, "Supplementary Note on Tel Duweir Scarab," *PEFQS* 68 (1936) 38.

Donald F. Brown, "A Graeco-Phoenican Scarab from Byblos," *AJA* 40 (1936) 345-347.

*A. Rowe, "Addendum No. 1 on Egypto-Canaanite Contacts (*A Catalogue of Egyptian Scarabs, &c., in the Palestine Archaeological Museum,* 1936)," *QDAP* 8 (1939) 72-76.

*Frederick O. Waagé, "Potters' Stamps in Samian and Pergamene Wares," *AJA* 41 (1937) 115-116.

R. Engelbach, "A new method of exhibiting scarabs and kindred objects," *ASAE* 40 (1940-41) 591-593.

R. Engelbach, "A 'Kirgipa' commemorative Scarab of Amenophis III presented by His Majesty King Farouk I to the Cairo Museum," *ASAE* 40 (1940-41) 658-661.

Rudolph Reitler, "A Theriomorphic Representation of Hekate-Artemis," *AJA* 53 (1949) 29-31.

M[argaret] A. Murray, "Some Canaanite Scarabs," *PEQ* 81 (1949) 92-99.

A. J. Arkell, "Scarab from Sennar," *Antiq* 25 (1951) 96.

J. Leibovitch, "Description of the Scarabs found in a Cemetery near Tel Aviv," *'Atiqot* 1 (1955) 13-18.

Olga Tufnell, "'Hyksos' Scarabs from Canaan," *AS* 6 (1956) 67-73.

Nimet Özgüç, "Seals from Kültepe," *A(A)* 4 (1959) 43-53.

Kemal Balkan, "Inscribed Bullae from Daskyleion-Ergili," *A(A)* 4 (1959) 123-128.

*Manfred Cassirer, "A Scarab with an Early Representation of Resheph," *JEA* 45 (1959) 6-7.

*J. Gwyn Griffiths, "Seth or Anubis?" *JWCI* 22 (1959) 367. (Rejoinder by A. A. Barb, pp. 367-371) [B. M. 48954 (gem)]

Alan R. Schulman, "Three Ship-wrecked Scarabs," *Exped* 3 (1960-61) #4, 24-25.

Dorothy Kent Hill, "Gem Pictures," *Arch* 15 (1962) 121-125. *[Scarabs]*

Siegfried H. Horn, "Scarabs from Shechem," *JNES* 21 (1962) 1-14.

*Henry G. Fischer, "Varia Aegyptiaca," *JARCE* 2 (1963) 17-51. [6. A Frequently Copied Scarab, pp. 39-41]

*W[illiam] A. Ward, "Cylinders & Scarabs from a Late Bronze Temple at 'Amman," *ADAJ* 8&9 (1964) 47-55.

*William A. Ward, "Scarabs, Seals and Cylinders from two Tombs at Amman," *ADAJ* 11 (1966) 5-18.

Siegfried H. Horn, "Scarabs and Scarab Impressions from Shechem—II," *JNES* 25 (1966) 48-56.

S. I. Hodzhash, "A Scarab of the Vizier Mont(u)hotp from the Pushkin Museum Collection," *VDI* (1967) #3, 64-65.

*William C. Brice, "Epigraphische Mitteilungen," *KZFE* 7 (1968) 180-181. [Cretan Glyptic and Cave Art, p. 180]

*Edith Porada, "Cylinder Seals from Enkomi, Cyprus, and a Re-appraisal of Early Glyptic Art in Cyprus," *AJA* 73 (1969) 244.

*Geoffrey T. Martin, "A Ruler of Byblos of the Second Intermediate Period," *Bery* 18 (1969) 81-83. *[Scarab]*

§217 ***2.5.9.13 Sceptres, Staffs, and Standards***

*H. D. Rawnsley, "Note," *PEFQS* 13 (1881) 124-125. *[Egyptian Staff head]*

C. G. Seligmann*[sic]* and Margaret A. Murray, "Note upon an Early Egyptian Standard," *Man* 11 (1911) #97.

C. G. Seligman, "The Uas Scepture as a Beduin Camel Stick," *JEA* 3 (1915) 127.

*Percy E. Newberry, "The Shepherd's Crook and the so-called 'Flail' or 'Scourge' of Osiris," *JEA* 15 (1929) 84-94. *[Symbols of Royalty]*

L. H. Dudley Buxton, Stanley Casson, and J. L. Myres, "A Cloisonné Staff-head from Cyprus," *Man* 32 (1932) #1-#3.

J. D. Beazley, "Narthex," *AJA* 37 (1933) 400-403. *[Staff]*

*G. A. Wainwright, "The Bull Standards of Egypt," *JEA* 19 (1933) 42-52.

Elie Borowski, "A Bronze Standard From Persia," *Arch* 5 (1952) 22-23.

*E. Douglas Van Buren, "The Sceptre, its Origin and Significance," *RAAO* 50 (1956) 101-103.

*Harald Ingholt, "The Parthian on the Augustus Statue of Prima Porta," *AJA* 64 (1960) 187. *[Standard]*

§218 ***2.5.9.14 Tools***

*R[ichard] F. Burton, "On Anthropological Collections from the Holy Land. No. II," *JRAI* 1 (1871-72) 321-342. [Note on the Implements from Bethlehem by John Evans, pp. 342-344 (Discussion, pp. 344-345)]

*C. F. Tyrwitt Drake, "Note on Collection of Flints and Skulls brought from Palestine," *JRAI* 4 (1874-75) 14-15 [Remarks by A. W. Franks, pp. 15-17. (Discussion, p. 18)]

John Lubbock, "Notes on the Discovery of Stone Implements in Egypt," *JRAI* 4 (1874-75) 215-222. (Discussion, p. 222)

Richard F. Burton, "Flint Flakes from Egypt," *JRAI* 7 (1877-78) 323-324.

A. J. Jukes Browne, "On some Flint Implements from Egypt," *JRAI* 7 (1877-78) 396-411. (Discussion, pp. 411-412)

*R. F. Burton, "Stones and Bones from Egypt and Midian," *JRAI* 8 (1878-79) 290-319. *[Tools]*

John Lubbock, "Note on a Stone Implement of Palæolithic Type Found in Algeria," *JRAI* 10 (1880-81) 316-319.

R. P. Greg, "I. Neolithic Flint Implements of the Nile Valley and Egypt," *JRAI* 10 (1880-81) 424-428.

[A.] Pitt Rivers, "On the Discovery of Chert Implements in the Stratified Gravel in the Nile Valley near Thebes," *JRAI* 11 (1881-82) 382-394. [Extracts of a letter by J. F. Campbell, pp. 394-397]

H. Villiers-Stuart, "Exhibition of Flint Instruments from Egypt," *SBAP* 5 (1882-83) 97-98.

*†E. A. [Wallis] Budge, "Bronze Mould for Arrow Heads, found near Mossul, and now in the British Museum," *SBAP* 6 (1883-84) 109-110.

*A. C. Merriam, "Ancient Terra-Cotta Whorls," *AJA, O.S.,* 1 (1885) 160-161. *[Goldsmith's Mold]*

( ) Greenwell, "Note on Ancient Axe-heads Found at Beyrout and Sidon," *PEFQS* 22 (1890) 45.

C. E. Haskins, "On Homeric fishing-tackle," *JP* 19 (1890-91) 238-240.

*J. William Dawson, "Notes on Useful and Ornamental Stones of Ancient Egypt," *JTVI* 26 (1892-93) 265-282. (Discussion, pp. 282-288) [7. Flint Flakes, Knives, Saws, &c., pp. 279-282]

Theodore F. Wright, "Palestine Exploration," *AAOJ* 15 (1893) 169-170. *[Flint Knife]*

J[ohn] L. Myres, "Copper and Bronze in Cyprus and South-East Europe," *JRAI* 27 (1897-98) 171-177.

*Walter L. Nash, "A Wooden Handle for Small Cymbals, from Egypt," *SBAP* 22 (1900) 117-118.

W. M. Flinders Petrie, "Egyptian Cutting-out Tools," *Man* 1 (1901) #123.

E. Towry Whyte, "Egyptian 'Foundation Deposits' of Bronze and Wooden Model Tools," *SBAP* 24 (1902) 191.

*Percy E. Newberry, "Extracts from my Note-Books. V.," *SBAP* 24 (1902) 244-252. [35. An Inscribed Bronze Axe-head, pp. 250-251]

Anonymous, "Discovery of an Interesting Egyptian Tool," *RP* 2 (1903) 32. *[A Cold-Chisel]*

W. L. Nash, "A Relic of Amenhetep III," *SBAP* 25 (1903) 101. *[axe-handle]*

H. W. Seton-Kerr, "Fayoum Flint-implements," *ASAE* 5 (1904) 145-186.

J. Dyneley Prince, "The Pierpont Morgan Babylonian Axe-head," *JAOS* 26 (1905) 92-97.

H. R. Hall, "Palæolithic Implements from the Thebaïd," *Man* 5 (1905) #19, #42.

*Arthur E. P. Weigall, "Upper-Egyptian Notes," *ASAE* 9 (1908) 105-112. [14. An Inscribed Copper Chisel, p. 111]

W. M. Flinders Petrie, "String Nets of the XVII Dynasty," *Man* 9 (1909) #76.

H. S. Cooper, "On a Series of Small Worked Flints from Hilwan, Egypt," *Man* 11 (1911) #5.

R. A. S[tewart] Macalister, "Palaeolithic Implements from Palestine," *PEFQS* 44 (1912) 82-84.

E[dith] H. H[all], "A Bronze Blade from the Dictæan Cave, Crete," *MJ* 5 (1914) 169-172.

J. Reid Moir, "Some Flint Implements of Rostro-Carinate Form from Egypt," *Man* 18 (1918) #2.

W. M. Flinders Petrie, "Egyptian Palæoliths," *Man* 21 (1921) #78. *[Tools]*

M[argaret] A. Murray, "Stone Implements from Gorg en Nadur," *Man* 23 (1923) #38.

*Pere Alois Mallon, "Flint Implements and Megalithic Monuments," *BS* 81 (1924) 271-275. *(Trans. by W. F. Albright)*

*G. Caton-Thompson, "Preliminary Report on Neolithic Pottery and Bone Implements from the Northern Fayum Desert, Egypt," *Man* 25 (1925) #96.

*R. W. Sloley, "An Ancient Surveying Instrument," *AEE* 11 (1926) 65-67.

Ludwig Keimer, "An Ancient Egyptian Knife in Modern Egypt," *AEE* 13 (1928) 65-66.

H. R. Hall, "Some Egyptian Axeheads in the British Museum," *AAA* 16 (1929) 23-24.

*R. Engelbach, "A Repaired Steelyard," *AEE* 14 (1929) 46.

E. A. Marples, "The Copper Axe," *AEE* 14 (1929) 97-100.

R. Engelbach, "Evidence for the use of a Mason's Pick in Ancient Egypt," *ASAE* 29 (1929) 19-24.

J. Reid Moir, "Flint Implements of Lower Palæolithic Types from Palestine," *JRAI* 60 (1930) 485-499.

Anonymous, "A Collection of Sino-Scythian Knives," *UMB* 2 (1930-31) 95, 98.

*H. R. Hall, "The Oldest Representation of Horsemanship (?). An Egyptian Axe in the British Museum," *AAA* 18 (1931) 3-5.

O. G. S. C[rawford], "Palaeolithic Axes from Transjordan," *Antiq* 6 (1932) 216-217.

Gisela M. A. Richter, "Note on the Running Drill," *AJA* 37 (1933) 573-577.

Margharita Lane, "The Pull-Saw in Egypt," *AEE* 20 (1935) 55-58.

Harold L. Cleasby, "Thumb and Finger Pestles," *AJA* 40 (1936) 116.

Joan Crowfoot, "Notes on the Flint Implements of Jericho, 1936," *AAA* 34 (1937) 35-52.

Stanley Casson, "Note on the Use of the Claw-Chisel," *AJA* 41 (1937) 107.

*Zaki Y. Saad, "Handles for copper piercers or gaming pieces?" *ASAE* 38 (1938) 333-344. (Reply by Walter B. Emery, pp. 345-346)

G. E[rnest] Wright, "Flint and Metal Implements in Palestine during the Historical Period," *JBL* 57 (1938) xviii.

E. Henschel-Simon, "The 'Toggle-Pins' in the Palestine Archaeological Museum," *QDAP* 6 (1938) 169-209.

James R. Stewart, "Toggle Pins in Cyprus," *Antiq* 14 (1940) 204-209.

C. G. Seligman, "An Unusual Flint Implement from Egypt, in the Seligman Collection," *Man* 42 (1942) #62.

T. K. Penniman and Francis Knowles, "An Unusual Implement from Egypt in the Seligman Collection," *Man* 42 (1942) #95.

*Gisela M. A. Richter, "The Drove," *AJA* 47 (1943) 188-193.

H. H. Coghlan, "The Evolution of the Axe from Prehistoric to Roman Times," *JRAI* 73 (1943) 27-56.

T. H. Gaster, "On an Iron Axe from Ugarit," *PEQ* 75 (1943) 57-58.

Percy E. Newberry, "The 'Formido' employed in Hunting by the Egyptians of the Middle Kingdom," *JEA* 30 (1944) 75-76.

M[oshe] Stekelis, "Note on Some Flint Implements from the Seven Wells (Sab'a Biyar)," *QDAP* 11 (1945) 44-46.

E. Mustaki, "An unpublished copper adze-head of Ahmosis I," *ASAE* 45 (1947) 121-122.

*Alexander Badawy, "A collection of Foundation-Deposits of Tuthmosis IIIrd," *ASAE* 47 (1947) 145-156. [I.-Description of the Collection; II.-Were Those Tools Intended for Practical or Votive Purposes? III.-To Which Monument were Those Tools Dedicated?]

[K.] Rachel Maxwell-Hyslop, "Western Asiastic Shaft-hole Axes," *Iraq* 11 (1949) 90-130.

K. R[achel] Maxwell-Hyslop, "Notes on a Luristan Axe in the Otago Museum, New Zealand," *Iraq* 12 (1950) 52.

J. Waechter, "Notes on the Flints from Nahariya," *QDAP* 14 (1950) 42-43.

Dorothy A. E. Garrod, "A Transitional Industry from the Base of the Upper Palæolithic in Palestine and Syria," *JRAI* 81 (1951) 121-130.

[K.] Rachel Maxwell-Hyslop, "Note on Two Western Asiatic Bronze Axe-Heads," *Iraq* 14 (1952) 118-119.

C. Hillen, "A Note on Two Shaft-hole Axes," *BO* 10 (1953) 211-215.

[K.] Rachel Maxwell-Hyslop, "Bronze Lugged Axe-or Adze Blades from Asia," *Iraq* 15 (1953) 69-87.

*P. V. Glob, "The Flint Sites of the Bahrain Desert," *Kuml* (1954) 112-115.

K. R[achel] Maxwell-Hyslop, "Note on a Shaft-hole Axe-Pick from Khurab, Makran," *Iraq* 17 (1955) 161.

*F. E. Zeuner, "The Identity of the Camel on the Khurab Pick," *Iraq* 17 (1955) 162-163.

*D[orothy] A. E. Garrod, "The Mugharet el-Emireh in Lower Galilee: Type Station of the Emiran Industry," *JRAI* 85 (1955) 141-162.

Dorothy Kent Hill, "A Class of Bronze Handles of the Archaic and Early Classical Periods," *AJA* 60 (1956) 178.

W. Needler, "The Flint Knife of King Djer," *JEA* 42 (1956) 41-44.

Dorothy Kent Hill, "A Class of Bronze Handles of the Archaic and Classical Periods," *AJA* 62 (1958) 193-201.

M. Stekelis, "An Obsidian Core Found at Kibbutz Kabri," *EI* 5 (1958) 85*. *[Tool?]*

Ephrath Yeivin, "The Flint Implements from Horvat Beter (Beersheba)," *'Atiqot* 2 (1959) 43-47.

*Viggo Nielsen, "The Al Wusail Mesolithic Flint Sites at Qatar," *Kuml* (1961) 181-184.

*Hans Jørgen Madsen, "A Flint Site in Qatar," *Kuml* (1961) 197-201.

Muzaffar [Süleyman] Şenyürek and Enver Bostancı, "A Hand-Axe Used as a Nucleus," *TTKB* 25 (1961) 309-310.

George E. Mylonas, "Three Late Mycenaean Knives," *AJA* 66 (1962) 406-408.

*Ruth Hestrin and Miriam Tadmor, "A Hoard of Tools and Weapons from Kfar Monash," *IEJ* 13 (1963) 265-288.

E. S. Higgs, "A Hand Axe from Greece," *Antiq* 38 (1964) 54-55.

Axel Steensberg, "A Bronze Age Ard-Type from Hama in Syria Intended for Rope-Traction," *Bery* 15 (1964) 111-139.

*C. Nylander, "The Toothed Chisel in Pasargadae: Futher Notes on Old Persian Stonecutting," *AJA* 70 (1966) 373-376. [Achaemenian Problems II]

Richard S. Ellis, "A Note on some Ancient Near Eastern Linch Pins," *Bery* 16 (1966) 41-48.

*C. Nylander, "Clamps and chronology (Achaemenian Problems II)," *IA* 6 (1966) 130-146.

R. Gophna, "A Crescentic Axehead from Kfar Monash," *IEJ* 18 (1968) 47-49.

Abdul Qadir al-Tekrili, "The Flint and Obsidian Implements of Tell es-Sawwan," *Sumer* 24 (1968) 53-55.

M. H. Newcomer, "The Chamfered Pieces from Ksar Akil (Lebanon)," *ULBIA* 8&9 (1968-69) 191.

C. C. Lamberg-Karlovsky, "Further Notes on the Shaft-hole Pick-axe from Khurāb Makrān," *Iran* 7 (1969) 163-168.

Sönmez Kantman, "A Microanalytic Studty of some Ground Stone Artefacts[sic]* from Tilmen Höyük and Gedïklï-Karahöyük (Southeastern Anatolia). Contributions to Functional Typology," *Anat* 3 (1969-70) 139-145. *[Tools]*

§219 ***2.5.9.15 Toys, Games, and Musical Instruments [See also: §84 Amusements, Athletics, Entertainment, Games, Recreations ←]***

*E. Towry Whyte, "Egyptian Musical Instrument," *SBAP* 21 (1899) 143-144.

*Walter L. Nash, "A Wooden Handle for Small Cymbals, from Egypt," *SBAP* 22 (1900) 117-118.

*E. Towry Whyte, "Types of Egyptian Draughts-men," *SBAP* 24 (1902) 261-263.

*W. L. Nash, "Ancient Egyptian Draughts-boards and Draughts-men," *SBAP* 24 (1902) 341-348.

*Waldo S. Pratt, "Music and Musical Instruments in the Bible," *HR* 57 (1909) 53-55.

Stephen B. Luce Jr.*[sic]*, "A Greek Jointed Doll," *MJ* 8 (1917) 186-187.

*N. de Garis Davies, "An Alabaster Sistrum dedicated by King Teta," *JEA* 6 (1920) 69-72.

*Sol Baruch Finesinger, "Musical Instruments in the O.T.," *HUCA* 3 (1926) 21-76.

*L. B. Ellis, "The Sistrum of Isis," *AEE* 12 (1927) 19-25.

*L[eon] L[egrain], "Old Sumerian Art," *MJ* 19 (1928) 221-247. [The Harp, pp. 235-241]

*H[enry] G[eorge] Farmer, "Ancient Egyptian Instruments of Music," *GUOST* 6 (1929-33) 30-34.

Kate McK. Elderkin, "Jointed Dolls in Antiquity," *AJA* 34 (1930) 455-479.

*Anita E. Klein, "Some Greek Playthings," *PAPA* 62 (1931) xxvii-xxviii.

*W[illiam] F[oxwell] Albright, "A Set of Egyptian Playing Pieces and Dice from Palestine," *Miz* 1 (1933) 130-134.

*E. Douglas Van Buren, "A Gaming Board from Tall Ḫalaf," *Iraq* 4 (1937) 11-15.

*Zaki Y. Saad, "Handles for copper piercers or gaming pieces?" *ASAE* 38 (1938) 333-344. (Reply by Walter B. Emery, pp. 345-346)

*M. E. L. Mallowan, "A Mesopotamian Trilogy," *Antiq* 13 (1939) 159-170. *(Review)* [Musical Instruments, pp. 167-170]

*R. G. Austin, "Greek Board Games," *Antiq* 14 (1940) 257-271.

*Nicholas B. Bodley, "The Auloi of Meroë," *AJA* 50 (1946) 217-240.

P. R. Kirby, "The Trumpets of Tut-Ankh-Amen and their Sucessors," *JRAI* 77 (1947) 33-45.

*P. R. Kirby, "The Trumpets of Tut-ankh-amen and their Successors," *Man* 49 (1949) #13.

A. J. Arkell, "The use of *Nerita* shells in early times," *ASAE* 50 (1950) 365-366. *[Whistle(?)]*

*Winifred Needler, "A Thirty-Square Draught-Board in the Royal Ontario Museum," *JEA* 39 (1953) 60-75.

*Henry R. Immerwahr, "An Inscribed Terracotta Ball in Boston," *GRBS* 8 (1967) 255-266.

§220 ***2.5.9.16 Weapons (Includes Knives) [See also: §101 Defense and Warfare ←]***

*W. St. Chad Boscawen, “Notes on an Ancient Assyrian Bronze Sword bearing a Cuneiform Inscription,” *SBAT* 4 (1875) 347-348.

[A.] Pitt Rivers, “On the Egyptian Boomerang and its Affinities,” *JRAI* 12 (1882-83) 454-463.

*†E. A. [Wallis] Budge, “Bronze Mould for Arrow Heads, found near Mossul, and now in the British Museum,” *SBAP* 6 (1883-84) 109-110.

F. G. Hilton Price, “Notes upon some Ancient Egyptian Implements,” *JRAI* 14 (1884-85) 56-64. *[Bronze Arrow Heads]*

*Henry W. Haynes, “Correspondence. Odysseus’ Feat of Archery,” *AJA, O.S.,* 6 (1890) 487.

Henry Balfour, “On a Remarkable Ancient Bow and Arrows believed to be of Assyrian Origin,” *JRAI* 26 (1896-97) 210-220.

J. E. Quibell, “Flint Dagger from Gebelein,” *ASAE* 2 (1901) 131-132.

*Percy E. Newberry, “Extracts from my Notebooks (IV),” *SBAP* 23 (1901) 218-224. [25. Handle of a Model Dagger (?) and a Plaque inscribed with the name of Bak-en-Khensu, p. 222]

Selah Merrill, “Ancient Arrows in the Castle of David,” *PEFQS* 34 (1902) 106.

*C. Clermont-Ganneau, “Archaeological and Epigraphic Notes on Palestine. 15. *The Depository of Ancient Arrows in the Castle of David,*” *PEFQS* 34 (1902) 136-137.

*A. H. Sayce, “Notes from Egypt,” *SBAP* 24 (1902) 86. *[Bronze dagger from Saqquara]*

A. H. Sayce, “Notes and Queries. 3. *The Bronze Scimitar,*” *PEFQS* 37 (1905) 88.

*Arthur E. P. Weigall, “Report on Some Objects recently found in Sebakh and other Diggings,” *ASAE* 8 (1907) 40-50. [Prehistoric Celt from Gebelên, pp. 42-43; Archaic Celt from Saḳḳâra, p. 43]

H. W. Seton-Kerr, "On a Maul from Upper Egypt," *Man* 7 (1907) #5.

*J. L. Myers, "A Tomb of the Early Iron Age, from Kition in Cyprus, containing Bronze Examples of the 'Sigynna' or Cypriot Javelin," *AAA* 3 (1910) 107-117.

*W. L. Nash, "A Scarab and a Leaden Sling-bolt from Samaria," *SBAP* 36 (1914) 278-279.

Walton Brooks McDaniel, "The So-Called Bow-Puller of Antiquity," *AJA* 22 (1918) 25-43.

Georges Bénédite, "The Carnarvon Ivory," *JEA* 5 (1918) 1-15, 225-241. *[Knife Handle]*

M[argaret] A. Murray, "The First Mace-Head of Hierakonpolis," *AEE* 5 (1920) 15-17.

*H. R. Hall, "The Discoveries at Tell el 'Obeid in Southern Babylonia and Some Egyptian Comparisons," *JEA* 8 (1922) 241-257. *[Mace Heads]*

V. Gordon Childe, "The Stone Battle-axes from Troy," *Man* 24 (1924) #51.

G. A. Wainwright, "A dagger of the Early New Kingdom," *ASAE* 25 (1925) 135-143.

Warren R. Dawson, "A Bronze Dagger of the Hyksos Period," *JEA* 11 (1925) 216-217.

Harold Peake, "The Stone Battle-Axe," *Man* 27 (1927) #112.

*E[phraim] A. Speiser, "Some Prehistoric Antiquities from Mesopotamia," *JQR, N.S.*, 19 (1928-29) 345-354. *[Stone Weapons]*

[W. M.] Flinders Petrie, "Daggers with Inlaid Handles," *AEE* 15 (1930) 97-102.

*William Nickerson Bates, "Two Inscribed Slingers' Bullets from Galatista," *AJA* 34 (1930) 44-46.

Sylvia Benton, "An unlucky Sword: the leaf-shaped blade from Mycenæ," *Man* 31 (1931) #134.

Anonymous, "Notes and Comments. The Resurrection of a Bronze Ægis in Boston after Nearly Three Millennia," *A&A* 33 (1932) 109-110.

Stanley Casson, "Battle-axes from Troy," *Antiq* 7 (1933) 337-339.

*O. H. Myers, "Two Prehistoric Objects," *JEA* 19 (1933) 55. *[Lance Head]*

E[phraim] A. Speiser, "An Inscribed Lance-butt from Tell Billah V," *BASOR* #50 (1933) 11-13.

R. W. Hutchinson, "Two Mesopotamian Daggers and their Relatives," *Iraq* 1 (1934) 163-170.

J. G. D. Clark, "Flint Arrow-Heads from the Grave of Mes-kalam-dug, Ur," *Antiq* 9 (1935) 210-215.

David Randall-MacIver, "The Iron Spear of Buhen,"*Antiq* 9 (1935) 348-350.

Theophile J. Meek, "Bronze Swords from Luristan," *BASOR* #74 (1939) 7-11.

[Alan H. Gardiner], "Tutʿankhamūn's Gold Dagger," *JEA* 27 (1941) 1.

Sarah Elizabeth Freeman, "A Copper Dagger of the Middle Bronze Age in Baltimore," *BASOR* #90 (1943) 28-30.

Harry Craig Richardson, "A Mitannian Battle Axe from Ras Shamra," *Bery* 8 (1943) 72.

*Helene J. Kantor, "The Final Phase of Predynastic Culture: Gerzean or Semainean(?)," *JNES* 3 (1944) 110-136. [Knife Handles showing Human Beings, pp. 119-127 (Note by Linda Braidwood, pp. 120-122)]

[K.] Rachel Maxwell-Hyslop, "Daggers and Swords in Western Asia: A Study from Prehistoric Times to 600 B.C.," *Iraq* 8 (1946) 1-65.

*Kurt Galling, "The Scepter of Wisdom, A Note on the Gold Sheath of Zendjirli and Ecclesiastes 12:11," *BASOR* #119 (1950) 15-18.

*Thomas T. Hoopes, "A Crested Helmet from Italy," *AJA* 56 (1952) 174.

Joseph Ternbach, "The Archaic Greek Helmet in St. Louis," *Arch* 5 (1952) 40-46.

Winifred Needler, "An Egyptian Battle-Axe," *Arch* 5 (1952) 48-50.

Henri Seyrig, "A Helmet from Emisa," *Arch* 5 (1952) 66-69.

Hugh Hencken, "Some Early Helmets," *AJA* 57 (1953) 107.

*J. T. Milik and Frank M. Cross Jr., "Inscribed Javelin-Heads from the Period of the Judges: A Recent Discovery in Palestine," *BASOR* #134 (1954) 5-15.

Claude F. A. Schaeffer, "A Bronze Sword from Ugarit with a cartouche of Minepth (Ras Shamra, Syria)," *Antiq* 29 (1955) 226-229.

F[rank] M. Cross Jr. and J. T. Milik, "A Typological Study of the el Khadr Javelin- and Arrow- Heads," *ADAJ* 3 (1956) 15-23.

*J. T. Milik, "An Unpublished Arrow-head with Phoenician Inscriptions of the 11th-10th Century B.C.," *BASOR* #143 (1956) 3-6.

Tahsin Özgüç, "The Dagger of Anitta," *TTKB* 20 (1956) 33-36.

S. Yeivin, "An Inscribed Bronze Arrow-Head from the Lebanon Baqʿa," *BIES* 22 (1958) #3/4, n.p.n.

G. Radan, "Helmet Found Near Ascalon," *IEJ* 8 (1958) 185-188.

Wallace E. McLeod, "*ΤΡΙΓΛΩΧΙΣ*," *AJA* 64 (1960) 370-371. *[Three-barbed Arrows]*

J. Vercoutter, "A Dagger from Kerma," *Kush* 8 (1960) 265.

*D. Thomas-Goorieckx and R. Lefève, "Examination and Treatment of a Bronze Dagger with Ivory Hilt (± 1800 B.C.); property of the Khartoum Museum no. 1228; length 56 cm (Plates XXXV-XXXVII)," *Kush* 8 (1960) 266-267.

*Walter J. Beasley, "Boomerangs, Babel and Blood Relations," *AT* 5 (1960-61) #1, 13-19.

*W[alter] J. Beasley, "Boomerangs, Babel and Blood Relations. No. 2," *AT* 5 (1960-61) #2, 7-8, 13-14.

G. Radan, "A Greek Helmet Discovered off the Coast of Turkey," *IEJ* 11 (1961) 176-180.

*Awni K. Dajani, "Some of the Industries of the Middle Bronze Period," *ADAJ* 6&7 (1962) 55-75. [Weapons, pp. 55-66]

Winifred Needler, "A Dagger of Ahmose I," *Arch* 15 (1962) 172-175.

*Ruth Hestrin and Miriam Tadmor, "A Hoard of Tools and Weapons from Kfar Monash," *IEJ* 13 (1963) 265-288.

* J. Birmingham, N. F. Kennon, and A. S. Malin, "A 'Luristan' Dagger: An Examination of Ancient Metallurgical Techniques," *Iraq* 26 (1964) 44-49.

*K. R[achel] Maxwell-Hyslop and H. W. M. Hodges, "A Note on the Significance of the Technique of 'Casting On' as Applied to a Group of Daggers from North-West Persia," *Iraq* 26 (1964) 50-53.

*Dorothy Kent Hill, "A Helmet Tomb-Group of the Trebenischte Type," *AJA* 69 (1965) 169.

*Ezat O. Negahban, "The Treasures of Marlik," *Arch* 18 (1965) 109-112. *[Mace Head]*

Keith Branigan, "Byblite Daggers in Cyprus and Crete," *AJA* 70 (1966) 123-126.

K. R[achel] Maxwell-Hyslop and H. W. M. Hodges, "Three Iron Swords from Luristan," *Iraq* 28 (1966) 164-176.

Robert L. Alexander, "Restoration of Figured Mace-head from Mari," *AJA* 73 (1969) 231.

Wallace [E.] McLeod, "Were Egyptian Composite Bows Made in Asia?" *AJA* 73 (1969) 242.

Keith Branigan, "A Minoan Dagger from Gournia," *Antiq* 43 (1969) 137-138.

Gayle Wever, "A Persian Puzzle from Teheran," *Exped* 12 (1969-70) #1, 24-27. *[Sword]*

§221 *2.5.9.17 Drawing and Writing Instruments*
[See also: §82 Development of Writing ←]

*E. Towry Whyte, "An Egyptian Painter's Palette," *SBAP* 23 (1901) 130-131.

†E. Towry White, "Palette," *SBAP* 23 (1901) 257-258.

*Anonymous, "Remains of Roman Ink," *RP* 8 (1909) 318.

Percy E. Newberry, "Two Prehistoric Slate Palettes," *AAA* 4 (1911-12) 140.

Winifred M. Crompton, "A Carved Slate Palette in the Manchester Museum," *JEA* 5 (1918) 57-60.

*H. R. Hall, "An Egyptian Royal Bookplate: The *Ex Libris* of Amenophis III and Teie," *JEA* 12 (1926) 30-33.

*C. Ainsworth Mitchell, "Marking-Ink in Ancient Egypt," *AEE* 12 (1927) 18.

S. R. K. Glanville, "Scribes' palettes in the British Museum. (Part I)," *JEA* 18 (1932) 53-61.

Ernest S. Thomas, "Note on an Early Egyptian Slate Palette," *Man* 34 (1934) #144. (Correction, #189)

*William C. Hayes, "A Writing-Palette of the Chief Stewart Amenḥotpe and Some Notes on its Owner," *JEA* 24 (1938) 9-24.

*Doreen Canaday Spitzer, "Ancient Ink-wells," *AJA* 46 (1942) 125.

William C. Hayes, "Writing Palette of the High Priest of Amūn, Smendes," *JEA* 34 (1948) 47-50.

*D. J. Wiseman, "Assyrian Writing Boards," *Iraq* 17 (1955) 3-13.

Erik Sjöqvist, "Morgantina: Hellenistic Inkstands," *AJA* 63 (1959) 275-277.

J. R. Harris, "A new fragment of the battlefield palette," *JEA* 46 (1960)104-105.

§222 *2.5.9.18 Artifacts - Unclassified*

*A. H. Sayce, "(I) Objects from the Tomb of a Pre-dynastic Egyptian King; (II) Some early Egyptian Seal-cylinders," *SBAP* 22 (1900) 278-280.

R. Sewell, "Tiles from Mycenae, with the Cartouche of Amenhetep III," *SBAP* 26 (1904) 258-259.

Harold R. Hastings, "A Bronze-Age 'Pocket' from Avgo (Crete)," *AJA* 9 (1905) 277-293.

Anonymous, "Nile Boat Models," *RP* 6 (1907) 272.

*Percy E. Newberry, "The Wooden and Ivory Labels of the Ist Dynasty," *SBAP* 34 (1912) 279-289.

*E. J. Pilcher, "Portable Sundial from Gezer," *PEFQS* 55 (1923) 85-89.

Stephen Bleecker Luce, "Recent Classical Accessions of the Rhode Island School of Design," *AJA* 28 (1924) 73.

R. Engelbach, "The treasure of Athribis (Benha)," *ASAE* 24 (1924) 178-185.

G. A. Wainwright, "Antiquities from Middle Egypt and the Fayûm," *ASAE* 25 (1925) 144-148.

H. R. Hall, "Objects of Tut'ankhamūn in the British Museum," *JEA* 14 (1928) 74-77.

*Percy E. Newberry, "Miscellanea," *JEA* 14 (1928) 109-111. [IV. A Label of the First Dynasty, p. 110]

E[phraim] A. Speiser, "Traces of the oldest cultures of Babylonia and Assyria," *AfO* 5 (1928-29) 162-164. *[Artifacts]*

*I. Sneguireff, "Some Unpublished Egyptian Objects from Kertch, Olbia and Tiflis," *AEE* 14 (1929) 101-103.

*S. R. K. Glanville, "Some Notes on Material for the Reign of Amenophis III," *JEA* 15 (1929) 2-8.

*Anonymous, "Notes and Comments. A Foundation-Box from Tell Abu-Maria in Iraq," *A&A* 30 (1930) 190-191.

Anonymous, "Notes and Comments. The Pliny Relics Located," *A&A* 31 (1931) 186-187.

*W[illiam] F[oxwell] Albright, "On the Map Found at Nuzi," *BASOR* #42 (1931) 7-10.

A. Lucas, "Artificial Eyes in Ancient Egypt," *AEE* 18 (1934) 84-98.

M. A. M[urray], "Artificial Eyes in Petrie Collection, University College, London," *AEE* 18 (1934) 98-99.

*Anonymous, "New Egyptian Acquisitions in the Metropolitan Museum of Art," *AJA* 39 (1935) 1-4.

W. D. van Wijngaarden, "Objects of Tutʿankhamūn in the Rijksmuseum of Antiquities at Leiden," *JEA* 22 (1936) 1-2.

Dorothy Kent Hill, "Source Material for Archaeological Study at the Walters Art Gallery," *AJA* 41 (1937) 111-112.

*Leicester B. Holland, "Axones," *AJA* 45 (1941) 346-362. *[Triangular wooden shafts on which the original laws of Solon were supposedly inscribed]*

*A. Lucas, "Notes on some of the objects from the tomb of Tut-Ankhamun," *ASAE* 41 (1942) 135-147; 45 (1947) 133-134.

I. J. Gelb, "Oriental Museum Notes. A New Clay-Nail of Hammurabi," *JNES* 7 (1948) 267-271. *[No. 6]*

*Alan J. B. Wace, "A Mycenaean Mystery," *Arch* 13 (1960) 40-43.

Kate Bosse-Griffiths, "Finds from 'The Tomb of Queen Tiye' in the Swansea Museum," *JEA* 47 (1961) 66-70.

Cyrill Aldred, "The Harold Jones Collection," *JEA* 48 (1962) 160-162.

*W. Winton, "Bagdad Batteries B.C.," *Sumer* 18 (1962) 87-88.

*Albert Al-Haik, "The Rabbou'a Galvanic Cell," *Sumer* 20 (1964) 103-104.

Pinakia Dikastika, "A Summary History of Greek Allotment Plates," *AJA* 71 (1967) 191.

Yasin Mahmoud, "A Clay Mould in the Iraq Museum," *Sumer* 23 (1967) 183-187.

E. Dabrowska-Smektala, "List of Objects Found at Der el-Bahari in the Area of the Thuthmosis III's Temple Seasons 1962-63 and 1963-64," *ASAE* 60 (1968) 95-130.

*John H. Kroll, "Bronze Allotment Plates from Aeolis," *AJA* 73 (1969) 239.

Sönmez Kantman, "A Microanalytic Study of some Ground Stone Artefacts[sic]* from Tilmen Höyük and Gedïklï-Karahöyük (Southeastern Anatolia). Contributions on Functional Typology," *Anat* 3 (1969-70) 139-145.

§223 ***2.5.10 Art - General Studies***

*Anonymous, "Art and Architecture," *DUM* 33 (1849) 151-168.

E. C. Ravenshaw, "On the Winged Bulls, Lions, and other Symbolic Figures from Nineveh," *JRAS* 16 (1854) 93-117.

Anonymous, "Some Remains of Greek Art," *DUM* 89 (1877) 612-620.

*†W[illiam] Houghton, "The Birds of the Assyrian Records and Monuments," *SBAP* 4 (1881-82) 57-60.

W. St. C[had] Boscanten*[sic]*, "Babylonian and Assyrian Art," *AAOJ* 5 (1883) 322-330.

*†Theo[philus] G. Pinches, "Babylonian Art, illustrated by Mr. H. Rassam's latest discoveries," *SBAP* 6 (1883-84) 11-15.

*William Houghton, "The Birds of the Assyrian Monuments and Records," *SBAT* 8 (1883-84) 42-142.

John Phelps Taylor, "Modern Glimpses of Assyrian Art," *AR* 2 (1884) 269-278.

Theo[philus] G. Pinches, "Babylonian Art, illustrated by Mr. H. Rassam's latest Discoveries," *SBAT* 8 (1884-85) 347-357.

*William F. Warren, "The Gates of Sunrise in Ancient Babylonian Art," *BOR* 3 (1888-89) 241-244.

Edward B. Tylor, "The Winged Figures of the Assyrian and other Ancient Monuments," *SBAP* 12 (1889-90) 383-393.

*W[illiam] H[ayes] Ward, "The Dragon Tiamat in Babylonian and Assyrian Art," *JAOS* 14 (1890) clxviii-clxix.

*(Mrs.) E. A. Finn, "Mosaic and Embroidery in the Old Testament," *PEFQS* 22 (1890) 189-193.

*B. T. A. Evetts, "The Canephoros in Early Chaldaean Art," *SBAP* 13 (1890-91) 153-159.

*W[illiam] H[ayes] Ward, "The Babylonian Gods in Babylonian Art," *JAOS* 15 (1893) xv-xviii.

W. St. C[had] Boscawen, "Note on Persian Art," *BOR* 7 (1893-94) 160-161.

*J. Offord Jr., "The Nude Goddess in Assyrio-Babylonian Art," *SBAP* 18 (1896) 156-157.

C[laude] R. Conder, "Greek Art in Asia," *SRL* 30 (1897) 340-361.

*William Hayes Ward, "The Hittite Gods in Hittite Art," *AJA* 3 (1899) 1-39.

W. C. Wilson, "Ancient Egyptian Art in the Museums of America," *AAOJ* 22 (1900) 245-252. [Note by Stephen D. Peet, p. 250-252]

*William Hayes Ward, "The Goddesses in Primitive Babylonian Art," *AJA* 4 (1900) 169-170.

Henry Proctor, "Chalcan Art (M. De Morga's Discoveries at Susa.)," *AAOJ* 29 (1907) 101-103.

Anonymous, "Origin of Babylonian Human-Headed Bull," *RP* 8 (1909) 244.

*William Hayes Ward, "The Representation of Babylonian Gods in Art," *AJA* 14 (1910) 83-85.

*Jean De Mot, "The Devil Fish in Ancient Art," *RP* 9 (1910) 276-278.

*[Paul Carus], "Battle Scenes in Ancient Art," *OC* 26 (1912) 443-446.

E[dith] H. H[all], "Examples of Mycenæan and Minoan Art," *MJ* 5 (1914) 145-168.

*Charles Whymper, "Birds in Ancient Egyptian Art," *AEE* 2 (1915) 1-5.

*Elizabeth Hazelton Haight, "The Story of Cupid and Psyche. I—In Ancient Art," *A&A* 3 (1916) 43-53.

[W. M. Flinders Petrie], "The Portraits," *AEE* 3 (1916) 188-192.

Albert T. Clay, "The Art of the Akkadians," *A&A* 5 (1917) 69-92.

George S. Duncan, "The Art of Sumerians," *A&A* 5 (1917) 93-100.

Joseph Offord, "Archaeological Notes on Jewish Antiquities. XXXIV. *The New Catalogue of Palestinian Antiquities in the Louvre*," *PEFQS* 49 (1917) 140-142.

C. Hercules Read, "Presidental Address. Primitive Art and its Modern Developments," *JRAI* 48 (1918) 11-21.

*Lillian M. Wilson, "The Contributions of Greek Art to the Medusa Myth," *AJA* 24 (1920) 232-240.

Frederick Poulsen, "Glimpses into Greek Art," *A&A* 11 (1921) 248-250.

*Guido Calza, "Art and Archaeology in Italy in 1921," *A&A* 13 (1922) 217-230.

Leon Legrain, "The Art of the Oldest Civilization of the Euphrates Valley," *MJ* 15 (1924) 151-170.

*Stephen Bleecker Luce, "Nicosthenes: His Activity and Affiliations," *AJA* 29 (1925) 38-52.

*Hans Henning v. der Osten, "The Snake Symbol and the Hittite Twist," *AJA* 30 (1926) 405-417.

*Joseph Pijoan, "Art and Archaeology in the Movies," *A&A* 25 (1928) 267-275.

*P. Hippolyte-Boussac, "The Typhonic Dog," *A&A* 25 (1928) 181-185.

*Mabel Lea Hedge, "Biology as Portrayed in Ancient Art," *A&A* 25 (1928) 292-300.

L[eon] Legrain, "Old Sumerian Art," *MJ* 19 (1928) 221-247.

E. J. Forsdyke, "Minoan Art," *PBA* 15 (1929) 45-72.

*Carl L. Steinbicker, "The Tabernacle and Mosaic Art," *SS* 5 (1931) 21-35.

David Moore Robinson, "Mosaics from Olynthos," *AJA* 36 (1932) 16-24.

Anonymous, "The Gallery of Italic and Etruscan Art," *UMB* 4 (1932-33) 149-175.

M. Rostovtzeff, "Early Christian and Judaean Art in Mesopotamia: Recent Discoveries at Dura-Europos," *PBA* 19 (1933) 319-321.

Dows Dunham, "A 'Palimpsest' on an Egyptian Mastaba Wall," *AJA* 39 (1935) 300-309.

*George W. Elderkin, "Architectural Detail in Antique Sepulchral Art," *AJA* 39 (1935) 518-525.

E. Douglas Van Buren, "Entwined Serpents," *AfO* 10 (1935-36) 53-65.

L. D. Caskey, "Recent Acquisitions of the Museum of Fine Arts, Boston," *AJA* 41 (1937) 525-531.

*Oscar Broneer, "Recent Discoveries on the North Slope of the Acropolis in Athens," *AJA* 42 (1938) 161-164.

Oscar Broneer, "Discoveries on the North Slope of the Acropolis in Athens," *AJA* 42 (1938) 445-450.

*Franklin P. Johnson, "Stamnoi," *AJA* 45 (1941) 89-90.

J. P. G. Rinch, "The Winged Bulls at the Nergal Gate of Nineveh," *Iraq* 10 (1948) 9-18.

*Kathleen M. Kenyon, "Neolithic Portrait-Skulls from Jericho," *Antiq* 27 (1953) 105-107.

John D. Cooney, "Egyptian Art in the Collection of Albert Gallatin," *JNES* 12 (1953) 1-19.

George M. A. Hanfmann and Benjamin Rowland Jr., "Ancient Arts at the Fogg Museum," *Arch* 7 (1954) 130-137. (With contributions by Andrée Luce and Stuart Cary Welch Jr.)

Francis Follin Jones, "The Princeton Art Museum: *Antiquities Received in Recent Years,*" *Arch* 7 (1954) 237-243.

*E. Douglas Van Buren, "The Sun-God Rising," *RAAO* 49 (1955) 1-14.

Dorothy Kent Hill, "The Roman Collections of the *Walters* Art Gallery," *Arch* 10 (1957) 18-24.

Dericksen M. Binkerhoff, "Greek and Etruscan Art in the Museum of Rhode Island School of Design," *Arch* 11 (1958) 150-157.

*Hazel Palmer and Cornelius Vermeule, "Ancient Gold and Silver in the Museum of Fine Arts, Boston," *Arch* 12 (1959) 2-7.

*E[velyn] Brandt, "Early Sumerian Art and Culture," *NOP* 2 (1961) 165-168.

P. M. Fraser, "Some Alexandrian Forgeries," *PBA* 47 (1961) 243-250.

Michael Avi-Yonah, "Oriental Art in Roman Palestine," *SSR* 5 (1961) 1-103.

Herbert Hoffmann, "Ancient Art in the Hamburg Museum für Kunst und Gewerbe," *Arch* 15 (1962) 38-45.

R. Ghirschman, "The Exposition of Iranian Art in Paris," *Arch* 15 (1962) 50-53.

Briggs W. Buchanan, "Ancient Near Eastern Art in the Yale Babylonian Collection," *Arch* 15 (1962) 267-275.

Michael Milkovich, "Ancient Art in the Worcester Art Museum," *Arch* 16 (1963) 154-161.

*Tahsin Özgüç, "The Art and Architecture of Ancient Kanish," *A(A)* 8 (1964) 27-48.

Rodney S. Young, "Early Mosaics at Gordion," *Exped* 7 (1964-65) #3, 4-13.

Dorothy Burr Thompson, "*ΠΑΝΝΥΧΙΣ*," *JEA* 50 (1964) 147-163. *[Plaster Cast]*

Unberto Paradisi, "Prehistoric Art in the Gebel el-Akhdar (Cyrenaica)," *Antiq* 39 (1965) 95-101.

‡Margarete Bieber, "New Trends in the New Books on Ancient Art, 1958-1964," *GRBS* 6 (1965) 75-142.

*K. de B. Codrington, "Art for Archaeologists," *BJRL* 48 (1965-66) 98-117.

Anonymous, "Art Treasures of Turkey," *Arch* 19 (1966) 190-198.

Emmanuel Anati, "Anatolia's Earliest Art," *Arch* 21 (1968) 22-35.

R. D. Barnett, "The Art of Bactria and the Treasure of the Oxus," *IA* 8 (1968) 34-53.

E. J. Peltenburg, "Assyrian Clay Fists," *OA* 7 (1968) 57-62.

*William C. Brice, "Epigraphische Mitteilungen," *KZFE* 8 (1969) 164-167. [Cretan Cave Art, p. 164]

Charles K. Wilkinson, "The Problems of Authenticity in Ancient Near Eastern Art," *AJA* 73 (1969) 287.

§224 *2.5.10.1 History, Motifs, Philosophy, Style, and Theory of Art*

John Smythe Menes, "Fine Art Among the Jews," *JSL, 1st Ser.*, 3 (1849) 50-73.

*E. F. Rockwell, "Superiority of the Greeks in Literature and Fine Arts," *SPR* 15 (1862-63) 198-204.

*J. Estlin Carpenter, "Art and Literature in Egypt at the Time of the Exodus," *URRM* 4 (1875) 441-470.

*William Houghton, "On the Mammalia of the Assyrian Sculptures," *SBAT* 5 (1876-77) 33-64, 319-383.

*A. C. Merriam, "Ancient Terra-Cotta Whorls," *AJA, O.S.*, 1 (1885) 160-161. *[Motif]*

*J. Leslie Porter, "On the Connexion Between Jewish, Phoenician, and Early Greek Art and Architecture," *JTVI* 21 (1886-87) 23-41, 51-52. (Discussion, pp. 41-50)

*George Birdwood, "The Empire of the Hittites in the History of Art," *IAQR, 1st Ser.*, 5 (1888) 190-212.

[Barr Ferree], "Comparative Art. The Historical Origin of Art," *AAOJ* 13 (1891) 225-228.

W. St. C[had] B[oscawen], "Egyptian and Assyrian influence in Archaic Greek work," *BOR* 7 (1893-94) 120.

Anonymous, "Hebrew Art During the Exodus," *MR* 77 (1895) 646-648.

*†Anonymous, "Aristotle's Theory of Poetry and Fine Art," *ERCJ* 188 (1898) 60-77. *(Review)*

Carleton L. Brownson, "A Philosopher's Attitude toward Art," *AJA* 4 (1900) 174-175.

*Percy E. Newberry, "Extracts from my Notebooks (III).," *SBAP* 22 (1900) 142-154. [14. The Cornflower in Egyptian Art, pp. 141-144; 15. The Poppy in Egyptian Art, pp. 144-146]

*E. P. Andrews, "Color on the Parthenon and on the Elgin Marbles, recently Discovered Facts and Resultant Theories," *AJA* 5 (1901) 21-22.

*Mitchel Carroll, "Aristotle's Theory of Sculpture," *AJA* 5 (1901) 24.

William Hayes Ward, "The Rule of Symmetry in Early Oriental Art," *AJA* 7 (1903) 86-87.

*Percy E. Newberry, "Extracts from my Notebooks VII," *SBAP* 25 (1903) 357-362. [56. The Daisy in Egyptian Art, p. 361]

Anonymous, "The Evolution of the Lotus Ornament," *RP* 3 (1904) 375-376.

(Miss) Alicia M. Keyes, "The Acanthus Motive in Greek Decoration," *AJA* 9 (1905) 76.

*William Hayes Ward, "The Origin of Babylonian Civilization and Art," *AJA* 9 (1905) 77-79.

*G. Frederick Wright, "Early Art in Egypt," *RP* 4 (1905) 367-372.

W. Arthur Heidel, "The Type as the Subject of Greek Art," *MR* 88 (1906) 565-577.

Samuel Allen Jeffers, "The Birth of Venus: A Greek Relief and a Renaissance Painting," *RP* 5 (1906) 204-213.

*Charles C. Torrey, "Traces of Portraiture in Old Semitic Art," *AJA* 11 (1907) 63-64.

Anonymous, "The Limitations of Egyptian Art," *ERCJ* 210 (1909) 400-425. *(Review)*

*Anonymous, "The Lion in Ancient Art," *RP* 8 (1909) 57.

George E. White, "Note on the Swastika in Asia Minor," *RP* 8 (1909) 91-92.

D. Gath Whitley, "The High Artistic Power of Primeval Man," *RP* 8 (1909) 83-91.

Anonymous, "Position in Spartan Art," *RP* 9 (1910) 123.

*Edmund von Mach, "Classic Myths in Art," *AJA* 15 (1911) 70-71.

*Arthur E. P. Weigall, "Miscellaneous Notes," *ASAE* 11 (1911) 170-176. [3. The long-necked lions of archaic times, pp. 170-171.] *[Design origins]*

*P. S. Ronzevalle, "Some Examples of the Hunchbacked Ox in Syrian Art," *RP* 10 (1911) 317-321. *(Trans. by Helen M. Wright)*

Thomas M. Stewart, "Suggestion as to the Significance of the Cone on the Head of the Defunct in Egyptian Judgment Scenes," *RP* 11 (1912) 93-95.

[Paul Carus], "Evolution of Artistic Observation," *OC* 27 (1913) 17-24.

John E. Granrud, "Characteristics of Roman Art," *RP* 12 (1913) 3-13.

L. W. King, "Some New Examples of Egyptian Influence at Nineveh," *JEA* 1 (1914) 107-109, 237-240.

H. R. Hall, "The Relation of Aegean with Egyptian Art," *JEA* 1 (1914) 110-118, 197-206.

T. Eric Peet, "The Art of the Predynastic Period," *JEA* 2 (1915) 88-94.

[Paul Carus], "Greece, the Mother of All Religious Art," *OC* 29 (1915) 32-41.

*Alan Ball, "The Comic Beast in Roman Art," *A&A* 3 (1916) 99-105.

*Alan Ball, "The Comic Beast in Roman Art (Concluded)," *A&A* 3 (1916) 153-163.

Ernest Mackay, "The Origin of Polychrome Boarders: A Suggestion," *AEE* 3 (1916) 169-173.

*Boyd Dawkins, "The Antiquity of Man and the Dawn of Art in Europe," *ERCJ* 224 (1916) 80-98.

Ernest Mackay, "Proportional Squares on Tomb Walls in the Theban Necropolis," *JEA* 4 (1916) 74-85.

F. B. Tarbell, "Centauromancy and Amazonomachy in Greek Art: The Reasons for Their Popularity," *AJA* 24 (1920) 226-231.

*Margaret C. Waites, "The Nate of the Lares and Their Representation in Roman Art," *AJA* 24 (1920) 241-261.

*Warren R. Dawson, "Egyptological Notes," *IAQR* 16 (1920) 337-340, 520-522. [4. The Critical Study of Egyptian Art, pp. 521-522]

*Rhys Carpenter, "Dynamic Symmetry: A Criticism," *AJA* 25 (1921) 18-36.

*Gisela M. A. Richter, "Dynamic Symmetry from the Designer's Point of View," *AJA* 26 (1922) 59-73. [Professor Carpenter's Reply, pp. 74-76; Rejoinder, by Gisela M. A. Richter, p. 76]

E. J. A. Mackay, "Note on a Scene in Tomb 85 at Thebes," *JPOS* 2 (1922) 171-174.

L[eon] Legrain, "The Sumerian Art Shop," *MJ* 19 (1923) 378-402.

*Kate Denny McKnight, "The Persistence of Egyptian Traditions in Art and Religion After the Pharaohs," *A&A* 17 (1924) 43-53.

F. P. Johnson, "Right and Left in Roman Art," *AJA* 28 (1924) 399-401.

H. R. Fairclough, "Greek Art as an Expression of Love of Nature," *AJA* 33 (1929) 100-101.

C. Leonard Woolley, "Notes on the Inlay Standard," *MJ* 20 (1929) 99-100. [Remarks by C. Leonard Woolley with a rejoinder by Leon Legrain, p. 100]

*Edith M. Guest, "The Influence of Egypt on the Art of Greece," *AEE* 15 (1930) 45-54.

Corinne Frazier, "Moukhtar and the Renaissance in Egypt," *A&A* 31 (1931) 207-212, 223. *[Influence of Egypt on Modern Art]*

Ernestine F. Leon, "Children in Ancient Art," *A&A* 33 (1932) 141-145.

H[enri] Frankfort, "On Egyptian Art," *JEA* 18 (1932) 33-48.

Elaine Tankard, "The art of the 'Amarnah Period," *JEA* 18 (1932) 49.

*E. T. Richmond, "'Loop Pattern' Decorating Lead Sarcophagi," *QDAP* 1 (1932) 36.

*E[dith] M. Guest, "Pathology and Art at El Amarna," *AEE* 18 (1933) 81-88.

*Stanley Casson, "Technique of Greek Sculpture," *AJA* 38 (1934) 280-284.

Neilson C. Debevoise, "The Essential Characteristics of Parthian and Sasanian Glyptic Art," *Bery* 1 (1934) 12-18.

*F. J. Stephens, "The Gesture of Attentive Humility in the Old Testament and in Babylonian Art," *JBL* 53 (1934) xi.

*E. Douglas Van Buren, "A Problem of Early Sumerian Art," *AfO* 10 (1935) 237-251.

Richard Bernheimer, "Sumerian Art and the Christian Lamb with the Cross," *AJA* 39 (1935) 112-113.

*George W. Elderkin, "Architectural Detail in Antique Sepulchral Art," *AJA* 39 (1935) 518-525.

*M. Narkiss, "The Snuff-Shovel as a Jewish Symbol. (A Contribution to the problem of Jewish decorative motifs)," *JPOS* 15 (1935) 14-28.

Michael I. Rostovtzeff, "Dura and the Problem of Parthian Art," *YCS* 5 (1935) 155-304.

Frank H. Blackburn, "An Optical Illusion at Khorsabad," *AJSL* 52 (1935-36) 114-116.

William F. Edgerton, "Neglect of the Unity of Time by Egyptian Artists," *AJA* 40 (1936) 124.

G. W. Elderkin, "A Dionysiac Personification in Comedy and Art," *AJA* 40 (1936) 348-351.

Hazel D. Hansen, "The Use of Wings as an Attribute in Greek Art," *AJA* 40 (1936) 120.

*D. Talbot Rice, "Art History as a Key to Racial Migration: A New Field for Research," *Antiq* 10 (1936) 146-153.

Clark Hopkins, "Aspects of Parthian Art in the Light of Discoveries from Dura-Europos," *Bery* 3 (1936) 1-30.

William F. Edgerton, "Two Notes on the Flying Gallop," *JAOS* 56 (1936) 178-188.

Paul Romanoff, "When Was Art (Mural and Mosaics) Legally Permitted to the Jews?" *JBL* 55 (1936) xvii.

*C. A. Robinson Jr., "The Development of Archaic Greek Sculpture," *AJA* 41 (1937) 110.

*George M. A. Hanfmann, "Gigantomacy," *AJA* 41 (1937) 113-114.

Kurt Pflüger, "The Art of the Third and Fifty Dynasties," *JEA* 23 (1937) 7-9.

*E. Douglas Van Buren, "The Scorpion in Mesopotamian Art and Religion," *AfO* 12 (1937-39) 1-28.

*C. A. Robinson Jr., "The Development of Archaic Greek Sculpture," *AJA* 42 (1938) 451-455.

Valentin Müller, "The Origin of the Early Dynastic Style (Studies in Oriental Archaeology II)," *JAOS* 58 (1938) 140-147.

J. W. Flight, "Art in the Period of the Judges," *JBL* 57 (1938) xix.

*D. H. Gordon, "The Buddhist Origin of the 'Sumerian' Heads from Memphis," *Iraq* 6 (1939) 35-38.

*R. D. Barrett, "The Hawk in Phoenicia," *Iraq* 6 (1939) 100.

Valentin Müller, "The Origin of Mosaic," *JAOS* 59 (1939) 247-250.

E. Douglas Van Buren, "The Seven Dots in Mesopotamian Art and their Meaning," *AfO* 13 (1939-41) 277-289.

*P. Romanoff, "Influence of the Temple on Ceremonial Objects and Art," *JBL* 59 (1940) xv.

Margarete Bieber, "Damophon and Pliny 34, 52," *AJA* 45 (1941) 94-95.

*Rachel Wischnitzer-Bernstein, "The Samuel Cycle in the Wall Decoration of the Synagogue at Dura-Europos," *PAAJR* 11 (1941) 85-103.

*C. A. Robinson Jr., "The Master of Olympia," *AJA* 46 (1942) 73-76.

*John Franklin Daniel, "Late Mycenaean Pottery with Pictorial Representations," *AJA* 46 (1942) 121.

Valentine*[sic]* Müller, "Studies in Oriental Archaeology IV. Progress and Reaction in Ancient Egyptian Art," *JAOS* 63 (1943) 144-149.

M. Avi-Yonah, "Oriental Elements in the Art of Palestine in the Roman and Byzantine Periods," *QDAP* 10 (1944) 105-151; 13 (1948) 128-165; 14 (1950) 49-80.

*Alan M. B. Little, "The Formation of a Roman Style in Wall Painting," *AJA* 49 (1945) 134-142.

Gisela M. A. Richter, "Greeks in Perisa," *AJA* 50 (1946) 15-30.

*W. L. Hildburgh, "Apotropaism and Greek Vase-Paintings," *Folk* 57&58 (1946-47) 154-178.

Helene J. Kantor, "The Shoulder Ornament of Near Eastern Lions," *JNES* 6 (1947) 250-274.

Dorothy Burr Thompson, "The Charmed Circle," *Arch* 1 (1948) 158-164.

*Elise J. Baumgartel, "The three colossi from Koptos and their Mesopotamian counterparts," *ASAE* 48 (1948) 533-553.

A. J. Arkell, "The Shoulder Ornament of Near Eastern Lions," *JNES* 7 (1948) 52.

*Lloyd W. Daly, "The Cow in Greek Art and Cult," *AJA* 54 (1950) 261.

Dorothea M. A. Bate, "The 'Shoulder Ornament' of Near Eastern Lions," *JNES* 9 (1950) 53-54.

Cyrus H. Gordon, "The Glyptic Art of Nuzu," *JNES* 7 (1948) 261-266. *(Review)*

E. Douglas Van Buren, "An Additional Note on the Hair Whirl," *JNES* 9 (1950) 54-55.

Helene J. Kantor, "A Further Comment on the Shoulder Ornament," *JNES* 9 (1950) 55-56.

Bernard Goldman, "The Allover Pattern in Mesopotamian Stuccowork," *Bery* 10 (1950-53) 13-20. *[Motif]*

Matthew I. Wiencke, "The Epic Theme in Greek Art," *AJA* 5 (1951) 155-156.

*Dorothy Kent Hill, "'Modern' Drawing on Greek Vases," *Arch* 4 (1951) 50-52.

G. D. Hornblower, "The Origin of Pictorial Art," *Man* 51 (1951) #2.

Robert L. Scranton, "Dimension in Greek Art," *AJA* 56 (1952) 176.

Ludmila Matiegka, "Individual Characteristics of Figures on the Egyptian Stelae," *ArOr* 20 (1952) 15-27.

*Pavla Fořtová-Šamalová, "The Egyptian Ornament," *ArOr* 20 (1952) 231-249. *[Design]*

Anne Vollgraff-Roes, "The Lion with Body Markings in Oriental Art," *JNES* 12 (1953) 40-49.

Briggs W. Buchanan, "The Cow and Calf," *AJA* 58 (1954) 144. *[Motif]*

George M. A. Hanfmann, "On Eastern Greek Geometric and Orientalizing Styles," *AJA* 58 (1954) 146.

Matthew I. Wiencke, "An Epic Theme in Greek Art," *AJA* 58 (1954) 285-306.

*Luisa Banti, "Myth in Pre-Classical Art," *AJA* 58 (1954) 307-310.

*Boaz Cohen, "Art in Jewish Law," *Jud* 3 (1954) 165-176.

E. Douglas Van Buren, "The Esoteric Significance of Kassite Glyptic Art," *Or, N.S.*, 23 (1954) 1-39.

*Chrysoula Kardara, "On Mainland and Rhodian Workshops shortly before 600 B.C.," *AJA* 59 (1955) 49-54.

*E. Douglas Van Buren, "How Representation of Battles of the Gods Developed," *Or, N.S.*, 24 (1955) 24-41.

*E. Douglas Van Buren, "Representations of Fertility Divinities in Glyptic Art," *Or, N.S.*, 24 (1955) 345-376.

*Franklin P. Johnson, "A Philosophic Allegory?" *AJA* 60 (1956) 57-61.

*Berta Segall, "Problems of Copy and Adaptation in the Second Quarter of the First Millennium, B.C.: Some Syrian and 'Syro- Hittite' Elements in the Art of Arabia and of the West," *AJA* 60 (1956) 165-170.

Carl H. Kraeling, "Narration in Ancient Art. A Symposium," *AJA* 61 (1957) 43. *[Introduction]*

Helene J. Kantor, "Narration in Egyptian Art," *AJA* 61 (1957) 44-54.

Ann Perkins, "Narration in Babylonian Art," *AJA* 61 (1957) 54-62.

Hans J. Güterbock, "Narration in Anatolian, Syrian and Assyrian Art," *AJA* 61 (1957) 62-71.

George M. A. Hanfmann, "Narration in Greek Art," *AJA* 61 (1957) 71-78.

Pter H. von Blanckenhagen, "Narration in Hellenistic and Roman Art," *AJA* 61 (1957) 78-83.

K. Weitzmann, "Narration in Early Christendom," *AJA* 61 (1957) 83-91.

*Thalia Phillies Howe, "Non-Classical Elements in Classical Vase Painting," *AJA* 61 (1957) 183-184.

*Emeline Hill Richardson, "The Recurrent Geometric Style in Early Etruscan Bronzes," *AJA* 61 (1957) 185-186.

Elmer G. Suhr, "The Spinning Aphrodite," *AJA* 61 (1957) 188.

Thalia Phillies Howe, "Sophokles, Milkon and the Argonauts," *AJA* 61 (1957) 341-349.

Alan Richard Schulman, "Egyptian Representation of Horsemen and Riding in the New Kingdom," *JNES* 16 (1957) 263-271.

Erik Iversen, "The Egyptian Origin of the Archaic Greek Canon," *MDIÄA* 15 (1957) 134-147.

Cecil Roth, "The Problem of 'Jewish Art'," *Jud* 6 (1957) 118-125.

*Elmer G. Suhr, "The Evolution of the Mesopotamian Cone and Spindle," *AJA* 62 (1958) 226-227.

Clark Hopkins, "The Origins of Etruscan Art," *Arch* 11 (1958) 93-97.

W[illiam] F[oxwell] Albright, "Was the Age of Solomon without Monumental Art?" *EI* 5 (1958) 1*-9*.

J. Leribovitch, "Egyptian and Hyksos Art," *EI* 5 (1958) 85*-86*.

*E. R. Goodenough, "The Paintings of the Dura-Europos Synagogue: Method and Application," *IEJ* 8 (1958) 69-79.

*G. A. Wainwright, "The 'Signet Royal' or Cappadocian Symbol," *Or, N.S.,* 27 (1958) 287.

*L. Y. Rahmani, "Transformation of an Ornament," *'Atiqot* 2 (1959) 188-189.

*R. Giveon, "King or God on the Sarcophagus of Ahiram," *IEJ* 9 (1959) 57-59. *[Motif]*

*Margarete Bieber, "Roman Men in Greek Himation (Roman Palliati). A Contribution to the History of Copying," *PAPS* 103 (1959) 374-417.

Mary M. C. Brennand, "A Glossary of Mosaic Motifs," *ULBIA* 2 (1959) 67-71.

Thalia Phillies Howe, "Expressionist Fragments of Pre-Roman Gaul," *AJA* 64 (1960) 186-187.

*Joseph V. Noble, "The Technique of Attic Vase-Painting," *AJA* 64 (1960) 307-318.

Bernard Goldman, "The Development of the Lion-Griffith," *AJA* 64 (1960) 319-328.

Donald M. Wilber, "The Off-Beat in Egyptian Art," *Arch* 13 (1960) 259-266.

*John Boardman, "The Multiple Brush," *Antiq* 34 (1960) 85-89.

Joseph Gutmann, "The Haggadic Motif in Jewish Iconography," *EI* 6 (1960) 16*-22*.

Rachel Wischnitzer, "The Moneychanger with the Balance, a Topic of Jewish Iconography," *EI* 6 (1960) 23*-25*.

*Helene J. Kantor, "Oriental Institute Museum Notes. No. 11: A Fragment of a Gold Applique from Ziwiye and Some Remarks on the Artistic Traditions of Armenia and Iran During the First Millennium B.C.," *JNES* 19 (1960) 1-14.

*E. Iversen, "A Canonical Master-Drawing in the British Museum," *JEA* 46 (1960) 71-79.

*Mario A. Del Chiaro, "A Decorative Motif Exclusive to Raliscan Red-Figure," *AJA* 65 (1961) 389.

Bernard Goldman, "An Oriental Solar Motif and its Western Extention," *JNES* 20 (1961) 239-247.

*Rutherford J. Gettens, "Minerals in Art and Archaeology," *SIR* (1961) 551-569.

G. Bagnani, "Pictura Compendiaria," *AJA* 66 (1962) 194.

Brunilde Sismondo Ridgway, "The Date of the So-called Jason," *AJA* 66 (1962) 199.

J. H. Young, "Commagenian Tiaras, Royal and Divine," *AJA* 66 (1962) 201-202.

*M. Lawrence, "Ships, Monsters and Jonah," *AJA* 66 (1962) 289-296.

Robert Houston Smith, "Near Eastern Forerunners of the Striding Zeus," *Arch* 15 (1962) 176-183. *[Style]*

*Abd El-Hamid Zayed, "Miscellaneous Notes," *ASAE* 57 (1962) 115-124. [I. Some Variations of the *rḫjj.t* Symbol, p. 115]

R. D. Barnett, "Median Art," *IA* 2 (1962) 77-95.

J. L. Benson, "A Problem of Orientalizing Cretan Birds: Mycenaean or Philistine Prototypes?" *JNES* 20 (1961) 73-84. *[Pottery Designs]*

Gisela M. A. Richter, "Late Hellenistic Portraiture," *Arch* 16 (1963) 25-28.

W. Tararkiewicz, "Classification of Arts in Antiquity," *JHI* 24 (1963) 231-240.

*Rudolf Anthes, "Affinity and Difference Between Egyptian and Greek Sculpture and Thought in the Seventh and Sixth Centuries B.C.," *PAPS* 107 (1963) 60-81.

Sabatino Moscati, "Historical Art in the Ancient Near East," *SSR* 8 (1963) 1-117.

Edith Porada, "Facets of Iranian Art," *Arch* 17 (1964) 199-204.

Stanisław Jan Gąsiorowski, "Interpretation of Nature in the Art of Ancient Mesopotamia," *FO* 6 (1964) 101-120.

John D. Cooney, "Persian Influence in Late Egyptian Art," *JARCE* 4 (1965) 39-48.

*Tariq Madhloum, "More Notes on the Near Eastern Griffin," *Sumer* 20 (1964) 57-62.

Christine Mitchell Havelock, "The Archaic as Survival versus the Archaistic as a New Style," *AJA* 69 (1965) 331-340.

*Brunilde Sismondo Ridgway, "Wounded Figures in Greek Sculpture," *Arch* 18 (1965) 47-54.

Cornelius C. Vermeule III, "A Greek Theme and its Survivals: The Ruler's Shield (Tondo Image) in Tomb and Temple," *PAPS* 109 (1965) 361-397.

Brunilde Sismondo Ridgway, "Greek Kouroi and Egyptian Methods," *AJA* 70 (1966) 68-70.

*Diane Lee Carroll, "The Heddle in Greek Art," *AJA* 70 (1966) 185.

Helene J. Kantor, "Landscape in Akkadian Art," *JNES* 25 (1966) 145-152.

John G. Griffith, "*Aegisthus Citharista,*" *AJA* 71 (1967) 176-177.

A. M. Bakir, "Remarks on some aspects of Egyptian art," *JEA* 53 (1967) 159-161.

Osamu Sudzuki, "Eastern Origin of Scythian Art—A Stylistic Approach," *Orient* 4 (1967) 1-16.

*Joseph Vogt, "Free Arts and Unfree People in Ancient Rome," *VDI* (1967) #2, 103.

John H. Betts, "Trees in the Wind on Cretan Sealings," *AJA* 72 (1968) 149-150.

*L. B. Schneider, "Compositional and Psychological Use of the Spear in Two Vase Paintings by Exekias: A Note on Style," *AJA* 72 (1968) 385-386.

Erik Iversen, "Diodorus' Account of the Egyptian Canon," *JEA* 54 (1968) 215-218.

P. P. Delougaz, "Animals Emerging from a Hut," *JNES* 27 (1968) 184-197. *[Mesopotamian Art Motif]*

*William C. Brice, "Epigraphische Mitteilungen," *KZFE* 7 (1968) 180-181. [Cretan Glyptic and Cave Art, p. 180]

R. North, "High-points in Mesopotamian Art," *Or, N.S.*, 37 (1968) 220-231.

S. P. Boriskovaskaya, "The Orientalising Style in the Art of Archaic Corinth," *VDI* (1968) #3, 115.

*Colin Renfrew, "The Development and Chronology of Early Cycladic Figurines," *AJA* 73 (1969) 1-32.

*J. T. Cummings, "The Michigan State University Kylix and its Painter," *AJA* 73 (1969) 69-71.

*Edith Porada, "Cylinder Seals from Enkomi, Cyprus, and a Re-appraisal of Early Glyptic Art in Cyprus," *AJA* 73 (1969) 244.

Charles K. Wilkinson, "Problems of Authenticity in Ancient Near Eastern Art," *AJA* 73 (1969) 287.

N. M. Nikulina, "The Question of 'East Greek' and 'Greco-Persian' Art," *VDI* (1969) #3, 120.

Philip P. Betancourt, "The Age of Homer: An Exhibition of Geometric and Orientalizing Greek Art," *Exped* 12 (1969-70) #1, 2-14.

*Pauline Albenda, "Expressions of Kingship in Assyrian Art," *JANES* 2 (1969-70) 41-52.

§225 *2.5.10.2 Drawings, Painting, Vase Painting, Color, Design and Perspective*

Anonymous, "Caricature in Ancient Art," *DUM* 67 (1866) 98-109. *(Review)*

*Carleton L. Brownson, "Papers of the American School of Classical Studies at Athens. The Relation of the Archaic Pediment Reliefs from the Acropolis to Vase-Painting," *AJA, O.S.*, 8 (1893) 28-41.

Richard Norton, "Andokides," *AJA, O.S.*, 10 (1895) 1-41. *[Vase Painting]*

*Maxime Collignon, "Polychromy in Greek Statuary" *SIR* (1895) 601-623. *[Color]*

C. M. Mulvany, "Colours in Greek. *ΧΑΝΘΟΣ*," *JP* 27 (1899-1900) 51-59.

*Percy E. Newberry, "Extracts from my Notebooks, III," *SBAP* 22 (1900) 142-154. [14. The Cornflower in Egyptian Art, pp. 142-144; 15. The Poppy in Egyptian Art, pp. 144-146]

John H. Wright, "The Composition of Apelle's Calumny," *AJA* 5 (1901) 21.

*E. P. Andrews, "Color on the Parthenon and on the Elgin Marbles, recently Discovered Facts and Resultant Theories," *AJA* 5 (1901) 21-22.

James W. Kyle, "The Maiden's Race on Attic Vases," *AJA* 6 (1902) 53.

*Arthur Fairbanks, "A Comparison of the Scenes on White Lecythiand on Grave Stelae," *AJA* 7 (1903) 84.

J. K. Crow, "Report on Samples of Colours scraped from the Monuments," *ASAE* 4 (1903) 242-243. *[Painting]*

F. Green, "Prehistoric Drawings at el-Kab," *SBAP* 25 (1903) 371-372.

W. N. Bates, "Scenes from the Aethiopis on a Black-figured Amphora from Orvieto," *AJA* 8 (1904) 87-88.

*P. C. V. Baur, "The Palace of Thetis on the François Vase," *AJA* 8 (1904) 88.

W. H. Goodyear, "Lotus Ornament on Cypriote Vases," *AJA* 9 (1905) 73-74.

*James M. Paton, "The Death of Thersites on an Amphora in the Boston Museum of Fine Arts," *AJA* 9 (1905) 82-83.

Oliver S. Tonks, "Exekias: a Master of the Black-figured Style," *AJA* 9 (1905) 84-85.

*James M. Paton, "Two Representations of the Birth of Dionysus," *AJA* 11 (1907) 65.

Eunice Gibbs Allyn, "The Evolution of the Greek Fret," *RP* 6 (1907) 210-215.

*Arthur E. P. Weigall, "A Report on Some Objects Recently Found in Sebakh and other Diggings," *ASAE* 8 (1907) 40-50. [6. Prehistoric Drawing from Maala, p. 49]

Anonymous, "Early Greek Paintings," *RP* 7 (1908) 258.

W. M. Flinders Petrie, "Roman Portraits in Egypt," *Man* 11 (1911) #91.

*W. M. Flinders Petrie, "Roman Portraits," *RP* 10 (1911) 303-315.

*N. de G. Davies, "A Foreign Type from a Theban Tomb," *AAA* 6 (1913-14) 84-86.

W. M. F[linders] P[etrie], "For Reconsideration.," *AEE* 1 (1914) 33-34. [Paintings of Prehistoric Towns]

David M. Robinson, "Two Unpublished Vase Illustrations of Homer," *AJA* 19 (1915) 78-79.

*Ernest S. Thomas, "On an unexplained object depicted on the walls of the tomb of Hesy at Saqqara," *ASAE* 16 (1916) 52-53.

N. de Garis Davies, "Egyptian Drawings on Limestone Flakes," *JEA* 4 (1916) 234-240.

*G. W. Elderkin, "Archaeological Studies," *AJA* 21 (1917) 397-408. [III. The Exergue in Cyrenaic Cyulices, pp. 404-406; IV. The Vine of Phytios and Andocies, pp. 407-408]

Ernest Mackay, "On the Various Methods of representing Hair in the Wall-paintings of the Theban Tombs," *JEA* 5 (1918) 113-116.

Stephen Bleecker Luce, "A Brief History of the Study of Greek Vase-Painting," *PAPS* 57 (1918) 649-668.

Arthur Fairbanks, "An Ionian Deinos in Boston," *AJA* 23 (1919) 279-287.

*Percy E. Newberry, "Extracts from my Note-Books. V.," *SBAP* 24 (1902) 244-252. [37. A Prehistoric Figure of an Elephant, p. 251] *[Drawings]*

Ernest Mackay, "Theban Borders of Lotus and Grapes," *AEE* 6 (1921) 39-41. (Note by [W. M.] F[linders] P[etrie], pp. 40-41)

(Miss) Mary Hamilton Swindler, "Drawing and Design on Greek Vases," *AJA* 25 (1921) 77-78.

N. de Garis Davies, "Mural Paintings in the City of Akhetaten," *JEA* 7 (1921) 1-7.

Stephen Bleecker Luce, "Heracles and the Old Man of the Sea," *AJA* 26 (1922) 174-192.

*Howard Carter, "An Ostracon depicting a Red Jungle-Fowl. (The earliest known drawing of the domestic cock.)," *JEA* 9 (1923) 1-4.

T. H. Greenles, "An ususual Tomb Scene from Dirâʿ Abu'l-Negâ," *JEA* 9 (1923) 131.

*Stephen Bleecker Luce, "Studies on the Exploits of Hercules on Vases," *AJA* 28 (1924) 296-325.

*Ernest Mackay, "The Representation of Shawls with a Rippled Stripe in the Theban Tombs," *JEA* 10 (1924) 41-43.

Miriam A. Banks, "The Survival of the Euthymidean Tradition in Later Greek Vase-Painting," *AJA* 30 (1926) 58-69.

N. de Garis Davies, "An Apparent Instance of Perspectival Drawing," *JEA* 12 (1926) 110-112.

E. S. Thomas, "A Comparison of Drawings from Ancient Egypt, Libya, and the South Spanish Caves," *JRAI* 56 (1926) 385-394.

*Henry Roy William Smith, "A Political Cartoon of the Sixth Century B.C.," *PAPA* 57 (1926) xxii-xxiii.

Edith Williams Ware, "Egyptian Artists' Signatures," *AJSL* 43 (1926-27) 185-207.

G. D. Hornblower, "The Spiral Design in Predynastic Egypt," *AEE* 13 (1928) 68-69.

Theodore Leslie Shear, "Color at Corinth," *AJA* 32 (1928) 300-332.

*D. Newbold, "Rock-pictures and Archaeology in the Libyan Desert," *Antiq* 2 (1928) 261-291.

J. D. Beazley, "Attic Black-Figure: A Sketch," *PBA* 14 (1928) 217-263.

[W. M.] Flinders Petrie, "The Egyptian Lily," *AEE* 14 (1929) 65-73.

*Stephen Bleecker Luce, "Studies on the Exploits of Herakles on Vases," *AJA* 34 (1930) 313-333.

*G. D. Hornblower, "Funerary Designs on Predynastic Jars," *JEA* 16 (1930) 10-18.

E. S. Thomas, "Note on a Decorated Gourd," *AEE* 16 (1931) 28-29.

Ingrid Strøm, "Some Groups of Cycladic Vase-Painting from the Seventh Century B.C.," *AA* 33 (1932) 221-278.

*G. D. Hornblower, "Blue and Green in Ancient Egypt," *AEE* 17 (1932) 47-53.

Harold L. Cleasby, "Wings in Red-Figured Pottery," *AJA* 36 (1932) 36.

G. Horsfield, A. Horsfield, and Nelson Glueck, "Prehistoric Rock-Drawings in Transjordan," *AJA* 37 (1933) 381-386.

G. W. Murray and O. H. Myers, "Some Pre-dynastic Rock-drawings," *JEA* 19 (1933) 129-132.

David M. Robinson, "A Red-Figured Vase Influenced by the Parthenon Frieze," *AJA* 38 (1934) 45-48.

Bessie Ellen Richardson, "The Geras Painter and Hartwig's Bald-Head Master," *AJA* 38 (1934) 187.

Gisela M. A. Richter, "The Menon Painter = Psiax," *AJA* 38 (1934) 547-554.

E[dith] H. D[ohan], "A Bell-Krater by the Christie Painter," *UMB* 6 (1935-37) #4, 126-128.

William Stevenson Smith, "The Paintings of the Chapel of Atet at Mēdūm," *JEA* 23 (1937) 17-26.

Franklin P. Johnson, "Oltos," *AJA* 42 (1938) 124.

Nina M. Davies, "Some Representations of Tombs from the Theban Necropolis," *JEA* 24 (1938) 25-40.

H. R. W. Smith, "Some Enigmatic Vases of the Lewis Painter (Polygnotos II)," *AJA* 43 (1939) 305.

R. F. Peel, "Rock Paintings in the Libyan Desert. An Appendix to Dr. H. A. Winkler's 'Rock-drawings of Southern Upper Egypt II'," *Antiq* 13 (1939) 389-402.

G. Ernest Wright, "Palestine's First Great Artist," *BA* 2 (1939) 16-20.

Hetty Goldman, "A Note on Two Painted Sherds from Tarsus with Representations of Birds," *BASOR* #76 (1939) 2-5.

Herbert Gordon May, "The Sacred Tree on Palestine Painted Pottery," *JAOS* 59 (1939) 251-259.

R. M. Dawkins, "The Colchicum Crocus at Knossos," *Man* 39 (1939) #90. *[Drawing of the flower on Pottery]*

*W. A. Heurtley, "A Palestinian Vase-Painter of the Sixteenth Century B.C.," *QDAP* 8 (1939) 21-37.

*C[hester] C. McCown, "The Underworld in a Painted Tomb in Transjordan," *JBL* 59 (1940) vi.

*Nina M. Davies, "Amenemḥab encountering a Hyena. *From the Tomb of Amenemḥab at Thebes* (no. 85)," *JEA* 26 (1940) 82.

*N. M. Davies and N. de G. Davies, "Syrians in the Tomb of Amunedjeḥ," *JEA* 27 (1941) 96-98.

*N. M. Davies, "Nubians in the Tomb of Amunedjeḥ," *JEA* 28 (1942) 50-52.

*Prentice Duell, "Etruscan Wall Paintings and Their Technique," *AJA* 47 (1943) 100-101.

Dietrich von Bothmer, "The Painters of 'Tyrrhen' Vases," *AJA* 48 (1944) 161-170.

Lindsley F. Hall, "Notes on the Colors Preserved on the Archaic Attic Gravestones in the Metropolitan Museum," *AJA* 48 (1944) 334-336.

Margarete Bieber, "A Tragic Chorus on a Vase of 475 B.C.," *AJA* 45 (1941) 529-536.

*Helene J. Kantor, "The Final Phase of Predynastic Culture: Gerzean or Semainean(?)," *JNES* 3 (1944) 110-136. [The Hierakonpolis Painting, pp. 11-119]

*Alan M. B. Little, "The Formation of a Roman Style in Wall Painting," *AJA* 49 (1945) 134-142.

*Doro Levi, "Gleanings from Crete," *AJA* 49 (1945) 270-329. [2. The Siren from Parisos, pp. 280-293]

Dorothy Kent Hill, "Bonn or Comar Painter (?)," *AJA* 49 (1945) 503-507.

D. A. Amyx, "A New Pelike by the Geras Painter," *AJA* 49 (1945) 508-518.

Otto Brendel, "Procession Personified," *AJA* 49 (1945) 519-525.

George M. A. Hanfmann, "Horsemen from Sardis," *AJA* 49 (1945) 570-581.

J. Gwyn Griffiths, "A Swastika from Ancient Egypt," *Man* 45 (1945) #51.

*Nina M. Davies, "An Unusual Depiction of Ramesside Funerary Rites," *JEA* 32 (1946) 69-70.

Semni Papaspyridi Karouzou, "Choes," *AJA* 50 (1946) 122-139. *[Pottery Painting]*

*M. Rostovtzeff, "Numidian Horsemen on Canosa Vases," *AJA* 50 (1946) 263-267.

J. D. Beazley, "Some Attic Vases in the Cyprus Museum," *PBA* 33 (1947) 195-243.

Osman R. Rostem, "Remarkable drawings with examples in true perspective," *ASAE* 48 (1948) 167-177.

*A. J. Arkell, "The Harpoon on Egyptian Pottery," *Man* 48 (1948) #128.

*Nina M. Davies, "Birds and Bats at Beni Ḥasan," *JEA* 35 (1949) 13-20.

*Sidney D. Markman, "A Correlated Chronology for Greek Sculpture and Vase Painting," *AJA* 54 (1950) 263.

*Dorothy Kent Hill, "Three Portraits of the First Century B.C.," *AJA* 54 (1950) 264.

Raymond S. Stites, "How the Greeks Got Their Black," *AJA* 54 (1950) 264-265.

*Andreas Rumpf, "Parrhasios," *AJA* 55 (1951) 1-12.

*Marie Farnsworth, "Second Century B.C. Rose Madder from Corinth and Athens," *AJA* 55 (1951) 236-239.

Chrysoula P. Kardara, "On Theseus and the Tyrannicides," *AJA* 55 (1951) 293-300. *[Painted Greek Bowls]*

*Dorothy Kent Hill, "'Modern' Drawing on Greek Vases," *Arch* 4 (1951) 50-52.

Elizabeth Riefstahl, "An Egyptian Portrait of an Old Man," *JNES* 10 (1951) 65-73.

*Pavla Fořtová-Šamalová, "The Egyptian Ornament," *ArOr* 20 (1952) 231-249. *[Wall Painting]*

Christoph Clairmont, "Danae and Perseus in Seriphos," *AJA* 57 (1953) 106. *[Painted Pyxis]*

Dorothy Kent Hill, "Heads by Athenian Artists," *Arch* 6 (1953) 66-67.

A. F. L. Beeston, "A Safaitic Hunting Scene," *BSOAS* 16 (1954) 392.

*Chrysoula Kardara, "On Mainland and Rhodian Workshops shortly before 600 B.C.," *AJA* 59 (1955) 49-54.

Franklin P. Johnson, "A Note on Owl Skyphoi," *AJA* 59 (1955) 119-124. *[Vase Painting]*

Sara A. Immerwahr, "Some Mycenaean Artists Reexamined," *AJA* 59 (1955) 172.

Wm. Stevenson Smith, "Paintings of the Egyptian Middle Kingdom at Bersheh," *AJA* 55 (1955) 321-332.

*Nina de G. Davies, "Two Pictures of Temples," *JEA* 41 (1955) 80-82.

Sara A. Immerwahr, "The Protome Painter and Some Contemporaries," *AJA* 60 (1956) 137-141. *[Vase Painting]*

M[argarete] B[ieber] and D. v[on] B[othmer], "Notes on the Mural Paintings from Boscoreale," *AJA* 60 (1956) 171-172.

Machteld J. Mellink, "Hunting Scenes in Late Phrygian Vase-Painting," *AJA* 60 (1956) 181.

J. L. Benson, "Some Notes on Corinthian Vase-Painters," *AJA* 60 (1956) 219-230.

Margarete Bieber, "Another Note on the Murals from Boscoreale," *AJA* 60 (1956) 283-284.

Nelson Glueck, "A Nabataean Painting," *BASOR* #141 (1956) 13-23.

J. L. Benson, "Corinthian Vase-Painters," *AJA* 61 (1957) 175-176.

*Christoph Clairmont, "The Stelai of Aristion and Lyseas: The Relationship between Sculpture and Painting in Late Archaic Greece," *AJA* 61 (1957) 183.

*Thalia Phillies Howe, "Non-Classical Elements in Classical Vase Painting," *AJA* 61 (1957) 183-184.

William Stevenson Smith, "A Painting in the Assiut Tomb of Hepzefa," *MDIÄA* 15 (1957) 221-224.

*Christoph W. Clairmont, "Studies in Greek Mythology and Vase-Painting," *YCS* 15 (1957) 161-178.

George E. Mylonas, "The Polyphemos Painter," *AJA* 62 (1958) 225.

*Vassos Karageorghis, "Myth and Epic in Mycenaean Vase Painting," *AJA* 62 (1958) 383-387.

A. D. Ure, "The Agros Painter and the Painter of the Dancing Pan," *AJA* 62 (1958) 389-395.

*E. R. Goodenough, "The Paintings of the Dura-Europos Synagogue: Method and Application," *IEJ* 8 (1958) 69-79.

Patricia Lawrence, "The Corinthian Chimaera Painter," *AJA* 63 (1959) 349-363.

*S. Yeivin, "Topographic and Ethnic Notes," *'Atiqot* 2 (1959) 155-164. [B. The Relief in Iny's tomb at Deshashe and the Date of the Execration Texts, pp. 159-163]

*Sylvia Benton, "Birds on the cup of Arkesilas," *Arch* 12 (1959) 178-182.

DeCoursey Fales Jr., "The New York Band-Cup Painter," *AJA* 64 (1959) 184.

J. L. Benson, "The Ampersand Painter," *AJA* 64 (1960) 281-283.

*Joseph V. Noble, "The Technique of Attic Vase-Painting," *AJA* 64 (1960) 307-318.

Alexander Cambitoglou, "The Woman Eros-Painter, A Late Apulian Artist," *AJA* 64 (1960) 365-366.

*John Boardman, "The Multiple Brush," *Antiq* 34 (1960) 85-89.

*E. Iversen, "A Canonical Master-Drawing in the British Museum," *JEA* 46 (1960) 71-79.

*D. A. Amyx, "The Medallion Painter," *AJA* 65 (1961) 1-15.

*Brian F. Cook, "Potters and Painters of Red-Figured Lekythoi," *AJA* 65 (1961) 188.

J. L. Benson, "Observations on Mycenaean Vase-Painters," *AJA* 65 (1961) 337-347.

*Mario A. Del Chiaro, "A Decorative Motif Exclusive to Raliscan Red-Figure," *AJA* 65 (1961) 389.

Nina M. Davies, "A Fragment of a Punt Scene," *JEA* 47 (1961) 19-23.

J. D. Beazley, "Some Fragments by the Panaitios Painter," *AJA* 66 (1962) 235-236.

Martin Roberton, "A Fragment by the Nikoxenos Painter," *AJA* 66 (1962) 311-312.

James Mellaart, "The Beginnings of Mural Painting," *Arch* 15 (1962) 2-12.

R. B. Serjeant, "A Note on the Rock Drawings from Wādī Hirjāb, Reported by G. F. Walford, Esq.," *BSOAS* 25 (1962) 149.

*Henry G. Fischer, "The Archer as Represented in the First Intermediate Period," *JNES* 21 (1962) 50-52.

Erika Simon, "Polygnotan Painting and the Niobid Painter," *AJA* 67 (1963) 43-62.

Elmer G. Suhr, "The Spinning Aphrodite in the Minor Arts," *AJA* 67 (1963) 63-68.

Miriam Balmuth, "The Birth of Athena on a Fragment in the Fogg Art Museum," *AJA* 67 (1963) 69.

Alan M. G. Little, "A Series of Notes in Four Parts on Campanian Megalography. A. The Composition of the Villa Item Painting," *AJA* 67 (1963) 191-194.

De Coursey Fales Jr., "An Unpublished Fragment Attributed to Kleitias," *AJA* 67 (1963) 211.

*Mariateresa Marabini Moevs, "From Campanian Black to Sigillata Red and the Rise of Orange Gloss and Metallic Gloss," *AJA* 67 (1963) 215.

Emily Townsend Vermeule, "Three New Illustrations of the Trojan War," *AJA* 67 (1963) 218-219.

Alan M. G. Little, "A Series of Notes in Four Parts on Campanian Megalography. B. Numerical Grouping at the Villa Item and the Balance of Opposites," *AJA* 67 (1963) 291-294.

*Marie Farnsworth and Ivor Simmons, "Coloring Agents for Greek Glazes," *AJA* 67 (1963) 389-396.

*Henry G. Fischer, "Varia Aegyptiaca," *JARCE* 2 (1963) 17-51. [1. Yellow-skinned Representation of Men in the Old Kingdom, pp. 17-22; 2. A Realistic Example of the Hieroglyph for 'Iw "Old", pp. 23-24]

*Robert North, "Ghassul's New Found Jar-Incision," *ADAJ* 8&9 (1964) 68-74. *[Drawing]*

Alan M. G. Little, "A Series of Notes in Four Parts on Campanian Megalography. C. The Boscoreale Cycle," *AJA* 68 (1964) 62-66.

J. L. Benson, "The Populonia Painter," *AJA* 68 (1964) 172-174.

D. A. Amyx and Patricia Lawrence, "*Adversaria Critica:* In and Around the Sphinx Painter," *AJA* 68 (1964) 387-390.

Alan M. G. Little, "A Series of Notes in Four Parts on Campanian Megalography. D. The Homeric Cycle and the Herculaneum Megalography," *AJA* 68 (1964) 390-395.

W. Eugene Kleinbauer, "The Dionysios Painter and the 'Chroninthio-Attic' Problem," *AJA* 68 (1964) 355-370.

Henry Riad, "Tomb Paintings From the Necropolis Of Alexandria," *Arch* 17 (1964) 169-172.

Olof Vessberg, "Recent acquisitions of Roman portraits," *MB* #1 (1961) 55-64.

R. Ross Holloway, "Conventions of Etruscan Painting in the Tomb of Hunting and Fishing at Tarquinii," *AJA* 69 (1965) 341-347.

Z[byněk] Žába, "Czechoslavak Discoveries of Inscriptions and Rock-Drawings in Nubia," *NOP* 4 (1965) 110-113.

Alan M. G. Little, "A Series of Notes in Three Parts on Greek Pictorial Composition. *A. Roman Megalographies and Greek Compositional Methods,*" *AJA* 70 (1966) 165-169.

Alan M. G. Little, "A Series of Notes in Three Parts on Greek Pictorial Composition. *B. The Cartoon of the Villa Item Painting,*" *AJA* 70 (1966) 283-286.

Marilyn Low Schmitt, "Bellerephon and the Chimaera in Archaic Greek Art," *AJA* 70 (1966) 341-347. *[Vase Painting]*

Alan M. G. Little, "A Series of Notes in Three Parts on Greek Pictorial Composition. *C. The Composition of the Achilles in Scyros Painting,*" *AJA* 70 (1966) 363-366.

Sami S. Ahmed, "Dura Europas Paintings—A Comparative Note," *IR* 23 (1966) #1, 17-28.

Z[enon] S. Pohorecky and T[im] E. H. Jones, "Recording pictographs," *Man, N.S.*, 1 (1966) 104.

Patricia Vinnicombe, "Recording rock paintings," *Man, N.S.*, 1 (1966) 559-560.

*G. Radan, "Attic Kylix with Four Warships," *Sefunim* 1 (1966) 35-39.

*Arie Ben-Eli, "Reconstruction of a Warship from a Wall Painting in a Catacomb in Jerusalem," *Sefunim* 1 (1966) 40-42.

Gloria Saltz Merker, "The Rainbow Mosaic at Pergamon and Aristotelian Color Theory," *AJA* 71 (1967) 81-82.

*R. G. Hood, "A Geometric Oenochoe with Ship Scene in Hobart," *AJA* 71 (1967) 82-87.

*John G. Griffith, "*Aegisthus Citharista,*" *AJA* 71 (1967) 176-177. *[Vase Painting]*

Richard C. Bronson, "The Chronology of Early Etruscan Tomb-Painting: The Campana Tomb at Veii," *AJA* 71 (1967) 184.

Mary B. Moore, "New Criteria for a Relative Chronology for Exekias," *AJA* 71 (1967) 192.

*Emily Vermeule, "A Love Scene by 'the Panaitios Painter'," *AJA* 71 (1967) 311-314.

P. R. S. Moorey, "Some Aspects of Incised Drawing and Mosaic in the Early Dynastic Period," *Iraq* 29 (1967) 97-116.

Winifred Needler, "A Rock-drawing on Gebel Sheikh Suliman (near Wadi Halfa) showing a Scorpion and Human Figures," *JARCE* 6 (1967) 87-91.

Zenon S. Pohorecky and Tim E. H. Jones, "Recording rock paintings," *Man, N.S.*, 2 (1967) 305-306.

A. R. Willcox, "Recording rock paintings," *Man, N.S.*, 2 (1967) 629-630.

Kyle M. Phillips Jr., "Perseus and Andromeda," *AJA* 72 (1968) 1-23.

Richard Holton Pierce, "The Rainbow Mosaic at Pergamon and Aristotelian Color Theory," *AJA* 72 (1968) 75.

Mary Aiken Littauer, "A 19th and 20th Dynasty Heroic Motif on Attic Black-figured Vases," *AJA* 72 (1968) 150-152.

Richard Daniel De Puma, "Preliminary Sketches on Some Fragments by Makron in Philadelphia and Bryn Mawr," *AJA* 72 (1968) 152-154.

D. A. Amyx, "A 'Corinthian' Forger Unmasked," *AJA* 72 (1968) 161.

Katherine Coleman, "Wall Paintings from Keos," *AJA* 72 (1968) 163.

*Mary B. Moore, "Horses by Exekias," *AJA* 72 (1968) 357-368.

*L. B. Schneider, "Compositional and Psychological Use of the Spear in Two Vase Paintings by Exekias: A Note on Style," *AJA* 72 (1968) 385-386.

Murray Schoonraad, "Recording rock painting," *Man, N.S.*, 3 (1968) 315-316.

J. S. Crawford, "The Figure Pose on the Tondo of the Michigan State University Kylix," *AJA* 73 (1969) 72-73.

Franklin P. Johnson, "Note on Hermonax," *AJA* 73 (1969) 73.

J. L. Benson, "The Three Maidens Group," *AJA* 73 (1969) 109-122.

Oscar Broneer, "Archaic Wall Paintings at Isthmia," *AJA* 73 (1969) 232.

Alexander Cambitoglou and A. D. Trendall, "Addenda to *Apulian Red-Figure Vase-Painters of the Plain Style*," *AJA* 73 (1969) 423-433.

Rodney S. Young, "Doodling at Gordion," *Arch* 22 (1969) 270-275.

*G. Lankester Harding, "A Safaitic Drawing and Text," *L* 1 (1969) 68-72.

§226 *2.5.10.3 Sculpture, Statuary, Friezes, and Reliefs (includes Terracottas)*

Anonymous, "The Nimroud Marbles," *BRCM* 4 (1847-48) 280-282.

Joseph Bonomi, "Note on an Egyptian Bust, formerly in the Harris Collection," *SBAT* 4 (1875) 332-333.

*William Houghton, "On the Mammalia of the Assyrian Sculptures," *SBAT* 5 (1876-77) 33-64, 319-383.

Gustav Hirschfeld, "The Sculptures in the Berlin Museum," *BQRL* 75 (1882) 375-396.

C[laude] R. Conder, "Notes from Constantinople. *The Gaza Jupiter,*" *PEFQS* 14 (1882) 147-148.

†Anonymous, "Greek Sculpture," *QRL* 154 (1883) 369-400. *(Review)*

†*Theo. G. Pinches, "Babylonian Art, illustrated by Mr. H. Rassam's latest discoveries," *SBAP* 6 (1883-84) 11-15. *[Sculpture]*

*Charles Waldstein, "The Panathenaic Festival and the central slab of the Parthenon Frieze," *AJA, O.S.,* 1 (1885) 10-17.

Alfred Emerson, "Two Modern Antiques," *AJA, O.S.,* 1 (1885) 152-156. *[Reliefs]*

Salomon Reinach, "Marble Statue of Artemis in the Museum at Constantinople," *AJA, O.S.,* 1 (1885) 319-323.

Wm. Hayes Ward, "Unpublished or imperfectly published Hittite monuments. I. The façade at Eflatün-Bünar," *AJA, O.S.,* 2 (1886) 49-51.

A. Furtwängler, "Note on Plate V, 2 of Volume I," *AJA, O.S.,* 2 (1886) 52.

*Alfred Emerson, "The portraiture of Alexander the Great: a terracotta head in Munich I," *AJA, O.S.,* 2 (1886) 408 -403.

J[oachim] Ménant, "Forgeries of Babylonian and Assyrian Antiquities," *AJA, O.S.,* 3 (1887) 14-31.

Augustus C. Merriam, "Painted Sepulchral Stelai[sic]* from Alexandria," *AJA, O.S.,* 3 (1887) 261-268. [Note on a Vase, p. 286]

William A. Ward and A. L. Frothingham Jr., "Unpublished or imperfectly published Hittite monuments. II. Sculpture Near Sindjirli," *AJA, O.S.*, 3 (1887) 62-69.

Alfred Emerson, "The Portaiture of Alexander the Great: a terracotta head in Munich II," *AJA, O.S.*, 3 (1887) 243-260. *[Includes Section III]*

Arthur H. Bagnold, "Account of the Manner in which two colossal Statues of Rameses II at Memphis were Raised," *SBAP* 10 (1887-88) 452-463.

Salomon Reinach, "An Inedited Portrait of Plato," *AJA, O.S.*, 4 (1888) 1-5.

*Alfred Emerson, "A laughing girl and a study of coiffure: a terracotta head in Munich," *AJA, O.S.*, 4 (1888) 165-168.

William Hayes Ward, "Unpublished or imperfectly published Hittite monuments. III. Reliefs at Carchemish = Jerablûs," *AJA, O.S.*, 4 (1888) 172-174.

C[onrad] Schick, "Statues at Askalon," *PEFQS* 20 (1888) 22-23.

L. R. Farnell, "The Origins and Earliest Development of Greek Sculpture," *ARL* 2 (1888-89) 167-184.

Charles Waldstein, "American School of Classical Studies at Athens. The Newly-Discovered Head of Iris from the Frieze of the Parthenon," *AJA, O.S.*, 5 (1889) 1-8.

*Carl D. Buck, "Discoveries in the Attic deme of Ikaria, 1888. II. Stele of a Warrior," *AJA, O.S.*, 5 (1889) 9-17.

M. L. Earle, "Papers of the American School of Classical Studies at Athens. Excavations at the Theatre of Sikyon. III. A Sikyonian Statute," *AJA, O.S.*, 5 (1889) 292-303.

Ad. Michælis, "The Thasian Relief Dedicated to the Nymphs and to Apollon," *AJA, O.S.*, 5 (1889) 417-422.

*Charles Waldstein, "Papers of the American School of Classical Studies at Athens. Report on Excavations near Stamata in Attika," *AJA. O.S.*, 5 (1889) 423-425. [II. Report on Excavations and Sculptures]

Carl D. Buck, "Discoveries in the Attic Deme of Ikaria, 1888," *AJA, O.S.*, 5 (1889) 461-477. [VIII. Sculptures]

Paul Wolthers, "*ΖΕΥΣ 'ΗΛΙΟΠΟΛΙΤΗΣ,*" *AJA. O.S.*, 6 (1890) 65-68. *[Sculpture]*

William Hayes Ward, "Notes on Oriental Antiquties. IX. A Babylonian Cylindrical Basrelief from Urumia in Perisa," *AJA, O.S.*, 6 (1890) 286-291.

A. S. Murray, "A Vase of the Mykenai Type in New York," *AJA, O.S.*, 6 (1890) 437-444.

C[laude] R. Conder, "New 'Hittite' Bas-Reliefs," *PEFQS* 22 (1890) 183-186.

[G.] Schumacher, "Sculptured Figures near Kânâ," *PEFQS* 22 (1890) 259-264.

C. R. Conder, "The Figures Near Kânâ," *PEFQS* 22 (1890) 264.

Charles Waldstein, "Papers of the American School of Classical Studies at Athens. The Mantineian Reliefs," *AJA, O.S.*, 7 (1891) 1-18.

*W. St. Chad Boscawen, "Statue of Gudea as 'The Architect'," *BOR* 6 (1892-93) 282-283.

F. B. Tarbell and W. N. Bates, "Notes on the Subjects of Greek Temple-Sculptures," *AJA, O.S.*, 8 (1893) 18-27.

*Carleton L. Brownson, "Papers of the American School of Classical Studies at Athens. The Relation of the Archaic Pediment Reliefs from the Acropolis to Vase-Painting," *AJA, O.S.*, 8 (1893) 28-41.

Herbert F. De Cou, "Papers of the American School of Classical Studies at Athens. II. The Frieze of the Choragic Monument of Lysikrates at Athens," *AJA, O.S.*, 8 (1893) 42-55.

A[ugustus] C. Merriam, "A Series of Cypriote Heads in the Metropolitan Musuem," *AJA, O.S.*, 8 (1893) 184-189.

[Charles Waldstein], "Papers of the American School of Classical Studies at Athens. Some Sculptures from the Argive Aeraeum," *AJA, O.S.*, 8 (1893) 199-204.

Rufus B. Richardson, "Papers of the American School of Classical Studies at Athens. I. A Torso from Daphne," *AJA, O.S.*, 9 (1894) 53-62.

N. E. Crosby, "A Bas Relief from Phaleron," *AJA, O.S.*, 9 (1894) 202-205.

Charles Waldstein, "Papers of the American School of Classical Studies at Athens. A Head of Polycleatan Style from the Metopes of the Argive Heræum," *AJA, O.S.*, 9 (1894) 331-339.

Henry S. Washington, "Papers of the American School of Classical Studies at Athens. On the Possibility of Assigning a Date to the Santorini Vases," *AJA, O.S.*, 9 (1894) 504-520.

Myron R. Snaford, "The New Faun from the Quirinal," *AJA, O.S.*, 9 (1894) 533-537. *[Statue]*

C[onrad] Schick, "Notes from Herr Baurath von Schick. Winged Figure from Palestine," *PEFQS* 26 (1894) 147-148.

*J. E.; Hanauer, "Notes on the Winged Figure at Jaffa, on Bether, &c.," *PEFQS* 26 (1894) 148-150.

Rufus R. Richardson, "Correspondence. Note to 'A Torso from Daphne'," *AJA, O.S.*, 10 (1895) 51.

Sarah Y. Stevenson, "Some Sculptures from Koptos in Philadelphia," *AJA, O.S.*, 10 (1895) 347-351.

†Anonymous, "Lost Masterpieces of Greek Sculpture," *QRL* 180 (1895) 61-87. *(Review)*

*Maxime Collignon, "Polychromy in Greek Statuary," *SIR* (1895) 601-623.

Rufus B. Richardson, "Papers of the American School of Classical Studies at Athens. Sculptures from the Gymnasium at Eretria," *AJA, O.S.*, 11 (1896) 165-172.

*Rufus B. Richardson, "Notes. Notes from Corinth," *AJA, O.S.*, 11 (1896) 371-372. [Statuary and Architectural Members, p. 372]

J. E. Hanauer, "Remarkable Sculpture at Mejdel," *PEFQS* 29 (1897) 33-35. *[Greco-Egyptian]*

J. E. Hanauer, "Notes by Rev. J. E. Hanauer. II.—Sculptured Stones from Na'aneh," *PEFQS* 30 (1898) 26-27. (Note by C. Clermont-Ganneau, p.157)

*Percy E. Newberry, "Extracts from my Notebook (I).," *SBAP* 21 (1899) 303-308. [4. A Statue of User, Vezîer of Upper Egypt under Thothmes III, pp. 306-308]

Edmund von Mach, "Hermes Discobolus?" *AJA* 4 (1900) 178-179.

(Miss) Susan Braley Franklin, "Reliefs on *κιονίσκοι*," *AJA* 4 (1900) 181.

*J. E. Hanauer, "Notes by the Rev. J. E. Hanauer," *PEFQS* 32 (1900) 250-251. [Sculptured Marble Slabs; Terra-cotta Coffins; Rock-hewn Vats]

Howard Crosby Butler, "Sculpture in Northern Central Syria," *AJA* 5 (1901) 5-6.

*E. P. Andrews, "Color on the Parthenon and on the Elgin Marbles, recently Discovered Facts and Resultant Theories," *AJA* 5 (1901) 21-22.

*Mitchel Carroll, "Aristotle's Theory of Sculpture," *AJA* 5 (1901) 24.

*Edmund von Mach, "The Statue of Meleager in the Fogg Museum of Harvard University," *AJA* 5 (1901) 29-30.

Karl J. Grimm, "The Polychrome Lion Recently found in Babylon," *JAOS* 22 (1901) 27-34.

*Percy E. Newberry, "Extracts from my Notebooks (IV)," *SBAP* 23 (1901) 218-224. [21. Statue of a Fan-bearer of the Body-guard of Amenhetep III, pp. 218-219]

Arthur Fairbanks, "On the So-called Mourning Athena Relief," *AJA* 6 (1902) 26.

James Tucker Jr., "Some Statues from Corinth," *AJA* 6 (1902) 26-27.

George A. Chase, "Some Terra-cotta Types from Heraeum," *AJA* 6 (1902) 40-41.

Edmund von Mach, "The Draped Female Figures from the Acropolis—An Attempt at Classification," *AJA* 6 (1902) 51-52.

D. Cady Eaton, "The Study of Greek Sculpture," *AJA* 7 (1903) 78-79.

*Arthur Fairbanks, "A Comparison of the Scenes on White Lecythiand on Grave Stelae," *AJA* 7 (1903) 84.

J. R. Wheeler, "Heracles Alexicacus," *AJA* 7 (1903) 85. *[Relief]*

Harold N. Fowler, "The Venus of Milo," *AJA* 7 (1903) 87.

Alfred Emerson, "Greek Sculpture in California," *AJA* 7 (1903) 97-99.

(Mrs.) Ghosu-el-Howie, "Rock Sculpture 'in the Westland'," *RP* 2 (1903) 140-144.

(Mrs.) Ghosu-el Howie, "Rock Sculptures at Hahr-el-Kelb," *RP* 2 (1903) 195-207.

Ghosn-el Howie*[sic]*, "Two Newly Discovered Sculptures in Coele Syria,"*JBL* 23 (1904) 211-214.

Paul Carus, "The Spinning Damsel," *OC* 18 (1904) 568-569. *[Bas-relief]*

A. H. Sayce, "Notes and Queries. 2. *Rock Sculpture at Lebanon,*" *PEFQS* 36 (1904) 286-287.

E. S. Banks*[sic]*, "Statue of the Time of King Daddu," *RP* 3 (1904) 316-317.

(Miss) M[argaret] A. Murray, "A Roman Terra-cotta Figure of an Apis Bull," *SBAP* 26 (1904) 294.

*Edgar James Banks, "The Oldest Statue in the World," *AJSL* 21 (1904-05) 57-59.

Paul V. C. Baur, "A Terra-cotta Tityrus in the Cincinnati Museum," *AJA* 9 (1905) 84.

Arthur E. Whatham, "The Meaning of the Ring and Rod in Babylonian-Assyrian Sculpture," *BW* 26 (1905) 120-123.

Anonymous, "Egyptian Statues," *MQR, 3rd Ser.,* 31 (1905) 383-385.

*G. Frederick Wright, "Early Art in Egypt," *RP* 4 (1905) 367-372.

C. C. Edgar, "Remarks on Egyptian 'sculptors' models'," *RTR* 27 (1905) 137-150.

George H. Chase, "Some Unpublished Terra-cotta Figures in the Boston Museum of Fine Arts," *AJA* 10 (1906) 79.

David M. Robinson, "Terra-cottas and Ointment Vases found at Corinth in 1902," *AJA* 10 (1906) 83.

David M. Robinson, "Terra-cottas from Corinth," *AJA* 10 (1906) 159-173.

*Edgar James Banks, "The Head of the Oldest Statue of a Semite," *OC* 20 (1906) 378-381. *[Sumerian-King Daddu]*

*Valdemar Schmidt, "Note on a peculiar Pendant shown on Three Statues of Usertsen III," *SBAP* 28 (1906) 268-269.

Harold N. Fowler, "The Beginning of Greek Sculpture," *AJA* 11 (1907) 57.

*Charles C. Torrey, "Traces of Portraiture in Old Semitic Art," *AJA* 11 (1907) 63-64.

Edmund von Mach, "Greek Draped Figure at Vassar," *RP* 6 (1907) 227-232.

Edmund von Mach, "Roman Portrait Head in Vassar College," *RP* 6 (1907) 292-298.

Anonymous, "A New Statue of Niobid at Rome," *RP* 6 (1907) 340.

*Arthur E. P. Weigall, "Upper-Egyptian Notes," *ASAE* 9 (1908) 105-112. [5. A Vase of Sebakhotep III from Dendereh, p. 107; 9. A Fragment of pottery from Edfu, pp. 108-109; 11. A. Pottery Vase from Fayûm, p. 110]

Richard Mahler, "The Niobid in the 'Banca Commerciale' of Rome," *RP* 7 (1908) 67-73.

Anonymous, "New Fragments of the Parthenon Sculptures Found," *RP* 7 (1908) 211.

(Miss) Elizabeth M. Gardiner, "A Group of Sculptures from Corinth," *AJA* 13 (1909) 62-63.

Arthur Fairbanks, "A New Marble in the Boston Museum of Fine Arts," *AJA* 14 (1909) 72.

L. March Phillips, "Greek Sculpture," *ContR* 98 (1910) 88-101.

W[illiam] N. Bates, "Mediterranean Section. Sculptures from Lake Nemi," *MJ* 1 (1910) 30-33.

*W. M. Flinders Petrie, "Roman Portraits," *RP* 10 (1911) 303-315.

William N. Bates, "Greek and Roman Sculptures in Philadelphia," *AJA* 16 (1912) 101-102.

Anonymous, "Gorgon at Corfu," *RP* 11 (1912) 104.

Lacey D. Caskey, "The Statue of a Mounted Amazon in the Museum of Fine Arts, Boston," *AJA* 17 (1913) 83.

*H. C. Tolman, "The Grave Relief of King Darius," *AJA* 17 (1913) 85-86.

E[dith] H. Hall, "A Sealed Dionysos," *MJ* 4 (1913) 164-167.

John E. Granrud, "Roman Historical Reliefs," *RP* 12 (1913) 75-84.

*W. M. F[linders] P[etrie], "The Portraits," *AEE* 1 (1914) 48. *[Amenemhat III]*

E[dith] H. H[all], "A Granite Sphinx from Memphis," *MJ* 5 (1914) 49-54.

R. Campbell Thompson, "An Egyptian Relief at Wadi Sarga," *SBAP* 36 (1914) 198.

Charles A. Weller, "A New Restoration of the Statue of Demosthenes," *A&A* 1 (1914-15) 47-51.

Anonymous, "Current Notes and News. The Venus Statue in the Royal Ontario Museum," *A&A* 2 (1915) 62.

[W. M. Flinders Petrie], "The Portrait," *AEE* 2 (1915) 144. *[Head of An Offical, XVIIIth Dynasty]*

H. R. Hall, "A Comparison of Chinese and Egyptian Tomb-Sculptures," *JEA* 3 (1915) 38-40.

*Charles Newton Smiley, "Athenian Thought and Life as Reflected in the Parthenon Sculptures," *A&A* 4 (1916) 27-46.

Alice Walton, "Painted Marbles from Thessaly," *A&A* 4 (1916) 47-53.

R. V. D. M[agoffin], "Current Notes and News. A Roman Sepulchral Relief," *A&A* 3 (1916) 122.

*James Henry Breasted, "Studio of an Egyptian Portrait Sculptor in the Fourteenth Century B.C.," *A&A* 4 (1916) 233-242.

George H. Chase, "The Sculptor Myron in the Light of Recent Discoveries I—The Discobolus or Discus-Thrower," *A&A* 3 (1916) 265-273.

Edgar James Banks, "Seven Wonders of the Ancient World. III—The Third Wonder: The Statue of the Olympian Zeus," *A&A* 3 (1916) 279-283.

George H. Chase, "The Sculptor Myron in the Light of Recent Discoveries II—Athena and Marsyas," *A&A* 3 (1916) 317-325.

F. W. Shipley, "Roman Portrait Sculpture," *AJA* 20 (1916) 92-93.

Alan H. Gardiner, "A New Masterpiece of Egyptian Sculpture," *JEA* 4 (1916) 1-3.

H. E. Winlock, "A Restoration of the Reliefs from the Mortuary Temple of Amehotep I," *JEA* 4 (1916) 11-15.

*Charles Ricketts, "Head of Amenemmēs III in Obsidian from the Collection of the Rev. W. MacGregor, Tamworth," *JEA* 4 (1916) 71-73.

*Charles Ricketts, "Head in Serpentine of Amenemmēs III in the possession of Oscar Raphael, Esq.," *JEA* 4 (1916) 211-212.

S[tephen] B. L[uce], "A Greek Torso," *MJ* 7 (1916) 87-92.

Caroline M. Galt, "A Marble Fragment at Mount Holyoke Collection from the Cretan City of Aptera," *A&A* 6 (1917) 143-154.

Edgar James Banks, "The Seven Wonders of the Ancient World.VI—The Sixth Wonder: The Colossus at Rhodes," *A&A* 5 (1917) 265-269.

G. W. Elderkin, "A Helmeted Head of Athena," *AJA* 21 (1917) 85.

G. W. Elderkin, "The Princeton Head of Athena," *AJA* 21 (1917) 292-295.

*G. W. Elderkin, "Archaeological Studies," *AJA* 21 (1917) 397-408. [II. Scenes from the Odyssey on an Etruscan Grave Stele, pp. 400-404]

*George A. Barton, "On the Identification of a Portrait Statue of a Semitic Babylonian King," *AJSL* 34 (1917-18) 204-206. *[Shargalisharri(?)]*

Alice Walton, "A Polyclitan Statue Wellesley College," *AJA* 22 (1918) 44-53.

A. L. Frothingham, "A New Mithraic Relief from Syria," *AJA* 22 (1918) 54-62.

A. L. Frothingham, "The Footgear of Immortality in the Redating of Roman Sculptures," *AJA* 22 (1918) 67.

L. D. Caskey, "The Ludovisi Relief and Its Companion Piece in Boston," *AJA* 22 (1918) 101-145.

Charles Ricketts, "Bas-relief Figure of a King of the Ptolemaic Period in Blue Faience," *JEA* 5 (1918) 77-78.

L. G. Eldridge, "An Archaic Greek Statue," *AJA* 23 (1919) 270-278.

C. Densmore Curtis, "Recent Archaeological Discoveries in Rome and Veii," *A&A* 9 (1920) 271-277.

W. M. Flinders Petrie, "A Mentuhetep Statue," *AEE* 5 (1920) 33-34. *[Ebony]*

E[rnest] Mackay, "Kheker Friezes," *AEE* 5 (1920) 111-122.

Charles T. Seltman, "Two Heads of Negresses," *AJA* 24 (1920) 14-26.

Theodore Leslie Shear, "A Marble Head from Rhodes," *AJA* 24 (1920) 313-322.

*W. E. Winlock, "Statue of the Steward Roy singing the Psalm to Rēʿ," *JEA* 6 (1920) 1-3.

[Alan H. Gardiner], "Another Statue of a Man named Roy as Worshipper of the Sun-God," *JEA* 6 (1920) 212-213.

*Jean Capart, "Some Remarks on the Sheikh el-Beled," *JEA* 6 (1920) 225-233

Eugénie Strong, "Greek Portraits in the British Museum," *QRL* 234 (1920) 22-40. *(Review)*

Ernest A. Gardner, "A Head of a Barbarian from Egypt," *AEE* 6 (1921) 42-43.

Roland G. Kent, "A Baffled Hercules," *AJA* 25 (1921) 80-81.

Jean Capart, "The Name of the Scribe of the Louvre," *JEA* 7 (1921) 186-190.

Harriet Boyd Hawes, "A Gift of Themistocles: Two Famous Reliefs in Rome and Boston," *AJA* 26 (1922) 81-82.

Harriet Boyd Hawes, "A Gift of Themistocles: The 'Ludovisi Throne'and the Boston Relief," *AJA* 26 (1922) 278-306.

*H. R. Hall, "The Discoveries at Tell el 'Obeid in Southern Babylonia and Some Egyptian Comparisons," *JEA* 8 (1922) 241-257. *[Relief]*

Anonymous, "Archaeological Notes and Comments. Two Heroic Egyptian Statues for the Metropolitan," *A&A* 15 (1923) 52.

Theodore Leslie Shear, "A Terra-cotta Relief from Sardes," *AJA* 27 (1923) 131-150.

*W[alter] R. Agard, "The Date of the Metopes of the Athenian Treasury at Delphi," *AJA* 27 (1923) 174-183.

(Miss) Elizabeth D. Pierce, "A Daedalid in the Skimatari Museum," *AJA* 28 (1924) 68.

Harold L. Cleasby, "The Victory in the Curia," *AJA* 28 (1924) 73-74.

Theodore Leslie Shear, "A Marble Copy of Athena Parthenos in Princeton," *AJA* 28 (1924) 117-119.

Elizabeth Denny Pierce, "A Daedalid in the Skimatari Museum,"*AJA* 28 (1924) 267-275.

Anonymous, "Head of Ariadne," *MJ* 15 (1924) 252-255.

L. D. Caskey, "The Metopes of the Sicyonian Treasury at Delphi," *AJA* 29 (1925) 17-19.

A[lexander] D[avid] Fraser, "An Athlete's Head in the Fogg Museum of Art," *AJA* 29 (1925) 70-75.

Gisela M. A. Richter, "Two Hellenistic Portraits in the Metropolitan Museum," *AJA* 29 (1925) 152-159.

A[lexander] D[avid] Fraser, "A Myronic Head in the Fogg Art Museum of Art," *AJA* 29 (1925) 314-320.

W. B. Emery, "A Relief from the Tomb of Ramōse at Thebes," *JEA* 11 (1925) 125.

A. W. Lawrence, "Greek Sculpture in Ptolemaic Egypt," *JEA* 11(1925) 179-190.

Anonymous, "Notes and Comments. A Roman Head of a Great Poet," *A&A* 21 (1926) 92.

K. Kourouniotis, "An Eleusinian Mystery," *A&A* 21 (1926) 113-117. *(Trans. by C. W. and E. D. Blegen) [Statue]*

William Bell Dinsmoor, "The Sculptured Parapet of Athena Nike," *AJA* 30 (1926) 1-31.

Cornelia G. Harcum, "A Statue of the Type of the Venus Genetrix in the Royal Ontario Museum," *AJA* 30 (1926) 83.

La Rue Van Hook, "An Athlete Relief from the Themistoklean Wall, Athens," *AJA* 30 (1926) 283-287.

H. F. Lutz, "A Stone of Amset and Hapi," *JAOS* 46 (1926) 312-313.

H[enri] Frankfort, "A Masterpiece of Early Middle Kingdom Sculpture," *JEA* 12 (1926) 143-144.

Cornelia G. Harcum, "Recent Acquisitions of Classical Sculpture in the Royal Ontario Museum," *A&A* 24 (1927) 55-62.

*H. J. Orr-Ewing, "The Lion and the Cavern of Bones at Petra," *PEFQS* 59 (1927) 155-156. *[Relief]*

*William Stuart Messer, "Classical Art from Ancient Shipwrecks," *A&A* 23 (1927) 147-159.

Dorothy Burr, "A Primitive Statue from Arkadia," *AJA* 31 (1927) 169-176.

H. R. Hall, "The Head of an Old Man (No. 37883) in the British Museum," *JEA* 13 (1927) 27-29.

*H. R. Hall, "Head of a Monarch of the Tuthmosid House, in the British Museum," *JEA* 13 (1927) 133-134. *[Tuthmosis III?]*

Leon Legrain, "The Stela of the Flying Angels," *MJ* 18 (1927) 75-98.

Leon Legrain, "Sumerian Sculptures," *MJ* 18 (1927) 217-247.

L[eon] Legrain, "Tomb Sculptures from Palmyra," *MJ* 18 (1927) 325-350.

Allen T. George, "A Unique Statue of Senmut," *AJSL* 44 (1927-28) 49-55.

Allen T. George, "More Data on Senmut," *AJSL* 44 (1927-28) 267-269.

Anonymous, "Notes and Comments. A Queen's Sphinxes," *A&A* 26 (1928) 53.

A[lexander] D[avid] Fraser, "Two Terra-cotta Heads of Hermes in Toronto," *A&A* 25 (1928) 150-155.

Gisela M. A. Richter, "The Right Arm of Harmodios," *AJA* 32 (1928) 1-8.

*Percy E. Newberry, "Notes on the Sculptured Slab No. 15000 in the Berlin Museum," *JEA* 14 (1928) 117.

H. R. Hall, "A Painted Terracotta Head in the British Museum," *JEA* 14 (1928) 209-210.

H. R. Hall, "A Ramesside Royal Statue from Palestine," *JEA* 14 (1928) 280.

J. M. Unvala, "Three Panels from Susa," *RAAO* 25 (1928) 179-185. *[Relief]*

Anonymous, "Notes and Comments. A Sea-God in a Net *(Translated by courtesy of the German Embassy from the Berliner Illustrirte Zietung),*" *A&A* 27 (1929) 89-90.

*Rhys Carpenter, "The Sculptural Composition of the Nike Parapet," *AJA* 33 (1929) 467-483.

*S. R. K. Glanville, "Some Notes on Material for the Reign of Amenophis III," *JEA* 15 (1929) 2-8. [I. Fragment of a statue of Amenophis, son of Hapu, pp. 2-5]

F. Ll. Griffith, "Scenes from a Destroyed Temple at Napata," *JEA* 15 (1929) 26-28.

G. D. Hornblower, "Predynastic Figures of Women and their Successors," *JEA* 15 (1929) 29-47.

Anonymous, "Notes and Comments. 125 Tons of Assyrian Sculpture," *A&A* 29 (1930) 93.

Ludlow Bull, "The Stelae with the Sing-Winged Sun Disk," *AJA* 34 (1930) 55.

G. A. Wainwright, "A Græco-Roman Glass Head," *ASAE* 30 (1930) 95-99. (Communication by F. A. Bannister, pp. 99-101)

H. R. Hall, "Two Middle Kingdom Statues in the British Museum," *JEA* 16 (1930) 167-168.

*W. R. Taylor, "Recent Epigraphic Discoveries in Palestine," *JPOS* 10 (1930) 16-22. [The Palmyrene Funerary Bust, pp. 16-17]

*I. Ben-Zevil, "Discoveries at Pekiin," *PEFQS* 62 (1930) 210-213. [(1) The Seven-branched Candelabrum; (2) The Door Tablet; (3) The Cluster of Grapes]

Anonymous, "A Hittite Tufa Eagle," *UMB* 1 (1930) #4, 26-27.

E[dith] H. D[ohan], "Two Greek Sculptures," *UMB* 2 (1930-31) 150-151, 153.

Anonymous, "Notes and Comments. Babylonian Lion at Yale," *A&A* 31 (1931) 142.

J. P. Droop, "Some Limestone Heads from Cyprus in the Liverpool Public Museums," *AAA* 18 (1931) 29-38.

Rhys Carpenter, "Symposium on the Hermes of Praxiteles. Who Carved the Hermes of Praxiteles?" *AJA* 35 (1931) 249-261.

Stanley Casson, "Symposium on the Hermes of Praxiteles. The Hermes of Praxiteles," *AJA* 35 (1931) 262-268.

Gisela M. A. Richter, "Symposium on the Hermes of Praxiteles. The Hermes of Praxiteles," *AJA* 35 (1931) 277-290.

Valentin Müller, "Some Notes on the Drapery of Hermes," *AJA* 35 (1931) 291-295.

William Bell Dinsmoor, "Symposium on the Hermes of Praxiteles. Architectural Note," *AJA* 35 (1931) 296-297.

F. Ll. Griffith, "Excavations at Tell el-ʿAmarnah, 1923-4. A. Statuary," *JEA* 17 (1931) 179-184.

E[dith] H. D[ohan], "A Head of the Youthful Herakles," *UMB* 3 (1931-32) 55-56.

Anonymous, "A Sculpture from Meydûm," *UMB* 3 (1931-32) 174-176.

H. P., "Notes and Comments. Egyptian Finds of American and German Excavators are Fitted Together," *A&A* 33 (1932) 159-161.

Herbert N. Couch, "The Illinois Minotaur," *AJA* 36 (1932) 41-42.

Franklin P. Johnson, "Three Reliefs," *AJA* 36 (1932) 276-283. *[Greek?]*

Gisela M. A. Richter, "The Relief in New York," *AJA* 36 (1932) 284-285. (Additional note by F[ranklin] P. J[ohnson], p. 286) *[Greek?]*

A[lexander] D[avid] Fraser, "The Restoration of the Ludovisi Gaul," *AJA* 36 (1932) 418-425.

Alexandre Piankoff, "Two reliefs in the Louvre representing the Gîzah Sphinx," *JEA* 18 (1932) 155-158.

*Anonymous, "A Collection from Tell Bella and Tepe Gawra," *UMB* 4 (1932-33) 17-20.

Anonymous, "A Marble Head from Minturnæ," *UMB* 4 (1932-33) 67-70.

Margaret Rickert, "A Rhodian Stele," *AJA* 37 (1933) 407-411.

*Percy E. Newberry, "A Statue and a Scarab," *JEA* 19 (1933) 53-54.

E. Douglas Van Buren, "A Clay Relief in the ʿIraq Museum," *AfO* 9 (1933-34) 165-171.

D. M. Vaughan, "Some Notes on the Dado-Sculpture of Sakjegeuzi," *AAA* 21 (1934) 37-41.

J. H. Iliffe, "A Copy of the Crouching Aphrodite," *QDAP* 2 (1933) 110-112.

*Horace C. Beck, "Notes on Glazed Stones," *AEE* 19 (1934) 69-83; 20 (1935) 19-37.

*Stanley Casson, "Technique of Greek Sculpture," *AJA* 38 (1934) 280-284.

W. L. Cuttle, "The Problem of the Hermes of Olympia," *Antiq* 8 (1934) 151-167.

Harald Ingholt, "Palmyrene Sculptures in Beirut," *Bery* 1 (1934) 32-43.

*Battiscombe Gunn, "The Berlin statue of Ḥarwa and some notes on other Ḥarwa statues," *BIFAO* 34 (1934) 135-142.

*R. O. Faulkner, "A Statue of a Serpent-Worshipper," *JEA* 20 (1934) 154-156.

R. Engelbach, "A Foundation-scene of the Second Dynasty," *JEA* 20 (1934) 183-184. *[Relief]*

B[attiscombe] G[unn], "A Head from an Egyptian Royal Statue," *UMB* 5 (1934-35) #3, 87-88.

E[dith] H. D[ohan], "An Italic Head," *UMB* 5 (1934-35) #3, 90.

E[dith] H. D[ohan], "A Statue of Athena," *UMB* 5 (1934-35) #6, 76-78.

*A[lexandre] Piankoff, "A Pantheistic Representation of Amon in the Petrie Collection," *AEE* 20 (1935) 49-51.

Valentin Müller, "An Attic Original of the Fifth Century," *AJA* 39 (1935) 248-253. *[Relief]*

M. S. Drower, "Egyptian Fragments," *Antiq* 9 (1935) 350-351. *[Reliefs]*

Vagn Hager Poulsen, "A Late-Greek Relief in Beirut," *Bery* 2 (1935) 51-56.

*L[eon] L[egrain], "The Museum's Gudea," *UMB* 6 (1935-37) #6, 6-8.

G. W. Elderkin, "The Seated Deities of the Parthenon Frieze," *AJA* 40 (1936) 92-99.

Lily Ross Taylor, "Seats and Peplos on the Parthenon Frieze," *AJA* 40 (1936) 121.

Margerete Bieber, "Aphrodite in Roman Copies of Greek Statues," *AJA* 40 (1936) 126.

Paola Zancani [Montuoro] and Umberto Zanotti-Bianco, "The Discovery of the Heraion of Hucania," *AJA* 40 (1936) 185-187. *[Sculpture]*

Oscar Broneer, "A Sandstone Head from Corinth," *AJA* 40 (1936) 204-207.

Gisela M. A. Richter, "A Greek Stele in the Metropolitan Museum," *AJA* 40 (1936) 301-304.

Gisela M. A. Richter, "An Early Terracotta Slab in the Metropolitan Museum," *AJA* 40 (1936) 304.

*[J.] Selim Levy, "A Statue of Gudea in the Iraq Museum in Baghdad," *AfO* 11 (1936-37) 151-152.

*C. A. Robinson Jr., "The Development of Archaic Greek Sculpture," *AJA* 41 (1937) 110.

Franklin P. Johnson, "A Statue at Corinth," *AJA* 41 (1937) 116.

A[lexander] D[avid] Fraser, "A Head of Demosthenes in Washington," *AJA* 41 (1937) 212-216.

Alexander Scharff, "Egyptian Portrait-Sculpture," *Antiq* 11 (1937) 174-182.

Herbert Maryon, "A Passage on Sculpture by Diodorus of Sicily," *Antiq* 11 (1937) 344-348.

Frederik Poulsen, "A Philosopher Head in the Museum of the American University, Beirut," *Bery* 4 (1937) 111-115.

*R. Campbell Thompson, "Fragments of Stone Reliefs and Inscriptions found at Nineveh," *Iraq* 4 (1937) 43-46.

*E[mil] G. [H.] Kraeling, "A Unique Babylonian Relief," *BASOR* #67 (1937) 16-18. *[Terra-cotta relief of Lilith]*

L. A. Mayer and A. Reifenberg, "Three Ancient Jewish Reliefs," *PEQ* 69 (1937) 136-139.

H[enri] Frankfort, "The Berney Relief," *AfO* 12 (1937-39) 128-135.

*Oscar Broneer, "The Lion at Amphipolis," *AJA* 42 (1938) 128-129.

Walter R. Agard, "Notes on the Siphnian Treasury Frieze," *AJA* 42 (1938) 237-244.

Sidney N. Deane, "A Statue in the Gardner Museum," *AJA* 42 (1938) 288-290.

G. W. Elderkin, "The Venus Genetrix of Arceilaus," *AJA* 42 (1938) 371-374.

*C. A. Robinson Jr., "The Development of Archaic Greek Sculpture," *AJA* 42 (1938) 451-455.

*R. Engelbach, "Some remarks on *Ka*-statues of abnormal men in the Old Kingdom," *ASAE* 38 (1938) 285-296. (Addendum, p. 399)

William Bell Dinsmoor, "The Lost Pedimental Sculptures of Bassae," *AJA* 43 (1939) 27-47.

Edward Capps Jr., "Two Archaic Poros Figures from Corinth," *AJA* 43 (1939) 301.

A[lexander] D[avid] Fraser, "The 'Capaneus' Reliefs of the Villa Albani and the Art Institute of Chicago," *AJA* 43 (1939) 447-457.

*Karl Lehmann-Hartleben, "Note on the Potnia Taurōn," *AJA* 43 (1939) 669-671.

*D. H. Gordon, "The Buddhist Origin of the 'Sumerian' Heads from Memphis," *Iraq* 6 (1939) 35-38.

Sidney Smith, "A Colossal Statue of the Nineteenth Dynasty," *JEA* 25 (1939) 145-147.

H[ermann] R[anke], "An Unfinished Statue of the Twelfth Dynasty," *UMB* 8 (1939-40) #2/3, 28-30.

*H[ermann] R[anke], "A Statue of the Goddess Hathor," *UMB* 8 (1939-40) #4, 10-12.

Elaine Tankard, "The Sculptures of Sakjegeuzi," *AAA* 26 (1939-40) 85-88.

George M. A. Hanfmann, "Later Etruscan Reliefs," *AJA* 44 (1940) 113.

Adelaide M. Davidson, "Some Unpublished Roman Portrait Heads," *AJA* 40 (1940) 114.

I. E. S. Edwards, "A Fragment of Relief from the Memphite Tomb of Ḥaremḥab," *JEA* 26 (1940) 1-2.

Alexander Scharff, "On the Statuary of the Old Kingdom," *JEA* 26 (1940) 41-50.

David M. Robinson, "A New Marble Bust of Meander Wrongly Called Virgil," *PAPS* 83 (1940) 465-477.

M. Avi-Yonah, "A Jewish Relief from Beth-Shan," *BIES* 8 (1940-41) #1, I-II.

R. F. S. Starr, "A Rare Example of Akkadian Sculpture," *AJA* 45 (1941) 81-86.

Georg Karo, "Early Dorian Friezes," *AJA* 45 (1941) 93.

Dorothy Kent Hill, "Sculpture Newly Exhibited in Baltimore," *AJA* 45 (1941) 153-158.

Gisela M. A. Richter, "Two Reconstructions of Greek Grave Monuments," *AJA* 45 (1941) 159-163.

Kurt Witzmann, "A Tabula Odysseaca," *AJA* 45 (1941) 166-181. *[Relief]*

William Stevenson Smith, "Old Kingdom Sculpture," *AJA* 45 (1941) 514-528.

C[harles] B[ache], "A Fragment of a Limestone Relief," *UMB* 9 (1941-42) #1, 28.

*C. A. Robinson Jr., "The Master of Olympia," *AJA* 46 (1942) 73-76.

Phyllis L. Williams, "A New Approach to the Sculpture of Southern Italy and Sicily in the Fifth and Fourth Centuries, B.C.," *AJA* 46 (1942) 119.

Franklin P. Johnson, "Notes on Bassai," *AJA* 46 (1942) 120-121. *[Acroterion]*

Frederick R. Grace, "Notes on the Daedalic Style," *AJA* 46 (1942) 122.

Anton E. Raubitschek, "The Potter Relief from the Akropolis, a Possible Work of Endoios," *AJA* 46 (1942) 123.

*Karl Lehmann-Hartleben, "Some Ancient Portraits," *AJA* 46 (1942) 198-216. [II. Portrait of an Early Roman Poet, pp. 204-216]

Frederick R. Grace, "Observations on Seventh-Century Sculpture," *AJA* 46 (1942) 341-359. *[Egyptian]*

Anthony E. Raubitschek, "An Original Work of Endoios," *AJA* 46(1942) 245-253. *[Relief]*

William Stevenson Smith, "The Origin of Some Unidentified Old Kingdom Reliefs," *AJA* 46 (1942) 509-531. [1. The Reliefs of Mery; 2. The Chapel of Tep-m-ankh; 3. The Archaic Chapel of Akhat-a'a; 4. The Reliefs of Hemiuwn; 4.*[sic]* The Architrave ofAkhy]

Neilson C. Deevoise, "The Rock Reliefs of Ancient Iran," *JNES* 1 (1942) 76-105.

*F. P. Johnson, "Three Notes on Bassai," *AJA* 47 (1943) 15-18.

*William B. Dinsmoor, "A Further Note on Bassai," *AJA* 47 (1943) 19-21.

[C.] A. Robinson Jr., "Observations on Seventh-Century Sculpture," *AJA* 47 (1943) 88.

*George M. A. Hanfmann, "The Evidence of Architecture and Sculpture," *AJA* 47 (1943) 94-100. *[Etruscan]*

R. Engelbach, "Statues of the 'Soul of Nekhen' and the 'Soul of Pe' of the reign of Amenophis III," *ASAE* 42 (1943) 71-73.

George G. Cameron, "A Photograph of Darius' Sculptures at Behistan," *JNES* 2 (1943) 115-116.

C. A. Robinson Jr., "Observations on Seventh-Century Greek Sculpture," *AJA* 48 (1944) 132-154.

Gisela M. A. Richter, "Two Greek Statues," *AJA* 48 (1944) 229-239.

Sterling Dow, "A Fragment of a Colossal Acrolithic Statue in the Conservatori*[sic]*," *AJA* 48 (1944) 240-250.

*Gisela M. A. Richter, "Polychromy in Greek Sculpture with Special Reference to the Archaic Attic Gravestones in the Metropolitan Museum," *AJA* 48 (1944) 321-333.

John D. Cooney, "A Relief from the Tomb of Ḥaremḥab," *JEA* 30 (1944) 2-4.

*Niels Breitenstein, "Analacta Acragantina," *AA* 16 (1945) 113-153. *[Statues and Reliefs]*

C. A. Robinson Jr., "The Zeus Ithomatos of Ageladas," *AJA* 49 (1945) 121-127.

*Niels Breitenstein, "Analacta Acragantina," *AA* 16 (1945) 113-153. *[Reliefs and Sculptures]*

John D. Cooney, "A Tentative Identification of Three Old Kingdom Sculptures," *JEA* 31 (1945) 54-56.

Phyllis L. Williams, "Amykos and the Dioskouroi," *AJA* 49 (1945) 330-347.

Karl Lehmann, "The Girl Beneath the Apple Tree," *AJA* 49 (1945) 430-433.

Henri Frankfort, "Achaemenian Sculpture," *AJA* 50 (1946) 6-14.

Elisabeth Jastrow, "Two Terracotta Reliefs in American Museums," *AJA* 50 (1946) 67-80.

Vladimir G. Simkhovitch, "Some Fifth-century Heads," *AJA* 50 (1946) 81-85.

Oscar Waldhauer, "Myron's *Anus Ebria* and the Drunken Woman in Munich," *AJA* 50 (1946) 241-246.

*M. Rostovtzeff, "Numidian Horsemen on Canosa Vases," *AJA* 50 (1946) 263-267.

D. B. Thompson, "Ostrakina Toreumata," *AJA* 50 (1946) 288. *[Sculpture from Corinth]*

Dieter Thimme, "The Masters of the Pergamon Gigantomachy," *AJA* 50 (1946) 345-357.

Rhys Carpenter, "A New Fifth Century Statue from the Athenian Agora," *AJA* 50 (1946) 404.

*M. Avi-Yonah, "Two Remains of our Ancient Art," *BIES* 12 (1946) I. *[Decorated limestone coffin; decorated marble screen]*

George H. Chase, "An Archaic Greek Sphinx in Boston," *AJA* 50 (1946) 1-5.

*H[enri] Frankfort, "Oriental Institute Museum Notes, Two Acquisitions for the Simkhovitch Collection," *JNES* 5 (1946) 153-156. [1. A Ewe's Head of the Proto-Literate Period, pp. 153-155; 2. An Assyrian Bronze Bowl, pp. 155-156]

*Labib Habachi, "A statue of Osiris made for Ankhefenamun, prophet of the house of Amun in Khapu and his daughter," *ASAE* 47 (1947) 261-282.

Dows Dunham, "Four Kushite Colossi in the Sudan," *JEA* 33 (1947) 63-65.

Gisela M. A. Richter, "A Greek Terracotta Head and the 'Corinthian' School of Terracotta Sculpture," *AJA* 52 (1948) 331-335.

Charles H. Morgan II, "Pheidias and Olympia," *AJA* 52 (1948) 379-380. *[On the Style of Greek Sculpture]*

David M. Robinson, "New Attic Sculptures and Inscriptions," *AJA* 52 (1948) 380-381.

George*[sic]* Karo, "Art Salvaged from the Sea," *Arch* 1 (1948) 179-185.

*Elise J. Baumgartel, "The three colossi from Koptos and their Mesopotamian counterparts," *ASAE* 48 (1948) 533-553.

*C. J. Gadd, "Two Assyrian Observations," *Iraq* 10 (1948) 19-25. [(a) A Sculpture in the Iraq Museum, pp. 19-21]

C. J. Gadd, "The Fan of Ba-ba," *Iraq* 10 (1948) 93-100. *[Relief]*

H. E. Taufiq Wahby, "The Rock-Sculptures in Gunduk Cave," *Sumer* 4(1948) 143-147.

Winifred Needler, "Some Ptolemaic Sculptures in the Yale University Art Gallery," *Bery* 9 (1948-49) 129-141.

Rhys Carpenter, "Two Old Women from New York," *AJA* 53 (1949) 149.

Saul S. Weinberg, "On Corinthian Terracotta Sculpture," *AJA* 53 (1949) 262-266.

*Victor Wolfgang von Hagen, "Frederick Catherwood in Egypt," *Arch* 2 (1949) 199-205. *[Colossi of Memnon]*

Homer A. Thompson, "Head of Nike from the Athenian Angora," *Arch* 2 (1949) 17-19.

*John D. Cooney, "A Souvenir of Napoleon's Trip to Egypt," *JEA* 35 (1949) 153-157.

*Rosalind Moss, "An Egyptian Statue at Malta," *JEA* 35 (1949) 132-134.

Faraj Basmachi, "The Lion-Hunt Stela from Warka," *Sumer* 5 (1949) 87-94.

Cleta Margaret Olmstead, "A Greek Lady from Persepolis," *AJA* 54 (1950) 10-18.

Kazimierz Bulas, "New Illustrations to the Illiad," *AJA* 54 (1950) 112-118. *[Relief]*

*Dorothy Kent Hill, "Three Portraits of the First Century B.C.," *AJA* 54 (1950) 264.

William Stevenson Smith, "Saite Sculpture," *AJA* 54 (1950) 256. *[Egyptian Sculpture]*

*Sidney D. Markman, "A Correlated Chronology for Greek Sculpture and Vase Painting," *AJA* 54 (1950) 263.

Edward Capps Jr., "Gleanings from Old Corinth," *AJA* 54 (1950) 265-266. *[Sculpture]*

Rhys Carpenter, "Tradition and Invention in Attic Reliefs," *AJA* 54 (1950) 323-336.

*Winifred Needler, "A Hathor from Eleventh-Dynasty Egypt," *Arch* 3 (1950) 194-195. *[Wall Relief]*

Edith Porada, "A Leonine Figure of the Protoliterate Period of Mesopotamia," *JAOS* 70 (1950) 223-226.

John D. Cooney, "Three Early Saïte Tomb Reliefs," *JNES* 9 (1950) 193-203.

*Helen Wade Smith, "Sculptural Style on Ptolemaic Portrait Coins," *Bery* 10 (1950-53) 21-36.

N. Avigad, "The Rock-carved Façades of the Jerusalem Necropolis," *IEJ* 1 (1950-51) 96-106.

R. D. Barnett, "Four Sculptures from Amman," *ADAJ* 1 (1951) 34-36.

George E. Mylonas, "The Figured Mycenaean Stelai," *AJA* 55 (1951) 134-147.

Saul S. Weinberg, "Terracotta Sculpture from Corinth," *AJA* 55 (1951) 148.

J. D. Beazley, "A Fragment of a Stele from Cyprus," *AJA* 55 (1951) 333-336.

*Charles Seltman, "A mine of statues," *HT* (Jan., 1951) 34-42. *[Herculaneum]*

*Ambrose Lansing, "A Head of Tutʿankhamūn," *JEA* 37 (1951) 3-4.

*Henri Wild, "A Bas-relief of Sekhemrēʿ-sewadjtowĕ Sebkḥotpe," *JEA* 37 (1951) 12-16.

Anonymous, "Some Opinions about an Unidentified Statue," *Sumer* 7 (1951) 73-76.

P. J. Riis, "The Pedigree of Some Heracles Figures from Tarsus," *AA* 23 (1952) 152-154.

*Sidney S. Schipper, "Cat or Marten?" *Arch* 5 (1952) 25-29. *[Relief]*

*R. T. O'Callaghan, "A Statue Recently Found in ʿAmmân," *Or, N.S.*, 21 (1952) 184-193.

*Herbert Hoffmann, "Lion at Didyma," *Arch* 6 (1953) 103.

Edith Porada, "An Ornament from an Assyrian Throne," *Arch* 6 (1953) 208-210.

Gustavus F. Swift Jr., "The Sphinx from Tell Tayinaat," *Arch* 6 (1953) 230-231.

Cyril Aldred, "The Statue Head of a Tuthmoside Monarch," *JEA* 39 (1953) 48-49.

Rhys Carpenter, "Two Postscripts to the Hermes Controversy," *AJA* 58 (1954) 1-12.

Harald Ingholt, "Parthian Sculpture from Hatra," *AJA* 57 (1953) 108.

P. L. Shinnie, "A New Kingdom head from Faras," *JEA* 39 (1953) 109-110.

Vagn Poulsen, "Odysseus in Boston," *AA* 25 (1954) 301-304.

*Margarete Bieber, "Romani Pallati," *AJA* 58 (1954) 143.

Bernard V. Bothmer, "Roman Republican and Late Egyptian Portraiture," *AJA* 58 (1954) 143-144.

William B[ell] Dinsmoor, "New Evidence for the Parthenon Frieze,"*AJA* 58 (1954) 144-145.

David M. Robinson, "Unpublished Classical Heads in the Robinson Collection," *AJA* 58 (1954) 149.

*Gisela M. A. Richter, "Acquisitions of the Fogg Art Museum: Sculpture and Figurines," *AJA* 58 (1954) 223-229.

Tahsin Özgüç, "Fragment of a Lion Statue Found in the Late Phase (Ib) of the Colony Period," *TTKB* 18 (1954) 445-447.

David M. Robinson, "Unpublished Sculpture in the Robinson Collection," *AJA* 59 (1955) 19-29.

Erik Sjöqvist, "A Cypriote Temple Attendent," *AJA* 59 (1955) 45-47.

*C. Vermeule, "Notes on a New Edition of Michaelis: Ancient Marbles in Great Britain. Part One," *AJA* 59 (1955) 129-150.

Thalia Phillies Howe, "Zeus Herkeios: the Triple-Bodied Monster of the Akropolis," *AJA* 59 (1955) 172.

Berta Segall, "Sculpture from Arabia Felix," *AJA* 59 (1955) 174.

Matthew I. Wiencke, "Sculpture from the East Frieze of Hephaisteion," *AJA* 59 (1955) 175.

John B. Stearns, "The Provenance of Assyrian Bas-Reliefs in American Collections," *AJA* 59 (1955) 177.

Berta Segall, "Sculpture from Arabia Felix. The Hellenistic Period," *AJA* 59 (1955) 207-214.

Thalia Phillies Howe, "Zeus Herkeios: Thematic Unity in the Hekatompedon Sculptures," *AJA* 59 (1955) 287-301.

G. A. Stamires, "From an Attic Grave," *Arch* 8 (1955) 121. *[Relief from a Marble Vase Fragment]*

*M. Cassirer, "A Granite Group of the Eighteenth Dynasty," *JEA* 41(1955) 72-74.

J. R. Harris, "The name of the scribe in the Louvre—a note," *JEA* 41 (1955) 122-123.

I. E. S. Edwards, "A Relief of Qudshu-Astarte-Anath in the Winchester College Collection," *JNES* 14 (1955) 49-51.

R. J. Riis, "Sculptured Alabastra," *AA* 27 (1956) 23-33.

*Franklin P. Johnson, "A Philosophic Allegory?" *AJA* 60 (1956) 57-61. *[Sculpture]*

Evelyn B. Harrison, "The West Pediment of the Temple of Hephaistos," *AJA* 60 (1956) 178. *[Sculpture Discoveries]*

*David M. Robinson, "A New Bust of the Empress Livia in the Robinson Collection," *AJA* 60 (1956) 181.

Louise Adams Holland, "The Purpose of the Warrior Image from Capestrano," *AJA* 60 (1956) 243-247.

*Cornelius C. Vermeule and D. von Bothmer, "Notes on a New Edition of Michaelis: Ancient Marbles in Great Britain. Part Two," *AJA* 60 (1956) 129-150.

W[illiam] B[ell] Dinsmoor, "The Sculpture Frieze from Bassae (A Revised Sequence)," *AJA* 60 (1956) 401-452.

Ruth B. K. Amiran, "A Fragment of an Ornamental Relief from Kfar Bar'am," *IEJ* 6 (1956) 293-245.

W. K. Simpson, "On the statue group: Amūn affixing the crown of the king," *JEA* 42 (1956) 118-119.

Cyril Aldred, "An Unusual Fragment of New Kingdom Relief," *JEA* 15(1956) 150-152.

J. M. Cook, "The Reliefs of 'Sesostris' in India," *TAD* 6 (1956) #2, 59-65.

Karl Lehmann, "Kallistratos Meets a Centaur," *AJA* 61 (1957) 123-127. *[Sculpture]*

*Carla Gottlieb, "The Pediment Sculpture and Acroteria from the Hephaisteion and the Temple of Ares in the Agora at Athens," *AJA* 61 (1957) 161-165.

Bernard V. Bothmer, "Some Graeco-Egyptian and Hellenistic Heads from Egypt," *AJA* 61 (1957) 182.

*Christoph Clairmont, "The Stelai of Aristion and Lyseas: The Relationship between Sculpture and Painting in Late Archaic Greece," *AJA* 61 (1957) 183.

Charles H. Morgan, "The Friezes of the Hephaisteion," *AJA* 61 (1957) 184-185.

David M. Robinson, "New Greek and Roman Sculpture in Mississippi," *AJA* 61 (1957) 186.

*J. Vercoutter, "Editorial Notes: *Hatshepsut, Tuthmosis III or Amenophis II?* (Khartoum Museum statue no. 30)," *Kush* 5 (1957) 5-7.

Dericksen M. Brinkerhoff, "The Identification of the Aphrodite Who Binds Her Sandal and Related Works of Hellenistic Sculpture," *AJA* 62 (1958) 222.

Quentin Maule, "Establishing a Sequence for Italic Warrior Sculpture," *AJA* 62 (1958) 224.

J. Walter Graham, "The Ransom of Hector on a New Melian Relief," *AJA* 62 (1958) 313-319.

R. Ross Holloway, "The Date of the Eleusis Relief," *AJA* 62 (1958) 403-408.

C. A. Burney and G. R. J. Lawson, "Urartian Reliefs at Adilcevaz, on Lake Van, and a Rock Relief from the Karasu, near Birecik," *AS* 8 (1958) 211-218.

George M. A. Hanfmann and Kemal Ziya Polatkan, "Three Sculptures from Sardis in the Manisa Museum," *A(A)* 4 (1959) 55-65.

*[Cornelius] C. Vermeule and D. von Bothmer, "Notes on a New Edition of Michaelis: Ancient Marbles in Great Britain. Part Three: 1," *AJA* 63 (1959) 139-166.

Evelyn B. Harrison, "The Relief Sculpture of the Temple of Ares in Athens," *AJA* 63 (1959) 188-189.

Elmer G. Suhr, "The 'Gatagusa' of Praxiteles," *AJA* 63 (1959) 191.

Matthew I. Wiencke, "New Studies of the Parthenon Frieze in Athens," *AJA* 63 (1959) 191-192.

*[Cornelius] C. Vermeule and D. von Bothmer, "Notes on a New Edition of Michaelis: Ancient Marbles in Great Britain. Part Three: 2," *AJA* 63 (1959) 329-348.

Seymour Howard, "On the Reconstruction of the Vatican Laocoon Group," *AJA* 63 (1959) 365-369.

K. R. Maxwell-Hyslop, "An Uratian Archer on the Zinjirli Chariot Relief," *ULBIA* 2 (1959) 65-66.

Cornelius C. Vermeule III, "Hellenistic and Roman Cuirassed Statues: A Supplement," *Bery* 13 (1959-60) 1-82.

Ellen Kohler, "An Etruscan Tomb-Guardian," *Exped* 2 (1959-60) #2, 25-27.

B. B. Shefton, "Some Iconographic Remarks on the Tyrannicides," *AJA* 64 (1960) 173-179. *[Greek Statues]*

Bernard V. Bothmer, "'Alexandrian' Portraits of the First Century B.C.," *AJA* 64 (1960) 183.

*Harald Ingholt, "The Parthian on the Augustus Statue of Prima Porta," *AJA* 64 (1960) 187.

Elmer G. Suhr, "The Spinning Aphrodite in Sculpture," *AJA* 64 (1960) 253-264.

Herbert Hoffmann, "Two Deer Heads from Apulia," *AJA* 64 (1960) 276-278. *[Terracottas]*

*R. D. Barnett, "Two Chance Finds from Ur," *Iraq* 22 (1960) 172-173.

*Bernard V. Bothmer, "The Philadelphia-Cairo Statue of Osorkon II. (Membra Dipersa III)," *JEA* 46 (1960) 3-11.

Mabel Lang, "Picture Puzzles from Pylos: First Steps in the Study of Frescoes," *Arch* 13 (1960) 55-60.

*D. J. Wiseman, "The Goddess Lama at Ur," *Iraq* 22 (1960) 166-171. *[Statue]*

Helene J. Kantor, "Oriental Institute Museum Notes. No. 12: A Fragment of Relief from the Tomb of Mentuemhat at Thebes (No. 34)," *JNES* 19 (1960) 213-216.

Seymour Howard, "Another Prototype for the Gigantomachy of Pergamon," *AJA* 65 (1961) 190.

Brunilde Sismondo Ridgway, "A Marble Head in California," *AJA* 65 (1961) 393-396.

Dorothy G. Shepherd, "An Achaemenid Sculpture in Cleveland," *Arch* 14 (1961) 102-103.

Alan [H.] Gardiner, "The Egyptian Memnon," *JEA* 47 (1961) 91-99. *[Statue]*

Labib Habachi, "A Statue of a 'Triton' from Gaza," *JNES* 20 (1961) 47-49.

*Alexander Badaway, "The transport of the colossus of Djeḥutiḥetep," *MIO* 8 (1961-63) 325-332.

*Henry G. Fischer, "A Provincial Statue of the Egyptian Sixth Dynasty," *AJA* 66 (1962) 65-69. *[Erratum, p. 226]*

J. R. McCredie, "Two Herms in the Fogg Museum," *AJA* 66 (1962) 187-189.

Margarete Bieber, "A Review," *AJA* 66 (1962) 237-244. *[Sculpture] (Review)*

Erik Sjöqvist, "A Portrait Head from Morgantina," *AJA* 66 (1962) 319-322.

T. B. L. Webster, "A Terracotta Head in the Metropolitan Museum," *AJA* 66 (1962) 333-336.

John L. Casey, "The Goddess of Ceos," *Arch* 15 (1962) 223-226.

*A. J. Arkell, "An early pet cat," *JEA* 48 (1962) 158. *[Relief]*

E. P. Uphill, "A New Kingdom relief from Memphis," *JEA* 48 (1962) 162-163.

Nicholas B. Millet, "A Fragment of the Hatshepsut Punt Relief," *JARCE* 1 (1962) 55-57.

*Margarete Bieber, "The Copies of the Herculaneum Women," *PAPS* 106 (1962) 111-134.

Bernard Ashmole, "Some Nameless Sculptors of the Fifth Century B.C.," *PBA* 48 (1962) 213-233.

*Faraj Basmachi, "Miscellania in the Iraq Museum," *Sumer* 18 (1962) 48-50. [An Assyrian Bronze Relief (I.M. 62197); Assyrian Marble Statue (I.M. 66456); Kudurru (A Boundary Stone) (I. M. 62269); A Marble Statue of a Girl (I. M. 63503); Limestone Relief (I. M. 56577); Decorated Marble Plaque (I. M. 66453); Gipsum*[sic]* Statuette (I. M. 64398); A Rough Limestone Statue (I. M. 66461)]

*Robert H. Dyson, "A Babylonian Lion in Toledo," *Exped* 5 (1962-63) #2, 14-15.

Lenore Keene Congdon, "The Mantua Apollo of the Fogg Art Museum," *AJA* 67 (1963) 7-13.

Dericksen Brinckerhoff, "Changing Methods in the Distribution of Sculpture in the Eastern Mediterranean Area during the Later Imperial Age," *AJA* 67 (1963) 208-209.

R. Ross Holloway, "Athena Archegetis in the Piraeus," *AJA* 67 (1963) 212.

*Harald Ingholt, "Colossal Head in Boston, Severan or Augustan?" *AJA* 67 (1963) 213.

Matthew I. Wiencke, "The Date of the Parthenon Frieze," *AJA* 67 (1963) 219.

*J. K. Anderson, "The Statue of Chabrias," *AJA* 67 (1963) 411-413.

*Ray L. Cleveland, "Cherubs and the 'Tree of Life' in Ancient Arabia," *BASOR* #172 (1963) 55-60.

*Harald Ingholt, "A Colossal Head from Memphis, Severan or Augustan?" *JARCE* 2 (1963) 125-145.

Olof Vessberg, "A Republican Portrait from Sabina," *MB* #3 (1963) 67-72. *[Statue Head]*

*Rudolf Anthes, "Affinity and Difference Between Egyptian and Greek Sculpture and Thought in the Seventh and Sixth Centuries B.C.," *PAPS* 107 (1963) 60-81.

P. J. Riis, "Etruscan or Modern? On the Authenticity of Certain Terracottas in Danish Collections," *AA* 35 (1964) 81-93.

Kim Levin, "The Male Figure in Egyptian and Greek Sculpture of the Seventh and Sixth Centuries B.C.," *AJA* 68 (1964) 13-28.

John H. Young, "Commagenian Tiaras: Royal and Divine," *AJA* 68 (1964) 29-34.

Christine Mitchell Havelock, "Archaistic Reliefs of the Hellenistic Period," *AJA* 68 (1964) 43-58. (Correction, p. 188)

Brunilde Sismondo Ridgway, "The Date of the So-Called Lysippean Jason," *AJA* 68 (1964) 113-128.

Seymour Howard, "Another Prototype for the Giantomachy of Pergamon," *AJA* 68 (1964) 129-136.

Evelyn B. Harrison, "Hesperides and Heroes, a Note on the Three-Figure Reliefs," *AJA* 68 (1964) 195.

Cornelius [C.] Vermeule [III], "Greek, Etruscan and Roman Sculptures in the Museum of Fine Arts, Boston," *AJA* 68 (1964) 323-341.

Cornelius C. Vermeule III, "Hellenistic and Roman Cuirassed Statues: A Supplement," *Bery* 15 (1964) 95-110.

J. H. C. Kern, "The Egyptian relief-fragment (Florence Museo Archaeologico no. 2566)," *BO* 21 (1964) 10-11.

C. De Wit, "Some remarks concerning the so-called 'Isis' in the Museum Vleeshuis, Antwerp," *CdÉ* 39 (1964) 61-66.

*Nelson Glueck, "Nabataean Dolphins," *EI* 7 (1964) 40*-43*. *[Sculptures]*

*Abd el-Mohsen el-Khachab, "Some Recent Acquisitions of the Cairo Museum," *JEA* 50 (1964) 144-146. [2. A charming glass bust; 4. Head of a woman, p. 145]]

Robert H. Dyson Jr., "A Stranger from the East," *Exped* 7 (1964-65) #1, 32-33. *[Wood Sculpture]*

*Ora Negbi, "A Contribution of Mineralogy and Palaeontology to an Archaeological Study of Terracottas," *IEJ* 14 (1964) 187-189.

J. E. Reade, "More Drawings of Assurbanipal Sculptures," *Iraq* 26 (1964) 1-13.

J. E. Reade, "Twelve Ashurnasirpul Reliefs," *Iraq* 27 (1964) 119-134.

*D. M. Dixon and K. P. Wachsman, "A Sandstone Statue of An Auletes from Meroe," *Kush* 12 (1964) 119-125.

Bengt Julius Peterson, "Two Royal Heads from Amarna: Studies in the Art of the Armana Age," *MB* #4 (1964) 13-29.

Cornelius C. Vermeule III, "Greek and Roman Portraits in North American Collections Open to the Public: A Survey of Important Monumental Likenesses in Marble and Bronze which have not been published extensively," *PAPS* 108 (1964) 99-134.

Brunilde Sismondo Ridgway, "The East Pediment of the Siphnian Treasury: A Reinterpretation," *AJA* 69 (1965) 1-5. *[Relief]*

Dericksen M. Brinkerhoff, "New Examples of the Hellenistic Statue Group, 'The Invitation to the Dance,' and their Significance," *AJA* 69 (1965) 25-37.

Elizabeth T. Wakeley and Brunilde Sismondo Ridgway, "A Head of Herakles in the Philadelphia University Museum," *AJA* 69 (1965) 156-160. [Addendum, p. 371]

Evelyn [B.] Harrison, "Who Was Who in the East Pediment of the Parthenon," *AJA* 69 (1965) 168-169.

*Brunilde Sismondo Ridgway, "Wounded Figures in Greek Sculpture," *Arch* 18 (1965) 47-54.

J. E. Wootton, "A Sumerian Statue from Tell Aswad," *Sumer* 21 (1965) 113-118.

Elizabeth T. Wakeley, "A Bibliographical Note," *AJA* 70 (1966) 70. *[Grave stela]*

*Otto Brendel, "A Diademed Roman?" *AJA* 70 (1966) 184.

Susan B. Downey, "A Statue of Hercules at Hatra," *AJA* 70 (1966) 187.

Miriam Ervin, "The Terracotta Statues from Keos," *AJA* 70 (1966) 188-189.

Elizabeth Theresa Wakeley, "The Harpy Tomb Frieze—A New Interpretation," *AJA* 70 (1966) 196.

Brunilde Sismondo Ridgway, "The Two Reliefs from Epidauros," *AJA* 70 (1966) 217-222.

G. Karl Galinsky, "Venus in a Relief of the Ara Pacis Augustae," *AJA* 70 (1966) 223-243.

George M. A. Hanfmann, "A Hellenistic Landscape Relief," *AJA* 70 (1966) 371-373.

Franklin P. Johnson, "On Believing Fioravanti," *AJA* 70 (1966) 373.

Elizabeth Gummey Pemberton, "A Note on the Death of Aigisthos," *AJA* 70 (1966) 377-378. *[Sculpture]*

*Brunilde Sismondo Ridgway, "Stone and Metal in Greek Sculpture," *Arch* 19 (1966) 31-42.

Cornelius C. Vermeule III, "Hellenistic and Roman Cuirassed Statues: Second Supplement," *Bery* 16 (1966) 49-59.

M. E. L. Mallowan, "An Alabaster Head from Timnaʿ, South Arabia," *Iraq* 28 (1966) 96-104.

N. Dorin Ischlondsky, "A Peculiar Representation of the Jackal-God Anubis," *JNES* 25 (1966) 17-26.

David Ussishkin, "On the Date of the Neo-Hittite Relief from Andaval," *A(A)* 11 (1967) 197-202.

Evelyn B. Harrison, "Athena and Athens in the East Pediment of the Parthenon," *AJA* 71 (1967) 27-58.

Werner Fuchs, "New Contributions to the West Pediment of the Parthenon: The Legs and the Action of Poseidon," *AJA* 71(1967) 187.

Brunilde Sismondo Ridgway, "The Banquet Relief from Thasos," *AJA* 71 (1967) 307-309.

*Otto Brendel, "A Diademed Roman? *For Richard Krautheimer*,"*AJA* 71 (1967) 407-409.

David Ussishkin, "On the Dating of Some Groups of Reliefs from Carchemish and Til Barsib," *AS* 17 (1967) 181-192.

Anonymous, "Two Treasures from Nimrud," *BH* 3 (1967) #1, 16-17. *[Sculptures]*

*R. Ross Holloway, "Panhellenism in the Sculptures of the Zeus Temple at Olympia," *GRBS* 8 (1967) 93-101.

J. E. Reade, "Two Slabs from Sennacherib's Palace," *Iraq* 29 (1967) 42-48.

Jean L. Keith, "Notes on a Marble Head of a Youth in the Brooklyn Museum," *JARCE* 6 (1967) 157-162.

*E. Danelius and H. Steinitz, "The Fishes and other Aquatic Animals on the Punt-Reliefs at Deir El-Baḥri," *JEA* 53 (1967) 15-24.

*Oscar White Muscarella, "Fibulae Represented on Sculpture," *JNES* 26 (1967) 82-86.

*H[assan] S. K. Bakry, "A stela of Horus standing on crocodiles from the Middle Delta," *RDSO* 42 (1967) 15-18.

Sami Sa'id Al-Ahmed, "Sculpture of the First Dynasty of Babylon," *Sumer* 23 (1967) 97-121.

H. M. Stewart, "A Monument with Amarna Traits," *ULBIA* 7 (1967) 85-88. *[Egyptian Statue]*

*G. R. H. Wright, "Recent Discoveries in the Sanctuary of the Qasr Bint Far'un at Petra. II. Some Aspects Concerning the Architecture and Sculpture," *ADAJ* 12&13 (1967-68) 20-29.

Carol Ward Carpenter, "Akrolithic Sculpture," *AJA* 72 (1968) 162-163.

Seymour Howard, "A New Veristic Portrait of Late Hellenism," *AJA* 72 (1968) 166.

*Brunilde Sismondo Ridgway, "A Head of Ptolemy VI in Providence," *AJA* 72 (1968) 171.

Cornelius C. Vermeule III, "Lifesized Statues in America," *AJA* 72 (1968) 174.

*Donald White, "Recent Discoveries from Archaic Cyrene II: The Dedicatory Sphinx and Bronze Plaques," *AJA* 72 (1968) 174.

Werner Fuchs, "A Late Hellenistic Group of Aeneas and Anchises," *AJA* 72 (1968) 384-385. *[Statues]*

Philip C. Hammond, "The Medallion and Block Reliefs at Petra," *BASOR* #192 (1968) 16-21.

*L. B. Kreitner, "Archaeological Notes. A Greek Arch and Parmenides' Head: *A report on Velia-Elea,*" *HT* 18 (1968) 129, 131.

Alan R. Schulman, "A Private Triumphal Relief in Brooklyn and Hildesheim," *JARCE* 7 (1968) 27-35.

*Gölül Öney, "Lion Figures in Anatolian Seljuk Architecture," *A(A)* 13 (1969) 43-67.

Henry S. Robinson, "Chiron at Corinth," *AJA* 73 (1969) 193-197.

Joseph Coleman Carter Jr., "Unpublishing Metopes from a Terentine Naiskos," *AJA* 73 (1969) 233.

Dorothy Kent Hill, "Polykleitos: Diadoumenos, Doryphoros and Hermes," *AJA* 73 (1969) 236-237. *[Statues]*

Jean Leslie Howarth, "A Palmyrene Head at Bryn Mawr College," *AJA* 73 (1969) 441-446.

Rhys [A.] Carpenter, "Belated Report on the Hermes Controversy," *AJA* 73 (1969) 465-468. *[Statue]*

Werner Fuchs, "Korai: A Review Article," *Arch* 22 (1969) 173-175. *[Sculpture] (Review)*

*G. A. Gaballas, "Minor War Scenes of Ramesses II at Karnak," *JEA* 55 (1969) 82-88. *[Relief]*

Margaret A. V. Gill, "The Minoan 'frame' on an Egyptian relief," *KZFE* 8 (1969) 85-102.

Arvid Andrén, "An Etruscan Terracotta Head," *MB* #5 (1969) 36-38.

Olof Vessberg, "A Roman Togatus," *MB* #5 (1969) 53-58. *[Statue]*

Pauline Albenda, "The Burney Relief Reconsidered," *JANES* 2 (1969-70) 86-93. *[Mesopotamian]*

§227 ***2.5.10.3.1 Metal Statuary and Castings (Especially Bronzes) [See also: Metal Artifacts §99 Metallurgy and §211 (Artifacts) Metal Articles ←]***

Charles C. Perkins, "The Siris Bronzes," *AJA, O.S.*, 1 (1885) 162.

*Salomon Reinach, "Inscribed base of an archaic bronze from Mount Ptous," *AJA, O.S.*, 1 (1885) 358-360. [Note by Michel Bréal, p. 360]

Alfred Emerson, "An Engraved Bronze Bull at Metaponto," *AJA, O.S.*, 4 (1888) 28-38.

Arthur L. Frothingham Jr., "Early Bronzes discovered on Mount Ida in Krete," *AJA, O.S.*, 4 (1888) 431-449.

A. L. Frothingham Jr., "Early Bronzes in the Cave of Zeus," *AJA, O.S.*, 5 (1889) 48.

*Oldfield Thomas, "Remarks on Facsimile of a Metal Mouse in the Collection of Baron Ustinoff at Jaffa," *PEFQS* 26 (1894) 189-190.

Walter L. Nash, "Bronze Figure of Isis, with Silver Head-covering," *SBAP* 17 (1895) 198.

Paul Wolthers, "Bronze-Reliefs from the Acropolis of Athens," *AJA, O.S.*, 11 (1896) 350-360.

*Walter L. Nash, "A Bronze Uraeus of unusual form," *SBAP* 20 (1898) 145-146.

*Walter L. Nash, "Ancient Egyptian Models of Fish," *SBAP* 22 (1900) 163-165.

J. R. Wheeler, "A Bronze Statue of Hercules in Boston," *AJA* 5 (1901) 29.

Anonymous, "Discovery at Suse," *RP* 3 (1904) 352. *[Bronze head of Marcus Vipsanius Agrippa]*

H. S. Cowper, "A Bronze Figure from Rakka," *SBAP* 28 (1906) 228.

*H. F. De Cou, "Jewelry and Bronze Fragments in the Loeb Collection," *AJA* 15 (1911) 131-148.

*Anonymous, "Ancient Bronze Statue Found at Cairo," *RP* 10 (1911) 116. *[Hittite Deity]*

*R. C. Bosanquet, "Second Interim Report on Excavations at Meroë in Ethiopia. Part III. On the Bronze Portrait-head," *AAA* 4 (1911-12) 66-71. *[Augustus?]*

Arthur E. P. B. Weigall, "A Silver Figure of a Cretan Bull," *JEA* 4 (1916) 187.

C. Hercules Read, "Two Bronzes of Assyrian Type," *Man* 18 (1918) #1.

W. M. Flinders Petrie, "A Negro Captive," *AEE* 6 (1921) 13. *[Egyptian Bronze Statue]*

Walter Woodburn Hyde, "A Terra-Cotta Head in the Loeb Collection," *AJA* 26 (1922) 426-429.

*H. R. Hall, "The Discoveries at Tell el 'Obeid in Southern Babylonia and Some Egyptian Comparisons," *JEA* 8 (1922) 241-257. *[Bronze Casting]*

*R. Engelbach, "Seizure of bronzes from Buto (Tell Far'aîn)," *ASAE* 24 (1924) 169-177.

Wilhelm Spiegelberg, "A Bronze Statue of a Cake-carrier," *JEA* 16 (1930) 73-74.

H. R. Hall, "An Eighteenth Dynasty Osiris Bronze," *JEA* 16 (1930) 235.

*H. N. Couch, "An Inscribed Votive Bronze Bull," *AJA* 35 (1931) 44-47.

J[ohn Story] J[enks], "Two Sculptures from Minturnæ," *UMB* 4 (1932-33) 9-12.

*Paolo Zancani [Montuoro] and Umberto Zantotti-Bianco, "Archaeological Notes. The Discovery of the Heraion of Lucania," *AJA* 40 (1936) 185-187.

M. E. L. Mallowan, "A Bronze Head of the Akkadian Period from Nineveh," *Iraq* 3 (1936) 104-110.

J. H. Iliffe, "A Hoard of Bronzes from Askalon. *c. fourth century B.C.*," *QDAP* 5 (1936) 61-68.

Gisela M. A. Richter, "Greek Bronzes Recently Acquired by the Metropolitan Museum of Art," *AJA* 43 (1939) 189-201.

Emeline Hurd Hill, "The Warrior Types in Etruscan Small Bronzes," *AJA* 44 (1940) 113.

George Mylonas, "The Bronze Statue from Artemision," *AJA* 45 (1941) 90-91.

*L[eon] L[egrain], "Nippur Again," *UMB* 9 (1941-42) #1, 9-14. [I. Sumerian Heads, pp. 9-10]

Gisela M. A. Richter, "Archaeological Notes. A Bronze Eros," *AJA* 47 (1943) 365-378.

George E. Mylonas, "The Bronze Statue from Artemision," *AJA* 48 (1944) 143-160.

Dorothy Burr Thompson, "A Bronze Dancer from Alexandria," *AJA* 54 (1950) 371-385.

*B. Ph. Loinski, "Eagle Symbols in Metal Work," *AJA* 56 (1952) 175-176.

Clay Lancaster, "Luristan Bronzes: Their Style and Symbolism," *Arch* 5 (1952) 94-99.

Rhys Carpenter, "A Reconditioned Bronze Masterpiece," *AJA* 59 (1955) 170.

E. F. Prins de Jong, "An Introduction to Etruscan Art: Metals," *A&S* 1 (1955-56) 169-204.

Giovanni Lilliu, "Small Nuraghian Bronzes from Sardinia," *A&S* 1 (1955-56) 268-290.

*M. A. Hanfmann and P. Hansen, "Hittite Bronzes and other Near Eastern Figurines in the Fogg Art Museum of Harvard University," *TAD* 6 (1956) #2, 43-58.

*Emeline Hill Richardson, "The Recurrent Geometric Style in Early Etruscan Bronzes," *AJA* 61 (1957) 185-186.

Donald P. Hansen, "A Bronze in the Semitic Museum of Harvard University," *BASOR* #146 (1957) 13-19.

*Aage Roussell, "A Hellenistic Terra-Cotta Workshop in the Persian Gulf," *Kuml* (1958) 198-200.

François Chamoux, "Une Tête de Dionysos en Bronze Trouvée à Méroë," *Kush* 8 (1960) 77-86. [English Summary: "A Bronze Head of Dionysus found at Meroe," pp. 86-87]

*Donald P. Hansen, "An Archaic Bronze Boar from Sardis," *BASOR* #168 (1962) 27-36.

K. R. Maxwell-Hyslop, "Bronzes from Iran in the Collections of the Institute of Archaeology, University of London," *Iraq* 24 (1962) 126-131. [Technical Report on the Bronzes, by H. W. M. Hcdges, pp. 131-133]

Ture J. Arne, "The Collection of Luristan Bronzes," *MB* #2 (1962) 5-17.

*Faraj Basmachi, "Miscellania in the Iraq Museum," *Sumer* 18 (1962) 48-50. [An Assyrian Bronze Relief (I.M. 62197), p. 48]

Mogens Gjødesen, "Greek Bronzes: A Review Article," *AJA* 67 (1963) 333-351. *(Review)*

Herbert Hoffmann, "Two Unknown Greek Bronzes of the Archaic Period," *AJA* 68 (1964) 185-188.

*Anonymous, "Recent Acquisitions by the Institute. A Bronze Cast of the Goddess Asherah," *BH* 1 (1964) #1, 8-9.

*P. R. S. Moorey, "A Bronze 'Pazuzu' Statuette from Egypt," *Iraq* 27 (1964) 33-41.

*Cornelius C. Vermeule III, "Greek and Roman Portraits in North American Collections Open to the Public: A Survey of Important Monumental Likenesses in Marble and Bronze which have not been published extensively," *PAPS* 108 (1964) 99-134.

*Brunilde Sismondo Ridgway, "Stone and Metal in Greek Sculpture,"*Arch* 19 (1966) 31-42.

Brian F. Cook, "The Goddess Cybele: A Bronze in New York," *Arch* 19 (1966) 251-257.

N. Dorin Ischlondsky, "Problems of Dating a Unique Egyptian Bronze," *JNES* 25 (1966) 97-105.

Brunilde Sismondo Ridgway, "The Lady from the Sea: A Greek Bronze in Turkey," *AJA* 71 (1967) 329-334.

Jeanny Vorys Canby, "The Pedigree of a Syrian Bronze in the Walters Art Gallery, Baltimore, and some Stylistic Crosscurrents in the Late Third Millennium B.C.," *Bery* 17 (1967-68) 107-122.

Brunilde Sismondo Ridgway, "The Bronze Lady from the Sea," *Exped* 10 (1967-68) #1, 3-9.

Jean Vorys Canby, "Who Made the Tiryns Bronze?" *AJA* 72 (1968) 162.

*Emeline Hill Richardson, "A Series of Votive Bronzes from Arezzo," *AJA* 72 (1968) 171.

*David Gordon Mitten and Suzannah Doeringer, "Master Bronzes from the Classical World," *Arch* 21 (1968) 6-13.

N. Dorin Ischlondsky, "The Saga of a Bronze and the Story of a Friendship," *JNES* 27 (1968) 51-60.

*Edith Porada, "Iranian Art and Archaeology: A Report of the Fifth International Congress, 1968," *Arch* 22 (1969) 54-65. [The Context of the Luristan Bronzes and Finds of the Median Period, pp. 62-64]

§228 *2.5.10.3.2 Statuettes and Figurines*

(Miss) Giovanna Gonino, "A Bronze Statuette of Osorkon I, in the Collection of Professor Lanzone," *SBAP* 6 (1883-84) 205-206.

Salomon Reinach, "Inedited Terracottas from Myrina, in the Museum of Constantinople," *AJA, O.S.*, 4 (1888) 413-420.

*Isaac H. Hall, "On a recently discovered Bronze Statuette now in the Metropolitan Museum of Art, New York," *JAOS* 15 (1893) cii-cvii.

*F. L. Griffith, "A Relic of Pharaoh Necho from Phoenicia," *SBAP* 16 (1893-94) 90-91. *[Bronze Statuette]*

Henry W. Haynes, "Grotesque Figurine," *AJA, O.S.,* 11 (1896) 150-151.

*Rufus B. Richardson, "Notes. Notes from Corinth," *AJA, O.S.*, 11 (1896) 371-372. [Archaic Terracotta Figurines, pp. 371-372]

George H. Chase, "Terracottas from the Argive Heraeum," *AJA* 4 (1900) 161-162.

*Walter L. Nash, "Egyptian Models of Fish," *SBAP* 21 (1899) 311-312. (Note by A. H. Sayce, *SBAP* 22 (1900) p. 86)

W. M. Flinders Petrie, "An Egyptian Ebony Statuette of a Negress," *Man* 1 (1901) #107.

*Arthur E. Weigall, "Egyptian Notes," *SBAP* 23 (1901) 13-15. [*A Statuette of Min-Mes, Chief Magician to Ramses II,* pp. 10-15]

F. G. Hilton Price, "Notes on a rare figure of Amen-Rā," *SBAP* 23 (1901) 35-36.

*Percy E. Newberry, "Extracts from my Notebooks (IV)," *SBAP* 23 (1901) 218-224. [23. A Priest of Astarte, pp. 219-220 (*figurine of Ptah*); 24. Some Egyptian Antiquities in the Dattari Collection, pp. 220-222 (*Statuettes*)]

Theodore F. Wright, "Figurines from Tell Sandahannah," *AJA* 6 (1902) 42-43.

*W. M. Flinders Petrie, "Prehistoric Egyptian Figures," *Man* 2 (1902) #14.

W. L. Nash, "Two Heads of Small Statues found at the Temple of Mutat Karnak," *SBAP* 24 (1902) 51.

*Percy E. Newberry, "Extracts from my Notebooks. VII," *SBAP* 25 (1903) 357-362. [57. Some Miscellaneous Antiquities, pp. 361-362 (*Statuette, p. 362*)]

*Percy E. Newberry, "Extracts from my Notebooks. VIII," *SBAP* 27 (1905) 101-105. [63. Some Small Inscribed Objects, pp. 103-105 (*Statuette, p. 103)*]

*Garrett Chatfield Pier, "An Egyptian Statuette with Sun Hymn," *AJSL* 22 (1905-06) 43-44.

F. Ll. Griffith, "The Egyptian Statuette from Gezer," *PEFQS* 38 (1906) 121-122.

P. Scott-Moncrieff, "Note on Two Figures found near the South Temple at Wady Ḫalfa," *SBAP* 28 (1906) 118-119.

*Charles C. Torrey, "Epigraphic Notes," *JAOS* 28 (1907) 349-354. [2. A Votive Statuette with a Phoenician Inscription, pp. 351-354]

Joseph Offord, "A Hittite Bronze Statuette," *AAA* 4 (1911-12) 88-89.

*Arthur E. P. Weigall, "Miscellaneous Notes," *ASAE* 11 (1911) 170-176. [10. A figure of a bird, p. 173]

Gisela M. A. Richter, "An Archaic Etruscan Statuette," *AJA* 16 (1912) 343-349.

*E. Mahler, "Notes on the Funeral Statuettes of the Ancient Egyptians, commonly called Ushabti Figures," *SBAP* 34 (1912) 146-151, 179.

Jean Capart, "A Naval Standard-Bearer of Amenhotep III," *SBAP* 36 (1914) 8.

Ernest A. Gardner, "A Cretan Statuette," *AEE* 2 (1915) 49-51.

L. D. Caskey, "A Chryselephantine Statuette of the Cretan Snake Goddess," *AJA* 19 (1915) 237-249.

Samuel A. B. Mercer, "Note on the Gorringe Collection," *AEE* 3 (1916) 49-52. *[Statuettes]*

John Abercromby, "Sculptured Figures from near Aden," *JRAI* 46 (1916) 438-440.

Stephen B. Luce, "A Tanagra Figurine," *MJ* 10 (1919) 20-25.

George A. Reisner, "Note on the Statuette of a Blind Harper in the Cairo Museum," *JEA* 6 (1920) 117-118. (Supplementary note by the editor [Alan H. Gardner], p. 118)

Charles Boreux, "On Two Statuettes in the Louvre Museum," *JEA* 7 (1921) 113-120.

*Stephen Bleecker Luce, "A Group of Terra-cottas from Corneto," *AJA* 25 (1921) 266-278.

*H. R. Hall, "The Discoveries at Tell el ʿObeid in Southern Babylonia and Some Egyptian Comparisons," *JEA* 8 (1922) 241-257. *[Statuettes]*

H. R. Hall, "A Wooden Figure of an Old Man," *JEA* 9 (1923) 80.

T. Zammit, "Neolithic Representations of the Human Form from the Islands of Malta and Gozo," *JRAI* 54 (1924) 67-100.

N. Flittner, "An Unpublished Wooden Statuette," *AEE* 10 (1925) 71-73.

Clarence H. Young, "A Bronze Statuette in the Metropolitan Museum of Art," *AJA* 30 (1926) 427-431.

*C. Leonard Woolley, "Babylonian Prophylactic Figures," *JRAS* (1926) 689-713.

L. B. Ellis, "A Graeco-Roman Apis," *AEE* 12 (1927) 9. *[Bronze Statuette]*

*S[tephen] Langdon, "Statuette of Gudea," *JRAS* (1927) 765-768.

*Henry Frederick Lutz, "Two Assyrian Apotropaic Figurines Complementing Kar. 298, Rev. 4-7," *UCPSP* 9 (1927-31) 383-384.

L[eon] Legrain, "Small Sculptures from Babylonian Tombs," *MJ* 19 (1928) 195-212.

H. R. Hall, "Some Early Copper and Bronze Egyptian Figurines," *AAA* 16 (1929) 13-16.

*I. Sneguireff, "Some Unpublished Egyptian Objects from Kertch, Olbia and Tiflis," *AEE* 14 (1929) 101-103.

Caroline M. Galt, "A Bronze Statuette," *AJA* 33 (1929) 41-52.

*S. R. K. Glanville, "Some Notes on Material for the Reign of Amenophis III," *JEA* 15 (1929) 2-8. [III. Seated figure of an ape in crystalline standstone, p. 6]

H. R. Hall, "Some Wooden Figures of the Eighteenth and Nineteenth Dynasties in the British Museum. Part I," *JEA* 15 (1929) 236-238.

J. H. Iliffe, "A Sumerian Gold Statuette from Egypt at Toronto," *A&A* 29 (1930) 157-159, 190.

H. N. Couch, "An Archaic Goddess and Child from Lokroi," *AJA* 34 (1930) 344-352.

*H. R. Hall, "The Bronze Statuette of Khonserdaisu in the British Museum," *JEA* 16 (1930) 1-2.

H. R. Hall, "Some Wooden Figures of the Eighteenth and Nineteenth Dynasties in the British Museum. Part II," *JEA* 16 (1930) 39-40.

E. Douglas Van Buren, "Two Statuettes of an Enthroned Goddess," *AAA* 18 (1931) 63-78.

*W. M. Crompton, "Two Glazed Hippopotamus Figures Hitherto Unpublished," *AEE* 16 (1931) 21-27.

*R. Engelbach, "Recent Acquisitions in the Cairo Museum," *ASAE* 31 (1931) 126-131. [II. Statuette of Thoth, pp. 127-128]

S. R. K. Glanville, "An Archaic Statuette from Abydos," *JEA* 17 (1931) 65-66.

S. R. K. Glanville, "An Unusual Type of Statuette," *JEA* 17 (1931) 98-99.

Mary Inda Hussey, "A Statuette of the Founder of the First Dynasty of Lagash," *RAAO* 28 (1931) 81-84.

W. R. Halliday, "A Statuette of Aremis Ephesia in the Possession of Dr. Robert Mond," *AAA* 19 (1932) 23-27.

Valentin Müller, "Note on the Bronze Statuette from Sardinia," *AJA* 36 (1932) 12-15.

*Alan W. Shorter, "Two statuettes of the goddess Sekhmet-Ubastet," *JEA* 18 (1932) 121-124.

Gisela M. A. Richter, "Two Bronze Statuettes," *AJA* 37 (1933) 48-51.

Wilhelmina van Ingen, "Types of Terracotta Figurines Found at Seleucia," *AJA* 37 (1933) 114.

D. B. Harden, "Three North Syrian Terra-Cottas," *AAA* 21 (1934) 89-92. *[Figurines]*

E. A. Gardner, "Egyptian and Greek Statuettes from Naucratis," *AEE* 19 (1934) 22-24.

*(Miss) M. A. Murray, "Female Fertility Figures," *JRAI* 64 (1934) 93-100.

J. H. Iliffe, "A Nude Terra-cotta Statuette of Aphrodite. *Fourth to Third Century B.C.*," *QDAP* 3 (1934) 106-111.

Wilhelmina van Ingen, "Bone Figurines from Seleucia on the Tigris," *AJA* 39 (1935) 112.

*R. Engelbach, "Statuette-Group, from Kîmâm Fâris, of Sebekḥotpe and his womenfolk," *ASAE* 35 (1935) 203-205.

Edith Hall Dohan, "A Bronze Statuette from Delphi," *AJA* 40 (1936) 520-521.

*Ludlow Bull, "Four Egyptian Inscribed Statuettes of the Middle Kingdom," *JAOS* 56 (1936) 166-172.

*Neville Langton, "Notes on Some Small Egyptian Figures of Cats," *JEA* 22 (1936) 115-120.

George E. Mylonas, "A Mycenaean Figurine at the University of Illinois," *AJA* 41 (1937) 237-247.

*E[phraim] A. Speiser, "Mesopotamian Miscellanea," *BASOR* #68 (1937) 7-13. [II. On Some Animal Figurines from Billa and Gawra, pp. 10-12]

Frederick R. Grace, "Archaic Boeotian Terracottas," *AJA* 42 (1938) 123. *[Figurines]*

D. H. Gordon, "The Age of Frontier Terra-Cottas," *Iraq* 5 (1938) 85-88.

*N. Langton, "Further Notes on Some Egyptian Figures of Cats," *JEA* 24 (1938) 54-58.

Guy Brunton, "Two faience statuettes," *ASAE* 39 (1939) 101-103.

A. Lucas, "Glass figures," *ASAE* 39 (1939) 227-235.

G. W. Elderkin, "Bronze Statuettes of Zeus Keraunios," *AJA* 44 (1940) 225-233.

Christine Alexander, "An Antefix and a Hekataion Recently Acquired by the Metropolitan Museum of Art," *AJA* 44 (1940) 293-296.

*Mary H. Swindler, "The Goddess with Upraised Arms," *AJA* 45 (1941) 87. *[Mycenaean]*

*E. Douglas Van Buren, "The *ṣalme* in Mesopotamian Art and Religion," *Or, N.S.*, 10 (1941) 65-92.

*Karl Lehmann-Hartleben, "Some Ancient Portraits," *AJA* 46 (1942) 198-216. [I. Philetairos, pp. 198-204]

Dorothy Kent Hill, "Two Unknown Minoan Statuettes," *AJA* 46 (1942) 254-260.

Hetty Goldman, "Two Terracotta Figurines from Tarsus," *AJA* 47 (1943) 22-34.

Zaki Y. Saad, "Statuette of God Bes as a part of a fan with the name of the King Taklot II .," *ASAE* 42 (1943) 147-152.

D. J. Beazley, "An Archaic Greek Statuette from South Arabia," *Man* 43 (1943) #68.

*Gisela M. A. Richter, "Five Bronze Recently Acquired by the Metropolitan Museum," *AJA* 48 (1944) 1-9.

Mohammad Ali Mustafa, "Kassite Figurines. A new group discovered near ʿAqar Qûf," *Sumer* 3 (1947) 19-22.

*Elise J. Baumgartel, "The three colossi from Koptos and their Mesopotamian counterparts," *ASAE* 48 (1948) 533-553.

*David M. Robinson, "New Mycenaean Figurines and Vases," *AJA* 53 (1949) 145-146.

*Bernard V. Bothmer, "Statuettes of Wꜣḏ·t as Ichneumon Coffins," *JNES* 8 (1949) 121-123.

Nimet Özgüç, "A Hittite figurine found at Dövlek, Anatolia (Summary)," *TAD* 5 (1949) 52.

M. Stekelis, "Some Remains of the Yarmukian Culture," *BIES* 15 (1949-50) #3/4, I. *[Figurines]*

*David M. Robinson, "A Small Hoard of Mycenaean Vases and Statuettes," *AJA* 54 (1950) 1-9.

*Saul S. Weinberg, "Neolithic Figurines and Aegean Interrelations," *AJA* 54 (1950) 256-257; 55 (1951) 121-133.

Dorothy Burr Thompson, "A Bronze Masked Dancer," *AJA* 54 (1950) 258. *[Statuette]*

George H. Chase, "Greek Terracotta Figurines," *Arch* 4 (1951) 159-161.

M. Stekelis, "Two More Yarmukian Figurines," *IEJ* 2 (1952) 216-217.

*Dorothy Kent Hill, "A Bronze Statuette of a Negro," *AJA* 57 (1953) 265-267.

*Manfred Cassirer, "An early faience statuette of a baboon," *JEA* 39 (1953) 108-109.

*Gisela M. A. Richter, "Acquisitions of the Fogg Art Museum: Sculpture and Figurines," *AJA* 58 (1954) 223-229.

Dorothy Kent Hill, "Six Early Greek Animals," *AJA* 59 (1955) 39-44. *[Greek Bronze Statuettes]*

W[illiam] K[elly] Simpson, "A Statuette of Anuḳet," *Sumer* 11 (1955) 131-132.

*Cyril Aldred, "The Carnarvon, Statuette of Amūn," *JEA* 42 (1956) 3-7.

M. A. Hanfmann and P. Hansen, "Hittite Bronzes and other Near Eastern Figurines in the Fogg Art Museum of Harvard University," *TAD* 6 (1956) #2, 43-58.

H. G. Fischer, "Prostrate Figures of Egyptian Kings," *UMB* 20 (1956) #1, 27-42.

*Rudolf Anthes, "Memphis (Mit Rahineh) in 1956," *UMB* 21 (1957) #2, 3-34. (Fig. 12. Toad, p. 34) *[Figurine]*

H. G. Fischer, "Further Remarks on the Prostrate Kings," *UMB* 21 (1957) #2, 35-40.

Margarete Bieber, "A Bronze Statuette in Cincinnati and its Place in History of the Asklepios Types," *PAPS* 101 (1957) 70-92.

Tahsin Özgüç, "The statuette from Horoztepe," *A(A)* 3 (1958) 53-56.

R. Ross Holloway, "A Terracotta from Gordion and the Tradition of a Seated Kybele," *AJA* 62 (1958) 223.

N. Tzori, "Cult Figurines in the Eastern Plain of Esdraelon and Beth-Shean," *EI* 5 (1958) 86*.

M. Cassirer, "An Early Statuette in Serpentine," *JEA* 44 (1958) 1-2.

L. Y. Rahmani, "A Lion-faced Figurine from Bet-She'an," *'Atiqot* 2 (1959) 184-185.

P.L. Shinnie, "A Gold Statuette from Jebel Barkal," *Kush* 7 (1959) 91-92.

*J. Leibovitch, "The Statuette of an Egyptian Harper and String-Instruments in Egyptian Statuary," *JEA* 46 (1960) 53-59.

*R. D. Barnett, "Two Chance Finds from Ur," *Iraq* 22 (1960) 172-173. *[Statuette]*

Elmur G. Suhr, "The Berlin Spinner," *AJA* 65 (1961) 389-391. *[Statuette]*

Ora Negbi, "On Two Bronze Figurines with Plumed Helmets from the Louvre Collection," *IEJ* 11 (1961) 111-117. *[Syrian]*

George M. A. Hanfmann, "A Near Eastern Horseman," *Syria* 38 (1961) 243-256. *[Statuatte]*

George M. A. Hanfmann, "A 'Hittite' Priest form Ephesus," *AJA* 66 (1962) 1-4. *[Bronze Statuette]*

George M. A. Hanfmann, "An Early Classical Aphrodite," *AJA* 66 (1962) 281-284. *[Bronze Statuette]*

George E. Mylonas, "Two Statuettes from Mycenae," *AJA* 66 (1962) 303-304.

Abd El-Hamid Zayed, "Some Notes on a Statuette of a cow from Sheik Abbada (Antinoe)," *ASAE* 57 (1962) 137-142.

*Peter J. Ucko, "The Interpretation of Prehistoric Anthropomorphic Figurines," *JRAI* 92 (1962) 38-54.

*Faraj Basmachi, "Miscellania in the Iraq Museum," *Sumer* 18 (1962) 48-50. [Gipsum*[sic]* Statuette (I.M. 64398), p. 50]

Margarete Bieber, "A Satyr in Pergamene Style in Kansas City," *AJA* 67 (1963) 275-278. *[Bronze Statuette]*

*Anonymous, "Recent Acquistions by the Institute. Baal, God of the Canaanites," *BH* 1 (1964) #1, 10-11. *[Statuette]*

Ora Negbi, "A Canaanite Bronze Figurine from Tel Dan," *IEJ* 14 (1964) 270-271.

P. R. S. Moorey, "A Bronze 'Pazuzu' Statuette from Egypt," *Iraq* 27 (1964) 33-41.

Elizabeth Thomas, "The Four Niches and Amuletic Figures in Theban Royal Tombs," *JARCE* 3 (1964) 71-78.

*Åke Åkerström, "A Horseman from Asia Minor," *MB* #4 (1964) 49-53.

*H. M. Stewart, "Egyptian Funerary Statuettes and the Solar Cult," *ULBIA* 4 (1964) 165-170.

H. M. Stewart, "Note on an Egyptian Statuette: Brit. Mus. 1735," *ULBIA* 5 (1965) 67-68.

Dorothy Burr Thompson, "The Origin of Tanagras," *AJA* 70 (1966) 51-63. *[Figurines]*

Patricia Preziosi, "Cycladic Objects in the Fogg and Farland Collections," *AJA* 70 (1966) 105-111. *[Figurines]*

Ora Negbi, "A Deposit of Terracottas and Statuettes from Tel Ṣippor," *'Atiqot* 6 (1966) 1-27.

Joan Oates, "The Baked Clay Figurines from Tell es-Sawwan," *Iraq* 28 (1966) 146-153.

Winifred Needler, "Six Predynastic Human Figures in the Royal Ontario Museum," *JARCE* 5 (1966) 11-17.

*Edward L. B. Terrace, "'Blue Marble' Plastic Vessels and Other Figures," *JARCE* 5 (1966) 57-63.

Ruth Amiran, "A Note on Figurines with 'Disks'," *EI* 8 (1967) 71*.

*H. M. Stewart, "Stelophorus Statuettes in the British Museum," *JEA* 53 (1967) 34-38.

M. Avi-Yonah, "A Reappraisal of the Tell Sandahannah Statuette," *PEQ* 99 (1967) 42-44.

*Helen Jaquet-Gordon, "A Statuette of Ma'et and the Identity of the Divine Adoratress Karomama," *ZÄS* 94 (1967) 86-93.

James B. Pritchard, "An Eighth Century Traveler," *Exped* 10 (1967-68) #2, 26-29. *[Statuette]*

Cornelius Vermeule,"The Basel Dog: A Vindication," *AJA* 72(1968) 95-101.

Cornelius Vermeule and Penelope von Kersburg, "Appendix: Lions, Attic and Related," *AJA* 72 (1968) 99. *[Figurine]*

David Gordon Mitten, "Some New Greek Geometric Bronze Statuettes," *AJA* 72 (1968) 169.

*Donald White, "Recent Discoveries from Archaic Cyrene II: The Dedicatory Sphinx and Bronze Plaques," *AJA* 72 (1968) 174.

H[assan] S. K. Bakry, "A Late-Period Statuette," *ASAE* 60 (1968) 1-6. *[Egyptian]*

*Elizabieta Dabrowska-Smektala, "List of Objects Found at Der el-Bahari in the Area of the Tuthmosis III's Temple Seasons 1962-63 and 1963-64," *ASAE* 60 (1968) 95-130. *[Statuettes]*

*Elise J. Baumgartel, "About Some Ivory Statuettes from the 'Main Deposit' at Hierakonpolis," *JARCE* 7 (1968) 7-14.

Ora Negbi, "Dating Some Groups of Canaanite Bronze Figurines," *PEQ* 100 (1968) 45-55.

*Colin Renfrew, "The Development and Chronology of Early Cycladic Figurines," *AJA* 73 (1969) 1-32.

*Donald P. Hansen, "Some Remarks on the Chronology and Style of Objects from Byblos," *AJA* 73 (1969) 281-284.

Trude Dothan, "A Female Mourner Figurine from the Lachish Region," *EI* 9 (1969) 135. *[English Summary]*

E. Sollberger, "Old-Babylonian Worshipper Figurines," *Iraq* 31 (1969) 90-93.

*Miroslav Verner, "Statue of Twēret (Cairo Museum no. 39145) Dedicated by Pabēsi and Several Remarks on the Role of the Hippopotamus Goddess," *ZÄS* 96 (1969-70) 52-63.

§229 ***2.5.10.3.3 Carvings, especially Ivory Carvings***

†*Theo. G. Pinches, "Babylonian Art, illustrated by Mr. H. Rassam's latest discoveries," *SBAP* 6 (1883-84) 11-15. *[Ivory Carvings]*

W. H. Rylands, "Egyptian Engraved Ivory in the British Museum [No. 18175]," *SBAP* 10 (1887-88) 570.

*F. G. Hilton Price, "Two Objects from prehistoric tombs," *ZÄS* 37 (1899) 47. *[Ivory Carvings]*

F. G. Hilton Price, "Some Ivories from Abydos," *SBAP* 22 (1900) 160-161. [Note by W. L. Nash, p. 161]

*W. M. Flinders Petrie, "Prehistoric Egyptian Figures," *Man* 2 (1902) #14.

W. M. Flinders Petrie, "Prehistoric Egyptian Carvings," *Man* 2 (1902) #113.

F. Legge, "The Magic Ivories of the Middle Empire," *SBAP* 27 (1905) 130-152.

F. Legge, "The Magic Ivories of the Middle Empire. II," *SBAP* 27 (1905) 297-303.

F. Legge, "The Magic Ivories of the Middle Empire. III," *SBAP* 28 (1906) 159-170.

*Percy E. Newberry, "The Wooden and Ivory Labels of the Ist Dynasty," *SBAP* 34 (1912) 279-289.

Georges Bénédite, "The Carnarvon Ivory," *JEA* 5 (1918) 1-15, 225-241.

*G. D. Hornblower, "An Humped Bull of Ivory," *JEA* 13 (1927) 222-225.

G. D. Hornblower, "Some Prehistoric Carvings," *JEA* 13 (1927) 240-246.

John Garstang, "An Ivory Sphinx from Abydos. (British Museum, No. 54678)," *JEA* 14 (1928) 46-47.

*S. R. K. Glanville, "Some Notes on Material for the Reign of Amenophis III," *JEA* 15 (1929) 2-8. [IV. Wooden head of a goat, pp. 6-7]

Anonymous, "Notes and Comments. Samarian Ivories," *A&A* 33 (1932) 273.

Ernest S. Thomas, "An Ivory in the Petrie Collection," *AEE* 18 (1933) 89-92.

J. W. Crowfoot, "On the Ivories form Samaria," *JPOS* 13 (1933) 121-127.

J. W. Crowfoot, "The Ivories from Samaria," *PEFQS* 65 (1933) 7-26.

Herbert G[ordon] May, "A Supplementary Note on the Ivory Inlays from Samaria," *PEFQS* 65 (1933) 88-89.

R. G., "Notes and Comments. Ivory Carvings from Samaria Received by Fogg Museum," *A&A* 35 (1934) 89.

*Anonymous, "New Egyptian Acquisitions in the Metropolitan Museum of Art," *AJA* 39 (1935) 1-4. *[Ivory Carvings]*

R. D. Barnett, "The Nimrud Ivories and the Art of the Phoenicians," *Iraq* 2 (1935) 179-210.

John A. Wilson, "The Megiddo Ivories," *AJA* 42 (1938) 333-335.

R. D. Barnett, "Phoenician and Syrian Ivory Carving," *PEQ* 71 (1939) 4-19.

Helen Pence Wace, "Notes on the New Mycenaean Ivories," *AJA* 45 (1941) 91-92.

*L[eon] L[egrain], "Nippur Again," *UMB* 9 (1941-42) #1, 9-14. [II. Archaic Engraved Stone Plaque, pp. 10-14]

Gisela M. A. Richter, "An Ivory Relief in the Metropolitan Museum of Art," *AJA* 49 (1945) 261-269.

*Helene J. Kantor, "The Final Phase of Predynastic Culture: Gerzean or Semainean(?)," *JNES* 3 (1944) 110-136. [Carving with Animals, pp. 127-131; Carved Limestone Disk, pp. 131-134; Carved Palette, p. 134-136]

*Elise J. Baumgartel, "The three colossi from Koptos and their Mesopotamian counterparts," *ASAE* 48 (1948) 533-553.

M. E. L. Mallowan, "Excavations at Nimrud (Kalḫu), 1949-1950. Ivories from the N. W. Palace," *Iraq* 13 (1951) 1-20; 14 (1952) 45-53.

Alan J. B. Wace, "Ivory Carvings from Mycenae," *Arch* 7 (1954) 149-155.

John D. Evans, "Bossed Bone Plaques of the Second Millennium," *Antiq* 30 (1956) 80-93.

Helene J. Kantor, "Syro-Palestinian Ivories," *JNES* 15 (1956) 153-175.

R. Giveon, "Notes on the Nimrud and Palestine Ivories," *BIES* 22 (1958) #1/2, v.

Anonymous, "Ivories from Nimrud," *AT* 4 (1959-60) #3, 6-7.

Ellen L. Kohler, "Phrygian Miniature Animal Carving," *AJA* 64 (1960) 187.

Helene J. Kantor, "Ivory Carving in the Mycenaean Period," *Arch* 13 (1960) 14-15.

Beatrice L. Goff, "Observations on Barnett's A Catalogue of the Nimrud Ivories," *JAOS* 80 (1960) 340-347.

*Helene J. Kantor, "Oriental Institute Museum Notes. No. 11: A Fragment of a Gold Applique from Ziwiye and Some Remarks on the Artistic Traditions of Armenia and Iran During the First Millennium B.C.," *JNES* 19 (1960) 1-14.

G. Roger Edwards, "An Ivory Gorgoneion," *Exped* 3 (1960-61) #3, 23.

Ray L. Cleveland, "An Ivory Bull's Head from Ancient Jericho," *BASOR* #163 (1961) 30-36.

P. Bar-Adon, "Another Ivory Bull's Head from Palestine," *BASOR* #165 (1962) 46-47.

Ray L. Cleveland, "Acknowledgement of the Bull's Head from Khirbet Kerak," *BASOR* #165 (1962) 47.

R. D. Barnett, "Hamath and Nimrud. Shell Fragments from Hamath and the Provenance of the Nimrud Ivories," *Iraq* 25 (1963) 81-85.

*Peter J. Ucko, "Anthropomorphic Ivory Figurines from Egypt," *JRAI* 95 (1965) 214-239.

*Harold L. Liebowitz, "Horses in New Kingdom Art and the Date of the Ivory from Megiddo," *JARCE* 6 (1967) 129-134.

*Elise J. Baumgartel, "About Some Ivory Statuettes from the 'Main Deposit' at Hierakonpolis," *JARCE* 7 (1968) 7-14.

*William C. Brice, "Epigraphische Mitteilungen," *KZFE* 7 (1968) 180-181. [Cretan Glyptic and Cave Art, p. 180]

*Machteld J. Mellink, "The Pratt Ivories in the Metropolitan Museum of Art—Kerma—Chronology and the Transition from the Early Bronze to Middle Bronze," *AJA* 73 (1969) 285-287.

*Ruth Amiram, "Canaanite Jars Depicted on Egyptian First Dynasty Wooden Labels and Ivory Inlays," *EI* 9 (1969) 137. *[English Summary]*

Elise J. Baumgartel, "Some Additional Remarks on the Hierakonpolis Ivories," *JARCE* 8 (1969-70) 9-10.

§230 2.6 Assyriology - General Studies

Anonymous, "Studies in Assyriology," *DUM* 83 (1874) 481-496. *(Review)*

†Anonymous, "Assyrian Discoveries," *LQHR* 46 (1876) 162-189. *(Review)*

Paul de Lagarde, "On Assyriology," *BS* 34 (1887) 563-569. *(Review)*

†Anonymous, "Assyriology," *LQHR* 49 (1877-78) 265-296. *(Review)*

O. D. Miller, "On Assyriology,—A Criticism [with Editorial Note and Reply.]," *BS* 35 (1878) 696-707.

Rufus P. Stebbins, "Recent Assyrian and Babylonian Researches," *URRM* 9 (1878) 610-636.

Bourchier W. Savile, "The Study of Cuneiform Archæology," *CM* 9 (1879) 257-272.

Hormuzd Rassam, "Late Assyrian and Babylonian Research," *JTVI* 14 (1880-81) 182-221. (Discussion, pp. 221-225)

Hormuzd Rassam, "Assyrian Discoveries near Bagdad," *PEFQS* 14 (1882)132-134.

Francis Brown, "Assyriological Notes," *PR* 4 (1883) 164-165, 420-424.

*D. G. Lyon, "Assyrian Research and the Hebrew Lexicon," *BS* 41 (1884) 376-385.

Francis Brown, "Assyriological Notes," *PR* 5 (1884) 131-134, 337-340, 510-513.

*R[obert] D[ick] Wilson, "Hebrew Lexicography and Assyriology," *PR* 6 (1885) 319-328.

‡Hugh M. Mackenzie, "Recent Assyriological Literature," *BFER* 35 (1886) 425-432.

*D. G. Lyon, "Assyriology and the Old Testament," *URRM* 28 (1887) 543-551.

‡D. G. Lyon, "A brief Account of some recent Assyriological Publications," *JAOS* 13 (1889) xxiii-xxiv.

[D. G.] Lyon, "On certain important recent Assyriological publications," *JAOS* 13 (1889) cxi-cxii.

*‡Paul Haupt, "On a new periodical devoted to Assyriology and comparative Semitic grammar," *JAOS* 13 (1889) cclxvii-cclxx. *[Beiträge zur Assyriologie und vergleichenden semitischen Sprachwissenschaft]*

Cyrus Adler, "Assyriology in Japan," *JAOS* 14 (1890) clxvii-cxlviii.

Robert W. Rogers, "Progress in Assyrian Research," *MR* 72 (1890) 53-64.

*Theo[philus] G. Pinches, "Notes upon some of the Recent Discoveries in the Realm of Assyriology, with Special Reference to the Private Lives of the Babylonians," *JTVI* 26 (1892-93) 123-171, 184. [(Discussion, pp. 171-177) (Remarks by C. R. Conder, pp. 177-181; H. G. Tomkins, pp. 182-183)]

A. A. Berle, "The Triumph of Assyriology," *BS* 52 (1895) 754-756.

D. G. Lyon, "A Half Century of Assyriology," *BS* 53 (1896) 125-142.

A. H. Sayce, "Assyriological Notes. No. I," *SBAP* 18 (1896) 170-186.

*A. H. Sayce, "Assyriaca," *ET* 9 (1897-98) 480.

*Charles L. Candee, "'Assyrian and Babylonian Archaeology and the Old Testament'," *CFL, N.S.*, 8 (1903) 169-176.

*Frederic Blass, "Science and Sophistry," *ET* 16 (1904-05) 8-15. [Knowledge and Science; Sophistry; Spread of Sophistry; Distinguishing Marks; Sophistry and Science (So-Called) of Religion; Assyriology and the Old Testament; Assyriology—History of Religion and the New Testament]

*C. H. W. Johns, "Assyriology and Inspiration," *ICMM* 1 (1905) 38-52, 125-132.

*C. H. W. Johns, "Assyriology and the Old Testament," *ICMM* 3 (1906-07) 70-78.

Gabriel Oussani, "The Story of Assyro-Babylonian Explorations," *NYR* 3 (1907-08) 516-544.

‡H. W. Hogg, "Survey of Recent Publications on Assyriology," *RTP* 3 (1907-08) 533-556, 605-629.

‡H. W. Hogg, "Survey of Recent Assyriology," *RTP* 5 (1909-10) 473-492, 533-553, 597-616.

‡C. H. W. Johns, "Survey of Assyriology," *RTP* 9 (1913-14) 189-200, 317-336, 377-392, 501-522; 10 (1914-15) 625-653.

*A. H. Sayce, "Assyriological Notes," *SBAP* 39 (1917) 207-212. [The Cherubim; The Hamathite God אלור; Baal and Yahveh; The God Kadmos; The Pig-God; The Nunnation in Arabic; The Ephod; Gopher-wood; Imperial Purple; The Shew-bread; The Hittite Code of Laws; The Name of the God Ea; The Babylonian Name of Nin-ip]

‡John A. Maynard, "A Survey of Assyriology During the Years 1915-1917," *JSOR* 2 (1918) 28-46.

‡John A. Maynard, "A Second Bibliographical Survey of Assyriology (1918-1919)," *JSOR* 4 (1928) 16-28.

‡John A. Maynard, "A Third Bibliographical Survey of Assyriology," *JSOR* 5 (1921) 18-35.

C. J. Gadd, "Thirty Years' Progress in Assyriology," *ET* 33 (1921-22) 392-397, 439-444.

‡John A. Maynard, "A Fourth Bibliographical Survey of Assyriology (Year 1921)," *JSOR* 6 (1922) 74-87.

‡John A. Maynard, "A Fifth Bibliographical Survey of Assyriology (Year 1922)," *JSOR* 7 (1923) 60-76.

‡John A. Maynard, "A Sixth Bibliographical Survey of Assyriology-Year 1923," *JSOR* 8 (1924) 135-166.

‡John A. Maynard, "A Seventh Bibliographical Survey of Assyriology. Year 1924," *JSOR* 10 (1926) 62-87.

T. Fish, "Assyriology in England During and Since the War," *BJRL* 13 (1929) 293-304.

E. R. Lacheman, "A Matter of Criticism in Assyriology," *BASOR* #80 (1940) 22-27.

Julius Lewy, "A Propos of Criticism in Assyriology," *BASOR* #81 (1941) 21. (Reply by E. R. Lacheman, p. 21; Postscript by W[illiam] F[oxwell] Albright, pp. 22-23)

M. E. L. Mallowan, "Recent Developments in Assyrian and Babylonian Archaeology," *Sumer* 11 (1955) 5-13.

§231 *2.7 Egyptology - General Studies*

†(   ) J., "Account of Egyptian Antiquities," *MMBR* 15 (1803) 397-401.

Anonymous, "Japanese Antiquities," *MMBR* 59 (1825) 136-137. *[Compared with Egyptian Antiquities]*

Anonymous, "Analogies of Mexican and Egyptian Antiquities," *MMBR* 59 (1825) 393-396.

Anonymous, "Remarks on Bunsen's Late Work upon Egypt," *BS* 6 (1849) 709-719. *(Review)*

Anonymous, "Egyptian Antiquities," *CR* 3 (1850-51) 8-27. *(Review)*

Isaac Denton, "Egyptian Archaeology," *MQR* 6 (1852) 43-78.

(   ) Q., "Egyptian Archaeology," *CRB* 18 (1853) 258-270. *(Review)*

*G. Seyffarth, "Three Lectures on Egyptian Antiquities, &c., delivered at the Stuyvesant Institute, New York, May 1856," *ER* 8 (1856-57) 34-104. [I. The Papyri,; II. The key to the Hieroglyphics; III. The Sacred Writings of Ancient Egyptians; IV. The Judicium Mortuorum, *(Judgment of the dead.);* V. The Demotic Documents; VI. The Phœnix; VII. The Apis-Mummies; VIII. The Astronomy of the Egyptians; IX. The Zodiac of Dendera; X. The Isis-Table *(Tabula Bembina);* XI. The Sarcophagus of Osimandya; XII. The Planetary Constellations of the Menes; XIII. The Planetary Constellations of the Greeks and Romans; XIV. The Planetary Constellations of the four Ages of the World; XV, The Planetary Constellations in the Alphabet; XVI. Defects of the Planetary Tables; XVII. The History of Egypt; XVIII. The Pyramid of Cheops; XIX. The Chronology of the Old Testament; XX. The History of The Greeks and Romans; XXI. The History of the New Testament; XXII. The Egyptian & Hebrew Measures of Capacity; XXIII. The Arabians]

*†Anonymous, "Egyptology and the two Exodes," *BQRL* 32 (1860) 440-479. *(Review)*

*[Joseph P. Thompson(?)], "Notices of New Publications," *BS* 19 (1862) 671-684. [Recent Works on Egyptology, Oriental Travel and Geography, pp. 671-678] *(Review)*

*[Joseph P. Thompson(?)], "Egyptology, Oriental Archaeology and Travel," *BS* 19 (1862) 881-890. *(Review)*

*Joseph P. Thompson, "Egyptology, Oriental Archaeology and Travel," *BS* 20 (1863) 650-660*(Review)*, 879-884; 22 (1865) 684-689.

*Joseph P. Thompson, "Egyptology, Oriental Travel and Discovery," *BS* 21 (1864) 425-435, 666-669. *(Review)*

*J. P. Lesley, "A Classified Catalogue of Antiquities Collected by Mr. Harris, and now in his Museum in Alexandria Egypt," *PAPS* 10 (1865-69) 561-582.

*Joseph P. Thompson, "Fresh Notes on Egyptology," *BS* 24 (1867) 771-775.

*Joseph P. Thompson, "Notes on Egyptology," *BS* 26 (1869) 184-191, 577-585; 28 (1871) 397-402*(Review)*; 29 (1872) 771-774; 30 (1873) 775-780.

Joseph P. Thompson, "New Studies in Egyptology," *BS* 27 (1870) 180-183.

Joseph P. Thompson, "Notes on Egyptology," *BS* 34 (1877) 537-545. *(Review)*

Bourchier W. Savile, "The Study of Egyptian Archæology," *CM* 9 (1879) 193-205.

G. Seyffarth, "Review of Important Egyptian Antiquities discovered since the Rosetta Stone," *JAOS* 10 (1880) clv-clvi.

*H. G. Tomkins, "Recent Egyptological Research in its Biblical Relation," *JTVI* 18 (1884-85) 72-88. [(Discussion, pp. 88-91) (Communication from Edouard Naville, pp. 87-88)]

Anonymous, "Recent Egyptian Discoveries," *JTVI* 21 (1886-67) 309-310.

W. M. Flinders Petrie, "Archæology in Egypt," *ARL* 1 (1888) 405-413.

Camden M. Cobern, "Egyptology.—No. I.—The Land of the Arabian Nights," *HR* 18 (1889) 27-31.

Camden M. Cobern, "Egyptology.—No. III. 'Œdipus Ægyptus.'," *HR* 18 (1889) 399-404.

*Camden M. Cobern, "Egyptology.—No. IV.—The Monumental Book of Revelation," *HR* 18 (1889) 494-500.

Camden M. Cobern, "Egyptology.—No. IV.*[sic]*—The Schools of the Pharaohs," *HR* 19 (1890) 31-36. *[Number IV duplicated in error]*

*Camden M. Cobern, "Egyptology.—No. V.—The Universities of Ancient Egypt," *HR* 19 (1890) 209-215.

*Camden M. Cobern, "Egyptology.—No. VI.—Bibliolatry and Monumentimania," *HR* 21 (1891) 311-318.

*Camden M. Cobern, "Egyptology.—No. VII.—An Ancient Bible Commentary," *HR* 21 (1891) 402-409.

J[ames] H. Breasted, "Scientific Egyptology," *BW* 1 (1893) 461.

*Camden M. Cobern, "The Higher Criticism and the Tombs of Egypt. Egyptology No. VIII," *HR* 22 (1891) 299-306.

James Henry Breasted, "Exploration and Discovery. The Latest from Petrie," *BW* 7 (1896) 139-140.

Anonymous, "Exploration and Discovery: The Latest from Petrie. (Illustrated)," *BW* 7 (1896) 292-295.

P. le Page Renouf, "Young and Champollion," *SBAP* 19 (1897) 188-209.

A. Wiedemann, "Observations on the Nagadah Period," *SBAP* 20 (1898) 107-122.

W. C. Winslow, "Progress of Egyptology," *AAOJ* 22 (1900) 187-190.

*(Mrs.) Sara Y. Stevenson, "Notes on Some Important Objects in the Egyptian Collection of the University of Pennsylvania," *AJA* 5 (1901) 34-35.

J[ames] H[enry] Breasted, "The Latest from Egypt," *BW* 23 (1904) 384-385.

James Henry Breasted, "Last Season in Egypt," *BW* 25 (1905) 66-69.

James Henry Breasted, "Exploration and Discovery," *BW* 26 (1905) 67-69. *[Egypt]*

James Baikie, "The Latest Discoveries in Egypt. A Review of Flinders Petrie's New Volume," *ET* 17 (1905-06) 89-92. *(Review)*

P. A. Gordon Clark, "The Egypt Exploration Report," *ET* 17 (1905-06) 381-382.

James Henry Breasted, "The First Season of the University of Chicago Egyptian Expedition," *BW* 28 (1906) 68-71.

Melvin Grove Kyle, "Archaeology Department—Egyptology," *CFL, 3rd Ser.*, 6 (1907) 139-140. *(Editorial Notes)*

Anonymous, "Egyptian Antiquities in Hungary," *AAOJ* 30 (1908) 280-281.

M[elvin] G[rove] Kyle, "Archaeological Department:—From My Egyptian Note-book of 1908," *CFL, 3rd Ser.*, 9 (1908) 154-157.

Melvin Grove Kyle, "Archaeology Department: Notes from the Field," *CFL, 3rd Ser.*, 8 (1908) 177-179.

*Melvin Grove Kyle, "Archaeological Resources—A Ground of Confidence," *CFL, 3rd Ser.*, 8 (1908) 342-344.

James Henry Breasted, "Oriental Exploration Fund of the University of Chicago: Second Preliminary Report of the Egyptian Expedition," *AJSL* 25 (1908-09) 1-110.

Melvin Grove Kyle, "Archaeology Department—From My Egyptian Note Book of 1908," *CFL, 3rd Ser.*, 10 (1909) 15-19.

Anonymous, "Exhibit of Results of the Work of the Egypt Exploration Fund," *RP* 8 (1909) 268.

Anonymous, "Egyptian Research Account, 1912," *RP* 11 (1912) 124-127.

K. Hamada and T. Chiba, "The Late Professor Tsuboi and Egyptology in Japan," *AEE* 1 (1914) 59-60.

‡F. Ll. Griffith, "Bibliography of 1912-13: Hellenistic Egypt," *JEA* 1 (1914) 124-128.

‡F. Ll. Griffith, "Bibliography of 1912-13-14: Ancient Egypt," *JEA* 1 (1914) 254-291.

W. M. Flinders Petrie, "The Egyptian Museum, University College," *AEE* 2 (1915) 168-180.

‡F. Ll. Griffith, "Bibliography: Graeco-Roman Egypt: C. Miscellaneous (1913-14)," *JEA* 2 (1915) 113-114.

‡F. Ll. Griffith, "Bibliography 1914-1915: Ancient Egypt," *JEA* 2 (1915) 234-254.

Anonymous, "Egypt at the British Association, 1915," *JEA* 3 (1916) 41-44.

‡F. Ll. Griffith, "Bibliography 1915-1916: Ancient Egypt," *JEA* 3 (1916) 257-277.

Joseph Offord, "French and Italian Egyptology," *AEE* 3 (1916) 15-21.

Joseph Offord, "Egyptology in France," *AEE* 3 (1916) 163-168.

W. N. Stearns, "The Egyptian Exploration Fund: A Plain Statement of Present Needs," *AJA* 20 (1916) 82-83.

Joseph Offord, "French Egyptology During 1916," *AEE* 4 (1917) 69-75.

B. P. Grenfell, "The Future of Graeco-Roman Work in Egypt," *JEA* 4 (1917) 4-10.

‡F. Ll. Griffith, "Bibliography 1916-1917: Ancient Egypt," *JEA* 4 (1917) 261-279.

‡F. Ll. Griffith, "Bibliography 1917-1918: Ancient Egypt," *JEA* 5 (1918) 286-302.

‡F. Ll. Griffith, "Bibliography 1918-1920: Ancient Egypt," *JEA* 6 (1920) 274-294.

W. M. Flinders Petrie, "The British School of Archaeology in Egypt," *AEE* 6 (1921) 33-34.

‡F. Ll. Griffith, "Bibliography 1920-1921: Ancient Egypt," *JEA* 7 (1921) 202-215.

W. M. Flinders Petrie, "Thirty Years in Egyptology," *ET* 33 (1921-22) 110-114.

W. M. Flinders Petrie, "The British School in Egypt," *AEE* 7 (1922) 33-39.

‡F. Ll. Griffith, "Bibliography 1921-1922: Ancient Egypt," *JEA* 8 (1922) 260-283.

‡F. Ll. Griffith, "Bibliography 1922-1923: Ancient Egypt," *JEA* 9 (1923) 201-225.

[W. M. Flinders Petrie], "The British School in Egypt," *AEE* 9 (1924) 33-38.

‡F. Ll. Griffith, "Bibliography 1923-24: Ancient Egypt," *JEA* 10 (1924) 306-323.

W. M. Flinders Petrie, "Recent Egyptian Discoveries," *ET* 36 (1924-25) 155-158.

‡F. Ll. Griffith, "Bibliography 1924-1925: Ancient Egypt," *JEA* 11 (1925) 299-319.

‡F. Ll. Griffith, "Bibliography 1925-1926: Ancient Egypt," *JEA* 12 (1926) 287-305.

[W. M.] Flinders Petrie, "Egypt Over the Border. The Work of the British School of Archaeology in Egypt," *AEE* 12 (1927) 1-8.

‡Jean Capart, "Bibliography (1926): Ancient Egypt," *JEA* 14 (1928) 159-179.

R. Engelbach, "The Aeroplane and Egyptian Archaeology," *Antiq* 3 (1929) 470-474.

Battiscombe Gunn, "Additions to the Collections of the Egyptian Museum during 1928," *ASAE* 29 (1929) 89-96.

‡Jean Capart, "Bibliography (1927): Ancient Egypt," *JEA* 16 (1930) 93-119.

Samuel A. B. Mercer, "Egyptology in Canada," *CdÉ* 6 (1931) 275-276.

Maurice A. Canney, "Egyptology in Manchester," *JMUEOS* #18 (1933) 27-36.

‡A. M. Blackman (ed.), G. A. Wainwright, N. de G. Davies, S. R. K. Glanville, L. P. Kirwan, I. E. S. Edwards, H. W. Fairman, R. O. Faulkner, M. F. L. Macadam, A. W. Shorter, R. W. Sloley, "Bibliography: Pharaonic Egypt (1936)," *JEA* 23 (1937) 230-237.

‡A. M. Blackman (ed.), G. A. Wainwright, N. de G. Davies, A. N. Dakin, S. R. K. Glanville, M. F. L. Macadam, I. E. S. Edwards, R. O. Faulkner, “Bibliography: Pharaonic Egypt (1937),” *JEA* 24 (1938) 213-241.

‡Jean Sainte Fare Garnot and Claire Lalouette, “Bibliographie des Eygptologes Français, 1940-1946. I,” *JNES* 6 (1947) 53-57.

‡Jean Sainte Fare Garnot and Claire Lalouette, “Bibliographie des Eygptologes Français, 1940-1946. II,” *JNES* 6 (1947) 164-168.

‡W. Federn, “Egyptian Bibliography (Jan. 1, 1939 - Dec. 31, 1947),” *Or, N.S.,* 17 (1948) 467-489; 18 (1949) 73-99, 206-215, 325-335, 443-472; 19 (1950) 40-52, 175-186, 279-294.

*Victor Wolfgang von Hagen, “Frederick Catherwood in Egypt,” *Arch* 2 (1949) 199-205.

*Herman Ranke, “The Egyptian Collection of the University Museum,” *UMB* 15 (1950) #2/3, 5-109. [A Guide to the Egyptian Collections, pp. 21-109]

M. Anis, “The First Egyptian Society in London,” *BIFAO* 50 (1952) 99-105.

Joan Gorell, “Treasures in Egypt,” *AT* 2 (1957-58) #1, 10-11.

Anonymous, “Egyptology,” *HT* 9 (1959) 371.

‡Makita Tominaga, “Books of Egyptology from the Terni Central Library,” *Orient* 1 (1960) 59-68.

*Henry G. Fischer, “Varia Aegyptiaca,” *JARCE* 2 (1963) 17-51.

William Peck, “The Egyptian Collection in the Cranbrook Academy Galleries,” *AJA* 68 (1964) 202; 69 (1965) 172.

Gun Björkman, “Egyptology and Historical Method,” *OrS* 13 (1964) 9-33.

‡Rosalind Moss, “By-products of Bibliography,” *JEA* 54 (1968) 173-175.